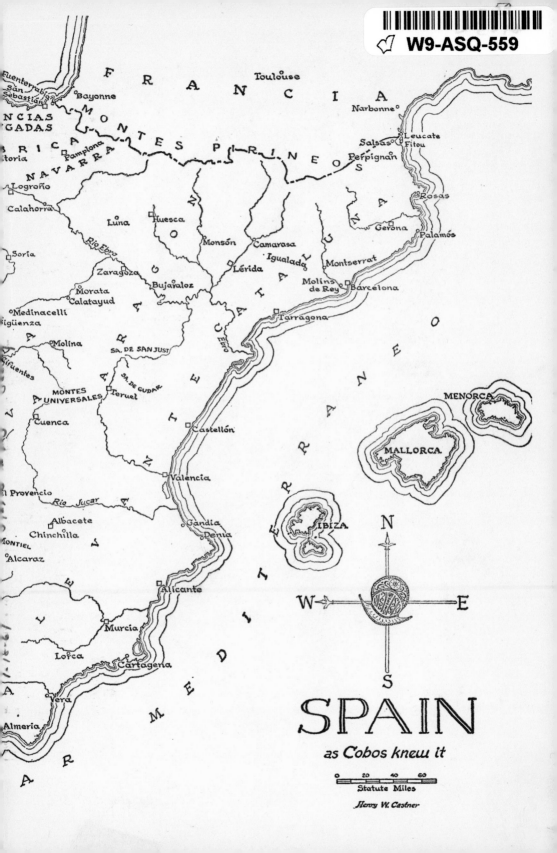

SPAIN
as Cobos knew it

```
0    20    40    60
```
Statute Miles

Henry W. Castner

FRANCISCO DE LOS COBOS

Francisco de los Cobos

SECRETARY OF THE EMPEROR

CHARLES V

by

HAYWARD KENISTON

UNIVERSITY OF PITTSBURGH PRESS

FOREWORD

My interest in Francisco de los Cobos was first awakened during
a study of the autobiography of Alonso Enríquez de Guzmán
by Don Alonso's frequent mention of Cobos' dominant rôle in
the counsels of Charles V and by his extravagant eulogies of
both Cobos and his wife, Doña María de Mendoza. Who could
this admirable couple be? A casual search quickly corroborated
Don Alonso's estimate of Cobos' importance in the affairs of
Castile, but surprisingly I could find no study of his life and
career. And so I started gathering material about him.

It soon became apparent that as chief secretary of the Emperor he must have left an abundant correspondence and that
some, at least, of these documents must still be available in
Spain. In the summer of 1954 an appointment as Guggenheim
Fellow made it possible for me to go to Europe. There I found,
not only in Spain—at Simancas, in Seville, in Madrid—but in the
archives of Belgium, England, France, and Italy, so voluminous
a body of documents that it explained, perhaps, why no one had
been so foolhardy as to undertake a study of Cobos' life. During
the next two years I gathered all the materials I could find, both
from manuscript and from printed sources.

Since my return to the United States I have devoted all my
spare time to organizing my loot of notes, microfilm, and photo-
stats into something like a coherent whole. It is my hope that out
of these scattered fragments there has emerged, as in the assem-

bled pieces of a jigsaw puzzle, the portrait of a man, set in the background of his time.

This book is, first of all, the story of Cobos' life and the little world of his family—his parents, his wife, his children. As far as possible, I have tried to see him as a human individual in his daily contact with people, to identify his hopes and ambitions, the standards of behavior that he accepted, the values he held dear. If the record is thin, it is the result of his secretiveness, which led him to destroy all of his personal correspondence. But in spite of the lack of intimate revelation on his part, the main traits of his personality are clear.

Because Cobos was, during his entire public career, a member of the royal secretariat, first under Ferdinand and Isabel and later under Charles V, I have devoted considerable attention to his contribution to the administrative structure of Castile, an area which has never been properly studied. The methods which he used in recruiting a staff, in developing an *esprit de corps,* and in conducting the affairs of office created a bureaucracy which was unique in the Europe of his day; their influence was felt long, both in Spain and the Indies.

For thirty years Cobos was associated intimately with the Emperor Charles V. Until the last years of his life he accompanied the Emperor on all of his travels and campaigns; in the end he was his most trusted Spanish advisor. The Emperor has, therefore, a large place in the story of Cobos' life. I have made no attempt to discuss Imperial policy, except in the few cases where there is clear evidence of the part that Cobos played personally in diplomatic negotiations. But here and there, in the letters of Cobos and his associates, one can catch a glimpse of the Emperor in his daily life, to help complete the picture of the most significant political figure of the sixteenth century.

Finally, I have tried to provide a setting for Cobos' life in the society of his time. The first half of the sixteenth century witnessed a momentous change in the standards and manners of Spain. The contact with the rest of Europe—the pageantry of Flanders, the sophistication of the French Court, the art of Italy —which came as a result of the Emperor's far-flung interests, almost overnight transformed Spain from an isolated, peninsular people into a member of a European community. At the same time, the influx of treasure from Mexico and Peru brought to many a Spaniard an undreamed-of wealth which made it possible for him to gratify his newly acquired taste for the refinements of social life. The era of austerity that marked the fifteenth century was replaced by an age of "conspicuous spending." Of this transformation the career of Cobos is a striking example. From the poverty and obscurity of a little Andalusian town he rose to wealth and world-wide power. The steps in that rise are the theme of this story.

September 21, 1958   H. K.
University of Pittsburgh

CONTENTS

ILLUSTRATIONS

CHAPTER I

THE YEARS OF PREPARATION

Ubeda

The broad valley that lies between the Guadalimar and the Guadalquivir is divided by a range of rolling hills that rise steadily from west to east. The central section of the range finally settles into a long slope, "La Loma," which ends abruptly, so that to the north, east, and south there is a drop of more than a hundred feet to the valley below. On the tip of this promontory stands the city of Ubeda.

The origin of the town is obscure; perhaps it existed already in Roman times, though it seems more probable that the first Roman settlement was on the bank of the Guadalquivir to the south, near the point now called "Ubeda Vieja." What is certain is that by the ninth century the Moors had founded a town on the top of the ridge. There they built a stout wall, following the curves of the ridge where the land fell away, and on the western side they constructed a high wall, strengthened with solid towers for defense in the one direction where the site was vulnerable. At the highest point on the eastern end of the town they raised the *alcázar* and hardby, the chief mosque of the community. The part of the present Ubeda contained within the ancient fortifications remains essentially Moorish in feeling, with narrow, winding streets, hardly more than alleys, wide enough for a man on horseback or a donkey laden with packs. And the older houses

1

are low, two stories at most, their windows guarded with a *reja,* gay in summer with flowering plants. One of the old gates, the "Puerta de Sabiote," with its horseshoe arch, set in an angle of the old wall, still evokes the memory of the primitive Moorish town.[1]

For four centuries the Moors held their village in comparative peace, protected from their Christian neighbors to the north by the rocky barrier of the Sierra Morena. But early in the thirteenth century Alfonso IX and his knights, led by the battling Archbishop of Toledo, Rodrigo Ximénez de Rada (Rodericus Toletanus), broke through the mountains and poured down into the valley. At Las Navas de Tolosa, on July 16, 1212, they won a decisive victory over the Moorish forces and pressing on, attacked Ubeda. The struggle was brief, for one Lope Fernández de Luna—so Rodericus Toletanus tells us in his chronicle—succeeded in scaling the wall, a feat that so disconcerted the Moors that they surrendered on July 23. The Castilians exacted a huge ransom in gold as the price for leaving the town in Moorish hands and then withdrew with their booty.

In the following years the Castilians reoccupied the town at least once, but were forced to withdraw by the plague. Again the Moors drifted back and the fortress remained in their hands until Ferdinand III, "el Santo Rey," undertook the reconquest of Andalusia. Baeza was taken in the '20's and on the day of San Miguel (September 29) in 1234 the Castilians captured Ubeda. This time the King was determined to hold his conquered territory, and to this end he granted lands in Baeza and Ubeda to three hundred of the *infanzones* under his command. We may judge the character of the allotments from the fact that Rodericus Toletanus received in 1238 a grant in Ubeda of fields, houses, a vineyard, and an orchard. And to assure a measure of municipal stability Ferdinand granted Ubeda the *fuero* of Cuenca as its basic system of law.

The new settlers proved to be anything but law-abiding. From the very beginning the town was rent with bloody feuds that were destined to keep it in turmoil until the early sixteenth century. Ubeda, too, like other Spanish towns, shared in the dynastic quarrels of the thirteenth and fourteenth centuries. In 1368, Pedro Gil, one of the supporters of Don Pedro who had been exiled from Ubeda by the supporters of Enrique de Trastamara, with the help of the Moorish King of Granada led an attack on the town. But the citizens took refuge in the *alcázar,* which proved too strong for the Moors to capture. Not until the end of the fifteenth century, when Ferdinand and Isabel completed the conquest of Granada, was the threat of the Moors finally dispelled. Ubeda had been granted the status of a "city" earlier in the century by Enrique IV; from now on it was a secure part of the kingdom of Castile.

The Family of Los Cobos

One of the Castilian *infanzones* who were settled in Ubeda by Ferdinand III after the capture of the town in 1234 was Ferrán Rodríguez (Roiz) de los Cobos. Nothing else is known of him, but it is probable that he came from Old Castile; later genealogists mention a Juan Cobos who appears in a royal document of 1137 as a resident of Santo Domingo de la Calzada and a Cobos family near Oña who were vassals of the lords of Tamayo. The house and lands which were granted to Don Ferrando were at the eastern edge of the town, north of the *alcázar,* high above the Moorish wall in the quarter that later became the parish of Santo Tomás. Though there is no mention of the family for more than a century, his descendants must have continued to live in their little estate, for the quarter ultimately became known as the "Cobos Quarter." [2]

There is a story—perhaps it is only a legend—that during the siege of Algeciras by Alfonso XI in 1344 a group of twelve knights from Ubeda, led by Hugo Beltrán, challenged and defeated twelve Moorish knights before the walls of the besieged city. One of the Christian combatants, who were called the "Twelve Lions of Ubeda," was a Lope Rodríguez de los Cobos; there is every reason to believe that he was a descendant of the original settler of the town. Perhaps a Rodrigo Rodríguez (Ruiz) de los Cobos who is mentioned as a loyal supporter of the bastard prince, Enrique de Trastamara, in 1366, was a son of Lope.

The first member of the family about whom we have more definite information was Pedro Rodríguez de los Cobos. He was chief constable of Ubeda and as ensign of the town carried its standard at the battle of Los Collajares in 1406. As a result of his participation in a feud in 1421 he was deprived of his municipal offices, and he was so truculent in his attitude toward the royal judge, Dr. Blasco Pérez Barroso, who had been sent to restore order in the town, that he was banished to a distance of forty leagues from the town.

By his marriage with Juana Rodríguez Mexía,[3] daughter of Juan Mexía and Juana Rodríguez de Mercado, Pedro had two sons: Juan de los Cobos, who was a councilman of Ubeda as late as 1456 and who died without issue, and Pedro Rodríguez de los Cobos, named for his father. This second Pedro was active in the affairs of his time. In 1439 he was warden of the town of Quesada; after 1443 he was *regidor* of Ubeda. On December 16, 1446 a royal court handed down a "decisión arbitraria," granting exemption from taxes to descendants of the original settlers of the town. No member of the Cobos family appeared in the list of knights and ladies who were granted this privilege. But three years later Pedro Rodríguez de los Cobos and other *regidores* appealed to the court, and having proved their claim, were added to the favored list.[4] The last mention of Pedro is in 1461 when he signed a homage to Prince Enrique.

About 1430 Pedro had married Isabel de la Tovilla, sister of the Comendador Tovilla. She bore him three children: a son, Diego de los Cobos, and two daughters, Leonor de los Cobos and Mayor de los Cobos. The son, Diego, who was said to have been almost a hundred years old when he died in 1530 or 1531, must have been born before 1435. We know nothing of his early years, but he took part in the final campaign of Granada between 1489 and 1492 and was granted lands in Benalúa by the Catholic Kings as a reward for his services. Late in life he was a *regidor* of Ubeda, like his father.

Diego de los Cobos married Catalina de Molina, granddaughter of Diego Fernández de Molina and Leonor González, and daughter of Diego de Molina, known as "el Paralítico," and Leonor de Arquellada.[5] When Diego's older sister, Leonor, married Pedro Fernández de Molina, his wife's uncle, the Cobos and Molina families were doubly tied together. Diego and Catalina had four children: three daughters, who bore the names of their grandmother, Isabel, and their aunts, Leonor and Mayor, and a son, Francisco de los Cobos. This is the boy, born in obscurity and poverty in a little Andalusian town, whose story we are going to tell, the story of his rise to fabulous wealth and power and to international fame in the service of the Emperor, Charles V.

Small Town Boy

Since no parish records of the fifteenth century in Ubeda have survived, it is impossible to establish the date of Francisco's birth. But in view of later events it is probable that he was born between 1475 and 1480; [6] if we assume the date of 1477, it will provide a convenient date from which to reckon. He must have been baptized in the parish church of Santo Tomás, situated a few rods down the street from his father's house, and perhaps, like other boys of the neighborhood, he first learned how to read and write from the parish priest.

Though his family could boast of a long line of noble ancestors, they had been reduced to straightened circumstances. Fernández de Oviedo, the only contemporary writer who knew Cobos as a boy, tells us that they did not have a penny of income.[7] And their poverty is corroborated by a story, told years later by a priest who had been curate of a parish in Torres, not far from Ubeda, of how Francisco, as a boy, used to come over to Torres to sell lace caps, which his sisters had knitted.[8] The story may be an invention, designed when he had become "Lord of Torres," to mark the contrast between his early poverty and his later wealth.

Certainly, all the men of his time were impressed, at the height of his power, with his humble origin—"ex honesto quidem sed humili loco," as Sepúlveda put it.[9] The Bishop, Pedro de Navarra, in his *Diálogos de la preparación de la muerte,* a fictionalized account of Cobos' last days written after his death, puts into the mouth of Basilio, who represents Cobos in the dialogue, the following confession:

> I was born a poor plebeian and I boast of being a rich courtier; I was born a servant to serve and I demand service from those whom I ought to serve; I was born in the status of a simple nobleman and I live at the height of knighthood; none of my ancestors ever had as many as ten servants to serve them and I have ten thousand for my service and profit; I was wont to prize a suit of good woolen cloth and now I scorn soft silks and precious cloth of gold.[10]

For a poor boy, life in Ubeda must have been drab. If we may judge by his later attitudes, Cobos had no taste for the street fights between the Molina "gang" and the Cueva "gang," in which the youngsters with sticks and stones imitated the more murderous feud of their elders. There were no books to read.

Almost the only diversions were the religious processions of
Holy Week and Corpus Christi. In 1489, it is true, there were
two momentous days. Ferdinand and Isabel had decided to undertake a decisive campaign against the Moors of Granada. On
May 7 the King passed through Ubeda on his way to the front,
and on November 5, the Queen, following him to the field of
battle, spent the night in Ubeda at the convent of Santa Clara,
close to the Cobos' house.[11] What a thrill it must have been for
Francisco and the other town boys to watch the Queen on her
white horse as she swept through the gate of Toledo, surrounded
by her knights!

Before she departed, the Queen left instructions that all those
who received the royal military stipend must now give service.
So the call went out. And on the appointed day the men of
Ubeda gathered under the leadership of Beltrán de la Cueva,
Duque de Alburquerque, at the Hospital of the Cofradía de San
Salvador, next door to the Cobos' house. Francisco's father, Don
Diego, though an old man, was one of those who answered the
call. Before the company started out, they all went to the Puerta
de Toledo to do reverence to the Virgen de los Remedios and to
implore her blessing.[12] With what misgiving Francisco watched
them ride away, leaving him alone with his mother and his three
sisters!

When Don Diego returned three years later, after the fall of
Granada, he may have brought some share of the booty; we
have already seen that he was granted lands in Benalúa. But this
did not solve the problem of Francisco's future. He was fifteen
years old now and he must be planning a career that would lift
him out of his family misery. He was of too peaceful a disposition to want to be a soldier; he had too little piety to feel a call
to the Church. "Iglesia o mar o casa real"—"Church or sea or
royal household," the saying went. But how was a boy without
family influence and friends to get started in the royal service?
From the little terraced vegetable garden behind his house he
could look out, beyond the fields of wheat and barley in the valley below, to the rolling hills where olive orchards marched up
in serried ranks to disappear above the crest, and far off, to the
southeast, to the ridge of Cazorla, hazy under the summer sun,
snow-capped in winter. Cazorla! It was like a magnet, pulling
him out to the unknown world that lay beyond, to the sea, to

fabled lands of wealth and beauty! Some day he would escape the dreary round of daily tasks and win his place in the world!

Apprenticeship

The opportunity for which he had been waiting came at last. His aunt, Mayor de los Cobos, had married Diego Vela Allide, who had been appointed accountant and secretary of Queen Isabel in the office of her chief accountants, the Licenciado Rodrigo and the Bachiller Serrano.[13] Now the uncle offered Cobos a place in his office. It was a petty post; the salary was surely trivial. But it was a start, and above all, it offered him a chance to leave Ubeda, for in those days royal officials followed the Court as it moved from town to town. So began the life of constant wandering which he was to live until his death.

During these first years of service in his uncle's office, Francisco learned the routines of a government official: how to copy a document in a legible, if not a calligraphic hand (Cobos' writing was always angular and jerky, quite unlike the neat orderly hand the Humanists were using in Italy); how to prepare a royal order in the proper formulae, correctly spelled; how to add the complex columns of *maravedís* in which the royal accounts were kept. He must, too, at this time have adopted the "rubric" which, attached to his signature or standing by itself, was to appear on so many thousand documents during his life.[14]

We have no record of his wanderings in these years. But it is certain that he made friends in the official circles at Court. He was a boon companion, anxious to please, and a hard worker. One of the officials with whom his work brought him into contact was the Queen's secretary, Hernando de Zafra, who in addition to his other appointments was chief accountant of Granada. Zafra was the dean of the Castilian secretaries; it was he who had drawn up for the Queen the terms of the surrender of Granada. Now, attracted by Cobos' personality, he offered him a post in his office. Cobos accepted this promotion with alacrity, and saying good-bye to his uncle, entered Zafra's service.[15]

Years later, an anonymous writer of the eighteenth century, having read in a manuscript of Oviedo that Cobos was once a "servant of Zafra," invented a romantic account of the circumstances of his appointment, telling how Zafra had met Francisco at an inn in the Sierra Morena and had induced him to follow him to Court.[16] In our own time the tale has reappeared with further embellishments. Zafra—so the story goes—secretary of Charles V, on his way to Jaén in 1528, stopped for the night at an inn in the Sierra Morena. He needed to write a letter but had no writing materials. Suddenly there appeared a lad of fourteen or fifteen, on his way to seek his fortune in Seville, with paper and ink, who offered to write the letter for him. This so delighted Zafra that he took the boy with him to Jaén and thence to Court. The boy—you have guessed!—was Francisco de los Cobos. And the story adds one further anachronism: when Charles V went to Flanders in 1540, Zafra recommended Cobos to the Emperor and so started him on his career! [17]

We do not know how long Cobos remained as an assistant in Zafra's office. But we come now to the first official document that mentions him. In the summer of 1503 the French had laid siege to the fortress of Salsas on the border of France and Cataluña. Ferdinand, after holding the Cortes of Aragon at Zaragoza and the Cortes of Cataluña in Barcelona, moved north to relieve the fortress, and at the same time the Queen sent a large force from Castile under the command of Fadrique de Toledo, Duque de Alba. The combined Spanish forces quickly forced the French to raise the siege. Ferdinand was in Perpignan, close to the border, on November 18, and on that day he issued a *cédula* (a "royal order") which is worth quoting as an example of the formula regularly used in such documents: [18]

> Don Fernando, by the grace of God, etc.
>
> To confer a grace and favor on you, Francisco de los Cobos, servant of Fernando de Zafra my secretary, and having regard for your competence and ability and for certain services which you have done me, it is my pleasure and I approve that now and henceforth for all your life you should be my royal scrivener *(escribano)* and my scrivener and notary public in my Court and in all my kingdoms and domains . . .
>
> Given in the town of Perpignan, on the 18th day of November of the year of the birth of Our Lord Jesus Christ, 1503.
>
> I the King.
>
> I, Fernando de Zafra, secretary, *escripsi.*
>
> He is competent. Licenciatus Petrus. Licenciatus Bermudes. Licenciatus Polanco.

Thus Cobos entered the official circle of the royal administration. The title of *escribano* was one granted to hundreds of public servants, but it was almost a necessity for members of the secretariat, since it authorized them to witness signatures and take depositions. Though the *cédula* does not mention his salary, we know from other sources that he was to receive 9,000 *maravedís* a year. Since the *maravedí* was worth, in modern purchasing power, approximately five cents or two pesetas, the salary of $450 or 18,000 pesetas was not princely, but it was surely the most that Cobos had ever earned. Before we take up the story of his advancement in the royal service, it will be well to glance for a moment at the organization of the secretariat that he was entering, for this was to be the world in which he operated for most of his life and his official colleagues were to be his closest friends.

The Secretariat of Ferdinand and Isabel

Though Aragon and Castile were in a sense united by the marriage of Ferdinand and Isabel, the two kingdoms remained separate and independent throughout their reign. This is strikingly evident in the difference of administrative organization, where each of the governments continued to operate in accordance with its traditional pattern.

Administration in Aragon was vested in a highly organized, bureaucratic Chancillery, directly responsible to the King.[19] The structure of the Chancillery had been established by the *Ordinances* of Pedro IV in the fourteenth century which had been confirmed by Ferdinand in 1481. The nominal head was the Chancellor, but this office was always honorific and assigned to a prelate. The actual administrative head was the Vice-Chancellor; it was he who countersigned all royal documents. Under him was a Protonotario, a sort of "office-manager" in charge of all the secretaries and clerks and responsible for the proper form of the documents. There were only three secretaries, whose task was to read communications to the King and to receive his instructions. The scribes of the Chancillery were divided into two classes: the *escribanos de mandamiento,* all of whom were notaries and who prepared the actual documents for the King's signature, and the *escribanos de registro,* a lesser breed who prepared copies for the file. The *Ordinances* also provided for a number of other officials: "regents" who were specialists in legal matters, and employees whose duty it was to heat the wax or to imprint the seal, or to carry mail, or guard the door.

The salaries of all officials and employees were prescribed by the *Ordinances* and although they were not high, appointments were eagerly sought for, since the King was accustomed to hand out special favors to his servants—gifts of money, appointments to offices which someone else could be hired to perform at small cost, even habits in one of the military orders. Moreover there was always the possibility of promotion from one of the humble posts to higher rank with an accompanying increase in salary. It is noteworthy that when Charles V came to rule in Spain he preserved the structure of the Chancillery in Aragon.

The Castilian administrative system was of a very different sort. Here, by tradition, the Consejo de Justicia, or Consejo Real, as it was sometimes called, was the body which was responsible for decisions, and the signature of at least three of its members was required on all official documents. The Consejo also nominated the judges of the Chancillery of Valladolid and later of Granada and the New World. The royal secretaries were the medium of communication between the sovereign and the Consejo; they prepared the agenda of problems which the Consejo was to discuss; they were responsible, through their assistants, for the redaction of all royal documents, and one of the secretaries countersigned all such documents.

There was no clearly defined hierarchy of lesser officials, but there were a number of *escribanos de cámara,* who drew up the documents for royal approval, and also other *escribientes* or copyists. In general, the Castilian administration was much more loosely organized than that of Aragon and hence was particularly subject to abuse or confusion of authority. The situation in Castile was made the more difficult because the provinces of the Indies were considered kingdoms of Castile and were staffed by a horde of officers appointed from Castile and loosely supervised by the royal authorities in Castile. Until the end of the reign of Ferdinand the affairs of the Indies, including the Casa de la Contratación in Seville, were administered by a subcommittee of the Consejo Real.

When Cobos entered the service in 1503 the chief officials of the Chancillery of Aragon were the Vice-Chanciller Alonso de la Cavallería, who had held office since 1479, and the Protonotario Miguel Velázquez Climent, who had succeeded his father in the office in 1500. The two senior secretaries were Miguel Pérez de Almazán and Juan Ruiz de Calcena. The former had been in service since 1488, when he was an *escribano de manda-*

miento. Ferdinand had showered him with favors; he was a commander of the Order of Santiago and Lord of Maella. Antonio de Lebrija was to dedicate his treatise *De liberis educandis* to him in 1509.[20] Calcena too had been long in service: he began as a handler of the seal in 1490.

On the Castilian side, Hernando de Zafra was the senior secretary, though no longer active in the dispatch of routine business. The secretary who signed most of the documents of this period was Gaspar de Gricio, who had succeeded Fernán Alvarez de Toledo in 1498.[21] A few months before the appointment of Cobos, one of the Aragonese officials, Lope Conchillos, who had been an *escribano de registro* and *escribano de mandamiento* since 1499, had been transferred to the Castilian secretariat. His first official appointment as secretary for Castile is dated December 21, 1503.[22] And it should be added that Pérez de Almazán occasionally countersigned Castilian documents. But it was undoubtedly from Zafra, Gricio, and Conchillos that Cobos received his training in the intricacies—and opportunities of his new job. He had mounted the first round of the ladder.

With its loose structure and its vague definitions of authority it is not surprising that the Castilian system was subject to criticism. At the very time when Cobos entered the service, an anonymous member of the Consejo, probably the loquacious Lorenzo Galíndez de Carvajal, wrote a memorandum on the steps which should be taken to avoid abuses in the government.

First of all all of the petitions which are presented for all sorts of action, both in matters of justice and in respect to royal grants, and almost all those who come to Court, go to the secretary Gaspar [de Gricio] and he sorts out the requests and sends them to the Consejo and to the accountants and to other persons who have charge of the affairs of Their Highnesses. Now this would be much better handled in the Consejo, because the members of the Consejo are better informed as to the importance of each question and what persons have charge of each type of business, in ignorance of which, matters of strict justice are handled outside of the Consejo.

These matters could be studied in the Consejo each week on a day appointed by Their Highnesses, where all requests could be examined and matters touching the Treasury could be referred to the *contadores* and those that deal with the approval of accounts to the persons encharged with them, and so on, as was the practice when Their Highnesses were in Seville [1500-1502]. Their Highnesses should instruct Gaspar to go to the Consejo every Friday with all the requests he has and there they should be read and referred, as I have said above.

There is another very serious disorder in the issuance of royal decrees

(cédulas) by some of the secretaries, especially Hernando de Zafra, the Treasurer Morales and Diego de la Muela, who dispatch many matters with the
King our lord and issue decrees without the approval of any member of the
Consejo, and with these decrees many excesses are committed throughout the
realm . . . Their Highnesses should instruct the members of the Consejo to
prepare the proper orders and approve them and they should tell Hernando
de Zafra and the Treasurer Morales not to bring any decrees for signature,
unless they have been authorized by the members of the Consejo.[23]

It is easy to see how this conflict of responsibility developed,
for the secretaries dealt directly with the King, who preferred to
reach his decisions without the interference or restraint of the
Consejo. After the death of the Queen in 1504, when Ferdinand
became governor of Castile, as well as king of Aragon, the authority of the Consejo was even further diminished.

There were even more serious abuses in the operation than
those pointed out by Carvajal. We have already mentioned the
practice of the kings of Aragon to hand out to their officials
special favors—gifts of money, appointments to office, expense
accounts—and this practice became firmly established in Castile
as well. Thus it was possible for an official to hold a long list of
offices for which he received a salary and whose duties he could
hire someone else to perform for a pittance. What is more, he
could sell or transfer any of these offices to another person at a
price. It is interesting that although the Cortes again and again
protested against these bad practices and though statesmen like
Cisneros and Gattinara later insisted that no man should hold
or be paid for more than one office and that no office should be
bought or sold, the bureaucrats were so solidly intrenched in
their privileges that no protests were of avail.

Finally, though it was not easy to present evidence, it was
widely believed that the secretaries received bribes in return
for favors they obtained, or promised to obtain, from the King,
and so were enriched. Describing the situation, Cisneros is reported to have said:

Many have come to the royal house with very little property and, once in
office, within four or five years were building great houses, buying estates,
establishing *mayorazgos*. And besides this, their ordinary expenditures were
so great that, even with the salaries they held in the royal accounts and the
special favors granted them, they far exceeded the amounts that they were
known to receive, so that what they bought and the estates they established
and the money that they gave in dowries they must have stolen, either from
the King or the kingdom. And it was a serious charge on the conscience of
the Prince to permit it, besides the harm it did his treasury.[24]

Climbing the Ladder

Such was the atmosphere of the official world which Cobos entered in 1503. We may be sure that in the first years his duties were humble ones—copying documents, later preparing the draft of royal orders for the approval of the Consejo and the secretary and for the signature of the King. But he was learning the trade, discovering how it was possible to add to the paltry 9,000 *maravedís* of his salary.

It does not seem probable that the Consejo and the Castilian secretaries accompanied King Ferdinand when he left for Aragon and Naples in the summer of 1506. Perhaps Cobos took advantage of the opportunity to return to Ubeda, for on September 13 he bought for his father some houses in the parish of Santo Tomás.[25] It may be, too, that at this time his father began the construction of the sturdy palace whose blackened façade still looks out on the narrow Calle de Francisco de los Cobos; in style, it seems to belong to the first decade of the century.

During the absence of the King in Italy both Hernando de Zafra and Gaspar de Gricio died, so that by the summer of 1507 Lope Conchillos is the only Castilian secretary whose name appears on the royal *cédulas*. And on December 24 of that year Ferdinand, now back in Spain, named Bishop Juan Rodríguez de Fonseca of the Consejo Real and Conchillos as the persons responsible for the conduct of all affairs affecting the Indies.[26] It is with the rise of Conchillos to a rôle of authority in the secretariat that Cobos begins to share in the distribution of favor. On January 14, 1508, a royal *cédula* of the Queen, Doña Juana, issued at the command of the King and countersigned at Burgos by Conchillos, appointed Cobos chief accountant *(contador mayor)* of Granada, a post left vacant by the death of Hernando de Zafra.[27] Although the *cédula* authorizes him to hold the office in person or to appoint a deputy to perform the duties, Cobos kept the post until the end of his life, when in accordance with the terms of his will it was transferred to his son. From 1508 on Cobos is known, both in official documents and to his contemporaries, as "servant" *(criado)*, or "officer" *(oficial)*, or "scribe" *(escribiente)* of Conchillos.[28]

Thanks to the influence of his chief, the record of the following years is studded with appointments and favors granted to Cobos by the King, and all countersigned by Conchillos. Before

the end of 1508 (October 3), Don Francisco was named councilman *(regidor)* of his home town of Ubeda, replacing Alonso
de Ribera "now dead and gone." [29] The royal decree does not
stipulate the salary, since it was undoubtedly paid by the municipal council of Ubeda, but that there was a salary is made clear
by another *cédula* of Ferdinand (February 15, 1509) in which
he instructs the city to pay Cobos' salary, as though he were
residing there, since he is occupied at Court in the royal service.[30]
Three years later he resigned the office in favor of his father,
Diego de los Cobos.[31] He must have been subsequently reappointed, for on June 12, 1518, Charles V authorized him to
transfer this and other posts to one of his sons or to any other
person who was not "a foreigner or infamous." [32] This time,
however, he continued to hold this office, too, until the end of
his life.

The only other favor *(merced)* granted to Cobos in 1509 was
an outright gift of two hundred ducats (75,000 *maravedís*)
from the King on May 15; [33] it was more than the salary he
received in eight years. But in the following year he received an
appointment which was to place him in a position where he could
wield a major influence in securing further appointments for himself and for his friends and relatives. On October 3, 1510, Ferdinand placed him in charge of recording all grants, offices, rewards, and payments of debts made by the King.[34] The salary
assigned was 35,000 *maravedís* a year, but apparently Cobos
had already been performing the duties of the office, for the pay
was made retroactive to March 1, 1510. He continued to receive this salary until 1515, when it was raised to 65,000
maravedís a year, a sum which was paid to him each year
through 1527, when he transferred the office to one of his
assistants, Juan de Enciso.[35]

The strategic importance of this post will readily be understood, for it placed in Cobos' hands the responsibility for recording all the royal decrees affecting individuals in Castile. Naturally, then, he was familiar with the salaries and emoluments
attached to each of the countless official posts in Castile and
the Indies; he was the first to be informed when a vacancy
occurred. The King could not be bothered with the burdensome
task of selecting the right man for each office. Hence it was
possible for Conchillos and Cobos to pick plums for themselves,
to do favors to their friends and relatives, and even to receive

a "gift" from office-seekers in return for an appointment. The historian Fernández de Oviedo recognized the importance of this new appointment when he wrote: "After the death of the secretary Zafra, Cobos entered the service of the secretary Lope Conchillos and there he was an excellent official and was placed in charge of the book of royal grants in Conchillos' house." [36]

Several years later (1516) there is a reference to the malpractices which grew out of this centralization of influence in the hands of Conchillos. In a *Memorial* addressed to Cardinal Cisneros, governor of Castile in the absence of Charles V, and perhaps written by Bartolomé de las Casas, among the long list of the offenses of Conchillos there appears the following charge: "Likewise it will be found that many abuses have been committed under instructions of Conchillos, if his books are investigated; for there is no other book of orders or dispatches except the one that he and an official of his [i.e. Cobos] keep, for everything was transacted by private decrees, from which he has derived a profit of more than four million *maravedís* each year." [37] But be it noted that the author of the *Memorial* brings no charge against Cobos.

Recently, in his volume on Bartolomé de las Casas, Giménez Fernández has quite without evidence created for Cobos the title of "Vice-Chancellor" in this new office. [38] But the title of Vice-Chancellor was never used in Castile in this period; it was an exclusively Aragonese title and office. As we shall see later, the Vice-Chancellor who was reported in Flanders in the summer of 1516 and whom Giménez identified as Cobos was certainly Antonio Agustín, Vice-Chancellor of Aragon. [39] It should be said in passing that Giménez's insinuation that Cobos shared with Conchillos in the loot has relatively little foundation. There is an occasional piece of evidence that he sold an office to which he had been appointed. But almost all the offices which he transferred to others went to his cousins and nephews or to his servants and assistants as a reward for their services. In this, within his little field, he was merely following the accepted practice of the Popes, Emperors, Kings, and Princes of his time.

It is not surprising that now that Cobos held so important a post in the official world of the Court, his reputation began to grow. In fact, before the end of October, 1510, the citizens of the ward (*colación*) of Santa Isabel in Granada elected him to the office of juryman (*jurado*), a post left vacant by the death

2. Guillaume de Croy, Seigneur de Chièvres, Grand Chamberlain of
Charles V (1509-1521)

By an unknown painter   *Bruxelles, Musées Royaux des Beaux-Arts*

3. The Palace of Bernardino Pimentel in the Corredera de San Pablo, Valladolid

This was the residence of Charles V during all of his stays in Valladolid. It later belonged to the Condes de Rivadavia and is now the Diputación Provincial.

4. The Church of San Pablo and the Palace of Pimentel in Valladolid

The frame of the door which led to the apartment of Juan Hurtado de Mendoza is visible on the north façade of the palace. Cobos' palace was on the opposite side of the Corredera, facing the church.

5. Coat of Arms of Cobos
Carved by Esteban Jamete on the façade of San Salvador, in Ubeda.

6. Coat of Arms of María de Mendoza

Carved by Jamete, San Salvador, Ubeda. It combines the arms of Mendoza and Sarmiento.

7. Charles V at the Time of his Coronation in Bologna (1530)
By Jan Cornelisz Vermeyen   *Bruxelles, Collection of Dr. Delporte*

8. Portrait Medal of Cobos
By Christoph Weiditz. Engraved at Brussels in 1531.

9. The Duke of Mantua Presents Titian to the Emperor (1532)

Pen and ink sketch by Titian. Since it was Cobos who urged the Duke to bring the painter to the Emperor's attention, the figure of the courtier at the right may be that of Cobos. *Besançon, Musée des Beaux-Arts*

uncertainty about the legality of the appointment and his prospects of collecting the tax, for he appealed to the King for a
confirmation of the grant, which was issued in the name of
Queen Juana on August 20, 1513.[44] His fears proved justified,
for the council of Granada protested. Eventually Cobos and the
city council submitted the question to the arbitration of the
Conde de Tendilla, who finally ruled in favor of the city on
condition that they make a single payment of two hundred
ducats to Cobos (April 5, 1519).[45] The latter assented to the
ruling at Barcelona a few months later (August 29).[46]

A much more important favor from the King came on April
19, 1513, when he was appointed clerk of the criminal court
(escribano del crimen) in Úbeda.[47] The municipal council seems
to have objected at first to the appointment, but on reconsidera-
tion they gave their approval on January 25, 1514. One of the
councilmen who signed the document was Don Diego, Cobos'
father, who, as we have seen, replaced his son in the council in
January, 1512. On receipt of the council's approval, Ferdinand
confirmed the original appointment, and after Charles V had
come to Spain Cobos again secured his confirmation; [48] in fact,
he held the office—and its salary—until his death. We may
guess that it was a profitable sinecure from the fact that the
similar post in the nearby town of Baeza yielded an income of
a thousand ducats a year.[49]

In the following months Cobos continued to pick up minor
grants and favors from the King—houses and lands in Avila,[50]
the privilege of collecting a tax on the washing and packing of
salt and fresh fish in Malaga,[51] the right to a commission on
fines imposed in Andalusia and Leon.[52] The last of these documents (June 16, 1514) is the first in which Bartolomé Ruiz de
Castañeda appears as secretary. Pérez de Almazán had died in
April, 1514,[53] and it was probably at this time that Castañeda
was added to the secretarial staff for Castile. In the conduct of
Aragonese affairs Almazán was replaced by Pedro de Quintana,
a protégé of Almazán and uncle of Lope Conchillos, who had
entered the service of Ferdinand in 1508 [54] as "heater of the
wax" *(calefactor)* and who had already been sent to France as
a special ambassador in 1513. The other Aragonese secretary
was Ugo de Urríes, who had been an *escribano de mandamiento*
since 1504.[55]

There are a few other documents of this period which give

a glimpse of Cobos' activities. At some time in 1513 he authorized his cousin, Francisco de Molina, to sell the property in
Benalúa which had been granted to his father as a reward for
his part in the final campaign against Granada.[56] On the last
day of the year he bought a mill-wheel from Aldonza de Perea,[57]
widow of Juan Vázquez, whose daughter married his nephew,
Jorge de Molina. His name must have been becoming known
even in the Indies, for on June 26, 1514, Vasco Núñez de Balboa, fresh from the discovery of the Pacific, named him as one
of his agents to protect his interests in Spain.[58] But even so, he
was evidently a vague figure to Balboa, for he does not mention
his first name and refers to him only as an "officer" of Conchillos.

At home, however, he was steadily gaining in prestige. On
May 8, 1515, the municipal council of Granada named him and
Juan Alvarez Zapata as their representatives (procuradores)
at the Cortes to be held at Burgos.[59] There is no record of the
part he played in the proceedings of the Cortes, but we may
be sure that he shared in the largesse which the King regularly
bestowed on the municipal representatives. The statement of
Oviedo that Ferdinand named him a scribe or secretary of the
Consejo Real is borne out by a document dated at Buitrago on
October 24, 1515, in which he was appointed a Court scribe
(escribano de cámara), "among those who are to reside in my
Consejo," at a salary of 9,000 maravedís a year.[60] He took the
oath of office on November 2, before the members of the Consejo. Oviedo adds that he sold this office and was then named
secretary of the Infante Don Fernando. The first part of his
statement is confirmed by a note on the cédula of appointment
that the post was transferred to one Juan de Oviedo at Cobos'
request. The latter part is not attested by any contemporary
document. If it is true, his duties must have been light, for the
Infante was then twelve years old. Perhaps it was only one more
sinecure. At least the paymaster's records reveal that this year
his salary as recorder of royal grants was raised from 35,000
to 65,000 maravedís, in addition to the 9,000 maravedís he received as scribe.[61] Now that his income was so handsome he was
able to indulge in a passion which was to continue throughout
his life—the acquisition of landed property; on June 30, 1515,
he bought a corral in the parish of San Millán in Ubeda.[62]

During the years from 1511 to 1515 there are many documents that attest his performance of the task of recording royal grants—instructions from the King or Consejo Real, notes on the back of *cédulas* that a grant had been recorded.[63] The last mention of his activity in this function is a marginal note on a document of December 15, 1515: "Cobos entered this memorandum without any date because none could be found." [64] Giménez believes that this is another example of Conchillos' skullduggery by which he antedated an appointment.[65] It is possible that he is right and that Cobos was a party to the trick. But it is also possible to interpret the statement literally, as an example of someone's failure to enter the proper date on the original document.

At the end of 1515 Cobos had been a dozen years in the royal service. He had risen steadily in influence and responsibility. If he had not yet achieved the title of secretary, he was at least Conchillos' chief assistant. He had acquired a comfortable income, and what was more important, he had become experienced in all the intricacies of operation within the secretariat. This experience was soon to serve him in good stead.

Hour of Decision

King Ferdinand's health had been failing in the spring of 1515. In June, after the Cortes of Burgos, he had been at the point of death and had made a new will in which he named his favorite grandson, the Infante Don Fernando, as his successor. But he recovered sufficiently to start once more on his restless wandering—to Aranda del Duero, to Segovia, to Calatayud (for the Cortes of Aragon), to Madrid, to Palencia.[66] Late in the year he started south, intending to spend the winter in Seville, to which he had already sent the President of the Consejo Real, Don Antonio de Rojas, Bishop of Granada, and most of the members of the Consejo.

Early in January, 1516, he reached the little village of Madrigalejo, near Trujillo, and here his condition suddenly grew worse. There was a rumor abroad that his illness was the result of a potion which his new Queen, Germana, had given him in hope that it would restore his virility and enable her to bear an heir to the throne. Ferdinand was at first unwilling to believe that the end was at hand. But he finally resigned himself and made his confession. Then he summoned his three most trusted

Castilian councillors, Carvajal, Zapata, and the Treasurer Vargas, to advise him concerning the future of his kingdoms. Reluctantly he yielded to their counsel, revoked and destroyed the will that he had drawn up at Burgos, and named his eldest grandson, Charles, as his heir, settling an income on the Infante Don Fernando from his Neapolitan possessions. Even more reluctantly he accepted their advice to name the aged Cardinal Cisneros as Regent of Castile, until Charles should come to take possession of his kingdom. As Regent of Aragon, Cataluña, and Valencia he nominated his bastard son, Alfonso de Aragón, archbishop of Zaragoza. The will was signed in the presence of the *protonotario,* Velázquez Climent, on the afternoon of January 22. Shortly after midnight that night he was dead.

It is probable that, as *escribano* of the Consejo Real, Cobos had accompanied the President and the other members of the Consejo to Seville and that, on the receipt of the news of the King's death, with them he hurried to Guadalupe, where the leaders of the kingdom were gathering to meet the crisis in the affairs of state. Many conflicting interests were represented in the group that assembled there in the last days of January. There was the Infante and his supporters, still ignorant of the change in Ferdinand's will and anxious to seize control; there was Adrian of Utrecht, who had been sent from Flanders by the advisors of Charles as his ambassador, with secret instructions to take over the government in Charles' name on the death of the King; there were the noblemen, like the Duque de Alba and the Marqués de Denia, determined to carry out the wishes of the King; there were councillors, prelates, and officials. And presently came the newly appointed Regent, Cardinal Cisneros.

The deathbed decision of Ferdinand had completely changed the prospects for the future. The Infante was discarded; the regency of Cisneros was valid only until the coming of Charles. Clearly any solution of the affairs of Castile must be a temporary one and clearly, too, all those who sought for favor and advancement must look to the young King Charles, a vague figure off there in the mists of Flanders.

Cisneros and Adrian arrived at a sort of compromise, and on February 1 they left for Madrid, where Cisneros had decided to establish the seat of his provisional government. Perhaps Cobos went with him. But like so many other Castilians and so many of his comrades in the secretariat of Ferdinand, he was

faced with the necessity of a decision with regard to the future.
Should he remain in the service of the Cardinal, or should he
try his fortune at the Court of Charles? He might well expect
preferment from Cisneros, for he was one of the few "old
Christians" in the secretariat of Ferdinand, which was so largely
made up of *conversos*. But he knew the inflexible integrity of
Cisneros and his intolerance of malfeasance and bribery in public office. There was slight prospect that he could look to him
for a continuance of the lavish favors he had received from
King Ferdinand. On the other hand, there was the possibility
of winning a place in the service of the royal youth in Flanders.
There were difficulties in the way—the long journey by land and
sea, his ignorance of French, the language of the Flemish Court,
his lack of any sure protector in that strange land. But his hopes
and ambitions were high. He was almost forty; he had had modest success in his career; he had gathered a little money. If ever
he was to achieve distinction, now was the time to gamble on
the future. And so he made the momentous decision, the decision that was to shape the rest of his life: he would try his
fortune in the service of the young King.

Two of his old associates elected to remain in the service of
the Cardinal: Lope Conchillos and Juan Ruiz de Calcena. Both
of them soon fell into disfavor under the watchful eye of Cisneros. Conchillos, overwhelmed by the charges of malfeasance
lodged against him by Bartolomé de las Casas, was dismissed
in June (the last document that he signed was dated June 4) [67]
and found his way to Flanders. He was replaced by Jorge de
Baracaldo who, if we may judge by his letters, was no less concerned for his personal preferment and profit than his predecessor.[68] Calcena was charged in October, 1516, with having
embezzled 30,000 ducats from the funds of the Inquisition in
the royal treasury, but in 1517 he was still on the payroll.[69]

Most of the other secretaries followed Cobos' example and
left for Flanders. Ugo de Urríes must have started immediately
after the death of Ferdinand, for on February 24 he wrote
from the Basque town of Iruiranzo that he had been forced to
turn back from Bayonne in France for fear of capture by the
French and that he was planning to make the journey by sea.[70]
He was in Brussels in April and was confirmed in his post as
secretary, for on April 19 he countersigned a royal *cédula*. A
few months later (August 29) Charles issued an instruction to

Cisneros to pay Urríes his salary for 1516, reminding him that he was to pay the salaries of the secretaries who were in service in Flanders as well as those who had remained in Spain.[71] Probably through his intervention the King issued an order on April 20, instructing Cisneros to release from prison the Vice-Chancellor of Aragon, Antonio Agustín.[72]

Agustín had been arrested at the order of the King immediately after the Cortes of Calatayud and since then had been confined in the fortress of Simancas. Historians differ in their account of the cause of his arrest. Abarca states that it was due to his efforts to dissuade the Cortes from granting the usual subsidy to the Crown.[73] Sandoval, on the other hand, charges that it was the result of his having made love to Queen Germana.[74] Whatever the cause, Cisneros must have complied promptly with Charles' instructions for his release, for he was in Flanders on July 28, when Cisneros' agent there, Diego López de Ayala, wrote to the Cardinal that the Chancellor had arrived and was in charge of Aragonese affairs as completely as in the lifetime of Ferdinand.[75] On June 9, 1517, Charles made him a grant of a thousand ducats to cover the expenses of his journey and his residence in Flanders.[76]

Of the other secretaries who made their way to the Court of the young King we need mention only Pedro de Quintana. He had been referred to as chief of the Aragonese secretaries in a list of officials prepared for Charles early in 1516,[77] and on his arrival in Brussels he was promptly confirmed in his post. The earliest cédula which he countersigned there is dated July 28, 1516,[78] but on July 12 López de Ayala had written to Cisneros: "Quintana is back in office, as before, except for the cipher of Rome and Your Lordship's affairs, for until I know what Your Lordship wishes, I have not been willing to have him attend to them." [79] On September 16 Charles instructed Cisneros to pay him his salary of 250,000 maravedís as secretary.[80] He continued in service until March 20, 1517, when he received permission to return to Spain, without loss of his salary, to visit his family.[81]

We do not know when Cobos reached Flanders. We have mentioned the difficulty which Urríes encountered when he attempted to pass through France. The historian Fernández de Oviedo tells us that he too left for Flanders immediately after the death of Ferdinand, but he was delayed on the journey by a series of mishaps. The ship on which he embarked was forced back to Spain several times by contrary winds; and having landed in England, he finally crossed the Channel from Dover to Calais, after a trip of almost four months.[82] Whether Cobos met similar *contretemps* we cannot tell, but it seems probable that he reached Brussels at some time during the spring. In the following months he must have been busy learning French. From a hint of Oviedo's we may surmise that it was Ugo de Urríes who introduced him to the Grand Chamberlain, Chièvres.[83] By the end of the summer he had entered the latter's service and was back on the royal payroll. On October 31 the King ordered Cisneros to pay Cobos his salary of 74,000 *maravedís,* explaining that "he came to serve us and has been and is here in our service." [84]

———————•◦⟨∞⟩◦•———————

CHAPTER II

SECRETARY OF CHARLES V

The First Appointment

It was through the influence of Chièvres that Cobos received
on December 12, 1516, the appointment that was to mark the
beginning of a new career: on that day he was named Secretary
of the King. Like all royal appointments of the time, the *cédula*
justifies the action on "the many and goodly services which you
have performed for the King and Queen our lords—God rest
their souls!—and for our royal crown." [1] It provides that he
was to continue his function in charge of the registry of royal
grants and for the present he was to receive a total salary of
100,000 *maravedís* a year. The *cédula* was approved by the
Grand Chancellor, Jean Sauvage, the Bishop of Badajoz, and
Don García de Padilla, and was countersigned by the secretary,
Antonio de Villegas. On December 20, Cobos appeared before
the Grand Chancellor and García de Padilla, took the oath of
office, and was approved.

The day before his formal appointment, December 11, Cobos
wrote to Cardinal Cisneros to announce his good fortune and
to offer his thanks for Cisneros' support. Since this is the first
personal letter that has survived, written in his own hand, we
should quote it here, for in spite of its stiff, awkward style it is
typical of hundreds of letters he was to write during his public
career.

Most Reverend and Most Illustrious Sir:

I have never written to Your Most Reverend Lordship since I came here, because there was nothing in which I could serve you; and what I now have to say is that the King our lord has been pleased to order that I be received as a secretary and I think that I will serve M. de Chièvres. A principal cause of this outcome has been the letter which Your Most Reverend Lordship has had written in my behalf and for this I kiss the hands of Your Most Reverend Lordship a hundred thousand times. I have nothing to offer, for I have always counted and now count myself as a servant of your Most Illustrious Lordship.

But very humbly I beg you to have confidence that wherever I may be, I shall count myself as such and that my desire is and will be to be able to serve Your Most Reverend Lordship in some way, since thereby God and the King are served. And for my own part I owe it to Your Most Reverend Lordship, because I always received from you many a mercy and favor.

From Brussels, 11th of December.

Your Most Reverend and Most Illustrious Lordship's

Very certain servant, who kisses your most reverend hands,

Francisco de los Cobos [2]

All of Cobos' contemporaries attribute his rise to power to the favor which he won with Chièvres, though Oviedo remarks that he bought his first appointment as secretary from a Flemish secretary.[3] How shall we explain his appeal to the dour Chamberlain of Charles, with his grim face and tight lips? In our own time Brandi has expressed the belief that Chièvres was attracted by his Andalusian wit and good humor.[4] But Cobos' letter to Cisneros makes it clear that he came with the Cardinal's recommendation. What is more, Chièvres must have been impressed by his long record of service in the affairs of Castile, by his intimate acquaintance with the members of the Consejo and the other officials, and by his capacity in handling financial matters. Perhaps too he was influenced by the fact that of all the officials who made their way to Flanders Cobos was almost the only one without a Jewish taint. From now on Cobos was a loyal servant and supporter of Chièvres; from him he was to receive favor after favor. But before we begin the story of his life as secretary, let us stop for a moment to take a brief glance at the new world into which he was entering at the Flemish Court.

The Court in Flanders

The young Prince Charles, known as the Duke of Luxembourg, had grown up virtually an orphan.[5] His parents, Philip the

Fair and Juana of Castile, had left him and his sisters, Eleanor and Isabel, in Flanders when they returned to Spain in 1505. A year later Philip died suddenly after a banquet, and Juana, swept over the brink of madness, was confined by her father in the castle of Tordesillas, where she was to spend the rest of her long, empty life. In 1507 Charles' grandfather, the Emperor Maximilian, placed his grandchildren in the care of their aunt, Margaret of Austria, who widowed a second time by the death of her husband, the Duke of Savoy, had returned to Flanders, accompanied by two of her Savoyard counsellors, Mercurino Gattinara and Laurent Gorrevod.

In the quiet town of Malines she built a sumptuous palace, which she adorned with works of art and rich hangings, as a residence for her little wards, and there she gave them a truly maternal affection and care. The atmosphere of her Court was essentially Burgundian; she and the children spoke only French. But Charles' grandfather was concerned with the training of the little boy who was to be the ruler of so many lands, for by a strange combination of dynastic marriages and untimely deaths, on his frail shoulders was to fall the weight of a world empire. From Maximilian he was to inherit the Hapsburg estates of Austria and the Tyrol; as heir of Marie of Burgundy he was to be the ruler of the Low Countries and even to hold a precarious claim on the Duchy of Burgundy, which had reverted to the crown of France; as son of Queen Juana he was heir presumptive to the throne of Castile; from his grandfather Ferdinand he would one day inherit the crown of Aragon and the Aragonese estates in Naples and Sicily; finally he would be the possessor of the still unsuspected treasures of the New World beyond the Atlantic which Columbus had discovered in the name of their Catholic Majesties.

As his teacher, Maximilian chose the devout and learned Dean of Louvain, Adrian of Utrecht, who had associated with him a group of scholars to instruct Charles in the rudiments of Latin and to teach him to love history. One of them was a Spaniard, Luis Cabeza de Vaca, but he seems to have taught Charles no Spanish. Even though he was a frail boy, his chief interests were in manly sports. With his Burgundian playmates he learned early to sit a horse well, to splinter a lance in the joust, to hunt with dog and falcon. When he was nine years old Maximilian appointed as his governor and Grand Chamberlain a distinguished

Burgundian nobleman, Guillaume de Croy, Lord of Chièvres, who was to remain as his chief counsellor until his death. By him he was initiated in the art of government. These three—Margaret, Adrian, and Chièvres—shaped his personality. From his aunt he acquired the sense of his divine right to rule and his obligation to promote the interests of his dynasty. If he showed any tendency to arrogance, it was restrained by Adrian, who developed in him a strong feeling of piety and of responsibility for the service of God and the Church. Finally, it was Chièvres who opened his eyes to the complexities and duplicities of international negotiation.

Charles was hardly fifteen years old when his grandfather decided to declare him of age and give him the authority in Flanders. On January 5, 1515, in the Parliament Hall of the castle of Brussels, he was proclaimed as ruler and took the oath of office before the assembled Estates. After a triumphal visitation to the cities of Flanders and the Netherlands, he returned to Brussels and took up his residence in the palace there, assigning to his elder sister Eleanor separate quarters in the palace.

Now began his real apprenticeship. Chièvres slept in the room with him and watched over his every step. He took him to meetings of the Council and began to discuss with him important matters of state. But except for ceremonial occasions he kept him isolated from the rest of the world. Charles was a shy boy and of no mind to exercise power. Years later he told the Archbishop of Capua: "The truth is that as long as he was alive, M. de Chièvres governed me." But Chièvres was moved by a high purpose in his efforts to train his young master. When the French ambassador, Genlis, asked him in 1515 why he made the young Prince work so hard, he replied: "My cousin, I am the keeper and guardian of his youth. When I die, I want him to be free to act, for if he did not understand his affairs, he would have to have, after my demise, another guardian, because he had not understood his affairs nor been trained to work, depending always on some one else."

The news of Ferdinand's death reached Brussels in nine days (February 1, 1516) and it brought about a radical change in the picture. Because of his mother's incompetence, Charles might now rightfully claim the throne of Spain. On the evening of March 13 a solemn procession issued from the palace gate—prelates, knights of the Golden Fleece, ambassadors, gentlemen of the Court, the young Prince, draped in mourning and mounted on a mule—and lighted by hundreds of torches, made its way to the cathedral of Sainte Gudule. The walls of the church were hung with black brocade, and thousands of tapers sputtered on the catafalque that occupied the crossing and on the high altar. There was a requiem mass and a sermon on the vanity of human ambitions. When the vespers were over the Prince and his company returned to the palace.

The next morning another procession moved from the palace to the cathedral. Down the main aisle went thirteen knights bearing the banners of King Ferdinand's kingdoms; they were followed by three knights carrying the symbols of his knighthood—a shield, a helmet, and a sword. Charles, still draped in mourning, came last and took his seat in the chancel. When the mass was over—it was sung that morning by a Spaniard, Alonso Manrique, Bishop of Córdoba—a herald of the Order of the Golden Fleece mounted the steps of the high altar, and turning to the throng that filled the church, called in a loud voice: "King Don Fernando!" From the depths of the church came an answer: "He is dead!" Three times the herald called; three times the answer came: "He is dead!" Then the knights who bore the royal symbols threw them to the floor and the herald cried: "Long live their Catholic Majesties, Queen Juana and King Charles!" At this the young King threw off his mourning cowl, and advancing to the altar received from the Bishop's hands a newly consecrated sword. Facing the congregation, he brandished the sword aloft, while the church resounded to the thousand-voiced cry: "Long live the King!" A week later, on the advice of Chièvres and his counsellors he wrote to the Consejo Real in Spain that he had determined to assume the title of "King of Spain."

The Court over which he ruled in Flanders was one of pomp and circumstance. The dominant figures were almost all members of the old Flemish and Burgundian nobility, and they lived in an atmosphere of extravagant display which was a last survival of mediaeval pageantry. Costumes, furnishings, ornaments were of the costliest kind. Charles himself is said to have spent the equivalent of $75,000 on clothes in eight months. Banquets, hunting-parties, tournaments were the order of the day. Before the end of 1515, Chièvres had reorganized the household of the Prince. The *Ordonnance* establishing the new structure (October 25)

has fortunately survived to give us some picture of the elaborate-
ness of Court ceremonial.[6] It is a formidable list, giving the
title and salaries of hundreds of the courtiers—the "Great
Chapel," the "Little Chapel," the Council, led by Jean Sauvage,
the Grand Chancellor, and Adrian of Utrecht, chaplains and
choristers, masters of the household, gentlemen of the bedcham-
ber, of the cellar and stables, squires, pages, officers of the guard.
The good burghers of Flanders must have had great pride in
their young lord to have voted the subsidies necessary to support
so lavish an establishment.

Spaniards in Flanders

In the list of members of the Prince's household there appear
the names of a few Spaniards. We must remember that after
the death of Philip the Fair in 1506 a number of his Spanish
supporters, like Juan Manuel, had left Spain and established
themselves in Flanders in the service of Charles. Sancho Cota,
in his still unpublished *Memorias de Carlos V*, gives a list of
scores of people who thus had joined the Flemish Court. Some
of them were clerics—Alonso Manrique, Bishop of Badajoz,
Luis Cabeza de Vaca, Pedro Ruiz de la Mota. Mota, "Master
of Sacred Theology," became Court preacher and counsellor of
the Emperor Maximilian, and one of the first requests that the
young Charles made to his grandfather Ferdinand was a recommendation that he nominate Mota to the vacant bishopric of
Catania (October 25, 1508).[7] After Charles' accession to the
throne, Mota became his chief Spanish advisor.

Few of the higher Spanish noblemen joined the Flemish
Court, but in addition to Juan Manuel there were members of
distinguished families, many of them younger sons, like Juan
de Zúñiga, Pedro Puertocarrero, or Diego de Guevara. These
were the men who occupied minor posts in the household of
Charles in the *Ordonnance* of 1515.

After the death of Ferdinand there was a general exodus
from Spain to Flanders. But again, almost none of the grandees
left the country. In fact, the contemporary historian, Santa
Cruz, wrote: "Many persons went where His Highness was,
most of them of lowly estate and little known in these parts, to
gain appointments in the King's household, and others to carry
on dubious business in which they had been engaged during the

lifetime of the Catholic King and to slander and speak ill of others toward whom they had no good will. And, in truth, for the good of the kingdom and the service of the King it would have been better if they never had gone there . . . And they did not fail to seek to buy appointments, so that often past services and good habits and experience in affairs were of no avail, unless they were accompanied by money. In this the Grand Chancellor, Jean Sauvage, was largely to blame." [8] From Flanders, too, there is evidence of the rush of office-seekers, for on June 23, 1516, the British ambassador, Tunstal, wrote to Cardinal Wolsey from Brussels: "Great numbers of Spaniards come here every day, petitioning for offices and fees. They are all told no grants can be made till the King go to Spain." Two weeks later (July 10) he wrote again: "The Spaniards daily increase. The Chancellor can never come to the Court but he is waylaid by 100 or 50 mules." [9]

Not all those who came were riffraff. On July 28 Diego López de Ayala wrote to Cisneros: "The day of Santiago (July 25) was celebrated in the chapel in the Spanish style; there were twenty-four commanders of the Order at vespers and at the mass." [10] Among the new arrivals there were also former counsellors of Ferdinand, such as García de Padilla, whom the King paid a thousand florins to keep him from going to Flanders [11] and who now was elevated to the post of advisor to Charles and, with Mota, made responsible for approving all royal orders. Another was Dr. Diego Beltrán, a member of the Consejo of Castile, of whom López de Ayala wrote: "Dr. Beltrán is back in the Council, they say through the door of sheer cash." [12]

During these months while the young King lingered in Flanders, waiting for his counsellors to terminate their negotiations with France and England, Cisneros and his associates in Spain were busy trying to find some way of extracting their new King from the hands of the Flemings and making him truly a King of Spain. The correspondence of his secretaries and agents is filled with their concern on this subject. Ayala believed that they would do well to support Mota as chief secretary because he spoke French and so could communicate directly with the King; besides, he was a loyal servant of the Cardinal.[13] But Alonso Manrique wrote Cisneros, as early as March, 1516, that they must be looking for a well-trained man of learning to assume the duties of prime minister, or at least have one ready when the King reached Spain.[14] Thus were laid the foundations for the struggle between the Spaniards and the Flemish advisors of the King which was to eventuate in civil war in Spain.

We have seen how most of the secretaries of Ferdinand had gone to Flanders and had been confirmed in their old offices— an action sorely distressing to Cisneros and his friends, who knew that they were venal and unscrupulously greedy. What was worse for most of these good churchmen: most of them were *conversos*. Let us look for a moment at the situation which they and Cobos found in the secretariat of Charles.

In his long letter of March, Bishop Manrique gave a detailed account of the organization.[15] A number of gentlemen—he explained—had been appointed to the post of secretary, even though secretaries were held in slight esteem and were called "clerques," because there were no other vacancies and a member of the royal household must have a title in order to receive a salary. At the time, there was no expectation that they would perform any duties. But in spite of their lack of qualifications, they had begun to serve as secretaries, a most unhappy situation, "because though they may be good persons for other things, it is not proper that they should perform the duties of this office, out of regard for the honor of the Prince and his conscience." According to the account-books there were ten secretaries of the Council in 1504 and 1508.[16] The *Ordonnance* of 1515 listed six full-time and fourteen half-time secretaries, the First Secretary and *audiencier* being Philippe Haneton, who alone was authorized to sign financial documents. At the end of the list is a note that no new appointments were to be made until the number had been reduced to six.[17] Nevertheless, on December 16, 1515, eleven men were appointed or reappointed to the post.[18]

Among those named in the *Ordonnance* were three Spaniards. The senior was Antonio de Villegas. With him in the conduct of the correspondence with Castile was Gonzalo de Segovia, who once had been master of the household of the Infante Don Fernando and whom Philip the Fair had made his first secretary.[19] Bishop Manrique had confidence in him and recommended him warmly to Cisneros as a person who could be trusted.[20] The third of the Spanish secretaries was Pedro Ximénez, who seems to have been in charge of the correspondence with regard to Aragonese affairs. The names of these three appear regularly

on official documents of 1516 and 1517. We have already mentioned the confirmation in office of Pedro de Quintana and Ugo
de Urríes; their names and those of Pedro de Barrionuevo and
Gáspar Sánchez de Orihuela also appear on the *cédulas* of the
period. There was at least one other Spanish secretary in Flanders, Sancho Cota, who was in the service of the Infanta Eleanor. In his *Memorias* he reports that when Chièvres received
word that King Ferdinand was dead, he summoned all the Spanish officials to his office and promised to confirm them in their
positions, to triple their salaries, and to do them other favors
in the future.[21] Clearly the Grand Chamberlain was determined
not to have them wooed away by any offers from the authorities in Spain.

One cannot but wonder what must have been the impact of
this brilliant, extravagant Court on the Spaniards who came
there. Both Ferdinand and Isabel had lived simply, almost
austerely; Spanish castles were bare; Spanish towns were for the
most part drab. Only her cathedrals and churches were enriched
with works of art. If the newcomers from Spain were for the
moment dazzled by the opulence of the world around them, like
good Spaniards, they quickly recovered their poise and took a
high resolve to have a share of these good things for themselves.
There was but one road to success: the service of the King.

New Duties

Cobos took up his new office as secretary on January 1, 1517.
He countersigned a royal order of January 25 at Brussels,[22]
and there are other documents with his signature in the following months, although Antonio de Villegas continued to sign most
of the Spanish papers of the King. Evidently he was gaining in
favor with Chièvres, for on March 3 Charles issued an instruction that, in spite of his earlier order that Cobos was to receive
a total salary of 100,000 *maravedís* (the regular stipend of the
secretaries), he now approved of adding to that amount the
65,000 *maravedís* which he had formerly received for his duties
in charge of the registry of royal *mercedes*.[23] On March 26 he
received another appointment: he was placed in charge of keeping the record of all sums received and paid by the royal treasurers of Castile. The salary assigned was 113,000 *maravedís*
(approximately 300 ducats) a year.[24] Apparently this sum was

to be paid by the Treasurer Vargas, not by the royal paymaster, if we may judge by a faint note on the margin of the document. His total salary of 278,000 *maravedís* was already greater than that of any of the other secretaries, even of Pedro de Quintana.

The paymasters in Spain were evidently taking their duties seriously, for they had refused to pay the salaries of the members of the Consejo and the secretaries who were in Flanders because the royal order referred only to the "Councillors and secretaries who reside in this my Court," without mentioning any names. As a result, the King issued a new instruction on June 26, specifically ordering the payment of Cobos' salary for 1517.[25] A month later he wrote to Cisneros from Middelburg, explaining why he had appointed Cobos to his new post, with a clear statement of his duties: "to take and keep the record of our income and finances and what is paid out and consigned to our treasurers and other persons, that all this might be done in conformity with what you had established and discussed." [26] Is it possible that Cisneros had recommended Cobos as a person competent to perform this function?

In view of his new duties, it is not surprising that it was Cobos who countersigned an instruction of April 21 to the Cardinal-Regent ordering him to turn over to the Treasurer Vargas 20,-000 ducats, to be taken from the money which he held, whether from the Indies, the Cruzada, or other sources.[27] Giménez Fernández believes that this was an intentional affront to Cisneros,[28] implying malfeasance, but it seems more probable that the language used is the formula regularly employed in issuing instructions for payments. The most significant aspect is the evidence it brings that thus, at the very beginning of his reign, Charles and his advisors were in financial straits, seeking money from every possible source.

As we have already remarked, Cobos' old protector, Lope Conchillos, had left Spain early in June, 1516. He was in Flanders by the end of July and was no doubt welcomed by his old friends Quintana and Urríes, as well as by Cobos. In Spain, the Cardinal and his followers were disturbed at the possibility of his restoration to favor. The Cardinal's secretary, Baracaldo, wrote to López de Ayala on October 14, 1516: "No news can come to the Cardinal which will displease him more than to hear that Conchillos has been received [as secretary], and in keeping with what the Cardinal wrote you on this matter, you must press this point in his behalf . . . In one way or another you must try to keep him from entering the service. Otherwise it would be a great mockery of the Cardinal." [29]

But Conchillos had too many friends at Court. He was back on the payroll as secretary in 1517. And presently new favors were bestowed on him. On May 2, 1517, he was granted an *ayuda de costa* of 50,000 *maravedís* a year; [30] on June 12 he was confirmed in his post as secretary of the Orders of Alcántara and Calatrava, [31] from which he had been removed by Cisneros. The news of this last appointment was a bitter blow to Baracaldo, for in October of the year before the Cardinal had nominated him for the post and had written to ask the King for his approval. [32] In Flanders, López de Ayala realized that he was fighting a losing battle. Writing to the Cardinal on August 30, 1516, with regard to the creation of a new "Consejo de Castilla" and a "Consejo de Aragón, Nápoles y Cecilia," he added: "Conchillos and the Vice-Chancellor [Antonio Agustín] are here and soon will be back in office; so too will all the rest who come." And bitterly he continued: "If I had not checked this gang of *conversos* [*la marranilla*] who are here, it would have become a synagogue by now. None of the men named in Spain will be approved; the King dislikes them." [33]

This was not the only case in which the Cardinal was overruled in Flanders. Several other nominations which he had made had been rejected and other men appointed. [34] This was a matter of grave concern to Cisneros. In the letter of October 14, 1516, already mentioned, Baracaldo had reported to López de Ayala how important it was that the Cardinal should have authority to fill vacancies in Spain, "because to have the power to take away and not the power to give is an office of the devil and makes a man the enemy of everyone." [35] By now it was clear that he had lost control. Thanks to Chièvres, the men whom he detested and whom he had scourged from office as unworthy public servants were back in power. For a man who loved authority as Cisneros did—albeit authority to promote some worthy cause—it must have been a bitter blow to realize that he could no longer cope with the King's advisors in Flanders. He was soon to have evidence of their power.

In all this unsuccessful struggle by Cisneros and his supporters to keep the "old gang" of secretaries from returning to office under the new régime, it is significant that the name of Cobos is never mentioned. Evidently Cisneros did not consider him one of the dangerous people; perhaps he even recommended him for preferment. The letter which Cobos wrote to him on the occasion of his appointment as secretary, then, is not merely a matter of formal courtesy, but may be interpreted as proof of cordial relations between the aging Regent and the newcomer in the royal service. Certainly we would not be justified in assuming that at this stage of his career Cobos had any decisive part in the relations between the Flemish Court and the Cardinal. Decisions were made, not by the King, but by Chièvres and his associates, including Bishop Mota and García de Padilla. It was Cobos' task to prepare the Spanish version of some of these decisions and to countersign them. But as long as he was in Flanders, he was one of the least of the Spanish secretaries.

Charles' First Visit to his Spanish Kingdoms

Almost from the day of King Ferdinand's death the Cardinal-Regent and the Council of Castile had been imploring the young king to come to Spain to govern his deserted and orphaned subjects. Although Charles repeatedly assured them of his intent to undertake the journey at the earliest possible moment, Chièvres and his associates felt it necessary to settle affairs in Flanders before they embarked on a new venture. Relations with France were patched up by the unrealistic Peace of Noyon (August 13, 1516), and on October 29 Charles's representatives signed a treaty of alliance with Henry VIII of England and the Pope, at the very time when the Chapter of the Order of the Golden Fleece was being celebrated with the usual pomp and ceremony in Brussels. The early months of 1517 dragged on with other political problems, but by May Chièvres had decided that it was time to undertake the trip to Spain. One wonders if Sancho Cota was close to the truth when he wrote that the long delay in reaching a decision was motivated by the desire of Charles's counselors to give him time to mature before he assumed his new duties.[36]

With his Court, Charles left Brussels for Ghent on May 4. There he remained for a month, during which he met with the Estates of Flanders on June 16 to explain the reasons for his departure and bid them farewell. On July 4 he reached Middelburg on the coast, where the fleet had already been assembled.

But the Fates were not propitious: for two months contrary winds made sailing dangerous. And so for two months Charles and his Court idled their time away, never far from the port. There were boat rides and visits to the fleet; there were rabbit hunts in the dunes around Westhoven. As the days grew shorter and the nights grew colder, many of the courtiers were convinced that the voyage would have to be postponed till the following spring; some of them started removing their baggage from the ships.

Then, suddenly, on the night of September 5 the wind shifted to the northwest and the sky was bright with stars. Early the next morning the pilots informed the King's counsellors that conditions were favorable and if they could sail at once they should be in Spain in six days. It was immediately decided to follow their advice. All day on Sunday and on Monday there was a mad rush to get the baggage aboard and to provide the necessary supplies of food and water. Late Monday afternoon Charles and his Court embarked on their appointed ships, to be ready for departure on the following morning.

It was a proud fleet that weighed anchor at five o'clock on Tuesday morning—forty ships large and small. The King's ship, the largest of all, was gaily painted green and red, with gold trimmings; the sails, too, bore paintings of the Crucifixion between the columns of Hercules with the device *Plus Oultre,* the Trinity, Our Lady with the Christ Child, and the saints—Santiago, St. Nicholas, St. Christopher with his feet in the sea. To keep the fleet together there was an elaborate set of sailing orders regarding lights and cannon shots.

Chief among the three hundred people who embarked on the King's ship was his sister, Eleanor. During the days of waiting on the coast, Charles had discovered that she was having a clandestine love affair with Frederick, Count Palatine, when he snatched from her a letter which she tried to hide in the bosom of her dress. Clearly it was not safe to leave her in Flanders; she was too valuable a pawn in Charles's dynastic schemes to waste on a petty nobleman. Her secretary, Sancho Cota, adds an amusing variant to the story when he relates that Charles had originally not intended to take her with him to Spain, whereat the Infanta was sorely grieved. And so, Cota, who had poetic ambitions, had written for her a *Canción de Tristeza,* a "Song of Sadness," which Eleanor sang in her garden and was answered (in song) by her ladies-in-waiting. And Cota adds that when Charles heard of this he relented and agreed to take her with him.[37] We may surmise that Cota was not informed that Eleanor's sadness had a different cause.

With Eleanor were her ladies-in-waiting and a great company of the gentlemen of the Court, headed by Chièvres. Of the Spaniards, we hear only of Bishop Mota, García de Padilla, and the secretaries, Antonio de Villegas, "et aultres," [38] among whom Cobos was certainly one. On the whole, it was an uneventful voyage. There were days of rough weather (the King was sea-sick one night); there were days when they were becalmed and so visited from ship to ship and watched the porpoises cavorting. Only one serious mishap occurred: one night the travelers were alarmed by a great glow of light on the horizon. The next morning it was learned that the ship which was carrying all the horses had been burned with all aboard. Perhaps some drunken stable boy had tipped over a candle in the straw.

Early in the morning of September 18, a sailor reported to the King that from the masthead he had seen the mountains of Viscaya in the distance, and he received the promised reward of wine. Most of the pilots, who were Basques, also believed that they were off the coast of Viscaya. But by the following morning, as they came closer to the shore, it was evident that they were mistaken: the mountains that rose before them were the mountains of Asturias. The King's advisors were uncertain as to what course they should follow. Should they try to make for Santander or Santiago, or should they land at once? The danger of being caught in a storm off this inhospitable coast led them to choose the safest way: to get the King ashore without mishap. And so that afternoon the royal barge was lowered into the water and furnished with cushions, tapestries, and banners. At five o'clock Charles and Eleanor, with the chief lords and ladies-in-waiting, the secretaries, and the necessary servants embarked in the barge. They passed by the sorry little village of Tazones and rowed up the tidal river that led to the town of Villaviciosa. Almost a mile from the town they disembarked and walked the remaining distance on foot. It was dark when they entered.

When the people of the town had seen this great fleet lying off the coast they were puzzled and terrified. Such ships never came there; they must be Turks, or French, bent on some evil. Hastily they retired to the hills, armed with sticks and staves and daggers, prepared to defend themselves against the invaders. As the royal company came ashore, the villagers sent out scouts to reconnoitre. Dodging behind bushes and thickets they came close enough to see the royal arms of Spain on the banners, and from some of the strangers who spoke good Castilian they learned that this was in truth their King, who had come to rule his people. Imagine the relief and delight of their fellow townsmen when they received the news!

The situation in which the royal party found themselves was not a pleasant one nor one to which they had been accustomed. Because of their haste to get ashore, they had not brought with them food or beds. And the village could provide neither. But these gallant gentlemen and fair ladies accepted the situation with good grace; as though they were on a picnic, they pitched in to prepare some sort of a meal. The Infanta Eleanor fashioned a tolerable ham omelet. There was good cheer and spirits were high, for after the perils of the voyage, all were safe ashore. The British ambassador, Spinelly, who was one of those in the company, wrote to his master Henry VIII that that night most of the company had to be content with straw or a bench for a bed.[39]

Even that first night on shore the secretaries were busy preparing dispatches, announcing to the Spanish noblemen and prelates, to the municipal councils and other authorities, the safe arrival of the King. Most of them were countersigned by Cobos.[40] In fact, from this time on, it is Cobos who was responsible for the royal correspondence in Castile. We must remember that he was already in charge of the records of all royal grants and of the receipts and expenditures of the Treasury. Now that they were in Spain, it was natural that Chièvres should have more and more depended on him for the conduct of the secretaries' office. Although he did not yet bear the title, he was in effect already the first secretary. From time to time Villegas or Conchillos signed a document, it is true, but we may be sure that they were both relegated to a place of secondary importance.

On the morning after their arrival the citizens of Villaviciosa came to pay obeisance to the King, bringing the only gifts they could offer: skins full of wine, twelve baskets of bread, six steers, twenty-four sheep. The chronicler of this *Premier voyage* of the young King, Laurent Vital, has left a vividly detailed account of their experiences in these first days in Spain.[41] His picture of the manners and customs of these Asturian village-folk, their strange clothes, their songs and dances, their bullfights—reveals an attitude singularly like that of the first chroniclers of the New World: for him these natives were semi-barbarous, outlandish folk—barefoot, primitive. Perhaps if he could have spoken their language, they would not have seemed so strange.

That same morning, gentlemen from the other ships, which had remained at anchor overnight, came to ask the King for instructions. After consultation with his advisors, they were ordered to proceed to Santander and there await the King who would travel overland to join them. During the next two days the King's quartermasters were busy trying to round up mounts and carts for the King and his suite. Their success was not great. The ambassador Spinelly reported that there were only forty horses and mules for two hundred people, so that many of the courtiers had to walk, while the fair ladies rode in oxcarts. Like a practical Englishman he had managed to find a "hobby" which he gave the King for the journey of the first four days.[42]

The road was a rough one through the mountains and progress was slow, for these city folk were not accustomed to life in the wilds. They reached the village of Llanes on September 26 and spent the following day there. Before they left, Chièvres prepared for the King an answer to Cisneros' letter of the twenty-third, which had arrived by courier.[43] It was Cobos who countersigned the letter. And we must bear in mind that since Chièvres did not know Spanish, Cobos must have been responsible for the language in which it was expressed, though the content was dictated by Chièvres. The letter began with an expression of the King's deep concern at the news of the Cardinal's illness. There followed his thanks for Cisneros' prompt execution of the instructions concerning the change in the household of the Infante Ferdinand. Then he explained that he was on his way to Santander, where he would join the rest of his Court. Meanwhile, since his plans were uncertain, the Cardinal and the Council of Castile should not attempt to join him, but should remain in Aranda till further instructions. It was a courteous, almost friendly letter, but it made clear that the King—or at least his advisors—were not ready to receive the old Cardinal.

So much has been written about this strange period when Charles and his Court were wandering through northern Spain, that we may well stop for a moment to consider the situation.

Contemporary Spanish chroniclers were convinced that the delay was due to fear on the part of the King's advisors that Cisneros would attempt to take over the government, and that knowing that he was on his deathbed, they deliberately dallied along the way to avoid a meeting with him. But it is not as simple as that. There can be no doubt that Chièvres and his associates were greatly worried about the reception their master would receive in Spain. The reports which they had received from their ambassadors, Adrian of Utrecht and La Chaux, had not been reassuring. They knew that the Cardinal was a man of unflinching integrity in the exercise of his authority. Undoubtedly they had read the *Memorial* he sent to Adrian, setting forth the principles of sound government.[44] Some of its thirty-two provisions, if accepted, would have spelled the ruin of their system of bribery and favoritism. They knew, too, that the nobles were lawless and the townspeople ready to take up arms in defense of their privileges. Above all they remembered that the Castilian Consejo had strongly opposed the proposal that Charles take the title of King during his mother's lifetime and had yielded only in the presence of a *fait accompli*. Could they count on the loyalty of the King's Spanish subjects?

Their fear of possible opposition was revealed in the instruction they sent to Cisneros on the eve of their departure from Middelburg (September 7), ordering him to replace the members of the household of the Infante Ferdinand with more reliable persons.[45] They were aware that the Infante had been his grandfather's favorite and that there were noblemen in Spain who would have been glad to see him on the throne instead of this Flemish stranger. If a coterie of supporters was centering in his household, it must be broken up and as soon as possible Ferdinand must be shipped out of Spain.

They had expected to land at Santander and thence proceed to the cities of Old Castile. But by the strange chance of their arrival far to the west, the Court was separated and all their plans were disrupted. And now a new complication arose. Toiling along the difficult coastal road the Court reached the fishing village of San Vicente de Barquera on September 29. There the King fell ill; the soft life of Flanders had ill-fitted him for such hardships; perhaps, too, the change in food and water was enough to explain his indisposition. Chièvres and his fellow-counsellors were well-nigh in a panic at this turn of events; for them, in fact for all Europe, everything depended on the survival of this lad. While they waited impatiently for the doctors to find some remedy, a few visitors reached San Vicente. Francisco de Vargas, the Royal Treasurer, sent by the Cardinal, came with money. He was gratefully received, but he was not confirmed in his appointment. Another who arrived was Antonio de Rojas, Archbishop of Granada and President of the Royal Council, who had defied the Cardinal's order to remain in Aranda. He was promptly dismissed and ordered to return to the Cardinal.[46]

When several days elapsed without any improvement in the King's condition, his physicians decided that it was the sea air that was causing his ailment and they recommended that he leave the coast and turn inland. The situation appeared so serious that Chièvres at once sent a messenger to Santander with instructions that the King's baggage be sent by boat to San Vicente and that the other members of his suite who were waiting there start for Valladolid. At the same time he ordered Zapata and Carvajal, two of the members of the old Privy Council, to stay at Aguilar de Campóo until the King's arrival there.[47] After a terrific struggle with rough water, the royal attendants finally landed the royal baggage. On the morning of October 12 the whole company started south. Because of rumors of a plague in Burgos it was decided to make direct for Valladolid.

The King was still ill; some days he ate little or nothing. And the weather in the mountains was terrible—fog in the valleys, blustering winds, rain and snow on the heights. One night, at Los Tojos, a violent storm broke at dusk and the King's physicians ruled that it was unsafe for him to sleep in his field-tent, which had already been set up. And so it was necessary to rig up a lean-to, sheltered from the wind against the wall of a house, for his bed. What with the King's weakness and the bad roads, it took three days to cover the short distance to Reinosa, where they came to the main road from Santander to Valladolid. Just outside of Reinosa they were met by the Grand Chancellor, Jean Sauvage, who had come overland from Flanders. It was a joyous reunion for all the courtiers. They stayed almost a week in Reinosa and there, at last, the King recovered, so that when they moved on to Aguilar de Campóo on October 21 the whole Court was in high spirits.

At Aguilar a large company was awaiting them. The Bishop of Burgos, Juan Rodríguez de Fonseca, and his brother, An-

tonio de Fonseca, one of the two royal *contadores,* were there;
so, too, were the Councillors Dr. Zapata, Dr. Carvajal, and
Hernando de Vega, Grand Commander of Castile. Besides, the
members of his suite from Santander must have arrived, for
there was a company of royal archers and a hundred German
noblemen who came out to escort him as he entered the town.
We do not know what transpired in these first meetings between
Chièvres, Sauvage, and the other Flemings and the Spanish councillors. At least we know that their request for confirmation in
their offices was denied and they were told that the King would
not consider the organization of his official household until he
reached Valladolid. But it is clear that Chièvres must have come
to fear more than ever the possibility that the Spaniards would
not accept Charles as their king and that it was necessary to
secure the Queen Mother's consent to his ruling in her stead.
This meant that they must by-pass Valladolid and make directly
for Tordesillas.

When the whole Court left Aguilar on October 27, they
moved more rapidly. At Herrera, where they spent the twenty-
eighth, they left the main road to Palencia and Valladolid and
traveled through little towns on the road to Tordesillas. Only at
Becerril did they spend a day, All Saints Day, where the Condestable, Iñigo Fernández de Velasco, accompanied by his kinsmen, all gorgeously arrayed in cloth-of-gold, came forth to pay
homage to the King and his sister and escort them into the town.
Late on November 4 they reached Tordesillas and were lodged
in the Queen's palace. That very evening Charles and Eleanor
had a brief, pathetic meeting with their mother, whom they had
not seen since they were tiny children and whom they could
hardly have remembered.

When they had been dismissed almost abruptly after the first
words of greeting, Chièvres returned for a long talk with the
Queen. Artfully he explained to her how fortunate she was that
her son was now a grown man, capable of conducting the affairs
of state and hence of relieving her of the heavy burden of responsibility of ruling her people. Perhaps the Queen was only
dimly aware of the meaning of his words, but inertia was a
characteristic manifestation of her form of mental disorder and
so she gave her consent. Chièvres was at last sure of his ground
and ready to go ahead with the assumption of royal authority
by the King.

One of his first acts was to draft in the name of the King a letter to Cisneros (it was countersigned by Cobos), in which he thanked the Cardinal for his past services and instructed him to meet the King at Mojados, where he could advise the King concerning the organization of his official household and then be relieved of further duties and enjoy a well-earned rest.[48] Cisneros had come from the monastery of La Aguilera to Roa near Valladolid. There his illness took a turn for the worse. The King's letter reached him on November 8 early in the morning; he died that afternoon. Contemporary Spanish historians early voiced the charge that it was this letter that caused the aged prelate's death. But it is doubtful if there is any truth in the charge. In the first place, it is by no means certain that he actually knew of the contents, for he was in his last agony when it arrived. But even if he saw it, it is hard to believe that a man of his character could have been broken by a rebuff of this sort.

Giménez Fernández has expressed the belief that it was Cobos who drafted this act of ingratitude and infamy.[49] Nothing could be more improbable. If Chièvres had sought the advice of any of the Castilians, he would have turned to Bishop Mota and Padilla, and not to a minor official like Cobos. It must be admitted that both Mota and Padilla must have been eager to see Cisneros eliminated. They owed their positions to Chièvres and Sauvage; the triumph of the Cardinal would have meant their dismissal and replacement. Almost since the death of King Ferdinand the Castilians and the Burgundian advisors of Charles had been engaged in a struggle for control. The letters of Cisneros and his associates to their agents in Flanders frankly express their purpose to take over the conduct of the King's affairs as soon as he reached Spain. But Chièvres and his group were in control of the King; his letter to the Cardinal is the definitive sign of their victory.

The King and his Court left Tordesillas for Mojados on November 12. There Charles and Eleanor found their young brother Ferdinand, whom they had never seen, with a great company of knights and prelates. On the following morning Chièvres met with the members of the Royal Council, who had also been summoned to Mojados, and now, sure of his authority, he did not hesitate to confirm them in their appointments; now they would be indebted to him for the royal favor and bound to his service. On the fourteenth the whole company moved on to the monastery of El Abrojo, where they waited while the preparations for the entry into Valladolid were being completed.

———————◦◦◦———————

CHAPTER III

IN HIS MAJESTY'S SERVICE

The Winter in Valladolid

Cobos had been in Valladolid many times while he was in the service of King Ferdinand, but surely he had never seen anything like the triumphal procession which entered the city on November 18. There were prelates in their scarlet robes, knights in armor, Flemish archers, German halbadiers, Spanish footmen, drummers, and fifers—all resplendent in their parti-colored uniforms. Then came the King, alone, in shining armor with a white plume in his black velvet cap, blazing with diamonds and pearls; and at the end the Councillors in their black gowns. Cobos must have been among the secretaries who followed inconspicuously in their wake. The procession halted while Charles stopped at Santa María to say a prayer. Then they moved on to his lodging in the house of Bernardino Pimentel, where the Infante had been taken as a little boy when the house still belonged to the Marqués de Astorga. It stood close beside the church of San Pablo in the Corredera. Just across the street, facing the church, were the houses of the Adelantado of Galicia, Juan Hurtado de Mendoza, and his wife the Countess of Rivadavia. Their oldest daughter, María de Mendoza, was then a little girl nine years old. One wonders if Cobos even saw her on this visit to Valladolid.

We need not rehearse the events of the next four months in

Valladolid. There was a constant round of banquets, jousts, and tournaments, in which the Burgundian courtiers strove to out-shine the Castilians. There was a mock trial at the Chancillery, where two teams of learned lawyers debated a legal issue in the presence of the King and his courtiers. Poor little King! He surely could not understand a word of their Castilian rhetoric. Most important was the first meeting of the Cortes which began on February 4 and which ended with the victory of Chièvres and Sauvage over the defenders of Castilian privileges, led by Dr. Zumel, one of the *procuradores* of Burgos. Cobos seems to have played no official part in the proceedings. Ruiz de Castañeda served as secretary of the Cortes and it was Antonio de Villegas who was called on to carry messages from the Flemish advisors to their Castilian opponents.[1] Cobos had been a *procurador* of Granada at the Cortes of 1515. This time the city was repre-sented by Antonio de Mendoza and Gonzalo de Medrano, who were among the few who refused to take the oath of allegiance to the King, until they were coerced into compliance by a threat of confiscation of all their property. Chièvres did not forget this when the next Cortes was called.

As soon as the *procuradores* had yielded and had granted a subsidy of 450,000 ducats for the next three years, the formal ceremony of recognition of Charles as King was held in the church of San Pablo. The Spanish noblemen insisted on accom-panying Charles on foot, in spite of the mud in the street, as he rode from his palace to the church.[2] There, before a throng of *procuradores,* gentlemen and bishops, the Infante swore alle-giance to his brother, followed by his sister Eleanor. The *grandes* were a little disturbed that the townsmen took the oath before them, but at last the ceremony was over and the vaults resounded with the *Te Deum Laudamus.*

During these months the figure of the King seems strangely like a puppet manipulated by Chièvres. Impassive and silent, he rode his restless horse in the processions. At public functions he sat unmoving on his throne, with Chièvres just behind, whis-pering in his ear what to do and what to say. He still knew al-most no Castilian. None of the Spaniards could get access to him; they must first meet with Mota and Padilla, who in turn spoke to Chièvres, who, alone, talked, or pretended to talk to the King and came back to relay the answer through Mota and Padilla. Small wonder that there was a rumor among the Spaniards that he was mentally deficient, incompetent like his mother. It was years before he demonstrated his capacity for personal rule.

Before he left Valladolid there was an episode which extended greatly Cobos' influence in the official world. Among those who had been confirmed in their former posts at Mojados in November were Bishop Rodríguez de Fonseca, who was once more in charge of the group of councillors who handled the affairs of the Indies, and Lope Conchillos, who was the secretary attached to that office. Conchillos was signing documents that related to the Indies in December 1517 and in January 1518.[3] Meanwhile, Fray Bartolomé de las Casas had returned from the Indies and he immediately renewed his charges against Fonseca and Conchillos to the Chancellor Sauvage. Sauvage was so shocked at his revelations that he at once ordered the suspension of all Indian affairs. But Fonseca called a meeting of his little group of Councillors and prepared a series of royal orders and instructions for the Chancellor's signature. When Conchillos appeared with the documents, Sauvage indignantly ordered him out of the room.[4] Las Casas tells us that it was Cobos who advised Conchillos to leave the Court at once and retire to his house in Toledo. The last paper signed by Conchillos was dated February 5, 1518; on February 10 Cobos' signature appears for the first time on one of the Indian documents.[5]

Las Casas paints an interesting portrait of Cobos as he appeared at this time. After explaining that he was one of those who went to Flanders in search of royal favor, he goes on:

But he surpassed all the rest in that M. de Chièvres became fonder of him than of any of the others, because in truth he was more gifted than the others, for he was very attractive in face and figure [and in his bearing he showed that he was prudent and calm]. He was also soft of voice and speech and so he was likable. He was likewise greatly helped by the information and experience he had in all the affairs of the kingdom, as one who had been trained in them for long years. He came with the King, as I have said, so close to M. de Chièvres that he discussed nothing with anyone but him, especially in matters that dealt with the affairs of the royal state. At his suggestion, Lope Conchillos left the Court and I think that he at once asked M. de Chièvres and the Grand Chancellor for the post as secretary for the Indies, either to perform the duties in place of Conchillos until the King made some other provision (knowing well that he would never let it out of his hands), or perhaps they gave him the definite appointment immediately. At any rate, he always held it and served for many years, until he gave it or transferred it or asked the King to grant it to Juan de Samano.[6]

Las Casas' account was written years later and his picture of Cobos' influence at this time may be colored in the light of his later power. But it shows that Cobos was beginning to exercise an important, if not a decisive part in the King's affairs. And there is further evidence of his increasing influence in the fact that the royal officials in Santiago de Cuba were writing fawning letters to him as early as October, 1517, begging him to show them favor.[7]

In the present case he certainly did everything possible in behalf of his old chief, who had fallen into disgrace. Through his intervention a royal *cédula* was issued on March 2 ordering the payment of Conchillos' *ayuda de costa* of 50,000 *maravedís*, even though he was absent from the Court.[8] On April 5 Conchillos wrote to the Consejo Real from Toledo, resigning his post as secretary in charge of Indian affairs on the ground of "certain occupations and ailments which have come upon him in the service of the royal crown." [9] And he added: "The secretary Francisco de los Cobos is very well informed in the field and he knows better than any other secretary what is best for the Indies and the policy which should be followed. I humbly beg Your Highness that in my place you entrust this office to the aforesaid secretary, that he may hold and perform it, as I have held and performed it." On the same day he also resigned his post as secretary of the Orders of Alcántara and Calatrava. A week later (April 14) he wrote to Chièvres, in answer to a letter concerning the archbishopric of Toledo, that he would continue to serve him with his life and worldly goods, as long as he lived.[10]

Cobos must have begun at once to perform the duties of the new office. Already on July 17 the Hieronymite fathers in Santo Domingo wrote to him that they had been instructed to send all communications to him,[11] although there is no official document which records his appointment until October 1, 1518, when the paymasters were ordered to pay him an *ayuda de costa* of 50,000 *maravedís*, as secretary, payable from the income of the Isla Española.[12] But he must soon have found his new duties too heavy to carry in addition to his other obligations. As his assistant and deputy he chose one of his old associates, Juan de Samano, who had been in the service of Conchillos as early as 1513 and had been granted some petty sinecures in Cuba.[13] Already commissioned as an *escribano* and notary,[14] he received his formal appointments as secretary for Indian affairs and as secretary of Cobos on November 15, 1519, at a salary of 40,000 *maravedís* a year.[15] He was to remain Cobos' most loyal friend and servant until the latter's death.

When the Duque del Infantado heard of Conchillos' dismissal, he wrote to Chièvres reminding him that Conchillos' wife, María Niño de Ribera, was his cousin and had married him with the approval of King Ferdinand. He begged now that she and her husband should not be deprived of the royal grants that they had received (April 30, 1518).[16] His plea bore fruit: on May 21 Conchillos' rights as *fundidor* in San Juan, paying 1 per cent on metal assayed there, were confirmed;[17] as late as 1520 he was still on the royal payroll as secretary, with a salary of 100,000 *maravedís* a year.[18] But his other affairs dragged on, though his wife, María Niño, followed the Court to Zaragoza to plead her cause. Las Casas met her one day on the stairs of the royal palace as she came down from an interview with Jean Sauvage and he later remembered how she had recognized him and had exclaimed: "God forgive you, father, for you have put my children in the poor-house."[19]

When the new *Ordinances* for the Indies were drawn up in the summer of 1518, Rodrigo de Figueroa was sent to the Indies to investigate conditions there. One of his first acts was to seize all of Conchillos' possessions.[20] Although a *cédula* was issued on January 13, 1520,[21] ordering a report on the value of the property taken from him, nothing seems to have happened when Conchillos died in May, 1521. His widow wrote to Cobos on June 2, asking that payments due her husband be made to their five children.[22] But it was not until 1522 that her cause was finally settled. On January 28 the Consejo ordered all debts in Cuba due her husband paid to her, and a few days later they granted her son, Pedro Niño de Conchillos, the income from the post as *fundidor* in San Juan, which his father had held, until the King decreed some other disposition.[23] Cobos had taken Conchillos' place in the leadership of the secretariat, but his unremitting efforts to protect the interests of his former chief and his family are typical of the loyalty which he showed to his friends and associates throughout his whole career.

Before the Court left Valladolid, Cobos secured his confirmation in some of the appointments which he had earlier received, as *escribano del crimen* in Ubeda [24] and as registrar of all treasury receipts and payments.[25] On the way to Zaragoza, at Aranda del Duero (April 10, 1518), he was granted a new *merced:* the privilege of shipping fifty negro slaves to the Indies; a little later the privilege was amended to provide that Cobos need not pay duty on their shipment.[26]

The Visit to Aragon and Cataluña

Although the King and his Court left Valladolid on March 22, their progress was slow, for at every town on the way there was an elaborate reception to mark this first royal visitation. Before they left Aranda del Duero (April 20), the Infante Don Fernando was shipped off to Flanders with a suite of Burgundian courtiers. It is clear that Chièvres felt that he was a potential threat to his brother's authority. The very fact that the Cortes had urged that he be allowed to remain in Spain until Charles had an heir made the danger more real; in case of a popular revolt he might easily become the rallying-point for the rebels. Outside of Aranda the two brothers said farewell; one day Charles was to more than repay him for this forced exile from the Spain that he loved and that loved him.

The Court did not reach Zaragoza until May 9. After the first days of joyous celebration the three "Estates" of the Aragonese Cortes began their deliberations. They proved far more obstinate than the Castilians in their refusal to give formal recognition of the King, during his mother's lifetime, and to grant a subsidy. The negotiations dragged on for months, so that it was January before the members of the Cortes finally yielded and granted the King's demands. There was one event during this period that was destined to change the course of European affairs—the death of the Grand Chancellor, Jean Sauvage, in July. In Spain his passing helped to ease the anti-Burgundian attitude of the Spaniards, for he was regarded as one of the most rapacious of the foreigners; he was said to have accumulated 50,000 ducats during four months in Spain. More important was the choice of his successor.

To replace him Chièvres called Mercurino Gattinara, who had been in the Burgundian service from the time he accompanied Margaret of Austria from Savoy to Flanders. He had served as an ambassador of the Emperor Maximilian in Spain in 1509 and 1513; at the time of his appointment he was President of the Parliament of Dôle. He reached Zaragoza on October 8 and took over the seals of office a few days later.

Gattinara brought to the King's entourage a wholly new point of view. Humanist and man of learning, he was imbued with the idea of world empire and for a dozen years he preached his doctrine to Charles and guided his steps, as far as he could, to the realization of his bold dream. We shall have frequent occasion to comment on his relations with Cobos.

Aside from his daily duties as secretary, the most important activity of Cobos mentioned in the records of the period in Zaragoza is his appointment to convey to the Marqués de Villafranca the King's decision in the long litigation between Antonio de Zúñiga, brother of the Duque de Béjar, and Diego de Toledo, son of the Duque de Alba, over the Priory of San Juan in the Order of Hospitallers.[27] Cisneros had decided the case in favor of Zúñiga and had sent troops to take possession of the Priory at Consuegra. But the Duque de Alba had appealed to the King for a rehearing. Now at last Charles made known his answer: he decreed a compromise, whereby the contestants were to share the income of the Priory. Chièvres was wise enough to realize that the King could ill afford to take sides in a conflict between two of the highest nobles in Spain. It may well be that Cobos' familiarity with the truculence of the Spanish *grandes* helped the King's counsellor to avoid a continuing feud.

One other new favor came to Cobos before they left Zaragoza, when he was authorized to transfer any of his appointments to one of his sons (he was not yet married!) or to any other person who was not a foreigner or infamous. Among the appointments listed was one that had not been mentioned in any of the earlier documents: that of chief *escribano de rentas* of the town of Alcaraz and its surroundings and the towns of the Campo de Montiel.[28] Trifling as each one of these posts was, together they brought in a considerable income.

The Year in Barcelona

The royal company finally left Zaragoza on January 24, 1519. At Lérida, (January 29-31) where they spent three days, a courier brought the news of the death on January 12 of the King's grandfather, the Emperor Maximilian. From then on the policy of the King's advisors took a new direction: his election to the Imperial throne. The Court reached Igualada on the morning of February 4, and when they started for the shrine of Montserrat the next morning, García de Padilla and Cobos were sent directly to Barcelona to conduct preliminary negotiations with the local authorities before the King's entry.[29] Late Sunday night (February 6) Cobos wrote the King to report his arrival: he had already talked to the Catalans and hoped that matters could be settled the next day, so that the King could come to Valdoncella on Tuesday. But the negotiations dragged. On Monday night Padilla and Cobos wrote to the King that they had met with the Vice-Chancellor and given him his instructions. Again, on the following night, Cobos wrote to Gattinara of the continuing discussions. The Grand Chancellor was evidently annoyed at their conduct, for on Wednesday night, at Molins de Rey, he sent a scolding letter to Agustín, Padilla, and Cobos, in the name of the King:

> I have your letters and I am greatly astonished at you, knowing my will and what I have written and instructed you to do in the investigation and execution of justice in the crimes that have been committed there, and at your negligence and heedlessness, since, as you know, my will has been and is that, until this matter is settled and decided, there should be no discussion of the Cortes or anything else. And you should have done that without meddling in anything else. . . . Early tomorrow come before me with an account of what you have done in all this and of what else should be provided. And as far as you are concerned, I think I might have been spared the necessity of writing this to you, for you knew my intention.

Only Gattinara could have penned such a contemptuous letter; clearly he had formed no favorable impression of Cobos' capacity to accept responsibility in this first assignment.

The three negotiators must have spent Thursday, the tenth, in consultation with Gattinara. But on Friday they were back in Barcelona. This time Dr. Carvajal of the Royal Council went with them; Gattinara felt the need of a more experienced and dependable representative. Friday night Cobos again wrote to the Grand Chancellor. It is significant that in recommending a grant of 200 ducats be made to the chaplain, Luis de Cardona, he added that he had discussed the matter with "Mussior," that is, with Chièvres. He still considered the Burgundian as his chief, perhaps too, as his protector.

Charles's entry into Barcelona was the most magnificent he had yet staged. The authorities had declared a three-day public holiday and had ordered the houses decorated and illuminated at night, the streets swept clean for his passage. The King spent the night of February 14 at the monastery of Valdoncella, outside the city. A contemporary chronicler says that after supper that night he could not restrain his curiosity and so slipped into the city, *incognito,* to see the illuminations and to witness the gaiety and rejoicing with which the people were celebrating his arrival.[30] The formal and official entry was made February 15.

Although the negotiations for the recognition of Charles as King, and the granting of a subsidy by the Cortes began almost immediately, the Catalans proved to be quite as obstinate as the Aragonese. Almost a year passed before the issues were finally compromised. During this period there were a few events in which Cobos was personally involved.

Since the death of the Emperor the contest for his throne between Charles and Francis I of France had come into the open; agents of both parties were actively soliciting the Imperial Electors with gifts and promises. Chièvres had always been eager to maintain good relations with the French. And now, in the spring of 1519, he made one more effort to arrive at a settlement of the problem of Navarre.[31] As early as October, 1518, Boissy had written to him, proposing a conference at Perpignan or Narbonne to discuss the revision of the Treaty of Noyon. On January 20, 1519, Chièvres replied that he was willing to go to Montpellier, taking with him Hernando de Vega, Dr. Carvajal, and his Flemish advisors.

There were difficulties and delays, proposals and counterproposals, but at last, on April 4 he left Barcelona with a great company of more than four hundred gentlemen. His chief advisors were the Grand Chancellor, Bishop Mota, Hernando de Vega, the Marqués de Villafranca, Pedro de Toledo, the Catalan Treasurer, Luis Sánchez, and Cobos.[32] There was further delay at Perpignan, while they waited for a safe-conduct, and it was not until April 28 that they reached Montpellier, where they found the French ambassadors, Boissy and Robertet, already arrived. But Boissy had fallen ill on the way and Chièvres was unable to see him until May 3. There were desultory conversations during the following days, in which it was patent that neither side could yield on the issue of the future control of Navarre. Then suddenly, on May 10, Boissy died and the Spaniards seized the opportunity to terminate the conference. They were back in Barcelona on May 24 and were received with great rejoicing, for many of the people had believed that they would be arrested by the French.[33]

The records of the conference, largely French, make no mention of Cobos' part in the negotiations, and there is no reason to believe that he played an important rôle. But we may be sure that, as secretary, he accompanied Chièvres to the various meetings. It was his first experience in the field of international diplomacy; he must have gathered some idea of the difficulty of reaching a settlement when the grounds for disagreement are deeper than the issues under discussion. Years later he was to face the same problem as a spokesman for the Emperor.

On July 6 a courier brought the news that Charles had been elected Emperor at Frankfurt on June 28. With the aid of huge loans from the banking house of Fugger in Augsburg Charles's agents in Germany had out-bribed the French representatives in winning the vote of the Electors. A few days later Gattinara drew up a long list of *Consigli* for the guidance of Charles in his new office.[34] It is a sort of treatise *De regimine principum,* the first of many such documents by the Grand Chancellor. He was already beginning to groom his master for the rôle he expected him to play in European affairs.

It is at this time we find the first intimate picture of Cobos in action in the affairs of the Court. A young Sevillan *hidalgo,* Alonso Enríquez de Guzmán, had come to Barcelona seeking an appointment in the royal household and a habit of Santiago. He came armed with letters of recommendation to important people, and the Duque de Béjar and the Almirante de Castilla accompanied him to an audience with the King, who promptly referred him to García de Padilla. The latter received him with fair words and promises, but nothing happened. So Don Alonso went to Cobos and gave him a letter from Rodrigo Ponce de León, Conde de Bailén, telling him who Don Alonso was. Cobos asked him what business brought him to Court and Don Alonso explained what he was seeking. But let Don Alonso tell the story in his own words:

He did not call me "Your Grace" *(Vuestra Merced),* though he is wont to call every one that, but he did me a far greater grace, if only I had known enough to recognize it. And he said to me: "Sir, I am not here to deceive or undeceive such as you. Because of what Don Rodrigo writes to me I am willing to take the trouble to spare you trouble, although I have plenty to do.

All the time you spend here will be wasted, because as for your appointment in the Emperor's household, he will not receive you at present, and even if he should receive you, you will have spent more money and honor, going from door to door requesting it, then you can gain from the appointment, the more so since you come at a very bad time, for because of this news about the Empire and because of the Cortes now in session the Emperor is not considering such matters. And I find the same and even greater difficulty in the question of the habit. It is my opinion that before you spend any more money, you should go back to your town, until you see that times are more favorable. And even then, do not think that merely because of your lineage you will gain what you are asking for, because other men who are of as noble birth as you and have served better than you have been here for many days in the same quest and cannot gain it. They must be dealt with before you, because they have a record of service.[35]

Don Alonso was displeased with Cobos' advice, but he thanked him. Two months later he had spent every penny he possessed and was forced to enlist as a soldier for the campaign against Los Gelves in Africa. He would have been better off if he had followed the wise and kindly, if blunt counsel of an older and more experienced courtier. We shall see him turning to Cobos for support again and again as the years went by.

Cobos himself must have received a habit of Santiago at about this time, for in a *cédula* of September 19, 1519, granting him the rights to lost cattle *(mostrenco)* in Alcaraz and its territory, he is styled "our secretary, knight of the Order of Santiago." [36] A little later he received what proved to be a far more remunerative privilege. The agents of Diego Velázquez had been in Zaragoza during the preceding summer, telling of his new discoveries on the mainland, and in August they had secured approval of his appointment as governor and *adelantado* of Yucatán. For a long time the post of *fundidor y marcador* of all the gold and silver found in the Indies had been considered valuable, though it paid only 1 per cent on metal assayed and minted. Hernando de Vega had long held the post in Cuba; [37] in San Juan it was Conchillos who possessed the privilege. Now that a new land was discovered it too offered possibilities, and on November 20, 1519, Cobos got his appointment as *fundidor y marcador* of Yucatán and the territory which Velázquez had discovered.[38] In the early years the annual income from the post must have been trifling. But from his position in the Consejo de las Indias Cobos was one of the first to learn of new discoveries and as each new area was opened, he quickly had his privilege extended to the new lands. As the treasures of Mexico and Peru came into the picture, this single appointment became the chief source of his ultimate wealth.

We have seen how Bartolomé de las Casas had come to Valladolid in support of his efforts to protect the Indians from the tyranny—as he called it—of the Spaniards. He had followed the Court to Zaragoza, and thanks to the favor of Sauvage and La Chaux, he thought that he had won his case, when the Grand Chancellor died. Nothing daunted, the battling friar started anew to press his cause with Gattinara and the other authorities at the Court in Barcelona. Although Las Casas had succeeded in eliminating Lope Conchillos, the Bishop of Burgos, Rodríguez de Fonseca, had managed to retain his post as chief councillor for Indian affairs—thanks to a generous payment to Chièvres, according to Las Casas—and it was against Fonseca that the friar now leveled his most violent attacks. There was as yet no formal Consejo de las Indias. Fonseca had associated with him a group of the Consejo de Castilla, García de Padilla, Hernando de Vega, Zapata, and later Peter Martyr, the humanist and historian. With Cobos as secretary they met in Fonseca's house to transact their business.³⁹

The debate between Las Casas and Fonseca became increasingly acrimonious, and Fonseca and his group finally drew up a list of thirty reasons why the friar's petitions should be denied, which they presented to the Royal Council. Las Casas went at once to Gattinara to request that he be allowed to see the charges and the Chancellor instructed Cobos to bring him the list. But Cobos failed to comply, offering one excuse after another: the list had not been copied; he had been too busy with other matters. At last the Chancellor insisted on their immediate delivery. But when Cobos turned them over to him, he exacted a promise from Gattinara that they would not leave his hands. It was only through a subterfuge that Las Casas was able to learn the content of the attack upon him.

There is no question that in all this conflict Cobos was a stout supporter of Fonseca. That was inevitable, for he was bound to him by long years of association and by the defense of their common interests. In this he was supported by Chièvres, and as Las Casas remarked rather bitterly, since Cobos was close to Chièvres who had no other light to guide him in the affairs of the kingdom and no one else whom he trusted, he approved of everything that Cobos and the Bishop said and desired.

Early in October, 1519, the King and his officials had moved out to Molins de Rey because of a plague in Barcelona. There Gattinara called the contestants to an audience before the King. In addition to members of the Consejo, Bishop Mota, Aguirre, and others, those summoned were Diego Colón, Admiral of the Indies, the Bishop of Tierra Firme, one of Las Casas' most vigorous opponents, and a Franciscan friar who had recently returned from the Indies and had aligned himself on the side of Las Casas, and finally Las Casas himself. The latter has left us a vivid picture of the audience in the royal lodging.

The King entered the hall and took his seat on the throne. A step below him the others were seated on benches; to his right were Chièvres, the Admiral, the Bishop of Tierra Firme, and Aguirre; to his left Gattinara, Bishop Mota, and the others. Las Casas and the Franciscan friar stood at the back of the room, against the wall. When all were in their places, after a long silence, Chièvres and Gattinara arose, mounted the step, and kneeling before the King on either side, whispered to him briefly. Then they stood up, bowed to the King, and returned to their places. Another silence followed before the Chancellor, addressing himself to the Bishop of Tierra Firme, said: "The King orders you to speak, if you have something to say about the Indies." This solemn procedure was repeated over and over with each of those who were asked to speak. When all had had their say the King arose and entered his private apartment. And that was all. There is every reason to believe that, as secretary, Cobos was one of those who sat on the bench at the end of the line, on the side of Chièvres. The cause of Las Casas was still unresolved.

Meanwhile Gattinara was busy putting the King's house in order. The special envoy of the Imperial Electors, Frederick Count Palatine, reached Molins de Rey on November 30, bringing the official notification of Charles's election and urging him to come to Germany at the earliest possible moment to receive his crown. A few days later the Chancellor drew up the schedule of the new formulae to be used in all official documents. They were to begin with the words: "Don Carlos, King of the Romans, Emperor-elect, *semper augustus,* and Doña Juana, his mother and the same Don Carlos, King and Queen of Castile and Leon, . . ." followed by all his other titles. On December 5 Cobos dispatched to all officials of the realm the new instructions, with a long accompanying letter to explain that in placing the title of Emperor first, the King had no intention of reducing the prestige and privileges of his Spanish kingdoms.[40] It is by no means sure that his Spanish subjects accepted this decision with satisfaction; what they wanted was a Spanish king of their own, not a foreign emperor.

At the same time Gattinara prescribed other changes in protocol. Hitherto, Charles had been called "His Highness"; now he was to be named "His Majesty." Letters to him had been addressed: "Very noble and very powerful Lord"; now they were to begin: "S. C. C. R. Magestad" (*Sacra, Cesárea, Católica, Real Magestad*), a formula that symbolized Gattinara's concept of empire. He also urged Charles to change the form of his signature, using merely his name "Carlos," instead of the traditional "I the King (*Yo el Rey*)", but this Charles failed to accept. Finally there were provisions for new seals and new coats of arms, even for new symbols on the royal coins. Nothing was too trivial for the Chancellor's orderly mind.

Before the departure from Barcelona for Castile he prepared a second memorandum for the King, setting forth his proposals for the proper organization of the kingdom of Aragon.[41] One of the measures which he urged was the creation of an office of "Comptroller of Finance," who would be responsible for recording all treasury transactions, and he added: "as Cobos does at present for the finances of Castile." At the end of the memorandum he suggested that they could discuss similar regulations for the affairs of Castile on the road to the new Cortes which was to be summoned.

The Return to Castile

As the months of negotiation with the Catalans dragged on, the King's counsellors became more and more restless, for it was urgent that he start for Germany, and they were anxious for an interview between Charles and Henry VIII before the projected meeting of the English and French kings. Already they had decided to abandon the plan for holding a Cortes of the kingdom of Valencia. Everything was therefore ready for their departure. On January 12, 1520, the Court moved back to Barcelona; a week later the Cortes was finally over. On January 23 the whole company started for Burgos. This time they moved more rapidly,

with only a day or two of rest along the road. By February 12
they were in Calahorra.

There Cobos dispatched messages to all the cities of Castile,
ordering them to send their *procuradores* to a Cortes to be held
at Santiago on March 20.[42] The purpose of the new call is clear:
the royal government was in financial straits and must have a
new subsidy to defray the expenses of the coming trip to England and Germany. Santa Cruz tells us that the expense of maintaining the Court during the year in Barcelona was greater than
the 300,000 ducats of subsidy granted by the Cortes. And although, with the aid of a bull from the Pope granting the King
a tithe of ecclesiastical revenues, he was able to extract 200,000
florins from the Spanish churches, that was not enough. On one
occasion in 1519 Cobos was instructed to prepare sixty-two blank
juros ("Treasury Notes" we would call them now) to be sold
to unnamed lenders.[43]

The reason for the choice of Santiago as the place for the
Cortes is not so clear. On December 23, 1519, Charles had informed the municipal council of Burgos of his intention to hold
a Cortes there. But his counsellors had already sent Bishop Rodríguez de Fonseca to La Coruña to prepare a fleet for the trip
to England; because of his long experience with the fleets of the
Indies he was especially qualified for the task. Chièvres' enemies
charged that Santiago was chosen because, fearing the possibility
of a popular uprising, he was anxious to be near a port and
escape with his loot. It is more probable, however, that he and
his counsellors, remembering the long wait at Middelburg in
the summer of 1517, wanted to be near a port of embarcation
which they could reach quickly, if weather conditions suddenly
became favorable.

The Court stayed only a week in Burgos (February 19-26) on
this first royal visit and then hurried on to Valladolid, which
they reached on March 1. There Chièvres tried to persuade the
municipal authorities to approve the immediate grant of a subsidy. For three days they were in almost constant session. Meanwhile the city was in a turmoil, for the representatives of
Toledo had come to town and were urging their colleagues to
join them in a movement of resistance. The air was rife with
rumors: the King was planning to leave Spain for good; he was
taking the Queen with him. Cries were heard in the streets:
"Long live the King! Death to the evil counsellors!" Then

someone rang the tocsin in the belfry of San Miguel and the people poured into the streets, ignorant of what had happened but ready for action.

It was a dark, rainy day and the King had been holding audience during the morning. One of his interviews was with Pedro Laso and Alonso Suárez, the Toledan agents. To their request that he listen to their petitions he replied that he was about to leave and that he would receive them after he left Tordesillas. When Chièvres heard the uproar in the street and was informed of its cause, he was seized with a panic and decided to depart immediately. He and the King mounted, and through the rain made for the city gate. A crowd of angry citizens had gathered there who tried to close the gate and prevent the horsemen from passing. But members of the royal guard dispersed them, and the King and Chièvres sped down the road to Tordesillas, where they arrived at the end of the afternoon, soaked to the skin and spattered with mud. The memory of the terror of that flight must have long lingered in the King's mind. Perhaps it explains the ruthlessness he later showed in the punishment of the leaders of popular revolt.

The other members of the King's suite joined him before he left Tordesillas on March 9. Two days later at Villalpando they found waiting for them the two Toledan representatives, who had now been joined by two *procuradores* of Salamanca. That Saturday morning, after mass, they went to the King's lodging, where they were received by Bishop Mota and Padilla. The latter insisted on knowing the nature of their request, to which the townsmen replied that they had instructions to deliver their message to the King in person.

Thereupon Mota and Padilla withdrew, presumably to consult with Chièvres. When they returned shortly after, they informed the delegates that unless they revealed the purpose of their coming, they would not be received by the King. As a result, they disclosed part of their petition and were then informed that they should return at two o'clock for their audience with the King. At the appointed hour they were ushered into his presence and briefly presented the petitions they had brought. The King listened, said that he had heard them, and would have a reply given to them. Later Mota and Padilla informed them that the King was leaving for Benavente on the morrow and that there he would consult with the Consejo. Pero Mexía says that among those who were present at these discussions was Francisco de los Cobos, "who was already taking part in the councils of state." [44]

At Benavente the *procuradores* of Toledo and Salamanca had no greater success. In fact, after a meeting of the Consejo they were given a scolding by Padilla and Antonio de Rojas, President of the Council, who told them, in substance, to go about their business and not meddle in the King's affairs. But they were determined to carry out the mission that had been assigned to them by their fellow-citizens and so they followed the King to Santiago.

The Cortes of Santiago-La Coruña

The Court reached Santiago on March 26 and the King was received with the usual ceremonies. On Sunday, April 1, the Cortes was convened, with Hernando de Vega as President and Padilla and Zapata as *licenciados*. This time Chièvres, remembering the experience in Valladolid two years before, had tried to secure the appointment of *procuradores* on whose subservience they could count.[44a] In fact, in two cases they succeeded: García Ruiz de la Mota, brother of the Bishop, was named one of the representatives of Burgos, and Cobos was again appointed *procurador* of Granada,[45] as he had been at the Cortes of Burgos in 1515. But for the most part their efforts were unsuccessful; the spirit of revolt was aflame in the Castilian towns and their agents came to the Cortes determined to press its cause.

The King appeared in person at the first session, where Gattinara and Mota presented the reasons for the King's departure and the necessity of a subsidy to meet his heavy expenses. But from the first there were grave difficulties. The delegates of Salamanca refused to take the oath unless their petitions were granted. For this act of contumacy they were dismissed from the Cortes. Pedro Laso insisted that the King must pay heed to the requests of the towns. For three days the Cortes was suspended while the discussion went on. A further difficulty arose from the demand of several of the Galician nobles that their towns should be authorized to send *procuradores* to the Cortes.

Meanwhile Pedro Laso had been actively urging the delegates of the other towns to join Toledo in her resistance and refuse to take part in the proceedings until the representatives of Toledo and Salamanca were admitted. On the night of Palm Sun-

day, Chièvres sent Cobos and Juan Ramírez, secretary of the
Consejo, to the lodging of the Toledans to inform them that the
King had ordered them to leave Santiago and retire to their
estates. Late that night, accompanied by Alonso Ortiz, the
Toledans had a long interview with Chièvres and tried to persuade him to have their banishment rescinded. As evidence of
their good faith and obedience, they agreed to retire to El Pa-
drón, four leagues from Santiago. On Tuesday, Ortiz returned to
Chièvres, but he was informed that the King had refused to lift
the ban on the Toledans. As was his usual custom, the King
retired to the monastery of San Lorenzo for Holy Week. When
Ortiz appeared there on Wednesday with new instructions from
Toledo, he was denied an audience with the King.

He therefore turned to Cobos for help,[46] and the latter reported the matter to Chièvres, who summoned Ortiz and asked
for the new instructions. Ortiz replied that he was to deliver
them only to the King. To that Chièvres answered that the
King had confessed that morning and received the Holy Sacrament and hence could not speak to him. After further wrangling
they parted. But a little later Cobos was sent to tell Ortiz that
Chièvres wanted to talk to him again. This time the Chamberlain
told him that he could not enter into any further discussion with
regard to lifting the banishment of the Toledans, and abruptly
left the room. Ortiz was left with Padilla, who again lectured
him on the evil behavior of the Toledans. Later that night Ortiz
visited Gattinara, but nothing came of a two-hour discussion.

On the day after Easter (April 9) Charles returned to Santiago, where the Cortes was still engaged in fruitless debate.
The following Thursday he started for La Coruña, ordering the
procuradores to transfer their meeting there. And so the debate
went on. Cobos and García de la Mota were the first to propose
that the Cortes vote the requested subsidy before the King had
granted their requests.[47] But the others were recalcitrant, and
even when a majority finally approved the subsidy, there were
six towns whose representatives refused to yield. Many of those
who did give their approval paid dearly for their betrayal of
their fellow-citizens when they returned to their homes.

Chièvres, and perhaps the King, too, was grateful to Cobos
for his support of the royal demands at the Cortes. On April 28
a *cédula* renewed his privilege of transferring his offices to anyone he wished, which was tantamount to authorizing him to sell

them or bestow them on a friend or relative. Such privileges were always granted in consideration of "many and continuous services." But in this case the justification is explicit: "in consideration of the services which you have performed and are performing every day, and the service which you gave as *procurador* of the city of Granada at the Cortes which you (!) held in the cities of Santiago and La Coruña in our kingdom of Galicia, this present year of 1520." [48] The value of the award meant little; it was merely the renewal of an earlier grant. But here was open recognition of his loyalty to the King's service. He was committed to that cause.

Chièvres' insistence on the granting of this new subsidy before the three-year period of the subsidy of 1518 had expired and in the face of the wellnigh unanimous opposition of the Castilian cities is hard to explain. Gattinara, in his *Vita,* says that he was opposed to the proposal but was unable to dissuade Chièvres. [49] As a matter of fact, the subsidy was never collected. Santa Cruz reports that even before the Court sailed from La Coruña, Francisco de Vargas, Treasurer for Castile, was ordered to borrow 400,000 ducats in bills of exchange to be paid out of future taxes. [50]

The last month which the Court spent in La Coruña was a crowded one for the secretariat, for there were countless decisions and appointments to be made before the departure. Schäfer has published a memorandum of agenda for a meeting of the Consejo which he believes was written by Cobos. In this he is surely mistaken, for the writing is wholly unlike that of Cobos and is one frequently found in other documents of the secretariat; it is probably the work of one of the many scribes. [51]

Before the Court left for England, the King signed a *cédula* appointing Pedro de los Cobos and Juan de Samano as the persons responsible for the business of the Consejo de las Indias during Don Francisco's absence, and instructing all officials to address their communications to them (May 17, 1520). [52] Pedro de los Cobos was Francisco's first cousin, the younger son of Diego Vela Allide, with whom Francisco had begun his apprenticeship. He had started his career as secretary of the Marqués de Comares. [53] In May, 1517 he had been named *regidor* of Ubeda, replacing his brother, Gerónimo Vela, who had resigned. [54] Two years later Gerónimo died and Pedro wrote to Francisco, asking him to have his salary paid to his widow. [55]

His appointment at La Coruña marks the beginning of his service in the royal secretariat, in which he was to continue, with increasing responsibilities, throughout his life. Of Juan de Samano we have already had occasion to speak. Francisco was beginning to build his own little empire of relatives and friends, dependent on him and as subservient to him as he was to the King.

Another matter which was settled at this time was the acquittal of Pedrarias de Avila from the charges brought against him for his actions in Darién.[56] It has interest to us because Pedrarias had written to his wife earlier in the year that he was counting on Cobos and García de Padilla to support his cause and that she should appeal to them for help.[57] Apparently he was not mistaken in his trust. One of the last documents that Cobos countersigned at La Coruña was the long-debated agreement with Las Casas.[58]

Since Chièvres was so largely responsible for Cobos' rapid advancement in the King's service, we should say a word about his behavior in the two and one-half years that he was in Spain. However much he trusted Cobos, for Spaniards in general he seemed to have only arrogant contempt. From the very beginning he flouted their traditions and their repeated requests. His initial affront was his appointment of his young nephew, Guillaume de Croy, already Bishop of Cambrai, as Archbishop of Toledo in place of the revered Cisneros; he was responsible too for the appointment of other foreigners to Spanish bishoprics and for the preference shown to Spaniards who had been with him in Flanders (like Mota and Manrique) in the distribution of high ecclesiastical honors. His last disregard of Spanish feelings was his naming of Adrian of Utrecht as governor of Castile on the eve of his departure for Flanders.

Karl Brandi has expressed the opinion that most of the Spanish complaints at the tactlessness, avarice, and self-interest of the Burgundians were voiced by the scholars and learned councillors of the time, like Peter Martyr and Carvajal, and by their plagiarists.[59] But there is ample evidence that the dissatisfaction was far more widespread. One need only read the petitions of the Cortes or the *Crónica* of Santa Cruz. There is also a rich documentation to show the extent to which Chièvres and his associates plundered Spain. For example, on the death in 1517 of Juan Velázquez de Cuéllar, one of the two *contadores mayores,*

Chièvres had himself appointed to the post, one of the richest sinecures in Spain, which he promptly sold to the Duque de Béjar for 30,000 ducats.[60] When his wife returned from Portugal, to which she had gone in the suite of the Infanta Eleanor on her way to marry the old Portuguese King, she came laden with gifts.[61] In September, 1519, the Diputación of Barcelona issued her a passport authorizing her to take out of Spain three hundred horses and eighty pack-mules, loaded with clothes, gold, silver, and jewels, and at the same time they permitted her to take out 3,000 ducats in cash for the expenses of her trip to Flanders by way of France.[62] A similar passport was issued to the wife of Charles de Lannoy, chief Equerry of the King.

Other Burgundians received valuable grants and privileges. Thus Laurent Gorrevod, Governor of Bresse, was granted the first license to send negro slaves to the Indies, a grant which he sold to Genoese bankers for 25,000 ducats, with the provision that the King would issue no further such licenses for eight years.[63] He was also appointed deputy to Chièvres as *contador mayor,* a post which he offered to sell to Juan López de Recalde of the Casa de la Contratación in Seville for 30,000 ducats, though he boasted that he had already received an offer of 40,000 ducats.[64] The list of such privileges is long enough to explain why Spaniards were saying:

> "Doblón de a dos, norabuena estedes
> Pues con vos no topó Xevres."

Even though there was undoubtedly exaggeration in the charge that the Burgundians carried off 2,500,000,000 *maravedís* from Spain, there can be no doubt that they exploited shamelessly their influence over the young King to secure fat plums for their own enrichment. Greed and the use of influence and bribery were the rule at the time everywhere in Europe and the Indies. Charles won the Imperial crown largely by open bribery; Popes sold cardinal's hats for a price; the Council of Ten of Venice instructed their ambassador to offer Chièvres 10,000 ducats if he was successful in promoting their cause, as well as smaller amounts to other courtiers, not to mention the silk cloth they sent to Gattinara.[65] If the Spaniards were fiercely resentful of Chièvres and his associates, it was not, then, merely because of their greed. It was because they were foreigners who were sacking the country. Spain has always been xenophobic.

Meanwhile, at La Coruña the fleet had been provisioned and ready for days. On May 19 the pilots announced that the wind had changed and was favorable for the passage to England. That night the King and his company went aboard. In addition to the Burgundian courtiers there were Queen Germana, widow of King Ferdinand, and her new husband, the Marquis of Brandenburg, Frederick, Count Palatine, the Principe di Bisignano, recently honored with the Golden Fleece at the chapter in Barcelona. Among the Spaniards who embarked were a few of the nobles: the Duque de Alba and his son, the Marqués de Villafranca, the Marqués de Aguilar, and some of the younger nobility who were already members of the King's household, like Pedro de Guevara and Juan de Zúñiga. The higher officials were Bishop Mota and Padilla; Alonso Manrique, Bishop of Córdoba, who had been named Chief Chaplain of the King; from the Consejo Real, Dr. Carvajal. The secretaries for Castile were Cobos, Antonio de Villegas, and Luis de Licerazo; for Aragon, Ugo de Urríes, Pedro García, Lope de Soria, and the Vice-Chancellor Antonio Agustín. Chièvres and Gattinara had won the loyal support of a little group of Spanish officials. At three o'clock on the morning of May 20 a gun was fired from the King's ship and the whole fleet weighed anchor. To the music of a choir of wood winds and a flourish of trumpets they sailed out of the harbor with great rejoicing, "leaving poor Spain"— as Sandoval put it—"laden with griefs and misfortunes." [66]

In Flanders, Germany, and England

During the two years which Charles spent in Flanders, Germany, and England, struggling with the problems of his Empire, there is little record of the official activities of Cobos, for in this period it was his French-speaking secretaries who conducted the royal correspondence, Jean Hannaert, now First Secretary and *audiencier* in Flanders, and Jean Lallemand, known in Spain as Juan Alemán. From the documents he countersigned we know that Cobos was constantly with the Emperor, even at his coronation at Aix-la-Chapelle. It is clear that in Spain he was regarded as the person of greatest influence in Spanish affairs at the Court; almost all the letters from Spain were addressed to him or passed through his hands, whether it was to ask for an appointment or a payment or a cipher for official correspondence. One of the first of these communications was a letter from the Condestable de Castilla, refusing to accept the favor of a cash gift which the King had ordered sent to him on the eve of his departure.

The royal fleet was hardly out of sight of land before the smouldering revolt of the Castilian towns burst into flame. City after city joined the *comuneros,* and Adrian and his associates were powerless to quench the fire. When the representatives of the towns gathered at the Junta de Avila on July 29, 1520, one of the demands presented by the *procuradores* of Burgos was that the King should dismiss Chièvres, Bishop Mota, García de Padilla, and Cobos and prosecute them because of the large sums of money they had carried off from Spain.[67] Later in the year one of the *regidores* of Soria reported that Hernando de Vega had written to the city council that they were responsible for sending delegates to Avila to demand the head of Chièvres and the banishment and disqualification of Padilla and Cobos; the *regidor* insisted that they had never thought of such a thing.[68]

On September 11 the Cardinal Adrian and the Consejo reported from Valladolid to the King the desperate situation in Spain, and this finally stirred Chièvres and Gattinara to action. On September 29 they appointed the Condestable de Castilla and the Almirante de Castilla as co-governors with Adrian. But long before the order reached Spain, the Junta had sent a force to Valladolid with orders to arrest the members of the Consejo and all the royal officials. Before their arrival some of them had fled: the President, Antonio de Rojas; the Treasurer, Francisco de Varges; Dr. Zapata; and Hernando de Vega. Among the rest who were carried off to Tordesillas was the secretary, Ruiz de Castañeda, and that night (September 30) Lope Hurtado de Mendoza wrote the King that they also carried away Cobos' deputy, Juan de Samano.[69]

Early in 1521, when the troops who were in the service of the *comuneros* in Valladolid threatened to desert unless they received their pay, the authorities, in despair, broke into the monastery of San Benito and seized 6,000 ducats which had been deposited there by private individuals for safe-keeping, and they seized a similar amount at the Colegio del Cardenal (Santa Cruz).[70] The Protonotary Frías wrote to Dr. Beltrán of the Consejo on February 15 that in the latter raid the *comuneros* had taken more than 2,000 ducats that belonged to Cobos.[71] Perhaps it was at this time too that the rebels attacked a negro servant of Cobos, named Alexo, and robbed him of more than twenty ducats, a gold ring set with a diamond and sixty-nine pearls, and the purse of silver thread in which he was carrying these treasures.[72]

Meanwhile in Germany the Diet and the problem of Luther's condemnation had kept the Emperor for six months at Worms. There, on May 18, 1521, occurred an event that had a profound effect on European affairs and also wrought a change in Cobos' relations to the Emperor—the sudden death of Chièvres in a plague that carried off many members of the Court. Charles replaced him as Grand Chamberlain with his old friend, Henry of Nassau. Although Nassau sat in the Privy Council of the Emperor, he was a soldier rather than a statesman and he never exercised the same influence as had his predecessor. From now on Gattinara was the sole architect of foreign policy. From now on, too, Cobos' rôle in Spanish affairs became increasingly important. Already on May 8 he had written to the secretary Ruiz de Castañeda in Spain: "I received your letter of April 24 and I assure you that I am concerned at your troubles. The true satisfaction is that you have done your duty, which is the principal obligation. I reported to His Majesty that you had returned there [to Valladolid] and he was glad to know it. There is nothing else to say at this time except that, if I can be of any service to you here, I shall do it with all my heart. God keep you . . ." [73] The significant revelation of the letter is that Cobos was now seeing the Emperor personally for the discussion of Spanish affairs. With the death of Chièvres he was soon to be indispensable.

The Court left Worms for Brussels at the end of May, 1521. On the way they stopped for a few days at Cologne and there, on June 9, the Emperor gave Cobos a precious relic: four heads of the Eleven Thousand Virgins, martyred at Cologne, together with a *cédula* validating the authenticity of the relic.[74] It was long a treasured possession of Cobos' chapel in Ubeda, but it has now disappeared. The summer was spent largely in Brussels. On July 9 Cobos wrote to Martín Ruiz de Avendaño another of the letters which show how he combined official business with personal relations.

Sir: I have received the letters which you have written me and I have reported them to His Majesty. His Highness is answering them, as you will see, and therefore there is nothing left for me to say, except that you have acted and are acting in such a way that His Majesty has been placed under the obligation of granting you favors; and so I hope that he will, as you deserve. In any way that I can serve you in this I shall be glad to do my best. Our Lord keep and increase your magnificent person and estate, as you desire.

From Brussels, July 9. Your servant, Francisco de los Cobos.[75]

Early in the fall the rivalry between Charles V and Francis I that had begun with their candidacy for the Imperial crown broke into open warfare on the Flemish border. Henry of Nassau was placed in command of the Imperial troops, and on October 22 Charles moved out to Audenarde to be nearer the front. A week later he bestowed on Cobos the greatest honor he had yet received, when he made him Commander of the Bastimentos de León in the military Order of Santiago.[76]

The habit of Santiago was an honor, but it was widely granted; Cobos, as we have seen, was already a knight of the Order. But commanderships were limited to a specific number of seats and hence were eagerly sought for, both for their prestige and for the income which went with them. In later years the Emperor reserved for his personal decision only two classes of appointment: the nomination of bishops and of commanders of the military orders. Cobos' appointment has, however, a very curious provision. He is to replace Gutierre Gómez de Fuensalida, who has resigned "for certain just reasons," but at Cobos' request, Fuensalida is to enjoy all the income and rights of the post during his lifetime; Cobos is to receive only the title. This is the first of a series of cases in which he revealed that his craving for prestige was greater than his desire for wealth.

On November 4 he sent to Spain one of his servants, Diego de Zárate, to complete the arrangements for the transfer of the title.[77] Zárate was another of the "old hands" of the secretariat of King Ferdinand. He had been appointed an *escribano* on June 19, 1509, and more recently (September 15, 1520) had been named a notary.[78] He remained with Cobos during the rest of his career as a sort of errand boy, though Cobos found him official appointments, first as *aposentador* ("billet officer") of the King and later as paymaster and then treasurer of the Casa de la Contratación in Seville.

As was the custom of the time, the messenger carried with him a list of instructions: "What you, Diego de Zárate, are to do—with the grace of Our Lord—on this trip to Spain is as follows . . ." It is a long document, thirteen folios written in a tight hand, and it is singularly important in its revelation of Cobos' personality—his concern with minute details, his caution and tact in dealing with people, his anxiety to curry favor with the great by the offer of his services, and most of all, his devotion to his family.

As soon as he landed in Spain, Zárate was to go wherever the Regents were (Cobos calls them "viceroys") and get the seal of the Order of Santiago from the secretary Zuazola, so that the royal provisions for his appointment might be sealed and recorded. If he saw the Regents or Antonio de Rojas or Dr. Zapata or Vargas he was to give them greetings and explain that he was in Spain on private business for Cobos. He must see Pedro de los Cobos, explain to him the mission he was on, and ask him to write often to Don Francisco's parents, since he (Don Francisco) wrote so seldom. He was to talk to Alonso de la Torre and tell him that he could not expect an appointment as secretary, but that Cobos would do everything possible to help him. Incidentally, Torre had been taking Cobos' place as registrar of fiscal transactions in Spain during Cobos' absence, and the Condestable had written to the King (June 11, 1521) asking that he be given Conchillos' post, explaining that "he is a servant of the secretary Cobos and from him he has learned well how to serve Your Majesty." [79] Finally, at Court he was to see Samano and thank him for his efficient services and his good relations with Pedro de los Cobos.

If he went through Burgos, he was to pay Cobos' respects to the Duquesa, to Doña Ana, and to the Conde de Haro. Even though the Conde had not believed, in the past, in his desire to serve him, he must now know that Cobos was his true servant.

From there he was to go straight to Ubeda and visit Cobos' father and mother and his sister Leonor and assure them that the principal reason for this trip was to tell them about Cobos' health and activities, so that they might rejoice and be relieved of worry. "God knows"—Cobos goes on—"how troubled I am at the concern they feel because of their desire, as true parents, to see me and how anxious I am, as a good and obedient son, to serve them and satisfy them in every way. And tell them that the only reason why I am eager to return to Spain is that I may in person console them, as I hope Our Lord will give me grace to do." Cobos hopes that they will be able to finish their business in England at least by April, and so he urges his parents not to worry or be troubled, but leave everything in the hands of Our Lord and his Glorious Mother, for trusting in them, God will fulfill their every desire and grant him the grace to do his duty. Finally he was to explain to them the purpose of this trip and the great honor which His Majesty had done him by this appointment, that they might be proud to know of it. And he was to visit Cobos' other kinsmen in Ubeda to bring his greetings.

This early demonstration of his devotion to his father and mother is of unusual interest, because, years later, Oviedo wrote that Cobos' greatest virtue was his love and care of his father. Cobos was so meticulous in his elimination of personal correspondence from his official file that not one of his letters to his parents has survived. But by chance, or oversight, there is preserved in the Archivo de Simancas an autograph letter from his father, probably written in 1518 or 1519, asking his son to do a favor for a friend.[80] It is written in a crabbed, shaky hand, beginning: "My beloved son" and ending: "From him who loves you dearly and longs to see you happy. Diego de los Cobos." Diego was an old man of ninety when Zárate came to visit him. It must have warmed his heart to know that his only son was winning a distinguished place in the favor of the King and that he had not forgotten his father and mother in the far away city of Ubeda.

In Granada, Zárate was to visit the Marqués de Mondéjar and tell him that at Court Verdugo was taking care of his interests. And Cobos names, one after another, the relatives that Zárate was to see, there and in Loxa, where his sister Isabel and her husband, Andrés de Torres, were living. Finally, he was given explicit instructions as to his negotiations in Malaga with Gómez de Fuensalida for the transfer of the commandership. The arrangements were complicated, involving payments of cash, ecclesiastical appointments, a habit of Santiago for Fuensalida's grandson, Gutierre Laso de la Vega, and a trip to the Priory of Uclés for the formal ratification of the contract. The details are not important here; what is significant is that Cobos was willing to pay for the title of Commander and to forego the income for the sake of the honor the title brought him.

As a matter of fact, Zárate was not successful in closing the deal on this trip. Not until two years later (November 23, 1522) did Fuensalida grant to Gómez Suárez de Figueroa a power of attorney to act in his behalf in the transfer of the title.[81] On February 10, 1523, Suárez de Figueroa appeared before the Prior of Uclés, Juan Sánchez de Salamanca, and with him came Zárate, bearing a similar power of attorney from Cobos, witnessed by three of his assistants, Juan Vázquez de Molina, Alonso de Idiáquez, and Gabriel Calderón.[82] There Figueroa, in the name of his principal, formally renounced the title and the Prior transferred it to Zárate, who kneeling before him, accepted it in Cobos' name.

To return to Zárate's instructions, when he had finished his negotiations with Fuensalida, he was to go back to Ubeda to report to Cobos' parents on what he had done and take a few days' rest. From there he was to return to the Governors, where he would find letters as to whether he was to return to Cobos or await his arrival in Spain. Finally, he was enjoined to keep Cobos constantly informed of his activity, for he was naturally worried about the outcome. One last point: when he was in Ubeda he was to get an account of all the money the royal paymaster, Cristóbal Suárez, had sent to Cobos there.

On the same day that Cobos dispatched Zárate to Spain he wrote to Ochoa de Landa, treasurer of Queen Juana, reminding him that a group of Court errandboys who had come to serve the King had not received their salaries and were in dire need. Would he please issue an order for their payment and have the money sent to them? And he adds: "In this, sir, you will do me a greater favor than I can express. And will you let me know what action you have taken?" [83] The surprising thing about the letter is that Cobos is issuing an order in his own name and not in the name of the King. Could it be that he had been authorized to act on his own initiative in such minor financial matters?

By the end of December the Court was back in Ghent and there, early in January, the Venetian ambassador, Contarini, received a letter from Vincenzo Priuli, captain of the Flanders fleet of the Serene Republic, with the news that one of his galleys had been seized at San Sebastián.[84] A few days later Contarini learned that Beltrán de la Cueva, commander of the Spanish forces in the north, was responsible for the seizure. On January 11 he wrote to the Signoria that he had received a copy of a letter from Henry VIII to Charles V, demanding the release of the galley. At the same time he reported that he had sent his secretary to read the letter to Bishop Mota and ask him to take action. It was Cobos who brought the Bishop's answer, which he had returned to Mota, with the request that one clause be expunged.

During the following months, in Flanders there is little mention of Cobos, except for one or two personal favors. In a long list of persons whose names were presented to the Emperor on May 11, 1522, as asking for an *ayuda de costa,* Cobos' name was naturally included.[85] A few days later (May 16) the Emperor extended Cobos' appointment as *fundidor mayor* from Yucatán to Cuba, Coluacán, and San Juan de Ulloa, called "New Spain." [86] It is surprising to find Cuba in this extension of his jurisdiction, since Hernando de Vega had had his appointment as *fundidor mayor* of that island confirmed on March 20, 1517,[87] and again at Zaragoza on July 27, 1518.[88] It may mean that Cobos now felt strong enough to take over the privilege for all the new found lands, except the now worthless privilege for the island of San Juan, which he left in the hands of Conchillos' son.

The Emperor had at last made up his mind to return to Spain. But first he must make his promised visit to England to carry out the arrangements which had been made at Bruges in August, 1521. The Court assembled at Calais on May 24 and sailed the next day. The Record Office in London has preserved a contemporary document intitled "A Boke of the Emperor's Trayne" which lists by name the persons who were to accompany Charles, with the number of their servants and horses.[89] In addition to the Flemish courtiers and the Spaniards who sailed from La Coruña in 1520 there are a few new names, like those of Antonio de Fonseca, "contador mayor" and Rodrigo Ronquillo, *alcalde de Corte,* who had fled from Spain to Portugal after their wanton burning of Medina del Campo in the conflict with the *comuneros* and thence had made their way to Flanders. In the list of Spanish secretaries appears the name of Cobos—"deux hommes, deux chevaulx." The total list numbered 2,044 persons and 1,126 horses; Charles had reported that he could not possibly bring any fewer. But the English authorities replied that they could not accommodate so many people, and so it was necessary to reduce the number; the Grande Chapelle was left in Flanders, half the courtiers were omitted, and of the Castilian secretaries, Licerazo was left out. The company, thus reduced, landed at Dover on the afternoon of May 25, where the Emperor was received by Cardinal Wolsey. The next day Henry VIII arrived in person and welcomed Charles to his kingdom.

During the whole month of June the Kings made merry at Greenwich, London, and Windsor with jousts and banquets and gay dances. Charles was delighted with his reception and he wrote to his old friend La Chaux with almost boyish enthusiasm, telling him how he and Henry had entered London, "both dressed in the same costume and with all the ceremonies which are customary here, as if I were to be received as the King of this kingdom, with such great joy and so many sumptuous decorations, that nothing more could be said." [90]

While the Kings played, Gattinara and Wolsey hammered out their political agreement for an alliance. It was Jean Lallemand, not Cobos, who accompanied the Grand Chancellor in these negotiations. Both the public and the secret treaties were completed by the end of June, and Charles and his Court sailed from Southampton on July 6. A few of his old Flemish courtiers went with the Emperor—Henry of Nassau, La Chaux, La Roche, and as secretary for Imperial affairs under Gattinara, Jean Lallemand. But it was a very different company from the foreign invasion of 1517. This time he came back to Spain with a tried and true suite of trained Spanish officials. Among them Francisco de los Cobos was rapidly rising to a leading place.

CHAPTER IV

RISE TO POWER

After an uneventful voyage the royal fleet reached Santander on July 16, 1522, where the Court remained for two days before they started for Valladolid. At Palencia, which Charles was visiting for the first time, they spent three weeks, so that they did not reach Valladolid until August.

Before they left England Bishop Mota had been ill with a fever, and he had not yet recovered when they reached Spain. At Herrera, as they moved south, his condition grew worse and he was unable to continue the journey. He died there some time in September. And so, as the King returned to his Spanish realm, he had lost the three chief advisors whom he had brought with him five years before: Chièvres, Sauvage, and Mota. It is true that he still had a Privy Council of Burgundians, but more and more, now that he was released from the tutelage of Chièvres, he was beginning to make his own decisions. At about this time La Roche wrote to Margaret of Austria that the King would not take the advice of anyone, but acted "as the spirit moved him." [1] And a little later Charles himself said to the Archbishop of Capua: "Think not that I communicate everything to the Council." [2]

For the administration of his affairs the King now had only three men on whom he could depend: Gattinara, assisted by Lallemand, for the conduct of Imperial business; in Castilian affairs, only Cobos, for García de Padilla was an insignificant figure, lacking in force and leadership; and Hernando de Vega, the only Spanish member of the Privy Council, who was timid and pliant. Martín de Salinas, who had joined the Court in England as ambassador of Ferdinand, now Duke of Austria, and whose penetrating letters provide such a complete picture of the time, was quick to recognize the importance of Cobos' position; on September 1 he wrote to the treasurer Salamanca: "Cobos is the man I can best judge as to what part he has in affairs, but the others each have their little corner." [3]

Of these three men, Gattinara, though of the minor Italian nobility, was a distinguished lawyer and scholar, friend of Erasmus. Jean Lallemand was a Flemish nobleman, Lord of Bouclans. Only Cobos was a "nobody," a clerk, an officeboy, uneducated, son of a village squire. We need not be surprised that among these associates he felt the need of prestige, that the title of "commander" meant so much to him. He was ambitious too for social recognition and now the opportunity was offered him.

Marriage

Back in Valladolid the King was lodged once more in the house of Bernardino Pimentel. And this time Cobos noticed a girl who lived across the street from the palace, María de Mendoza. She was a distant cousin of Don Bernardino; perhaps Cobos met her at his house. At the time, Doña María was fourteen years old, old enough to be married according to the laws of the time; Cobos was in his forties, but December and June marriages were common in the sixteenth century. We do not know whether Cobos courted her; at least we know that he courted her parents. On October 19, 1522, Francisco de los Cobos, Commander of the Order of Santiago, Secretary and Member of the Council of the Emperor, and Juan Hurtado de Mendoza and María Sarmiento, Count and Countess of Rivadavia, signed a marriage contract whereby Cobos agreed to marry their daughter, María de Mendoza y Pimentel, the betrothal to take place on that day and the marriage ceremony to be celebrated before Christmas.[4]

Marriage agreements in those days were complicated financial deals, and this was no exception to the rule. In the first place, the Count and Countess agreed to provide for their daughter a dowry of 4,000,000 *maravedís*. Of this amount the first million was to be handed over at once by the transfer to Cobos of the town of Hornillos, with its fortress, vassals, and other rights, which belonged to the Countess, but with the provision that, if within two years they paid Cobos 1,000,000 *maravedís* in cash, he would return the town to them, but if they failed to make payment, Dr. Pedro López and Dr. Francisco de Espinosa were to appraise the property and return to the Count and Countess any excess in value over 1,000,000 *maravedís*. The other 3,000,000 *maravedís* they promised to pay to Cobos within six months either in cash or securities.

Cobos, for his part, agreed to provide his bride with a dower of 2,000 ducats (750,000 *maravedís*), "of good gold and just weight," swearing that this sum was within the tenth part of his total possessions. The Archivo de Camarasa once had a copy of the inventory which Cobos presented to prove this statement, but unfortunately it has disappeared from the bundle in which it was catalogued. This meant that Cobos had already amassed a tidy little fortune of at least 20,000 ducats, the equivalent of about $360,000 in today's money. Although his total salary in the last three or four years had amounted to almost a thousand ducats a year, it is not possible that he could have saved this sum out of his salary and his other privileges and appointments. There must have been some truth in the charge of the *comuneros* that he had used his official position for his personal enrichment. It should be added that the payment of the dower of Doña María did not leave him in financial straits, for on November 7 he bought from the royal *argentier,* Jean Adurza, a *juro* of 4,000 ducats, at 7 per cent, to help the King pay the wages of the troops posted in Navarre and on the French frontier in the effort to recover Fuenterrabía.[5]

Curiously enough, however, on the same day the parties involved agreed to a modification of the original contract.[6] Cobos now agreed to accept, instead of the 4,000,000 *maravedís,* the sum of 3,000,000 and in addition, one half of the property which belonged to the Count and Countess in the Corredera de San Pablo, facing the church of San Pablo, with a stone arch at the doorway, a property which had belonged to the late Count of Rivadavia, who died in 1522, and also 100,000 *maravedís'* worth of tapestry, to be appraised by the Conde de Benavente. Again there was a supplementary provision that if the Count and Countess decided within six months to build a house on this land, which was adjacent to their other holdings, they were to pay Cobos 150,000 *maravedís* in lieu of the property. For some reason Cobos had been willing to reduce his original demands.

Martín de Salinas, who knew everything that was going on at Court, wrote on November 4:[7]

On October 20 Secretary Cobos was betrothed to the daughter of Don Juan de Mendoza, granddaughter of Ruy Díaz de Mendoza, who lives in the houses that belonged to the Condesa de Rivadavia in the Corredera de San Pablo in this town of Valladolid. She is a lovely lady, a girl of about fourteen years. The most distant relatives she has are the Condestable and the Almirante and the Conde de Benavente, with all the others related to them, and no one of them is less than an uncle. Her marriage was and is left in the hands of the Conde de Benavente, to decide what he thinks best, because between Don Juan and Cobos they couldn't come to an agreement, for one wants four and the other offers three—millions I mean. He is betrothed and the marriage is still to be settled. Many of us think that he made a mistake in this, that it would have been better for him to have an ass that would carry him rather than a nag that would dismount him. She is the person I describe. You and his friends will have to decide.

It is uncanny how exactly Salinas knew the details. And except for the whimsical exaggeration, he was right about her family relations.[8] Her father, Juan de Mendoza, was Adelantado de Galicia, an appointment that had been in his family for several generations. Her mother, María Sarmiento, had inherited the title of Condesa de Rivadavia on the death of her sister, Francisca Sarmiento. Her grandmother, María Pimentel, belonged to the family of the Conde de Benavente, Alonso Pimentel. Her aunt, Francisca Sarmiento, had married Enrique Enríquez and thus was related to the Almirante, Fadrique Enríquez, and through Don Enrique's mother, María Velasco, she was kin of the Condestable, Iñigo Fernández de Velasco.

Even though the Sarmientos and Mendozas belonged in the highest social circle, they were not well off. The county of Rivadavia was considered one of the poorer estates, with an income of only 6,000 ducats a year, as compared with an estimated 60,000 ducats of the Conde de Benavente.[9] Besides, Doña María was one of eleven children, the oldest of five daughters, and it was not easy to support such a family with so modest an income. We may well believe that her parents hoped through this alliance to have access to royal favors, even though Cobos had no social standing. Even in the sixteenth century impoverished noble families deigned to marry their daughters to *nouveaux-riches*. We may be equally sure that for Cobos it meant admittance to the social élite of Castile. On December 11 no less a person than Luis de Córdoba, Conde de Cabra and grandson of the Gran Capitán, Gonzalo Hernández de Córdoba, wrote to him from Badajoz, where he had been sent to receive the widowed Queen Eleanor,[10] to congratulate him on his marriage and send good wishes to him and to Doña María.[11]

But the Conde de Benavente did not accept him. Alonso Pimentel was a grandee of the old school, proud and arrogant. At the chapter of 1519 in Barcelona he had refused to accept the collar of the Golden Fleece, saying that he was very Castilian and cared not for foreign honors, since there were as good, or even better in Spain.[12] During the struggle with the *comuneros* he had been one of the King's stoutest supporters and once he had sent a *memorial* to Charles, reminding him that Chièvres and Cobos had told him that the King had promised to reward him for his services.[13] Perhaps he came to dislike and distrust Cobos during the negotiations regarding the marriage contract. At any rate, the same priest who told the story of Cobos' peddling lace caps as a boy related that the Conde de Benavente gave the Emperor a list of two hundred charges against Cobos, swearing that he would pledge his whole estate for any one of them that he could not prove.[14] Luckily for Cobos the old Conde died.

Although there is no record, Cobos and Doña María were undoubtedly duly married before the end of the year, probably in the church of San Pablo. And we may surmise that they made their home in her parents' house. Now that we have him settled down as a married man, we must return to his public life.

The Comuneros *Pardoned*

One of the first concerns of the government after their return to Valladolid was the restoration of confidence and security among the Castilians. On October 28 Cobos drew up, in the King's name, a general pardon.[15] It was a long document, citing in detail the offenses committed by the *comuneros,* not the least of which was *lèse-majesté,* and granting pardon to those who had taken part in the rebellion. On All Saints Day, after hearing mass, the King repaired to the Plaza Mayor, where a platform had been erected, draped with cloth of gold and silk. The King, dressed in a long robe, like a judge, took his seat on the platform, surrounded by the nobles and the members of his Council. Then Cobos stepped forward and read the pardon in a loud, clear voice.[16]

Though the general pardon did not emphasize the point, some two hundred and ninety of the leaders were excepted.[17] Of these a few were executed, others had their property confiscated, some were finally pardoned. In the Archivo de Simancas there is a document containing a list of persons whose property was confiscated, with marginal notes by Cobos indicating the value of their possessions. Cobos' name does not appear on another list of persons asking to be granted the property thus confiscated. But more than a year before, when the Governors, at the King's command, had granted a pardon to the city of Ubeda for the disorders that had taken place there, one of the offenses listed is that "you deprived Francisco de los Cobos, my secretary, of his post as *escribano del crimen* of the city and gave it to other *escribanos*." And one of the conditions of the pardon was that they restore the office to the person or persons who held it in Cobos' name—since he had been granted the privilege—in order that he might hold the office, as he had before.[18]

Perhaps it was in restitution of the damage done that Cobos was permitted, in May, 1521, to purchase from the receiver of confiscated property, Juan de Vozmediano, a house in the parish of Santo Tomás, adjoining his father's house, for the sum of 24,000 *maravedís*.[19] There is still a house in the Calle de Francisco de los Cobos in Ubeda from whose stone escutcheon the armorial bearings have been effaced; local tradition identifies this as one of the houses confiscated after the revolt.[20]

Government Reforms

Early in 1523 Gattinara took up again the problem of the organization of the King's official household which he had been forced to put off because of their hasty departure in 1520. The most urgent problem was that of finances. Although the Flemish Estates had voted a subsidy that covered the expenses of the Emperor's coronation at Aix-la-Chapelle and of his trip to England, there was still a serious deficit. Even before the Emperor's return to Spain the Treasurer Vargas had reported that he owed

the Fuggers 152,753 ducats for advances made at the time of
the Imperial election and for current expenses and had urged
that funds be found to pay the debt and thus avoid the high
interest charges.[21] On the eve of his departure from England
Henry of Nassau told Salinas that the King did not have a
penny.[22] And the Treasury in Spain was no better off, for the
Governors had pledged the income of the Crown for two years
ahead to meet the expenses of the civil war.

The first step was to secure from the *contadores* a statement
of the estimated income and expenses of the current year. It
was not reassuring, for it revealed that there was a deficit of
70,000,000 *maravedís* on arrears of indebtedness from preceding
years. On January 29 Charles sent the Consejo the financial estimates he had received and called upon them to study the problem and propose ways for balancing the budget, so that he might
not be forced to alienate the royal patrimony in order to raise
the funds necessary for all the regular and extraordinary expenses—the army, the royal household, the government officials,
etc.[23] There is no record of what the Consejo proposed; in
reality one of the chief sources of difficulty was the King himself,
with his personal extravagance and his Imperial obligations.

At the beginning of February the King issued a series of
orders consolidating the management of financial affairs. The
first action was the creation of a "Consejo de la Hacienda"
which was to pass on all expenditures.[24] The persons appointed
to this Consejo were Henry of Nassau, Juan Manuel, and
Jacques Laurin (who had just come from Flanders),[25] as Councillors; Francisco de Vargas, as Treasurer; Cobos, as Secretary;
and Sancho de Paz, as *escribano de finanzas*. With the appointment went a detailed instruction as to their duties. The Consejo was to meet every day; they were to receive and study all
estimates of income and expenditures, including monies derived
from the Indies and from the sale of confiscated property; each
year they were to submit a budget for the following year. In
addition, Cobos was instructed to countersign all orders, provisions for payments, and other fiscal documents. Sancho de Paz,
who had already been serving as Cobos' deputy in keeping the
records,[26] was to register all payments. A similar instruction
was issued to Vargas, describing his duties.[27]

The news of the King's decision must have been a shock to
some members of the Court, for rumors had been going around

that Alonso Gutiérrez, a protégé of Gattinara, was to be placed in charge, together with the Vozmediano brothers, and that Vargas was out.[28] The actual outcome, whereby Cobos and his assistant Sancho de Paz were given the administrative posts, in a sense, was a victory for Cobos. And apparently Gattinara was not happy at the solution, for a little later he wrote to Charles: "in this new reform of your finances they have left me out entirely and have settled everything without my signature," and he added that the King should have followed the advice of Alonso Gutiérrez in financial matters.[29]

The new Consejo began to function on February 25, 1523; the first documents, signed by the new Councillors and countersigned by Cobos, are dated February 27.[30] But the organization did not long survive. On October 4 Salinas wrote that Nassau and Juan Manuel were tired of the job, that Laurin had died. He even lists those who had replaced them.[31] But in September, 1524, he wrote that Nassau, Juan Manuel, and Cobos were still in control.[32] The Treasurer Vargas was certainly out before that time, for early in the morning of July 21, 1524, as he was leaving the convent of Las Huelgas outside of Burgos after spending the night, like Calisto departing from the garden of Melibea, he fell from the wall and was killed.[33] He was probably replaced by Gutiérrez, for Cobos notes in a memorandum that he had consulted him about a financial matter.[34] But he did not hold the title of Treasurer. During the next years Jean Adurza is *argentier* of the Emperor; not until 1529 does the title of "treasurer" reappear.

At the same time that the King was reforming the treasury he was also occupied in the re-ordering of the Consejos. A document in Cobos' hand records some of the changes.[35] In the Consejo Real, Dr. Palacios Rubios was to be retired on a pension because of old age and ill-health. Alonso de Castilla, who was to be appointed Bishop of Calahorra, could no longer serve. Dr. Tello was transferred to the Consejo de las Ordenes, which had charge of the military Orders, and hence could not serve in two Councils. The name of Dr. Beltrán is left blank; Salinas, who also reports most of these changes, explains that it was because he was said to have loaned money to the *comuneros*.[36] In the Consejo de las Ordenes, Dr. Calvete was to be relieved of office and given a half pension. The four men named to the Consejo de Guerra were the Marqués de Aguilar, the Marqués de Denia, Alonso Téllez, and Rodrigo Manrique.

Another contemporary document establishes the schedule of meetings of the Consejos:[37] the Consejo de Justicia (de Castilla), every Friday (as in the days of King Ferdinand); the Consejo de Cámara (the Privy Council), every other Monday, alternating with the Consejo de Aragón; the Consejo de Guerra, daily in emergencies, regularly every other Wednesday, alternating with the Consejo de las Ordenes; the Consejo de las Indias, every other Sunday. Cobos was now secretary of all the Councils except Aragon, Ordenes, and Guerra. As Salinas remarked: "He has full charge of the Council of State of Castile and in truth it is considered in this Court that he is high in His Majesty's favor and all matters of these kingdoms are dispatched by his hand. You may well believe that he is prospering."[38]

Gattinara was indefatigable in his efforts to direct the course of his young master. Later in 1523 he prepared another of his long letters of advice, which was discussed by the members of the Privy Council, consisting of Henry of Nassau, La Chaux, La Roche, Gorrevod, and one Spaniard, Hernando de Vega.[39] We need not discuss here the details of the document, but it is worth noting that under the question of implementing the wills of Ferdinand and Isabel, the Emperor noted in the margin: "Have Cobos write a letter instructing my Confessor to make inquiry and find out what I am under obligation to do." No detail was too insignificant for the Grand Chancellor: he urged the Emperor to meet with his Consejo de Estado every day, at 7:00 A.M. in winter, at 6:00 A.M. in summer; he should empower the Consejo to act in his name and have a stamp made for his signature, without "cracking your head and wearing out your mind" over details.

And he ended his seven chapters of advice: "If you observe well these seven articles, they will be for you the seven gifts of the Holy Ghost; and on the contrary; if you disregard them, they will be for you the seven deadly sins, for which you will later be accused and blamed."

Royal Favors

Among all these public activities Cobos' personal affairs were not being neglected. Early in January, 1523, he secured the appointment of Francisco Chirino, brother-in-law of Pedro de los Cobos, as *regidor* of Ubeda;[40] before the end of the month he transferred his office as *veinticuatro* of Granada to the younger Hernando de Zafra.[41] During the summer the Emperor renewed the order for the payment of 113,000 *maravedís* to Cobos as his salary for recording financial transactions.[42] On August 20, Juan de Mendoza transferred to his daughter, María de Mendoza, a *juro* with an annual income of 74,550 *maravedís* which he had received from his father, Ruy Díaz de Mendoza.[43] The principal of this *juro,* worth a little over 1,000,000 *maravedís,* was probably a payment on account of his daughter's dowry.

On November 12, the British ambassadors, Sampson and Jerningham, wrote from Pamplona to Cardinal Wolsey: "Franciscus de los Covos, the fyrst secretarie, hath not only at all tymes beyn very willing to do us such pleasur as he might for the service that he oweth to the King's Highness, but allso he is at this tyme in such favor that very few men in Spaine may doo bettyr service."[44] They go on to explain that his wife is "with chylde" and ask the King to command his ambassador to christen the child in the King's name, as the Emperor Maximilian had once provided for the christening of a child of Brian Tuke. The expected child, a boy, must have been born in December or January, for he was eleven years old in February, 1535.[45] He was christened Diego de los Cobos, after his grandfather, whether by the British ambassador we do not know. There were other evidences at this time that Cobos' star was rising. On January 6, 1524, Antonio de Guevara wrote to the Condestable: "The news from this Court are: the Secretary Cobos is in high favor; the Governor of Bresse [Gorrevod] is silent; La Chaux is grumbling; the Almirante is writing; the Duque de Béjar is saving; the Marqués de Pliego is gambling."[46] And Pero Mexía commented: "At that time the Emperor was placing great trust in Francisco de los Cobos, his secretary, and most of the public business passed through his hands."[47]

Cobos had accompanied the Emperor when he went north in the autumn of 1523 to be nearer the front in the war on the border and so must have been absent from Valladolid at the time of his son's birth. On the way back to Burgos in the spring of 1524, after the recovery of Fuenterrabía, the King decided to negotiate with the King of Portugal with regard to the possession of the Moluccas.[48] On March 5 Cobos dispatched a letter to Ruiz de Castañeda, the secretary, ordering him to report at Court immediately, to serve as secretary of the commission of experts which the Emperor was sending to Badajoz to meet with the Portuguese representatives.[49] The negotiations proved difficult; on April 21 Juan de Samano sent Castañeda a copy of the Bull of Alexander VI which had established the boundaries of the newly discovered territories. A few days later he wrote to congratulate him on his skill in conducting the business, and before the end of May, Cobos also sent his congratulations and thanks.[50] But the negotiators were unable to reach an agreement.

Royal favors continued to fall on Cobos. When the property seized from María Pacheco, leader of the Toledan *comuneros,* was appraised, it included a gold chain that weighed 322 *castellanos* and a gold necklace, worth about 93 *castellanos.* At Burgos, on June 20, the King gave these to Cobos as a reward for his services.[51] A month later he granted him a much greater favor. Before the end of 1523 a report had reached Spain that cochineal *(grana)* had been found in abundance in Mexico and that it would be a rich source of royal revenue.[52] The King at once ordered Hernán Cortés to look into the matter. His reports were so favorable that it gave promise of being a profitable venture. Cobos, as usual, saw in this an opportunity for his own profit, and on July 15, 1524, he secured from the King a royal order granting him 2,000 ducats a year for the next ten years, payable at the Casa de la Contratación from the net income of all cochineal produced in New Spain and adjacent territory.[53] Unfortunately, the expected profits did not materialize and Cobos had to take other measures to secure his annual 2,000 ducats.

While the Court was in Valladolid in August that Sevillan adventurer, Alonso Enríquez de Guzmán, turned up again, still seeking his habit of Santiago. He had been a-soldiering for five years and he was charged with hideous crimes—murder, rape, plundering—while he was a captain in the island of Ibiza. This time he went straight to Cobos' house, where he found him at nightfall. They looked at each other, "he with his eye on me and I with my eye on him," and at first Cobos was silent. Then he upbraided him for his misdeeds and suggested that he would be wise to leave the Court. But Don Alonso explained that the charges against him were false. And so Cobos took him on the crupper of his mule to the house of the old Duque de Alba, who said, on seeing Don Alonso: "Why have you got that ne'er-do-well with you?" [54]

Thanks to the support of Cobos and the Duque, Don Alonso was finally acquitted of the charges by Hernando de Vega and Dr. Carvajal, who had been appointed to investigate his case, and when he had an audience with the Emperor, the latter said: "Speak to Cobos and tell him to take care of your affairs." The upshot was Don Alonso's appointment as a Gentleman of the Royal House. He was profoundly grateful to Cobos and in the *Libro de su vida* he wrote:

> I did not have to importune him greatly, for he was concerned with my affairs and all those of the kingdom, especially of those who had served well, both out of regard for the honor and conscience of his master, the King, and because of his noble nature, for his goodness was so great that I can assure you that I have never seen his equal in the world, nor do I think that anyone has, because the Emperor never had anyone like him and he governed through him to the good order and harmony of his kingdoms.

The Emperor's Plans for the Future

That summer the King fell ill with a quartan fever that lasted for several months and official business was almost at a standstill. When the King left for Tordesillas at the end of September to complete the arrangements for the marriage of his young sister, Catalina, to King João III of Portugal, Gattinara, Cobos, and the other officials remained in Valladolid and did not rejoin the Court until December, after the King had reached Madrid. Some time in October Cobos drew up a memorandum of "What has been done after His Majesty left." [55] The first item is the preparation of the dispatch providing for the departure of the new Queen of Portugal. Most of the other matters reported deal with finances: negotiations for a loan of 200,000 ducats from the Genoese bankers Agustín and Nicolás Grimaldo; discussions with the Chancellor, Alonso Gutiérrez, and Juan de Vozmediano about money matters; a recommendation that 200,000 ducats of the income for 1525 be set aside for the payment of the armed forces and that Alonso de Baeza be placed in charge of these payments; the provision of 2,000 ducats as a gift to the Portuguese ambassadors, who had negotiated the marriage of the Infanta Catalina and Don João.

There are, however, two topics of exceptional interest in the report. All through the summer of 1524 there had been persistent rumors in the Court that the Emperor was planning to go to Italy. Contarini, the Venetian ambassador, had reported them to the Signoria, adding that 300,000 ducats had been set aside for the expenses of the trip.[56] Salinas also had mentioned them, though he did not think them well-founded.[57] The memorandum under discussion makes it clear that definite plans had already been made for the absence of the King from Spain. There are a series of questions as to whether each of the Consejos should "go or stay"; the Archbishop of Toledo must be informed as whether he would go or stay or remain in his see during this time, since he wanted to spend Holy Week in his church. Should any of the nobles go with him?

Evidently Dr. Carvajal had also been consulted on the problem, for he prepared a memorandum, which is preserved in the British Museum, entitled: "Opinion of Dr. Carvajal on what the Emperor should do when he leaves Spain and how the matter of the Consejos should be handled, and who will go with him." [58] Carvajal, loyal to the past, recommends that Queen Juana be named regent and that the Councils reside with her. Only the Consejo de Guerra should go with the Emperor. As for the Consejo de la Hacienda, he thinks that in its present form it served no useful purpose; Francisco de Mendoza could handle its affairs. In fact, Carvajal believes the Consejo more likely to ruin than to benefit the Treasury. Finally he remarks that the Emperor himself will have to decide whom he wants to take with him.

The second point of interest in the document are the specific references to the "Empress." "With what person or persons will the Empress discuss problems of government that may eventuate, in addition to matters of the Consejo and the household?" "If someone in addition to the person whom the Emperor is to name for the Empress is to stay with Her Highness, it will be well to call the Duque de Béjar." [59]

The question of the marriage of the Emperor had been a matter of concern from the day when he first came to Spain. He had arranged to marry a succession of French princesses and, later, Mary, the daughter of Henry VIII. But these alliances had collapsed and the choice had finally narrowed down to the Infanta Isabel of Portugal. As early as July, 1520, the delegates of Valladolid at the Junta de Avila had included among their demands that Charles marry Isabel of Portugal; in the following month the Regent Adrian had written him urging him to marry the Infanta. In 1521 the secretary Cristóbal Barroso was in Lisbon, sounding out the possibilities of a match. At the end of 1522 a Portuguese embassy was at Court, openly urging the marriage. The present document proves that Charles had made up his mind early in the autumn of 1524 and that the famous memorandum in which he set forth the problems that he was facing was written several months before the date usually assigned. In it he had said:

> To remedy all this, I see no better means than straightway to arrange for the marriage of the girl from Portugal and myself, in order that she may come here as quickly as possible, and at the latest in the month of May; and that the money which they will give me with her should be the largest possible amount in cash; and if it seems wise, to discuss the question of the spice-lands, either at the same time or separately, or to say nothing about them for the present.[60]

All things considered, he could find no better way than to go to Italy and "leave the girl from Portugal, who then would be my wife and their queen, as governor of these kingdoms, to rule them well with the advice of the Consejo and those whom I would leave with her, and also to handle financial negotiations and other matters which I shall not have been able to finish before my departure."

However intimate the confession was, people at Court seemed to have heard about his plans. Contarini wrote to the Signoria on December 4, 1524, that the Archbishop of Capua, who had recently arrived in Madrid, had been urging the Emperor to marry Isabel, and on January 9, 1525 he reported that the Florentine ambassador had told him that Gattinara thought that he would marry her.[61] But it was a long time before his marriage and his journey to Italy, now so definitely formulated, were to come to fruition.

That fall, probably before Cobos left Valladolid for Madrid, his wife gave birth to another child, a daughter, who received the name of María Sarmiento. She must have been born before November 30, for she had reached the minimum age for consent, fourteen years, when she was betrothed on November 30, 1538.[62] No other children blessed the wedlock of Don Francisco and Doña María. And she was still only sixteen years old! That winter in Madrid Don Alonso Enríquez met her for the first time and he tells an amusing story of an experience with her.[63] It seems that one day Doña María with two of her friends, Isabel de Quintanilla and Catalina Laso, and her brothers went out to a garden for a picnic. After they had eaten, the men stripped down to small-clothes and jerkin and started playing "tag." Don Alonso slipped and fell with such force that he was knocked senseless. The ladies came running up, crying, and Doña María sat down and took Don Alonso in her lap, bemoaning her misfortune in coming. The Archbishop of Toledo, Alonso de Fonseca, and the Confessor, García de Loaisa, who had come out to look at the garden, arrived just in time to witness this touching scene, and Loaisa, thinking that Don Alonso was dead, said: "That's the end this fellow should have expected. Now run along, Your Ladyship." And so Fonseca took Doña María away. But Don Alonso had come to, sufficiently to hear the Confessor's remark, and although the Archbishop later tried to excuse him on the ground that he hated to see Doña María crying, Don Alonso was not to be mollified and bore a grudge against Loaisa till his dying day. With equal constancy from this day on he was a devoted worshipper of Doña María, whom he always thought of as "La Excelente."

If Don Alonso was profuse in his admiration for Cobos, he was even more prodigal in his praise of Doña María.

> This lady was so discreet and gracious, so sensible and honorable that no wise man was or is dissatisfied with her goodness,—honoring everyone, dishonoring no one, doing good to many and ill to none, protecting and aiding all those who put their trust in her. She was a devout Christian, affable and approachable, very merciful, very beautiful and comely, very chaste, though gay, suiting her behavior to the season. She seemed like the sister of her husband, so alike they were in disposition and in purpose and manners. Because of this and my own judgment, diligence and restraint, I was admitted into their favor, both his and hers, though she, as a woman, outwardly showed more feeling, both by her tears and words, when my affairs were going ill, and by her delight, when they were going well. And so, with presents and luncheons and snacks and shirts and towels, she always provided for me, as if I were one of her brothers, whom she loved so dearly.[64]

Turning, now, to public affairs, Dr. Carvajal's recommendation of Francisco de Mendoza seemed to have had immediate effect. In a new "shake-up" of the Consejo de la Hacienda in January, 1525, he was named as the chief councillor.[65] The other new members of the Consejo were the *contadores* Martín Sánchez de Araiz and Cristóbal Suárez. Of the original group only

Cobos as secretary, and Sancho de Paz as recorder, survived, with Jean Adurza still as *argentier*. Gradually the Consejo was being transformed from a policy-making body, controlled by the King's Burgundian advisors, into a bureaucratic group of government employees. Francisco de Mendoza, brother of the Conde de Cabra, was the only "outsider," and he too withdrew when he was appointed Bishop of Zamora in 1528.[66] Cobos remained more than ever the dominant figure in financial affairs.

Martín de Salinas was aware of Cobos' increasing influence. And now he recognized the emergence of another personality in the life of the Court. As early as August, 1523, Charles had begun to confess with García de Loaisa, General of the Dominicans, whom he was soon to name President of the Consejo de las Indias and Bishop of Osma.[67] In December, 1524, Salinas wrote to the Treasurer Salamanca: "The Confessor of His Majesty is rising at full speed and I wish that His Highness [Duke Ferdinand] would pay some attention to him." [68] Twice in the spring of 1525 he wrote urging that Ferdinand should cultivate the favor of Cobos and the Confessor.[69] Salinas himself, however, seems to have had little contact with Cobos; he relied almost wholly on Jean Lallemand, which was natural since Lallemand was the secretary, under Gattinara, in charge of foreign affairs.

Because of his concern with financial matters it is not surprising that Cobos was appointed, with Hernando de Vega and Dr. Carvajal, as member of a commission to settle the affairs of Atanasio de Ayala, son of the Conde de Salvatierra, who had been one of the leaders of the *comuneros* and whose estates had been confiscated.[70] The Emperor, hard pressed for funds, was more and more inclined to commute the sentences of the former rebels in return for cash.

The news of the victory of Pavia and the capture of the French King reached Madrid early in March, and for days Cobos was busy writing letters to the grandees and to the municipalities to inform them of this act of Providence. One of the letters went to King João of Portugal, and it was Don Alonso Enríquez that Cobos chose as the bearer of the message.[71]

The Chapel of La Concepción

When the Emperor decided in the spring of 1525 to fulfill a vow by a pilgrimage to the shrine of Our Lady of Guadalupe,

Cobos took his first vacation in many years.[72] With his wife he left Madrid for Ubeda, probably on the day when the Emperor departed. His mother had died and he had not seen his old father since 1515. For María de Mendoza it was her first visit to her husband's home. While they were in Ubeda, Cobos took his first steps toward building a burial chapel for his father: in those days, all distinguished people built chapels. Naturally he wanted it attached to his parish church of Santo Tomás and for 4,000 *maravedís* he secured a piece of property adjacent to the church, occupied only by the ruins of an old chapel.

On Good Friday (April 4) he went over to Jaén to see the "Verónica" (it is still a revered relic in the Capilla Mayor of the Cathedral) and on Easter Sunday he returned to Ubeda with the Bishop of Jaén, Gabriel Merino. In the following days the Bishop gave his approval to the foundation of the chapel, to be known as the "Chapel of the Conception of Our Lady" and attached to it two benefices which had formerly belonged to Fernando de Ortega, who was named chaplain of the new chapel. The Archivo de Camarasa has preserved scores of Papal Bulls, confirming this and other privileges and indulgences granted to the chapel.[73]

Before he left Ubeda, Cobos completed the arrangements for building the chapel. Two local architect-builders *(canteros)*, Alonso Ruiz and Bartolomé Copado, were given the contract for the building, under the supervision of Alonso de Segura, Cobos' majordomo. It was to consist of a main structure with a sacristy and a tribune at the side. While it was under construction, the chaplain and a sacristan were to say mass for Don Diego in his house or in the church of Santo Tomás, when he was able to attend. Thus filial piety, religious devotion, and personal distinction were combined in a single foundation. Don Francisco and Doña María must have started back to Madrid with real pride and satisfaction at what they had accomplished.

They reached the Court on May 1 and Cobos was at once busy sending out the summons to a new Cortes to be held early in June at Toledo. When the *procuradores* assembled, under the presidency of Gattinara, it was Cobos who read the address from the throne, setting forth the needs of the Emperor.[74] This time, though they renewed their old petitions, the *procuradores* granted an exceptional subsidy to cover the expenses of the Emperor's expected marriage. During the following months Cobos was with the Court as it moved from place to place. At Segovia, in September, he was present, with the Viceroy of Naples, when the Vice-Provincial of the Mercedarians pled the cause of Pedrarias de Avila before the King.[75] That winter he was again in Toledo.[76]

When the long drawn out negotiations with Francis I were at last terminated by the Treaty of Madrid (January 14, 1526), the Emperor was free to carry out the plans for his marriage with Isabel; the Court left Illescas on February 21 for Seville. But before they reached their destination there came an unexpected piece of news: the Bishop of Zamora had murdered the warden of his prison at Simancas in an attempt to escape and was under close confinement.[77]

The Bishop of Zamora

The Bishop of Zamora, Antonio de Acuña, had been one of the most violent leaders in the revolt of the *comuneros*. After the defeat of Villalar he had tried to escape into France but had been apprehended near the border and at the Emperor's command had been imprisoned in the fortress of Simancas. Charles had been particularly resentful in his attitude toward the Bishop. On January 10, 1523, he had written to the Duque de Sesa, his ambassador in Rome, instructing him to ask the Pope for a *breve* which would authorize the Archbishop of Granada and the Bishop of Ciudad-Rodrigo to put Acuña to torture, until he told the truth, and threateningly he added: "If His Holiness should not do that, we shall be forced to take whatever other steps seem advisable." [78] Sesa promptly carried out his instructions, but without success. Shortly thereafter the Bishop asked permission to have certain books for his study and consolation. A *cédula* of April 25, 1523, granted his request, on condition that Cobos approve the list and examine each volume, page by page, to ensure that no letters or papers were inserted in them nor anything written on the margins or on the cover by way of notes.[79] Salinas had commented that the Bishop was very anxious to be released and had even offered to pay 60,000 ducats in cash, but that the Emperor had refused, badly as he needed the money.[80]

Thwarted in his efforts, the Bishop finally plotted to escape, suborning a young priest and one of the servants to aid him.

Early one morning in March, 1526, he walked into the office of the warden, Mendo Noguerol, who was seated at his table. As the warden looked up the Bishop seized a brazier full of hot embers that stood on the table and dashed it in the warden's face. While he was thus blinded, the Bishop drew a brick from the sleeve of his robe and cracked the warden's skull. Then, as he turned to flee, he was met at the door by the warden's son, who had heard his father's scream and who now tackled the Bishop and brought him to the floor, where he was quickly overpowered.

The Emperor had been reluctant to take action against the Bishop on the basis of his rebellious activities, but this murderous act was too much. As soon as he reached Seville he ordered the Alcalde Ronquillo to go at once to Simancas and take appropriate action. Ronquillo began his investigation on March 20. Put to torture, the Bishop finally revealed the names of his fellow-plotters and admitted his own guilt. On March 23 Ronquillo passed sentence: death by the *garrote* on the very battlement of the fortress from which he had planned to escape. And that same day, after the execution, Ronquillo wrote to the Emperor that he had carried out his commands. A similar letter went to Cobos, with the added request that he seek absolution for what he had done to the Bishop, torturing him and executing him, and also for torturing his accomplice, the priest Bartolomé Ortega. On March 28 Cobos answered, expressing the Emperor's satisfaction, and on the thirty-first the Emperor wrote to him personally, thanking him for his faithful service.[81]

This gory tragedy took place in the midst of the gay celebration of the Emperor's wedding. He had entered Seville a week after the arrival of the Infanta. As this was his first visit to Seville, the town had prepared a sumptuous reception with triumphal arches and song and dance.[82] On the night of his arrival Charles and Isabel were married in the great hall of the Alcázar that is now called the Sala de los Embajadores. Now, on receipt of the message from Ronquillo, the Emperor as a good Catholic considered himself excommunicated and absented himself from mass. The Papal Nuncio at the Court, Baldassare Castiglione, wrote to the Archbishop of Capua on April 9 that the Emperor had shown exemplary obedience to the Pope by thus abstaining from divine services, and he justified the Emperor's action in thus "punishing by justice so wicked a man, who so often and with such extreme criminal acts made himself unworthy of enjoying the privileges and favors that are granted to bishops, that they may use them, not for the harm but for the benefit of the faithful." [83] That year, for the first time the Emperor failed to make his Holy Week retreat, and not until he had received absolution from the Pope at the end of April did he retire to the convent of San Gerónimo, outside of Seville.

There is no question but that the Emperor accepted full responsibility for Ronquillo's act. On March 26, as soon as he received the news, he wrote to the Duque de Sesa: "The thing is done and in truth it was ordered by us, not thinking that it was as serious a matter as it afterward proved to be, rather feeling sure that God would be greatly served by the elimination from this world of a thing so foul and that had done so much harm." [84] This is borne out by a report from the Marqués de Villareal, the Portuguese envoy at the Court of Charles, to King João III, that the Emperor had told him that in ordering the death of the Bishop, he had had no other purpose than the service of God.[85] Villareal adds that he believed that the real motives for his action were his hatred for the Bishop and his fear that, if he lived, he might start another revolt, for he considered him the chief cause of the rebellion of the *comuneros* and of the attack which Francis I had made on the frontier.

As usually happens in such cases, it was his subordinates who were held to blame: Cobos for having advised the execution and Ronquillo for having carried it out. Hence they were the ones who had difficulty in securing absolution. Charles wrote to his secretary in Rome, Juan Pérez, on November 16, asking him to press the Pope for the absolution of Cobos and Ronquillo.[86] Pérez reported on December 15 that the Pope would absolve Cobos, if he established a fund with an income of twenty ducats a year for the cathedral of Zamora; he was not willing to absolve Ronquillo until he appeared in person before the Pope.

Cobos did not receive the notice of his absolution until early in March, 1527, when Castiglione wrote Clement VII from Valladolid that "it had been received as devoutly and with as much humility as one could desire, so that the said Secretary has set an example as a most obedient and devout Christian." [87] Finally, the official commutation of the penance imposed on Cobos and the absolution of Ronquillo and the others arrived,[88] and at Palencia, on September 8, all of the guilty came in penitents'

robes from the convent of San Francisco to the Cathedral, where
they were absolved by the Bishop, Pedro Sarmiento.[89] A manuscript of the British Museum tells a story from the Archbishop
of Zaragoza, Fernando de Aragón, that Cobos did his penance
in the chapel of Nuestra Señora de la Antigua in the cathedral
of Seville, holding a lighted candle before the altar at vesper
service. But it is hardly possible that Cobos was in Seville in
1527. Probably there was confusion with the penance of Palencia; the ceremony may have been held in the Capilla Mayor
Antigua of the cathedral there. At least it is good to know that
the Pope is reported to have said: "At any rate Cobos seems to
be a good Christian, since he is doing penance for the offence
done a Bishop." [90]

Seville and Granada

During these weeks in Seville, Cobos was busy working out the
details of the financial agreement between the Emperor and
King João with regard to the marriage contract. The Portuguese
ambassador, Antonio Azevedo Coutinho, wrote the King on
March 24: [91]

Cobos told me that he had learned that Your Highness said that he was
not taking good care of Your Highness' affairs, and that I knew how diligently he had dispatched everything that came to his hands and how devoted
a servant of Your Highness he was, and he asked me to defend him from
this charge. Your Highness may be sure that he appears to be a great servant
of Your Highness and he has become a good friend of mine and I too have
tried to have his friendship. He takes rapid care of all your dispatches and
sends them to my house and asks for nothing . . . He is a great friend of the
Confessor, who in my opinion is not favorable to us, and nevertheless, in the
last two or three months Cobos has shown that he is a good friend of mine,
and so also has Dr. Beltrán, who is in the Consejo de las Indias, a good friend
of Cobos and the one who knows most about the affairs of the Indies, though
even he knows but little. . . . And so, sir, I have found Cobos a servant of
Your Highness and I am grateful to him; and in the negotiations with France
he has acted very well and I hope that he will in these other matters.

What a clear light this throws on Cobos' eagerness to win the
good will of the men with whom he had to deal!

The newlyweds and their Court left Seville on May 14, arriving at Granada on June 4. These honeymoon months at Granada
in the summer and fall of 1526 were the happiest in Charles's
life; the "girl from Portugal" had turned out to be something
more than a source of money for Imperial plans: she was a

lovely and lovable woman. For many of the courtiers and ambassadors too they were days of idyllic delight, as they strolled in the gardens of the Generalife. Charles's marriage had not dampened his enthusiasm for hunting, and once during the summer he got lost while on the trail of a wild boar in the mountains. When he had not returned at nightfall, the whole Court was in a panic. Torches were lighted on the towers of the Alhambra, lights were placed in all the windows, and searching parties were dispatched in all directions. Late that night the Emperor appeared, guided by a *morisco* whom he had met in the mountains.[92] What a relief for Cobos and all the other courtiers, who were so utterly dependent on him, to have him back, safe and sound!

Not all was play that summer. From France, from Austria, from Italy came alarming news. And closer at hand there arose the problem of the *moriscos* of the kingdom of Granada, who came now to protest at their treatment by the Inquisition. The Emperor appointed an investigating committee to study their complaints, and the report of the committee was referred to a large commission of prelates, to which García de Padilla and Cobos were added as representatives of Charles's government. One of the seven decisions of the commission was the transfer of the office of the Inquisition from Jaén to Granada; another forbade the *moriscos* to wear their traditional garb. When the *moriscos* appealed from these two decisions, offering to add 80,000 ducats a year to their contribution to the treasury, the Emperor relented and yielded to their request. It was said that part of the money landed in the hands of the Emperor's favorites. At least 18,000 ducats were allotted to the construction of the abortive palace which Pedro de Machuca was building for the Emperor within the precincts of the Alhambra.[93]

In September it was announced that the Empress was pregnant and plans were laid to move north. On December 5 Cobos issued the dispatches calling for another Cortes at Valladolid in February[94] and on the tenth of the month the Court left Granada. Moving slowly because of the Empress's condition, they reached Ubeda on December 16.

The Royal Visit to Ubeda

This was the Emperor's first visit to the city, and as everywhere,

he was received with elaborate ceremony. At the Puerta de Toledo, he was met by the royal governor, Don Alvaro de Lugo,
and the councilmen of the city, and there the local authorities
begged him to confirm the rights and privileges which had been
conferred on the town by his predecessors as a reward for their
faithful services against the Moors. Then, while Cobos held in
his hands a Book of the Gospels and a silver crucifix, the Emperor took off his cap, kissed the cross, and placing his right
hand on the Gospels, swore in the name of God and Holy Mary
and by the cross and the Gospels that he would preserve all the
rights and privileges of Ubeda and hereby he confirmed them.
Cobos requested a notary to bear witness to the act. And so, in
the presence of Alvaro de Lugo and Francisco de Loaisa, his
deputy, and of the councilmen of the city, Juan Vázquez de
Molina and Pedro de los Cobos, the *escribano* Luis Peláez drew
up and signed the official document. That night the Emperor and
the Empress were lodged in Cobos' house.[95]

The Palace in Valladolid

After a few days in Madrid, the Court reached Valladolid on
January 14, 1527. And this time Cobos was able to move into his
new home. We have seen how a clause of the marriage contract
of 1522 had provided that the Count and Countess of Rivadavia would turn over to Cobos half their property on the Corredera de San Pablo, with the condition that within six months
they could recover the land by payment of 150,000 *maravedís*.
They had not availed themselves of this privilege and late in
1524 Cobos had decided to build a house of his own on the lot.
It is probable that he had also acquired the house of his parents-
in-law, for in the spring of 1527 they were living in part of the
house of Bernardino Pimentel, across the street.[96]

As the architect of his new house Cobos appointed Luis de
Vega. The little we know about its construction is found in a
letter which Vega sent to Cobos on October 26, 1526.[97] In it he
reported the progress of the work: they were putting on the
roof; he thought that no one had ever seen a better façade. As
soon as it was finished, which should be in December, he wanted
to go home to Madrid, for he had been away for two years.
Would Cobos have his agent Saldaña pay him his bill? He adds
a number of details: a property of Alvaro Daza, which Saldaña

had bought, had made it possible to make a number of changes: to put windows in the stairway, to introduce a chapel into the plan, to enlarge an inner room, to open windows in three of the bedrooms, to build kitchens and add a *corral*. In closing, he remarked that no matter how soon Cobos returned to Valladolid, he would have a good new house to stay in, as well as a good room in the old house [that had belonged to the Count and Countess?], which could be added to the new one.

It is impossible to tell what state the house was in when Cobos returned in 1527. The body of the building must have been completed by 1528, for in that year Luis de Vega entered into a contract with Dr. Beltrán and his wife to build a palace in Medina del Campo (the present Palacio de los Dueñas), and when the owners made a contract with the iron-worker, Cristóbal González, on April 12, 1529, he agreed to make the *rejas* exactly like those he had made for the house of Cobos in Valladolid.[98] Certainly Cobos continued to add to its ornamentation in later years with mural decorations and sculpture. Today the only part that has survived in anything like its original form is the patio, which is now the main court of the Capitanía General. The quaint capitals, with their ornamentation of *putti*, were often attributed to Berruguete;[99] it is now clear that they were designed by Luis de Vega. The medallions, with their heads of Roman emperors, were probably carved by Jamete in the following decade.[100] The paintings which once adorned the walls have long since been effaced. But in its day it was one of the great palaces of Valladolid; late in the 30's Cristóbal de Villalón called it "imperial."[101]

The first weeks in Valladolid were crowded with the preparations for the gathering of all the Estates of Castile, for this time the Emperor had summoned the nobles, the clergy, and the knights of the military orders, as well as the *procuradores* of the towns. On February 11 Cobos read to the assembled clergy the Emperor's plea for financial aid.[102] But the prelates turned a deaf ear: they had no money to give. In the course of the meeting there arose a conflict between the Archbishop of Seville and the Archbishop of Santiago over their order of precedence.[103] The question was referred to the Emperor for decision and on March 2 he called a meeting of his Castilian advisors: the Archbishop of Toledo, García de Padilla, Dr. Carvajal, and the Lic. Polanco; and in the presence of Cobos, summoned the two archbishops who had been waiting in the ante-room. Thereupon he announced that neither one should have precedence; they would sit on one side or the other; they could take turns in the order of speaking, now one, now the other. When they had accepted this proposal, he ordered them to present to him within six months any relevant documents or papers, so that he might pass judgment on the substantial question. Cobos placed his rubric on the document that recorded this solemn farce.

On the following day the Emperor presided over the Chapter of the Order of Santiago. As "Trece" of the Order and Commander of the Bastimentos de León, Cobos was one of those who took part.[104] But in response to the Emperor's request for funds, the knights replied that they were bound by their vows to accompany him in case he went to war; if he did not go in person, they would support him with a fifth of their income.[105]

On March 30 the Grand Chancellor, Gattinara, left Court; ostensibly he had a three months' leave to visit Montserrat in payment of a vow. But everyone knew that he was thoroughly dissatisfied, that he was going to Italy and might not return.[106] What was the cause of his dissatisfaction?

CHAPTER V

———··❮∞❯··———

RIVALS FOR FAVOR

Conflict with Gattinara

The Grand Chancellor had been annoyed at being left out of the picture in the reform of the finances in 1523, and from this time on there are constant references to his dissatisfaction with the conduct of the Emperor's affairs. In the spring of 1524 he had planned to go to Rome to negotiate with the Pope, but it was La Roche who was finally sent.[1] Marco Foscari wrote to the Signoria of Venice that the Chancellor had refused to go because the Emperor would not grant him full power to act.[2] In August Contarini commented on the difficulty of dealing with him, saying that he had a very small brain and when once he had formed an opinion he became stubborn.[3] It must be said, however, that when Contarini made his formal *Relazione* to the Council of Ten in the following year, he expressed a very different impression, praising him for his immense capacity for work and the skill with which he conducted all of the Emperor's affairs.[4]

Gattinara had not been happy at the handling of the negotiations between Charles and Francis I; he had even refused to place his seal on the Treaty of Madrid, in January, 1526. Later in the spring he was in conflict with the King [5] and in July he offered his resignation, but he returned to his office in a few days.[6] Shortly after the Court reached Granada, he wrote a long

letter to his secretary, Jean Lallemand, asking him to appeal to
the Emperor for help in solving his financial problems: he was
burdened with debts and would have to discharge all of his servants, unless Charles granted him some favors.[7] For some reason
Lallemand did not carry out his mission and on June 17 the
Chancellor wrote directly to the Emperor, describing in detail
his financial needs and possible ways in which the Emperor could
relieve him. The only immediate result was a petty grant of
50,000 *maravedís* a year as an *ayuda de costa*.[8] That summer
Salinas reported that he was again in serious conflict with the
Emperor.[9]

Matters came to a head after the Court returned to Valladolid. In February and March there were persistent rumors that
Gattinara was planning to return to his home in Italy and had
asked the Emperor for a leave, that the Emperor was willing to
let him go.[10] Brandi has written that "Gattinara's journey to
North Italy is wrapped in mystery." [11] But there is considerable
evidence that casts light on the mystery.

At some time in March Gattinara wrote a bitter letter to the
Emperor, outlining his grievances. He had never been rewarded
properly for his services and he was not one of those who had
been corrupted by gifts; even the silk cloth which he had received
from Venice he had accepted only because of the Emperor's command. What was worse, he had far less authority than the Chan-
cellors of France and England, nay even of Burgundy. He
protests:

> Your Majesty pays no respect to my office, but reather demeans it, granting
> audience to others of lesser stuff and handling through their hands what
> should belong to my office and tolerating in your presence things that your
> predecessors would not have tolerated, by chastising those who should be
> chastised; often summoning me and making me remain for an hour or two,
> without doing anything, while I wait for those who ought to wait for me;
> and often stopping to talk to insignificant people, when Your Majesty might
> without trouble be dispatching important matters. . . . In a word, it seems
> that I am nothing but a tavern sign.

He goes on to demand that all appointments should have his
approval and that it should not be in the power of the secretary
or anyone else to report them to the parties concerned, but this
should be done only through him and by his word of mouth.
Finally he insists that members of the Consejos must be subject

to his commands and must come to him at his summons, under penalty of losing their salary.

This letter was apparently given to the Grand Master, La Roche, for delivery to the Emperor. But La Roche returned it to him with the suggestion that it was "a little choleric" and might be expressed differently. At the same time La Roche assured him that the Emperor was desirous of keeping him in his service, in spite of the leave that he had granted him, and that he was ready to correct the offenses against his office and reward him for his services. That night the Chancellor thought it over and prepared a new statement of the conditions under which he was willing to continue in the Emperor's service. It is a long document, written in Gattinara's tight hand, and contains ten main demands. They cast so clear a light on the source of his dissatisfaction that they deserve to be summarized here.

(1) The first demand was that in order to restore his good name which had suffered by the public announcement of his leave, the Emperor should order all the Consejos to consider him as their head and obey him and grant him all the rights and privileges of his office.

(2) That all the secretaries should be subordinate to him and not presume to propose anything in the Consejo or make reports or present memoranda without the Chancellor's orders; that the secretaries should not prepare papers of any kind for the King's signature without orders from the King or the Chancellor and without the Chancellor's signature; that His Majesty should not issue any orders, unless the Chancellor was present, except when he was sick and unable to attend; and if any secretary failed to observe these rules, he be punished and the Chancellor be authorized to report infractions to His Majesty and have him punished.

(3) That no secretary or other person dare to dispatch mail or receive and open pouches, without the Chancellor's orders and in his presence; that all mail should be received and dispatched by the Chancellor and that ambassadors and viceroys be instructed to address their correspondence directly to the Emperor and not to any secretary; and, to prevent private correspondence, all mail pouches should have lock and key and only authorized persons should open them.

(4) That all grants of favor or appointment should be made in the Chancellor's presence.

(5) That, in conformity with the laws of recent Cortes, no councillor or secretary be permitted to hold more than one office nor to appoint a deputy to perform the duties of an office nor to derive profit from the appointments to the offices in their charge, lest the desire for personal gain lead them to do something unjust and unreasonable.

(6) That in matters affecting Aragon the old rules be preserved.

(7) That the Chancellor should have the authority to make minor appointments without consultation.

(8) That the Emperor should give him a special evidence of love and confidence by authorizing him to come to his bedroom each morning to report and to receive instructions.

(9) That the Emperor appoint someone to help him in the performance of his duties and to take his place, if his gout come back, so that there will always be someone prepared to transact the necessary business, "because the exercise of practice and experience makes men, who are like gold, which can be judged only when it is proven."

(10) That the Emperor instruct the *argentier* to pay him his salary for six months and also grant him an additional sum, so that he may settle his affairs and marry off his niece.

In a final paragraph Gattinara explains that in none of these demands did he have any intention of limiting the Emperor's right to make any decision he chose.

These documents present a very different side of the Chancellor's character from the selfless statesman whom Brandi has portrayed. Here he appears arrogant, vain, and petty; in his appeal for money he is groveling. In reality, the King had been generous to him in rewarding his services. In the autumn of 1524 he had paid him 14,628 ducats at one time.[12] It was reported that the Duke of Milan had given him an estate with an income of 7,000 ducats a year.[13] Between 1519 and 1528 a long list of royal grants was made to him and members of his family in Italy.[14] Obviously his demands were based upon his belief that someone was usurping his authority. Now who are these "insignificant people of lesser stuff" who keep him cooling his heels in the King's ante-chamber? Surely not García de Padilla, Grand Commander of Calatrava, or García de Loaisa, Bishop of Osma, or even his secretary, Lallemand, Lord of Bouclans. Who is this secretary who is presuming to overstep his bounds and assume functions and privileges unbecoming his station? The only person possible is Francisco de los Cobos.

From the time that the Emperor returned to Spain in 1522, Gattinara and Cobos had been engaged in an unconfessed struggle for the control of the machinery of government. As Cobos gained in influence and intimacy with the King and placed his assistants in all of the key administrative posts, the Chancellor was naturally disturbed and resentful. It is of particular interest that in the Archives du Royaume in Brussels there is a copy of Gattinara's demands which contains in the margins the Emperor's comments. To many of them he replies that the authority he seeks is not a part of the function of the Chancellor, but belongs to the administration of Castile; to others he says only that he will do "what seems best to him." He does, however, agree to advancing him his pay for six months.[15] Clearly the Emperor was not inclined to take away from Cobos the post of responsibility and trust which he had won in the conduct of Castilian affairs nor deprive him of the privileges and favors which he had showered on him, albeit in disregard of the laws of the Cortes.

The Emperor's decisions were not satisfactory to Gattinara, and on March 30 he left for Montserrat and Italy, taking with him all his personal possessions. He traveled slowly. But if he thought that the Emperor would recall him, he was mistaken. Charles was now sure of himself; he would not be beholden to any man. From Italy Gattinara continued to write to him about affairs of state. By the end of the summer his indignation had cooled down; at the end of October he was back at Court, ready to take up his old job, with no conditions attached.[16] His influence with the Emperor was already beginning to wane.

The Birth of Philip II

The news of the birth of a son and heir to the throne on May 21, 1527, at Valladolid, was received with universal rejoicing in Spain.[17] As on earlier occasions, the Emperor and Empress were lodged in the house of Bernardino Pimentel. The main entrance to the palace was on the western front, but on the northern side, facing the church of San Pablo, there was another door that opened into the staircase which led to the apartment where Juan Hurtado de Mendoza and his family were living. From this doorway a passage-way was built across the street, straight to the main portal of San Pablo. It was gaily trimmed with greens and roses, oranges and cherries; at intervals there were arches and tabernacles. At eight o'clock on the morning of June 5, Henry of Nassau, as master of ceremonies, summoned to the church the principal functionaries: La Chaux, the Bishop of Elna, Cobos, the *alcaldes de Corte,* to see if everything was in order for the christening. A little later the Emperor came to mass and gave his approval of the arrangements.

That afternoon the procession began. Accompanied by all the nobility and the prelates, the Condestable carried the newly-born baby down the stairs from Mendoza's apartment and they moved across the street into the church, while all the musicians played and children, dressed as angels, sang from the tabernacles *Gloria in excelsis Deo.* With what pride the Emperor watched the scene, as he looked down from the upper window of the Palace! Was María de Mendoza, as lady-in-waiting of the Empress, one of those who, dressed all in black satin and black velvet, rich with pearls and golden beads, followed in the train of Queen Eleanor? The church, hung with tapestries and brocade, was jammed with people as the procession moved down the aisle to the baptismal font. There the Archbishop christened the baby, who screamed lustily as the water fell on his head, and a herald proclaimed: "Hear ye, hear ye, hear ye! Don Felipe, Prince of Castile, by the grace of God!" The old Duque de Alba would have had him called "Fernando," in memory of Ferdinand the Catholic. But Charles had preferred the name of his Burgundian father, Philip the Fair. That night there was a gala ball, and for days after there were jousts and tournaments in the city. At one of these, held in the Corredera of San Pablo on Sunday, June 16, Doña María's oldest brother, Diego Sarmiento de Mendoza, was one of the five gentlemen who fought against the Emperor's side.[19]

Though we know from documents which he signed that Cobos was with the Court in the following months, as it moved to Palencia, to Burgos, and back to Madrid, there is little evidence of his participation in the affairs of state. But he was busy exploiting his personal interests. In August he secured from the King an extension of his jurisdiction as *fundidor y marcador mayor* to the whole coast from Florida to Panuco and from Darien to the gulf of Venezuela.[20] When the two agents of the

Welsers, Heinrich Ehinger and Hieronymus Seiler, came to Spain to arrange for the colonization of Venezuela, Cobos entered into a contract with them to pay them a percentage of his rights as *fundidor* on any mines they might develop there (February 12, 1528),[21] and before they left he pledged his income as *fundidor* as security for a loan of 1,000 ducats which they had made him.[22]

Cobos had managed to secure the appointment of his son Diego as a knight of Santiago. The *prueba de nobleza* to test his fitness took place at Burgos on November 2, 1527.[23] Though the witnesses all testified to knowing Diego's parents and grandparents, none of them mentioned his age. Which was just as well: he was then four years old! At about the same time Cobos had a share in obtaining another appointment as knight of Santiago.

Don Alonso Enríquez, still on the quest for his habit, had turned up again, armed this time with a letter of recommendation from the Prior of San Juan, Diego de Toledo, to his old enemy the Bishop of Osma. When he reached Burgos, Don Alonso went to the house of the Bishop, who invited him to stay to dinner. Just as they were finishing the meal, Cobos came in. Don Alonso turned him a cold shoulder, but Cobos insisted upon embracing him, saying that when he knew the facts, he would not lay on him the blame for his failure to receive his habit. The Bishop and Cobos agreed to speak to the Emperor again. For the moment, Cobos asked Don Alonso to have supper with him and his wife, saying that Doña María was astonished and annoyed that he had not come to stay at their house as was his custom. So that night Don Alonso went to their lodging, where he was well received by Doña María, because, as he said: "she was as good as goodness and goodness not such as she." Encouraged by the reports of Cobos and the Bishop, Don Alonso visited the Emperor to present his plea, and again the Emperor said: "Speak to Cobos." Within a week Cobos was able to tell him that the Emperor had at last consented to grant him the long-coveted habit.[24]

Pedro de Alvarado

Not long before this, Pedro de Alvarado, the lieutenant of Hernán Cortés in the conquest of Mexico, had reached the Court and had quickly made friends with Cobos, who supported him vigorously in his efforts to secure recognition. The eight-year privilege for the exportation of negro slaves to the Indies, which Laurent Gorrevod had received in 1518, had expired, and on November 15, 1527, the Emperor granted to Cobos and to Dr. Beltrán the right to export two hundred slaves each.[25] A month later they entered into a contract with Alvarado to form a company for the exportation of six hundred slaves to work the mines in Guatemala, each party to contribute his share of the cost of the slaves, at ten *pesos* each, and all to share in the profits.[26] Cobos' commitment therefore amounted to 900,000 *maravedís,* or 2,400 ducats. Perhaps it was to meet part of this payment that he borrowed the 1,000 ducats from the two Germans.[27]

Three days after the signing of their contract (December 18, 1527), Alvarado was appointed Governor and *adelantado* of Guatemala at a salary of 562,500 *maravedís* (1,500 ducats).[28] And at the same time he was named a Commander of the Order of Santiago. Remesal tells a story that when he was first in Mexico, Alvarado used to wear an old velvet jerkin that had belonged to his uncle and which still showed the traces of the cross of Santiago, so that the soldiers used to call him mockingly the "Commander." Now he had won the right to wear the cross. Before he left Spain, he married Beatriz de la Cueva, niece of the Duque de Alburquerque. It was commonly said that Cobos had arranged the marriage because she was his close relative. While their kinship was remote,[29] rather than close, there is reason to believe that he did use his influence to promote the marriage, for on March 20, 1529, he wrote to his nephew Juan Vázquez de Molina, asking him to appeal to Elvira de Mendoza for help in securing a dowry for Doña Beatriz from the old Queen Juana.[30]

When Alvarado returned to New Spain he fell on evil days. Hardly had he landed when his wife died, and shortly thereafter he was arrested by the Audiencia of Mexico. But he was soon released and made his way to Guatemala. From there he sent Cobos a gold pitcher and a cup as a gift and Cobos ordered Samano to have them assayed and the money paid to Alvarado out of his income as *fundidor;* they were assayed as worth 167,-902 *maravedís* on August 21, 1530. Muñoz cites this as an example of Cobos' integrity and even adds that he told Samano

that he would rather risk his property than his conscience.[31]
Alvarado had already written to Cobos, on July 28, 1530, revising the contract of 1527 and reducing the amount to be paid for each slave from ten to three *pesos*.[32] A month later Luis de Bivar wrote to Cobos from Guatemala that Alvarado's imprisonment had delayed his work on the contract, but that he was now proceeding diligently, "to your great profit, remembering the honors he has received from you." [33] One more detail of his relations with Alvarado should be recorded: it was he who was responsible for securing the dispensation which permitted Alvarado to marry his first wife's sister, Francisca de la Cueva, who came to such a tragic end in the earthquake of 1541.

Before the end of 1527 Cobos picked up another favor when the King granted him seventy acres of land in the Cañada de la Nava, which was under the jurisdiction of Medina del Campo.[34] The municipal council gave their approval to Cobos' agent, the banker Rodrigo de Dueñas, on January 24, 1528. Subsequently they seem to have reversed their decision and for several years Cobos kept securing confirmation of the original grant. The last of these, dated July 7, 1530, specifically excluded Cobos from the instruction revoking earlier *mercedes* on the ground that "because of his quality, merits and services it was just that he be excepted from the provisions of the royal order." [35]

Early in 1528 the Emperor decided to make his first visit to Valencia. Cobos drew up in his own hand a long list of matters which must be settled before his departure: provisions for the powers to be granted to the Empress and the persons who were to attend her, methods of handling state business, of filling vacant posts, decisions concerning the persons who were to accompany the Emperor, and the preparation of the necessary wagons and pack-mules for the journey.[36]

Shortly after Easter the Court left Madrid, and at the end of May reached Monzón, whither the Emperor had summoned the representatives of Aragon, Cataluña, and Valencia for a joint Cortes. On June 7 there arrived at Court the herald of the King of France, who had come under safe-conduct to deliver to Charles the challenge of Francis I to a personal combat. That night he lodged in the house of Jean Lallemand and the next morning he appeared before the Emperor and the assembled leaders of the Court. Although Lallemand did not mention

Cobos in his official account of the act, Santa Cruz names him among those present.[37] Certainly it was Cobos who was charged with the messages which the Emperor sent to the nobles and prelates of Castile, seeking their advice as to whether he should accept the challenge.[38] Many of their replies were addressed directly to Cobos; in other cases they wrote both to Cobos and the Emperor. Thus the President of the Consejo wrote to Charles: "In order not to be troublesome in this matter, I refer Your Majesty to Cobos, to whom I am writing in greater detail." And the letter of the Condestable, almost certainly addressed to Cobos, said: "If what I have said seems good to you, show it to the King; and if it seems bad, I beg of you to tear this letter up, since I am talking to you as unrestrainedly as I would to one of my sons." Cobos' answer to the Duque del Infantado is typical of his official style: "Illustrious Sir"—it begins—"The Emperor our lord has received Your Lordship's opinion and he has approved highly of all that you have said in it. His Majesty is answering Your Lordship, as you will see. There is nothing else for me to say, except that if there is anything in which I can serve you, I shall count it a favor, if you will command me. Monzón, June 24." And in a postscript in Cobos' own hand: "Your Lordship's servant has shown great diligence, for His Majesty received your letter on Monday, June 22. I kiss Your Lordship's hands. Your very certain servant. Francisco de los Cobos." [39] Let it be recorded that Charles did not accept his rival's challenge.

The Visit of Hernán Cortés

At this same time there appeared at Monzón a notorious figure —Hernán Cortés, conqueror of New Spain, back in his homeland for the first time since his great exploits. Cobos had never seen him before, but he had been the recipient of his gifts. When Cortés sent his first shipment of treasures to Spain (they reached Molins de Rey early in December, 1519),[40] Cobos was one of the long list of courtiers who were to receive personal gifts. His were: "three shields: one with a blue field, with a gold and feather monster in the middle; another with a green field, with a gold serpent; another, white, with a knot of feathers and some gold shells." [41] On October 15, 1524 Cortés wrote to Charles that he was sending him further treasures, including a silver culverin on which he had spent 27,500 *pesos* (33,000 ducats) in metal and workmanship.[42] Díaz del Castillo said that the value of the gold sent was 80,000 *pesos* and that the culverin was called "The Phoenix," because of the figures on it and the inscription: "This bird was born without equal; I without a second in serving you; you without an equal in the world." [43]

On June 1, 1525, Contarini reported to the Venetian Signoria that some caravels had reached Seville bringing treasure for the Emperor and a piece of artillery of gold, silver, and other metals, the whole of a value of 100,000 ducats.[44] In September Navagero wrote that the cannon had arrived, that it was about the size of a demi-culverin, but the metal was of very base alloy and worth little.[45] Díaz del Castillo in his *Verdadera historia* says that in Mexico they had heard that the Emperor had given it to Cobos, who had promptly had it melted down in Seville and derived more than 20,000 ducats from the metal.[46] If his history is really "true" in this case, it was indeed a precious gift that the Emperor made to Cobos.

Returning to Spain, Cortés landed at Palos in December, 1527, and passing through Seville went on to the shrine of Guadalupe. There he paid his devotions to Our Lady, gave alms to the poor, and ordered masses said for the souls of his father and his wife and for his friend Gonzalo de Sandoval, who had died shortly after arriving in Spain. With him he brought as an *ex-voto*, made when he was bitten by a scorpion, a magnificent gift for Our Lady—a golden jewel containing the body of the scorpion, encrusted with green, blue, and yellow mosaic, and ornamented with forty-five very large, clear emeralds and several pendant pearls, with two of exceptional orient clasped in the claws of the insect.[47]

Now it happened that that spring María de Mendoza had come to Guadalupe, presumably for her annual Holy Week retreat, bringing with her a large company of noble ladies, among them her lovely young sister. Cortés, with his followers, went at once to pay his respects to Doña María and the other ladies. And presently he began to bring them gifts: quaintly wrought golden jewels, plumes of green feathers, set with gold, silver, and pearls. It was, above all, Doña María and her sister that he showered with presents—gold beads, amber and balsam, even a pair of pack-mules for the litter of the little sister. In fact, he was so attentive that Doña María thought—so the story goes—

that he might marry her sister and she wrote to her husband, singing the praises of Cortés and urging him to support his cause with the Emperor.

Unfortunately, however, it turned out that Cortés was engaged to Juana de Zúñiga, niece of the Duque de Béjar, and so Doña María's dream vanished. There were some who said that it was this rebuff which was responsible for Cortés' failure to receive all the honors he sought. Díaz del Castillo nowhere mentions the name of the "little sister," but modern writers have called her "Francisca de Mendoza." [48] Doña María's only sister of that name was Francisca Sarmiento, who had already married Fernán Díaz de Rivadeneira, *regidor* of Toledo, in 1526,[49] and who could not have been eligible as Cortés' bride. If there is any truth in the story—which is doubtful—she may have been another sister, Beatriz de Noroña, who later married Alonso Luis Fernández de Lugo, *adelantado* of the Canaries and governor of Santa Marta.

At Court, Cortés was graciously received by the Emperor. He came to the audience accompanied by the Almirante de Castilla, the Duque de Béjar, and Cobos. But the Emperor declined to bestow any honors on him. Grave charges had been lodged against Cortés; even before he left Madrid, the Emperor had ordered the Audiencia of Mexico to take his *residencia*. And so for months Cortés followed the Court, hoping for a decision. Relying on the support of the Almirante, the Duque de Béjar and Henry of Nassau, he paid little attention to the Bishop of Osma and the other members of the Consejo de las Indias, or even to Cobos and his wife. Many of the courtiers thought that he was putting on airs; once, when he arrived late for mass, he walked by all the others and took his place beside Henry of Nassau. But the Duque de Béjar defended him, saying that he and his companions had made the same sort of conquests as had their own ancestors, from whom they derived their titles and estates.[50] Another reason for his failure to receive recognition that was rumored was that the Empress was annoyed with him because he had brought his fiancée an emerald of far greater worth than the jewel he gave to her.

Many of these stories are probably only Court gossip, heard in garbled form in New Spain. The source of the Emperor's delay was undoubtedly his unwillingness to reach a decision until the investigation in Mexico was completed. At Zaragoza, on

April 1, 1529, he specifically refused to name him as Governor of New Spain, although he did grant him the title of "Captain General." [51] Finally, at Barcelona, on July 6, 1529, he granted him the title of "Marqués del Valle de Oaxaca," with 23,000 vassals, as well as two islands in the lagoon of Mexico, and at the same time confirmed his title as "Captain General." [52] The implication that Cobos was hostile to Cortés is wholly unfounded. To the end of their lives he was a loyal friend and supporter of Cortés, even when he had fallen into disfavor.

Cobos spent a good deal of time in the spring and summer of 1528 on his own financial affairs. The grant of 2,000 ducats a year from cochineal, made in 1524, had not panned out, and on April 22 he secured a decree transferring the source to overdue debts to the Crown, fines paid to the Treasury, and the income from brasil-wood.[53] To make sure of the collection, the treasurers in the Indies were informed of the amount which each one was to contribute every year, but even so, there were difficulties. Well into the 30's Cobos was still securing orders from the Emperor and from the Consejo de las Indias requiring payment. On the same day he was granted another royal favor. Back in 1526 he had been made a *regidor* of Valladolid and now he received permission to transfer the office. At some later date he exercised the privilege and gave the post to one of his kinsmen, Juan Mosquera de Molina, but in his last will he revoked the transfer and left the position to his son.[54]

During the summer he picked up another *merced* from the Emperor: the grant of all the saltmines in the Indies, for himself and his descendants, with the condition that he pay one-fifth of the income to the Crown.[55] In September he had the grant confirmed and instructions sent to all the officials in the Indies to collect the income for him. But this was another of the fine schemes that failed to produce results. The Indians would not cooperate, but produced only enough salt for their own use. Cobos' agents regretfully reported to him that he could expect little from this source. Yet years later the Emperor still thought that this was one of the greatest favors that he had bestowed on Cobos.[56]

The Downfall of Lallemand

In the autumn of 1528 the Court was shaken by a shocking piece of news: Jean Lallemand, the secretary, had been arrested on the charge of treason. It must have happened early in October, for Lallemand was signing warrants for payment till the end of September; he countersigned documents on October 9.[57] On October 13 he wrote a pathetic letter to the Emperor, begging him to believe in his loyalty.[58] At first he was exiled to a village near Toledo under house arrest. When the emperor left for Barcelona on March 9, 1529, he was allowed to return to Toledo to the Court of the Empress.[59]

The formal trial began on March 18, when the royal prosecutor presented twenty-nine charges against him.[60] The first was the most serious: that he had been in secret communication with people in France. The others dealt with various forms of malfeasance in the conduct of his office: changing the language of dispatches, eliminating or inserting documents, all for his own profit. Two of the charges dealt with his improper conduct in revealing to the Papal Nuncio, Castiglione, the content of the *Diálogo de Lactancio y el arcediano,* the manuscript of which Alonso de Valdés had shown to him. There was a long list of witnesses—the Grand Chancellor, La Chaux, Pedro de Guevara, and other courtiers. Of the secretaries only two were called, Ugo de Urríes and Alonso de Valdés. The latter was the one witness whom Lallemand challenged, as being notoriously his enemy. Many of the witnesses testified that it was a common practice to give gifts to persons who had influence with the Emperor, and Lallemand himself pointed out that if charges were brought against every official who had received gifts, few would escape. The wheels of justice ground slowly in those days and Lallemand finally wrote to the Emperor, imploring him to order the Fiscal to hand down a decision.[61] But two years passed before the Court rendered its verdict: acquittal on the main charge of treason, conviction on the other charges and a penalty of the confiscation of a quarter of his property, and banishment to a distance of five leagues from the Court.

In December, 1531, Lallemand turned up in Brussels and the Emperor commuted his sentence: the banishment was now limited to the Court itself. He returned to Spain and then retired to his estate in Burgundy.[62] As late as March, 1534, Salinas reported that he was still hanging around, trying to get his job back, charging that Granvelle was hostile to him, and that the Emperor would not listen to him.[63] He never recovered his post as secretary.

López de Gómara in his *Anales* stated that Cobos was responsible for the downfall of Lallemand.[64] But there is no evidence that this is true. Santa Cruz says that it was Laurent Gorrevod who brought the charges against Lallemand and he even quotes Francis I as saying: "Jean Lallemand, who is in my employ at the Emperor's Court, is worth more to me than the twenty thousand people that he is paying against me in Italy." [65] Salinas also reported that Gorrevod and Gattinara were both to blame for the action against him, hoping to promote their own interests, if they could eliminate him from his position of confidence with the Emperor.[66] In view of the violence of feeling against him that Valdés reveals in his letters, it is not impossible that he had a share in the accusations.[67]

Portrait of a Secretary

Valdés had entered the service as an *escribano* in Gattinara's office in 1522; he was on the payroll in 1526, concerned with the Latin correspondence. In the struggle between the Emperor and Pope and the French king, he proved to be a vigorous defender of the Imperial cause. In this connection it is worth recalling that in his *Diálogo de Mercurio y Carón* he introduced the shade of a French secretary, who is supposed to have represented Jean Lallemand. But the picture he draws might apply to any secretary of the time, including Cobos. For example, the *Anima* says: [68]

In less than ten years I amassed 80,000 ducats . . . The first thing I did was to give everyone to understand that I had such influence with the King that I could do anything I wanted to with him and that he made no decisions without me. In that way I made everyone come to me for help and to those who gave me something I spoke with my cap in my hand and gave them audience at any hour of the day; to the rest I turned a sour face, till I got something from them. If there was an office vacant or something had to be provided and two or three people asked me for it, I promised to help them all, if they promised to pay me for it; and at times I did not speak in behalf of any one of them. But when the offices were filled, though I had done nothing, I carried off the whole amount promised, pretending that I had done it, though often it had been the opposite. So that from everything that went through my hands, and at times through other people's hands, I got my pickings. And in this way, promising both parties, nobody could escape me. Besides this, if something was decided in the Consejo in favor of someone, I at once made it known to him, giving him to understand that "So and so" was against him, but that I was the only one to support him . . . In this way I had the Court so tyrannized that some gave me silk, others silver, others goodly ducats. And so, gaining much and spending little, which is the true alchemy, I soon became rich. Listen, brother, my whole intent was to leave a great estate and to do that, I had no better way than this. No, sir; be good and you'll live poor all your life.

Is it possible—Charon asks—that at the Court of a Christian prince they tolerate a pest like you?

On the contrary—replies the shade—these and similar acts are necessary at Court.

And are there no laws to punish such great evils?

Yes, there are. But who will dare to make an issue with the favorite of a prince?

All of this satire would seem to be as appropriate a description of Cobos as of Lallemand; almost every detail fits what we know of his career. Like the secretary in the *Diálogo*, he was passionately concerned with accumulating an estate and handing it on to his heirs. But there was a great difference between Lallemand and Cobos: Lallemand made enemies; Cobos made friends. And so Lallemand was eliminated and Cobos advanced to greater influence. Apparently they were never closely associated, for Lallemand was wholly concerned with foreign affairs, while Cobos was at the time limited to the problems of Castile. It is, then, almost certain that Cobos was not involved in his downfall; he was not even called as a witness at the trial. But it is also true that he must have viewed his departure without great regret. The men who succeeded him in charge of the French correspondence, Anthoine Perrenin and Jean Bave, were men of lesser stature and slighter influence. With the disappearance of Lallemand, Cobos is left as the only secretary who enjoyed the confidence of the King.

The Mayorazgo

A striking demonstration of Cobos' determination to insure the future of his estate is found in a *cédula* of February 26, 1529, which granted to him and his wife the privilege of establishing a *mayorazgo,* an entailed estate handed on only through the eldest son.[69] The craze for founding a *mayorazgo* is characteristic of the period. Years ago Gounon-Loubens observed: "Nothing is more respectable nor more interesting than the efforts by which men try to attach themselves to the generations which precede them and those that follow them, to enlarge in this way the narrow field of their existence and to rise above the very laws of nature. No people has sought to satisfy this impulse with more ardor than the Spaniards, among whom there was not a father of a family who did not aspire to found his dynasty on the model of the royal house; even insignificant people, anxious to imitate the great lords, were seeking the privilege of founding a *mayorazgo*." [70]

The privilege of Cobos and Doña María is couched in the customary formula of the time: "Considering that the republic is more honored and is preserved and enhanced because there are in it possessors of entailed estates which are indivisible and subject to restitution, and attain through them more power to give defense and succor when it is necessary and likewise have more forces with which to serve their king and lord,"—and so on, citing the precedent of ancient sages and Holy Writ, as well as of the Spanish Kings,—"now, having regard for the many, continuous, praiseworthy, pleasant and noteworthy services which you, Francisco de los Cobos, have performed and are performing every day and which we hope you will perform, in order that there may remain a greater memory of you and of María de Mendoza, your wife, and that your descendants may be more honored and may have wherewith better to serve the royal Crown of these kingdoms, and to do you a grace and favor, we give you hereby permission and faculty . . . to establish a *mayorazgo* of all your towns and villages and fortresses and vassals and rentals and mines and salt-licks and any other real or personal property that you have or may acquire, in order that your eldest, first-born son, Diego de los Cobos, a knight of the Order of Santiago, may have and inherit it, and after him his legitimate and illegitimate descendants, and lacking them, your daughter, María Sarmiento." There was a provision that they might provide a dowry of 4,000,000 *maravedís* for their daughter out of property not included in the *mayorazgo*.

One wonders why Cobos and his wife sought the privilege at this time. They held little real property, except the estate of Hornillos and the house in Valladolid, and they did not exercise the privilege for ten years. Perhaps it was because of their desire to be on the safe side, in case something happened to the Emperor on his trip to Italy. It should be noted that in this document Cobos is called for the first time "Commander of Azuaga in the Order of Santiago." We have seen how he had foregone the income of the *encomienda* of the Bastimentos de León in 1521. This time he did better, for the *encomienda* of Azuaga was the richest in Spain, with an annual income of 9,000 ducats.[71]

Early in 1529 the Emperor was at last ready to undertake the long-projected trip to Italy. If the question of the administration of Castile was important the year before, when he made his brief visit to Valencia and Monzón, this new journey raised far more serious problems, for there was no telling how long he would be absent from Spain. The Archivo de Simancas has preserved a variety of memoranda on the subject, prepared by the King's advisors.[72] There is a brief one in Gattinara's hand; a long one from Dr. Carvajal, who had presented his opinion on the same subject four years before. But most of them were drawn up by Cobos.

The first action that he proposed was that the Emperor draw up his will, in case of death, or "arrest" (Cobos had not forgotten what happened to the French King at Pavia), or other mishap. This the Emperor did—it was his second will—and signed it at Toledo on March 3 in the presence of the secretaries Cobos and Perrenin.[73] We need not discuss the details of these memoranda; they cover hundreds of problems: the powers of the Empress, the defense of the frontiers, the payment of troops and public officials, the appointment of persons to carry out specific tasks, the question of who should stay in Spain and who should accompany the Emperor. Their chief interest to us is their revelation of the mass of detail which Cobos had to handle in the administration of his various offices. The documents in question are the originals which Cobos used in his consultations with the Emperor and he scribbled in the margin of almost every paragraph a note of the action to be taken. These comments give new evidence of the difficulty the Emperor always had in arriving at decisions—in his youth his motto was "Non dum." In most cases he referred the question to one of the Consejos or to the President of the Consejo Real. In others the note says: "Have a memorandum prepared" or "The Majordomo and the Secretary will attend to this." In all too many cases the comment is "His Majesty will think about it," or "Handle this matter when we get there." But eventually decisions were made, and on March 3 the Emperor signed the orders naming the Empress as Regent and providing the necessary instructions for administration during his absence.[74]

Before the Court left Toledo Cobos had a number of personal matters to clear up. On February 19 he secured from the Emperor a *cédula* authorizing him to transfer his post as *fundidor* to his son Diego,[75] though he was only five years old, far below the minimum legal age of fourteen. Once more, to be safe, he had the Emperor renew his appointment as secretary.[76] On March 6 he issued a power of attorney to Juan de Samano, authorizing him to collect his income from the grant of 2,000 ducats a year, from the salt mines, and from his position as *fundidor*.[77] At the same time he sent Samano a list of all the money which he was to collect for him during his absence.

Income in 1529

On the basis of this list it is possible to estimate the income which Cobos and his wife expected to receive in 1529, as he started for Italy. Some of the items can only be estimates. For example, it is difficult to tell how much he received in 1529 from his post as *fundidor*. But Haring and Hamilton are in agreement that in the years between 1525 and 1530 the average receipts of gold and silver from the Indies were approximately 100,000,-000 *maravedís* a year. On this Cobos received 1%. Similarly, the salaries which he received as *regidor* of Ubeda and Valladolid and as *escribano del crimen* of Ubeda must be based on those paid to others in similar posts. Moreover, in the list which he sent to Samano he did not include a number of important items, such as his income from the *encomienda* of Azuaga and from his investments in property and *juros;* probably these were handled by other agents. Finally there are several items for which it is not possible to hazard a guess. But the total is impressive: 6,688,200 *maravedís*.[78] At the rate of 2 pesetas or $.05 to a *maravedí,* this is equivalent to 13,376,400 pesetas or $334,410. For a poor boy, he was doing very well!

Included in the instruction to Samano are a few unpaid debts and a request that he try to buy a *juro* of about 15,000 *maravedís* which he would like to give to his chapel in Ubeda as an endowment. The architects had gone ahead with the construction after the necessary ecclesiastical privileges had been granted and Cobos had ordered a gilded *reja* to separate it from the church.[79] The chapel of La Concepción has long since disappeared, but one wonders if his *reja* was as lovely as the one that

his chaplain, Fernando Ortega, had made for the chapel he endowed in the church of San Nicolás in Ubeda. On January 8,
1530, Pope Clement VII gave his approval to the dedication of
the chapel and granted a number of special indulgences to those
who attended mass on the day of Holy Trinity and the Immac-
ulate Conception.[80]

On March 8 the Court started for Barcelona. On the road, at
Calatayud, Cobos wrote a long personal letter to his nephew,
Juan Vázquez de Molina, who had remained in Toledo as secretary of the Empress.[81] We should say a word about this new
kinsman of Cobos who had entered the royal service. The first
mention of him is found in a letter, dated at Valladolid on November 1, 1522, when he was living in Cobos' house in Ubeda; [82]
he was already a *regidor* of Ubeda. In 1523, as a "servant" of
Cobos, he witnessed his signature.[83] In the following year he
was reported to have passed through Toledo; by this time he
was called a "secretary." [84] He had married Antonia del Aguilar,
daughter of Francisco de Aguilar, *alcaide* of Ciudad-Rodrigo,[85]
and on April 22, 1528, he was named a knight of Santiago.[86]
Now, on the eve of the Emperor's departure, he had been appointed secretary of the Empress, at a salary of 65,000 *maravedís* for handling the affairs for which Cobos was regularly
responsible; in addition he received 45,000 *maravedís* a year as
a gentleman of the Empress' household.[87]

Although Cobos always referred to him as his "nephew," he
was in reality the son of Cobos' cousin, Jorge de Molina, so that
we should call him a "second cousin." Oviedo says that Cobos
trained him and treated him like a son.[88] It is clear that he saw
in him a young man of far greater promise than his other cousin,
Pedro de los Cobos, who never rose to important responsibilities. And Juan Vázquez quickly became one of his most trusted
assistants. His appointment now as secretary of the Empress
further strengthened Cobos' control of the administration of
Castile.

It is amusing to see how anxious Cobos was that he do a good
job in his new post. The letter from Calatayud began: "I am
astonished that you have not sent the dispatches"—which is as
close to a scolding as public officials ever came. And the letter
is filled with detailed instructions as to people he must see, dispatches he must forward, reports he must make. Cobos was taking no risks with his young protégé. From now on it is to

Vázquez that he addressed all of his personal correspondence.

While Hernán Cortés and Pedro de Alvarado were still at Court, another *conquistador* arrived in Spain—Francisco Pizarro—with his fabulous account of the land of Peru. Like the others, he came seeking new powers and support; like them, he came bringing strange gifts—llamas and chinchillas—as well as a treasure of gold and silver. Some of these landed in Cobos' hands, as had the cannon of Cortés, for at Zaragoza on April 19 the Emperor issued an order to Captain Pizarro to turn over to Cobos or his representative the five "rams and sheep" which he had brought to Toledo and at the same time he sent another order to the officials of the Casa de la Contratación, instructing them to send to Azuaga, of which Cobos was Commander, the "sheep and rams" which they still had from Pizarro's shipment and also the sheep which Sebastian Cabot had sent.[89] Apparently the poor animals did not long survive; at least we hear no more of them.

One of the many unsettled problems with which the Emperor had long been struggling was that of the "Spice Islands" of the Moluccas, over which he and the King of Portugal had been negotiating for years. Now, driven by his desperate need for money, he decided to relinquish his claim in return for a cash payment; Salinas understood that he expected 350,000 ducats.[90] And so, on the day that he departed from Zaragoza, he left behind Gattinara, Loaisa, Padilla, and Cobos, with instructions to negotiate an agreement with the Portuguese representatives. In this they were successful, and Juan de Samano was sent to Lisbon to collect the money. The Spanish negotiators did not rejoin the Court until after it had reached Barcelona.

The composition of this commission shows how greatly the group of Charles' Castilian advisors had changed since he came back to Spain in 1522. With the exception of Padilla and Cobos, all the original company had disappeared. We have already mentioned the death of Bishop Mota. Bishop Rodríguez de Fonseca died at the end of 1524 and was replaced, as Bishop of Burgos, by Antonio de Rojas, who was succeeded at that time as President of the Consejo Real by Juan Tavera, Archbishop of Santiago. Rojas, too, died in 1527. Hernando de Vega, Grand Commander of Castile, died in 1526 and his post was given to Antonio de Fonseca, brother of the Bishop. Amid all these changes, Cobos had survived, closer than ever to the Emperor, rich now in experience as well as in worldly goods. How indispensable he had become is reflected in an anecdote that when King João III of Portugal chided his ambassador for his failure to accompany the Emperor when he left Toledo for Zaragoza, the ambassador excused himself by saying: "Not even Cobos went!" [90a]

When the Court reached Barcelona, on April 30, there emerged a new figure in the councils of the Emperor—Nicholas Perrenot, Lord of Granvelle. He had come from a modest Burgundian family—it was even said that he was a blacksmith's son—, but he was well educated, a doctor of laws and a good Latinist. Like Gattinara he had received his political apprenticeship at the Parliament of Dôle. From there he entered the service of Margaret, the Regent of Flanders, who sent him to Spain as her agent in 1526.[91] He was ambassador in France in 1527 and 1528; [92] after the break between Charles and Francis in the spring of 1528 he came to Spain and was one of those present when the French herald delivered the challenge to the Emperor at Monzón in June.[93]

Immediately after the downfall of Lallemand, Charles appointed him a member of the Council of State.[94] While he was, in a sense, a replacement of Lallemand, he never bore the title of secretary, but from the first held a post of authority. Now, in Barcelona, he began to take a leading part in the conduct of foreign affairs. With Gattinara and Louis de Praet he negotiated the league between the Emperor and Pope Clement VII, which was signed on June 29.[95]

All through these months the Emperor was busy assembling his fleet, his soldiers, and the suite that was to accompany him— the "flower of Spain," as one contemporary chronicler called them.[96] On June 19 Andrea Doria, who had deserted the cause of Francis I to enter the service of the Emperor, sailed into the harbor with his fleet and was received with a thunderous salute from the batteries of all the forts. The following Sunday, with a suite of two hundred gentlemen, he paid his respects to the Emperor, who embraced him and presented him with 20,000 ducats for his expenses.[97]

Meanwhile, the Spanish officials had been busy in Lisbon collecting the cash from the King of Portugal. On June 1 Gómez de León wrote to Cobos that he had finally got together 125,000 ducats, largely in silver, and that he was starting out with forty-two pack-mules; and he added: "Can you imagine me, accustomed only to watching Samano prancing ahead of me on his blossom-colored horse, riding for a month straight among forty mules?" [98] A few days later, the Spanish ambassador in Lisbon, Lope Hurtado de Mendoza, reported to the Emperor the dispatch of 150,000 ducats in specie, to go by way of Toledo; it should be in Barcelona before July 10. The shipment was assayed at the mint in Toledo on June 11 and sent on to Barcelona. Promptly on schedule it reached there on July 7 in thirty-seven loads.[99]

Busy as the days were in preparation for the departure, Cobos found time to attend to his personal affairs. On April 10 García de Lerma, governor of Santa Marta, had written to the Emperor to report the discovery of some Indian tombs in which they had found gold ornaments worth 4,000 *pesos*.[100] Cobos at once secured from the Emperor a *cédula* (July 10, 1529) granting him all further sums thus found for a period of twenty years [101] and the Emperor also wrote to Lerma, approving of his having taken a third of the treasure for himself, but instructing him in the future to turn over to Cobos all gold thus recovered.[102] Unfortunately this proved to be another will o' the wisp, like the cochineal of Yucatán. For it turned out that there were no more tombs and no more gold; Lerma had got all there was.[103]

Grand Commander of Leon

On the very day that the fleet sailed, Cobos entered into a strange contract.[104] We have seen how, early in 1529, he had secured the *encomienda* of Azuaga in the Order of Santiago. Hernando de Toledo, brother of the old Duque de Alba, had long held the title of Grand Commander of Leon in the Order; his nephew, Pedro de Toledo, was Commander of Monreal. Now, on June 27, the three Commanders agreed, subject to the Emperor's approval, to swap their titles: Cobos, to transfer the *encomienda* of Azuaga to Hernando de Toledo and to receive in return the *encomienda mayor* of Leon; Hernando de Toledo to transfer the title of Azuaga to Pedro de Toledo; and Don Pedro to transfer his title of Monreal to García de Toledo, son of Don Hernando. The title which Cobos relinquished had an income of 9,000 ducats a year; the *encomienda mayor* which he received paid only 6,000 ducats.[105] What could have induced him to sacrifice so large a sum?

There seems to be but one possible answer: the title meant more to him than money. We have seen how in 1521 he was willing to go without the income of the *encomienda* of the Bastimentos de León for the sake of the title. The title which he now acquired was a far more distinguished honor. There were only two Grand Commanders in the Order of Santiago, one of Castile, the other of Leon. On the death of Hernando de Vega, the former title had gone to Antonio de Fonseca. García de Padilla was Grand Commander of the Order of Calatrava. In a word, it was the highest title a courtier could receive, short of a patent of nobility, such as his wife and her family held. Is it possible that there was a sentimental reason, too, for wanting this particular title? that his own coat of arms—five lions *or* rampant on an *azure* field—were in his mind? There is a document of July 28 which he countersigned in the usual way: "Francisco de los Cobos, secretary." [106] On August 1, at Palamós, he signed for the first time: "Cobos, Grand Commander." [107] As the fleet set sail, the jester, Francesillo de Zúñiga, conjured the galley of the King to bear him safe to shore "by the power of Cobos." [108]

————•◦◦◦◦———

CHAPTER VI

IMPERIAL MINISTER OF STATE

The First Italian Journey

The seven years that Charles V had spent in Spain had made him a truly Spanish king; he had won the respect and admiration of his people; the language of Court and Council had become Spanish. With his departure for Italy begins a new phase of his career—defense of his Empire. For Cobos, these years had witnessed his gradual rise to a place of influence and power in the affairs of Castile. For him too the trip to Italy marked the beginning of a new period in his life—his activity as an international diplomat. For both of them, for all the Court, there was a strange outward symbol of the change. Until then the Emperor had always worn his hair long, in a "page-boy bob," and had been clean-shaven. A miniature in the Bibliothèque Nationale shows him in 1527 as still boyish, in his broad-brimmed velvet hat.[1] Now, on the eve of his departure, he had his hair cropped and started to grow a beard. Many reasons have been offered for the Emperor's action—a head-ache, a skin disease, the discomfort of long hair under a helmet. No one seems to have suggested the most natural explanation. Charles was going to Italy to be crowned as Emperor, and Gattinara, filled with his memory of the busts of Roman emperors—Julius Caesar, Augustus, Trajan—could not find one with long locks. What more natural than that he should have persuaded Charles how

silly the Imperial crown would look, mounted on a shock of hair?
For us the significant thing is that, following his example, the
whole Court cut their hair and stopped shaving. From now on
we must think of Cobos as wearing a beard, scraggly at first,
like that of Charles in portraits of the period,[2] but steadily
growing more opulent, as the years went by.

The great fleet of Andrea Doria sailed out of the harbor of
Barcelona on July 28, the Emperor and his advisors aboard the
flagship. Following the coast at first, they crossed the Mediterranean to Monaco and reached Savona on August 8. There they
waited for four days while preparations for the entry into Genoa
were being completed. The Emperor had been brought up to
love pageants, and this was a spectacular one.[3] As the fleet entered the harbor on August 12, two hundred small boats came
out to meet them. At a given signal they lowered their sails and
a great shout went up: "Carlo, Carlo! Imperio, Imperio! Cesare, Cesare!" The authorities had built a long pier for the
reception, hung with tapestries and cloth of gold, and as the
Emperor stepped ashore, clad all in white, with a cloth of silver
cape, a great ball appeared, with an eagle on top; a door opened
and showered perfume on him; and then a youth, symbolizing
"Justice," stepped forth and handed him the keys to the city.
He was lodged in the ducal palace and it is amusing to learn
that, before his arrival, his *aposentador,* Figueroa, had written
to him to ask him to send some tapestry hangings for his apartment, since they did not use them there.[4]

To greet the Emperor a group of distinguished visitors came
to Genoa: three cardinals sent by the Pope, the Duke of Ferrara, Alessandro de' Medici, still an exile from Florence. Before he left the city he dispatched Luis Sarmiento to Spain with
messages for the Empress.[5] He reached Madrid on September
3, and the next day he saw Juan de Samano, to whom he brought
a letter from Cobos. In the Archivo de Indias there is an unsigned letter, which is certainly Samano's answer. It gives such
an intimate picture of Cobos' family in Spain that it must be
recorded:[6]

Sir: After my banishment I came here to Madrid on Saturday, September
4, which was the day after Sarmiento arrived. With Don Luis I received a
long letter from you, which was for me such a joy—the letter and the news
of your health and the success of the Emperor's journey—that it was another
resurrection for me, like the past one, because we were greatly worried that

so many days had passed since you left without any news of your arrival. God grant that we may always have such news and that affairs there will turn out as His Majesty desires, in order that you may return quickly with the good health that I desire for you! And I am sure that that is your desire too.

I came through Valladolid to pay my respects to My Lady and the children—God bless them!—They are the cutest youngsters in the world, for Don Diego, now that he is over the quartan fever, looks like a different boy from what you have known and Doña María is the cutest thing in the world, for I swear to God that I don't think that you could find anyone like her anywhere. Only, she doesn't like her father, for you can't get her to call herself anything but 'de los Cobos' and she tears her hair, if they tell her her name is 'Sarmiento' or 'Mendoza.' She has another very funny trick that twenty times a day they must show her her 'Mamo,' which is the painting of Our Lady where your portrait is. And when she saw me, she thought her father was coming and with great glee she took me see her 'Mamo.' I tell you it's something to see. She has grown a lot and is very much prettier. God bless her, as you desire, and grant you the grace to enjoy them! I am writing more details about Doña María than about Don Diego, because we must always show preference for the ladies and because you know what Don Diego is like, though to tell the truth, he was never the way he is now. He has grown a lot.

I saw the house and I was amazed, and all I can say about it is that you can boast that nobody in the world has a house and a daughter like yours. One thing only is lacking: that God will grant you the time to enjoy it, for a whole lifetime seems little to enjoy such a house, which is not like any other that I have seen. It is so healthy and gay that it has given new life to the children, for running around those galleries Don Diego got rid of his fever, although My Lady the Countess says that it was because they fed him everything he wanted.

My Lady was so glad to see me that she kept me there for six days; they entertained me more royally than had parents and children. And though they were calling me from here, I stayed there, because My Lady was so worried at not hearing from you and so troubled at your absence that it is hard to believe and she was glad to talk to me about it. Believe me that, though she is well, she is very troubled. I found Her Ladyship so changed in her dress that I was astonished, for she was wearing a black woolen skirt and a very heavy head-dress and a sloe rosary. That was all. Her only pastime is spending three or four hours a day with her children, playing in her room. God keep them all, that they may enjoy you for many years!

Cobos' heart must have lifted as he read this letter about the folks at home.

As Charles and his Court moved on to Piacenza, there came disturbing news from his brother Ferdinand with regard to the threat of the Turks in Hungary. And there was also the problem of the Lutherans which must be faced. During the month and a half that he spent in Piacenza he reached a number of decisions. The first was that he must settle affairs in Italy as quickly as possible. Gattinara, who had at last picked up his cardinal's hat,[7] was sent to Cremona to negotiate with Francesco Sforza, Duke of Milan.[8] On October 26 he wrote from Casalmaggiore to Charles, recommending that he send a safe-conduct for Sforza.[9] A few days later, in answer to a letter from the Emperor, in which he asked his opinion regarding the necessity of taking the Iron Crown of Lombady and referring to the correspondence which had been addressed to Cobos, the Chancellor remarked rather peevishly that, not having seen the correspondence, he could hardly express an opinion.[10]

The second problem with which the Emperor was confronted was that of funds to pay his armies. On September 9 Cobos negotiated a loan of 100,000 *scudi,* payable in Genoa or Milan, with the banker Tomás de Forne.[11] Early in October the Emperor had decided to send the Bishop of Ciudad-Rodrigo to Spain to see if money could be raised there.[12] On October 30 Cobos drew up the instruction to the Bishop, in which for the first time he proposed levying a general sales tax *(sisa)* in Spain.[13] When the Bishop reached Madrid, the Empress called a meeting of the Consejo to consider the proposal. The draft of her reply, drawn up by Juan Vázquez de Molina and with his emendations, is still preserved at Simancas.[14] Addressed to Cobos, it explains that, great as is her confidence in the messenger, Antonio de Mendoza, she prefers to have Cobos deliver her message in person to the Emperor. The Consejo is unanimously of the opinion that the imposition of a sales tax is unwise. Under any circumstances, it would be necessary to summon a new Cortes and even if it were approved, it might be disobeyed, to the detriment of royal prestige. They had not yet forgotten the rebellion of the *comuneros.*

The last decision of the Emperor was that in view of the situation in Germany and Austria, he could not afford to take the time to go to Rome for the coronation, but must ask the Pope to crown him in Bologna.

Meanwhile, he had given to Cobos the final evidence of his confidence, when he named him a member of the Council of State on October 4.[15] The group of intimate counsellors of the Emperor which he now joined was a wholly new "team," with the exception of Gattinara. At Granada, in 1526, the Emperor had tried the experiment of adding the Duque de Alba and the Duque de Béjar to his Privy Council.[16] But he always distrusted the grandees of Spain and he soon dismissed them. The Council now consisted of García de Loaisa, still Bishop of Osma, Gabriel Merino, Cobos' old friend, Archbishop of Bari and Bishop of Jaén, Granvelle, Padilla, Louis de Praet, who had just returned from a diplomatic mission to the French Court, and Cobos, the chief Spanish layman in the group.[17]

When the Emperor learned that the Pope had reached Bologna on October 23 for their interview, he himself started for the city. Between Parma and Reggio the Duke of Ferrara came to meet him,[18] and on the night of October 31 in Reggio Cobos was lodged in the house of Madonna Tovia Sobola.[19] The Emperor and his Court spent the night of November 4 at the Carthusian monastery outside of Bologna. He made his formal entry into the city on the following day.

The Coronation of Charles

This was one of the most impressive shows Charles had ever staged,[20] for he came with an army of German, Spanish, and Italian soldiers—foot and horse—under the command of his old general, Antonio de Leiva, so ailing that he had to be carried in a litter. The procession was led by twenty pages, clad in velvet uniforms of yellow, gray, and purple. They were followed by the mounted gentlemen of the household, trumpeters, princes, treasurers scattering golden ducats and medals, the Marqués de Astorga, the Emperor, mounted on a white horse under a baldoquin carried by the learned doctors of the University, then Henry of Nassau and the dukes. After them came the Council and the secretaries—Cobos, Urríes, Zuazola, Pedro García—and a great company of courtiers, all in rich costumes.[21] A Venetian engraver pictured the scene in a magnificent series of folio woodcuts that somehow caught the grandeur and excitement of that day.[22] That night Cobos and the other secretaries were lodged in the Bonasoni palace, opposite the palaces of the Bombelli and the Dall'Armi.[23]

Charles had hoped to be quickly through the ceremonies of the coronation so that he might start for Germany to hold the Diet. But the negotiations moved at a snail's pace. On December 23 Gattinara, Granvelle, Louis de Praet, and Cobos signed the treaty between the Emperor, the Pope, Duke Ferdinand, Venice, and Milan; other states were invited to join the

League.[24] At the same time they signed the agreement which restored the duchy of Milan to Francesco Sforza. It was Alfonso de Valdés who witnessed the Latin document.[25] Thus peace was restored for the moment in Italy. Only Florence was left out, for Charles had yielded to the demand of the Medici Pope that Alessandro de' Medici be given back his duchy, by force if necessary. In January, Cobos informed the ambassadors of the Florentine republic that they must come to terms with the Pope, since the Emperor had made up his mind.[26] The Prince of Orange and his army were summoned to enforce the decision.

As soon as the treaties were signed, Cobos sent the Empress an account of their terms and at the same time he wrote to Juan Vázquez, reporting on recent events and adding that the Pope had approved the transfer of titles in the Order of Santiago. In a postscript in his own hand, he said: "I am sending a letter of mine for the Queen of France [Eleanor]. Give it to her and send Doña María hers. Offer my excuses to the Bishop of Zamora and the Bishop of Ciudad-Rodrigo." [27]

Cobos took advantage of his interviews with the Pope to secure a few personal favors. On the same day (January 8, 1530) that the Pope approved of the foundation of Cobos' chapel in Ubeda, he also issued a *breve* granting Cobos and his family and friends a series of indulgences and special privileges in such matters as fasting, early mass, and the like.[28] The list of persons who were to share in these favors is revealing in its reflection of the people that Cobos thought important. It begins, naturally, with Doña María and their two children; next came his wife's parents and her brothers and sisters; then Cobos' father and his two sisters, Leonor and Isabel (Mayor must have died before this), and two of Don Diego's grand-daughters. There follow the names of several of Doña María's kinsmen and then some "Important People": Francisco de Borja, heir to the duchy of Gandía, and his wife; Juan de Mendoza, Lord of Morón, and his wife; Iñigo López de Mendoza, heir to the duchy of the Infantado; Alvar Pérez de Osorio, Marqués de Astorga. At the end, Cobos had remembered his associates: María Niño, widow of Conchillos; Pedro de los Cobos; Juan Vázquez de Molina; Cristóbal de Saldaña, his agent in Valladolid; and Juan de Samano, each with his wife. The indulgences were valid for all of these and for their children and grandchildren and, in addition, to any other twelve persons that Cobos might name. One of the most interesting of the privileges is that Doña María, or any of the other women named, might visit the nuns of San Francisco, even the "Claritas," once a month.

Social prestige meant much to Cobos. He was proud, even if a bit envious of his wife's noble family; he had made friends himself among some of the *grandes*. It was Francisco de Borja who secured the approval of the Spanish translation of the *breve* at Ocaña on January 21, 1531, from the Bishop of Zamora, Francisco de Mendoza. But he was loyal to his more humble comrades in the administration of royal business. It must have meant a lot to Juan de Samano and his wife, Juana Castrejón, to have been included in this select group.

Charles V was behind schedule all his life and so the days drifted by early in 1530 without any action. Cobos was busy writing letters,[29] interviewing people, attending public functions. When Martín de Salinas conveyed to the Emperor Ferdinand's request that he pardon the Spaniards who had left Spain to enter his service, Charles referred the question to Cobos for study and report.[30] Salinas, watchful as always to discover who could best support Ferdinand's cause, wrote to his master February 2:

> Your Highness should understand that he must grant favors to some of the persons who are close to His Majesty, especially to those who have served Your Highness in the past and who can serve now and in the future, men like Cobos and Granvelle. I think Your Highness must give some present to these two and if Your Highness approves, it might be that there would be an opportunity to win their support with a gift of sable cloak-linings, for they are coveted by everybody. To these two, Your Highness must not fail to do favors, both for what you owe them and what you hope from them, for they are men who can repay them seven-fold.[31]

On February 14 a special mass was sung in the church of San Salvatore which was attended by the Emperor and one hundred and twenty knights of the Order of Santiago, all dressed in long white robes with the red cross of Santiago on their breast and all carrying staffs. After the mass they visited the refectory attached to the church to see the mural paintings by two local painters, Bartolomeo da Bagnacavallo and Biagio Pupini.[32]

Cobos must have been impressed by the decorative value of murals in churches and private houses in Italy, and seeing the beauty of the paintings in San Salvatore, he thought of his own house in Valladolid. And so he sought out the two painters and engaged them to come to Spain. The contract which was drawn up provided that Cobos would pay each of them 100 ducats for a year of work, to be deposited as a guaranty with the Rector of the Colegio de los Españoles in Bologna, and in addition, 25 ducats each for their travel expenses, as well as travel expense for their return to Italy. For their part Bagnacavallo and Pupini agreed to go directly to Valladolid, to take no other job during the year, to work every day except holidays, to provide their own colors, and to paint whatever "histories" or other things that Cobos might order.[33] For some reason, the contract was never signed nor executed. But Cobos did not give up the idea; later he found two other painters to embellish his houses in Valladolid and Ubeda.

By February 20 the elaborate plans for the double coronation were completed. A wooden passageway was built from the Palazzo del Podestà, where Charles and the Pope were lodged, across the square to the great church of San Petronio. So covered with laurel and ivy was this walk that not a board could be seen; the sides were brilliant with the arms of Emperor and Pope. All the palaces of the town were hung with tapestries; the streets were jammed with the holiday crowd. On the twenty-first the magistrates of Monza arrived with the Iron Crown of Lombardy, and the next day the ceremony of the first coronation was held in San Petronio.

We need not give here the details of the ceremony, of which there are so many accounts.[34] But it is of interest that a contemporary chronicler, in his narrative of the event, mentions among the gorgeously dressed gentlemen who took part "the counts of Saldaña, Altamira, Fuentes and Aguilar; Alfonso Téllez; Juan Pacheco; the Marqués de Villafranca; Francisco de los Cobos, who was also an Imperial Councillor; the Marqués de Cenete [Henry of Nassau], the Grand Chamberlain . . . all of whom stayed close to Caesar to serve him, and they were magnificently dressed and we shall also see them in the solemnities of the Imperial coronation." [35] Another contemporary account, printed in a *pliego suelto,* gives a specific picture of Cobos' costume: "a suit of mulberry-colored cloth-of-gold, lined with mulberry velvet, a gold chain, and a tunic of the same material." [36] The little boy from Ubeda had made the "Society Column!"

Two days later Charles received the Imperial crown. Early that morning his army entered the city—foot, horse, and artillery—and were posted in the Piazza Maggiore, occupying all the entrances to the square. Two fountains were built—a lion from whose mouth white wine poured all day and an eagle whose breast yielded red wine for the populace. In one corner of the square was a whole roast ox, stuffed with game; from the windows around the square came showers of fruits and sweets. No wonder the Emperor needed money! Presently the Pope, emerging from the Palace, borne on a litter and followed by a throng of cardinals, archbishops, and bishops, moved across the passage to the church. When he had entered he sent two cardinals to escort the Emperor. And so the Imperial procession started across the square: gentlemen of the household, princes and heralds, the bearers of the insignia—the Duke of Savoy, the Duke of Bavaria, the Duke of Urbino, the Marquis of Montferrato— then the Emperor in his Imperial robe, the Marquis of Cenete holding his train. To close the procession came the archers of the guard. There was a narrow escape from disaster, for as the archers crossed the gangway it collapsed and one of them was killed.

Once more our chronicler, who was fascinated with clothes, describes the costumes of those present: "The Marqués de Villafranca, Don Pedro de Toledo, son of the Duque de Alba, was richly dressed in cloth of gold and blue, with a velvet lining of the same color, as well as his tunic: his pages wore the same colors. The Grand Commander of Leon, the councillor Don Francisco de los Cobos, in a suit of rich gold brocade lined with sable and a tunic with trimmings of gold and crimson velvet." [37] Santa Cruz tells us the Marqués de Moya, the Marqués de Astorga, the Conde de Saldaña, the Conde de Aguilar, the Grand Commander of Leon, His Majesty's secretary, and other gentlemen wore clothes of different colors, of silk and brocade and cloth of gold and silver every one of the four days from February 22 to February 25. [38]

After the ceremony the Emperor returned to the Palazzo to dine; Ulloa includes Cobos among those invited to the banquet [39] and we may assume that he shared in the festivities of the following days. Bologna was crowded with distinguished ladies: the Queen of Naples, the Marchesana di Mantua, with their train of ladies-in-waiting, who were entertained by the Spanish courtiers. There were banquets and jousts, *juegos de cañas,* and dances. Cobos must have felt that he had really "arrived."

Another month elapsed before the Emperor was ready to

start for Germany. During this period he made a decision which has always puzzled historians. García de Loaisa had been one of his most trusted advisors ever since he was chosen as the King's confessor in 1524. Now, on March 9, he was given a cardinal's hat and sent off to Rome.[40] Many reasons for this action have been proposed. Perhaps the most likely is that the Emperor was tired of Loaisa's constant criticism of his personal habits—his indolence, his procrastination, his self-indulgence. Certainly Loaisa felt that his transfer to Rome was an exile and he long continued to beg the Emperor to allow him to return to his service. Though for many years he was unsuccessful in his pleas, he remained a loyal servant in Rome, negotiating at the Vatican in the Emperor's behalf and carrying on a voluminous correspondence with him.

The Court finally left Bologna on March 22. At Correggio the next day they were received by Veronica Gambara, Lady of Correggio, who had had a new road built from the highway to the door of her palace in honor of the Emperor. On March 25 they entered Mantua, where they were received by the Marchese in the magnificent vestibule of the Palazzo del Te, which Giulio Romano had designed and decorated. For almost a month the Emperor lingered in Mantua, hunting with the Marchese, resting from the long struggles of Bologna before he started for a new world of strife. He showed his gratitude by elevating the rank of the Marchese to that of Duca di Mantova and arranging for his marriage with Margherita, daughter of the Marchese di Montferrato.

It was during these weeks, perhaps in Holy Week (April 14-17), that Cobos became involved in an affair that deserves a section by itself.

Amorous Interlude

At one of the gay parties in Bologna or Mantua, Cobos met a vivacious young woman, the Countess of Novellara. She was a devoted supporter of the Emperor—her husband was fighting in the Imperial army at Naples—and she invited Cobos and some of his friends to visit her at Novellara, a little town set in a flat plain not far from Reggio, with the castle of the Counts of Novellara, "La Rocca," as its only feature—a squat fortress then, surrounded by a deep moat. During that visit Cobos met a protégée of the Countess, Cornelia Malespina, one of the ladies in waiting of the Countess Isabella de' Pepoli, in Bologna, and had a fleeting affair with her.

There is no record of these few days, yet they must have been memorable for all these people. For a dozen years Cobos continued to write to these two women and they to him; for years his friends in Italy, Spaniards and Italians, talked about them in their letters to Cobos. It is proof of Cobos' secretiveness that not one of their letters to him has survived, nor have the archives of Italy yielded any of his correspondence with them. The little that we know must be gleaned from passing remarks in the letters of other people. Why did these women have such an effect on him? Was he dazzled by their brilliance, so different from the style of women he knew in Spain? Was it a brief return to the romance of youth? He was over fifty now.

The letters of Luis de Avila, reminiscing years later, give us a glimpse of that first visit. After telling of his arrival at Novellara, he goes on: "I went into the parlor, where they observe Lent, as you know, and from there into the bedroom where the illustrious ladies used to sleep. I sat down by the fire and undressed, as though I were at home, and pulled off my riding-boots and put on a dressing gown." After he had told of his talk with the Countess, he adds: "and we remembered how you laughed that night when we were sitting on the bed and the illustrious Pedro [González de Mendoza?] saying that in Venice they don't wear swords. The same bed is there, covered with the same coverlet." [41]

From another letter of Avila's we may get a vague idea of what Cornelia was like at that time. In Rome, in 1539, he saw a girl that reminded him of her and he wrote to Cobos: "A girl from Florence has come here—tall, very beautiful, with eyes like Cornelia's; she's a marvelous thing: seventeen years old. I saw her once and Rábago saw her too. I'm reminding you, so that you can ask him about her when he gets there." [42] He must have thought that Cobos too would be interested in reviving the memory. Though we know almost nothing about Cornelia, the Countess was a well-known person.[43]

Costanza d'Austria was the daughter of Giberto X, Lord of Correggio, and Violante Pico della Mirandola. Her mother died when she was a little girl and in 1508 her father married Veronica Gambara, one of the best known poetesses of her time.

When her father died in 1518, leaving to Veronica the care of his daughters by his first marriage, one of her first concerns was to marry Costanza to Alessandro Gonzaga, Count of Novellara, on September 16, 1518, providing her with a dowry of 7,000 ducats. By her marriage Costanza had four children, three boys —the eldest Francesco—and a daughter who became a nun. Her husband was one of a large family, with three brothers and four sisters, one of whom, Camilla, was also a poetess.

Count Alessandro was active in the service of the Emperor, and in the spring of 1530 was serving in the war in Naples. On July 23 Ferrante Gonzaga wrote from Florence to his brother the Duke of Mantua that the Count of Novellara was at the point of death, but two days later he wrote again to report that news had come from Naples that he was out of danger and would recover.[44] However, on August 27 the Countess wrote to the Duke of Mantua that her husband was dead. His brother, Pirro, died in the same campaign.[45]

Left a widow with her four small children, the Countess dedicated herself to the management of her little domain. The local chronicler of Novellara comments on the skill with which she steered her course between the warring factions. Her situation was a delicate one, since her own sympathies were with the Imperial cause, while one of her brothers-in-law, Annibale Gonzaga, had long been in the service of the French King. He was back in Italy in 1533, when Antonio de Leiva wrote to Cobos that he was causing trouble to the Countess.[46] And on November 28 Lope de Soria wrote to him that she was afraid that Annibale would try to steal her fortress from her.[47]

The summer of 1533 was one of drought and poor crops in Northern Italy, and the Countess appealed to Charles V for help. Perhaps through the intervention of Cobos the Emperor sent her 380 *scudi* and permission to have 500 tons of wheat shipped to her from Sicily by way of Genoa. Cobos wrote to the Duke of Mantua on September 25 that the Emperor had granted his approval,[48] and on December 5 Soria reported that she had received the money. And he added: "Certainly Her Ladyship would give a good reward to anyone who brought her the news that His Majesty is returning to Italy or is sending an army of Spaniards to Lombardy, for she lives in terror of her brother-in-law, Annibale." [49] Perhaps it was out of gratitude for this favor that she used to send him—the chronicler says—boxes of quince paste, made with her own hands, of which the Emperor was very fond.[50]

Annibale, the dangerous brother-in-law, soon returned to the service of Francis I. On March 19, 1536, he was reported to have passed through Turin with messages from the French King to the Emperor.[51] Shortly thereafter he was captured by the Imperial troops, and their commander, Antonio de Leiva, wrote him an apologetic letter, saying that the Emperor desired to show every courtesy to the servants of Francis, but that he must remember that these were troubled times and that strangers might easily be suspected.[52] As captain of 1,500 French troops Annibale captured the town of Botiglera early in 1537.[53] He was killed in action in the campaign of the Marchese del Guasto in Piedmont on August 12, 1537.[54]

Donna Costanza's oldest son, Francesco, while still a lad, fought in the Imperial army in Provence in 1536. He soon brought distress to his mother by falling in love with his cousin, Barbara di Correggio, who had entered a nunnery. He was a determined young man, finally secured the annulment of her vows and married her. It may be that it was while he was in Rome soliciting the annulment from the Pope that Cobos wrote to the Spanish ambassador there, the Marqués de Aguilar, asking him to do everything he could to help the Count.[55]

Of the later years of the Countess we know very little, except that she was busy developing her estate—a second story on the "Rocca," the arcades in the town square, a casino in the country. A number of affectionate letters to her from her step-mother, Veronica Gambara, have been printed.[56] Cobos and his friends also knew Veronica. Luis de Avila and Lope de Soria often mention her in their letters; so for example, Avila: "I came to Correggio, where I had luncheon. I saw Veronica in bed, with a very ornamental night-cap and a very embroidered coverlet." [57] Veronica also wrote a letter to Cobos, which has been published in her *Lettere,* in behalf of her son Ippolito. It is a perfect example of the ornate epistolary style which was cultivated in the sixteenth century.

She asks her messenger to remind Cobos "that the roots of your memory, together with my infinite obligation, grow greener again each day in me, forever cultivated by your great courtesy, and I live with the intense desire that I may be so worthy as to show you in some way my gratitude . . . I shall not say anything

about my Countess of Novellara, because she herself is writing
to you. But she is well and so are all of her children. Seldom
does an hour pass that she and all of us do not recall the sweet
memory of the benefits and courtesies we have received from
Your Excellency. God keep you safe and happy." [58]

It is not surprising that the Countess, brought up in the literary circle that gathered around her step-mother, should have
been something of a "blue stocking" herself. One of her contemporaries, Ortensio Landi, in a strange book called *Paradossi,*
has this to say under the quaint *Paradox* XXV: "That woman
is of greater excellence than man: Among the gay and charming
ladies of Lombardy I have always revered Lady Costanza di
Novellara, a lady of the most perfect manners, brilliant mind
and more than average literary talent." [59] We are also told that
she knew Latin, Greek, and Spanish and that she "cultivated
piety and letters to the end of her days, which happened on
August 19, 1563." [60] She must have had a sharp tongue as well
as a facile pen, for Soria once remarked that when she was
annoyed at the Marchese del Guasto for his failure to pay her
son, "she says wonderful things on this subject in a better style
than Aretino," [61] or again: "I am very glad that the Countess
of Novellara was not here when I received your letter, because
I think that, since there was none for her, she would have cursed
all Spain and even the Order of Santiago . . . God save me from
her wrath!" [62] After this long, and perhaps unnecessary digres-
sion, it is time to return to Cobos and his relations with these
fair ladies.

The first mention of Cornelia, after the visit in the spring of
1530, is found in a letter of the Duke of Mantua to the sculptor,
Francesco Bologna, dated on July 6, in which the Duke asked
him to make a portrait of Cornelia, one of the ladies of the
Countess de' Pepoli in Bologna, a small picture of her head and
bust, as good a likeness as possible.[63] The Duke must have given
a similar commission to Titian at the same time, for on July 8
he wrote to the Countess that he was sending Titian, "a rare and
excellent painter," to her and asking her to provide him with an
opportunity to paint a portrait of Cornelia, her servant.[64]

On the twelfth Titian wrote to the Duke: "This lady Cornelia
is not here in Bologna. The Countess has sent her to Novellara
for a change of air, because she has been ill, and they say that
she has been somewhat upset by the illness, though she is better

now. When I learned that, I was afraid that I could not do her justice, and since I have been bothered by the heat and a little indisposed, I did not go ahead." But he was sure that he could paint so good a picture of her that anyone who knew her would say that he had painted her many times. If the Duke would send him the portrait of her that the other painter had made, he could finish his in ten days. And after the Duke had seen it, if he found it unsatisfactory, Titian would be glad to go to Novellara and correct it, but he did not think that that would be necessary.[65]

He must have completed the painting during the summer, for on September 26 the Duke wrote to Sigismundo della Torre, his agent at the Emperor's Court: "Today the mule-driver of M. Antonio Bagarotti left here with the arms that we are sending to Don Pedro de la Cueva and the portrait of Cornelia for the Grand Commander." [66] Was this one of the four pictures that Cobos' servant Zárate took back to Spain from Germany in the spring of 1533? [67]

The illness of Cornelia that summer is mentioned in a letter from the Countess of Novellara to the Governor of Modena (August 9):

> Monday morning the Marchese del Guasto sent here a messenger with letters for me and for Cornelia from the Commander, and he wrote me to send the reply to His Excellency and so I am sending it to him today . . . I have not written to you since you left Novellara and I have waited so long because I did not want the Commander to receive the unpleasant news that Cornelia was ill and so I did not let you know, so that you would not write to him. She is cured now and in good health, more beautiful than ever. Constantia da Gonzaga.[68]

From Flanders, early in 1531, Cobos wrote to the Duke of Ferrara, asking him to show favor to the Countess and her brother-in-law, Giulio.[69] Throughout that year and the next few years every letter of Lope de Soria mentions the Countess and Cornelia—letters they have received from Cobos, letters they have written to him.

The Emperor and his Court returned to Italy at the end of 1532, and in February, 1533, Cobos again wrote to the Duke of Ferrara, sending him a copy of the investiture of Novellara and asking him to execute it in favor of the Countess.[70] At Genoa, on the eve of embarking for Spain in April, 1533, in another letter to the Duke, he reported the marriage of Cornelia to Giovanni Pietro de' Vecchi, who had some property in Reggio; and he asked the Duke to show him favor, knowing as he does, how much this will mean to Cobos.[71] Before Soria went to Venice as ambassador, he visited Novellara and wrote that he found Cornelia very unhappy, swearing that she would not live long away from Court.[72] (Had she been in Bologna that winter?) In the same letter Soria explained the arrangements he had made for handling the ladies' correspondence with Cobos: they would send their letters to the warden of the castle of the Countess of Flisco, who would forward them to Figueroa, the Spanish ambassador in Genoa; Cobos could use the reverse method. The plan was put into effect at once, for Figueroa wrote to Cobos on August 26 that he was sending a second batch of letters from the Countess. Would Cobos please acknowledge their receipt? [73]

Before the end of the year the General of the Augustinians in Venice gave Soria a large glass bottle, covered with fine straw and ornamented with mother-of-pearl, to send to Cobos. But Soria was afraid to ship it by post, lest it get broken, and he suggested that maybe Cobos would like to have him give it to Cornelia. For his part he would be glad to fill it with "musk scented water from his apothecary shop." [74] The Emperor was not the only one who received table delicacies from the Countess. The Conde Cifuentes, on his way to Rome as ambassador, wrote to Cobos that a messenger from the Countess had come with letters, which he was forwarding, and also a gift of Parmigiano cheese and two boxes, one of sausages and the other of quince paste.[75] They say that the way to a man's heart is through his stomach!

In June, 1535, the Marchese del Guasto wrote to Cobos that he expected to be in camp near Modena, where he understood Cornelia was, and he would be able to send her letters to him. And he adds: "In my youth I am glad to serve as a go-between for Your Lordship, in spite of García, and both in Novellara and there [in Spain] I will use every caution." [76] Another distinguished general of the Emperor, Antonio de Leiva, wrote to the Countess from Milan on March 29, 1536: "The Grand Commander of Leon has begged me most urgently to show you and your brother favor, if opportunity occurs; and being anxious to please the Commander, I shall try to serve you with speed and good will." [77] By now, Cobos was in Italy again, and on May

13 Pedro de la Cueva wrote to him from Mantua: "I am staying with the Marchesana, where you would have been entertained, if fortune had brought you here, for there are some sweet Cornelias here. And lest you think that I am spending my time with them, I am being purged tomorrow." [78]

Aside from a letter which the Marqués de Aguilar, on his way to Rome, wrote to Cobos from Genoa in January, 1537, saying that he would write to Cornelia,—"La Illustre" he called her [79] —there are no documents that refer to her in the next few years. Cobos was more and more involved in diplomatic negotiations in this period. But at the end of 1539 Luis de Avila joined the Marqués in Rome and was soon swept along in the round of gay parties. Writing to Cobos on December 6 he described a supper-party at the house of the Marchesana di Massa at which Aguilar and Cardinal Farnese were vying for the attention of the hostess, glaring at each other every time that she spoke to one more than the other.

They are wonderful people and you would have laughed more than you did that night in Novellara over the story of the Venetians . . . The *courtisanes* go to banquets to sing, as they did last night at the Marchesana's. One of them told me that she had sung and played and danced before the Pope—or at least, sung and played. And off there in our Old Castile we are shocked if a perfectly respectable lady from Seville goes out to supper with a gentleman. "O brutto paese tramontanaccio!"—as they say in Florence.[80]

Early in January Avila sent further news of his social life. At a supper-party which he attended with the Princess of Sulmona, they happened to start talking about Cornelia and the Princess said: "That love of Cornelia's must have been a real one, since it still lasts, though the Comendador Mayor is so *lontano,* off in Spain." "I said that Your Lordship did not forget so quickly someone that he cared for." [81] This time he promised that he would soon visit Novellara. Actually he left Rome almost at once, and a few days later was in Correggio, where, as he said, Cobos "was written in the hearts of all the people." [82] It was only seven miles from there to Novellara, so he decided to make the detour. His account of this visit is especially revealing:

Although I had sent a messenger ahead, they were not expecting me. But they opened the gate of the castle and came out to meet me: Quintin in front and a brother of his, then Count Giulio, then the Countess, with three or four other people. And since I came from the Comendador, they received me with great delight . . . Giulio went out to see about some supper and I stayed there with the Countess, waiting for the illustrious Cornelia, who

was a long time in coming. Finally she came, in a black skirt of Milanese silk
that looked like gossamer, with a black head-dress and an embroidered blouse,
and gloves on—not the old kind—with one finger torn, and those white fingers
of hers! I felt bad for her and I said to myself:

> Other gloves she used to wear,
> Gloves that are no longer there.

As a matter of fact, she has three children, and two that are dead; that makes
five.

She is thin, but her eyes, that you have seen in other days, and her mouth
and her speech and her complexion! In short, she's pretty, and extremely annoyed and complaining at you. I said that if she could see the Commander,
she would make peace and she shook her finger. I tell you, sir, that if you
saw her, you would make peace too, even if you were annoyed with her.
She's pretty, but you, who saw her when she was better and enjoyed her
when she was better—I mean back in those childish days—would not find
her as lovely. I told her that you had told me to tell her that you would
feel bad, if you thought that she believed that you no longer had her written
in your memory, more now than ever. She said: "Si vede alla dimostrazione."
I tried to appease her anger and she finally agreed that she would make peace,
if she saw you.

I said a lot more, but what she would really like is a message from you—
"muito dolce," or, as they say in Italian—"molto amorevole."

The little Countess is plump, prettier than María de Mongaya . . . She
showed me your portrait and—so help me God!—I was glad to see it. It's
hanging beside her bed and it was Cornelia who lifted the veil that covered
it. I said—but it was to myself: "This girl knows how to lift the clothes of
this gentleman." Then we sat down again and the Countess says that you
don't remember her, she's sure. I said that she was mistaken.

So it really was a love affair!

From Novellara Avila went on to Piacenza and Milan, on his
way to join the Emperor's Court in Flanders. Everywhere he
was royally entertained and he felt that he was really Cobos'
guest, "because everywhere they are so fond of the 'Boss' of
Leon, whom I love as truly as I ought, and I wish that I did not
owe him so much, that my affection for him might be attributed
to my virtue rather than my obligation." [83]

That spring Lope de Soria was in Milan, and in June the
Countess, with Cornelia and her husband, came there for a visit.
They started back to Novellara on July 1 and on the way out of
town they stopped for a moment at Soria's lodging. Cornelia and
her husband told him that the young Count, Francesco, was
treating them very badly and asked him to persuade Cobos to
intervene.[84] Already, in June, Soria had written to Cobos:

Cornelia is very well and very funny in her remarks, but she seems very
dissatisfied, saying that you have wholly forgotten her. I swore to her that

you hadn't, and I don't think that I swore falsely, and I assured her, and the Countess too, how eager you were to come to Italy, just to see them and show them with deeds how mistaken they are in thinking that you have forgotten them. They were glad to hear it, but I know that they would be even gladder to see you, and I no less than they.

In a postscript he added that he had offered to give Cornelia money, if she needed it.[85]

It must have been during this spring that Doña María, Cobos' wife, discovered in a letter of Diego Hurtado de Mendoza about Cornelia. When Cobos wrote to him about it, Mendoza replied: "I never in my life have laughed so much as I did at the shock to the magnificent 'Patrona,' I'll take care of the bill and the business about Cornelia." [86] But it was no laughing matter for Cobos and he suggested to the Marchese del Guasto that he might help him out. So the Marchese wrote to Doña María that his wife had said that Cornelia was so ugly that she was surprised that Cobos had ever liked her.[87] On July 19 Cobos thanked the Marchese for his letter, with the comment: "Doña María thinks that it was always like that." [88] When the Countess of Novellara somehow heard of this, she was outraged at the insult to her protégée and wrote Cobos a diatribe against the Marchese.[89] As Soria remarked: " 'Tis the custom of women not to praise any as fair, though envy of favors reigns everywhere."

Cobos had not accompanied the Emperor to Flanders and so had more time for his own affairs. All through 1540 and early 1541 he wrote frequently to the two women and to Soria and del Guasto about them. But on March 21, 1541 Soria had bad news to send:

I can't tell you how much I dislike to send you the latest news, because I know how badly you will feel when you read it. It has pleased God to take to His Heaven good and blessed Cornelia. Praised be His name in all things! I couldn't tell you how badly I feel about it for every reason, because really I loved her like a daughter. I don't need to remind you to show your usual prudence and patience. Please write to the Countess, for I am sure that she needs someone to console her for this loss.

P. S. I don't need to say how badly I feel about poor Cornelia's death.[90]

Later in the year the young Count of Novellara wrote to Cobos—and this is the only mention of Cornelia's family name:

What the Countess wrote you about the poor Malespina girl is unfortunately true and I assure you that it grieves me so that I can't make up my mind to go to Novellara. But since these are things that cannot be remedied and recalling them increases and renews the pain, may Our Lord grant peace to her soul.[91]

With the death of Cornelia, the correspondence peters out. Early in 1543 the Countess was still complaining that Cobos had forgotten her.[92] Perhaps he had. It is hard to explain the nature of the Countess's relations with Cobos. He could hardly have been her lover. Was it merely a sort of pride that the councillor of the Emperor had fallen in love with her protégée? Or was she just a calculating female, anxious to use this relationship to secure favors? These are questions we cannot answer. But these scattered shreds of evidence make it clear that for both Cobos and Cornelia Malespina those few days at Novellara in the spring of 1530 were a deep and moving experience. Cobos' marriage to María de Mendoza was for both parties a *marriage de convenance;* according to the standards of the time, he was a devoted husband. But love comes with overwhelming power. To the end of his life the memory of this tall, lovely girl that he had enjoyed for one fleeting moment—her eyes, her mouth— was written in his heart.

Problems of Empire

After almost a month of sumptuous entertainment at the Court of Mantua, on April 18, 1530, the Emperor started for Germany. As so often happened, Cobos was left behind to clear up unfinished business. On April 20 he wrote, in the Emperor's behalf, to the Duke, asking him to pay Giambattista Castaldo, the Imperial captain, the 3,000 ducats that were due him, and he added his personal request for action: "because of the friendship I have for Juan Baptista and my desire that he may prosper." [93] Two days later, following the Emperor's steps, he was in Verona, where he wrote to the Condestable, forwarding a letter from Charles.[94] He probably overtook the royal suite at Trent and with them continued the journey to Innsbruck, which they entered on May 4. There the Emperor was joined by his brother Ferdinand and his sister Mary and began his preparations for the Diet of Augsburg.

A month later the Grand Chancellor Gattinara suffered a stroke and died the next day.[95] In spite of waning influence, Gattinara had retained his post as chief advisor of Charles in matters of foreign policy. Now the Emperor was faced with the necessity of choosing his successor. When the Cardinal Loaisa, in Rome, heard of Gattinara's death, he wrote to Charles, urging him to be his own chancellor and to depend on Cobos and Granvelle as his chief advisors.[96] Loaisa had retained a high regard for Cobos from the days when they worked together in Spain. On July 6 he wrote to the Emperor:

> I always held that the Secretary Cobos was the coffer of your honor and your secrets, who knew how to make up for your carelessness in your dealings with people and in defense of his master. He loves you with the highest loyalty and he is extraordinarily prudent, and he does not waste his brains saying clever things, as others do, and he never gossips about his master and he is the best liked man that we know.

And Loaisa added a word of praise for Granvelle—a trained lawyer, a good Latinist, and a good Christian, though not as easy a person to talk to as Cobos.

Loaisa's respect for Cobos was revealed in another letter which he wrote to him a little later.

> I read your letter to the Pope . . . and in truth, to judge by what he says, His Holiness gets more pleasure from hearing your letters than from all those that the Ambassador shows him, because he says that they are cordial and that in a few words you put a lot of meaning and all expressed with great discretion and no deceit. I answered him: "Holy Father, he has greater worth and more influence with His Majesty because he is virtuous, prudent, and of sound and solid counsel than because he is a secretary." The Pope replied, saying that the Emperor was fortunate to have such an official, who was beloved by all and was so faithful and useful in his service.[97]

Whether or not he was moved by Loaisa's advice, the Emperor decided not to replace Gattinara; from now on he assumed personal responsibility for the conduct of foreign policy, using Cobos and Granvelle as his aides. They were his advisors, though he often disregarded their advice; they served as a sort of buffer to whom he could refer ambassadors, when he was unready to make a decision; they were his agents and representatives in the conduct of diplomatic negotiations. For years these two labored together with notable harmony in the service of their master. Both were wholly dedicated to the Emperor, ready to subordinate themselves to his will, disinclined to press their point of view or become peevish, as had Gattinara, when their advice was over-ruled. Both were men of peace, preferring compromise to force, in personal as well as public affairs. And finally, both were ambitious for wealth and realized that they could gain more by working together than by rivalry for Imperial favor.

The death of Gattinara left his secretary, Alfonso de Valdés, without a protector. Loaisa wrote to Cobos on June 27, 1530, urging the appointment of one Marcello as Latin secretary. "At any rate I beg you to find a good Latinist, and Valdés is not one. People here make fun of his Latin and say that the letters he writes here in Latin are full of blunders." [98] But Cobos was more sympathetic to Valdés. He wrote to Henry of Nassau: "His Majesty should, if it be his pleasure, sign the appointment of the secretary Valdés. It is not an important post nor one in which His Majesty has anything at stake. Lest he despair, I have not told him that his appointment was not signed. As His Majesty knows, nothing is ever done for him and he works and serves well." [99] Cobos' plea was successful, for Valdés name appears from now on, on Spanish, not Latin documents.[100]

The two and a half years that the Emperor spent in Germany and Flanders, trying to solve the religious and political problems of his Empire, were busy years for Cobos. With Granvelle and the members of the Privy Council—Nassau, Praet, Padilla, and Merino—he was involved in all of the negotiations; this we know from the correspondence of ambassadors and Papal legates. But there is no record of the particular part that he played. He was still given special responsibility in the handling of finances. At Augsburg on October 31, 1531, for example, he and Granvelle, Padilla, and the Treasurer Zuazola signed a contract with Bartolomé Welser for a loan of 200,000 ducats, secured by income from the military orders.[101]

For the most part the documents of the period which refer to him deal with routine matters: perfunctory letters to the Empress, all couched in much the same vein: "The Emperor was delighted to receive your letters. He is well—thank God!—and in good spirts, but eager to return to Spain. He is too busy to write personally." There are lengthy letters to Juan Vázquez in Spain with minute instructions as to matters that must be handled. As always there are the letters to individuals—to some whom he cannot help, to others for whom he would have liked to do more, to still others whom he promises to serve. Thus when Gerónimo Zurita, the future historian, was appointed a *contino* in July, 1530, Cobos wrote to his father that he had tried to get a larger stipend for him, but it could not be done ("no hubo lugar") ; he would always be glad to serve him in any way possible.[102]

There is, however, one document of singular importance as revealing the methods by which Cobos and Granvelle conducted the affairs of the Emperor. As usual, Charles left the Court for a Holy Week retreat at Groenendael early in April, 1531, leaving Cobos and Granvelle in Ghent. An April 4 Cobos wrote to the Emperor:

The mail for Italy will be dispatched at once, although we thought that, in order that it might not go without letters from the Legate [Campeggio] and these ministers of the Pope, it should be held till tomorrow. Today M. de Granvelle and I have been with the Legate and the ministers and we have told them everything Your Majesty ordered us. They asked us to give them a copy of it. We said that we had a commission only to talk to them and that for the sake of confidence we had been willing to bring them in writing what is happening and also that we might not change the words in any way. They insisted and because Gambara said that he wanted to go to Your Majesty to beg it from you, we agreed that we would consult with Your Majesty and in the morning we would give them the reply. We think that the substance of what is being written to Rome should be given to them, and so in the morning we will give it to them, but not the part about France, because it might be that M. de Praet would not have time to negotiate so soon with the King of France, both because it is Holy Week and for other reasons, and there would be a chance that before we knew his answer, the representatives of the Pope might tell him.

On this we will give him the best excuse we can, unless Your Majesty gives other orders. They wanted to discuss the matter with us. We answered that our commission was limited to giving them the reply with regard to the Council. The mail will be dispatched tomorrow, so that it will not go with their letters.[103]

There are several other paragraphs: news from Italy; they are preparing the dispatches which Idiáquez is to carry to Spain. One interesting note is: "I am sending the memorandum of what Your Majesty is to write to the King [Ferdinand] and to the Empress. In the letter to the Empress you can add the news about Venice." Evidently the advisors were dictating this sort of communication. In the margins and at the end of the letter Charles wrote his comments in his scrawly hand.

At some time during this year there came to Flanders an Augsburg engraver named Christoph Weiditz. In Brussels he made a number of medals of people of the Court: Alfonso de Valdés, Hernán Cortés, Bishop Merino, and one was of Cobos.[104] It was dated "MDXXXI" and it must have enjoyed some popularity, for in the following year Weiditz got out a "second edition" by adding a "I" to the date. It is one of the two portraits of Cobos that have come down to our day.

By the end of 1531 the Emperor had settled most of his Flemish problems. His brother Ferdinand was crowned "King of the Romans" in January; late in November he held another chapter of the Order of the Golden Fleece at Tournai, where he named twenty-one new knights. First was his infant son, Philip; there were other Spaniards: the Duque de Calabria, the Duque de Alburquerque, the young Condestable de Castilla, and the Conde de Miranda, and three Italian friends of Cobos: the Marchese del Guasto, Andrea Doria, and Ferrante Gonzaga. During the Emperor's visit to Tournai Cobos stayed behind in Brussels to dispatch business.[105] There were collars of the Order for the *grandes;* there were cardinal's hats for the clergy who served well. For ordinary folk like Cobos and Granvelle the only possible rewards were money, and more money. But there were occasional sops: at a banquet in Brussels, after the Emperor's return, to which only twenty-four courtiers were invited, Cobos was one of the guests.[106] Finally, after meeting with the Estates of all the Low Countries in Brussels, Charles departed on January 17, 1532, for Germany, reaching Ratisbonne at the end of February.

For six months the Emperor remained there, while the Diet wrangled without success over the thorny religious and political questions. In the spring the Emperor had a series of ailments: in April an inflammation of the eye that spread to his whole face in May; in June a bad leg that came as a result of a hunting accident. Between June 24 and July 11 he was taking the cure at the baths near Ratisbonne; the Venetian ambassadors reported that they could not see Cobos, because he was with the Emperor.[107] Meanwhile, the threat of the Turkish invasion became more imminent and Charles, accepting his responsibility as the defender of Christendom, summoned his forces from all his lands. In spite of the advice of the Consejo, he even had the Empress call a new Cortes at Segovia to secure a new subsidy. On September 2 he started for Linz and from there moved on to Vienna. But before the Imperial forces had an opportunity to join battle, the Sultan Suleiman suddenly withdrew his forces. The Emperor promptly disbanded his own army.

While they were in Vienna, Alfonso de Valdés died.[108] The ambassador in Rome, Miguel Mai, wrote twice to Cobos, urging him to appoint Juan de Valdés in his brother's place. And Cornelius Schepper, who had just been on a special mission to the Swiss cantons, was also a candidate for the post. But Cobos decided not to make a definite appointment; for the present he turned the conduct of Neapolitan affairs over to one of his assistants, Alonso de Idiáquez. Schepper was outraged that a person like Idiáquez, who possessed neither letters nor talent, should be given such a responsibility, but he explained it on the ground that he was a favorite of Cobos and had been his majordomo. Here again Cobos used his power to promote the interests of one of his henchmen.

Still, it was necessary to have someone to take care of the Latin correspondence, and Cobos found this person in one of the *escribanos* of Valdés, Gonzalo Pérez. Pérez had been in service for several years with Valdés, at Bologna, in Flanders, and in Vienna. In his last will, signed at Vienna on October 5, 1532, Valdés had left him a horse and 200 ducats and had given this instruction: "I wish him at once to take possession of all my papers and do with them whatever the Comendador Mayor de León commands. And for this reason I beg His Lordship to make use of his services and to consider him as recommended." [109] Cobos accepted this recommendation and assigned Pérez duties in his office, though he gave him no formal title. Thus far, all of Cobos' associates had been men who had grown up in the government service, without education. Now for the first time he brought into his official entourage a man of learning who knew Latin and who also was a man of letters. But it was years before he gave him any signal recognition.[110]

———••◦◦•———

CHAPTER VII

HAPPENINGS AT HOME

During the years when Cobos was absent from Spain he kept up a steady correspondence with his family and friends at home. Doña María and the children spent most of their time at their palace in Valladolid. Don Alonso Enríquez visited her there and so did Juan de Samano, who wrote to Cobos: "My Lady is well and so are the young folks—God keep them!—and young Mistress Mary is the funniest thing in the world with her stories about the Court." [1] The Condestable and the Conde de Miranda and other friends reported to him that his family was well.[2] Early in 1530 Doña María was in Toledo for a while with her father, the Conde de Rivadavia, who had been *corregidor* of the city since 1526, and Don Alonso stopped to see her there.[3] In October, 1531, Cobos sent Captain Andrés de Prada to stay with her and serve her; he was sure that he was a wise and honorable person and the Emperor had approved.[4]

He also managed to pick up a few small favors for his family. His wife had been a lady in waiting of the Empress from the time of her arrival in Spain, and Cobos had added the name of his mother-in-law to a list of ladies who should be appointed.[5] Both Doña María and her parents were granted mine rights in the area where they held property.[6] At Bologna, on March 8, 1530, the Emperor granted the Count and Countess the right to establish a *mayorazgo,* a privilege which they exercised on May 11 in favor of their eldest son, Diego Sarmiento de Mendoza.[7] The Count Juan Hurtado de Mendoza must have died during that year, for in a letter to Cobos written on September 10, Loaisa reported that he had heard of the Count's death.[8]

Even the children came in for their share of honor: Don Dieguito was named a page of the Emperor (he was seven!), and Doña Mariquita, a lady in waiting of the Empress (she was six!). Doña María complained to Cobos that they were not receiving their salaries because he had not sent an instruction to the paymaster. Cobos answered to Juan Vázquez that he thought that this was just a pretext for not paying them; after all, there wasn't much loss involved. But he would send the order.[9] What were 9,000 *maravedís* a year (a page's salary) to a man with Cobos' income? But the honor was important.

The most striking favor that Cobos received for his little boy was his appointment as Chanciller de las Indias, to fill the post left vacant by the death of Gattinara. From Cologne, on January 28, 1532, Charles sent an instruction to the Consejo de las Indias to prepare the necessary papers for transfering the seal of the Indies to Diego.[10] The official documents were signed at Ratisbonne on August 10 and 12, naming him Chanciller and Keeper of the Seal, with the proviso that his father was to perform the duties of the office until Diego was of age.[11] For good measure the Consejo de las Indias provided on December 24 that he was to receive back pay from the date of Gattinara's death, June 5, 1530, minus one-fourth for office expenses.[12] Cobos promptly appointed Martín Ortiz de Urbina as his deputy and granted to Juan de Samano a power of attorney to act in his behalf, a power which Samano at once transferred to the treasurer and paymaster of New Spain.[13] Charles seemed to have forgotten that one of the most insistent demands of every Cortes and of Gattinara had been that no man should be allowed to hold more than one office nor engage another person to perform the duties of an office. And speaking of multiple appointments, we might add that in July, at Ratisbonne, the Emperor had added another 100,000 *maravedís* a year to Cobos' salary in recognition of his duties in finances.[14]

There was, however, one temporary set-back for Cobos. On August 9, 1529, the Consejo de Castilla had granted to him and Juan de Vozmediano the right to all the mines in the archbishopric of Toledo.[15] Later the Consejo decided that this was an alienation of the royal patrimony and revoked the grant.[16]

When Cobos heard of this in Flanders, he wrote to Juan Vázquez: "As for the mines, there is nothing to say except that
those gentlemen have done what they think is best for His
Majesty's service and that I am glad of it." And in his own hand
he added: "Please let me know what they have decided." [17]
But attached to the *cédula* revoking the grant is a slip of paper
which explains that the original grant was exactly like those
made to Dr. Carvajal, Francisco Pacheco, the Licenciado Zapata,
Lope Conchillos, and other persons, and that the royal treasury
would profit more by this privilege than by leaving the metal
under ground. Evidently Vázquez would not let the matter lie,
for on November 21, 1531, at Medina del Campo, the Consejo
renewed the grant to Cobos and Vozmediano; [18] his share was
listed in the final inventory of his estate.[19]

Cobos did not forget his kinsmen and associates in the secretariat. For Juan Vázquez de Molina he secured an appointment
as Comendador de Estriana in the Order of Santiago. In this,
he enlisted the support of the Empress, who wrote a personal
letter to her husband in his behalf,[20] and of García de Padilla,
who was with him in Flanders.[21] Cobos was able to write to his
nephew on October 23, 1531, that the order for his appointment
was being dispatched.[22] For his cousin Pedro de los Cobos he
won an appointment as knight of Santiago.[23] Don Pedro was
anxious to be appointed Treasurer of Queen Juana, but on several occasions Cobos informed him that, hard as he had tried, he
had not been able to secure it.[24] Even Juan de Samano came in
for a little recognition when he was accorded the privilege of
shipping 100 negro slaves to the Indies.[25]

The Palace in Ubeda

Cobos' father, Don Diego, died some time in 1530. The last
documents which mention him are early in the year when he exchanged property with the Monasterio de la Trinidad [26] and
when he received a power of attorney from his son to restore
Fernando Ortega as chaplain of the Capilla de la Concepción.[27]
He was a very old man when he died—Oviedo says that he was
more than a hundred years old. And he tells the story that at
the end he was so weak that he could not eat and had to be fed
by two wet nurses, and every night his two granddaughters slept
with him to keep him warm.[28]

As heir to his father's estate, Cobos soon began to think of extending the family house. He had been buying adjacent property between 1518 and 1526 and now, in the spring of 1531, his agents purchased two more parcels of land next to his.[29] Once more he engaged as his architect Luis de Vega, who had built his palace in Valladolid. At the same time, through Micer Mai, the ambassador in Rome, he ordered a stone fountain for the patio of his house. Mai reported on December 13, 1531, that he was having difficulty in finding transportation for it; if Cobos could have it picked up at Alicante, there were frequent ships. And he added that he was sending a marble bust of Apollo, "one of the good pieces of Italy." [30] To provide water for the fountain, Cobos secured from the municipal Council of Ubeda a grant of water from the fountain at the Puerta de Toledo, with the privilege of carrying it to his house through any streets he thought best.[31] Some of the citizens protested at this highly personal favor and Cobos wrote to Juan Vázquez on October 23 that he was sending the Emperor's approval to Ubeda and that he must defend the right, since the water was already at the house. Again he added in his own hand: "Do your best not to get into a lawsuit." [32]

Luis de Vega visited Ubeda late in 1531 or in the spring of 1532 and drew a rough plan, which still exists at Simancas,[33] of the additions to the house. In view of the present ruined condition of the palace, it is impossible to speak with certainty about the changes. But it is clear that the principal new construction was a wing on the east side of the house, inclosing the patio and providing a *mirador* overlooking the valley. In the piles of debris there are still the white marble floor tiles and pieces of the slender marble columns which once ornamented the *mirador*. On July 15, 1532, Cobos' business agent in Granada, Francisco de Biedma, wrote that he had just visited Ubeda and had been able to purchase the houses of Luis de Elviruela. He was tremendously impressed with the changes already made and felt that Cobos had done a favor to Ubeda. He only hoped that Cobos would live to enjoy it for fifty years. The fountain was working and it made the house so delightful and cool that it seemed like a different place.[34]

On August 1 Fernando Ortega, the chaplain, wrote Cobos a long letter about affairs in Ubeda—his sisters' health, the benefices for the chapel, their worry over the threat of the Turks, and the solemn procession of devotion to the Cross through the streets of the city to implore divine aid. He discusses in detail the work of construction: the width of the foundations, the stone vaults to provide cooler rooms, the windows that looked out on the garden and the Calle de Tovaria. He was still trying to secure a piece of ground from Martín Ortega which would permit them to extend the building. Would the Comendador like to have a tower built at the back, even if it was not a high one? [35]

If we may judge by the fragments of carved capitals, gargoyles, and architraves that still lie on the ground, it must have been a very grand house. In 1601 Cobos' grandson, Francisco de los Cobos y Luna, said that it was as good as or better than his palace in Valladolid.[36] There is a description of it in an inventory of Camarasa property made in 1752:

> The house in the street that they call "de los Cobos" is fifty-nine *varas* long (I paced it off as sixty yards) and eighty *varas* deep, including thirty-eight *varas* of garden. Two stories, upper and lower. On the ground floor: an entrance way with two stables and a straw loft, a rectangular patio, a drawing room with three bedrooms, a wine cellar, a kitchen; another drawing room with two bedrooms, two yards with their garden, a wine room. Second floor: a drawing room and anteroom, with two bedrooms, another drawing room with two more bedrooms, a passageway and a sun gallery; another sun gallery; another drawing room with its kitchen and two bedrooms, its porches and gallery. . . . Besides, in the patio it has a fountain, with its own water.[37]

Today the fountain, badly worn by time and weather, is still flowing in the Plaza de Juan Vázquez de Molina, in front of the chapel of San Salvador. Of the palace, all that remains is the long, dark façade, with a few rooms clinging to it; the rest was destroyed by fire some years ago. The façade must once have been typical of Spanish palaces of the early sixteenth century, with a single door in the center and one large window on the second story in each wing. At a later date the entrance was widened and a window opened above it, bearing the arms of Cobos' son Diego. Small windows were also opened at the ends of the upper floor and on the ground floor. The masonry is of carefully cut stone, each with a mason's mark, laid in regular courses. The windows are screened with *rejas;* those on the large windows may be the original ones. Inside there are two or three rooms still occupied on the ground floor; one has a tiny fireplace in the corner. Upstairs, all that is left is one of the *salas,* a fine room about thirty feet long with a beamed ceiling.

It is hard to understand why Cobos lavished so much time and money on this palace. He almost never visited it, until he came there to die. It is true that it provided a home for his sisters, Leonor "la Beata" and Isabel, with her two daughters. But they did not require so lavish an establishment. Was it because he felt the need for a distinguished ancestral home, like the castles and palaces of his noble friends—the Condestable de Castilla in Burgos, the Conde de Benavente in Valladolid, the Duque del Infantado in Guadalajara? Or was it merely a reflection of the almost universal craze for building private, and even royal palaces that swept Spain in the sixteenth century? Perhaps the most that we can say is that for Cobos, as for most Spaniards, and for that matter, for most Europeans of his time, a palace was the hallmark of distinction.

Italy Again

When Charles V with his Italian and Spanish troops came down from the Brenner into the Italian plain in the autumn of 1532, there was a rumor abroad that he was planning to visit Venice. In fact, the municipal council of Treviso voted on November 4 to make a gift of 300 ducats each to Cobos and the Marchese del Guasto when they came to town.[38] But the Emperor made straight for Mantua, and so Cobos missed this little gratification. The Emperor's stay in Mantua was brief, but long enough for him to become impressed with the talent of Titian. He had met him at Bologna in 1530, but at that time he had paid little attention to him. Now, perhaps encouraged by the Duke of Mantua and by Cobos,[39] he sat for his portrait and was so pleased with the result that from this time on, Titian was his only painter. Apparently Cobos stayed on in Mantua after the Emperor left on November 7, for he signed documents there until December 6.[40] Perhaps he found time in these weeks to make a visit to his friends in Novellara.

There is a story that during these months the Duke of Ferrara, Alfonso d'Este, was making every effort to win the support of Cobos and instructed his envoys to pay whatever price was necessary.[41] Knowing that Cobos was interested in paintings, he engaged Titian to work on him; perhaps Cobos would like to have some of the pictures in the Duke's collection. There were portraits of the Emperor, of the Duke himself, of his son and heir, Ercole; there was a Judith, a St. Michael, a Madonna. After the Court reached Bologna, the Duke's agents, Jacopo Alvarotti and Matteo Casella, continued to tempt him: he could have any of the pictures he wanted. Cobos now gave them a list of the pictures that Titian had suggested; the one that he was most anxious to have was that of the Duke. On January 23, 1533, Alvarotti and Casella delivered the portrait to Cobos; the others were being shipped to Genoa. A few days later Cobos met Casella and told him that the Duke's portrait was already hanging in the Emperor's room. On February 12 the ambassador in Genoa, Suárez de Figueroa, acknowledged the receipt of a large picture and another small box of paintings from the Duke,[42] and on March 4 he wrote Cobos that he was sending them, together with the paintings that Cobos had shipped from Germany, to Barcelona, in charge of Zárate.[43]

When Charles reached Bologna, he found the Pope waiting for him and at once took up with him the vexed question of the Church Council.[44] On December 16 he appointed a commission to work with the Papal representatives, consisting of Granvelle, Cobos, Mai, and Merino who had just received his cardinal's cap. In the hours between their discussions, Cobos found time to write his usual letters to the Empress[45] and to ask further favors from the Duke of Ferrara.[46] Finally, on February 24, the conferees had patched up an agreement whereby envoys were to be sent to France and the German Protestants to explore the possibilities of a Council; Granvelle and Cobos signed for the Emperor, Jacobo de' Salviati and Francesco Guicciardini for Clement VII.[47] Three days later they also signed a treaty between the Emperor, the Pope, and the Italian states, creating a defensive league against aggression; this time Florence was included in the league.[48] On the next day, now that the chief business of his visit was over, the Emperor started for Spain.

As so often happened, he moved slowly, making a long detour to Milan and the battle field of Pavia. On the way down to Genoa, on March 21, at the little village of Piedracaya, Cobos and Granvelle dispatched Pedro González de Mendoza to Ferrara with detailed instructions for his negotiations with Queen Isabel of Naples for the marriage of her daughter, the Infanta Donna Giulia, to Giangiorgio, Marchese di Montferrato; both counsellors signed the orders.[49] From March 28 to April 9 the

Court remained in Genoa, whence they at last embarked for Spain. The voyage was a stormy one, but they reached Rosas on April 21. There Charles went ashore, and accompanied only by the Duque de Alba, the Conde de Benavente, and a few other gentlemen of the household, hurried on by land to join the Empress. The rest of the fleet reached Barcelona on April 25.

Return to Spain

The Empress, with her two children and the members of her suite, had arrived at Barcelona almost a month before.[50] Cobos' wife, as one of her ladies in waiting, had come with her. As early as March 8 the ambassador in Rome, Micer Mai, had heard that she was planning the trip and wrote to Cobos offering him and his wife the hospitality of his house in Barcelona.[51] Whimsically he remarked that his wife had promised not to pester them with her religious devotions. And so in Barcelona Cobos was reunited with his wife and children for the first time in almost four years. He quickly reported to the Duke of Mantua that he had found them in good health.[52]

The Emperor left for Monzón on June 10; Cobos and Granvelle, having finished the dispatches, followed two days later.[53] On the morning of June 18 Charles opened the Cortes, but that very day he learned that the Empress was ill and immediately left for Barcelona; it was almost the only time in his life when he traveled fast: forty-three leagues in twenty-four hours. On June 22 he wrote to Cobos about the condition of the Empress and asked him to send him a copy of her will.[54] Cobos had planned to return to Barcelona with Louis de Praet, but on the twenty-seventh the Emperor instructed him to remain at Monzón.[55] Again on July 9 he wrote Cobos and Granvelle that he had received their recommendation that the Duchess of Savoy, the Empress's sister, should not be invited to come to the Court that year. He had consulted with the Empress and he now ordered them to send the messages at once by Gutierre López de Padilla, who was leaving on Friday, July 11.[56] Already on June 15 he had written to the Duke of Savoy to congratulate him on the birth of his child and to invite him, but not the Duchess, to come to Spain.[57]

The session of the Cortes at Monzón was even more prolonged than usual; it was almost six months before a settlement was reached and a subsidy voted. They were, for Cobos, months filled with routine duties. Most of the ambassadors in Italy addressed their letters directly to Cobos, who in turn discussed them with the Emperor. To all he wrote personal answers. And then there was the correspondence with his Italian friends—the Duke of Ferrara, the Duke of Mantua, not to mention the ladies of Novellara. His daily chore of letter-writing was prodigious. Fortunately he had the assistance of Idiáquez; many of the minutes and marginal notes are in his tiny, crisp hand.[58]

Martín de Salinas had been absent from the Court for almost two years in Spain. On August 6 he rejoined the Court at Barcelona and was cordially received by the Emperor, as well as by Cobos and Granvelle.[59] Already, at Valladolid, on June 20, he had received news from the Court and had written to the King's secretary Castillejo:

> The Grand Commander, according to what they say, is greatly favored by His Majesty and this is generally believed in Castile, because they say that he has great influence and is likely to have more, so that everything will be under his control. Zuazola has been named general Treasurer and they have removed him from his post as Secretary of War and given it to Juan Vázquez, whose father-in-law has died, and he will also serve as Cobos' deputy in the affairs of Castile. Idiáquez has received the habit of Calatrava and they have given him the post of Naples which Valdés had and he is to help Cobos in the business of the Council of State. So that everything related to correspondence and administration is under Cobos' hand. People here are amazed at his power, and in view of his ability and goodness, he deserves it.[60]

As usual, Salinas was informed about affairs before they were officially announced. Idiáquez was not granted his habit in the order of Calatrava until May 11, 1534;[61] on December 2 of that year he was named secretary of the Orders of Calatrava and Alcántara.[62] But he was right in his estimate of the extent to which Cobos had gained control of all the administrative posts. Either in his own right or through one of his assistants he now held a decisive power in all of the affairs of the Emperor and the Empress in Castile; in addition he was responsible for the relations with the Pope and the Italian states.

During the first months after his arrival at the Court, Salinas was more and more impressed with the growing influence of Granvelle. In his letters to Castillejo he repeatedly urged that Ferdinand should write to him and to Cobos to express his gratitude for their support. It might be well, too, to send them presents; Granvelle would be glad to receive some sable furs and

Cobos must not be forgotten.[63] Just as Lallemand had been his chief contact in the days before his downfall, Granvelle now became his best source of information. Late in December he wrote to King Ferdinand that he had delivered to Granvelle the King's message regarding the investiture of Montferrato, but he had not handed Cobos his letter, because Cobos was a close friend of the Duke of Mantua and was already suspicious.[64] Between the lines one can read a growing hostility toward Cobos, though Salinas continued to cultivate him because of his power.

The most exciting news reached the Court at the end of December. On August 1 the Licenciado Gaspar de Espinosa had written to Cobos from Panama about the fabulous exploits of Francisco Pizarro and Diego de Almagro in Peru—the capture of Atahualpa and the vast treasure they had acquired: more than 2,000,000 *pesos* of gold and 50,000 marks of silver, strange objects, and gold nuggets that weighed eight or ten pounds. All told, it amounted to more than a billion *maravedís*. Hernando Pizarro was bringing a part of the treasure to His Majesty; and he went on: "The offices which you hold in these provinces are and will be of great profit. If it be your desire, I will take charge of receiving here the income and profits which come to you and send them to Pedro of Speyer, or wherever you say, and to serve you in any possible way." [65] Cobos' share, 1 per cent on specie, suddenly loomed large. It was long before the Indies fleet reached Seville; on December 7 the Consejo de las Indias wrote to Cobos that they too had received the glad news, but that the fleet had not appeared.[66] Meanwhile it was annoying to have to sit down with Granvelle, Padilla, the Conde de Miranda, and M. de Noircarmes to discuss a projected attack on Corón.[67]

Charles had sent the Empress to Zaragoza and had hoped to spend Christmas with her there, but the Cortes was not over until December 27, so that he did not reach Zaragoza until New Year's Eve. When they left two weeks later, Cobos did not go with them; this we know from letters written to him by Juan Vázquez in January and early February. From them we learn that Don Luis [de Avila?] and Lope Hurtado de Mendoza were with Cobos. The only evidence as to his whereabouts is found in a letter from the Marqués de Denia to Charles, written at Tudela del Duero in February, in which he reported that Cobos had passed through there and had delivered his message.[68] It is possible that his mission was to discuss with the Marqués the question of Queen Juana's last will, to which Salinas refers in a letter to King Ferdinand.[69]

Vázquez's letters, written along the road from Medinaceli to Madrid in the company of the Emperor, are full of entertaining comments on the life of the Court. He had not been able to deliver one of Cobos' letters to the Emperor because the Emperor spent most of the day playing cards with the Conde de Benavente, the Marqués de Aguilar, Pedro de la Cueva, and Pedro González de Mendoza; González and Aguilar had won all the money. And after that, the Emperor had tried out some new guns, so that it was bedtime before he was free. Incidentally, a few nights later Aguilar lost all he had won and González came out 600 ducats ahead. (Note: there were stiff penalties for gambling under the laws of Castile!) Would Cobos please send the Emperor 500 ducats to meet the expenses along the road? In Guadalajara there was a great rumpus, because the Emperor would not let the Marquesa de Lombay and the Marquesa de Aguilar stay in the Palace, but insisted that they stay with their husbands. At Medinaceli they would have had good cheer, if only the Duque had had good wines; at least, he gave the Emperor two fine horses. He had heard that Doña María had passed through Guadalajara without stopping and was going straight to Novés; she and the children were well.[70]

In Alcalá they found the Congregation of Bishops in session, studying the question of the new taxes on the churches which the Pope had authorized. The Emperor addressed them in person and graciously assented to accepting the same subsidy that they had granted in the past. At the same time he threatened that if they did not give their approval—and quickly—he would forbid them to return to their sees and would order their churches not to pay them their income. Vázquez thought that they would yield.

There are several matters in these letters which concern Cobos personally. Thus, for instance, for the first time in the record, there is a mention of an illness; he had been suffering from a pain in the back and chest. A week later he had written that his back was better. But of far greater importance was the news of the illness of the Archbishop of Toledo, Alonso de Fonseca. Already, at Medinaceli, Vázquez had heard that he was at the point of death. When they reached Alcalá he was still alive, but so weak and so swollen with dropsy that he was a pitiful sight.

On February 4, the day after the Emperor left to go hunting in El Pardo, he was dead. There are several veiled references in Vázquez's letters to show why this was important to Cobos; there is even one specific mention of the "business about the *adelantamiento*." We shall have to go back to reconstruct the story.[71]

The Adelantamiento *of Cazorla*

Since the thirteenth century, when the archbishop of Toledo, Rodericus Toletanus, had recovered it from the Moors, the frontier province of Cazorla had been an appanage of the Archbishops of Toledo, governed by an *adelantado* who received his appointment from the Archbishop. In 1527, on the death of García de Villarroel, Fonseca had appointed his nephew, Alonso de Acevedo, as *adelantado,* subject to a pension of 700 ducats a year payable to La Chaux. For Cobos, Cazorla was a part of his world. As a boy he had looked out to its distant ridge; he knew of the wealth that came from its heavy forests and fertile fields. Knowing the Emperor as he did, he could not hope, with his modest origin, to receive a title of nobility. But he could aspire to the title of *adelantado;* his father-in-law, Juan de Mendoza, and his forbears had long been successively *adelantados* of Galicia.

Now, as Fonseca's health began to fail, he started to prepare the way for his appointment to the post when Fonseca was gone. Confidentially he talked to Granvelle and to Juan Tavera, Archbishop of Santiago; both of them assured him of their support. During the days of Fonseca's last illness, he even took definite steps to achieve his purpose. He sent his errand-boy, Diego de Zárate, to Toledo to persuade the Chapter of the Cathedral to turn the title over to him, as soon as Fonseca died, and Zárate won the support of the *maestrescuela* of the Cathedral to take the lead.

When Juan Vázquez received letters from Zárate and the *maestrescuela* of Toledo, asking for instructions as to the next step, he was perplexed as to what to do. If they acted now, *sede vacante* and everyone absent, people would say that they had taken the post away from the Conde [de Osorno?], without the Emperor's approval, particularly because the latter had ordered a letter written to the Chapter to take no action until his arrival. Thus in doubt, Vázquez talked to Tavera, who advised him to present the matter frankly to the Emperor and, if he approved, to ask him to withdraw his instructions to the Chapter. The Emperor evidently did not approve and matters were at a standstill. This was the situation when Vázquez wrote to Cobos on February 8.

There were three candidates for the post at Toledo left vacant by the death of Fonseca: Alonso Manrique, Archbishop of Seville; García de Loaisa, the former Confessor, now Cardinal of Sigüenza; and Juan Tavera.[72] In length of service, Manrique was the leading aspirant; he had been with the Emperor in Flanders before his first visit to Spain. Many people at Court thought that he was certain to receive the appointment. But there was a story current that Cobos had approached him with an offer of support in return for the appointment as *adelantado* and that Manrique was so sure of success that he rebuffed him. Besides he had another count against him: back in 1529 he had had the effrontery to sponsor and bless the marriage of his nephew, which the Emperor had forbidden. Loaisa had been permitted to return to Spain but he had never recovered the confidence of the Emperor. That left Tavera; it was to him that Cobos decided to look for support.

On February 6 Vázquez wrote to Cobos that the day before, at El Pardo, when he went to consult with the Emperor, he found him opening a letter from Tavera and the Emperor asked him to tell him what it was about: it dealt with the question of Church taxes. In the letter was a slip of paper, in Tavera's own hand, and when Vázquez took it out to read, the Emperor, laughing, said: "This must be *it*." It proved to be a plea to the Emperor to keep him in mind in this new situation brought about by Fonseca's death. The Emperor instructed Vázquez to write to him that he would not forget him, but that he would make no decision until he reached Toledo.

Cobos must have rejoined the Court before the end of February and we may be sure that, aided by Granvelle, he continued to press his case and that of Tavera. By the end of March the Emperor had made up his mind about the appointments to bishoprics. As he was leaving Toledo on April 1 for his Holy Week retreat at San Jerónimo, Tavera accompanied him to the gate of the city and asked permission to go with him. With that fine sense of theater which he so often showed, Charles turned to him and said: "Go back, Archbishop of Toledo, and wait for my return." Cobos had fulfilled his share of the bargain. On May 19 Tavera completed his part by appointing Cobos as *adelantado* of Cazorla "in consideration of your prudence and merits and the love and good works which we owe you." [73] Word of what was happening must have got around, for Juan de Zúñiga wrote to his mother-in-law from Molins de Rey on May 8 that he would not be surprised if Cobos were appointed *adelantado* of Cazorla, because it was near his home town.[74] But the appointment was only the beginning of a struggle that was to occupy the rest of Cobos' life.

Meanwhile, Hernando Pizarro had reached Seville on January 14 and the Consejo de las Indias reported this to the Emperor at once.[75] During his absence from Court Cobos had recommended that the Casa de la Contratación should impound all the gold and silver that he brought and the Emperor had approved. In March, Pizarro came to Toledo, bringing samples of the gold and silver vessels from the treasure of Atahualpa, bringing too strange animals and huge nuggets of gold. Far away in Austria King Ferdinand heard about those nuggets and asked Salinas to get him one to give to the Duke of Hesse. When Salinas spoke to the Emperor about it, the latter said that there had been one big one that weighed 4,000 *pesos,* but that it had been broken up by private parties; he would ask Cobos to try and find one. But the best that Cobos could find was one worth 212 *castellanos,* which he had put aside for himself and which he now gave to Salinas for the King.[76]

It is hard to conceive of the effect on the public mind of these fantastic stories and treasures of the New World. People were ready to believe that anything was possible. It is not surprising that a story spread through Spain that seventy great ships had arrived at Laredo on the north coast, with ten thousand Amazons aboard who had come to seek fathers for their children among the brave men of Spain and were offering fifty ducats apiece for every pregnancy, on condition that boys born as a result would remain in Spain, but girls would go back with them to Amazonia.[77] Cobos was of a more practical turn of mind: on May 4, 1534, he had his privilege as *fundidor* extended to cover all of South America as far as the Strait of Magellan.[78] You never could tell what might happen in that strange New World.

All during these months in Toledo, Salinas continued to culti-

vate Granvelle and Cobos. On March 16 he was happy to report to Castillejo that the gifts for them that he had so long
been urging had at last arrived. There were sables for Granvelle, a little spoiled in transit but still good, and a jewel for
Cobos' wife. When he gave the gift to Granvelle,

> he wanted to know if they were sending something for the Comendador
> Mayor and I said "Yes" and showed him the jewel, talking it down a little
> so that he would appreciate his sables more. I went to give my letter to the
> Comendador Mayor and before I talked business, I mentioned the commission
> I had for María de Mendoza, his wife. This I did to make him more favor-
> able to what I was going to propose to him later. He was grateful for the
> gift, though he did not see it at the time, because there were people there.
> I received his permission and presented it to Doña María according to your
> instructions. Her Ladyship received it with both hands and even if it had
> been heavier, she would have picked it up from the floor. She sends infinite
> thanks to the Queen, as is the custom of all those who receive something. I
> think that they will pay it back in good works.[79]

A little later he answered a comment of Castillejo's that King
Ferdinand had noticed that he was not cultivating Cobos, saying
that since the Emperor had placed all foreign affairs in Granvelle's hands, he was the only person who could help him to
perform his duties. If he saw Cobos at all, it was merely a matter of courtesy and tact. There were two reasons why he seldom
had contact with him:

> Ever since Cobos came back to Spain and is with his wife, he is so hard
> to get at and to see that I assure you that it is easier to see the Emperor.
> The only time when you can see him is at dinner, and not every day then,
> for at that time the lords and other folks who want to pay court to him go
> to his house, and as I am not of that profession, I don't do it, because it would
> mean losing the little reputation I still have, and I never have an opportunity
> to do it, without this difficulty. Yet even so, I sometimes try to do it. When
> Luis de Tovar was here and had to transact his business with the Comenda-
> dor Mayor, he was careful to observe all these times, and even with good
> ducats, paying the doorman to let him in.[80]

Salinas was the first person to comment on the inaccessibility
of Cobos, but he was not the only one. Juan Ginés Sepúlveda,
in his grave Latin, says that he aroused hostility "quod se iam
non facile aditi convenitique sinebat, quae res ut conficiendis ex-
pediendisque negotiis moram, sic ea gerentibus magnam moles-
tiam et dispendium afferebat." [81] Another of his contemporaries,
Pedro de Navarra, in his fictional dialogue which depicts Cobos,
had one of his interlocutors say:

When I first came to Court, I went to your house twice a day for a month and in all that time I never got by the first door, until, remembering that Horace says that money breaks down cliffs, I gave the outside doorman two ducats to let me in, and even that profited me little. I waited in that room for another month, without success. And the next device I used was a medal that I gave to the second doorman, who let me in even farther a few times and still I could not speak to you. Finally, bored at having wasted my time and my medal and my ducats, I held you up one day in company with a duke and this so recklessly that it was considered as bad breeding. But I preferred to have shame in my face rather than pain in my heart.[82]

How little Court life had changed from the 14th century when Pedro López de Ayala wrote his *Rimado de Palacio!*

Salinas reports another episode that reveals the sort of conflict which so easily arose among the Emperor's counsellors. Pedro González de Mendoza had received a dispatch from King Ferdinand for the Emperor and when he presented it to him the Emperor said to take it to Granvelle. González, either by mistake or intentionally, replied: "Did you say to take it to Cobos?" The Emperor answered: "No, to Granvelle." When the Emperor told Granvelle about it, the latter took it as a slight. But Salinas was able to patch up the misunderstanding and restore peace.[83] It is astonishing that Cobos and Granvelle did not more often come into conflict; perhaps it can be explained by the Spanish proverb: "Dos alevosos y tres al mohino."

The Emperor had never visited Avila and Salamanca, and on May 22 he left Toledo with his Court. At Segovia, at the end of the month, Cobos obtained a leave of absence to permit him to visit his new domain of Cazorla. On the morning of June 5 he was about to leave for Valladolid when a courier arrived from King Ferdinand with a message of such importance that the Emperor felt that a meeting of the Consejo should be called. The Cardinal of Sigüenza, Loaisa, was also leaving for Valladolid, and the Marqués de Cenete, Henry of Nassau, was persuaded to go along, although he was not on good terms with Cobos. So, with Granvelle, they proceeded to Valladolid to hold the meeting there. On the following day they all rejoined the Court at Avila to hold another meeting and report to the Emperor their recommendation that 100,000 *scudi* be sent to Ferdinand. This time Cobos was able to get away on his leave.[84]

We do not know what he found at Cazorla, but at Ubeda, where he stopped on his way and saw for the first time his rebuilt palace with its fountain, there were important developments. In spite of all his efforts to build a worthy chapel at Santo Tomás and to secure privileges and indulgences from the Pope, things were not going well. The parish priest was complaining that the services and singing in the chapel, so close to the high altar, were disturbing the regular masses of the church.[85] Now that his income was sure to be increased so greatly by his share of the treasure of Peru, Cobos was beginning to think of more ambitious plans. If the priests of Santo Tomás did not like his chapel, why should he not build a church of his own?

The Chapel of San Salvador

If this was an era of palace building, it was also an age of chapel building. Usually they were attached to a church, like the magnificent chapel of the Condestable in the Cathedral of Burgos, or like Cobos' own chapel in Santo Tomás. Even his chaplain, Fernando Ortega, was already building a chapel in the church of San Nicolás in Ubeda. But there was one notable exception: the Royal Chapel in Granada which Ferdinand the Catholic had had built as a burial-place for Isabel and himself. This example must have been in Cobos' mind, as he laid his plans for the future.

Already on January 11, 1534, he had had his agents buy a piece of property from the Brotherhood of the Honored Old Men of the Holy Saviour,[86] a sort of asylum for the aged that had been endowed long since by Pero Yáñez. Their house was only a few rods down the street from his palace; it was ideally suited for his purposes. And now he began to discuss with them the possibility of acquiring enough of their land to provide space for his church. When he left Ubeda he commissioned his chaplain to continue the negotiations.

He was back in Valladolid on June 27, when he reported his return to the Emperor and Juan Vázquez.[87] Two days later Charles and the Court arrived there; after three weeks they went on to Palencia. Ortega had been successful in his dealings with the Brotherhood and they had written to Cobos to express their readiness to cede him the land he needed. On August 21, at Palencia, he answered their letter, outlining some of the conditions of the contract. He agreed to transfer to the new church, for the benefit of the old men of the Brotherhood, the value of the dowry of one of the maidens that the Pope had granted to the chapel of La Concepción and to ask the Pope to approve of the transfer. As for the special jubilees of the chapel, he would prefer, for the moment, to leave them there, but he would seek new indulgences and privileges from the Pope.[88]

A month later Ortega sent him the formal acceptance of the Cofradía. They too described the conditions of the agreement. Cobos was to undertake to build a church with a main chapel on the site where there was an altar, taking as much land, front and back, as was necessary, the church to be of the same length and width as the church of San Pablo in Ubeda, not counting the lateral chapels. He was to grant them an alms of 100 ducats of annual income, derived from the sum that the Pope had conceded to the chapel of La Concepción to provide each year a dowry for certain poor maidens, the 100 ducats being the amount of one dowry. And this money was to be used to feed and care for the poor in the hospital of the Brotherhood. They considered their action a "donation," whereby Cobos was to be the owner of the property, with the right to be buried in the church, with any others he might elect, and with the privilege of free access to the church at any time, either through the main door or through any other door.[89] On February 2, 1535, the Pope issued a bull, transferring to the new church all the benefits and privileges of the old one.[90] But other more pressing problems prevented Cobos from going ahead at once with the plans for his new church.

CHAPTER VIII

SERVICE IN TUNIS, ITALY, AND PROVENCE

For months the western Mediterranean had been hearing with alarm of the raids of Barbarossa on the coasts. When the news of his capture of Tunis in August, 1534, reached Spain, the Emperor decided that he must take action against him, not only to defend the coasts of Spain, Sicily, and Naples, but also to check this onslaught of Islam against the Christian world. Secretly he sent messengers to Flanders, to Austria, to Italy to begin the gathering of a vast army and navy. In Spain he moved to Madrid and held a Cortes of Castile, with Tavera and Cobos as its presidng officers.[1] The Castilians proved far more docile than the Aragonese and the Catalans; Cobos had learned how to be sure of the compliance of the *procuradores* by handing them out a few favors and gifts. They promptly voted for 1535 an extra subsidy of 200,000 ducats. Aside from their usual requests, they approved of the *pragmática* which Charles had issued, forbidding gentlemen to ride on mules.

He also called meetings of all the military orders to enlist their support. At the Chapter of the Order of Santiago, which met at the monastery of San Gerónimo on November 25, Cobos, as Grand Commander, had a leading rôle. It was a solemn sight as the Emperor entered the church and took his seat at the foot of the steps that led to the high altar. To his right were the knights of Castile, seated in order of seniority, the Grand Commander wearing a black choir cape and biretta, the other knights in white robes, and the clerical members in surplices; to the left were Cobos and the other knights of Leon in similar garb. Even here his power was exercised, for Juan Vázquez de Molina was secretary of the Chapter.[2]

The Emperor's Castilian advisors were strongly opposed to the whole idea of the African campaign; they had no faith in his Imperial schemes. The Cardinal Tavera, now President of the Consejo, wrote a long memorandum setting forth his objections to the project as personally dangerous to the Emperor and certain to yield him little gain.[3] And Salinas wrote to Castillejo that he had not delivered a letter to Cobos because Cobos had not laughed once since the decision to leave Madrid had been announced; he would wait until Cobos was in a better mood.[4] A few days later he wrote that Cobos was so surly over this new trip that he didn't know where his hands and feet were. What was more, when the list of commanderships in the military orders was announced, not one of Cobos' candidates was named. For that matter, there were very few people who were happy about this new campaign. They were all tired and hard up and dubious about the prospects. Besides, the decision had been taken so suddenly that no one had time to get ready.[5]

A few days later Cobos himself gave evidence of an irritability which had hitherto been unknown in his correspondence. In a letter to Juan Vázquez, written on May 18, he had expressed the hope that Almaguer, one of his assistants, was satisfied with what he had done for him. But before he finished the letter, another courier arrived from Madrid, with further news about him. At the end of his letter Cobos now added:

I am astonished at what you write about Almaguer. If he thinks that I am so dependent upon him that he can hold me up in this way and do what he wants, he is mistaken, for just as I am glad to have him attend to my affairs, I will have him drop them and go where he wants to. He has been in service all his life and you know how far he has got and he is not satisfied that I have done more for him in three days than he ever earned up to now. Put him straight and tell him that he can't push me around like that, and that even if more than money were at stake, I shan't be moved and if he won't be satisfied with that job, it's his hard luck, for he won't get it that way.[6]

On March 1, 1535, Charles issued the formal orders providing for the Regency of the Empress during his absence, and that same day the Empress signed her will in the presence of Cobos.[7] On March 2 the Emperor started for Barcelona, leaving Cobos in Madrid to clear up the unfinished business. Most of the problems were financial, and Cobos drew up a statement of the resources available. The main item was the sum of 800,000 ducats which Charles had ordered seized from private persons who had brought back gold from the Indies, against which he issued *juros*. The total amount received from the Indies that year was a little over 1,000,000 ducats. The other sources of revenue were the subsidy from the Cortes, the ecclesiastical contribution and small amounts from the military orders, the Mesta, and the silk tax in Granada. The total seemed formidable.

But it was typical of the deficit financing of Charles's reign that almost half the available resources were already committed. About 500,000 ducats were ordered sent to Barcelona to help defray the costs of the campaign. Cobos, on March 9, signed a contract for 120,000 ducats in payment for a loan in Flanders.[8] Money was set aside for the maintenance of the royal household. By including in current income the amount expected from the churches in the following year it appeared that there was a balance of a little over 1,000,000 ducats.

However, after the Emperor left Madrid a long list of additional charges appeared: payments for the fortresses and the fleet, loans made in Genoa, the dowry of the Princess of Denmark, the balance due on a loan from the Welsers. When these items, amounting to 123,000 ducats, were subtracted there seemed to be still a balance of 825,000 ducats. Whatever portion of this was in specie was to be sent to the Mota of Medina del Campo for safekeeping.[9] In the meantime, orders had been sent to Seville to dispatch the gold and silver from the Indies to Barcelona; by the end of March the treasurer of the Casa de la Contratación reported that he had sent 290,000 ducats.[10] From the Mota of Medina another 185,000 ducats' worth of gold was sent from the treasure of Pizarro, which had been stored there since it arrived in Spain the year before.

By the middle of March Cobos had put everything in order; on the sixteenth he started for Barcelona. Along the way he carried on a steady correspondence with Juan Vázquez, who had remained with the Empress, and with the Idiáquez, who was with the Emperor. At Guadalajara, Sigüenza, Zaragoza, and

Bujalaroz he reported on his progress: it was slow, for he was tired and so were the horses. Just before they reached Zaragoza, Juan de Samano, who was with him, had a fall and had to be left behind. Easter he spent at Bujalaroz. But slow as was his progress he gained on the Emperor; he reached Barcelona on April 5, two days after the Emperor's entry.[11]

Barcelona, 1535

He had been concerned about where he was to be lodged in Barcelona. He wrote to Idiáquez expressing the hope that they could find a place where they would not be pestered. He also sent Zárate ahead to see what he could find. Zárate prepared a long report on possible houses, with detailed descriptions of situation, facilities, and the space available for Idiáquez.[12] Even before Zárate arrived, the Archbishop of Zaragoza had written to Cobos (March 10), telling him of two good houses that he could have: one was the house of the Treasurer Puch, where the Archbishop of Toledo had stayed, the other was that of Marguet in the Carrer Ample.[13] We do not know which one Cobos chose. Let us hope that it was the one with a garden full of orange trees that Zárate described.

The two months in Barcelona were full of excitement as the forces gathered there—Andrea Doria with his fleet, the Infante Luis with the Portuguese contingent, the Marqués de Mondéjar and the fleet and troops from Malaga, and all the Castilian lords and their followers. Almost to the very end the Emperor made no public statement of his plans; people at Court were asking Loaisa and Cobos to find out what was to be the destination and who would be the general in command.[14] But rumors were abroad: the Emperor was taking the field in person against Barbarossa. The money from the Indies began to arrive to finance the campaign: twenty-two cart loads on April 29,[15] twenty mules, heavily laden, on May 22.[16]

Busy as he was, Cobos found time for his personal affairs. Some of them were trifling: a chinchilla (they called it a "cat") that María de Mendoza sent to the Queen of Hungary died on the way; Cobos would try to get another one.[17] He tried in vain to find a map of the Indies that Salinas wanted to send to King Ferdinand.[18] Others were more important. To be sure of his payments, he had the source of his salary as secretary for the

Indies transferred from the Isla Española to the Casa de la Contratación.[19] Once more he had his privilege as *fundidor y ensayador mayor* confirmed to cover all of South America.[20] His mine rights in Azuaga were extended for twenty years.[21] He was one of the many who helped to provide the Emperor with cash by purchasing from the Treasurer Alonso de Baeza a *juro* of 1,030,500 *maravedís* at 5 per cent, through his assistant, Francisco de Almaguer.[22]

The most significant favor that he received was from the Archbishop of Toledo, who yielded to his request and transferred the title of *adelantado* of Cazorla to his eleven-year-old son Diego, thus assuring that the boy would inherit the post.[23] Tavera was reluctant to take the step and consented only because he feared that a refusal would involve him and his church in trouble. Even so, he recorded that he was acting under protest and that the appointment was valid only so long as was his will. The Pope confirmed the appointment on May 15, and the Emperor ratified it on May 28. Cobos did not draw up a will before he left, but he did have his privilege to establish a *mayorazgo* confirmed.[24] Just on the eve of his departure he gave a proxy to his wife, with authority to collect in his and Diego's name all of their income from the various sources in the Indies.[25]

On May 13 the Emperor held a formal review of his forces. Early in the morning they gathered outside the Perpignan gate, and at ten o'clock they started to file by the Emperor in all their gayest trappings. At a table beside the Emperor sat the Treasurer Zuazola and the secretary Juan de Samano, representing the Consejo de Guerra, to take down the names and numbers as they rode by. The chroniclers of the sixteenth century loved to describe the costumes of distinguished folk at public occasions. And so we can catch a glimpse of Cobos, "unarmed and dressed in a black velvet tunic without a cloak, wearing a heavy gold chain," as he came up to join the Emperor. According to some accounts this was the occasion when Charles finally answered the questions regarding his plans. Unfurling a banner that bore the figure of Christ Crucified, he cried to the assembled nobles: "This is your captain-general! I am his standard-bearer!" [26]

Amid all the preparations for war, there were still complicated international problems to be handled: France must be held in check; the old question of the Church Council was being taken up again by the new Pope Paul III. Most of these matters were in Granvelle's care, but at the end of May two missions arrived from Florence, one sent by the Duke, Alessandro, the other representing the republican exiles, who were still seeking restoration. Both groups were received by the Emperor and both were referred to Cobos and Granvelle, who listened graciously to their story but replied that there was no time to discuss their pleas.[27] When the second group appeared, Cobos is said to have remarked: "This is a concert!" [28] Five days later the great fleet, one of the largest that generation had seen, sailed for the rendez-vous in Sardinia.

The Campaign in Tunis

Although we know that Cobos took part in the expedition to Tunis, and the Emperor later testified to the services that he performed there at the risk of his life,[29] there is almost no record of his actual participation. The other secretaries who went with him were Miguel Mai, Vice-Chancellor of Aragon, who was in charge of the affairs of Sicily and Naples; Juan de Comalonga, for Catalan affairs; Anthoine Perrenin, Granvelle's secretary; and Idiáquez, as Cobos' personal aide.[30] The only episode in which we know that he took part is tucked away in an obscure Latin work by Joannes Berotius, *Commentarium, seu potius Diarium expeditionis tunetanae*. The author tells us that on June 18, just before dawn, a ship was trying to enter the harbor of La Goleta, when it was discovered by the Emperor's fleet, and one of the boats, the "Aguila," gave chase and forced the enemy ship ashore. Now the "Aguila" was the boat on which Granvelle and the other counsellors and secretaries were traveling, so that we may be reasonably sure that Cobos took part in this enemy action.[31]

For the rest, we know only that Cobos signed documents along the way, and after their arrival on the African coast that the Emperor frequently discussed matters with him.[32] After the capture of Tunis and the release of the twenty thousand Christian captives there, the Emperor returned to La Goleta and on August 6 signed a treaty restoring Muley-Hassan to the throne which Barbarossa had taken from him. Cobos was one of the witnesses to the signing of the treaty.[33] When the Emperor took the oath to abide by the terms of the treaty, he placed his hand on the cross of Santiago on the cloak of one of the gentlemen at his side;[34] it may well have been the cloak of the Grand Commander of Leon.

On August 16 the Emperor went aboard his galley, off La Goleta, and that night dispatched a long series of letters, countersigned by Cobos, to announce his departure for Sicily.[35] He had hoped to capture the town of Africa on the way, but contrary winds prevented the ships from reaching shore, and so he continued his voyage to Trapana on the Sicilian coast, where he arrived on August 22.

Imperial Triumph

The Emperor's progress through Sicily and Italy in the following months was in truth a triumphal return, reminiscent of the days of Imperial Rome; Charles was greeted everywhere as "Carolus Africanus." Local chroniclers took delight in describing the triumphal arches and the crowds of prelates and nobles which welcomed him on this, his first visit to the Kingdom of the Two Sicilies. Most of the inscriptions on the elaborate arches were in Latin, which Cobos could not read, but Granvelle was there to translate them for him.[36]

After crossing Sicily, the Emperor spent a month in Palermo, where he held a meeting of the Estates and was granted a subsidy of 150,000 ducats. When he left on October 13, Cobos stayed behind, as usual, to attend to the unfinished business. But his stay was prolonged by an attack of dysentery; on October 17 he wrote to Idiáquez, who had gone on with the Emperor, that the doctor said it was good for him.[37] Even Salinas had heard at Pozzuoli that he was very thin and that he was planning to wait in Palermo till Andrea Doria returned.[38] Doria had been sent on a mission to strengthen the defenses of La Goleta. On November 11 he sailed from Puerto Farina, and after stopping at Trapana, sailed on to Palermo.[39]

In spite of his indisposition Cobos had been as busy as ever during these weeks: raising money, providing for the payment of the troops, provisioning the fleet.[40] To Ferrante Gonzaga, who had just been named Viceroy of Sicily, he sent a long memorandum on the situation there, with recommendations for appointments; he had hoped that Gonzaga would arrive before he left.[41] Perhaps his ill health had made him irascible, for he wrote to Idiáquez on October 24: "I am astonished that the courier had not arrived there when you last wrote. You must tell M. Felipe [de Taxis?] to correct the situation and give a good scolding to the couriers, because the negligence that they show every day is no longer tolerable." [42] With Dr. Guevara and some other officials who had stayed in Palermo, he embarked with Andrea Doria and reached Naples on November 26.[43]

Proceeding slowly overland and stopping frequently along the way, the Emperor had made his triumphal entry into Naples the day before and was lodged in the Castel Nuovo. On the afternoon of the twenty-sixth, Salinas had an appointment with the Emperor, and when he reached the Palace he found him standing at the window that overlooks the Bay, watching the fleet of Doria enter the harbor. As soon as Doria and Cobos had landed, they were warmly received by the Emperor and had a long talk with Granvelle.[44] We do not know where Cobos stayed in Naples, but during the preceding summer Lope de Soria had written to him from Venice, offering him his house in Naples: "It is gay and comfortable and big enough for all your household and aides and horses. It is close to the Palace in the pleasantest quarter of Naples. And there won't be any landlord or landlady to grumble at you." [45] He must have been quartered in the same house as Granvelle, for Salinas wrote to the Cardinal of Trent that he should not refuse the offer of Cardinal Salviati's house, since it was close to the Palace and next door to the house of Granvelle and Cobos, with whom he would have to be dealing.[46]

The Winter in Naples

The winter of 1535-1536 was one of the most memorable in the reign of Charles V. The weather was propitious—spring-like days without a cloud, so balmy that the roses could not wait for April.[47] To greet the Emperor the élite of Europe had flocked to Naples, cardinals and princes, dukes and bishops, ambassadors of kings and city states. The Pope had sent his son, Pier Luigi Farnese, to welcome the Emperor and to discuss with him matters of common interest. The Viceroy, Pedro de Toledo, and the Neapolitan nobles, anxious to show their wealth and power, provided a series of brilliant entertainments for the visitors. On December 18 the Viceroy gave a banquet for the Emperor in the garden of the Poggio Reale that lasted all night. There were no less than a hundred and fifty ladies there, including seven princesses, and one of the features was the performance of an "Eclogue, or Pastoral Farce." On Sunday, January 3, there was a bull-fight in the Piazza Carbonara in which the Emperor distinguished himself.

We may be sure that Cobos, as the Emperor's chief counsellor, shared in these festivities. The historian, Paolo Giovio, records that on December 11, 1535, he had dinner at Cobos' house; the other guests were the Marchese del Guasto, Pedro de Córdoba, and Lope Hurtado de Mendoza.[48] Perhaps it was at this time that Cobos gave Giovio an Aztec manuscript, bound in a tiger skin, which must have been a gift to Cobos from Hernán Cortés.[49] On the Feast of the Epiphany a number of the courtiers—Granvelle, Pedro de la Cueva, Diego Hurtado de Mendoza, and Perrenin among them—made a trip to the hot springs of Pozzuoli. On the way they came to a cavern which belched fumes which were said to be lethal. To test it, they threw Granvelle's dog into the cave and pulled him out, apparently lifeless. But the next day he turned up, none the worse, at Granvelle's lodging.[50] It is tempting to suppose that Cobos was one of the other people "non obscuri nominis" who were in this group of his friends and associates. But it is possible that he stayed in Naples, for that afternoon there was a *juego de cañas* in which the Emperor took part, dressed in a Moorish costume, and that night there was a gala dance.[51]

Dances for the entertainment of the ladies were an important part of the festivities, and the Emperor was so active in them that husbands were said to have been jealous of their wives because of his attentions. Particularly during Carnival week there was a round of masked balls.[52] At one of them there was an episode that casts an amusing light on Cobos' fame. On the road to Naples the Emperor had spent several days at the estate of the Prince of Bisigniano and his dashing young wife. When the Emperor resumed his journey, he had ridden part of the way in the litter of the Princess. Taking advantage of this intimacy, the Princess had asked the Emperor to pardon a friend of hers who had been convicted of murder. When the Emperor replied that he could not intervene in matters of justice, she reminded him that mercy was the special privilege of rulers. To that the Emperor answered: "I will consult with Cobos." At one of the masked balls the Emperor recognized the Princess, in spite of her domino, and gallantly asked her for a bunch of flowers that she was carrying in her hand. Quickly she retorted: "Sir, I will consult with Cobos." To which replied the Emperor: "The favor you asked me for has been granted." [53]

For Cobos and Granvelle not all the winter was gaiety. Never before had they been faced with so many serious problems; in fact, Cobos was so busy that Salinas reported it was impossible to secure an audience with him, unless it was a matter of great urgency.[54] The most crucial issue was the relations between the Emperor and the King of France. The death of Francesco Sforza (November 1, 1535) had opened anew the old question of the duchy of Milan, for the marriage of Sforza and the child princess of Denmark had not resulted in the birth of an heir and the duchy had reverted to the Emperor. The latter had hardly reached Naples when he was confronted with a demand from the French ambassador, Velly, that he at once cede Milan to Francis I.

It is difficult to be sure what were the real intentions of the Emperor, though in the light of subsequent events it seems probable that he never seriously considered alienating the duchy from his possessions. Nevertheless, he authorized Cobos and Granvelle to enter into negotiations. Francis I was not the only candidate for the investiture. King Ferdinand would have been glad to see it fall to him and he authorized Salinas to offer Granvelle a pension of 6,000 ducats a year in case the decision was favorable. At the same time he sent Salinas a letter for Cobos, probably containing a similar offer, but on the advice of Granvelle, it was not delivered to him.[55] There was talk, too, of naming Don Luis of Portugal, the Emperor's brother-in-law, an appointment that would have been pleasing to the Empress and her sister Beatriz, Duchess of Savoy. But it is certain that the Emperor had other plans for him—a marriage with Princess Mary of England.

The real matter of negotiation was the possibility of granting the duchy to one of the sons of Francis I. From the beginning he had insisted on the appointment of his second son, the Duke of Orleans. This Charles was unwilling to consider; he would, however, discuss the possibility of naming the King's third son, the Duke of Angoulême, and on this point he had the support of the Pope. But as early as January, 1536, the Emperor's agents in France were reporting the King's preparation for the invasion of Savoy and an attack on Milan. From this time on the Emperor's policy was one of temporizing, till the situation became clarified. As the earlier reports were confirmed and the invasion of Savoy became a reality in March, 1536, avoidance of an open break became even more necessary, while he made preparations to meet the attack by force of arms. Even the Pope realized that he was "stalling" for time.

In these months there is increasing evidence of a sharp divergence between Charles and his ministers. Both Cobos and Granvelle were convinced that peace must be attained, even at the cost of compromise. Their reasons were different. Cobos, as chief financial minister, realized that Charles was on the verge of bankruptcy and that a continuation of the military expenditures could only result in financial ruin. Granvelle, on the other hand, felt that a cessation of hostilities on both the Flemish and Italian fronts was necessary in order to free the Emperor for a settlement of the conflict with the German Protestants. Charles, however, though he had no thought of accepting a compromise, encouraged them to continue their negotiations with the French ambassador. Yet, with a growing secretiveness, which he had already shown on the eve of his departure for the Tunisian campaign, he failed to inform his representatives of his real intentions.

As a result, Cobos and Granvelle, anxious for a solution, indicated to Velly that they were ready to accept the designation of the Duke of Orleans as the Duke of Milan. This is borne out by the fact that when the Cardinal of Lorraine on his way to Rome met the Emperor at Lucca in April, 1536, and reminded him that he had agreed to grant the duchy to Orleans, the Emperor replied that he had never personally ("de sa bouche") made any such promise. At that, Velly, who was present, angrily interrupted and asked the Emperor not to make him appear to be a liar. The only answer that Charles could give was that he had instructed his ministers and his ambassador in France, Jean Hannaert, to express his readiness to approve of the appointment of Orleans, but that Francis had rejected the offer and that he had now withdrawn it.[56] We shall presently see other evidences of the failure of communication between the Emperor and his ministers.

A second problem that occupied the attention of Cobos and Granvelle in these months was that of Florence. We have seen that when an embassy of Florentine exiles went to Barcelona in 1535 they were given a friendly hearing by the two ministers. Now Filippo Strozzi and the Florentine cardinals came to Naples to plead the cause of the exiles and seek the restitution of the city to their hands. They were prepared to make appealing offers to the Emperor, and they found Cobos and Granvelle well disposed to their cause. The Florentine historian, Varchi, is authority for a story that Pedro Zapata, the Emperor's representative in Florence, had entered into a deal to support the cause of the exiles and that a large sum of money had been deposited in the convent of San Domenico in Naples which was to be paid to Zapata, if the Emperor granted their plea. Zapata, in turn, had made a bargain to share the profits with one of the principal agents of the Emperor (this must have been either Cobos or Granvelle), if they helped him to win the case of the exiles.[57]

Meanwhile, Alessandro de' Medici, the rival claimant for the duchy of Florence, had arrived in Naples with a brilliant suite to press his case and remind the Emperor of the agreement that he had made at Barcelona in 1529 to grant him the hand of his illegitimate daughter, Margarita. In the end it was Alessandro who won, and on February 28, 1536, the Emperor granted him the title of Duke of Florence and approved his betrothal to Margarita.[58] In this case Varchi again attributes his victory to the lavish gifts he made to the Emperor's agents.[59] While this may be the explanation, for bribery was an accepted part of negotiations in the sixteenth century, it seems more probable that the Emperor's decision was made without regard to the opinions of his advisors and was based on the 200,000 florins which Alessandro paid him in satisfaction of the dower, on his general suspicion of popular government, and on his need for a loyal and subservient ruler in Florence in the event of future complications in Italy.

Another issue in which Cobos and Granvelle were involved was the old question of a Church Council, for which the Emperor had been pressing since 1529, as a first step in the solution of the problem of the Lutherans in Germany. There were talks with Pier Luigi Farnese and with the Papal Legate, Vergerio, and this time they found the attitude of the Vatican more favorable. Closely related to this question was the problem of the Pope's position in the strife between Charles and Francis: the Em-

peror and his counsellors were making every effort to persuade
the Pope to abandon his neutrality and give open support to
Charles. Vergerio had several meetings with Cobos and Granvelle in February and reported to Ricalcati that he was surprised
that during one of their conversations Cobos had said: "His
Holiness loves the Emperor without any fear that he will lose
Spain from their obedience to him, and he also loves the King
of France, though he is afraid of losing it, so far as one can
see." And Cobos went on to say that a son whose love and
obedience was certain and constant should be loved and held
more dear than one who was uncertain and doubtful. In short,
he concluded quite openly, he was not at all satisfied, if a Pope
who was so good, in this case was determined to remain—and he
used this word—neutral. To which Vergerio replied that though
the Pope held Charles dear, he could not, as leader of all Christians, take sides and so become involved in leagues and wars.[60]

Rassow has pointed out that in thus contrasting Spain and
France, rather than the Empire and France, Cobos was thinking
of his master as primarily King of Spain and thereby revealed
how far his ideas were from those of the Emperor.[61] In this,
Rassow is undoubtedly correct. He might even have gone further,
for to the end of his life Cobos was stoutly opposed to the Imperial ventures and on every occasion urged Charles to stay at
home in Spain and rule his people in peace and prosperity.

Not all was conflict during this momentous winter. The meeting of the Estates of the Kingdom of Naples was happily and
quickly concluded with the granting of a huge subsidy, no less
than 1,500,000 ducats.[62] Another source of difficulty, the divorce
by Henry VIII of the Emperor's aunt, Queen Catherine, was
solved by the death of the Queen on January 7, 1536, since
Charles was thereby released from his obligation of hostility to
the English King. A few days after her death the Imperial ambassador in London, Eustace Chapuys, wrote to Granvelle that
in her last illness the Queen was continually asking him for news
of Granvelle and Cobos. "Her last words and commendations to
me were that I should write and plead her excuses with His
Imperial Majesty, as well as with you and Cobos, if her illness
and the close confinement in which she was kept prevented her
from writing." And he added in cipher: "I was to write to the
Emperor, her nephew, and beg that he would request you and
the Commander, for God's sake, to put an end to her sufferings,

one way or another." [63] There was hardly an event in all Europe in which Cobos and Granvelle were not involved.

In addition to all these activities, Cobos was responsible for the necessary instructions for the provisioning and dispatch of the fleet and the armed forces. As the French threat became more clear, this involved a complete realignment of the troops that had originally been assembled for the projected invasion of Algiers in the following year and their dispatch to the front in Northern Italy. Besides, there were all the little personal matters, favors to friends, in which Cobos was always involved. Salinas reported that when Cobos and Granvelle went to talk to the Emperor on New Year's Day, 1536, Cobos had a favor to ask in behalf of one Iñigo de Mendoza and that he had been so sure that it would be granted that he had not bothered to consult Granvelle about it. Great was his chagrin when the Emperor indignantly refused the request.[64] In the same letter to Castillejo, in answer to a request for information, Salinas explained that there had been no change in Cobos' title since the post as *adelantado* of Cazorla had been transferred to his son. But he went on to say that Iñigo de Mendoza had expressed surprise that Castillejo in his letters to Cobos addressed him as "Illustrious and very magnificent sir," whereas Spanish grandees always wrote "Very illustrious sir," leaving the "magnificent" in the inkwell. Salinas felt that Cobos was not the sort of person who paid much attention to such niceties, but still, Castillejo would do well to follow the usual practice. One wonders how Cobos could find time for all his little personal affairs; the Archivio di Modena contains a series of letters he wrote to the Duke of Ferrara during these months, asking him to show a favor or grant a pardon to some one or other of his protégés.[65]

Rome, 1536

The Emperor had originally planned to leave Naples at the middle of January,[66] but a host of new developments had forced him to delay his departure. It was March 22 when he finally started for Rome. On April 4 he reached the outskirts of the city and spent the night at San Paolo fuori le Mura.[67] That night Cobos and Granvelle went into the city and had dinner with the Cardinal Campeggio to discuss the final arrangements for the

official entry. The next morning they had an audience with
the Pope.[68]

For months Paul III had been preparing for the Emperor's
reception. From a special tax imposed on the city he had collected
over 50,000 ducats, almost half of which was spent on the erec-
tion of triumphal arches and statues along the line of march.[69]
To make the entry more impressive he had ordered the construction of broad, new streets, which involved the demolition of a
large number of buildings. François Rabelais, who happened to
be in town, wrote to one of his friends that more than two hundred houses and three or four churches were torn down. " 'Tis a
pity"—he commented—"to see the ruins of these churches, palaces and houses which the Pope has had demolished." [70]

The entry of the Emperor on April 5 was the most magnificent triumphal procession of his Italian visit. At the Porta
Capena the Vicar of the Pope came to receive him. Then, accompanied by a small army of his veteran foot and horse, by his
commanders—the Duque de Alba, the Marchese del Guasto, the
Conde de Benavente, and their suites, arrayed in gorgeous costumes of cloth of gold and many-colored silks, and by a host of
Roman prelates and nobles, he started down the new street (today the Via di S. Gregorio) that led straight to the Arch of
Constantine. When the procession turned at the Arch to cross
the Roman Forum, the crowd that thronged the arches of the
Colosseum roared their applause. As they crossed the bridge
over the Tiber, the artillery in the Castel S. Angelo thundered
a greeting. On the steps of St. Peter's the Pope was waiting.
Dismounting, the Emperor knelt to kiss his hand.[71]

During the following days the Emperor and his counsellors
were engaged in discussion with the Pope of the main issues that
demanded decision—the calling of a Council to settle the affairs
of Germany and the question of the Pope's position in the conflict between Charles and Francis. Even the Marchese del Guasto
was sent to the Pope to urge him to declare his support of the
Emperor. Benvenuto Cellini gives an amusing account of his
failure. It seems that the Pope had commissioned Cellini to make
a "Book of Hours," richly bound in gold and jewels at a cost of
6,000 scudi, as a gift for the Emperor. When Cellini brought
the "Book" to the Pope for his approval, the latter asked him
to make a ring for a diamond which the Emperor had just given
him. A few days later, returning with the diamond duly mounted,

he found the Marchese del Guasto with the Pope. Cellini surmised that he must have been pressing the Pope to do something that he did not want to do, for he heard the Pope say: "I tell you 'no,' because I must be neutral and nothing else." Then, turning to Cellini, the Pope talked to him for an hour, deliberately disregarding the Marchese, who finally stalked out in high dudgeon.[72]

Charles piously fulfilled all the duties of Holy Week—the washing of the feet, the visit to the Seven Churches. On Easter Sunday, clad in a new and lighter imperial crown and robe, he attended mass at St. Peter's. Sad to relate, during the ceremony he lost one of the jewels from the sleeve of his imperial robe.[73] And now he came to the climax of his visit with the Pope.

On Monday morning, April 17, the Emperor invited the cardinals, the foreign ambassadors, and the members of his own suite to meet with him in the Sala dei Paramenti of the Vatican. When the whole company was assembled, the Pope, returning from mass, entered the room and took his seat. Then Charles stood up and taking his place beside the Pope, began to speak. The harangue, delivered in Spanish and without a prepared manuscript, lasted over an hour. We do not know the exact words he used, for in those days there were no stenographers; contemporary accounts differ and the printed versions published at the time were certainly edited. But the general character of the speech is clear. After a detailed account of the long conflict between him and Francis I, Charles turned to a vehement denunciation of his rival's failure to keep his pledged promises and his constant efforts to stir up discord among the Christian states. He (the Emperor) had reached the end of his endurance; if the French King refused to accept the Emperor's conditions and make peace, he was prepared to make war. As an alternative to war, with all that it involved in the loss of innocent lives, he was ready to submit the issue to a personal trial-at-arms between him and Francis, the prize to be Burgundy, if he was victorious; Milan, if Francis won.

This unexpected attack on Francis, which was tantamount to an ultimatum, struck the assemblage like a bombshell. And no one was more surprised and dismayed than Cobos and Granvelle, who had not been consulted and who had no inkling of what their master would say. As the company left the room, the faces of the two counsellors reflected their displeasure, and they told the

French ambassadors that they had not expected the Emperor to preach such a sermon, but that they should heed only the first part of the speech.[74] The British ambassador reported exactly the same reaction: "We did mete in coming oute with the Sieur de Granvelle and the commandeur Cauves, which said unto us that they loked not that their maistre should make such a sermon, but that the first partie onely was to be taken." [75]

It is not easy to explain what prompted Charles to take this step. In part it stems from the flush of self-assurance and power which his African victory had given him. He had come back with great plans for the unification of Christendom and a concerted campaign to put an end to the threat of the Turk. And now, once more, Francis stood in the way. The news of the occupation of Turin on April 3 was a last straw. The time for negotiations was over. Francis must be defeated.

The decision placed Cobos and Granvelle in an impossible situation. In defense of their own integrity and sincerity during the months of negotiation with the French ambassadors, they were driven to repudiate their master's words. Thus, once more, the gap that separated their thinking from the Emperor's and the slight confidence he placed in their counsel became abundantly clear. They must have expostulated with him concerning his address, particularly the proposal for a duel, for the next morning, when the Emperor met with the Pope and the French ambassadors, he was at pains to explain that he was still eager for peace and that, if he had suggested a single combat as a solution, it was only as a last resort. Late that night he left Rome on the way to Siena and Florence, leavng Cobos, Granvelle, and their secretaries to complete the negotiations with the Pope regarding the calling of a Church Council.[76]

Two days later, April 20, they sent Idiáquez to the Emperor, reporting satisfactory progress in their discussions.[77] He overtook the Emperor at Pienza on the twenty-second and at once wrote to Cobos: "They have been bringing additional pressure on His Majesty to make war. Your presence and that of M. de Granvelle are very necessary in every respect. Once you are here, matters can be properly directed." [78] Peace, not war, was the goal of the Emperor's advisors.

Meanwhile the conferences continued in Rome. The Emperor's spokesmen had not been able to persuade the Pope to take sides. In fact, on April 24, he issued a public proclamation of his determination to maintain the strictest neutrality in the war that now seemed imminent.[79] But with regard to the Council they were more successful. The Pope accepted the proposals which Granvelle and Cobos formulated for the terms of the Papal bull to summon the Council and for the appointment of a commission to draw up the summons.[80] The bull was actually issued on June 4, 1536, calling for a Council at Mantua on May 23, 1537.[81] It should be added that when the German Protestants refused to attend a Council on Italian soil, the meeting was canceled.

From Siena, Idiáquez wrote again to Cobos on April 25, saying: "His Majesty desires greatly to have you and M. de Granvelle here, and certainly it is important for the dispatch of business." [82] This is borne out by the fact that in letters to his representatives in France and Flanders, written at Acquapendente on April 21 and at Siena on April 24, the Emperor had to explain that he was writing in Castilian, rather than in French, because neither Granvelle nor Perrenin were with him.[83] Cobos and Granvelle had hoped to leave Rome April 24, but their business was not concluded till the end of the day.[84] Accompanied by a suite of five hundred mounted troops, to assure their safety, they bade farewell to Rome on the morning of April 25.[85]

They reached Siena April 27, and after spending the night there, hurried on in the Emperor's wake.[86] They must have reached Florence on the twenty-ninth, shortly after the Emperor entered the city for another elaborate reception.[87] Their stay there was brief, though they remained for a day after the Emperor's departure for Lucca to catch up on unfinished business.[88] By May 6 they were in Lucca, and the next day the city council voted to make gifts to the Emperor and to Cobos and Granvelle —1,800 *scudi* to Charles, 400 *scudi* each to his counsellors. In addition they decided to present them with silk cloth and certain "noble paintings" which they viewed with great pleasure.[89] On May 8, the town elders appointed delegates to visit the principal members of the Emperor's suite. It is noteworthy that in the long list of persons who were thus to be honored the names of Cobos and Granvelle come first, followed by such minor personages as the Marchese del Guasto, the Duke of Ferrara, the French ambassador, the Duke of Florence, Ferrante Gonzaga, the Duque de Alba, *et al.*[90] These good citizens knew who were the men that would be most influential in supporting their cause.

While the Court was in Lucca, the Cardinal of Lorraine, on

his way back from Rome, came to town and conferred with the Emperor. Though he was dismissed without receiving any hope of concessions from the Emperor, he traveled with the Court for a day and a half after they left Lucca on May 10, hoping to persuade him to enter into new peace discussions. But it was clear by now that the die was cast; Charles had decided for war. From now on all of his energies were devoted to the gathering of his forces on land and sea for an attack on France. In this he was encouraged by his two chief commanders, Andrea Doria and Antonio de Leiva, while the plan for the invasion of France was opposed by the Marchese del Guasto and his civilian counsellors. But as always, in the end the decision was his own and there can be little doubt that he was led to the notion of a joint attack by land and sea by the success of his operation against La Goleta the year before.

War with France

When he reached Sarzana, on the border of Genoese territory, Andrea Doria came to meet him. At the same time the Genoese banker and money-lender, Ansalmo di Grimaldo, came two miles out of town to meet Cobos and Granvelle, presumably to discuss the question of financing the campaign.[91] As he hurried to the front, the Emperor, accompanied by Cobos and Granvelle and a few gentlemen of his household, turned aside one day (May 21) to visit the widowed Duchess of Milan and the Duchess of Savoy, who came out from Milan for the interview, at Arena.[92] From May 26 to June 21 the Emperor remained at Asti, maturing his plans; at Savigliano (June 23–July 16) he finished gathering his forces.

Of Cobos' activities during this period we know very little, except that he was so busy that Salinas was unable to see him to ask for a book that Castillejo had requested.[93] Late in June the Emperor sent him and Granvelle to Nice to convey his condolences to the Duke of Savoy on the death of his son and daughter.[94] Cobos was in Genoa on July 3, when he wrote to the Duke of Ferrara to ask a favor for the Conde de Novellara.[95] On the following day he and Tomás de Forne negotiated a loan of 100,-000 scudi with Grimaldo.[96] We may be sure that he was back with the Emperor when he left Savigliano with all his forces on July 17. A week later they crossed the border into France.

There is no need to tell here the story of the disastrous campaign in Provence. Montmorency's strategy of the "scorched earth" brought defeat to Charles, without French losses in men and munitions. For a month the Emperor lay in camp at Aix, hoping that the French would come forth to challenge him, but too weak to risk a frontal attack upon them. During this long month disease was taking its toll and tempers were frayed. There were frequent quarrels among the courtiers, one of which took place in Cobos' tent between a nephew of the Cardinal of Toledo and a son of Pedro López de Guevara; there were insults and blows, but happily peace between the contestants was restored.[97] By September 3 Charles had decided to retreat, though he kept his decision carefully a secret.[98]

Again the Pope renewed his efforts to bring about peace. He had sent Cardinal Trivulzio to the French Court as his legate, and early in September Francesco Guicciardini and Giovanni Guidiccione, Bishop of Fossumbruno, arrived at the Imperial camp at Aix. The situation had changed greatly because of the death of the Dauphin at Avignon on August 10; as a result, the Duke of Orleans had succeeded to the title of Dauphin and Angoulême had become Duke of Orleans. Both Papal representatives conferred at length with Cobos and Granvelle and found them disposed to peace. On September 6 Guicciardini wrote to Trivulzio that he had had a long conference with Cobos and had told him what a mistake the Emperor had made by his refusal to discuss terms of peace, to which Cobos replied by way of explanation that in view of Francis' demand that the county of Asti and the duchy of Milan be turned over to him in person, the Emperor could not do otherwise. When Guicciardini expressed the opinion that the Emperor would have done the same thing, if Francis had not asked for either one, Cobos insisted that this was not true. Both he and Granvelle assured him that if Francis would make a reasonable offer, their sincere desire for peace would become manifest. But when Guicciardini suggested that he invite Trivulzio to come to Aix for further conferences, they asked him to postpone the invitation, since they did not want it known that they were giving their consent to the negotiations.[99]

On September 7 the Emperor's old commander-in-chief, Antonio de Leiva, died. Guidiccione, knowing that Leiva had been one of the chief advocates of war, at once appealed to the Emperor's counsellors to take up again with him the question of peace. After a two hours' talk with the Emperor, they reported that if Francis was willing, peace was possible. Guidiccione then wrote to the Grand Master, Montmorency, asking him to come to Aix with the Cardinal of Lorraine and the Papal legate to meet with the Emperor's representatives; if Aix was undesirable, he proposed a meeting half-way between Avignon and Aix. Guicciardini repeated the invitation and added the suggestion that Charles himself might be willing to advance to a place near the meeting place, in order to hasten the agreement. But the plans fell through. Montmorency wrote to Granvelle on September 11, assuring him that both he and the King were eager to achieve a just and lasting peace. The next day Granvelle answered in a similar vein.[100] That day the Emperor broke camp and started on the long road back to Genoa.

During the weeks while Charles lingered in Italy, settling his affairs there and preparing for his voyage to Spain, his ministers were still studying the possibility of peace. Granvelle told Martín de Salinas that he was convinced all was lost, unless they could come to an agreement with the French, granting Milan to the Duke of Orleans and arranging for his marriage with the second daughter of King Fernando. He had earlier believed that Cobos favored the claim of Don Luis of Portugal, but when he presented his proposal to Cobos, he found him wholly in agreement.[101] They therefore prepared a memorandum for the Emperor, setting forth the alternatives: war, an armistice, or peace. War would certainly bring about the ruin of both sides; an armistice would probably be used by the French merely to advance their own interests. As for peace, they reminded the Emperor that he had been willing to grant Milan to the Duke of Angoulême, but that Francis had refused. If, now that Angoulême had become the Duke of Orleans, he would renew the offer, they felt that it would open the door to successful negotiations.[102] We do not know what was Charles's answer; we do know that nothing happened.

One of the matters which was at last settled before they left Genoa was the adjudication of the duchy of Montferrato to the Duke of Mantua, with the proviso that he divorce his wife, Giulia de Aragón, and marry the sister of the late Duke of Montferrato, a matter that had been in the hands of a court of justice, since the death of the Duke in 1533. The Duke of Savoy had been one of the claimants for the title, and when he heard of the decision, he went to the Emperor to protest at his stripping him of his rightful possessions. When Charles replied that the case was closed and not open for further discussion, the Duke started to walk out of the room in indignation. But Cobos and Granvelle, who were present at the interview, ran after him and persuaded him to stop, while they placated him with fair words and promises.[103] Blessed are the peacemakers!

Spain Again

The fleet sailed from Genoa on November 16, and after a long, rough voyage reached Palamós on December 5. That night the Emperor had a long conference with Cobos and Granvelle and after midnight started for Barcelona, accompanied only by the Duque de Alba and a few courtiers.[104] After one night in Barcelona he hurried on to join the Empress, who was waiting for him at Tordesillas with the old Queen Mother.

Cobos and Granvelle remained for four days at Palamós, arranging with Andrea Doria the disposition of the fleet and the Spanish infantry who had remained in Italy.[105] Thence they moved on to Barcelona, where they stayed another four days, occupied with the dispatch of other business. One of their orders was an instruction to Alvaro de Bazán to proceed with six of his Spanish galleys to winter at Malaga. Off the coast of Valencia they were caught in a storm and all six galleys were lost with all aboard, except the captain. The loss of property was also great, including personal property of Cobos said to have been worth 12,000 ducats.[106] It probably represented all the gifts that he had received in Italy; the silk and paintings given him by the city of Lucca were surely only a part of his acquisitions.

Just before Cobos and Granvelle left Barcelona, there was an amusing incident that involved Cobos. He was at the time lodged in the palace of the Archbishop of Zaragoza, who had just been named Viceroy ("luoctinent") of Cataluña. On December 13 Cobos sent a messenger to the *Consellers* of the city, summoning them to meet with him. This raised at once a question of protocol, for the municipal councillors had a rule that they were subject to the call only of the King, the Queen, the Infantes, or the Viceroy. After consultation with the town elders they informed Cobos that by the rules of their office they could not accept his summons.

The next day, however, when they went to the Palace to take the oath of allegiance, they found Cobos with the Viceroy and so, as their diary records: "they were under the necessity of saluting the Comendador Mayor, who was present with the Viceroy, something which they would not have done, had he not been present there." [107] And so the ceremonial of the city was preserved!

The two ministers left Barcelona at the middle of December. They did not progress with anything like the speed the Emperor had shown, in part because they ran into heavy snow in the mountains. They took time, too, to carry on a correspondence with Italy and with the Emperor, who had moved from Torde-sillas to Valladolid on December 28. But at last, with their suite, they entered Valladolid on the day after Epiphany.[108] For the first time in almost two years Cobos was reunited with his wife and children in their lovely palace.

During his absence the palace had been further ornamented. At some time in 1535 the French stone-carver, Etienne Chamet (Jamete), had come to Spain from his home town of Orleans and had worked for two or three months at the palace of Dr. Beltrán in Medina del Campo, carving medallions, coats of arms, gargoyles, and other ornaments. From there he went to Valla-dolid and worked for a month and a half on Cobos' house.[109] Though there is no record of the actual work he performed, it may well be that the vigorous medallions of Roman emperors' heads in the spandrels of the first floor of the patio are by his hand. It might even be that the single female head in the group is a stylized portrait of María de Mendoza.

Cobos may also have found the walls of the main hall of the palace newly decorated with mural paintings. We have seen that he had thought of bringing the Bolognese painters, Bagnacavallo and Pupini, to Valladolid, but for some reason had abandoned the project. He had not given up the idea: Francisco Pacheco, in his *Arte de la pintura*, tells us that it was Cobos who brought to Spain two painters, Julio and Alejandro, to decorate his house in Ubeda and that afterwards they were engaged in mural painting at the Alhambra. Pacheco had evidently seen their work, for in commenting on the innovations that they brought in the use of *tempera* and *al fresco*, he remarks "it is this kind of painting that has given the good light which it still has today in both places." [110] Years ago the elder Gómez Moreno identified the two painters as Julio de Aquiles (*alias* Julio Romano) and Alejandro Mayner.[111] Now we know that Julio de Aquiles was working in Valladolid in 1533, when he was named by Alonso Berruguete as his expert in adjudicating the value of his work on the now famous *retablo* of San Benito el Real.[112] Though there is no contemporary record of his having worked on Cobos' palace, the fact that it was Cobos who brought him to Spain and that he was interested in decorating his dwelling makes it very probable that he devoted some of his time to this task. If so, it must have been before 1537, since he began his work at the Alhambra in that year.

The compelling motives in the Emperor's return to Spain were to see the Empress and, if possible, beget another offspring, and to raise funds from the Cortes of Castile and Aragon. In both he was successful, although the Infante Don Juan, born at Valladolid in October, 1537, probably in Cobos' palace, died a few days after his birth. The Castilian Cortes met at Valladolid in April and May and after the usual haggling over details, granted a large annual subsidy of 200,000 ducats. The Archbishop of Toledo, Tavera, and Cobos were once more the presiding officers,[113] and on June 30 Charles made a gift of 200,000 *maravedís* to Cobos in recognition of his services at the Cortes.[114]

Lord of Sabiote

When Cobos returned to Spain he found his personal finances in a most prosperous state. The huge influx of gold and silver from Peru in 1535 and 1536 had increased his income as *fundidor* ten-fold and this continued in 1537 and 1538. Up to now he had had his palaces in Valladolid and Ubeda, but he possessed no landed estate which would give him the title of "Lord." In his desperate need of money, the Emperor had succeeded in persuading the Pope to issue a bull which gave him the right, as Grand Master, to "dismember" any of the property of the military orders, in other words, to expropriate their lands and sell them to the highest bidder, the money to be used in the war against the Turk.

A few miles east of Ubeda lay the town of Sabiote, with a

massive fortress which had belonged to the Order of Calatrava. Probably because it was close to his home town, Cobos now offered to buy the property. And to help finance the down payment he and his wife sold the town of Hornillos, which Doña María had brought as part of her dowry, for 8,000 ducats to Pedro Fernández de Portillo, *regidor* of Valladolid.[115] On July 1, 1537, the Emperor agreed to sell Sabiote to Cobos.[116] Ten days later the latter accepted the terms: a down payment of 3,830,- 928 *maravedís,* to be used to pay off a mortgage note to Ansaldo di Grimaldo, and the mortgage then to be re-issued to the Order of Calatrava in compensation for their loss of income, and a payment on account of 7,500,000 *maravedís* (20,000 ducats) eight days after Cobos had taken possession.[117] On the same day the Emperor ordered the Commander of Sabiote in the Order of Calatrava to turn the town over to his agent, Fernando de Bustillo; [118] on August 7 Bustillo took possession of the town in the Emperor's name.[119]

During the following months the details of the deal were worked out. One of the issues at stake was the right to receive lodging in the town at any time. When Cobos inserted a clause in the sales agreement stipulating that this right was to be included in the sale price, the members of the Consejo Real, when asked to give their approval, expressed their dissent on the ground that it was improper for the King thus to renounce a royal privilege; [120] but their objections were overruled. Finally, on November 16, the sale was completed. The total price was 18,509,751 *maravedís* (over 40,000 ducats). In addition to the down payment and a first payment of 7,500,000 *maravedís,* Cobos had agreed to pay the balance of 7,178,823.5 *maravedís* at the fair of Medina del Campo in October.[121] On the same day the Emperor instructed Bustillo to hand the town over to Cobos; [122] on November 17 Cobos authorized his cousin, Pedro de los Cobos, and Dr. Peñalosa to act in his name in the affairs of the town.[123] Peñalosa took possession on December 20; [124] in the following year (September 26) Ortega, Cobos' chaplain, notified the municipal council of Sabiote that the Pope had ratified the sale.[125]

The news of Cobos' acquisition of this new estate was soon known at Court. Salinas, writing to Castillejo in answer to his query, replied: "His title is still 'Grand Commander of Leon and member of His Majesty's Council of State,' and if you wish, you can add 'Lord of Sabiote.' " [126] Even in Italy it was reported in embellished form. Diego Hurtado de Mendoza, the ambassador in Venice, wrote playfully to Cobos: "Will Your Excellency [a form of address used only to princes] write to me if it is true that we can label you 'Duque de Sabiote,' though I have heard you referred to at other times as 'Highness' and 'Majesty?' " [127] Cobos replied: "The story about the title of Duque de Sabiote is not true, nor has it ever entered my head. I have enough titles without adding that one." [128] But in view of his persistence in securing the title of *adelantado* of Cazorla for himself and his son and his satisfaction at the marriage of his daughter to a duke, it is hard to believe that he was quite frank in this modest denial.

The Contract for the Chapel

The Emperor left Valladolid on July 23 for Monzón, where he had summoned the representatives of Aragon, Cataluña, and Valencia for another Cortes. It seems probable that Cobos did not accompany him on this trip, for there are no official documents which bear his signature during this period; and Salinas, who was with the Court, had frequent conversations with Granvelle and with Idiáquez, but does not mention Cobos until after his arrival at Monzón. Perhaps he took advantage of this respite for a hasty trip to Ubeda and Sabiote. There was certainly a reason why he should have wanted to visit Ubeda, for the plans for the building of his chapel, which he had initiated in 1534, had now taken definite form.

Before he left Naples in March, 1536, Cobos had secured a copy of the Papal bull authorizing the construction of the chapel; this he sent to Suárez de Figueroa, the ambassador in Genoa, who answered on March 26 that he was sending it to Juan Vázquez de Molina in Spain by the first courier.[129] We know that Cobos' wife, Doña María, was in Ubeda on May 28, when she exercised her power of attorney to transfer the right to collect Cobos' fees as *fundidor* in Santa Marta from the two Germans who had been appointed in 1528 to her brother-in-law, Alonso Luis Fernández de Lugo, recently appointed governor of Santa Marta.[130] Perhaps she made the trip as a result of her husband's request that she make the arrangements for beginning the construction of the chapel.

On September 18, 1536, Fernando Ortega, in behalf of Cobos, signed a contract with two *canteros*—as architect-builders were called—Alonso Ruiz of Ubeda, and Andrés de Vandelvira of Alcaraz, to build the chapel of San Salvador on the site given to Cobos by the Hospital, within six years, for a fee of 12,800 ducats.[131] Ruiz had been one of the builders of Cobos' chapel of La Concepción in Santo Tomás; Vandelvira was still a young man, but since 1530 he had been working on the chapel which Ortega himself had founded in the church of San Nicolás. By the terms of the contract, Ruiz and Vandelvira undertook to construct the church in accordance with the design which had been prepared by Diego de Siloee, who was at the time the chief architect of the Cathedral of Granada. Since Siloee's drawings were not complete, the builders were to proceed with the work according to the verbal instructions they had received from him.

The contract specifies in detail the provisions for the work. The material was to be finished Ubeda freestone of the best quality available; the mortar was to be of earth, not sand, the lime to be provided by Ortega. The overall length was 157 feet, the width, at the level of the tower and sacristy, 90 feet. Provision was made for the cylindrical *contre-forts* at the corners of the façade and for the tower, which was to rise 130 feet in stone and terminate in a metal spire. Windows, mouldings, and other details were specified, but there was no mention of the carving and ornamentation.

If Cobos visited Ubeda in August, 1537, he must have found the construction of the chapel well under way, for the builders had agreed in the contract to complete, during the first year, the foundations and outer walls, to a height of nine feet. But the rest of the work did not progress as had been planned, for Cobos soon began to have misgivings about the undertaking. While he was in the midst of the negotiations at Salsas, he sent an urgent letter to Ortega.[132] Although the letter has not survived, Francisco de Olaso, one of his servants, wrote to Juan Vázquez at the end of January, 1538, that Cobos had instructed Ortega to go slow with the work and was thinking of suspending it altogether.[133] Vázquez had even suggested that he should build the chapel in Sabiote, rather than in Ubeda. On February 13 Cobos wrote to him that there were difficulties in that; he hoped that God would soon give him freedom to go to Ubeda and decide what was the best course of action.[134] And so, for more than a year work was at a standstill.

Cobos managed to get to Ubeda for a brief visit at the end of April, 1539, and at that time, in view of the cessation of the work, Ruiz and Vandelvira asked to be reimbursed for the expenses they had already incurred in tearing down the buildings of the Hospital, laying the foundations, and paying for the stone, which had already been delivered. Cobos referred the matter to his financial agent, Francisco de Almaguer. The latter, on the advice of Luis de Vega, now *maestro de obras* of the Emperor,[135] perhaps through Cobos' influence, and with the approval of Ortega, agreed to a payment of 783,117.5 *maravedís*. The agreement was signed at Ubeda on May 9, 1539; on June 9, at Toledo, Cobos gave his approval.[136] A year later he was ready to take the matter up again.

CHAPTER IX

PEACE NEGOTIATIONS

In spite of earlier failures, Pope Paul III continued throughout 1537 to urge further negotiations between Charles and Francis with a view to achieving peace. On February 15 he wrote to the Emperor that he was sending the Bishop of Reate to discuss the matter.[1] The Bishop, who brought letters of recommendation to Cobos and Granvelle, was in Valladolid in March and on the seventeenth Charles prepared an answer, pointing out that he had always been anxious for peace and that while he was in Italy he had made definite offers to Francis, who had not even acknowledged them.[2] A few days later Salinas reported the Emperor's reply to King Ferdinand;[3] once more the Papal legate's mission was in vain.

Again on June 16 both the Pope and the College of Cardinals addressed an appeal to the Emperor to appoint plenipotentiaries to start negotiations.[4] The Emperor did not reply until after he reached Monzón, when once more he defended his position and insisted that the next move must come from Francis.[5] Meanwhile the representatives of Francis and of María, the Regent of Flanders, had signed a truce on July 30 at Bomy, providing for a cessation of hostilities on the Flemish front for a period of ten months. María promptly sent Cornelius Schepper to Spain to secure the Emperor's ratification. He was at Monzón early in September; Cobos wrote to Queen Eleanor on September 12 to report his arrival[6] and on the fifteenth Charles sent a long

194

dispatch regarding his mission to his ambassador in Rome, the Marqués de Aguilar.[7]

Schepper had passed through France, thanks to a safe-conduct, and on the way he had an opportunity to talk to the King and Queen and to the Grand Master, Montmorency. He reported that he had found them all, especially the Queen and Montmorency, more anxious than ever to find a way to peace and that they had suggested a meeting between Eleanor and María of Flanders as a possible solution. The Emperor did not approve of this, but he at once sent Schepper back to France, with a proposal that he and Francis, together with their representatives, should meet at Perpignan or Narbonne and try to reach an agreement. On September 26 Schepper reported that Francis was still disposed to negotiate and was sending an ambassador to discuss details. The courier bearing his report reached Monzón on October 5;[8] he was followed a few days later by the French ambassador, Claude Dodieu, Seigneur de Velly.

After ten days of discussion with Granvelle and Cobos, they had reached an agreement as to the terms of the interview: the representatives of Francis would be the Cardinal of Lorraine and Anne de Montmorency; Granvelle and Cobos would represent the Emperor. The Emperor was to be in Barcelona on November 20, his agents at Perpignan; on the same day Francis would be in Avignon, while his spokesmen would be at Narbonne. An armistice was to be approved, whereby the French troops would be withdrawn from Italy during the negotiations.[9]

In another document Granvelle and Cobos reported to the Emperor the terms of the agreement. They added that they had insisted that the Duke of Savoy be restored to his estates, but that Velly had replied that his instructions were limited to arranging for the interview. They also reported that Velly had explained the King's choice of representatives on the ground that the Cardinal had always shown his desire for peace and that Montmorency was the person best informed as to his master's intentions. Velly left on October 19, promising to be back with the King's reply by November 5. But he did not arrive until the eleventh.[10]

Francis' reply was favorable, so that it was possible to reach an agreement quickly. On November 16 Velly, Granvelle, and Cobos signed the document; the only change was one made necessary by the delay: the representatives of both sides were to be at the appointed places on December 17, instead of November 20; Francis would be at Montpellier instead of Avignon. The truce was to last for three months.[11] On November 18 the Cortes finally closed its sessions with the usual plea to the Emperor that he stay in Spain and with the grant of the usual subsidy. The following day the Emperor left hurriedly for Valladolid to visit the Empress and to complete his preparations for the meeting on the French border.

Before he left Monzón, Granvelle and Cobos drew up a list of questions on which they needed his instructions, if they were to negotiate properly. It is a long list, of one hundred and eight paragraphs, discussing every possible aspect of the matters under dispute, beginning with the problem of Milan and touching all parts of the Empire.[12] As a result of their conferences with the Emperor, they now prepared a list of his chief demands, under some nineteen paragraphs. The order of their presentation is significant: they begin with the actions which Charles called on Francis to undertake: to join in the Church Council, to join in the war against the Turks, to restore the Duke of Savoy, to confirm the treaties of Madrid (1526) and Cambrai (1529), to desist from attacks on Charles and his brother Ferdinand. Not until we come to the eighth item is there mention of the question of Milan: a proposal for the marriage of the Duke of Orleans and the second daughter of Ferdinand, the Infanta Ana, then nine years old, and the ultimate investiture of Milan in the Duke.[13] It is undoubtedly this list which was to serve as a guide to Granvelle and Cobos in the actual negotiations.

They left Monzón for Barcelona on November 23. Early in December Cobos wrote to Juan Vázquez that there were no new developments, except that reports from France indicated that they wanted peace. "We'll soon know the secret," he added.[14] During the following days they were busy completing the final details with the French ambassador Velly. On December 12, escorted by a gallant troupe of courtiers, they started for Perpignan, where they arrived on the appointed day. On December 20 they moved on to Salsas. The next day a representative of the French came to report that the French ambassadors were at Leucate. On the nineteenth Granvelle and Cobos dispatched Francisco de Mendoza, bishop-elect of Jaén, and Gutierre López de Padilla to Leucate to make the final arrangements for the conference.[15]

Fitou

Lying across the then border between France and Spain is a long lagoon, separated from the sea by a narrow sandbar. At the northern end of the lagoon was the village of Leucate; at the southern extremity was Salsas, with its important fortress. Halfway between the two towns, on the sandbar, at a place called Fitou, were a few fishermen's cabins, and here, in this "no man's land," they agreed to hold their meetings.[16] Each side was to come with only fifty attendants, unarmed except for their swords. Cobos preserved the list of those who were to accompany him and Granvelle: fourteen gentlemen with Granvelle, including Martín de Salinas, and forty gentlemen and attendants with Cobos. It is striking that the only prelate in the group was Francisco de Mendoza and that not one of the Spanish grandees was present. Most of them were kinsmen or henchmen of Cobos.

On Friday morning, December 21, the envoys of both sides started for the rendezvous. The French arrived first at the cabins, and as the Spanish group approached, the Grand Master, mounted on a mule and accompanied by a goodly company of prelates and courtiers, came out a few hundred yards to meet them. After some discussion as to who should lead the way, he finally joined the Spanish group and they proceeded together to the meeting place. As they rode along, there was a fair exchange of mutual respect and a common desire for peace. When they came up to the cabins, the Cardinal of Lorraine, with a group of priests and gentlemen, came out to greet them with evident signs of pleasure, and as soon as they had dismounted, the four envoys went into one of the cabins, where the Cardinal had prepared a little room as a chapel, the walls hung with crimson satin tapestry, decorated with bands of cloth of gold and with the Cardinal's arms.

As soon as they were seated at a table, two on each side facing each other, the Cardinal made a little speech: Our Lord had said that where two or three were gathered together in His name, there would He be also. And now there were four of them, in a church, for the lofty purpose of peace, and the Cardinal firmly believed that God would be present, especially in view of the good will of the Emperor and the King and the desire of the Grand Master and himself, which he was confident that Granvelle and Cobos shared. He was particularly hopeful, he said, because the Emperor had named as his representatives Cobos, whose reputation (here, Cobos originally wrote "fame") they had heard of, and Granvelle, with whom they had long been acquainted.

To this Granvelle made appropriate answer, assuring him of their own desire for peace and their confidence in the Cardinal and the Grand Master. And well he might be hopeful, for, as we have seen, Montmorency had repeatedly shown his readiness to negotiate, and the Cardinal of Lorraine, on his mission to Italy in the spring of 1536, had actually ordered the French commander in Piedmont to withdraw his forces to Turin, in order to keep the door open for further discussion. Surely, if peace had depended only on the good will and sincere desire of these four men, the negotiations would have had a happy outcome.

The French asked Granvelle and Cobos to present their views first, and they stated their position in conformity with their instructions. But almost at once the issue turned to particulars: the restoration of Savoy and the town of Hesdin, recently captured by the French, and the investiture of Milan. The French envoys, in behalf of their King, insisted that, as a first step, the Emperor must turn Milan over to Francis; when that was done, he would consent to discuss the other problems. And so, for more than four hours they debated the issues at stake, amicably enough, but with no meeting of minds. In fact, Granvelle and Cobos were so discouraged that they proposed returning to Perpignan, but the French persuaded them to wait till Sunday; by that time they hoped to have received further instructions from Francis, who was at Montpellier. And so they returned to Salsas, where Velly came to visit them that night to apologize for his failure to accompany them on their return and to report that he had sent a dispatch to the King. After his conference with the Spanish envoys, Velly returned to Leucate to tell his associates what he had learned, and on Saturday he again came to Salsas with further suggestions for a compromise.

The French messenger had not returned on Sunday, and the Spaniards remained in Salsas, lodged in the town, not in the fortress, for they were afraid that the French would take advantage of the opportunity to reconnoitre the strength of the fortress. As a matter of fact, that is exactly what happened, for Montmorency succeeded in getting one of his servants into the fortress in disguise and so secured a report on its armament. Early Monday morning the secretary of the Grand Master came to Salsas to report the arrival of the King's messenger. Since it was Christmas Eve and a fast day, they agreed to meet at noon in the cabin. This time the Spaniards arrived first, and they returned the compliment of the French by going out to meet them and escorting them to the meeting-place. The King had not changed his position: Milan must be handed over as a preliminary to further discussion. Granvelle and Cobos now proposed a personal meeting between Charles and Francis. The French appeared to be favorable; they even raised the question as to whether Queen Eleanor should be invited too. And so they adjourned to meet on Christmas; but again that night Velly came to Salsas to say that they were sending for further clarification.

The Grand Master was ill on December 26, but they met again on the twenty-seventh. This time the French raised certain new issues. One was the "red herring" of Navarre; for Francis now suggested that he might return Savoy to the Duke, provided that he raze the fortresses between Milan and the Alps and that Henri d'Albret's long-standing claim to Navarre were favorably settled. As for Hesdin, he might restore the town to the Emperor, if the latter would give him back Asti or Tournai. In the matter of Milan, he was prepared to hold it for five years and then turn it over to the Duke of Orleans. He saw no reason for a personal interview with Charles, until their envoys had reached an agreement.[17] Granvelle and Cobos now presented a written statement of their minimum terms. The three major points were the transfer of Milan to the Duke of Orleans at the end of three years, French aid against the Turks, French support of the Church Council. Faced with this impasse, Granvelle and Cobos now decided to consult with the Emperor. On December 31 they dispatched Idiáquez to Barcelona (the Emperor arrived there that day), with a detailed account of the proceedings thus far and a request for instructions concerning their future course.

There was another meeting of the delegates after Idiáquez left on December 31, and on January 1 Granvelle and Cobos wrote again to the Emperor, urging him to consult with the cardinal of Sigüenza, Loaisa, and send his reply promptly, because the French were learning too much about the Spanish fortifications on the frontier. Idiáquez reached Barcelona late on

January 2, and at midnight the Emperor sent him back to Salsas
with oral instructions,—a renewal of the original terms, a proposal for a truce and for a meeting between Francis and the
Emperor. Idiáquez was back at Salsas on January 4, and the
Emperor's reply left his representatives troubled and perplexed.
In their anxiety they once more sent Idiáquez to the Emperor,
proposing certain minor compromises and asking for an immediate, specific answer. On Wednesday morning, January 8, Idiáquez sent two letters to his superiors.[18] He had delivered their
letters to the Emperor and the Cardinal of Sigüenza had read
them. But nothing that they had said would move the Emperor
to change his mind. In fact, he was ready to terminate the conference, saying that there was no use in talking about anything
except a truce, until they reminded him that he must at least
answer his representatives' questions. And so he was sending a
clear, but unyielding reply. And Idiáquez noted that the Cardinal
wished to have it recorded that he would have approved the proposal to grant the duchy of Milan to the Duke of Orleans within
a year, as Granvelle and Cobos had suggested.

In a second letter to Cobos, Idiáquez made the interesting
comment that in the course of the discussion the Emperor had
said that he had thought of other courses of action, but that it
was not yet time to state them, nor would he reveal them to his
counsellors, nor even to his wife, until the opportune moment
came. When the Cardinal suggested that at least he should
inform his representatives, to guide them in their negotiations,
the Emperor replied that if he could, he would hide them from
his own mind, and he would not reveal them. As Idiáquez remarked: "You, sir, who know him better than anyone, can interpret what he means." A few days later, in another letter to
Cobos, he returns to the same theme: "His Majesty"—he wrote
—"has thought up some great speeches and undertakings that
every now and then start to appear and then he closes up again."
We shall have occasion later to revert to these dark sayings.

The Emperor's clear and uncompromising reply was dispatched by special courier on the evening of January 8 and
reached Salsas at nightfall on the ninth. The next morning Granvelle and Cobos met with the French and conveyed to them the
Emperor's decision. That night they wrote to Idiáquez: "We
are troubled that the negotiation has not turned out as we desired, yet we are satisfied that we have done everything within

our power, in accordance with His Majesty's intention and command, and that we have kept him clearly informed of what was transpiring and of our thoughts and opinions, with the fidelity and good will which we have always shown in his service. God grant that he has chosen the wise course."

This marks the end of the negotiations for peace. All that could be salvaged now was a truce. The commissioners met at the cabin for the last time on January 11. The French proposed a truce for a long period and in this Granvelle and Cobos concurred. But in spite of the support of the Cardinal of Sigüenza, who argued for a minimum of two years of truce, Charles was adamant and refused to consider anything other than a brief period. Undoubtedly he had set his heart on an early meeting with Francis at Nice in which the Pope would participate. The French delegates departed for Narbonne on the night of the eleventh. On the fourteenth Granvelle and Cobos had received the Emperor's decision and dispatched Cornelius Schepper to carry to the French ambassadors their proposal that a truce until June 1 be approved. That afternoon they left Salsas for Perpignan. The next day came a letter from Schepper that the French had offered no objections, but must consult with the King, who had already left Montpellier for Lyons. On the sixteenth they instructed him to proceed to the French Court to complete the truce.[19] Before they left Perpignan, the Papal legate, Jacobazzi, on his way to Barcelona, had a long conference with them and once more reported the strong desire for peace he had found in France; a compromise on Milan was possible.[20] And so the door to the meeting at Nice was still open. A week later the Spanish company had returned to Barcelona.

In all this discussion the most striking feature is the Emperor's desire for a "summit" meeting with his rival. Already in September, 1537, he had written to his sister Eleanor suggesting that she use her influence to persuade her husband to agree to a meeting at Narbonne or Perpignan.[21] When a truce and the plans for a conference of the ambassadors were agreed upon at Monzón on November 16, the Emperor at once set about plans for the meeting. He must come to the interview with all the pomp and majesty possible. At Valladolid on December 7 he negotiated a loan with three Genoese bankers[22] and he started gathering the necessary equipment—tapestries, livery for his attendants, and other evidences of splendor. It was said that it took one hundred and fifty carts to transport all of his finery to Barcelona. At the same time he instructed several of the great nobles—the Condestable de Castilla, the Duque del Infantado, the Duque de Nájera, the Marqués de Villena—to go to Barcelona with their suites, to accompany him with proper ceremony to the interview.[23] So great was his eagerness to arrive in time that he did not wait to spend Christmas with the Empress, but left Valladolid on December 21. He made the trip to Barcelona in the almost record time of ten days.

Events at the border conference soon disillusioned him; on January 14, convinced that there was no possibility of a meeting, he wrote to the Empress and to the four grandees whom he had summoned that the plans were cancelled. Thereupon three of the noblemen, who were already on their way, returned to their homes. But the Duque de Nájera received permission to continue his journey to Barcelona. There, in the following weeks, the Duke celebrated a series of magnificent entertainments—banquets, jousts, and masked balls.[24] After the tension of the preceding weeks, the Court seems to have given itself up to a period of revelry. In later years, Cobos' friends looked back with nostalgia to those gay days in Barcelona.

Barcelona in the Spring of 1538

During these festive months in Barcelona there are a number of documents which cast light on the personal affairs of Don Francisco. In several letters which he wrote to Juan Vázquez he mentions a lady to whom he refers only as "La Ilustrísima." On November 22, before he left Monzón, he had commented: "I don't know whether I will write to La Ilustrísima, for I am cross with her, because she is behaving in the way that Don Diego de Mendoza ascribed to her. Still, I beg you to serve her in any way you can." [25] After he reached Barcelona he wrote again: "I kiss the hands of La Ilustrísima, *mia cara,* a hundred million times. In this town they are saying all sorts of evil things about her, but Doña Guiomar Gralla has told me a very good story about what happened with two masqueraders who came to her house when Her Ladyship and Don Lorenzo were there." [26] On his return from Salsas he wrote:

Tell La Ilustrísima that I kiss her hands, though she is no longer *mia cara,* since she won't answer my letters, though I have begged her to. Don Lorenzo has been long in coming, for I had hoped to find him here to settle the principal business, because I don't like some little things that I have heard from Jovenet, who is offering excuses that his family is causing difficulties. . . . As soon as he arrives, I will do what is necessary and I shall not fail, as is right, for I will have the advantage over La Ilustrísima that I will always serve her with the best of good will, without expecting from her anything more than what could come from something I have lost. I swear that Don Diego was not far wrong in what he said about Her Ladyship. I know that I do not need to urge you to give her this message, but I beg you to keep it secret, lest they kill all of us.[27]

Again, in a letter of February 13, in a postscript in his own hand, Cobos wrote: "The delay of Don Lorenzo has caused a lot of damage to La Ilustrísima, because they are making trouble here about her business. I am doing everything I can, but I don't know whether it will do any good, though right now the situation is better than it was. I don't want to write to her for the reason that she knows." [28] The last reference to her is a footnote to a letter of March 3: "I am writing to La Ilustrísima. I'll bet she doesn't show you my letter, although she wrote to me that she wanted to show the letters I wrote to her." [29]

It is not possible to give any clear meaning to these rather cryptic statements. Since he calls her "mia cara," one suspects she was Italian. It is possible that the Don Lorenzo was Lorenzo Manuel, who had been the Imperial agent in Casalmaggiore and other towns in Northern Italy. The title "Her Ladyship" certainly indicates that she was a noblewoman of rank. On the other hand, since she was in Valladolid at the time, she cannot be the Condesa de Novellara, who was in Italy in this period. Whoever she was, Cobos surely had business matters to consider in her behalf and the bantering tone of his comments on her lead one to believe that this was no affair of the heart but a mere display of gallantry.

One of Cobos' servants, Francisco de Olaso, however, was disturbed at Cobos' behavior with regard to women. On January 30, 1538, he wrote to Juan Vázquez from Barcelona:

I don't think that you would want to offend His Lordship, but as he approaches old age, his servants no longer tell him certain things they rightly could about his behavior. And if he would stop doing some of the things he does, there wouldn't be all the talk there is. All things should be pardoned in the name of love—well and good! But in old men they say it is a disgrace, and unless we can cut it short by joining with My Lady, it certainly doesn't look well. If you would be willing to prod him, I think he would take it well. I regret this more than other people do, and so I would like to see it remedied. . . . Would to God that we might soon be together, for I think that if you were here, the little matters that trouble me, because the "Boss" is not behaving as I would like to have him behave, would soon be remedied. For I know that you would talk to him in a different way from the rest and that as a result he would respect you.[30]

Juan Vázquez must have received other reports on Cobos' behavior in Barcelona, for before he could have received Olaso's letter of January 30, he had written to Cobos about his masquerading. In his reply of February 13, a long letter in which he took up, point by point, all the matters which Vázquez should attend to, Cobos added:

As for my masquerading, if I thought that it was wrong, either I would not do it or else I would do it in such a way that no one knew about it. But it can perfectly well be done without seeming wrong, and when I do it, everybody sees it. I know that I am not the President of the Council nor a doctor-of-laws nor a bishop. If people there are gossiping about it, I am not disturbed. I am sorry that I do not get much fun out of doing it; if I did, I would do it more often, for it does not conflict with my obligation. What they say about my coming in at midnight is a lie. I did go there one night as a masquerader after a banquet, when we first got there, and also here to a party that the Duque [de Nájera] gave; and to another, with the Emperor. And since His Majesty enjoys it, the gossip doesn't have much weight. I have already said that I am sorry that I don't derive much pleasure, or I would do it more often, for even the Legate who is here [Jacobazzi] is not blamed if he does it. And so, do not offer excuses for me, for I will confess it to all those who want to know about it.[31]

These episodes are significant, not because of any specific evidence of wrongdoing, but because they help to explain why it was that in later years Cobos had the reputation of being fond of women. Because of his caution, none of Cobos' intimate personal correspondence has survived. In fact, aside from the ladies at Novellara and a few Italian women who wrote to him to ask for his help in securing favors from the Emperor, there is almost no mention of the part that women played in his life. It is true that some of his friends in their letters referred to a certain María Artal; the last comment on her was that she was getting fat and ugly.[32] But that is all.

During these months Cobos continued to receive special favors from the Emperor. When the Duque de Béjar, who was one of the Contadores Mayores of Castile, had died some years before, Cobos had prepared a list of persons who had applied for the post. In the margin of the document which was presented to the Consejo he wrote the prudent comment "We'll discuss this in

Valladolid." [33] Since then his assistants had been performing the duties of the office. On November 17, 1537, at Monzón, the Emperor instructed the paymasters to pay Cobos 1,500 ducats a year for the years 1536 and 1537 as an *ayuda de costa* for his services in this function. The 3,000 ducats were paid at Valladolid on March 2, 1538, and at the end of the month (March 30) the Emperor issued a new order providing for a similar payment for the year 1538.[34] By another royal *cédula* of February 10, 1538, Charles extended the authority of Cobos' son Diego, as Chanciller de las Indias, to the Audiencia and Chancillería which he was about to establish in Panama, in addition to those already operating in Santo Domingo and Mexico.[35] The official order for the new Audiencia was issued on February 26.[36]

The Emperor and Cobos must have been thinking already of establishing an archive for royal documents at the fortress of Simancas. Henry of Nassau (Marqués de Cenete) had been warden of the fortress since 1526; on February 13, 1538, Cobos wrote to thank Vázquez for sending him a copy of the terms of his appointment.[37] And in a letter of March 3 Cobos reported that his plans for Simancas were going well: he had talked to the Marqués and his wife and they were willing to transfer the title of warden to him, without recompense. He would let Vázquez know what happened.[38] The actual letter of appointment does not seem to have survived, but we may be sure that it was issued during that year and that it carried a salary with it.

Cobos had not even completed the deal for the purchase of the fortress of Sabiote before he was thinking of acquiring other strongholds that belonged to the military orders. Writing to Vázquez from Monzón on November 22, 1537, he reported: "I think I wrote you that they had told me that the wife of Diego de Carvajal was planning to sell her estate and see if she could buy Torres and Ximena. You know what we have discussed on that subject and so you are warned." [39] Torres and Ximena were fortresses of the Order of Calatrava in the province of Jaén, about fifty miles southwest of Ubeda. Just west of Ubeda was another fortress, Canena, which was the joint possession of the Orders of Calatrava and Santiago. After discussion with the Emperor, Cobos now undertook to purchase both Canena and Torres.[40] In the spring of 1538 Charles approved of the sale and started the necessary steps to carry the deal to a conclusion. This involved securing the approval of the commanders of the two Orders and an appraisal of the value of the properties. In August he ordered the Clavero of Calatrava to turn over to Cobos all the papers dealing with Canena, Torres, and Sabiote.[41] An unexpected difficulty was a protest from the citizens of Torres against the separation from the Order of Calatrava and the sale to Cobos. But they were disregarded, and on December 24, at the same time that he announced the "dismembering" of the fortresses, the Emperor issued an order uniting the two municipal councils of Canena. The formalities were at last completed and on February 21, 1539, the properties were turned over to Cobos on payment of 21,796,316 *maravedís* (about 58,000 ducats).[42] At the same time he was granted the privilege of lodging *gratis* in either town. He could now feel that his palace in Ubeda was protected by a ring of fortified outposts against any hostile attack.

There are numerous evidences of the high favor with the Emperor which Cobos enjoyed in these days. While he and Granvelle were still at Salsas he had written to congratulate them on the judgment and loyalty they had shown in the negotiations. It is not surprising, then, that he continued to receive so many favors nor that the Emperor accepted his advice in granting favors to others. Salinas gives us some idea of his methods in a letter to Castillejo, who had asked him to enlist the support of Granvelle in his request for a bishopric. After explaining that the Emperor was very cautious and consulted Granvelle and Cobos on all matters, he went on: "But M. de Granvelle is not accustomed to meddling in appointments, except by way of advice; they are left exclusively in the hands of Cobos. His method of operation is to yield to the will of the Emperor, but at the same time he stands firm in his support of the person he wants and he leads the Emperor to have the right will, if he doesn't come to it by himself." [43] Clearly implied in Salinas' remark is a "gentlemen's agreement" between Cobos and Granvelle as to their spheres of activity. This is borne out in a *consulta* which they jointly addressed to the Emperor on March 13, 1538, with regard to further negotiations with the French. "Under the circumstances"—they wrote—"it seems that there is nothing else to be done for the present, except to draw up the dispatch for Cornelius [Schepper]. I, Granvelle, will take care of that; while I, Cobos, will attend to the affairs of Castile." [44] This division of labor and of jurisdiction, whereby each of the ministers left the other free to operate in his special field, explains how it was possible for them to live in friendly harmony, instead of trying to cut each other's throats. In fact, Cobos had so little taste for these foreign negotiations that Salinas reported he wanted to stay in Spain, under the pretext that he must try to raise money for the Treasury.[45] But the Emperor had other plans for him.

Nice

The failure of the conference at Fitou had not lessened the Emperor's desire for a personal interview with Francis. At a conference with the French ambassador Pressiu, early in February, it was the theme to which he recurred again and again.[46] Leaving his counsellors in Barcelona, he spent the last two weeks in February on a trip to visit the fortifications on the frontier, including a day's visit at Salsas. By the time he returned to Barcelona, the situation had become clearer. The French King had been reluctant to agree to an interview, least of all in the presence of the Pope. But the reports of the Papal legates in France and in Spain had been so encouraging that by the end of February Paul had decided to go in person to Nice and there attempt to find a common ground between the rival sovereigns. Charles had been willing from the first to accept the Pope's invitation. Now Francis also yielded to the pressure of opinion and agreed to attend the meeting, although as late as March 17 the French ambassador Velly was suggesting that it might be well for the King to send the Cardinal of Lorraine and Montmorency to the Isle d'Hyères for a preliminary meeting with the Emperor and his advisors.[47]

Once the decision to hold the meeting had been made, there were countless details to be settled in preparation for the trip—instructions to the noblemen who were summoned to accompany the Emperor, orders to Andrea Doria regarding the fleet and the troops in Italy, the assemblage of equipment and supplies, and, as always, the provision of money to defray the expenses. It was late in April before all was ready. On April 25 the Emperor and his suite embarked in Doria's galleys. The voyage was slow because of bad weather which several times forced the fleet to take refuge in coastal waters. Off Marseilles there was a brief skirmish with some French ships. But they reached Villefranche, close to Nice, on May 9.[48]

As soon as he reached Villefranche, the Emperor sent M. de
Bossu with thirteen galleys to Savona, where the Pope was awaiting his arrival. He had originally intended sending Cobos and
Granvelle, but changed his mind, in order not to seem to be
trying to influence him.[49] The Emperor had been met by the
Duke of Savoy as he landed at Villefranche. The Duke at first
agreed to permit the Pope to lodge in the castle of Nice, and
Cobos and Granvelle were sent to Nice to complete the arrangements. Almost immediately Cobos returned to Villefranche, leaving Granvelle for further discussion, for the Duke had begun
to offer difficulties, saying that the soldiers had kidnapped his
son and occupied the castle and that they would not permit the
Pope to enter. Granvelle wrote to Cobos daily about the obstacles he was finding,[50] and after the Venetian ambassadors had
come to visit Cobos, they reported to the Doge that when they
raised the question as to what was going to happen about the
castle of Nice, Cobos replied:

> That devil is causing a lot of trouble. First he says "Yes"; then he says "No,"
> so that there is no possibility of being sure of the outcome. He has invented
> as a last impediment that the infantry who are in the castle are not willing
> to deliver it up, unless they are paid a certain sum of money. And so I have
> now sent 3,000 *scudi,* and M. de Granvelle is there to see if he can arrange
> the matter. God grant that no new snag will develop.[51]

In spite of their efforts, the Duke would not yield; so that
when the Pope reached Nice on May 17 and learned of the
Duke's decision, he refused to land at the pier which the citizens
of the town had built for his reception and continuing along the
coast, disembarked on the beach near the Franciscan monastery
of Les Cordeliers on the outskirts of the city, where he was provided with lodging. The cardinals and other members of his suite
found quarters in the city. The next day Charles came along
the coast from Villefranche with his galleys and landing near
the monastery, accompanied only by a few of his courtiers, had
an hour's conference with the Pope in the cloister of the monastery. That same day he renewed for another three months the
truce which had been made at Fitou in January.[52]

Two days later they met again, this time in a gay pavillion
pitched in an orange orchard between Nice and Villefranche.
And this time the Emperor came by land, escorted by five hundred arquebusiers, while the galleys followed along the coast
to be ready in case of an attack. It was a long conference, marked

by a violent rainstorm that drenched the courtiers who were waiting outside, and it even penetrated the pavillion and soaked the distinguished conferees inside. When the conference was over both parties returned to their lodgings through a sea of mud.

The only inkling we have of what transpired is a report from the Venetian envoys that while they were discussing the question of the League and the Emperor's plans to remain in Italy, Granvelle turned to Cobos, asking him to speak and the latter made a sign to him that he should answer. When the Venetians insisted on the importance of the Emperor's remaining in Italy, Granvelle and Cobos kept interrupting them, and Cobos said: "You have been discussing your plans since February and reproving us for delay, making it clear that you were not satisfied with our proposal that the Emperor should remain in Italy." When Granvelle remarked that the Emperor had never made up his mind to stay, Cobos added: "If His Majesty were to come back, we would think that the Signoria should assign Andrea Doria, if he were in Venice, for the protection and security of his Royal Person." There was further debate and finally Cobos said, laughing: "I see that you want to be treated as kings, and we will grant that to you. And we will make proper arrangements for the fleet. Tomorrow we will meet again and decide about the infantry, because meanwhile we can get a better idea of the agreement." [53] Such must have been the issues which the Pope and the Emperor were striving to solve.

After long delay King Francis arrived at Villeneuve, west of Nice, on May 28. He came with a brilliant company—Queen Eleanor, his daughter-in-law, Catherine de' Medici, and the ladies of their Court, courtiers and prelates, to say nothing of a body-guard of ten thousand Swiss soldiers. The very next day the Emperor sent to greet him three galleys, his representatives, the Duque de Alburquerque, Granvelle and Cobos, and a group of gentlemen, all gallantly arrayed, wearing gold chains about their necks. The King received them, cap in hand, and embraced them all. After a brief conversation, the three leaders asked permission to go and kiss the hand of the Queen. She too received them graciously, with tears in her eyes, and took them to visit the ladies of the Court. Returning to the King, they were served with a grand banquet and once more joined the ladies. So happy was the evening that it was two in the morning when they returned to Villefranche, where people were beginning to worry lest some mishap had befallen them. A similar visit of courtesy brought the Cardinal of Lorraine and Montmorency, now Grand Constable, to greet the Emperor at Villefranche.

Francis held his first conference with the Pope on June 2 at a house between Villeneuve and Nice which he had ornamented with flowers and rich tapestries. Their talk lasted four hours before they returned to their respective lodgings. On the following day the Emperor again came to talk with the Pope; he too came this time with a bodyguard of two thousand troops, who surrounded the pavillion during the long conference. Finally, on June 4, the French and Imperial commissioners met with the Pope for the first time. Once more, then, the men who sat together in the cabin at Fitou met to seek a solution of their masters' conflict; once more the old obstacles remained unchanged. A second meeting on June 5 was no more successful. As one contemporary said: "Ea die cecidit spes pacis." [54] A final interview between the Pope and the Emperor on June 9 produced no results, and the Emperor, writing to Lope de Soria, his ambassador in Venice, expressed his belief that there was little hope of peace.[55]

During these days there were disorders in Nice, where the citizens were openly hostile to the Emperor's followers. A kinsman of Andrea Doria was shot as he stood at the window of his house, and a little later, one day when Cobos and Granvelle were visiting with the Marqués de Aguilar, the chamberlain of the Marqués was killed just outside the house. The two ministers were so outraged that they at once summoned the officials of the city and warned them that if they did not put a stop to such disorderly acts, the Emperor would have the city burned.

Before the conference broke up, however, there was one more gala event. On June 11 Queen Eleanor and the ladies of her Court came to visit her brother. The sixteen galleys which served as her escort were met by the Imperial fleet under Andrea Doria, and together they sailed to Villefranche, where the Duque de Nájera, the Conde de Benavente, and the Archbishop of Santiago came out in a small boat to receive the visitors. The Emperor had had a long wooden pier built, so that they might land directly from the galleys, and he was waiting at the end of the pier as they came close to shore. As the queen and her ladies stepped onto the pier, the Emperor embraced and kissed each one. There was such a crowd of people trying to get a glimpse of the Queen that all of a sudden the pier collapsed and they were all thrown into the water. Fortunately the water was shallow, so that no one was lost, but the Archbishop of Santiago was up to his neck and many of the ladies were wet up to their waist. The Emperor himself was thrown in, but he caught the Queen and led her ashore; in the excitement he lost his cap! A French observer remarked: "There you would have seen the gentlemen who most desired to serve the ladies throwing themselves into the sea, lifting them in their arms and carrying them ashore." [56]

Led by the Emperor and Queen Eleanor the whole company repaired to the Emperor's lodging, where those that were drenched changed into dry clothes. Some of the gentlemen sent their servants to fetch dry underdrawers for the ladies. After all the excitement and confusion they settled down to enjoy the party; there was much to talk about that afternoon. The Emperor and his sister had supper with the Cardinal of Lorraine and Montmorency, and afterwards some of the ladies and gentlemen went off to Cobos' lodging, where there was a supper, dancing, music, and games; others were invited to the lodging of the Duke of Mantua.

Among the ladies who went to Cobos' house was Mme. d'Estampes, the King's mistress. Pedro de Gante, in his account of the party, described her as well-built and pretty, and he was impressed by the fact that her breasts were uncovered, like those of the other French ladies. Demurely he added: "They are by no means as modest as our women and they wear no make-up." Another contemporary tells the story that the Queen confessed to her brother that she was humiliated by her husband's open attentions to Mme. d'Estampes and begged him to pay court to her, so that all might see. Whereupon the Emperor got up and kissed her, saying many sweet things to her, such as: that he wished that he might become the object of her affections and that he meant to surpass even King Francis in his devotion. It was late that night before all the festivities were over. At last the Emperor accompanied the ladies back to the pier. As the Queen embarked in her boat, there was sorrow on her face.

During the following days the four negotiators continued to meet with the Pope. Several times the conference was on the point of breaking up, but Paul insisted on their trying to find a compromise. In despair at their inability to reach a solution, both sides finally placed the matter in the Pope's hands. At their last meeting on June 17 he proposed a ten years truce, which was accepted by both parties. It was late at night when all was settled, and the Pope, who was an old man, was thoroughly exhausted, but even so, he said that he rejoiced more at this truce than he had on the day of his election to the Papacy.[57] It could have brought little comfort to the four men who had so long been striving to find a road to lasting peace. And it left the Emperor still unsatisfied in his desire for a meeting with the King.

The Emperor approved the truce on June 18. Three days later, at Villeneuve, Francis signed the agreement.[58] The Venetian ambassadors reported that before he left for France he sent Cobos and Granvelle gifts of the value of 12,000 ducats.[59] On the twentieth the fleet bearing the Emperor and the Pope sailed for Genoa, where they continued their discussion of the Council and the League against the Turk for several days. Andrea Doria and his fleet took the Pope to a harbor near Leghorn, and on his return the Emperor and his suite embarked for Spain on July 4. Of Cobos' activities during these days we know only that he was so busy that he did not even have time to discuss with the banker Tomás de Forne an offer to purchase his pension of 1,500 *scudi* in the duchy of Milan.[60]

Aigues-Mortes

When Queen Eleanor had a final talk with her brother at Villefranche on June 19, she had urged him once more to have a personal meeting with her husband. In Genoa the Emperor received a message from her in which she reminded him of her desire, and at the same time came a definite invitation from the King. Charles thereupon agreed that he would meet with Francis off Marseilles, and he left Genoa on the appointed day. On July 8, while they were at anchor off the island of Santa Margarita, a French galley came out bringing the ambassador M. de Velly with the news that the King had not been able to stay at Marseilles because of his health, but that he would like to meet with the Emperor at Aigues-Mortes, a port a little way to the west of Marseilles. To this the Emperor assented, and he reached the island of Pomègues off Marseilles on July 13; there a French delegation came out to his galley, offering him the keys of the city.

The fleet sailed that night. The next day dawned with a thick
fog and navigation was almost impossible. The Emperor's galley
ran ashore on a shoal and was rammed in the stern by another
ship, wrecking the rudder. But at noon the fog lifted, and by mid-
afternoon they were off Aigues-Mortes.[61] The fleet had hardly
anchored when the Grand Constable with a group of courtiers
came out in a small boat to welcome the Emperor and tell him
that the King was awaiting his arrival. As soon as he left the
Emperor sent the Duque de Alba, Cobos, and Granvelle
to return the visit and suggest to the King that if he would come
out in a galley, they could talk together from ship to ship. But
just as the three messengers were approaching the town on the
little river that joined it with the sea, they met the King, with
his two sons and a goodly company, coming down the river in
six gaily decorated barges. There was time only for a brief
word of salutation from boat to boat as the King continued on
his way without stopping.

The Emperor was taken by surprise as the French boats drew
aside his galley, but he stood at the top of the ladder and gave
Francis a hearty embrace as he stepped onto the deck. Hand in
hand they walked to the poop, and there, being presently joined
by Cobos and Granvelle and by the Cardinal and Montmorency,
they all talked together for nearly two hours. As Francis was
about to leave for the shore he urged the Emperor to visit him in
Aigues-Mortes on the next day; he even took him by the arm
and said to the Cardinal: "Let's take him with us!" It was getting dark when they left.

After this display of friendliness and good will on the part of
Francis, it is puzzling that the Emperor hesitated to accept the
invitation. Perhaps he was still thinking of the long captivity of
Francis and feared that the King might retaliate. But after talking to the Duque de Alba and his counsellors and finding that
they were all agreed that he could not let the French King outdo
him in confidence and courtesy, he decided to go ashore the next
day. Early the next morning, Salazar, one of Cobos' aides, went
from ship to ship in a small boat with instructions that his chief
courtiers should be ready to go ashore with not more than four
attendants at the given signal and that no one else should leave
the ships. At ten o'clock the fleet of small boats started for the
town. As the Emperor disembarked, he was greeted by the King
and Queen and their sons and was taken to his lodging close to

the King's. There was a great banquet at noon in a hall hung with mauve velvet and satin, spangled with gold fleurs-de-lis; this was the sort of splendor that Charles had hoped to provide for the meeting at Perpignan.

When the meal was over, the Emperor retired to the house of Archambaud de la Rivoire to rest. Before long the Queen, Granvelle, and Cobos arrived and shortly thereafter came the King with a few courtiers. He presented the Emperor with a diamond ring, worth 30,000 *écus,* inscribed "Dilectionis testis et exemplum." Charles, having nothing to give him in return, took off his collar of the Order of the Golden Fleece and hung it around the King's neck. The latter gallantly returned the compliment by placing his own collar of St. Andrew on the Emperor. After wine had been served, all the company departed except the Emperor, the King and Queen, and the four negotiators, who by now must have felt like old friends. After an hour's talk they called for more wine and all went off together for supper. But first the Emperor dispatched a messenger to Doria to tell him that he had decided to stay in Aigues-Mortes that night and would return to the galley on the morrow.

After supper there was a dance, which Charles left early in the evening to retire to his apartment. A little later he was joined by the King and they had a long private talk. As Francis left for his own quarters, he saw the four negotiators sitting in an adjoining room and still talking business. "I will not allow such conversations"—he said to them—"as long as the Emperor is under my roof, no other business should be done save that of attending to his pleasure and comfort. There will be plenty of time hereafter to discuss such subjects." The only record of what he and the Emperor talked about is found in the latter's letters to the Empress and to his ambassadors. It is a strange picture, for it is clear that they talked only in general terms, carefully avoiding all the critical issues which had so long prevented peace. The main theme had been that henceforth they would be brothers; nothing would come between them.

One topic that had long been on the Emperor's mind certainly did come up for discussion: his proposal for a new Crusade against the Turks that would involve an attack on Constantinople. It is said that Francis promised to contribute thirty well-equipped galleys for the proposed expedition and to take part in person, if the Emperor should decide to go. It was even reported that the Dauphin and his brother had an argument as to which of them might take part in case their father could not go in person. The Emperor himself refers to it guardedly in a letter to his wife: "It was agreed to proceed with a numerous and highly efficient force, not only to the defense of Christendom and the repulsion of the Turk, but likewise to offend and attack him in his own territory, if deemed necessary or convenient." Perhaps this was the secret plan which he would not reveal to his counsellors or to his wife in January. But for the rest there was no decision; all matters of detail were left to the now familiar negotiators. They did not meet again.

After dinner on the sixteenth Charles returned to his galley, accompanied by Francis, his two sons, and several gentlemen. They all had supper together, served on the poop deck. Perhaps this was the occasion when the Emperor said to the Dauphin: "For God's sake, let not you and my son Philip be such fools as your father and I have been." Supper over and the last courtesies and embraces exchanged, Francis and his suite left for the town. That very night the Spanish fleet weighed anchor and started for Barcelona. But a sudden storm came up with such heavy seas that they were forced to turn back to Aigues-Mortes, where Queen Eleanor came out on Wednesday for a last visit with her brother. On the eighteenth they set sail again and reached Barcelona two days later. The Emperor spent a week there before he left to join the Empress in Valladolid.

His Daughter's Betrothal

Although there is no specific evidence, we may assume that Cobos returned to Valladolid with the Court. On August 9 the Consejo de las Indias approved a number of extensions to the privileges he already held in the New World,[62] and on the same day the Empress signed an order, granting him a profit on exchange amounting to 34,851.5 *maravedís*.[63] Cobos was always ready to accept the most trifling gratification! We know from letters of Juan Vázquez that he was away from Court at the end of September and early October, when he visited Simancas, Velliza, and Escalona.[64] We have already mentioned his interest in securing the post as *teniente* of the fortress of Simancas. This may have been his first visit to Velliza since he purchased the town from the Conde de Luna on April 1, 1535, for 3,262,500 *maravedís*, completing a deal which had originally been made on September 13, 1532.[65] Cobos never showed great interest in this property, although he continued to hold it throughout his lifetime. Agapito y Revilla, however, has suggested that a *custodia* still preserved in the church of Velliza may have been a gift from Cobos.[66] The visit to Escalona was possibly for the purpose of negotiating an agreement with the Duque concerning their conflicting claims to certain mine rights in Cartagena. At least we know that in the following year he transferred his half of the rights to the Duque in return for a *juro* of 140,000 *maravedís* a year.[67]

As soon as he arrived in Spain, the Emperor had begun to plan for raising the necessary funds to carry out his projected attack on the Turk. As a first step, Cobos was instructed to prepare budget estimates for the next four years. The result was a distressing picture: the projected income was inadequate to provide even the ordinary expenses of the kingdom. The Crown was already in debt, on loans, to the extent of 1,120,000 ducats; the estimated deficit for 1539, not including interest on outstanding loans, was 865,000 ducats.[68] Faced with the realization that there were no new sources of income, the Emperor decided to appeal to his Spanish subjects to rescue him by accepting the imposition of another tax, the *sisa* (a general sales tax).

On September 6 he sent out the summons for another Cortes in Toledo. And this time, for the first time, the call went to all three "Estates" of the realm—the nobles, the clergy, and the municipal representatives.[69] The Cardinal Tavera presided at the meeting of the *procuradores* and Cobos was one of the *asistentes*. But the chief interest of the Cortes lay, not in the assembly of the townsmen, but in the stormy session of the nobles. The story of the Emperor's futile attempt to impose the *sisa* on the nobles has been so often told that the details need not be repeated here.[70] But we should comment briefly on the part that Cobos played in the proceedings.

When the nobles met for the first time on November 1, in the presence of the Emperor, at the house of Diego Hurtado de Mendoza, Conde de Melito, it was Juan Vázquez de Molina who read the address from the throne, setting forth the desperate state of the finances and calling on the nobles for aid in this dire need. As soon as he finished, several of the nobles stood up and said: "We kiss His Majesty's hands." But Cobos interrupted: "Listen, gentlemen; His Majesty wishes to speak." Very briefly the Emperor urged them to act quickly and to say no words that would jeopardize a satisfactory outcome. He gave no hint as to what steps they should take.

The next day they met again at the chapel of San Juan de los Reyes. The first tasks were to establish rules of procedure, methods of electing committees and approval of credentials. There was some question as to the right of Don Luis de la Cerda to take part, since he held no landed property in Castile. At this point Cobos appeared with a message from the Emperor, asking them to admit Don Luis, as a personal favor to the Emperor. To this they acceded, though Don Luis never availed himself of the privilege. Their first official action was to expel the Secretary of the Consejo Real, Gáspar Ramírez de Vargas, from the proceedings; only nobles could take part.

In the next few days there was general discussion of the problem of providing the help the Emperor had requested and one of their first decisions was to ask him to grant them permission to consult with the *procuradores* of the towns in the effort to find a common solution. This the Emperor refused; he could not risk a coalition of the nobles and the commoners. And now he informed the spokesmen of the nobles that he had decided that the only way out of the difficulty was the imposition of a general sales tax *(la sisa),* applicable to all citizens, including the nobles. Several times before he had suggested this measure, but each time he had been dissuaded by the strong opposition of the Consejo. This time he was determined to put the issue to test. On November 6 the nobles elected a committee of twelve to study the proposal and report to the entire assembly.

The committee again asked for permission to consult with the *procuradores* and again were refused. And so the days went by in futile debate. On November 25, the Emperor sent the Cardinal Tavera, Cobos, García de Padilla, and Dr. Guevara and the Licenciado Girón of the Royal Council to urge them to take prompt action, renewing his request for approval of the *sisa.* But the nobles showed no signs of yielding.

At this point in the deliberations there was, for Cobos, a momentous interruption: on November 30 his daughter, María Sarmiento, was betrothed to the young Duque de Sesa, Gonzalo Hernández de Córdoba, grandson of the Gran Capitán,[71] whose duchy was considered the richest in Spain. Martín de Salinas, always informed of events at Court, had written to

Castillejo several days before that he understood that Pedro de Córdoba, the Duke's uncle, had arranged the match and would get as a reward the appointment as *contador mayor de rentas.* And with regard to Cobos' power, he added: "This gentleman seems to have the power of St. Peter: he absolves those that he wants to absolve, and to the rest: 'Ite, maledicti!' " [72]

Salinas and Santa Cruz have given us the most detailed accounts of the festivities of the betrothal.[73] The actual ceremony took place in the Royal Palace, and since Toledo was crowded with all the nobility who were attending the Cortes, there was such a crush of people who were anxious to see the show that the Emperor had to rise from his chair and order the crowd back. It was the Cardinal Tavera who pronounced the blessing. That night there was a great throng who came to Cobos' house to pay their respects, in spite of the mud in the streets. "Anyone who failed to turn up"—Salinas commented—"was considered hopeless, except me, who do not belong to this world." The next day, a Sunday, the Emperor and all the Court came to watch a tournament in the square, which Salinas said was dedicated to the bride, although they had been planning it for a long time. On Sunday night all the grandees went to supper at Cobos' house.

As part of the celebration, the nobles decided to hold a bullfight and a *juego de cañas* in honor of the Duke, and even more, in honor of his father-in-law.[73a] Since there were so many gentlemen who wanted to take part and the *plaza* was so small, they had an arena with stands for the spectators built outside the city in the Vega of San Bartolomé, and there they celebrated their contests. Juan Vázquez de Molina took part—Salinas says—on two accounts: because he was a kinsman of the bride and also because he was Secretary of the Council of War.[74] But the betrothal did not end the story.

When the assembly of nobles reconvened on December 3, Cobos appeared with a message from the Emperor authorizing the committee to consult with the financial experts: Juan de Vozmediano, Alonso de Baeza, Cristóbal Suárez, and Sancho de Paz. Before the end of the month the nobles elected a new committee of ten to seek alternatives to the *sisa.* This time the Duque de Alba was not included. On January 6, 1539, the Condestable de Castilla visited the Cardinal and the Duque de Alburquerque visited Cobos, in behalf of the committee, urging them once more to use their influence to persuade the Emperor to permit a joint conference with the representatives of the towns. Once more they were unsuccessful.

By now it was clear that a large majority of the nobles, led by the Condestable de Castilla, was unalterably opposed to the *sisa,* and the Emperor had not softened their resistance when he told them arrogantly that he had not summoned them to give him advice but only to receive their approval of the *sisa.* There was, however, a minority of younger men, led by the Duque de Alba and the Duque del Infantado, who were ready to find a compromise that would be acceptable to the Emperor. And now there occurred an episode that was intimately related to the deliberation of the nobles.[74a]

They had decided to hold another tournament in the arena in the Vega de San Bartolomé, which had been built for the celebration of the betrothal of María Sarmiento and the Duque de Sesa. On Sunday, January 12, a great crowd gathered to see the spectacle, though this time only fifty knights were taking part. The Duque del Infantado and his retainers arrived just as the police were pushing the crowd back to clear the field. A mounted alguazil, swinging his staff, struck the horse of the Duque, making him rear. Thereupon the Duke roared at him: "Do you know who I am?" The policeman replied: "I know very well who you are. You are the Duque del Infantado." At that the Duque drew his sword and slashed the bailiff on the head. The poor policeman, thinking that he was done for anyhow, also drew his sword and struck the Duke's horse.

The Emperor had always been intolerant of quarrels in his presence, and when the officer came up, dripping with blood, to protest, the Emperor was doubly outraged at the offense to one of his officers and at once ordered the Alcalde de Corte, Ronquillo, to place the Duque under arrest. By this time a great crowd had rushed to the scene, and when Ronquillo rode up to carry out his orders, the Condestable de Castilla and the Duque de Alba pushed him aside, saying that this was their responsibility. And so, accompanied by all the nobles, they escorted the Duque to his lodging. The Cardinal and Cobos were the only persons left standing beside the Emperor. The next morning, when the assembly was supposed to meet again, not one of the nobles appeared. When the Emperor asked: "Where are the *grandes?*" he was told that they were with the Duque del Infantado and would not return without him.

The situation was embarrassing, for the Emperor could not afford to alienate one of the small group that was supporting him. And so, on the following day he pardoned the Duque. When the latter came to thank him for his clemency, Charles went so far in his retraction as to say: "Is it possible that that knave had the effrontery to strike you? He deserved to be hung on the spot." Thus was justice maintained!

As the meetings of the assembly continued without result, the Emperor finally sent a message that the nobles must vote publicly their stand on the issue. When the message was delivered, one of the nobles, Juan de Saavedra, rose and said that he had just received a note from Cobos: it was an announcement that the congregation of the clergy had voted to approve the *sisa*. But this piece of strategy had no effect. And now at last the committee of ten reported their recommendations to the assembly: the nobles would not approve the *sisa,* as an infringement of their traditional privilege of freedom from taxation; to meet the financial situation they proposed that the Emperor make peace with France, stay in Spain, and cut down his personal spending.

When the vote on the recommendation was taken, two-thirds of the nobles approved; a minority group, consisting of the Duque de Alba, the Duque del Infantado, and seventeen others, dissented and presented a motion that the assembly approve a proposal to impose a tax on the export of merchandise from Spain, but the motion was voted down. Thoroughly disgusted at his failure, the Emperor summoned them anew on February 1. At that time, Tavera, Cobos, and the other counsellors appeared before the assembly and Tavera read a message from the Emperor. "Gentlemen"—it said—"I called Your Lordships together, thinking that, as the needs were common to all the kingdom, so the remedy should be common to all. In view of what has happened, I see no reason for detaining Your Lordships here any longer, but suggest that you go home, or anywhere else you think best."

When Tavera finished reading the message, he turned to Cobos and asked: "Have I forgotten something?" Cobos answered; "No." Thus, curtly, the nobles were dismissed. The Emperor had been able to overcome the resistance of the townsmen by a combination of bribery and coercion; with the nobles he had no such instruments of control. From this experience in Toledo he learned his lesson: he never again attempted to win their approval of his policies. In all this debate, it is hard to believe that Cobos, knowing as he did the almost unanimous objection to the *sisa,* could have approved of the proposal. But in this, as in all things, he had no choice; he was committed to carry out his master's commands.

Two months later, early in April, Cobos left the Court to visit his newly acquired estates of Canena and Torres,[75] and, as we have already seen, it was on this trip that he suspended work on his chapel in Ubeda. The news of the death of the Empress on May 1 probably led him to return at once to the Emperor. Perhaps, on the road, he passed the funeral procession, led by Francisco de Borja, Marqués de Lombay, which was escorting her body to the Royal Chapel in Granada. When the Emperor moved to Madrid in July, Cobos was with him and found lodging in the house of Luis Núñez.[76] During the following months the only news we have of him are the usual sucession of royal favors. As before, he received a special grant of 200,000 *maravedís* as a reward for his services at the Cortes.[77] On July 1 he was appointed Secretary of the young prince Philip, now twelve years old, which added another 100,000 *maravedís* a year to his salary.[78] The most important appointment that came to him was that of *Contador mayor.*[79] As we have already remarked, he had been receiving an annual salary of 1,500 ducats a year for his services as an interim appointment; the actual income from the post, in salary and perquisites, was approximately equal to this amount. By now, his income from salaries alone amounted to 1,150,000 *maravedís* a year.[80]

On the same day that he received the appointment as *contador* (November 1, 1539), Cobos entered into an agreement with the Emperor that was ultimately to have an important effect on his family's income. The assignment by the Cardinal Tavera of the *adelantamiento* of Cazorla to Cobos and his son, in perpetuity, had been confirmed both by the Pope and the Emperor. In view of this permanent addition to his income, the Emperor now called on Cobos to agree to accept a reduction in his income as *fundidor mayor* of the Indies on the death of the Cardinal. It is clear that Cobos accepted this decision with reluctance. He put his trust in the Emperor's "benignancy, clemency, and virtue"; he hoped that he will exercise his right with moderation, knowing with what good will and fidelity he has served in the past and hopes to serve in the future.[81] It seems that the Emperor had decided that Cobos was carrying too far his plans to provide for the future of his son; if he was to enjoy the perpetual grant of Cazorla, he must yield part of his expectation from the Indies.

It is difficult to find any consistent order or pattern in Cobos' activities in this period. We know, for instance, that he and Granvelle were still discussing the problem of peace with the French ambassador, the Bishop of Tarbes.[82] Matthias Held, whom Charles had sent to Vienna as his agent, told the Papal nuncio, Morone, that both Granvelle and Cobos believed in the sincerity of the French and were anxious to promote peace. Rather maliciously he added: "Perhaps they are motivated by the same reasons as was M. de Chièvres, when he was alive." At the same time Held told Morone that the Emperor had few advisors, and no good ones. "Granvelle"—he explained—"yields to Cobos in everything, because he wants to keep his post and reap the profits." [83]

There were other duties that Cobos was called upon to perform. On August 10, 1539, the Emperor appointed him, the Cardinal Tavera, and Loaisa, President of the Consejo de las Indias, as a commission to revise the ordinances of the Casa de la Contratación in Seville, in order to settle a variety of jurisdictional disputes that had arisen.[84] Late in the year he and Loaisa made a report to the Emperor on another jurisdictional problem: the rights and privileges of the Admiralty of the Indies which should be assigned to the Virreina, María de Toledo, widow of Diego Colón. Their recommendation limited the permanent rights of the office to the ports of Santo Domingo, Puerto Rico, Santiago de Cuba, Jamaica, Nombre de Dios, Veragua, and Cartagena; in other ports, the Almirante should have jurisdiction only when he was in actual residence. By a divided vote, the Consejo de las Indias, which had been asked to review the case, approved the recommendation on April 14, 1540.[85]

CHAPTER X

ELDER STATESMAN

The news that reached Spain from Flanders in the autumn of 1539 was alarming: Ghent was in open revolt; there was danger that the unrest would spread to other towns. At this threat the Emperor determined to return to the Low Countries and set his house in order. At Aigues-Mortes Francis had urged him to pass through France, if he should go again to Flanders. But Charles was hesitant until a new and formal invitation came from the French King. Now that the Empress was dead, he decided to leave the nominal responsibility for the government of Castile with Prince Philip, twelve years old, but he named Tavera and Loaisa as Regents during his absence.[1] Granvelle was sent ahead on November 1 to make the necessary arrangements in France [2] and on the tenth, the Emperor sent letters to his representatives in Italy, telling of his decision, and adding that he was leaving Cobos in Spain for a few days to settle various financial matters.[3] Even before that, Salinas had written to King Ferdinand that Cobos was to remain behind to clear up the question of finances, and he remarked that he might be there for a long time in view of the slight prospect of finding money, especially in large amounts.[4] Salinas' conjecture proved to be well founded; Cobos did not join the Emperor in Flanders. In fact, from this time on he remained in Spain, even when the Emperor was abroad, leaving to Granvelle, Vázquez de Molina, and Idiáquez the provision of secretarial service outside of Spain.

223

By the beginning of December Cobos' friends in Italy had heard of the decision and they all wrote to him to express their satisfaction.[5] The Treasurer Rábago, who was conducting various personal negotiations for Cobos in Rome with regard to the bulls for his chapel and his new estates, wrote on December 5:

> We have learned that you are staying in Spain during the absence of His Majesty. I beg you, as one of your servants, that even though there may be some unpleasantness, you will show the prudence with which you have governed for so many years; and I hope to God that you will govern the whole world, with universal satisfaction, for it seems certain that this change will not prevent the continuing increase of the favor and regard which you enjoy, as your services deserve.[6]

And two days later he wrote again:

> People here are saying that although the title [of Regent] is in the Cardinal, everything will remain, as always, in your hands. God knows how glad I am![7]

Luis de Avila reached Rome on a special mission just at this time, and his letters to Cobos, in spite of their mocking tone, reveal a real affection for him. Thus, in reporting he had heard that Cobos was not going to Flanders, he said: "To think that I shall not find you in Flanders and that after I have reached there, it will be long before you come, has taken from me half the spurs that made me want to hasten my arrival."[8] A few days later he wrote: "Don't think that I am joking when I say that everything I see makes me wish that you were here, till it is almost a sickness. And that is true of all of us who know that our 'Boss of Leon' is a *bonissimo compaño,* when he wants to be."[9]

In the weeks following the Emperor's departure Cobos was desperately trying to raise money for the necessary expenditures. The only immediately available source was new loans from the Genoese bankers. It is noteworthy that one of the loans which he negotiated was payable in Flanders, which is evidence that Spain was now being called upon to support the Emperor's expenses there. The only possible security that he could offer was the gold and silver that had come or was expected from Peru. But this was inadequate to cover all that was due. As a last resort Cobos asked the Emperor to approve of using part of the treasure at once, to appease the bankers and not jeopardize their future credit.[10]

In the letter which Cobos dispatched to the Emperor on No-

vember 25, detailing the financial problems, he reported that he
had not been able to consult with Tavera and Loaisa with regard
to the best residence for the Infantas, because he had been suffering from a cold and fever which had prevented him from
leaving his house.[11] He must also have informed his friends of
his indisposition, for on January 28, 1540, Francisco de Borja
wrote to him that he was glad to hear he was feeling better.[12]
This is the first mention of any ill health since the brief attack
of dysentery at Palermo in 1535. In a way, it marks an important change in his life, for from this time on he was increasingly troubled by a variety of ailments. It must have been at
about this time that there arrived in Spain a man who pretended
to possess a number of medical secrets.

The Maestre de Roa

On his return to Spain in 1538, the Emperor had notified his
viceroys of the successful conclusion of his peace talks with the
French. One of these messages, sent on August 23, was directed
to Antonio de Mendoza, Viceroy of New Spain.[13] The news of
peace was received with great rejoicing in Mexico and was celebrated with an elaborate *fiesta*. One of the men who took an
active part in the celebration was a misshapen dwarf with a large
goiter, called the Maestre de Roa, whom Hernán Cortés had
brought from Spain to see if he could cure an arm which he had
broken in a fall from a horse. After the *fiesta* was over, the
Maestre started back to Castile where he met María de Mendoza, Cobos' wife, and promised to give her potions which
would enable her to bear a child. Doña María agreed that if he
was successful she would give him 2,000 ducats and would use
her influence with the Consejo de las Indias to secure him grants
in Mexico.[14] Evidently both Don Francisco and Doña María had
been troubled by their failure to have any more children after
the son and daughter born in the first years of their marriage.
Early in 1540, Lope Hurtado de Mendoza wrote to Cobos from
Rome: "I have been thinking about the wretched life you lead
and how you never have time for anything. You must find time
to beget a son and don't think that the fault lies with My Lady;
the fault is yours. Just recently the wife of the Pope's physician,
who hadn't had a child for eleven years and was almost forty,

became pregnant. I'm glad to send you this good news amid all the bad news I send from here. Tell Doña María." [15]

Our friend from Mexico also persuaded the President of the Consejo de las Indias, Loaisa, that he could cure him of his gout, and managed to extract from him the grant of a number of Indians in Mexico. And he offered to cure Cobos of some other ailment.[16] But alas! The hot potions of sarsaparilla that he gave to Doña María were ineffectual; the Cardinal of Sigüenza did not recover from his gout nor Cobos from his ailment. But the charlatan returned to Mexico with richer rewards than the real *conquistadores* had won with their true services!

Early in 1540 the Moors made a raid on Gibraltar, and although they quickly withdrew with a few prisoners, there was almost a wave of panic in Andalusia at the prospect of new attacks. Cobos was one of those who were moved to take steps for defense, and on April 23 he wrote to Juan de Luna, chatelain of the fortress of Florence, that Duke Cosimo had informed him he had founded certain pieces of artillery for a fortress which Cobos was strengthening, presumably Sabiote. Would Luna make arrangements, without publicity, to have the cannon shipped to Genoa, in care of the ambassador, Figueroa, who would send them to Spain? [17] For a boy whose father had fought in the war in Granada, the Moors were still a very real threat.

A few weeks later the anniversary of the death of the Empress was celebrated by a solemn ceremony in the church of San Juan de los Reyes which was attended by all the dignitaries of the Court, led by Prince Philip. The church was draped in mourning and a catafalque with a crown upon it was erected in the center of the high chapel. Cobos was one of those who sat on the Gospel side of the high altar, along with the Cardinal Tavera, the Duque de Escalona, the Conde de Osorno, Don Juan de Zúñiga, Comendador Mayor of Castile, and other noblemen.[18]

Amid all these public activities Cobos still found time to think about his personal affairs. And now, in spite of his earlier decision to hold up further work on his chapel in Ubeda, he made up his mind to go ahead again. On May 20, 1540, Hernando Ortega, his chaplain in Ubeda, and Luis de Vega, as expert, signed a new contract to complete the chapel, but this time the *canteros* were Domingo de Tolosa, of Jaén, and Florentino Gerantón, of Porcuna, who undertook to complete the structure for 8,900 ducats, plus an advance payment of 100 ducats. However, the original architects, Alonso Ruiz and Andrés de Vandelvira, now appeared and protested that they had already done a considerable amount of work and had ordered the stone for the chapel. As a result, on June 12 Cobos' agents entered into a new contract with them to complete the chapel for the sum of 8,781 ducats. There were a number of new provisions: the main entrance was to be similar to the Puerta del Perdón, which had recently been built in the Cathedral of Granada, but at no additional cost; there were to be doors on the sides, a sacristy, balconies with balustrades, paving in all the chapels, as well as in the church. Furthermore, they undertook to provide the coats of arms, both outside and inside the church, and to make such other additions and changes in the original plans as Ortega should provide.[19]

All this time Cobos had been urging his agent in Rome to secure the Pope's formal approval of the foundation of the chapel. On December 13, 1540, he wrote to Francisco de Valenzuela to acknowledge the receipt of a special indulgence for the church of Cazorla and to protest again at the Pope's delay, pointing out that the construction of the chapel involved a total expenditure of more than 20,000 ducats, a large part of which had already been spent.[20] But in spite of the constant efforts of his agents in Rome, the Papal *breve* was not signed until February 10, 1542.[21]

Local News

At the end of June, 1540, an old friend of Cobos and his wife, Don Alonso Enríquez de Guzmán, turned up in Madrid. Don Alonso, who had been in Peru for almost six years, came back, summoned by the Emperor, with serious charges against him of having been responsible for the bitter struggle between Diego de Almagro and Hernando Pizarro. Immediately on his arrival in Madrid, he was placed under house arrest by the President of the Consejo de las Indias. But Don Alonso tells us that as soon as his protectress, Doña María de Mendoza, heard of his plight, she sent him a messenger with six trout in two silver plates and a cake and a note which said: "My Lady sends this to you and says for you not to be troubled, for no evil will befall you, as long as she is alive; and that tomorow she will put on her cloak and go to the members of the Consejo, and if her plea does not avail, the next day she will put a rope around her neck and go and demand justice." The latter was not necessary, for the next day the Consejo authorized Don Alonso's transfer to a house which had been the lodging of her majordomo, Romain, and which she now turned over to Don Alonso. There she sent him food and presents. And Cobos himself came, which excited considerable comment in the Court, because he was not accustomed to visit anyone, in his almost royal function as regent.[22]

One night that summer, while Don Alonso was still awaiting trial, there was great excitement in Madrid when a fire broke out in the house of Diego de Vargas in the Plazuela de la Paja, where Loaisa, the President of the Consejo de las Indias, was staying. It spread so rapidly that it cut off escape from the upper rooms and the Cardinal, who was still suffering from gout, had to be carried up to a terrace and from there lowered to the ground. The air was filled with smoke and cinders and a great crowd gathered. Among those who hurried to the scene was Cobos, and he took Loaisa to his house, where Prince Philip and the Cardinal Tavera came to visit him. Eventually Cobos found lodging for him in the house of Luis Núñez, which he had formerly occupied.[23]

From the time that the Emperor had left Spain in November, 1539, Cobos carried on a voluminous correspondence with him, Granvelle, Idiáquez, and the Imperial ambassadors all over Europe. These letters provide a cross-section of European affairs and above all, of the issues which involved Spain. Naturally financial matters held an important place, and it is amusing to find Cobos protesting at the Emperor's purchase of jewels worth 30,500 ducats in France, when he had not yet paid for the jewels he bought as gifts in Rome and in Nice.[24] It was difficult to balance the budget, when Charles had the power at any moment to spend anything he saw fit without asking how it was to be paid for. There were problems, too, with regard to the Indies, and Cobos discussed the question of sending a new governor to straighten out the conflict in Peru.[25] At the Court there was a petty quarrel between the Cardinal Tavera and Valdés, the President of the Consejo de Castilla, over their respective powers, where Cobos was called on to act as peace-maker.[26] And always there were the vacancies to be filled and appointments made, each one of which had to receive the formal approval of the Emperor and his signature on the proper *cédula*.

As was always the case, Cobos was busy trying to raise new funds for the Emperor. Once more he had recourse to a measure which had been used with some success before: that of borrowing money from the *grandes*. Cobos prepared a memorial, listing all the persons who were to be asked to make a loan; the richest were put down for 10,000 ducats, the rest for 5,000 ducats each. Cobos' name was included among the latter, but a marginal note recorded that he had offered 10,000 ducats.[27] Actually he paid the Treasurer Baeza 10,000 ducats on June 17, 1541 and another 5,000 on June 21. Not until May 8, 1545 did he receive from Philip, then Regent, a *juro* of 375,000 *maravedís* (1,000 ducats) a year in payment of the loan.[28]

This was not his only investment in payments to the Emperor. When he had purchased the fortresses of Sabiote, Canena, and Torres, the *alcabalas* which the towns paid each year had been expressly reserved. These he now proceeded to buy. On April 22, 1540, he paid the Royal Treasurer 44,240 ducats for the *alcabalas* of Sabiote and on December 22 he paid an additional 21,000 ducats for those of Canena and Torres.[29] Since most of his investments in royal *juros* were at the rate of 7 per cent interest, we may assume that Cobos expected to derive at least that much from these new investments; at that rate, they would have added another 1,700,000 *maravedís* to his annual income. It should be aded that with these new payments his total investment in these three properties amounted to more than 172,000 ducats, the equivalent of more than $3,000,000 in present values. And still the money continued to flow into his coffers. *In absentia,* King Francis gave him another 4,000 ducats in silver at the time when he was handing out a largess to the members of the Emperor's company.[30] Nor did he scorn such modest contributions as a grant of 300 ducats, which had originally been assessed as a fine against his brother-in-law, Alonso Luis de Lugo.[31]

Margarita de Parma

One of the most interesting problems in which Cobos was involved in this period was the marriage of the Emperor's natural daughter, Margaret, to Ottavio Farnese, grandson of Pope Paul III. Her marriage to Alessandro de' Medici in February, 1536, was ended less than a year later by the assassination of her husband; at fifteen she was a childless widow. Her father at first thought of marrying her to the new Duke of Florence, Cosimo de' Medici, but he soon decided that politically and financially it was wiser to accede to the Pope's urgent request and marry her to the young Ottavio, then thirteen years old. As her chief chamberlain and her lady-in-waiting he appointed Lope Hurtado de Mendoza, who had been ambassador in Portugal, and his wife, Margarita de Rojas, until such time as the marriage was completed.

The Duchess proved to have a mind of her own and at first refused to go ahead with the proposal, even revoking a power of attorney which she had granted to the Marqués de Aguilar, authorizing him to act in her behalf.[32] She did, however, move from Prato to Rome, accompanied by Lope Hurtado and his wife, and was received with great honor by the Pope and his family. Although a marriage agreement was signed early in 1539, Margarita refused to cohabit with Ottavio, alleging that he was a mere child, incapable of acting as a husband, and— what was worse—that he was a bed-wetter. There can be no doubt that Hurtado and his wife supported her in her refusal, thereby bringing down on their heads the violent hostility of the Pope and the Imperial ambassadors in Rome. In one of his many letters to Cobos with regard to the situation he makes the wry comment: "What did you think of the portrait I sent? Andalot and I think that he made Madama look small and Ottavio look big. Would to God that were true!"[33]

All sorts of charges were leveled at Hurtado and his wife; a certain friar even accused them of having bewitched the Duchess, though he later withdrew the charge. Cobos, who had long been a friend of Hurtado, was greatly troubled at these events and supported him warmly against the charges brought against him. While he was willing to approve of transferring him to another post, he urged the Emperor to make it clear that he had not failed in any respect to perform the proper duties of his assignment. In particular, he backed Hurtado's suggestion that Ottavio should be sent to the Emperor's Court, in order that he might have time to grow up, and he wrote to Poggio, objecting to the Pope's refusal to send his grandson to the Emperor.[34] In fact, his influence was so great that Andalot, whom the Emperor had sent to straighten out the affair, wrote that no one dared to speak ill of Hurtado for fear of offending Cobos.[35]

Further evidence of his influence is found in a letter of the Marqués de Aguilar in which he reported that Giovanni di Montepulciano had told the Pope that the failure to settle the case of Hurtado to his satisfaction was due to Cobos' intervention. When His Holiness heard that, he exclaimed: "Is it possible?" And then he frowned and beat his brow and said: "I dare say it is. I have no doubt that the person who is making war on me is the Grand Commander of Leon." Montepulciano explained that nothing was done at the Imperial Court without Cobos' advice, especially in matters relating to Rome. And he went on to say that even Luis de Avila had lost favor with Cobos, because he had made an unfavorable report on Hurtado.[36] Cobos must have heard of the Pope's remarks, for he wrote to the Nuncio Poggio in Ghent that the charge had no foundation.[37] And a little later he asked the Cardinal Farnese to use his influence to keep him in the favor of the Pope, since he had no more devoted servant than Cobos in Spain.[38]

The long debate was finally settled in October, 1540. On the thirty-first of the month Aguilar wrote to Cobos that Margarita had at last relented and that the marriage had been consummated. All that was needed now to make the Pope completely happy was the news that she was pregnant.[39] Hurtado was assigned to another post.

The Marriage of His Daughter

The marriage of Margarita and Ottavio was not the only one that raised difficulties. Although María Sarmiento and the young Duque de Sesa had been betrothed at the end of 1538, a number of problems remained unsettled. On March 4, 1539, the Duke was authorized by the Emperor to pledge one of his estates, the town of Doña Mencía, as security for the payment of his dower to the bride.[40] When Cobos and his wife had modified the terms of their *mayorazgo* in 1535, they had provided that they might assign 4,000,000 *maravedís* to their daughter as a dowry—the amount that Cobos had demanded of the Condes de Rivadavia at the time of his marriage. But the Duke's uncles, Pedro de Córdoba, Alvaro de Córdoba, and Juan de Córdoba, who had engineered the marriage, were driving a hard bargain. And so, on March 10, 1540, Cobos and his wife received permission from the Emperor to increase the dowry to 10,000,000 *maravedís,* with the provision that his daughter thereby renounce all other claims to her inheritance. At the same time the Emperor gave her 1,000,000 *maravedís,* in the form of a *juro* of 125,000 *maravedís* a year for life, in special recognition of the services which her father had rendered and was rendering.[41]

Cobos' acceptance of the terms makes it clear that, in spite of his statement he was not interested in titles, the marriage of his daughter to one of the grandees of Spain meant a great deal to him. And this is borne out by the many letters he wrote to announce the forthcoming marriage—to Granvelle and to all of his friends in Italy.[42] But another more serious difficulty had arisen. The young Duke had been betrothed to another girl, and it was in part to break up this marriage that his uncles had intervened. At the command of the Emperor the boy had yielded, but he was still resentful and showed no desire to make a success of his marriage. In fact, he was so critical of Cobos and his wife that they wished that they had never undertaken the match. But the deal had been made and it was necessary to go through with the arrangements.[43]

Cobos wrote to Juan Vázquez, then in Flanders with the Emperor, on January 27, 1541, that the Duke had reached Madrid, in conformity with the agreement, and that his aunt, Doña Felipa, the wife of Pedro de Córdoba, had also been duly received. Within a week or ten days the wedding would take place and then they would see what could be done to remedy all the damage there had been and still was: "God help us in this business!" He went on to discuss further details. But let him say it in his own words:

These people (the Duke's family) are so full of airs and vanity that they wanted the Prince to be the *padrino* at the wedding and that has been arranged. And because in such cases the Prince or His Majesty or the Catholic King have never come to the bride's house, because the ceremony has taken place in the Palace, when there was an Empress or Queen, it has been decided to hold the ceremony in the church, because His Highness can go there. I think that the Condesa de Palamós, mother of Doña Estefanía, will be the *madrina,* since she is a lady-in-waiting, and His Highness will go back to the Palace to dine. After dinner there will be a *fiesta.* I assure you that none of this pleases me because of the way things are going and because His Majesty is absent, without whom nothing is wholly satisfying . . . Doña María and I are doing everything we can to make it a success for the sake of the Duchess, who is so lovely and who knows so well what she must do . . .

The Duque de Nájera is in town on business and he will stay for the wedding. I think the Duque del Infantado will come and the Duque de Alba and perhaps the Marqués de Villena. The Almirante of Naples is staying with us. God knows how anxious I am to have this business finished and be free from all these ceremonies.[44]

Even so, he could not help being flattered at the idea of all these great lords doing him honor, and in his letters to the Marqués de Aguilar in Rome and to Pedro de Toledo in Naples he did not fail to mention the names of some of the expected guests.[45]

The wedding on Sunday, February 6, was a gala event.[46] Cobos was living at the time in a house in the Calle Ancha (now the Calle Mayor) next door to the church of Santa María de Almudena and opposite the palace of Juan de Vozmediano (now Los Consejos). The Prince with his attendants came to Cobos' house, and having dismounted in the patio, walked with the company to the church, which was richly decorated with silk, brocade, and cloth of gold. The ceremony was performed by Juan de Córdoba, Dean of the Cathedral of Granada, the uncle of the groom, before a great congregation. The Cardinal of Toledo was there and six bishops; there were dukes, the young Prince of Ascoli (son of Antonio de Leiva), Hernán Cortés, Marqués del Valle, the grand commanders of the military orders, counts and royal counsellors, not to mention all the fair ladies—in a word: "All Madrid."

As they came out of the church on the way back to Cobos' palace, there was a great salvo of artillery and the air was filled with the sound of wind instruments, trumpets, and drums. The palace was sumptuously decorated with tapestries of silk and gold; brocade canopies hung over the tables, richly arrayed with vessels of gold and silver. The courtiers ate in the great hall on the first floor—one hundred and fifteen sat at the main tables; the rest ate with Cobos in an inner room. Upstairs fifty-five of the ladies sat in the main room; the overflow were with Doña María in another room. It was a memorable banquet.

When the feasting was over the whole company moved outside. Against the wall of the house they had built a sort of grandstand from which they watched the games and jousts in the Calle Ancha. The leaders were Doña María's oldest brother, Diego Sarmiento de Mendoza, and the young Duke's uncle, Gabriel de Córdoba; and among those who took part were Prince Philip, the Duke himself, Cobos' son Diego, and a host of others. The games were followed by a series of pageant-like masques. After this part of the *fiesta* the whole company adjourned to the lodging of the Duke, where there was dancing until suppertime, when they returned to Cobos' house. That night there was music and dancing with more masques, one of them organized by Hernán Cortés. It was after midnight when the revelry was over and the last candle snuffed. Looking back at the celebration the anonymous chronicler of the affair expressed the fear that not all the ladies had obeyed the *pragmática* which set strict limits to the finery they could wear and that the police might confiscate their costumes. But he added: "I suspect that this once they will be pardoned."

With such a throng of courtiers in Madrid, the round of parties went on for weeks, in spite of the fact that it was Lent, and Cobos wrote to Juan Vázquez on March 24 that he was tired out.[47] Troubled as he was at the turn of events, he was at pains to inform all of his friends of the marriage of the Duchess, and letters of congratulation poured in from every quarter— from Francisco de Borja and his wife, Leonor de Castro; from Andrea Doria; from Pedro de Toledo, Viceroy of Naples; from the Imperial ambassadors in Rome, Venice, and other cities. None of them could have given him greater satisfaction than a letter from the Emperor in which he said: "I have been glad to hear of the marriage of the Duchess, as I rightly should for the sake of your peace of mind . . . God grant that you may see its rightful fruits, so that your pleasure may be complete." [48] A little later the Emperor wrote to Philip's chief counsellor, Juan de Zúñiga, approving of his son's participation in the *fiestas* that attended the wedding, though he added slyly: "I have no doubt that the judges who awarded him the prize on the day when he competed in the 'ring game' [*la sortija*], did not judge the matter with the rigor that you describe." [49] Cobos promptly thanked the Emperor for his good wishes, with the pious hope that all would turn out well.[50]

The newly-weds remained in Madrid until early June, when they started for the Duke's estate in Baena, accompanied by Doña María and a group of courtiers. After a few days getting her daughter settled in her new home, Doña María returned to Jaén, where she was royally entertained by the Bishop, Francisco de Mendoza, a distant kinsman, before going on for a brief visit in Ubeda, Sabiote, and Canena. She was back in Madrid on June 29.[51]

Don Alonso Enríquez at Jaén

One of the gentlemen who accompanied the Duchess and her mother on this trip was Don Alonso Enríquez, who after nine months on trial had been released on bail. One night at a banquet at the palace of the Bishop of Jaén, one of the men at the table, a "born fool with a running nose," named Tamayo, made a remark which offended Don Alonso, who promptly picked up a pickled partridge from the table and slapped Tamayo in the face with it. This seems to have annoyed him, for he grabbed a long table knife and plunged it a full span into Don Alonso's chest, so that everyone thought that he was doomed. Doña María was greatly upset and began to cry, as well she might, since this mishap had occurred while he was in her service. "So I went to Her Ladyship"—Don Alonso explained—"honored and comforted by her expression of grief, and I said to her: 'My Lady, although my good will deserves all this display of feeling and though this disaster has happened while I was in your service and company, let it go no farther, for it might be that I would be more concerned with it than with the salvation of my soul, which would not be pleasing to God or to Your Ladyship. The more so, because I do not believe that the wound is as deadly as it seems.' "

The knife was now pulled out and laid on the table, and when no blood came the physicians were sure that it was a mortal wound, and insisted that Don Alonso must make confession, receive the sacrament, and make his will. All this he did, but when it came to the will, no one would believe him when he said that he had only 10,000 ducats, knowing, as they did, that he had just returned from Peru. They begged him not to conceal his possessions, lest he go straight to Hell, but Don Alonso remained obdurate in his statement. And so they sent for Doña María, hoping that she could extract the truth from him. She came into the room and sat down on the bed beside Don Alonso. "Don Alonso," she said, "do you remember how you often asked me what I would do, if you were to die, and how I always replied that I would tear my hair and weep bitterly? And do you remember how you would say 'If I could only live to see that!'? Well, now you do see it." The upshot of the matter was that they did cure Don Alonso, and in four days he was out of danger. Presently there came a letter from Cobos, who had been informed of the mishap:

"Sir"—it began—"if you are dead when this arrives, God forgive us! And I shall have to find consolation in the thought that there was nothing that anyone could have done for you, although the Prince our Lord and the Cardinal of Toledo and everyone else at Court has regretted to hear the news, I not least. And if you are alive, congratulations! And remember that the relapses are always worse than the lapses." [52]

In reality, Cobos was greatly disturbed at what had happened to Don Alonso, and after he learned that he had returned to Seville completely recovered, he wrote to Gutierre López de Padilla how great was his relief, for he could never have forgiven himself if the accident had proved fatal.[53] He even added the information that that man Tamayo had formerly been a servant of the Conde de Osorno.[54]

We know little of Cobos' activities during his wife's absence. With Philip and Blasco Núñez Vela he made a brief visit to Aranjuez.[55] From Rome the Marqués de Aguilar wrote that Granvelle had informed him that during Doña María's visit to Baena, Cobos had enjoyed himself thoroughly. "There's nothing like taking a good time when you can"—he wrote—"for bad times come of themselves." [56] But it is by no means certain that Cobos was in a mood for gaiety. For some time his health had been increasingly bad. As early as April, 1540, he was complaining of a touch of gout.[57] In September he wrote to Idiáquez that he had had a cruel attack of pain in his kidneys and groin, which lasted only a day but left him upset for several more.[58] In April, 1541, shortly after the marriage festivities, he reported that he had had an attack of rheumatism in his arm.[59]

A few days after Doña María's return he wrote to Diego Hurtado de Mendoza in Venice to announce her arrival, with the comment: "She found me with a pain in the groin that had hit me the day before. What a help for the reception!" Mendoza had written to Cobos about his own ailments and now Cobos replied:

I was sorry to hear about your cold in the head and not so sorry to hear about the trouble with your testicle, because I think that you are having that merely to keep me company, for one of mine is still swollen and I've decided to pay no attention to it, for there is nothing that can be done to remedy it . . . God knows how I envy the people that are getting ready to go over to Italy and how I would like to be with you, for here everything is toil and trouble. The Duque de Alba is here as my guest and Enrique de Toledo came with him. We are doing our best to give them a good time, but compared with the life you lead, everything here is full of trouble.[60]

During the summer Cobos' health grew steadily worse. He was still troubled by the ailment in his kidneys and groin; early in August he suffered an attack of dysentery with a severe headache, followed by a siege of tertian fever that kept him in bed for three weeks. He was so exhausted and weak that he was not able to write, even to the Emperor, and he signed the necessary dispatches only with the greatest difficulty.[61] By the beginning of September, after being purged, he was feeling better; Ledesma, one of his assistants, wrote to the Duque de Alba that the fifth attack had passed without serious chills.[62] From Spezzia, where he was about to depart for the expedition against Algiers, the Emperor wrote to Cobos on September 27, expressing his concern at his indisposition, and urging him to keep away from things that troubled him and try to recover his health. At the same time he thanked him for his diligence in having the Spanish fleet sent to the rendezvous in Mallorca.[63] Granvelle, too, wrote to convey his hopes of an early convalescence.[64]

In reality, Cobos had already taken advantage of the absence of his wife on a pilgrimage to Our Lady of Guadalupe to rest from his work at the convent of San Gerónimo, outside of Madrid.[65] On her return from Guadalupe, Doña María also had a brief bout with tertian fever,[66] but by the middle of October Cobos was able to write to Idiáquez that they were both better, although he was still suffering at times from a painful headache, "relics of my illness and my old age." [67]

In the Archivo de Simancas there are the rough drafts of two unaddressed and unsigned letters, dated October 15, which cast a revealing light on his illness. It is probable that they were intended for Juan Vázquez and Idiáquez and that they were both written by Gonzalo Pérez, for one of them contains a Latin quotation and Pérez was the only one of Cobos' associates who knew Latin. The content of the two letters is almost identical. After commenting on the improvement in his health, in spite of a continuing headache, the writer goes on: "The cause of the Grand Commander's illness has undoubtedly been his worries over the marriage of the Duchess that you have heard about. And they are not over yet." [68]

Let us look back for a moment at the conflict between

Cobos and his son-in-law. Not long after Doña María returned to Madrid from Baena at the end of June the Duke also came to Madrid, and Cobos wrote to Juan Vázquez in August:

> He is in every way so changed that you would be surprised. I am sure that if those uncles and aunts of his would only leave him alone, he would not fail in any way to give me satisfaction. Since he is the person that he is and has the wife he has, I have always wanted to serve him and have him well treated and favored; now, more than ever I want to.[69]

But other difficulties arose, and some time in October Cobos wrote again to Vázquez a letter which shows how deeply disturbed and irritated he was at the turn of events. It is at once an explanation of his illness, and his irritation is a reflection of his illness. As an intimate revelation of Cobos' feelings it is almost unique and deserves to be quoted in full:

> I wrote to you how the Duke had come here, apparently corrected of all the past things, showing his eagerness to please me in every way. And as I have no other purpose except what would help to make him forget what has happened, I had persuaded him to go and serve His Majesty on this expedition, thinking that a person of his quality who was my son should take part in it. During the days that he was here, we discussed the matter and made the preparations for what was needed on the trip, and we treated him in this house as you can imagine. At the same time he was seeing his aunt. She is so ill-intentioned, as we have always seen, that she did not fail to attract him to her schemes. And among other things she had him convinced to leave to her husband, Don Pedro, the entire management of the Duke's estates, without paying any more attention to my daughter than if she were not the Duke's wife.
>
> I heard about it and when the Duke came to talk to me about it, although at the time my health was not good enough to warrant my losing my temper, I told him my opinion in such violent language as the situation demanded, in the presence of Don Juan de Córdoba, his uncle, telling him how forgetful he was of his honor and duty and of what people were saying about him and Doña Felipa, and that such behavior was knavish and childish and that I would not tolerate it, especially his wanting to leave the management of his estates in the hands of the person who was the cause of all the past troubles and would be the cause of others that were worse, expatiating on the theme as it deserved.
>
> He took it patiently and obediently, because, in truth, if they would leave him alone, he has good judgment and I am sure that he would be a good husband and we should not have to worry about these upsets. After this talk we agreed that the management should be given to the Duchess and that she should have with her as her counsellor, to sign her orders, Fray Francisco de la Cerda, another of the Duke's uncles. And in conformity with this, the Duke has sent her his power-of-attorney. That is how things stand here and in Baena they have accepted the arrangement . . .

Doña Felipa is thinking of going to Baena and though she appears very submissive, saying that they will serve the Duchess and not do anything for which I could take offense at them, I replied that for my part I could not approve of Doña Felipa's going there, for I know that she will put my daughter in confusion and annoy her and even kill her, if she could. And as I have no other daughter, I cannot fail to regret it and try to do everything I think best to remedy it. But I can't prevent them from going where they want to. And so, sir, they are leaving. Knowing how important it is to prevent it, as you have so often written me and as I myself realize, and how shameless they have been and where the matter has come to, I really believe that when they get to Baena, they will soon furnish a cause for breaking wholly with them and finding some way of remedying the situation.

You can understand what a pretty thing it would be to let that woman go and not be willing to let my daughter live in her own house and upset her and lead her a dog's life, when there is no excuse for it, except what people say about the Duke and her, all of which is honest and justified. I have written in detail to you about it, in order that you may be informed in case of what may happen.

With regard to the Duke, I have learned that both in Cartagena and on the way there he has behaved very honorably and was well accompanied by many gentlemen. I am glad of that, because I hold him in esteem and I shall continue to do so. I have written to His Majesty before and I am writing to him now what I think about these matters, begging him to let the Duke know that he was sorry for what had happened in the past, for it was right that he show greater respect for the Duchess, because she was his wife and had been a lady of the Empress and had been married with His Majesty's approval and was our daughter, making clear to him that he knows the fault was not his; and that if in the future he did not mend his ways, he would be displeased and could not fail to make provision for a remedy. Although I have informed the Duque de Alba and Don Enrique de Toledo, so that they may mention it to His Majesty, do not fail to do the same, if an opportunity arises. I beg of you to show every attention to the Duke, favoring him and going to visit him in his tent or lodging, because his uncles are so punctilious you cannot leave anything undone, although, as I have said, I cannot consider him as other than my son and appreciate any favor that is shown him.

I wanted you to be warned about these matters, because I think that these people will write that they are going to Baena with my approval, so that you will know the truth about what has happened and can tell it, if necessary. And if there is an opportunity you might speak to the Duke about it. His uncle, Don Gabriel, is there with the Duke, and though in these matters they are all alike, do not fail to show him attention and tell him that I have great confidence in him; and you may even tell him how badly I feel about this visit of Don Pedro and Doña Felipa, for I think that it would not be ill received. Don Sancho de Córdoba is there too; you know how much I have always liked him. You can speak to him at greater length about these matters, for he wants the Duke to do what he should. And you will tell him that in this and in all things I have in him the confidence that he has deserved and that I shall always be grateful to him and try to serve him.[70]

There is corroboration of Cobos' resentment against the Duke's family in one of the unsigned letters to which reference has already been made, for the author wrote: "Against his will, Don Pedro de Córdoba and Doña Felipa, 'horum caput et causa malo ruant,' have gone to Baena, at which he is greatly annoyed, and rightly, believing that they are going to upset his daughter and even do worse. . . . I have nothing to say about it, except that the shamelessness and pettiness of these people is such that it cannot be endured." [71]

Cobos' hope for the solution of his daughter's problems and his confidence in the Duke proved to have been well-founded. We know that the Duke took part in the unfortunate expedition to Algiers. Francisco Duarte wrote to Cobos at the end of September that they were expecting him in Italy [72] and Diego de Mendoza saw him in Genoa in October. He was with the fleet when they returned to Cartagena in December, 1541.[73] In his uncouth epic on the Emperor, *Carlo famoso*, Luis Zapata even reports that the Emperor showed him especial honor:

> "Del puerto acá y allá sin detenencia
> Se van todos donde yr cada uno ordena.
> El buen duque de Sesa, que la ausencia
> De su esposa le afflige y le da pena,
> Al alto Emperador pide licencia,
> Que a la Duquesa andar quiere a Baena.
> Le honrra Carlo al partir, licencia dada,
> Que pocos vee como él en su mesnada." [74]

Zapata goes on to recount a series of fantastic adventures which befell the Duke on his way home from Cartagena. But at last

> "Y con gozo de todos a Baena
> Llegó, con gran tristeza antes estando;
> Todos le van a dar la norabuena
> A la gentil señora, él llegando."

For Zapata, the Duke appeared to be a model husband. And ultimately Cobos too became convinced that he had mended his ways. Three years later he wrote to Juan Vázquez: "Relations between the Duke and the Duchess of Sesa are getting better and better every day—thank God! You couldn't believe the harmony and great love there is between them. The Marqués [Don Diego] has been visiting them and will stay there until October, when he will come back by way of Ubeda." [75] At about the same

10. The Patio of Cobos' Palace in Valladolid

Designed by Luis de Vega (1526). The Palace, reconstructed when it became the Palacio Real under Philip III, is now the Capitanía General. The patio is the only part of the original structure that has survived. The partitions between the columns of the second story are a modern addition.

12. Illuminated Manuscript of the Bill of Sale of Sabiote to Cobos (November 16, 1537)

The coat of arms at the bottom of the page is that of Cobos' son, Diego (Los Cobos-Molina-Mendoza-Sarmiento).

Sevilla, Archivo de Camarasa

11. Holograph Letter of Cobos to Juan Vázquez de Molina

Valladolid, June 27, 1534. Note the rubric after the signature.

Archivo de Simancas

13. The Castle of Sabiote (Jaén)

Purchased by Cobos in 1537.

14. The Castle of Canena (Jaén)

Purchased by Cobos in 1539.

15. Patio of the Castle of Canena
Probably designed by Andrés de Vandelvira.

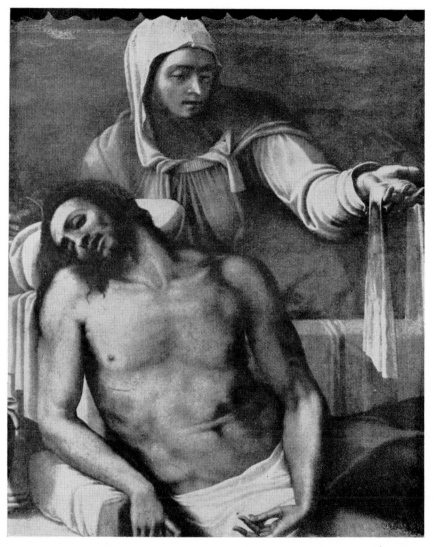

16. Pietà

By Sebastiano del Piombo. Commissioned by Ferrante Gonzaga and presented
to Cobos in 1539. *Sevilla, Duques de Alcalá Collection*

17. Portrait of a Secretary

This portrait, by an unknown painter, was long considered to be a portrait of
Cobos.   *Madrid, Museo del Prado*

18. Francisco de los Cobos

This is an Eighteenth century copy of a portrait by an unknown painter.

Sevilla, Duques de Alcalá Collection

19. A Reliquary of Cobos

It may once have contained the heads of the virgins presented to Cobos by Charles V at Cologne in 1521.

time, Gonzalo Pérez wrote: "The Duke has been here for several days, very obedient and reformed from what he was and very much in love with My Lady, the Duchess." [76] And even the historian Santa Cruz, in his *Crónica* reported: "As time went by, at the Emperor's command, he accepted his wife and lived maritally with her and loved her dearly." [77] So ended the bitterest crisis in Cobos' life.

The Mayorazgo *Established*

Perhaps it was the marriage of their daughter that led Don Francisco and Doña María to exercise at this time the privilege of establishing a *mayorazgo* in favor of their son Diego, which had originally been granted in 1529 and which they had twice modified to provide for her dowry. The official document, signed at Valladolid on November 9, 1541, was witnessed by Valdés, President of the Consejo Real; Alvaro de Mendoza, Chaplain of the Capilla de los Reyes in Toledo (María de Mendoza's brother); Gregorio López of the Consejo Real; Lope de León; and Francisco de Almaguer, Cobos' business agent. It is of singular importance in that it lists all their real estate and investments, as well as a number of their valuables which they prized sufficiently to keep them forever in the family. Although much of it is written in the conventional legal formulae of the period, it will be illuminating to outline its main provisions. [78]

The document begins with the conventional phrases:

In the name of the Most Holy Trinity, Father, Son, and Holy Ghost, who are three persons and one true God, and in praise of the ever Virgin Mary, Our Lady, and in honor of the glorious apostle Santiago, whom we count as our advocate, let all men know that we, Don Francisco de los Cobos, Grand Commander of Leon and Chief Accountant of Castile, member of the Council of State of the Emperor Don Carlos and Queen Juana his mother, Lord of the towns of Sabiote and Torres and Canena, and Doña María de Mendoza, his wife, considering that all men desire to perpetuate and renew their being, but in this present world the brevity of life and the corruption of death do not permit it and because no one can live beyond the natural limits, it is proper that he strive to live in memory in times to come, and in order that this memory be praiseworthy, which principally requires temporal wealth that has been justly gained without offense to God or prejudice to his neighbor, and that this be united and entailed in perpetuity, in such wise that it cannot be dissolved or diminished, and although these and other causes move us to make this disposition of our property, nevertheless our principal trust is in God Our Lord, in whom we hope that, as it was His pleasure to grant us this property, so He will conserve and increase it for His glory and service, accepting the admonition of the glorious Apostle St. Paul, who writing to his disciple Timothy says: "Let not the rich of this world be proud nor boastful nor trust in the uncertainty of wealth, but let their trust be in God, who giveth all things in abundance."

And so, placing in Him all our hope and trust, desiring as rightly as possible, without offense to Our Lord and without charge or risk to our consciences, to enhance our house and lineage and to establish together a *mayorazgo* and entailment of the property which God in his infinite goodness has given us and may in the future give us, whereby we may better serve Him, using the faculties which the laws give us and likewise those which Their Majesties have granted us to create a *mayorazgo* of our property, we hereby establish a *mayorazgo* in favor of Don Diego de los Cobos, Adelantado de Cazorla, our eldest son, and his descendants, and in defect of them, of our daughter, Doña María Sarmiento, Duchess of Sesa, and her descendants, and in defect of them, in other persons.

There follows a list of the property which he had acquired since he entered the royal service, a poor young man, in 1503. It begins with his real property:

The town of Sabiote with its fortress and all its appurtenances, and the rights to its taxes, the title of patron of its churches, and all the other lands and houses in Sabiote, Ubeda, Baeza, El Mármol, and Santistevan which Cobos had bought, and all their improvements.

The towns of Torres and Canena, with all similar rights and privileges, with specific mention of such properties as mills, olive and mulberry orchards, gardens, even the right to sell wood in the area of Torres to make charcoal.

The family palace in the Calle de los Cobos in Ubeda, with all the other houses, lands, vineyards, and olive orchards which he had acquired within the jurisdiction of the city.

The salt mines of Pinilla, which he had received from the Duque de Escalona, at the time when he transferred to him half the rights to the alum mines in Cartagena, with an annual income of 273,570 *maravedís*. In this case he grants to the Duke the right to recover the salt mines within eight years of February 15, 1539, on payment of 8,205,000 *maravedís*. If payment is made, the money is to go into the estate.

The town of Velliza, which he bought from the Conde de Luna, together with a *juro* of 51,500 *maravedís* a year, based on the *alcabalas* of the town, for which he had paid 1,030,000 *maravedís*.

The palace in Valladolid, with its gardens, yards, servant quarters, and adjacent buildings.

The garden that had belonged to Cristóbal de Saldaña on the bank of the Pisuerga, beside the road from Valladolid to Simancas, which he had permitted his widow, Isabel de Cuéllar, to occupy during her lifetime.

The village of Valloría, which he had acquired for 1,600,000 *maravedís* from Antonio de Fonseca, who in turn had received it as property confiscated from the *comunero,* the Conde de Salvatierra—the son of the Conde, Francisco de Ayala, having subsequently sold him the rights to the village.

The seventy acres in the Cañada de la Nava (Medina del Campo) which the Emperor had given him.

In addition to these pieces of real estate, he also lists certain other rights and investments:

A mortgage of 120,000 *maravedís* on a house in Medina del Campo which he purchased from Cristóbal de León.

A long list of mine rights in Azuaga, Cartagena, Lorca, the archbishopric of Toledo, Cazorla, Iruela, Cuenca, Sigüenza, Osma, Canena, Ximena, and Recena.

The rights to the salt mines in the Indies.

A pension of 1,500 *scudi* a year in the duchy of Milan, until a total of 15,000 *scudi* were paid.

There now follow in the document a number of items of personal property which were to be included in the *mayorazgo.* They are of special interest because they reveal what kinds of possessions were held in high esteem at the time.

The first is a "state bed," a magnificent treasure which is described in detail:

The canopy is of brocade, three breadths wide, and in the middle is an embroidered shield, with our arms. There are four valances of the same brocade, half a yard wide, double on two sides, single on the other two, with gold and scarlet fringe trimming, lined with blue buckram. With the valances, the canopy is four and two-thirds yards long and four yards wide, with yellow frieze edging, on which the hangings are fastened. It has three side panels, with another embroidered shield like the canopy, five and a sixth yards long and four yards wide, lined with blue buckram, with yellow frieze edging for the fastening. The fourth panel is the same, except that it is four fingers shorter. The two curtains of red taffeta have six panels each, five and an eighth yards long, with their fasteners, without any other ornament. The three-ply brocade coverlet has four side panels of brocade, with a border of a different brocade all round, five and a third yards long in all and four yards wide, with a gold and scarlet silk border and lined with red buckram.

The next items listed are eight wall-hangings, "of cloth of gold, with a strip of crimson velvet between the panels, a span wide, and another strip of the same material for a border. Each hanging has four panels of cloth of gold, plus the velvet strips, and is three and three-fourths yards long, not counting the strips, which are lined with buckram, with pieces of frieze on which they are fastened. Besides, there is a window drape of two panels of the same material, with its crimson strips, three yards of cloth, plus the crimson."

A similar item is a dais of rich brocade, with a crimson velvet border and silver points and gold and silk edging, with valances of the same brocade, lined with crimson satin, with the edging of scarlet and gold.

Of unusual interest are the three great rugs that had belonged to Barbarossa, which the Emperor gave to Cobos at the time of the capture of Tunis. The largest was seven yards long and almost four yards wide, with purple and yellow embroidery surrounded by white stripes. The two smaller rugs were of similar pattern.

The last of these decorative articles was a set of five tapestry panels, seven yards long from the top to the bottom, representing the *Triumphs* of Petrarch, which Cobos felt worthy of preservation "because they are of such fine design and material as they are." [79]

The final object of value which Cobos and his wife included in the *mayorazgo* was a gold ring, with a flat diamond worth 1,500 ducats, which the Emperor had worn on the day of his coronation at Bologna in 1530 and which he had given him on that very day, at the same time that he granted him a privilege of knighthood, sealed with his royal gold seal. "Wherefore"—says Cobos—because such a favor is worthy of perpetual memory, we include and incorporate in this our *mayorazgo* the aforesaid ring with its diamond and the privilege." And he added that it must never be sold or alienated.

The rest of the document is given over to setting forth the terms for carrying out the provisions of the *mayorazgo*. They are so detailed that they make the instrument to all intents and purposes a last will and testament. Two of the clauses refer to his daughter María. In the first he recalls that in her marriage contract with the Duque de Sesa, it had been provided that if she died without issue, two thirds of her dowry of 10,000,000 *maravedís* should revert to her parents. Cobos now modified this to permit her to bequeath 4,000,000 *maravedís* for the repose of her soul and other pious purposes; the remaining 6,000,-000 *maravedís* were to be invested and incorporated in the *mayorazgo*. In a second paragraph Cobos pointed out that they had given María a dowry of 10,000,000 *maravedís*, had presented her with gold, silver, jewels, and clothes worth 496,306 *maravedís*, had also provided her with a *juro* of 125,000 *maravedís* for life (this from the Emperor), and finally had expended large amounts on her betrothal and wedding; therefore she must not expect anything more from their estate.

The care with which Cobos tried to foresee every possible contingency is typical of his concern with detail. Thus he included in the *mayorazgo* all property they might acquire up to the time of their death, all payments to their account after their death, all cash, jewels, and other valuables remaining in Spain or in the Indies at the time of their death, though he did permit either one of them to withhold small amounts for the repose of his soul or to meet current obligations; the rest must be invested in real estate or perpetual *juros*. All cash and valuables were to be deposited in the monastery of San Francisco in Ubeda in a chest with three different keys: one to be held by Cobos or his wife, the second by the Guardian of the monastery, and the third by the Prior of the monastery of Santo Domingo in Ubeda. This system, common in the sixteenth century, made it impossible to open the chest except when all three persons were present. In another chest there must be a bound book for keeping a record of all cash and all transactions and for all the papers, documents, etc. which were involved. This provision was certainly carried out, and these papers still provide the nucleus of the Sabiote section in the Archivo de Camarasa.

The most extended section of the *mayorazgo* is that which deals with the succession to the estate in the event that Diego should die without a legitimate male heir or María should die without issue. It is interesting that in this case the first claimant should be an illegitimate son of Diego or the eldest son of an illegitimate daughter. If these fail, then Carlos de Mendoza, Doña María's youngest brother, becomes eligible, provided that he marry some woman of the Cobos family, beginning with the eldest daughter of Isabel de los Cobos (Don Francisco's sister) and running through a list of nine or ten families. If Carlos cannot meet this condition, then nephews of Doña María become eligible, always providing that they marry some woman in the Cobos family and that no person might be Conde de Rivadavia and also hold the *mayorazgo*. As a last resort the eldest sons of Juan Vázquez de Molina and Pedro de los Cobos are to be in line.

There were, moreover, certain persons who were automatically disqualified from holding the estate: one who was stark mad or an idiot "without lucid intervals," or one who took holy orders, although this did not mean membership in the military orders of Santiago, Calatrava, and Alcántara. An heir who was convicted of a major crime, heresy, or lese majesty was also ruled out, since this would involve confiscation of his property. And finally, any son who was guilty of ingratitude toward his parents forfeited his claim (was Cobos worried about Diego or was this a conventional provision?). After all these precautions it is pleasant to record that Diego did have two sons; the eldest inherited the *mayorazgo;* the second eventually became the Conde de Rivadavia.

One of the most significant sections, in its revelation of the ideals of the time and of Cobos in particular, is the one that deals with the family name and the coat of arms. "Because it is the desire of us both"—it begins—"to enhance and preserve the fame and name and lineage of Los Cobos, because it is noble and ancient in the city of Ubeda, where the members of this lineage have their ancestral mansion, we order that Don Diego and all his successors must bear the name of 'Los Cobos.' " If he bore two family names, that of Los Cobos must come first. Furthermore, in the family coat of arms those of Los Cobos (five golden lions rampant on an azure field) must always be placed on the right. To such a height of dignity and prestige had Cobos risen!

Since Cobos and his wife had provided so munificently for their son Diego, they called upon him to assume the responsibility for the payment, out of income, of all debts and bequests "in discharge of conscience." If he or his successors failed to do this, they authorized the Emperor to sequester whatever was necessary to fulfill their obligations. They reserved the right, during their lifetime, to change the provisions of the *mayorazgo* by joint action. Finally, they begged the Emperor to confirm the document, "in order that now and henceforward forever more, it may be preserved and fulfilled and have complete effect." The Emperor complied with their request at Valladolid on February 10, 1542.[80]

In a sense the document of establishment of the *mayorazgo* is a summary of Cobos' life and ambition—his pride in the titles and emoluments that he had won for himself and his son, the wealth that he had acquired and the few personal objects that he prized, the gifts from the Emperor, the sumptuous bed, the dais, the hangings, the tapestries, as tokens of the splendor of his household. It is striking that he did not mention any works of art. We know that he had a number of paintings, some of them by Titian, and a few works of sculpture. Perhaps he considered them merely a part of the decoration of his palaces, like the murals that Julio and Alejandro had painted in Ubeda and Valladolid, or even as household furnishing, like his rugs and tapestries or the gold and silver vessels for his table. The document also reveals the meticulous care with which he managed his affairs: he had even kept a record of every *maravedí* he gave his daughter. In planning for the future no detail was too insignificant to be left to chance or uncertainty. But the most revealing aspect of the document is the picture it gives of his tremendous desire to survive beyond the confines of this present life. Fame was a characteristic goal of the sixteenth century, and in his craving to assure that the memory of his name and fame should not perish with him, Cobos was a typical son of the Renaissance.

CHAPTER XI

———————··⟨∞⟩··———————

THE EMPEROR RETURNS TO SPAIN

At the beginning of November, 1541, Cobos learned that the Emperor had decided to abandon his campaign in Algiers and was returning to Spain; Cobos had instructions to proceed at once to Cartagena to meet him. A few days later the Marqués de Lombay, writing to Cobos from Barcelona, remarked that he had no doubt the good news of the Emperor's return had restored his health.[1] In the following days Cobos was busy with the preparations for the trip.[2] At first he had thought of taking with him Loaisa, now Cardinal of Seville, but it seemed wiser for Loaisa to return to his diocese. And so, having settled the question of the *mayorazgo,* he left Madrid on November 11.[3]

On the fifteenth one of his servants, Juan de Enciso, wrote from Madrid that he was sending him three horses—not very good ones—and he added: "My Lady Doña María is well and I gave her your message. She asked me as many questions as if a year had passed since you left. Herewith are letters from her and from Ledesma." [4] The next day Doña María wrote to him again, and by some strange chance her autograph letter has been preserved in the Archivo of Simancas, the only one of hundreds which we know that she sent him during the course of their married life. Ordinarily Cobos took great care to keep his personal correspondence out of his official files. But this time, perhaps because he was so busy on the trip, he must have overlooked it and some one of his clerks included it among his official papers.

There are, it is true, a number of her letters, prepared for her signature by the royal secretariat, conveying her thanks for a gift or congratulating some one on their marriage. But this is written in her own hand.

It must be admitted that it is a very awkward hand, hardly more than a scribble and barely legible. This is true of the writing of most of the Spanish lords and ladies of the time. Antonio de Guevara, in his *Epístolas,* frequently mocks at the penmanship of his correspondents. Thus, to the Condestable of Castile he writes: "I have received your letter and even though it had not been signed, I would have recognized that it was by your hand, because it had few lines and many blots." [5] Doña María's writing must have been particularly bad, for the Duke of Alba once wrote to Cobos: "The Duchess sends you her greetings and we both send greetings to Doña María, although at the moment she has caused us much trouble, trying to read a letter which she wrote to the Duchess—and this is no jest, but the truth." [6] Fortunately some expert modern paleographer at the Archivo has deciphered her letter, in all its unconventional spelling. It deserves to be quoted here.

Sir: By a courier that Juan de Enciso sent I wrote to you everything there was to tell here, but because I didn't want any to go without a letter of mine, I am writing again, and also to beg you to let me know by every courier you send how your trip is going, for I suspect that it won't be with much peace of mind, since we know nothing about His Majesty. God bring him safely back, for his long delay has been a cause of worry to us all.

They tell me that Samano came to see me this morning, but I wasn't up. I must send for him right away to find out what kind of a life you are leading on the way. Mine is, as usual, crowded with visitors and the ones that never leave the house are Doña Isabel de Orosco and Doña Isabel de Carvajal and her daughter, with whom Perico de Santernas is madly in love—and not joking, but in earnest; you would die laughing to see him.

I am still not eating well, though better than when you left. Tell Rábago that if he doesn't look out, he'll be getting a letter of excommunication in reply to his letter, for everyone here that he mentioned in it wants to reply. I send my greetings to Don Alvaro, for I am very glad that he is joining you, for after what you wrote to me, I was afraid to see him come in the door, with that frown on his face.

Our Lord keep you, as I desire. From Madrid, on November 16.
Your servant
Doña María de Mendoza.[7]

The "Perico" whom Doña María mentions is almost certainly the famous buffoon of the Conde de Benavente, frequently quoted for his pert sayings in the chronicles of the time. His portrait, by Antonio Moro, still hangs in the Museo del Prado.[8] "Don Alvaro" is probably her brother, the chaplain of the Capilla de los Reyes in Toledo.

Cobos had reached Albacete by November 20 and there he wrote to Ledesma that the horses which Enciso had sent had not arrived, but that he was grateful for those that Ledesma had sent and would pay him back at the next fair. The next day he was in Chinchilla and on the twenty-fifth he came to Murcia, where he waited for a week to have news of the Emperor's plans.[9] Actually the latter reached Cartagena on the evening of December 1 and Cobos did not arrive until the following day. For Cobos, at least, it must have been a glad reunion. The Emperor and his suite stayed only four days in Cartagena before starting for Toledo on December 5. By December 13 they had reached El Provencio, and from there Cobos wrote to Ledesma that he should come to Ocaña, where he expected to find Doña María, who had written of her plans to leave Madrid.[10] The Infantas had been living at Ocaña for some time, in care of the Conde de Cifuentes, and now Prince Philip came from Madrid to meet his father. The whole Court reached Ocaña on December 18 and the Emperor enjoyed a week with his children, eating frequently with them. On the last day of the year they all reached Toledo.

The first months of 1542 were uneventful. As usual, the Emperor's first thought on returning to Spain was raising more money from his Spanish subjects. Even before he reached Toledo he sent a summons from Ocaña to the towns of Castile for another Cortes at Valladolid. There was the usual haggling with the municipal councils over the powers they were to grant to their *procuradores*. But when they gathered on February 10, most of the towns had yielded to royal pressure and the individual representatives were further softened by open bribery; Cobos prepared a list of the special favors which each one of them had requested.[11] There was the usual debate over grievances and reforms, but on April 4 they finally voted an exceptionally large subsidy of 400,000 ducats a year. And, as usual, Cobos was presently rewarded with a grant of 200,000 *maravedís* for his services at the Cortes.[12]

On the day after the conclusion of the Castilian assembly, the Emperor issued the summons to the realms of Aragon, Cata-

luña, and Valencia for a Cortes at Monzón. But he did not leave
Valladolid until May 22, when he started for Burgos with his
Court, accompanied this time by Prince Philip. This time, too,
Doña María went with her husband and they were both guests
at a banquet which the Condestable de Castilla offered the Em-
peror in his Casa del Cordón in Burgos late in May. Among the
others present were the Duque de Alba and Philip's majordomo,
Juan de Zúñiga.[13]

Barcelona—Valencia

Leaving Burgos on June 2, the Emperor made a quick visit to
inspect the defenses of Navarre and reached Monzón June 22.
He found the Cortes already assembled, and the next morning
he appeared before them and took his place on the throne. After
the Protonotary Climent had read the royal address, setting
forth the desperate needs of the Emperor and urging prompt
action, Charles announced that he was leaving Cobos, Granvelle, and the Vice-Chancellor Mai to conduct the deliberations
and then retired to his lodging.[14]

The meetings of the Cortes dragged on all through the summer. Not until the end of August did they finally consent to vote
the subsidy the Emperor demanded. At the middle of August
Cobos had another attack of tertian fever, and as late as September 16 he wrote to Juan de Vega, the Viceroy of Navarre,
that he had been too ill to attend to affairs of state.[15] Meanwhile, the Emperor had been arranging for the public recognition of Philip as heir to the throne, and in a series of separate
ceremonies between September 14 and October 6 the representatives of Cataluña, Valencia, and Aragon took the formal oath
of allegiance.

The Emperor reached Barcelona on October 16, and on November 8 Philip made his formal entry into the city and received
the oath of the city councillors. Although Charles was preoccu-
pied with the preparations for the renewal of the war with
France, which had become certain with the receipt of the formal
declaration of war by Francis (July 10, 1542), he found time
for a round of gay parties, banquets and tournaments in celebration of Philip's visit. Doña María had gone directly to Barcelona, where she was probably the guest of the Duchess of
Soma, for the latter had written to Cobos that she could hardly

wait to see them both.[16] On November 12 the Duke and Duchess of Soma presented an elaborate *fiesta* in their palace and on the sixteenth the Condesa de Palamós offered a banquet and dance which was attended by seventy ladies. After the banquet the Emperor came in disguise, dressed in purple and yellow velvet, and the dance went on until three in the morning.[17] We may be sure that Cobos and his wife were present at both these parties, for they were close friends of the hosts. In fact, on November 19 Doña María and the Condesa de Palamós were the godmothers at the christening of the infant son of the Duke and Duchess of Soma.[18]

At the beginning of December the Court moved on to Valencia for another round of parties in honor of the young Prince. On the evening of the eighth, the Duchess of Calabria, Doña Mencía de Mendoza, wife of the Viceroy and former wife of Henry of Nassau, "gowned in cloth of gold, borne in a litter covered with cloth of gold and followed by twelve ladies, went to Cobos' lodging for supper," [9] and on the twelfth, at a banquet which the Duchess offered in honor of Charles and Philip, María de Mendoza was one of the many guests.

Cienfuegos, the pious biographer of Francisco de Borja, tells the story that it was at this time that Doña María de Mendoza commented to Leonor de Castro, Borja's wife, on the humble clothes she wore, so unbefitting her age, and that Doña Leonor replied that she was following her husband's example.[20] Certainly Doña María must have rivalled the Duchess of Calabria in splendor, if we may judge by the jewels which her servant, Juan Pérez, took to Valencia for her:

A collar of gems and pearls, to wit: four diamonds, two of them flat cut—one large and one small—another pointed, another triangular, six rubies, one of them flat cut, eleven pearls, some bigger than the others and all very good, so that in all there are twenty-two pieces, not counting another, without any pearl at the end, where the collar is fastened.

A fleur-de-lis of five diamonds, one large, the others smaller, to form the flower, with three pendants of six pearls, three large and three small, because the pendants are like little gourds. The piece on which the fleur-de-lis is set is in colored enamel in the antique style.

A ribbon with gems and pearls, set on black velvet, with the following pieces: a buckle (?) in relief, with three large rubies and six big round pearls, together with twenty-five gold pieces and twenty-five rubies of different sizes, all from Calcutta, and twenty-four gold pieces with three pearls in each piece, not as large as those on the buckle (?) but all very round and matched and white, with very good color.[21]

On December 16 the Court left Valencia to return to Castile. After spending Christmas with his children at Alcalá de Henares, the Emperor was back in Madrid again on the last day of the year. Doña María returned with the Court; on January 8 the Duchess of Calabria wrote to Cobos, telling him how much she and the Duke missed them both.[22] Amid all these activities and festivities, the Emperor was busy with his preparations for war. Instructions were sent to the viceroys and commanders of fortresses on the Navarre and Roussillon borders; the nobles were notified to be ready in arms with their followers in case of invasion. The burden of work on the secretariat must have been extremely heavy. And since Granvelle had been sent to Italy to negotiate with the Pope, Cobos remained as the only major advisor of the Emperor. Perhaps this explains why so many of the official *cédulas* of the period were countersigned by Idiáquez. The threat of war also aroused the nobles to think about strengthening their defenses, and a long list was drawn up, authorizing many of them to build or rebuild their fortresses. Cobos was one of those who received permission to rebuild his fortresses of Sabiote, Torres, and Canena, or build new ones, if he preferred.[23]

In fact, ever since he became Lord of Sabiote and the other towns, Cobos had been thinking in military terms. We have seen how he had ordered cannon from Florence. And in 1540 he also ordered suits of armor and saddles from Milan, through the Marqués del Guasto, which Lope de Soria shipped in thirty-four bales to Cartagena. They arrived there in March, 1541, and at the same time came three cases of corselets which Guasto had sent him. The latter he ordered sent to Madrid.[24]

On September 1, writing to his brother-in-law, Juan de Mendoza, who was about to join the Emperor, he expressed his regret that he could not give him a good suit of armor because, the day before, he had given the only one he had left to Hernán Cortés, Marqués del Valle. However, he explained, he still had some suits of armor in Ubeda which the Marqués del Guasto had sent him and he could have one of them; there was one especially good one of gilded wrought iron.[25] Again, in October, 1542, the ambassador in Genoa wrote him that he was sending with Doria's galleys a shipment of arms, lances, and saddles, and also artillery ammunition.[26] Cobos was determined to be equipped, in case it proved necessary to take the field.

Reforms in the Affairs of the Indies

While the Emperor was still in Barcelona, another matter came to a head. Several years before (1539), in Valladolid, Charles had appointed a large representative commission to study the administration of affairs in the Indies; the chairman was Loaisa, President of the Consejo de las Indias; Cobos was the secretary, as well as Chanciller of the Indies, representing his son. They made their recommendations to the Emperor while he was still in Monzón in the summer of 1542, but he was too busy at the time to give them his attention and postponed the matter until he reached Barcelona. There he appointed a small sub-committee, consisting of Loaisa, Dr. Guevara, the Regent Figueroa, Fray Diego de Soto, his confessor, Granvelle and Cobos to review the proposals and make a final report. Their recommendations received the Emperor's approval and were officially promulgated on November 20, 1542.[27]

This is not the place to study in detail the new ordinances. Suffice it to say that in many respects they represent the reform of the treatment of the Indians which Bartolomé de las Casas had been preaching for twenty-five years. There was, however, one provision of which several members of the Consejo de las Indias disapproved—the Cardinal, the Bishop of Lugo and Cobos among them—namely the law which prohibited members of the clergy and government officials from receiving *encomiendas* or allotments *(repartimientos)* of Indians to work as their servants or slaves. León Pinelo records that he had seen an opinion of Cobos in which he said: "In my judgment the laws which provide for the allotment of Indians are not satisfactory and I was always afraid that difficulties and damage would result from them." [28] Events of the next few years in Peru proved how sound his opinion was.

While the study of the new ordinances was going on, the Emperor had appointed the Regent Juan de Figueroa to make a special investigation of the charges of malfeasance among members of the Consejo de las Indias, and his report was presented at the same time. It was plain that there had been many irregularities in the performance of their duties, that bribery had become almost the rule. The President, Loaisa, was not mentioned, although it was known that he had received many gifts of gold. Suárez de Carvajal, the Bishop of Lugo, was removed from the

Consejo and ordered to pay 12,000 ducats which Diego de Almagro had sent him from Peru as a dower for his son Diego, who was to marry Carvajal's daughter; when the boy was killed, Carvajal had kept the money. Dr. Bernal was acquitted of wrongdoing, but he was ordered to be more affable in his treatment of litigants. The one who was most rigorously treated was Dr. Diego Beltrán, the oldest member of the Consejo, who was convicted on all counts, dismissed from all his offices, and fined 17,000 ducats. Exiled from Court, he returned in disgrace to Medina del Campo and entered a monastery. His wife brought suit against him to recover her dowry.[29]

Finally the secretary, Juan de Samano, was exonerated. Santa Cruz interprets this action by saying: "He explained the large sums of money which he had received, saying that he had no part in the decisions of the Consejo, but only kept the record of what was ordered, and that anything that he had received had been given to him of their own free will by people who came to do business with the Consejo and not because of anything improper that he might do for them. Because of this and because of the plea of the Grand Commander of Leon and other gentlemen that his appointment should not be taken from him, he was allowed to remain in office." [30] Once more Cobos' influence was strong enough to protect one of his assistants. As for himself, although he was officially the secretary of the Consejo, he was not even investigated!

By the time the Emperor reached Madrid he had already made up his mind that he must return to Flanders and Germany to do what he could to settle affairs there in person. More and more he had come to depend upon his own judgment in matters of policy; less and less did he rely upon Cobos and his Castilian counsellors for advice. In fact, even before, while Granvelle was in Italy, he had written to his sister Mary, Regent of Flanders, that there was no one with whom he could discuss matters: "In this Council of Castile, as you will readily believe, there is not a soul who imagines that I have any intention of leaving these kingdoms. If they knew, they would try to prevent me." [31] But Cobos remained his chief financial advisor and was busier than ever in the effort to secure new funds to defray the expenses of the forthcoming campaign.

The necessary preparations had been completed by the end of February, 1543, and on March 1 Charles left Madrid with

Philip, who accompanied him as far as Alcalá de Henares. After a few days in Zaragoza the Court reached Molins de Rey on March 29, where they remained for almost two weeks. During their stay there Gerónimo Zurita came to consult the Emperor in behalf of the Inquisition on a matter regarding the Moriscos and he was referred to Cobos,[32] who years before, in 1526 at Granada, had been on a commission concerned with the same problem. Before they left, the Bishop of London also came to Court to receive the Emperor's confirmation of the secret treaty between Henry VIII and Charles which had been signed on February 11. The ceremony took place on April 8 in a room overlooking the garden, in the palace of Juan de Zúñiga, which had been set up as a chapel, and there, cap in hand, the Emperor took the formal oath. The original Latin document, on a great sheet of parchment, is still in the Record Office in London,[33] witnessed by the Duque de Alba, Cobos, Joaquin de Rye, Enrique de Toledo, and Montfalconnet. The notaries were Alonso de Idiáquez and Gonzalo Pérez; it was probably the latter who prepared the Latin text.

After three weeks in Barcelona the Emperor embarked on May 1, but he put in at Palamós on the second and remained there until the twelfth, before sailing for Genoa. This time he took with him as secretaries both Juan Vázquez de Molina and Idiáquez. To help Cobos in the conduct of affairs in Spain, two of his associates were raised to the rank of royal secretary— Juan de Samano and Pedro de los Cobos. Another, Gonzalo Pérez, was named secretary of Philip. A fourth secretary, Francisco de Ledesma, who had been attached to the office of Cardinal Tavera, had gone to Barcelona with Cobos, and the Cardinal wrote to the Grand Commander that they could not conduct any business in Valladolid, because there were no secretaries. Would he please send Ledesma back?[34] Samano had long served as Cobos' deputy in the Consejo de las Indias, but this was the first time that he had to accept personal responsibility. Before Cobos returned to Valladolid, Samano wrote to him: "I am working as hard as I can not to make many mistakes in these matters in which Your Lordship has ordered me to serve, but as a man without experience in such matters there cannot fail to be plenty of them, though unintentional."[35]

The Emperor had issued the formal instructions for the administration of Spain on May 1.[36] Philip was to act as Regent,

with the support of a group of three chief advisors: Cardinal
Tavera, the Duque de Alba, in matters of defense, and Cobos, in
charge of finances. But of the three Cobos undoubtedly had the
widest influence because he, or one of his deputies, was a member
of all the Councils and so had a hand in the transaction of all
state business. In addition to this public document, while he was
at Palamós Charles prepared in his own hand two famous instructions for his son Philip.

The Emperor's Instructions to Philip

The first of these, dated May 4, is commonly called the "Intimate Instruction." [37] It deals primarily with Philip's personal
life—the virtues which he must cultivate and his relations with
the girl that he was soon to marry. Rarely has a father portrayed a higher ideal for his son than is set forth in these moving
pages. Cobos—he wrote—would bring him a copy of the general
orders for the conduct of business and the duties of each of the
Councils. In all matters he was to consult with Tavera and
Cobos, "treating each of them as is befitting the quality and authority of their persons and the confidence which I place in them,
urging them to counsel you as to what is proper, in complete harmony and unmoved by false modesty, passion and confusion."
This, he added, was particularly important in the appointment
of municipal *corregidores*. All orders issued by the several Councils he was to sign on his own responsibility, although Charles
did not object to the Cardinal's being present. Other communications and correspondence must first be read and approved by
Cobos, who was to advise him concerning the problems involved.

As his confidential advisor the Emperor urged him to turn to
his majordomo, Juan de Zúñiga, in whose judgment and loyalty
he could put entire trust. Especially in matters in which he felt
uncertain he should look to him for loyal counsel. In addition he
should rely on Cobos:

> Because you see what confidence I have in Cobos and the experience he has
> in my affairs and because he is better informed and more familiar with them
> than anyone, in these and other matters where you think that you may need
> his information and advice, turn to him.

Finally he should look to his former tutor, now his confessor,
the Bishop of Cartagena, for guidance in all spiritual matters.

He concludes—

"God grant you understanding, will and strength—that you may so act that He will be served and that you may deserve, after long years, His Paradise. This I beg of Him to grant you, with all prosperity, which is the desire of your good father. I the King."

The second instruction which Charles sent his son on May 6 is called the "Secret Instruction," [38] because it contained an evaluation of the individual members of Philip's entourage and was to be kept carefully locked up. If the first instruction is a revelation of the Emperor's ideals of conduct, the "Secret Instruction" is equally clear evidence of his uncanny gift of judging the men around him, recognizing in each their virtues and their weaknesses. It has been so often published and so often discussed that we need here to consider only the parts which concern Cobos and his relations with the other advisors of Philip.

Charles was well aware of the rivalries between the men whom he left with his son: "for that reason"—he explained—"I have named the Cardinal of Toledo, as President, and Cobos, so that you may take counsel with them in matters of government. And though they are the heads of the rival cliques, nevertheless I decided to appoint them both, so that you might not be left in the hands of either one of them." As for the Duke of Alba, the Emperor was suspicious of his ambition and he warned Philip not to give him or any other grandees an important place in civil government; in military affairs he could rely on him.

Cobos—*he goes on*—I consider faithful. Up to now he has been little involved in rivalries; now I think he shows some signs of it. He is not as hard-working as he used to be; his age and ill health are responsible. I believe that his wife harasses him and is responsible for involving him in rivalries. And she even gives him a bad reputation by accepting gifts, though I believe that he does not accept anything of importance. A few little presents given to his wife are enough to discredit him. I have spoken to him about it; I believe that he will mend his ways. He is experienced in all my affairs and thoroughly informed about them. I am sure that you will find no one whom you can better use in all matters concerning them. I believe that he will act well and honestly. God grant that rivalries and the causes that prompt him to them may not make him lose his judgment.

It will be well for you to use him as I do, not exclusively nor giving him more authority than that provided for in the instructions. In conformity with them, show him favor, for he has served well, and I believe that lots of people hold a contrary opinion, which he does not deserve nor is it proper. I am sure that he will try to win your favor, as everyone will, and since he has been fond of women, if he saw any inclination on your part to play around with them, he might help you, rather than hinder you. Watch out for it, for it is not proper.

I have done him many favors and sometimes he would like to have more; he makes it a point of honor, as the others do, and he says that I fail to grant him favors, because people are gossiping about him. He does have one very important privilege—too important a privilege: his right to collect revenue as *fundidor* of the Indies. I have told him that his son is not to have it. He secured from the Pope some bulls granting him the Adelantamiento of Cazorla and he has signed a paper (Granvelle has it), that if the bulls are carried out and his son is given the Adelantamiento, his appointment as *fundidor* can be taken from him. Granvelle has the *cédula* and if I die, you can ask him for it and use it in conformity with this. He also has the grant of salt mines in the Indies. Right now it does not amount to much; in time it might become important. If I die, you will do well to take it away from him and from anyone else who holds similar privileges.

In matters of finance he is an excellent official, and if some people think that he is the one who dissipates and wastes the public funds, the fault in not his, nor even mine, as I have said, but the course of events. If they would permit it, I believe that he would be as good a reformer as anyone else. The post as *contador mayor* he holds only during my absence. When I came back, I could have taken it away from him, but I decided not to do him that disfavor. If I should die, you will do well to confirm him in the appointment and make use of him. In these matters of finance it is not desirable that he should be left alone, as I have left him, and for that reason I cannot think of anyone whom you might better associate with him than Don Juan de Zúñiga, The post should not go to the Duque de Alba nor to the sons of Cobos or Zúñiga, for it is one that requires great experience.

The marriage which Cobos has arranged in Aragon for his son—*the Emperor continues*—and the fact that I have named as viceroy of Aragon the Conde de Morata, who is a kinsman of his daughter-in-law, will cause a lot of talk. In reality I could not find in Aragon anyone who was better than he and since the Council of Aragon is never so perfect that there is not plenty to correct in it, I am sure that there will be many complaints. This I have set down in this secret letter with regard to Cobos.

As for Cobos' relations with the other counsellors, the Emperor remarks that the Vice Chancellor of Aragon, Miguel Mai, is an old man, wholly dependent on Cobos. The President of the Consejo de Castilla, Hernando Valdés, Bishop of Sigüenza, is not an able man, but he gets on well with Cobos; unfortunately Cobos is more inclined to support him in his weaknesses than to try to correct them. Juan de Zúñiga is highly dependable, but he is jealous, particularly of Cobos, but also of the Duque of Alba. He resents the favors done to Cobos, considering his own higher social status (he was the son of the Conde de Miranda) and his long years of service. Like Cobos he is anxious to secure the future of his children. We shall not try to summarize here the Emperor's comments on the others: Philip's confessor, Juan Martínez Siliceo, Bishop of Cartagena, the Cardinal of Seville, President of the Consejo de las Indias, the Conde de Osorno, President of the Consejo de las Ordenes, and Granvelle, his chief advisor in international affairs.

The Emperor had been working with Cobos for twenty-five years. He had come to respect him and have confidence in him because of his loyalty and his capacity for handling public affairs, particularly in financial matters. One of the striking traits of Charles' personality is the unswerving confidence that he placed in his ministers. With the exception of the brief transfer of his confessor, García de Loaisa, to Rome in 1530, he never dismissed any of his chief advisors. In succession Chièvres, Gattinara and, after 1530, Cobos and Granvelle remained constantly in his service until their death. In the case of the two latter, their usefulness to the Emperor may have been their readiness to accept his decisions and to do their best to implement them. But they were not wholly passive instruments of his will; they regularly expressed to him their own opinions and made their own recommendations, which gave him a balance in his own decisions.

If the Emperor recognized the good qualities of the men who worked with him, he was equally aware of their personal weaknesses—their ambitions, their craving for wealth and power, their jealousies and rivalries. The counsel he gave to Philip was the fruit of a lifetime of experience and of penetrating insight into human nature. His analysis of Cobos, in a sense, is a summary of the traits which we have tried to illustrate in detail in the story of his life.

CHAPTER XII

THE SECOND REGENCY

When Charles embarked on May 1 he left the Duque de Alba and Cobos in Barcelona to complete the unfinished business. There were many problems to be settled: preparations for the defense of the frontiers in Navarre and Roussillon, orders to be promulgated, like the instruction as to who in Castile had the right to pack animals and lodging—a long list of members of the royal family, members of the Councils, and other officials.[1] On May 12 the municipal councillors paid a visit to the Duke, who was lodged in the house of the Duque de Segorve, to consult him about the fortifications of the city; Cobos and the Vice Chancellor Mai were present at the discussion.[2]

There were personal matters, too, that occupied their attention. In spite of his wealth, the Duque de Alba did not scruple to ask the Emperor for an *ayuda de costa* in view of his new duties.[3] The Emperor replied that he could receive his salary of 5,000 ducats a year as majordomo of the royal household, even *in absentia,* but he could not have both that and his salary as captain-general.[4] Cobos, too, was busy trying to clear up a conflict with Juan de Vega, Viceroy of Navarre, who had charged that Cobos had tried to prevent his appointment as ambassador in Rome in order that the post might be given to the Marqués de Mondéjar. Cobos was able to demonstrate that the charge was unfounded; in fact, he had always been a good friend of Vega. He was particularly worried that if Vega went to Rome with this feeling of animosity, he might try to influence the Pope to change his mind with regard to Cobos' possession of the *adelantamiento* of Cazorla, and he even wrote to the Emperor asking him to tell Vega not to meddle in the affair when he went to Rome. As late as August he was still worrying and wrote to Juan Vázquez a detailed account of his part in Vega's appointment.[5]

Alba and Cobos had finished their business my May 19, but they were held up by the Duke's attack of fever, so that they did not leave Barcelona until the day after Corpus Christi. Cobos had already written that they were planning to be in Zaragoza early in June, that Doña María and the Adelantado would meet them there, and that they would celebrate the marriage of their son.[6] Along the way they wrote almost every day to the Emperor and to Prince Philip, reporting their progress.[7] Doña María reached Zaragoza on June 4, and Cobos must have arrived there at the same time.[8] It would be well to stop briefly to look at the story of Don Diego whose marriage was about to be celebrated.

The Marriage of Don Diego

Cobos had been particularly successful in securing appointments and privileges for his son, even while he was a mere child. At the age of four he was made a knight of Santiago; three years later he was a page of Prince Philip and the Empress. He was only eight years old when he was named Chanciller of the Indies; he was eleven when he was appointed *adelantado* of Cazorla. In 1538 he was *regidor* of Ubeda.[9] And each of these appointments carried with it a salary. Cobos, naturally eager to have him win the favor of the young Prince, arranged to have him join him in his studies. Juan de Zúñiga wrote to Cobos that though he was further advanced than Philip, it would do him no harm to review the elementary work.[10]

As early as May, 1540, Cobos was beginning to plan for a suitable marriage for his son and he wrote to Juan Vázquez that his agents in Seville were negotiating a marriage between Diego and the sister of the Duque de Arcos and hoped that the outcome would be favorable.[11] But the deal fell through and Cobos turned to a less distinguished union. On January 26, 1543, Diego was betrothed in Madrid to Francisca Luisa de Luna, Marquesa de Camarasa.[12] She came from an old Aragonese family—she was a relative of Pedro Martínez de Luna, Conde de Morata, and lived in his house in Zaragoza—but she was poor, so poor that Cobos had to accept a mortgage on her estates in lieu of a dowry. The important thing was that she was heiress to the title. And on February 18 the Emperor granted Diego the title of Marqués de Camarasa, in his own right. When one remembers the passionate concern that Cobos showed with the marriage of his daughter, it is puzzling that he betrayed no more than a casual interest in his son's marital affairs. Was he disappointed in him and his lack of initiative?

The only account we have of the wedding festivities in Zaragoza is found in the autobiography of Don Alonso Enríquez. Don Alonso had come back from Seville to the Court and was in high favor with the Prince, a good fortune which he attributed wholly to the influence of Cobos and his wife, the "Excellent Lady." In the rambling *Libro de su vida,* he tells an absurd story of an experience early in May, 1543, at the house of María de Ulloa, dowager Condesa de Salinas, in Santiago el Real, where he was left alone in the dark with the Countess's lovely granddaughter, Marina de Aragón. Doña María, her sister, Francisca Sarmiento, and her brother, Alvaro de Mendoza, were there too and Don Alonso declared that they would vouch for the truth of his story.[13]

Doña María, accompanied by Don Alonso, left Madrid on May 15, and on May 17 they reached Alcalá de Henares, where they were entertained by the Infantas and their ladies. Don Alonso went every day with Doña María to the Palace, where they played bowls and other games with the princesses, amid much pleasant conversation. Continuing on their journey on May 21, they were lavishly entertained along the way by the Duque del Infantado and the Duque de Medinaceli. They reached Zaragoza on June 4. Five leagues outside the town they were met by a distinguished company: Cobos, the Duque de Alba, the Viceroy, the Conde de Morata, the Condes de Aranda, Nieva, and Luna, the Archbishop of Zaragoza, and other important persons. Together they entered the city, where three triumphal arches had been erected in the main square and a list prepared for tournaments. The Archbishop performed the marriage ceremony that night. The festivities continued for a week, with dances and evening parties, banquets and suppers, jousts and bull-fights.[14] When the celebration was over, Cobos and his wife, the Duque

de Alba, and Don Alonso started for Valladolid, where they arrived on June 29.[15]

Don Alonso also gives a detailed account of a tournament
which he and Doña María's brother, Juan de Mendoza, organized shortly after they reached Valladolid. The judges were
Cobos; the Grand Commanders of Castile, Alcántara and Calatrava; and Sancho de Córdoba. The Prince was one of those who
fought on Don Alonso's "team" and it was he who won the first
prize.[16] On July 15 the Duque de Alba left for a brief visit with
his wife at Alba de Tormes, taking Don Alonso with him. On
July 19 he reported his safe arrival;[17] ten days later he wrote
to Cobos that the Emperor had ordered him to return to Valladolid and that he was starting at once.[18]

Imperial Finances

Cobos' first problem on reaching Valladolid was to raise money.
On July 19 he wrote to the Marqués de Aguilar, now Viceroy of
Cataluña: "I am envious of the life you are leading there with
Rábago; that will have to stop when the Marquesa gets there . . .
Here all is trouble and difficulty in raising money, for I don't
know what will be enough nor where we can get so much." [19]
Early in August he wrote the Emperor an even more despairing
letter:

> The difficulty of finding money is so great that there never has been any-
> thing like it. I assure Your Majesty that no way can be found to get money,
> because there isn't any. The 150,000 ducats in cash which went to Portugal
> (for Philip's dower) have caused great damage; some wealthy and important
> bankers were on the verge of bankruptcy. And afterwards, to provide 18,000
> ducats every thirty days for the defenses of Perpignan, Fuenterrabía, San Se-
> bastián and Navarre, as well as Malaga and Cartagena, has been and is
> extremely difficult, because the only way to provide money for that is by bor-
> rowing it and what is worse, none can be found, for as Your Majesty knows,
> the securities which were left to meet these obligations were ecclesiastical
> "half fruits" and the Cruzada and the sale of knighthoods in the military
> orders and of local tax rights and *juros*. And nothing can be done in this way,
> because no one will buy them. And as for the "half fruits," a large part of
> them have already been committed as security for bills of exchange.
>
> I am truly very perplexed and I do not see any way to provide for this; and
> I do not know how we can meet payment on the bills of exchange which have
> been acquired, both before Your Majesty left and since then, for they in-
> volve a large sum and to meet them, there is nothing but what Your Majesty
> already knows. God knows that I do not like to tell Your Majesty of these

difficulties and to find new troubles. But Your Majesty must realize that we are in such a crisis that there cannot fail to be a serious deficit.[20]

In spite of his discouragement, Cobos continued to make every effort to find funds. Once more he prepared a list of persons who were to be solicited for a loan. A few of them replied favorably: the Cardinal Tavera subscribed 16,000 ducats; Cobos himself loaned 8,000 ducats more, in addition to the 19,000 ducats he had advanced two years before. But many of the nobles declined; the Duque de Alba replied that "he would serve the Emperor with a pike in his hand." [21] Cobos also proposed to the Emperor other possible sources of income: the creation of new municipal offices which could be sold to individuals; the issuance of permits to ride mules, which had been forbidden by a *pragmática,* at fifty ducats each. By August 25 he was able to report to the Emperor that he had succeeded in raising 420,000 ducats, part of it from a shipment of gold and silver from the Indies.[22]

Not the least of his difficulties arose from the fact that the Emperor was constantly borrowing money from bankers, without any provision for security. On September 9 Cobos wrote to protest, as vigorously as he dared, at the loans he had made in Genoa to pay Diego de Mendoza and Juan de Vega and for the purchase of a diamond at 4,000 ducats. He would, he said, make provision for payment, even though the other financial needs were so great and there were so many things for which provision must be made. And he added: "Your Majesty should order that, as far as possible, no money should be borrowed in Genoa on bills of exchange, because there are no securities on which to base them and no way of repaying them." This was the nearest that Cobos could come to saying: "Do not borrow any more money!" At the end of the letter he remarked that he had been in bed for several days with a bad bump on his shin that had temporarily incapacitated him.[23]

The Marriage of Philip II

Before he left Barcelona, the Emperor had abandoned his plans for a dynastic alliance with England or France and had made up his mind to marry Philip to the Infanta María of Portugal. Was he moved by a desire to please his Spanish subjects or was he thinking in terms of the financial possibilities or did he remember his own happy marriage with another Portuguese princess? Perhaps all these thoughts were in his mind. When Cobos returned to Valladolid, he brought with him detailed instructions regarding the marriage. The date was set for October or November; the Duque de Medinasidonia and the Bishop of Cartagena were to go to the Portuguese border to receive the Infanta and conduct her to Salamanca. During the early fall Cobos and the other members of the Regency were busy working out the details.

These details had been complicated by Philip's not unnatural desire to catch a glimpse of the girl he was going to marry, before the actual ceremony. And so it had been necessary to make plans whereby the Prince might be at some point on the road along which the Princess was to travel. This meant the most exact timing, and Cobos and the Duque de Alba were working on the problem for weeks.[24]

The arrangements were finally settled and on November 2 the Prince left Valladolid with the Cardinal Tavera, the Almirante de Castilla, Juan de Zúñiga, and a few other courtiers. After a brief visit at Tordesillas, to receive the old Queen's benediction, they moved on to Medina del Campo, where they were joined by the Duke and Duchess of Alba and Cobos. That night they all reached the village of Cantalapiedra. From there, the Prince with a small group of attendants, including the Duque de Alba, the Conde de Benavente, the Almirante de Castilla, and other members of his household (Don Alonso Enríquez was one!), started for Alba de Tormes; the rest of the Court went on directly to Salamanca.

One of the Duke's properties, El Abadía, was on the road from Cáceres to Salamanca and there, one morning, Philip and his escort, hidden behind sheets, watched the Princess and her retinue as they passed along the road. It was even said that the young couple exchanged one fleeting glance of recognition. The Princess and her company reached the outskirts of Salamanca on Saturday, November 10, and shortly after, the Prince and his group were joined there by Cobos and the other members of the Court. On Sunday Cobos, Juan de Zúñiga, and his wife, Doña Estefanía de Requeséns, made a formal visit to pay their respects to the Prince.[25] All day on Saturday and Sunday there was coming and going between the gentlemen of Philip's suite and the leading citizens of Salamanca.

The Prince made his formal entry into Salamanca on Monday. The city was gaily decorated with five triumphal arches and the streets were crowded with citizens who had gathered to welcome their young lord. Philip was lodged in the house of the Licenciado Lugo, and from the windows of the house he and his followers, their cloaks over their faces, had another chance to see the Infanta as she passed down the street a few hours later on her way to her lodgings in the house of the *contador* Cristóbal Suárez. This time Cobos and Zúñiga were in the group that peeked out of the windows.

After the Prince and the Infanta had time to change their clothes (the Prince into white silk and gold), they were formally betrothed by the Cardinal of Toledo. There were parties and dances until late that night, when the Cardinal pronounced the marriage benediction. The Duke and Duchess of Alba were the sponsors. Among the brilliantly dressed company who witnessed the ceremony, Cobos was recorded as wearing "a suit of sable and brown satin and a tunic of the same material, with many jeweled buttons on the sleeves." [26]

The newly-weds and their suite started almost immediately for Valladolid, stopping at Tordesillas for another visit with Queen Juana. They reached Valladolid on November 22, and there too they were received with great pomp, the city having provided for the construction of a series of triumphal arches, designed by Antonio Vázquez and Gaspar de Tordesillas, one of them in the Corredera de San Pablo in front of Cobos' palace.[27] And it was in his palace that the Prince and Princess were lodged.[28]

The months after the return of Philip's Court to Valladolid were relatively uneventful. In December Cobos was in bed for some time with a bad cold.[29] In December, too, there was a flurry of excitement at Court when it was reported that a gold mine had been discovered near Alicante. The Marqués de Lombay and his wife, the Duque de Calabria, and the Conde de Oliva all wrote to Cobos asking him to grant them the right to the mine. Cobos wisely declined to make a decision, saying that he must ask the Emperor for his approval. But in the end it proved to be a false rumor: when the samples of supposed ore were assayed they turned out to be nothing but black dirt.[30]

Cobos' Evaluation of Philip and His Counsellors

It must have been in this period that Cobos wrote to the Emperor his analysis of the activities of Philip in his new rôle as Regent and of the several members of his advisory staff. The letter in question, preserved only in an eighteenth century copy now in the Biblioteca Nacional in Madrid,[31] is certainly the work of Cobos, for only he could have possessed the intimate knowledge of details which it reveals. But it presents some puzzling problems.

The first is the question of the date. The letter begins: "In a letter of Your Majesty, dated at Palamós on the 15th of the present month, you order me to report to you and give a secret account of King Philip's method of governing at home and abroad and of other important matters of these kingdoms." It ends: "Aranjuez, February 6, 1543." Now these dates do not make sense. The Emperor was not at Palamós on the fifteenth of any month in any year; a letter dated on the sixth cannot be in answer to one of the fifteenth of the same month; on February 6, 1543, the Emperor and Cobos were still in Madrid.

The content of the letter makes it clear that it was written some time after Cobos' return to Valladolid on June 29, 1543. It must have been written before September, 1545, for the Duque de Alba, who is reported as present, left for Flanders at that time. But Cobos could not have been at Aranjuez on February 6 in either 1544 or 1545, for in both of those years he was in Valladolid. A possible explanation of the dates given is that they were garbled by the copyist; he must have made some changes in the original text, for the title of "King" as applied to Philip was never used in this period; he is always referred to as "the Prince" or "His Highness." But even this explanation is unsatisfactory, for it seems little likely that the copyist would have made an error twice, both at the beginning and at the end of the latter. Is it possible that someone in the secretariat of Cobos deliberately changed the dates because of the confidential character of the document?

The other puzzling feature of the letter is the style in which it is written. Cobos' communications were always couched in a simple, straightforward style, without any trace of literary sophistication. But the present letter is elaborate, even pretentious in language. Again, it is possible that the form may be the result of the eighteenth century copyist's revision. Another possibility is that Gonzalo Pérez, the secretary of Philip, collaborated with Cobos in preparing the document, for Pérez was a man of letters and knew what a formal style was. But these questions of date and style are of minor importance. The significance of the letter lies in what it has to say about Philip and his advisors; in respect to the latter, it forms a pendant to the Emperor's "Secret Instruction" to Philip. As the only extensive expression of Cobos' opinion about the men with whom he worked, it deserves to be quoted in full.

After the opening sentence, cited above, the letter continues:

In obedience to Your Majesty's instruction and counting it one of the many favors which I confess and shall confess that I owe him, I shall try to comply with the clarity and truth which Your Majesty knows by long experience that I am accustomed to use in all my affairs.

First of all, sir, King Philip my lord is already so great a king that his knowledge and capacity have outstripped his years, for he seems to have achieved the impossible by his great understanding and his lofty comprehension. His diversions are a complete and constant devotion to work and the affairs of his kingdom. He is always thinking and talking about matters of good government and justice, without leaving room for favoritism or idleness or flattery or any vice. His relations and conversations are always about these matters with mature men of the highest reputation. At times he asks questions about matters in which he is informed, and this is no doubt his greatest quality, for he does it so as not to err in his commands.

In the most important affairs, where it is necessary to hold meetings to discuss them, he listens to the opinions of each one with the greatest gravity and attention; after he has heard and understood them all, with every consideration and judgment he disapproves of what does not seem good, rarely making a mistake, and afterwards he reaches his own decision, taking the best from each one, which is a source of wonder to all. And so in all this he is doing astonishing and admirable things.

He frequently is closeted with me for hours at a time to discuss important matters of state. Afterwards he does the same thing with the President of the Council [Valdés], to study the problems of justice, and with the Duque de Alba to talk about questions of war, and with other people to talk over other very different questions and to inform himself in detail about his distant dominions. And afterwards he has me write out his orders and decisions in each one of these things, which he dictates to me. And although I have express instructions from Your Majesty—and he knows it—to reprove him and to advise actions more likely to achieve good, I assure Your Majesty I not only do not have to reject anything that he decides, but I am astonished at his prudent, well-considered recommendations, which are more fitting in a man trained all his life in state and other affairs than in a ruler who is so new in it, in years and in authority.

He is, sir, devoted to virtue and justice, scorning all that is contrary to them. Wherefore we all accept and respect his advice, because in the midst of the gravity and restraint with which he gives it and points out the errors, it is accompanied by a natural majesty and authority which is terrifying. Your Majesty may be sure that the King my lord was born only to be a great king.

Your Majesty is familiar with the qualities and spirit of the Duque de Alba. In spite of that, it happened one day last month that His Highness asked the Duke something about the war with France. The Duke, with his accustomed impetuosity, replied that as long as the Emperor and he were alive, they would soon take care of France. The King my lord, very quietly but with all his majesty, said to him: "After the Emperor, no one holds a place before me. I am of the opinion that anyone who does not understand that and boasts in my presence either does not know me or is trying to displease me. This should let you know who I am." With that His Highness turned his back, and the rest of us who were there were amazed at his angry reply. We all had to intervene to restore the Duke to his favor.

In one hand he holds punishment for the guilty and in the other, reward for the deserving. He rules his kingdoms with such prudence and justice that nothing is hidden from him and he is familiar with everything. At public audiences he is so quiet and humane that by his gentleness and affability he encourages those who come with pleas. He listens attentively to everyone, which is most praiseworthy. For some he makes suitable provision; others he sends to the proper official; those who make improper requests he dismisses sternly and majestically.

He is watchful for the honor of God and the welfare of these his kingdoms. He requires that in the courts only right and justice shall prevail. He demands that offices in them shall be given only to those who are competent to fill them and he tries in every way to find out whether this is being done. Finally, sir, the King my lord is acting and thinking at so high and just a level that without the aid of anyone he is capable of maintaining his kingdoms in great glory and fame and of winning for himself the name of a great king.

So much with regard to King Philip, my lord and Your Majesty's glorious son. Last of all, with regard to the other matters of these kingdoms, it will suffice to say that with such a ruler all will be well. Nevertheless it is still necessary to tell Your Majesty some other things that are happening, since although the King my lord is so honest and grave and invincible, he is human and can easily become subject to the rivalries, flattery and counsel of those who seek to win his whole regard for themselves, with no other purpose than to rule and control him wholly, from which there might arise the evils and harm which Your Majesty knows very well.

For that reason and being sure that there are many who desire this, it is right that I should tell it and explain it to Your Majesty, not only to carry out the instruction Your Majesty has given me, but also that Your Majesty may provide the remedy which is most proper and necessary.

The Cardinal Tavera is ceaselessly trying to win the whole love of the King my lord, using for that end methods which are not very honorable, such as provoking people to talk, so that he may hear them and then report them and others of their ilk.

The Duque de Alba is moving in the same direction, adding a few authorities of his own, and even, in order to achieve his purpose, inciting the King to diversions which are not at all proper.

Don Juan de Zúñiga is working hard for himself. I do not mean to say against me, lest I become suspected by this comment. He wants complete control, without regard for the services and loyalty of the rest, and to gain this he does everything he can to get the King to make him his only privy counsellor, to such a point that his ambition is widely known, and nothing good was ever done by that. The sternness and rigor with which he brought His Highness up has been changed into sweetness and gentleness, all of it arising from flattery to help him attain his goal.

The Conde de Osorno, in his silent way, does everything he can to the same end and he even looks at me in a different way. He has frequent conversations with Zúñiga and the Duque de Alba. Nothing reasonable can be expected from that triumvirate.

Siliceo, the Bishop and confessor of His Highness, is not far behind them; they sometimes join with him and I am almost prepared to tell Your Majesty that between the three of them they have offered him a cardinal's hat, if he will dispose the mind of His Highness to something that I cannot tell Your Majesty about, because I am not very sure of it, but I will, as soon as I am sure, for I am working diligently in the service of Your Majesty and His Highness, as I always have been accustomed, in the sight of everyone.

The Cardinal Tavera carries on his affairs in another way and with other people. Those that he is most intimate with are the Cardinal of Seville and the Licenciado Paramo and Catalán. What they discuss, they only know, but judging by the authority which the Cardinal and those of his party are secretly assuming, I cannot believe that their talks are intended for purposes that are important for Your Majesty and His Highness, as they should be, for their temperaments are so well known that no one can help believing something else, which is not very reasonable.

Besides these, there are other cliques, but these are the principal ones. And although His Highness gives his attention to everything, he cannot understand all the problems. I have called some things to his attention and I do not know how he has received it. Your Majesty, who is familiar with such things and such people, will realize that these cliques and gatherings cannot be reasonable nor good for these kingdoms nor the King my lord.

Your Majesty with his lofty discernment will be able to provide what is proper, so that each one of us may live and work in his own field, serving Your Majesty and His Highness in our necessary duties, without seeking other intimacies and promotions than those which our industry and effort deserve, avoiding secret meetings, because they give a bad impression to those who observe them, even though they are not evil in themselves.

Without presuming to offer Your Majesty advice, for your great understanding does not need my poor, limited contribution, I do think that it would be right and proper for Your Majesty to intervene in this matter. And for that, it would be very useful if the clergy in each of the two groups would leave the Court to govern their churches and feed their flocks, for they badly need it, and would leave worldly matters as alien to their character, rank and station. In this way I am sure that we would avoid the cliques and secret meetings, or at least for the most part, and His Highness would be rid of the purple robes which never, as Your Majesty once said, go well with gentlemen's ruffs. In this and in all the rest, Your Majesty will decide what he thinks most appropriate.

Day before yesterday Figueroa was transferred to the Royal Council, where I am sure that he will prove very valuable, for as Your Majesty knows, he is a man of sound learning, very honest and in official matters nothing will deflect him an iota from what is right. I have been very glad of Your Majesty's choice, for he will serve well. Though I did not ask for his appointment, I have not learned who did advise Your Majesty; it was certainly a very right and Christian piece of advice.

Last week Sanabria was also transferred from the Council of the Orders to that of Castile. Your Majesty knows that he should have been there long ago because of his learning, his piety and his merits. From what I have heard he obtained the transfer because he wrote to His Highness to remove him from the Council of the Orders for certain personal reasons; and if His Highness did not approve of this action, to accept his resignation from the post. The outcome of this was the change which I have reported to Your Majesty.

Although Sanabria did not give, in his communication to His Highness, the reasons for this request and though they had never been made known, it would be necessary to consider them just in a man of his high integrity. But afterwards they were learned and they were that he could no longer stand the harshness with which the President, Osorno, treats the Council, for he has all the Councillors so under his thumb that they have no freedom to make decisions, and so everything is settled in accordance with his will, a situation which does not seem desirable, and for that reason I ask Your Majesty to intervene, so that the Count may be restrained and the Councillors may reach their decisions and cast their votes as is their duty, and not as he demands.

All this is what I can tell Your Majesty in conformity and obedience to your instructions. And although at present the affairs of these kingdoms are quiet and peaceful, with the conflicts of these cliques nothing good and justified can be expected. And for this reason my insistence is so great, for I desire only the glory of the King my lord and the peace and prosperity of these kingdoms and his vassals, as I think I have demonstrated to Your Majesty after so many years in which I have had the privilege and honor of serving you.

God grant Your Majesty wise guidance in this and that he may conquer the enemies that he is now planning to fight, and grant him too the long years of life which Christendom needs.

Sir, always at the royal feet of Your Majesty,

Your most humble and loyal servant
Francisco de los Cobos.

Cobos' letter is a document of capital importance both as an intimate picture of Philip and the Court rivalries that beset him, and as a revelation of Cobos' own personality. It has been remarked that in his characterization of the Prince he stressed those traits which he knew would please his father; [32] certainly the portrait he draws is a forecast of the man he was to be— dedicated to his duties, prudent, and arrogant. The vignettes of his counsellors correspond closely with those that the Emperor had sketched in his "Secret Instruction." Not unnaturally Cobos paints himself as a wholly disinterested and faithful servant. But it must be pointed out that if the Emperor had followed his advice and ordered the prelates to return to their dioceses, it would have eliminated not only Tavera, Siliceo, and Loaisa, but also Valdés, President of the Council of Castile, who was bishop of Sigüenza, and would have left Cobos, the Duque de Alba, and Juan de Zúñiga in complete control of the Regency. One wonders if the Emperor also asked Tavera for his opinion on the situation at Philip's Court. If he did, it would be interesting to know what he thought of Cobos.

Throughout 1544 Cobos continued to carry on his usual voluminous correspondence. There were almost daily letters to the Emperor, Juan Vázquez, and Idiáquez; there was the normal exchange with the ambassadors in Italy and Portugal. Most of them deal with routine matters of business, but now and then there are other topics. Cobos was still disturbed at the heavy cost of the Emperor's military campaigns, and on February 14 he wrote to him: "If Your Majesty, as His Highness writes, could find a way to peace or to a truce, that we might have a breathing space, it would be a great boon, and though I know that Your Majesty desires and wants peace and it is no longer in his power, still I cannot help begging you, as humbly as I can, to bear in mind the great service you will do to God, if you can achieve it." [33] At the same time Philip wrote to his father that he had discussed the financial situation with the Council and that in view of the impossibility of raising any more money, they urged the Emperor to make peace, or at least a truce, with France. We may be sure that Cobos drafted that letter for his signature.[34]

Early in 1544 Juan Vázquez was ill in Flanders and Cobos wrote to Francisco de Madrid, who was temporarily taking over some of his duties, to keep in touch with Idiáquez and to behave in all matters with due modesty and restraint.[35] Shortly thereafter (March 26), he wrote to Vázquez that Zárate had sent him enough "China wood" and sarsaparilla for a treatment, but that the little bag of "China wood" had got lost on the way; he was sending the sarsaparilla and would order more "China wood." [36] It was, however, Francisco de Eraso, a protégé of the Regent Figueroa, who was assigned the task of assisting Idiáquez during Vázquez's absence from the Emperor's Court.

Although Cobos and the Council had opposed calling the Cortes again, after a lapse of only two years, the Emperor had insisted and so the *procuradores* met again in Valladolid in March, 1544. This time their meetings were held in the great hall of Cobos' palace, where Philip was living; it was Gonzalo Pérez who prepared the address of the Crown in Philip's name and who read it to the assembly in a "loud, intelligible voice." When the delegates procrastinated, Cobos brought pressure on them, saying that the Prince must get away at once for his Holy Week retreat and that he wanted their decision before he left. And so submissively they voted the ordinary subsidy, but they could not be induced to approve additional funds. As *asistente* of the Cortes, Cobos shared in the distribution of payments to the participants to the extent of 50,000 *maravedís;* even his doorkeeper, Murga, received 2,250 *maravedís* for his services.[37]

Conflict with the Duque del Infantado

During that spring Cobos became involved in a controversy with the Duque del Infantado. In August, 1543, a vacancy had occurred in the post of *corregidor* of the Duke's city, Guadalajara, and he had asked for the appointment of his son, Don Enrique.[38] There were many applicants for the post, and the Council, in spite of the Duke's protests, recommended to the Emperor that decision be postponed until his return to Spain.[39] The Duke believed that Cobos was responsible for this action and wrote him a violent letter of denunciation. Cobos showed the letter to the Duque de Alba, who wrote to the Duque del Infantado in October, 1544, a warm letter of exoneration:

> What you wanted the Grand Commander to do is a matter outside his control and one in which he had always done everything possible. You must remember that in questions that come before the Council not only Cobos but the Emperor himself has no more influence than the sorriest squire in the kingdom, if they want something to which the Council does not take a fancy. Quite apart from what I have told you, because I have seen it, that the Grand Commander has done what he could in this affair, if we take the ques-

tion by itself, in a man like him whom we have always seen and will see inclined to do good, never having found in him evidence of serving his own interests or anyone else more than you, which would impel him not to do what you wish, why should you believe that he would fail to do what he has done all of his life, even for those who were not his friends, to say nothing of you, for whom he has always had and has such respect?

Alba chided Infantado for his impolitic language and told him that he had advised Cobos not to answer the letter, and he ended: "You should write to him again and try to keep him as truly a father as he has been up to now and as I know he still is." [40] Núñez de Castro, in his history of Guadalajara, tells us that the dispute was finally settled by an agreement that the Emperor would appoint some one acceptable to the Duke.[41]

The Archivo de Simancas

During the summer of 1544 Cobos completed the preparations for the establishment of an archive of official documents at the fortress of Simancas.[42] The Spanish kings had long been concerned with the preservation of state papers. Enrique IV had ordered them placed for safekeeping in the castle of Segovia; others were in the Mota of Medina del Campo. On March 24, 1489, Ferdinand and Isabel had issued an instruction that further documents were to be deposited in the Chancillería of Valladolid; meanwhile those at Segovia and Medina del Campo were to be kept in good order. When the secretary Gaspar de Gricio died in 1508, his widow was ordered to turn his papers over to his successor, Lope Conchillos.[43]

The first official "Keeper" of the papers was the Licenciado Salmerón, a member of the Council, who served from 1509 to 1519. He was followed by Francisco de Galindo (1519-1526) and the Licenciado Acuña (1526-1544).[44] There was as yet no official depository, and during his regency the Cardinal Cisneros wrote to the King on the desirability of designating such a place.[45] The need of a secure spot was amply demonstrated during the war of the *comuneros,* when the house of García Ruiz de la Mota in Burgos was sacked by the rebels, who carried out and burned in the plaza all the official papers which his brother, the Bishop Mota, had placed in his care.[46] Doubtless many others were lost through carelessness or fire.

With the coming of Charles to Spain the interest in the preservation of official documents continued. On the death of Con-chillos, in 1522, his widow in turn was instructed to deliver his papers to Cobos.[47] A related interest was revealed in the instruction issued on December 7, 1526 to all those having papers of Peter Martyr to turn them over to the royal chronicler, Antonio de Guevara.[48] The royal secretaries, too, were becoming conscious of the importance of their official correspondence. When Alonso de Valdés died in 1532 he left a clause in his will that all his papers be sent to Cobos.[49] And Cobos himself, on the eve of his departure for Tunis in 1535, sent a chest full of documents to Juan Vázquez, which the latter delivered to the Cardinal Tavera.[50] Unfortunately the ambassadors and viceroys did not often preserve their correspondence, but this lack was in part made up by the practice of preserving in the secretariat a rough draft of letters sent to Imperial representatives.

Shortly after his appointment as *alcaide* of Simancas, in 1538, Cobos and the Emperor began to study the need of a suitable depository. Simancas was selected as the most desirable site, partly because of the strength of its fortress, partly because it was close to Valladolid. Cobos' old friend, Luis de Vega, was named as the architect to draw the plans for the necessary construction of a section of the castle to receive the papers. In 1539 Cobos wrote to his majordomo, Hernando Bernaldo, that he was to work with Juan Mosquera de Molina, whom Cobos had appointed as his deputy in charge of the castle, to carry out Luis de Vega's plans.[51] Between 1539 and 1543 Bernaldo was authorized to make payments of a total of 895,132 *maravedís* for the costs of construction;[52] part of the funds came from money paid by individuals for licenses to export negro slaves to the Indies.[53]

On June 26, 1540, Cobos wrote to Juan Vázquez:

> I do not think that the papers which the Licenciado Acuña had are being properly cared for. I am sending you a blank instruction for them to be turned over. You will consult with His Majesty as to the person to whom he wishes them given, while we are setting up the Archive, which I will have put in order this summer in Simancas. Find out whether they should be left for the present in the hands of Mosquera or someone else, provided that His Majesty must not think that the intention is to give him the title of "Keeper" of the Archive. If he approves, have Figueroa prepare the instruction there, so that no one will think that we engineered it here.[54]

The work did not proceed as rapidly as Cobos had expected.

On January 26, 1543, Mosquera reported that work on the first two floors of the Archive was finished and that there was enough money to complete the third floor.[55] It was a tiny affair, housed in one of the north towers of the fortress, but Luis de Vega had designed an exquisite interior in pine, rising in three levels to a pointed ceiling, crowned with the arms of the House of Austria. Even today it remains one of the gems of Renaissance woodwork in Spain.[56] None of the work of Luis de Vega as royal architect of the *alcázar* of Madrid has survived, but the few remnants that have come down to us—the Palacio de los Dueñas in Medina del Campo, the patio of Cobos' palace in Valladolid, and the *cubo* of the fortress of Simancas—prove him to have been a designer of refined taste, worthy of a place among the leading architects of the day.

The transfer of documents to their new quarters began almost at once. On February 19, 1543, the Chancillery of Valladolid was ordered to deliver to Simancas the papers that had come from Medina del Campo.[57] During 1544 a series of orders continued the process. On February 11, the monastery of San Benito in Valladolid was instructed to turn over all its patents of nobility, and other monasteries received similar orders.[58] In June the Consejo de las Indias was ordered to send all its papers to Simancas, and at the same time Cobos was instructed to have a special chest made for them with two keys, one for himself, the other for Juan de Samano.[59]

The task was finished by the end of the summer of 1544, and on September 17 Valdés and Cobos wrote to the Emperor that his instructions had been carried out. They had made a visit to Simancas ten or twelve days before, to see the rooms that had been prepared and to study the plans for their use. They were well satisfied with what they found and felt that all was well planned. They asked the Emperor to instruct all persons possessing papers to deliver them to the Archive.[60]

At the same time they recommended the appointment of the Licenciado Catalán (was this a sop to Tavera?) as Keeper of the Archive, at a salary of 100,000 *maravedís,* without any requirement of service, and also the assignment of 40,000 *maravedís* a year to the deputy *alcaide* [Mosquera] for his services in the care and maintenance of the collection. The appointment of Catalán was approved on November 30,[61] and on March 25, 1545, Cobos sent the necessary papers for his appointment and that of Mosquera; he would at once take steps to have all the papers in Spain brought to Simancas.[62] Finally, on August 25, Philip issued the formal order, calling on all officials and official bodies to turn over their documents.[63] Thus was initiated the Archive of Simancas, largely the creation of Cobos, which one day was to become one of the greatest documentary collections in Europe.

The Peace of Crépy

Meanwhile, thanks to the funds which Cobos had managed to scrape together in 1543, the Emperor had been waging a successful military campaign against Francis on the Franco-German border. His successes had forced the French King to enter into negotiations for peace, and at Crépy on September 14 and 18, 1544, Granvelle and Ferrante Gonzaga, in behalf of Charles, signed two treaties—one public, the other secret. The major points at issue had not changed greatly since the negotiations of 1537-1538; but this time Charles was a victor and Francis was vanquished. The public treaty provided for the confirmation of the treaties of Madrid and Cambrai, French aid against the Turks, and the marriage of the Duke of Orleans to the Infanta María of Spain, with the Netherlands as their inheritance on the death of the Emperor, or to the Infanta Ana of Hungary, now sixteen years old, with the investiture of Milan a year later. The Emperor was to decide which of these two marriages he deemed best, and he at once dispatched messengers to consult with Philip and with Ferdinand of Hungary.[64]

It was the secretary Idiáquez who was sent to lay the matter before Philip. He reached Valladolid on November 1,[65] and Philip immediately called a meeting of all his advisors to discuss the question of the marriage. The long report of that discussion records the opinions of all those who took part: Tavera, Alba, Loaisa, Hernando Valdés, the Conde de Osorno, the Vice Chancellor of Aragon, Miguel Mai, Dr. Guevara of the Council of Castile.[66] It is comforting to know that they thought that the person most concerned, the Infanta María, should also be consulted. Cobos' name does not appear on the list of speakers; it is possible that he was not able to attend the session. He had written to Juan Vázquez on October 31 that he had had another attack of his groin trouble and was incapacitated.[67] On November 7 the Duque de Calabria wrote to Cobos that he was sorry to hear of his illness, but he hoped that, now that he had passed a "little stone," he would soon be better.[68]

In reality, the Emperor never had to reach a decision with regard to the marriage, for the Duke of Orleans died on September 9, 1545, and Charles promptly decided to grant the investiture of Milan to his son Philip. In view of his hedging over all the long years of discussion, it is difficult to avoid the conclusion that he never seriously considered alienating Milan as a fief that belonged to his dynasty.

The Statutes of San Salvador

Ever since the renewal of construction of his chapel of San Salvador, in 1540, Cobos had continued to show his interest in its progress. At Madrid, on October 31, 1541, he entered into a contract with a Toledan silversmith, Francisco Martínez de San Román, to make a number of objects for the services of the chapel: a monstrance, two chalices (one partly gold-plated), an altar cross, candelabra, etc., of a total value of 138 silver marks. Martínez was required to give security to Diego López de Ayala, canon of the cathedral of Toledo, and to deliver the vessels at Court within a year and a half. For his part, Cobos agreed to an advance of 100 ducats on account. If there was disagreement as to the value of the work done, a jury was to decide. Luis de Vega was one of the witnesses who signed the contract.[69]

Between 1541 and 1544, Jamete, the sculptor, worked for two years and a half on carvings of the chapel;[70] his subtle hand is largely responsible for the beauty of its decoration. When the Pope finally confirmed the privilege of the chapel on February 10, 1542, he also authorized Cobos to found a university at Ubeda, "with all the privileges and rights that have been granted to the universities of Salamanca, Paris, Bologna, and Alcalá de Henares." At the same time he authorized him to establish a monastery in Ubeda. A week later he approved of the use of the income, for a five-year period, to complete the construction of the church.[71]

Although the work was far from completion, Cobos presently made up his mind to draw up the constitution or statutes which were to govern the operation of the church. At Valladolid, in the house of Juan Mosquera de Molina and in the presence of

Prince Philip, the document was signed on October 13, 1544.[72] For many reasons it is of unusual interest, in part because it provides a summary of the development of the chapel and also because it illustrates Cobos' care and mastery of minor details. It is too long to quote in full, but certain details are worthy of mention. After the conventional invocation to the Heavenly powers, Cobos goes on:

> Turning over in my mind the many great favors and benefits which up to now I have received from almighty God, for which I always gave, give and will give to Him such thanks as I can, with the strength and devotion that he has granted me, desiring to put my soul in a good state and to exchange temporal for spiritual blessings, moved by humility and devotion, in correction and satisfaction of my faults and sins and those of my wife, Doña María de Mendoza, and in order that God may pardon my father and mother and my kinsmen, my successors and benefactors, using the privileges granted by our Holy Fathers Clement VII and Paul III, I have ordered the construction of a church which I have begun to build, dedicated to the Saviour, in the city of Ubeda on a piece of ground which I acquired from the Hospital of San Salvador . . . in which I wish the Holy Sacrament to be constantly revered, and it is my will that the divine offices be celebrated in the form and manner set forth in the following statutes and ordinances.

He had already established a chapel of the Conception—he tells us—in the church of Santo Tomás, but it had proved too small for the proper celebration of the services; hence he had decided to build a larger edifice, where the aged poor of the Hospital would be able to enjoy the offices of the Church. Pope Paul III had authorized the transfer to the new church of all the privileges, indulgences, and benefices of the earlier chapel. But even when the new structure was finished, one mass a day was to be sung in the chapel of Santo Tomás, of which he and his heirs were to be the patrons. Cobos also renewed the assurance of his intention to establish a university and a monastery in Ubeda at an early date. For the present the income of the church was to be used to complete the construction.

He now proceeds to provide in detail for the operation of the church—the qualifications and duties of the chaplains, the sacristan, the acolytes, the organist. Rules for attendance, fines for absence, the proper vestments to be worn, days of special observance, hours of the masses—a bewildering list which his head chaplain, Hernando Ortega, must have helped him to compile. Thus, for example, he provided that on All Souls' Day all the chaplains and acolytes shall stand around his tomb, holding lighted candles in their hand, during high mass and vespers, and that in addition to the usual candles, four large candles be lighted and extra incense be provided. It is noteworthy that in the service of the canonical hours he provides that they be sung "in the same order and manner as in the Royal Chapel of the Catholic Kings in Granada." Another interesting provision is that on the first days of the three *pascuas,* if the patron or his wife were in Ubeda, the chaplains were required to "go to his house and bless the table and give thanks to God because He permitted me to build this church, for I have not thanked Him as I should, since I was so busy in the service of His Majesty; and the patron and his wife shall be obliged to give to each of the chaplains on Christmas, a pair of chickens, on Easter, a quarter of lamb, and on the Day of the Holy Spirit, a half a kid."

On the ground that "because of human weakness, spiritual things cannot long endure without temporal support," Cobos describes in detail the endowment and income of the church— the *juros,* benefices, and other grants which have been given to it, either by himself or by the Popes. The total income is 612,500 *maravedis* a year and one of the chaplains must keep a record book of all receipts and expenditures. Special provision is made for the payment of 100 ducats a year to feed the poor in the Hospital and the dowry of 100 ducats for the two orphaned damsels, to be named, one on the day of the Conception, and the other on the day of Our Saviour.

After his death, his son Diego and his successors, as provided in the *mayorazgo,* are to be the patrons of the church. He and his wife and any of their heirs who so desire are to be buried in the main chapel, in front of the high altar. As a special evidence of his affection he also approves of the burial of his chaplain, Hernando Ortega, in the main chapel; other chaplains may be buried in some other part of the church. He requests that his heirs shall not place any effigy in the main chapel, which he reserves for himself and his wife, as founders of the church; they may, however, erect burial monuments in the walls of the church.

Finally he provides that his heirs shall continue to serve as patrons and protectors of the chapel which Hernando Ortega has established in the church of San Nicolás in Ubeda, "because of the obligation, love and kinship which I feel for the aforesaid Dean and for all that he has labored and created in the construction and foundation of this my church by his good industry and prudence."

It is melancholy to think that all this magnificence and ceremony which Cobos tried so hard to establish "forevermore" has vanished with the years. The income has dwindled; revolutions have stripped the church of most of its treasures. But something still remains. At Christmastime the choir of local boys, trained by the devoted chaplain, still sing their *villancicos* to the accompaniment of castanets, and at the *misa del gallo,* the midnight mass on Christmas Eve, the icy church is crowded with the faithful, as the crucifer, in his white wig and deep purple robe, stands before the high altar on the very spot beneath which Don Francisco and Doña María lie buried.

Tragedy at Home

The year 1544 was a tragic one for María de Mendoza and Cobos. In January Doña María's mother, María Sarmiento, died.[73] She had inherited the title of Condesa de Rivadavia on the death, without issue, of her older sister, Francisca Sarmiento, wife of Enrique Enríquez. Since the death of her husband, Juan Hurtado de Mendoza, in 1530, she had been a widow.[74] Now the title passed to her eldest son, Diego Sarmiento de Mendoza. In September, Doña María's brother, Juan de Mendoza, died suddenly. On the seventeenth Cobos wrote to Juan Vázquez:

> After I finished the letter that goes with this dispatch, it has been God's will to take to Himself my brother-in-law, Juan de Mendoza (may he have eternal rest!) in the most unfortunate situation. For after he had been hit in the head by a wand in a *juego de cañas* and it was thought that he had recovered, a fortnight later a fatal illness killed him. I am terribly troubled and grieved, both because of the person he was and because of my affection for him, for, as you know, I loved him like a true brother. Doña María was and is greatly afflicted, especially because this comes in addition to other misfortunes and losses.[75]

Before the end of the year death came again to the family. Doña María's oldest brother, Diego Sarmiento, had been in ill health for some time. In July, 1541, he had had a fall,[76] and in October one of Cobos' assistants (the letter is unsigned) wrote to Juan Vázquez: "You have probably heard about the ailment of the Adelantado de Galicia. They have brought him here and he is certainly a pitiful sight. Doña María does not know about it yet." [77] Two years later, on his way from Barcelona to Zaragoza, Cobos asked Juan de Samano to let him know about the health of Don Diego and his wife, Leonor de Castro.[78] The ailment from which he was suffering was plainly mental, and on August 25, 1543, we was officially declared insane and a guardian appointed for him.[79] In November, 1544, he was dead.[80]

In the midst of a letter filled with gossip and mockery which Don Alonso Enríquez wrote to Doña María from Seville on December 8, he suddenly interrupts his nonsense to turn philosopher: "Why should you blame me, if I pay little heed to a thing that is so certain as death, when those who fear it most may rightly be called crazy? Since we are all born with this condition, we ought rather to be glad and thank God, when our husbands and wives and brothers die before us, because God allows those of us who are left to live, in order that we may witness it and be left to pray to Him for their souls and emend our ways." [81]

Early in January Doña María answered his letter:

I received your letter and you may be sure that I was glad to have it. I am sure that you wrote to me to console me for the death of my mother and my brothers that God has sent me, as a discreet person who is fond of me, by similes and other comparisons. I am consoled, because God knows what is best and He does not send me as many afflictions as I deserve, through His infinite goodness and mercy. The Grand Commander and I are well and so anxious to see you that it will be ingratitude and inhumanity, if you fail to visit us. The Duque de Alba sends his greetings and says that he will show you a favor. I suspect that your threats are rather a sign of affection than anything else, for I know that you will not fight about it, since it is so clear that you are both fond of each other, as you should be. In order to give you some desire to see me, I won't write at great length. God keep you . . .[82]

We have had frequent occasion to mention the constant interest that Cobos showed in securing special grants and appointments for his own kinsmen. But he was no less zealous in using his influence with the Emperor and his officials to promote the interests of his wife's family. We have already mentioned the appointment of his mother-in-law as lady in waiting of the Empress and the mine rights granted to her and her husband. It will be of interest to trace his activities in behalf of Doña María's brothers and sisters.

Don Diego Sarmiento de Mendoza, her oldest brother, long played an active part in the life of the Court. At the tournament in Valladolid, in 1527, to celebrate the birth of Prince Philip,

he was one of the five knights who fought on the side against
the Emperor's team and he was named the best of all the contestants.[83] In 1532 he was in Venice and with the Spanish ambassador visited the Doge.[84] He took part in the Tunisian
campaign and he accompanied Cobos when he went to Salsas in
December, 1537. In the festive days in Barcelona in the spring
of 1538 he took a leading part.[85] On November 21, 1539, the
Emperor named him Comendador of Monasterio in the order
of Santiago,[86] and in 1543 appointed him Adelantado of Galicia, succeeding his father.[87]

In a burlesque *romance,* ascribed to Luis de Avila, he is described as follows:

> "No se nos quede en olbido
> Ese un llando furión;
> Parece mastín bermejo,
> También parece cabrón.
> Muchos le tienen por bravo,
> Mas el que lo conoce, non,"

along with his brother, Juan de Mendoza,

> "Si no, dígalo su hermano,
> Ese peladillo hurón,
> Galguillo que le ahorcaron
> Porque hizo una trayción." [88]

Doña María's second brother, Juan de Mendoza, was also
early in the Emperor's service. He too was with Cobos at Salsas
and in Barcelona in 1538. In August, 1541, Cobos sent him with
messages to the Emperor,[89] and after the Emperor left Barcelona in May, 1543 he was sent to carry messages to the Portuguese Infanta.[90] Cobos had also used his younger brother,
Bernardino, as a carrier of messages: he sent him to the Marqués
del Guasto in 1541; [91] he was in Genoa in 1542.[92] He had also
secured for him an appointment as *trinchante* of Prince Philip.[93]

When Don Juan died in September, 1544, Cobos wrote to
Juan Vázquez urging him to beg the Emperor to give Bernardino the *encomienda* of the Corral de Caracuel in the Order of
Calatrava which had been granted to Don Juan. Cobos reminded
him that Don Bernardino had served well in the campaigns of
Tunis, Lombardy, and Algiers; he was one of three brothers
who were left with nothing to eat, for Don Juan had been providing for them and the Emperor had refused to renew the *juro*

which had lapsed on the death of his mother, the Countess. He was sending Don Bernardino in person with the letter; since he was inexperienced in affairs, would Vázquez do everything he could to help him? [94] The Emperor did not grant him the favor that Cobos had requested, for the latter wrote again to Vázquez on December 14 that he would have to accept the Emperor's decision, although he could not fail to regret his lukewarm attitude toward him in all of his affairs; he only hoped that the Emperor would do better in the vacancy in the appointment that Don Diego had held as *comendador*.[95]

The fourth brother of Doña María, Alvaro de Mendoza, had entered the Church. Cobos had secured for him an appointment as head chaplain of the chapel of Los Reyes Nuevos in Toledo, and in 1538 he wrote to Juan Vázquez that he could not at present do anything more for him.[96] Ultimately he became successively bishop of Palencia, Jaén, and Avila. He was a stout supporter of Santa Teresa in the establishment of her first house of the Carmelites in Avila.

Another brother, Ruy Díaz de Mendoza, seems to have been a constant source of trouble. Already in April, 1535, Cobos wrote to Vázquez that he was sorry he was behaving so badly.[97] A month later Cobos saw him in Barcelona and Don Rodrigo insisted that not only was he innocent of any wrongdoing, but that he deserved favors.[98] On October 15, 1539, he received an appointment as *comendador* in Malta [99] and he and his wife, Doña Guiomar, sailed for Palermo. Early in 1540 they embarked in a small vessel for Naples, but they were driven back by a storm to the island of Lipari, and there Doña Guiomar gave birth to a daughter.[100] They finally reached Naples, and there Cobos still tried to befriend him, writing to the Viceroy to ask him to show him favor: he had overstayed a leave of absence on account of the wedding of his niece.[101] The last we hear of him was a letter he wrote to Cobos from Naples on June 5, 1542:

I have reached such a pass that, remembering the evil reputation I have or have had with Your Lordship, I cannot fail to confess that I feel proud when I see in this kingdom men in important posts, old and held in repute, involved in such shady affairs that if I were in the least of them, knowing Your Lordship as I do, I would throw myself into a well in despair. I beg Your Lordship to help me, not as a member of your family, for I do not have that good fortune, but as a stranger, if it is shown on sound evidence that I am doing what I should, and perchance even more than some people.[102]

Of Doña María's youngest brother, Carlos de Mendoza, there is no record other than the mention of him in the *mayorazgo* of Don Francisco and Doña María.

Doña María also had four sisters. Of the eldest, Beatriz Sarmiento de Mendoza, who married her kinsman, Juan Sarmiento, Lord of Salvatierra, we know nothing more. Another sister, Francisca Sarmiento, had married the Mariscal Fernando Díaz de Rivadaneira, *regidor* of Toledo, in 1526. At that time Cobos was one of those who appeared to offer security for the payment of her dowry.[103] Years later he was endeavoring to secure preferment for their son in Rome.[104] A third sister, Beatriz de Noroña, married Alonso Luis Fernández de Lugo. Cobos was certainly responsible for securing his appointment as *adelantado* of the Canaries and later as governor of Santa Maria, just at the time when Don Alonso Enríquez thought that he was to be the commander of the forces in that province.[105] We need not discuss here his scandalous conduct in the Indies. But Herrera reported that when Gonzalo Ximénez returned to Spain in 1539 he did not dare to go to Court because of his fear of Lugo, a kinsman of Cobos and María de Mendoza.[106] Bartolomé de las Casas was violent in his condemnation of Lugo, whom he called "one of the most cruel tyrants, a most irrational and bestial man, of little sense and worse conscience than that of Barbarossa." And he added that Cobos would have to give account to God for appointing him, for he knew what an evil person he was.[107] Of Doña María's youngest sister, Ana de Mendoza, there is no record; perhaps she died early.

It was a big family and they were not rich. But no one could have done more than Cobos did to secure every possible favor and privilege for his wife's relatives. In those days everyone who was in a position of power imitated the Emperor in promoting the interests of his dynasty.

CHAPTER XIII

THE LAST YEARS

The early months of 1545 were filled with the usual round of daily tasks—conferences with Philip, with Tavera and the Council, correspondence with the Emperor and the secretaries about the health of the Infantas, the vacancies to be filled, and the appointments to be made,[1] with the ambassadors at foreign Courts. As always, financial matters were a constant cause of concern. On March 25, Cobos wrote to Charles that he could find no source of new funds, for all revenues were committed until 1548. It was idle to call the Cortes again during the Emperor's absence; the year before they had made every effort to secure a larger appropriation but had failed. The Emperor must not count exclusively on Spain, but must seek support elsewhere. The device of selling offices had proved a failure, for no one was willing to pay. As for himself, Cobos added: "Believe me, Your Majesty, there is not a damned office that I want to add to my list nor have I any other aim or concern, except Your Majesty's service in all matters." [2]

Increasingly he felt the weight of his responsibilities. To Juan Vázquez he confided:

Loaisa is ill and Tavera has gone to his diocese in Toledo for Easter. They are all badly needed, though in the end everything falls on me. I am so troubled that I do not know what to do. I swear that I have not ill deserved the favors His Majesty has done me. And I am still doing much, since I take on all this toil and trouble, without expecting any new favors, for my

287

son does not yet have any appointment. I will not go on with what I had to
say about this, until you rejoin His Majesty. And what I have said I beg you
to keep to yourself alone. I have said it only as a relief.[3]

There were, however, some moments of pleasure. In March
their old friends, Francisco de Borja and his wife, Leonor de
Castro, came to Valladolid for a visit with Don Francisco and
Doña María. Doña Leonor had come to Spain in the suite of the
Empress in 1526. Don Alonso Enríquez had met her at the Portuguese Court in 1525 and left a burlesque account of their
amorous conversations.[4] At the Court of the Empress she met
Francisco de Borja, then nineteen years old, heir to the duchy of
Gandía, and with the Emperor's approval, they planned to
marry. But the old Duke was opposed. At the time Borja ex-
plained to Cobos:

My father, who has never left his little corner of Gandía, cannot get used
to the customs that are current here. Perhaps he fears that it is contrary to
the laws of the kingdom of Aragon, if I were to marry outside the kingdom.
But if His Majesty is willing to have the matter go ahead, I will open an
easy way. Have His Majesty write to my father that he needs him at Court
for certain matters in his service and that he must come to Court. With that,
the Duke will lay off of me, in return for not leaving his peaceful life and
coming to Court.[5]

Cobos presented the proposal to the Emperor, and the latter
sent an instruction to the Duke, who reacted as his son had
prophesied. Don Francisco and Doña Leonor were married in
March, 1529; at that time Charles named Don Francisco the
Marqués de Lombay, though the formal decree was not issued
until July 7, 1530. Between 1539 and 1543 Borja was Viceroy
of Cataluña. But when the Emperor left Spain in May, 1543,
he had made up his mind to appoint Borja as majordomo of the
Princess María and Leonor de Castro as her chief lady in waiting. And so the Marqués de Aguilar was named to replace him
as viceroy. Unfortunately the King of Portugal refused to agree
to their appointment in charge of his daughter's household and
so they had remained at Gandía, awaiting a solution. The early
pregnancy of the Princess made it seem unwise to force a decision, so that there could be no objection to their visiting the
Court, even though the Princess was living in Cobos' house. We
do not know how long their visit lasted. But on March 20 Cobos
wrote to Lope Hurtado, now ambassador in Portugal, "The
Marqués and his wife started home yesterday. Doña María and

I rode out with them as far as my garden on the river and there we parted. We shall miss them sorely." [6]

Cobos spent Easter Week in retreat at the monastery of El Abrojo, outside of Valladolid. There is an interesting letter at Simancas from the Guardian of the monastery to Philip, written on Palm Sunday, reminding Philip that only he and his sisters were to have the privilege of opening certain doors and windows of the monastery. And now he had heard from Cobos' servant, Hernando Bernaldo, that Cobos was coming to El Abrojo with the intention of opening them, which would be a dangerous precedent, since every great lord in the kingdom would presume to do the same thing. Would Philip order Cobos not to open any doors or windows? [7]

In Flanders Juan Vázquez had been slow in recovering from his illness, and Cobos' letters in February and March were full of concern and fatherly advice. He should not try to go with the Emperor to Germany, but should remain in Brussels for treatment until he was wholly recovered.

> I beg of you to remember how ill you have been and how important it is to rest, if you are to get well. If you had done that in Barcelona, your illness would not have become so serious. I think that you should rest there until you are well, for it is a good climate in the summer, and later, if you are not as strong as you should be, do not join the Emperor, but come back here, for your home surroundings will help more than anything else. Remember that without health you can do nothing.

Meanwhile he was anxiously awaiting the return of Bernardino de Mendoza with detailed information about his condition.

Cobos had already sent Eraso to Flanders, and he now approved of Figueroa's suggestion that he be given a temporary appointment as a substitute for Vázquez at an appropriate salary. But he added:

> I do hope that you will soon be well of all these troubles, for surely we need a more competent person than Eraso. But if the situation continues and you come back here, we will discuss what we should do and I will do what I can, for I am thinking about the future and what is best for you, rather than for me, for I am no longer fit for these tasks. So have no other thought than to recover your health; with that, all will be well.[9]

Vázquez evidently sent a favorable report on Eraso, for Cobos later wrote:

> Eraso can remain in your place, and since you have so much confidence in him, he will do whatever you say and I will help him from here, and there

will be no change without your approval, since that is what Figueroa seems
to want in order to have more authority, although in view of all that he
owes me, I think that he will not be ungrateful.[10]

We do not know what were the determining causes—whether
Vázquez's continuing ill health or reports to the Emperor from
Spain of Cobos' declining strength—but in July Vázquez was
back in Spain. On July 21 Eraso was appointed temporary secretary during his absence. Beginning with January 1, 1546 he
was a regular secretary at a salary of 100,000 *maravedís*.[11]

Birth of the Infante Don Carlos

On July 8 the Princess gave birth in Cobos' palace to a son,
named Don Carlos for his grandfather.[12] Cobos and the others
sent the glad news throughout the Empire. At Worms, on July
22, the Emperor attended a solemn *Te Deum* in honor of the
event.[13] But four days after the birth, on Sunday, July 12, the
Princess died and the rejoicing was changed to mourning. Alfonso de Ulloa, in his *Vita* of Charles, tells the story that the
blame for her death rested on two of her Spanish ladies in waiting, the Duchess of Alba and María de Mendoza. For on that
Sunday they left the Princess to witness an auto-da-fe of the
Inquisition against some Lutheran heretics, and during their absence the Portuguese attendants of the Princess gave her some
appetizing things to eat, especially a lemon, as a result of which
she suffered a convulsion and choked to death. "And so"—Ulloa
continues—"when these ladies returned to the Palace, gay with
the spectacle they had seen, they found the Princess dead, which
perhaps would not have happened, if they had not left her, and
they were blamed by many because at such a time, they had deserted the Princess and gone off for entertainment." [14] There may
be some truth in the account, but there is little reason to believe
that the lemon was the cause of her death, rather than a post-
puerperal fever, which was also the cause of the Empress's death.

The body of the Princess was buried in the church of San Pablo
on July 13,[15] and Philip at once retired to El Abrojo. But the
place was so unhealthy that he returned to Valladolid on August
4 and remained in seclusion in Cobos' house, although he continued to transact necessary business.[16] Before he returned, Don
Carlos was quietly baptized on August 2 in the chapel of the
Rosario, which was attached to Cobos' house, of which he and

Doña María were the patrons. The ceremony was performed by the Bishop Siliceo.[17] Before the chapel was destroyed there was a plaque on the wall that read: "The Infante Don Carlos was baptized here on August 2, 1545." [18]

Cobos was one of the throng of courtiers and officials who attended the memorial service for the Princess,[19] and he was named as one of her executors, along with Siliceo and two of her Portuguese attendants, Fray Tomás de Santa María and Manuel de Melo.[20] When Philip left for Madrid in September he ordered Cobos to remain in Valladolid to settle her affairs.[21] The plump little Princess was a pathetic figure. In his "Intimate Instruction" Charles had warned his son not to spend too much time with her, lest he yield to the temptations of the flesh. A few months after their marriage, Lope Hurtado wrote that people in Portugal were commenting on Philip's failure to show her any signs of affection. And so she had lived alone with her maids and ladies in Cobos' house. Even the son she bore was destined to be a tragic failure. Like so many of the Emperor's hopes and dreams, this too was shattered by the whim of fate.

The Adelantamiento *of Cazorla Again*

On August 1, 1545, Cardinal Tavera died in Valladolid, after ten years of service as the Emperor's chief official in Spain. The next day, in a letter to the ambassador St. Mauris, Cobos wrote: "He was so important a person, of such goodness and authority, that all of us miss him greatly." [22] And on August 13, writing to the Emperor of his death, he said: "I talked to him a few hours before he died and he was in as good a Christian state and of as clear an understanding as when he was in perfect health, telling me of the satisfaction he felt that Our Lord had brought him to his high estate. His only regret was that he could not kiss Your Majesty's hand, before he passed on." Of the 24,000 ducats which he had loaned the Emperor, he gave one half to him; the other half he requested should be given to the hospital where he was to be buried.[23]

We have seen how Tavera had named Cobos as *adelantado* of Cazorla on May 18, 1534.[24] Cobos appointed the Licenciado Ayvar as governor, and when he resigned to become chief *alcalde* of Ubeda, he named the Licenciado Rivas to the post. Almost at once he began to press Tavera to transfer the title to his son

Diego. At first the Cardinal objected: the boy was only eleven years old. But he finally yielded, perhaps fearing that a refusal would annoy the Emperor, "in view of the great damage and irreparable harm which would probably ensue for our church and dignity and its important interests, if we were to refuse the appointment, because of the indignation and offense it would incur, and because it seems to us that for the present it cannot and should not be refused." This decision—he explained—was under protest and valid only for such time as was his will. The document was signed on February 28, 1535; it was confirmed by Pope Paul III on May 15 and by the Emperor on May 28.

Cobos now set about securing from the Pope, without Tavera's knowledge, a bull which would grant to Diego and his descendants the possession of Cazorla in perpetuity. On July 25, 1537, the Emperor wrote to his ambassador in Rome, the Marqués de Aguilar, asking him to intercede with the Pope in support of Cobos' request. On November 11 Paul III granted the extension, with the proviso that each year the *adelantado* should pay the Archbishop of Toledo 300 ducats and that with each change in either party, the *adelantado* must request the Archbishop to renew the investiture and give him a white horse worth 100 ducats. This ruling was not satisfactory to Cobos, and again the Emperor wrote to Aguilar (June 25, 1538), asking him for further support for Cobos, "whose great and outstanding services deserve even greater reward and honor." [25] Perhaps it was in this connection that the Emperor wrote an account of the services which Cobos had up to then performed.

From Cobos we have received many and outstanding services from the beginning of our reign, especially the first time that we went to Spain, where in Castile and in the Cortes which we held in the kingdom of Aragon he served us with hard work, fidelity and loyalty. And he came with us to Flanders and Germany, when we received the first crown in the city of Aix-la-Chapelle and during that trip, for all that was necessary to provide, in order to settle and pacify the uprisings in Castile, he worked and served well, being, as he was, in charge of all the affairs of these kingdoms. And after we returned to them, he was active in all matters of our service, both in war and government, with fidelity, care and industry, until it was necessary for us to make the trip to Italy in 1529 to remedy the affairs of Christendom. There he served us, not only in general matters, as he had up to then, but also in matters of foreign policy. He was with us at our coronation in Bologna and on the expedition we afterwards made to Hungary to drive back the Turk, enemy of our Holy Catholic Faith, who came with great power to damage and destroy Christianity; and likewise in the expedition to Barbary, where we won the kingdom of Tunis and drove out Barbarrosa, and all that happened until we returned to our kingdoms of Spain, the said Francisco de los Cobos served us personally, not only in public affairs but in everything else, risking his person like a good knight, at all times accompanied by worthy people and incurring great expenses in our service.[26]

Cobos' agents in Rome, Valenzuela and Rábago, as well as the Marqués de Aguilar, continued to work on the formulation of a new bull and on December 6, 1539, the Pope issued the desired document, whereby the possession of Cazorla was defined as, not one of "Infeudación," but of "Gracia bajo censo." When the Emperor confirmed this at Speyer on January 25, 1541, Cobos felt reasonably secure in his possession, but he must have had still some misgivings, as was evidenced by his fear that Juan de Vega might meddle in the matter, when he went to Rome as ambassador in 1543.

As soon as Tavera died Cobos immediately went into action. Early in the morning of August 2 he sent Gonzalo Pérez to El Abrojo to show Philip the Papal bulls he had received and to ask him to instruct the Chapter of the cathedral of Toledo to obey the bulls and grant Cobos possession of Cazorla. Bishop Siliceo was with the Prince when Pérez arrived and he urged him to refer the question to the Royal Council, for it was a serious matter and they could reach a wiser decision than the Prince alone. Philip approved, but when the Council decided that it was a matter for legal decision, the question was referred back to Philip and he issued an order to the Chapter to obey the bulls. Siliceo later charged that Cobos had summoned the individual members of the Council to his house to urge their approval of his cause, a thing that had never been seen or heard before— that a private person, no matter how great he was, should call members of the Council to his house in a matter on which they were to vote. Naturally it provoked a great deal of talk.[27]

Philip had issued a temporary order to Cobos on August 1 to continue to exercise the office of *adelantado,* and he at once dispatched a courier posthaste to Hernando Ortega in Ubeda. Ortega appeared before the *regidores* of Cazorla on August 5 with Philip's instruction and the authorities accepted the provision.[28] On August 13 Cobos wrote to the Emperor:

I must thank Your Majesty for the *adelantamiento* of Cazorla, because with the death of the Cardinal—may he have eternal glory!—I have made known the favor which Your Majesty did me and I have sent to take possession anew, for so Your Majesty had instructed me. Please God that I may serve Your Majesty in return for this favor, for I assure you that it has not been forgotten nor treated with ingratitude.[29]

The next day, in the presence of the Bishop of Lugo, Juan Suárez de Carvajal, Cobos had all the papal and royal grants duly notarized and attested,[30] and on August 21 he and his son appointed Juan Vázquez de Molina (who had now reached Spain), his chaplain, Hernando Ortega, and his majordomo, Hernando Verdugo de Henao, as his authorized agents to take formal possession of Cazorla. On August 29 they arrived there and carried out their instructions.[31]

On August 25 Philip sent Gonzalo Pérez to Toledo with copies of the documents and with letters to the Dean and Chapter of the cathedral, to Pedro de Córdoba, *corregidor* of the city, and to the Bishop of Coria, asking them to accept the provisions and grant their approval. And so Pedro de Córdoba and his wife, Doña Felipa, the Bishop, Gutierre López de Padilla, and others appeared before the Chapter, which quickly gave its assent, with only one dissenting vote, that of Dr. Berzaval.[32] The Emperor is said to have remarked to Cobos later that he should not be surprised that there was one honest man in the company. Siliceo also commented that the Prince's letters were certainly dictated by Cobos in his own interest. And he adds that Doña Felipa afterwards boasted that she was largely if not wholly responsible for winning the favorable decision of the canons and other dignitaries.[33]

The Emperor wrote to Cobos on September 14 that he was anxious to fill the vacancy in the archbishopric of Toledo.[34] We do not know what suggestions Cobos made. Back in 1540, when there was a vacancy in the bishopric of Cartagena, he had written to Juan Vázquez that he was not ready to make a recommendation, but he did think that the Emperor should rightly consider appointing the tutor of the Prince (Siliceo) to some episcopal chair.[35] It was Siliceo who was named Bishop of Cartagena.

On October 23 the Emperor wrote to Siliceo that in view of his long services to the Prince he had decided to appoint him Archbishop of Toledo; Cobos would convey to him the detailed instructions.[36] Cabrera, in his biography of Philip, expressed the belief that it was Cobos' recommendation which had won Siliceo the post, and this seems to be the most reasonable explanation.[37]

But this is qualified by a note among the papers of Florián de Ocampo that there was a rumor that Cobos had secured the appointment in order to win his support in the possession of Cazorla, which he desired to add to his *mayorazgo*.[38] It is possible that Cobos still cherished the hope of finding Siliceo on his side.

In the letter of October 23 already mentioned the Emperor had taken up in some detail Cobos' claim to the *adelantamiento*:

You undoubtedly know that His Holiness, with our approval and permission, granted his bulls in such fashion that the Grand Commander might have and hold, he and his successors in perpetuity, the *adelantamiento* of Cazorla and that after they were issued, we approved and confirmed it for our part and ordered the necessary instructions so that it might be fulfilled and put into effect. And when the very reverend Archbishop of Toledo died, he made use of them with our permission. Now we have learned how unanimously the Chapter of Toledo has accepted them and that he has again taken possession and holds the *adelantamiento,* whereat we are rejoiced, that the favor which we did him may be fulfilled and carried out, without litigation and delay. And because the right and obligation for this is such as the many, continuous services of the Grand Commander merit, we urge you to approve what has been done by His Holiness and by us, that it may be observed and fulfilled, without any impediment or alteration, for even if matters were not in their present state because of what has transpired, you will do us in this great pleasure and service.[39]

A few days later the Emperor wrote to the Pope, asking him to confirm his earlier action.[40] At the same time he requested his ambassador, Juan de Vega, and the Cardinal Farnese to support Cobos' request, and he informed the Archbishop-elect of his action. Siliceo was enthroned in the episcopal chair on January 30, 1546, but he showed no signs of complying with the Emperor's request. Two months later Cobos wrote to Charles:

In the matter of the *adelantamiento,* I wrote to Your Majesty how well the Archbishop answered me and two or three times he told the Prince that he would do what Your Majesty ordered. Afterwards, pretending that he had some complaints against me, he put it off, saying that during his lifetime he would make no changes with me or my son. I made no comment, waiting for what Your Majesty would reply. And even though the desired answer came, he still postponed taking action. I think that it must be that he wants to be sure of Your Majesty's will. Since so much thought was given to this grant, both on Your Majesty's part and that of His Holiness, and since afterwards it was obeyed by the Chapter of Toledo, where the bulls and grants were seen by eight learned dignitaries and canons of the church and by other theologians who gave it as their opinion that they could not fail to be obeyed with a charge of conscience, with that and with the Archbishop's realizing that it is Your Majesty's will, it seems clear that he will approve. I beg Your Majesty to write to him, so that he will see that Your Majesty desires it, in order that I may no longer be importunate in the matter.[41]

As a result of Cobos' plea the Emperor wrote again on April 24, repeating what he had said in his earlier letter and adding:

because we have heard that you are still postponing action and are unwilling to approve, we again urge you greatly to take action as completely as is necessary, so that the order may at once take effect without further delay and without your placing any impediment, since none is warranted, knowing that this is and has been our definite will. In this you will do us a real pleasure and service, because of our desire that this satisfaction be done to the Grand Commander. You will let me know how you carry out this instruction.[42]

For his part, Cobos wrote to the Pope on May 3, humbly asking him to confirm the earlier bulls. By June 25 he had heard from the Bishop of Coria that the Pope had reached a favorable decision and he wrote to express his thanks.[43] The actual bull, *Perinde valere,* was issued on July 9, confirming the earlier bulls, in spite of the fact that Tavera had not been informed.[44] But Siliceo was not moved, either by the Emperor's almost peremptory letter or by the Papal decree. He now wrote to the Emperor a long detailed letter on the situation, rehearsing what had happened and justifying his own failure to comply:

"For twelve years"—he began—"the Commander has been trying to gain this grant in perpetuity and my predecessor would never agree to it. I suspect that the thought which both Your Majesty and His Holiness have given to this grant of the *adelantamiento* has been based only on the opinions of those persons who were anxious to please the Commander." He was—he insisted—ready to grant his approval of the concession to Cobos and his son, valid during his lifetime, but he could not commit the future decisions of his successors. He had heard that some people were reporting Cobos as saying that he was on ill terms with Cobos and that he showed it when he deprived him of his staff of office as *alguazil mayor* of Talavera, a favor which he had received from Siliceo's predecessor.

It is true—*he wrote*—that one of the good deeds I have done in my life, both for Talavera and its territory and for the Grand Commander, was to take the staff away from the man who held it, because after I appointed a new *corregidor* and *alguazil mayor,* the town has been peaceful and freed from the rivalries and tyranny it was suffering. The 70,000 *maravedís* which the Commander was receiving was a small matter for him.

The charge that he was on ill terms with Cobos had arisen only because of his refusal to approve the alienation of Cazorla in perpetuity. "I cannot fail to suspect that long before now the Commander has been on ill terms with me; the reason is in part well known and in part not understood by many people. God knows how little cause he has for it, and Your Majesty too will know some day." And now the Archbishop waxes eloquent in defense of his position:

I cannot make out what Christian heart can find it right to strip Our Lady of her dignity and estate, that some one who never deserved it should possess it. I should like to know the important things that the Grand Commander has done in the service of Our Lady of Toledo. I do not think that one will be found. Up to now I have never heard of any service that he has done to the Church Militant of Spain or anywhere else. The favors that the Emperor has received from Our Lady far outweigh all the services of Cobos; in fact, Cobos has received so many rewards that if the question were left to justice, he might have to give back much that he has received.

And finally he declares:

I would never have believed that Your Majesty felt such love and concern for the Grand Commander of Leon, until I saw the sternness of the letter you wrote me and what has happened afterwards in Rome in the matter of the *adelantamiento*.[45]

Faced with the determined resistance of the Archbishop, who belonged in the stout tradition of Cisneros, Cobos became more and more discouraged and exasperated. On August 23 he wrote to the Emperor: "The Archbishop still insists that he cannot in good conscience grant the concession. I do not know what to ask for or what to say about it, but I hope that since Your Majesty granted me the favor, he will order that it be put into effect." [46] And again, on October 10, he wrote even more bitterly: "I am very sorry that Your Majesty has lost the authority he has always had to require the Archbishop of Toledo to obey his instructions, especially when appointments are being made. As for my relations with him, I need not try to deal with him, except through the courts, where, with the favor of Your Majesty, I think that the justice of my cause will be very clear." [47] And so the conflict remained unsettled when Cobos died.

The ambassador in Rome, Diego de Mendoza, who had received his appointment through Cobos, wrote to Prince Philip, as soon as he heard of Cobos' death, that he had spoken to the Pope and Cardinal Farnese about the *adelantamiento,* and asking him to intervene in behalf of Cobos' son.[48] Philip thanked Mendoza for his good offices and assured him of his support.[49] Mendoza, in reply, expressed gratification at Philip's interest.[50]

As late as October 19, 1548, the Emperor was still concerned about the matter, but by then he had decided to leave the issue to the courts:

> In the matter of the *adelantamiento* of Cazorla, I cannot fail to tell you that I always intended to favor and help the Grand Commander of Leon, because of the love and affection I felt for him, for his great and constant services. And for the same reason I desired to favor the Marqués his son, especially since the grant was made after such long consideration on our part. Although we should have been very glad, if you had accepted what we wrote to you several times, as we would be glad now, since you feel that you could not accede in good conscience for the reasons which you mention and since you request it so urgently, in a matter that so affects my own conscience, it would not be right to deny you an appeal to the courts and not leave you free to present the case wherever and in whatever way you deem proper. But I must warn you that I cannot escape the obligation of doing whatever I can to support the cause of the Marqués, for the reasons that I have mentioned.[51]

And so, in the Curia of Rome and the Chancillery of Valladolid, the case of the Archbishop and the Marqués dragged on through the years. One by one the original principals died. When, at last, in 1604, the case was finally settled, it was a new Archbishop, Rojas y Sandoval, who won the award against Cobos' grandson, Francisco de los Cobos y Luna. In the final settlement, the Archbishop agreed to pay the Marqués and his heirs an annual pension of 7,000 ducats a year from the income of the *adelantamiento*.[52] When we remember that this was obviously only a small part of the total income, it is easy to understand why Cobos' heirs fought so long to retain the title.

If Cobos could have known the ultimate outcome of the suit, it would have been the bitterest disappointment of his life. He had set his heart on handing on the title to his son and his descendants. For years he dedicated much of his time and thought to this end, openly and secretly. To assure its possession he was even willing to accept the loss of part of his income as *fundidor* of the Indies. In the end, in spite of having tried to forestall every possible *contretemps*, his hopes were destined to failure.

The Last Visit of Don Alonso

Before the end of November, 1545, Cobos had finished settling the affairs of the Princess and had joined Philip and the Court in Madrid. At the beginning of January he went to Alcalá de Henares for a few days' visit with Philip, who was spending the holidays with his sisters.[53] A little later he and Doña María received a last visit from Don Alonso Enríquez, who was preparing to try his fortunes once more at the Court of the Emperor. Let us listen to Don Alonso's own account of the visit.

As usual I was well received by the illustrious lady, Doña María de Mendoza; by her husband, not as other times, but lukewarmly and with restraint. I was dissatisfied with that, although the "excellent" lady, his wife, consoled me, saying: "Don't pay any attention to that, Don Alonso, for I am here. Don't fail to talk to the Commander, for when he sees your good will, you can do anything you want with him, for he is well disposed, as you know, since you have known him for twenty five years." With the encouragement of this great lady, the next night, when the Grand Commander was alone, I went in to speak to him. With great courtesy he asked me to sit down, he with his cap in his hand and I with mine. I said to him: "Sir, I wrote Your Lordship a letter which has annoyed you, when I was only jesting, counting on your good will and toleration. And now it seems that you have taken offence, considering me ungrateful. I am not so foolish or so evil as that, for I know and have always remembered that you have done me favors, and I do not think that you have erred. But if Your Lordship thinks that I have, I beg your pardon."

He replied: "You are mistaken, for I do not remember any such letter nor am I annoyed with you." I said to him: "Why then do you address me as Your Grace? [the formal salutation]" And nevertheless he called me that several more times. I was angry and insulted, for I prefer the love of people I like to any show of courtesy. And I said to him: "By God, sir, you consider me too crazy to give me a *corregimiento* [Don Alonso had failed to receive an appointment as *veinticuatro* of Seville], and too sane to stand my foolishness." I walked out and went to tell the Prince what had happened. His Highness said to me: "Nonsense, Don Alonso. Don't be upset, for I will make you friends with the Grand Commander, as you were before." I said to him: "Sir, I am not interested. Do whatever you will. Time will tell and he will see that he has no friend left who is older than I."

Then his wife sent for me. "Listen, Don Alonso"—she said—"don't stop coming to have dinner and supper every day with the Commander and me. Have confidence in his goodness and my diligence and good will." I said to her: "I don't know whether I can bring myself to it, or whether I will offend him even more." She said: "How silly you are, Don Alonso! Do what I tell you." And so I did, for when this lady calls you silly, which is the worst thing that can be said, you are left happy and honored. And she so maneuvred things that within two days the Commander was sharing his food with me and making me drink out of his cup, for his goodness and her good will and my intentions were all joined. Amen! So that I was back in my old place with him, which couldn't have been better. The Prince was very glad of that, and most other people too, though there were few who were sorry.[54]

And so, with a glad heart, Don Alonso set forth for Germany on his last adventure.

During the following months Cobos was busy with the usual routine of correspondence. It is typical of his rôle as a peace-maker to find him writing to Granvelle, who had become involved at Court in a conflict with the Duque de Alba, urging him to forget their differences and treat the Duke as he always had, "for you know what we have to go through every day in such matters and how necessary it is to put up with it." [55]

New Financial Problems

Much more urgent, however, was the financial situation. Cobos wrote to the Emperor on January 28, proposing once more that he be authorized to sell privileges to ride on a mule at 50 ducats each; if a thousand persons would pay, it would bring in a handsome sum.[56] But the plan fell through; Cobos explained in May that it had aroused too many protests.[57] By this time the situation had become even more critical. On April 24 the Emperor wrote from Ratisbonne to Philip that he had made up his mind to take the field against the German Protestant princes. For this he would need large sums of money, and he was secretly negotiating loans, pretending that the money was for the expenses of his household, with bankers in Nuremberg, Augsburg, Genoa, and Antwerp.[58]

He now instructed Philip to explain the situation confidentially to Cobos and have him undertake negotiations in Spain with the agents of the Fuggers, the Welsers, and the Genoese and Florentine bankers, even though he was already negotiating with their representatives in Germany. If there was an overlap, the contract signed first was to be effective. As security for these loans he proposed to pledge the shipments of gold and silver from the Indies for a total of 600,000 scudi.

The Emperor was certainly over-optimistic in his estimates of receipts from this source. If the figures given by Laiglesia have any validity, the total receipts of Indian treasure in 1545 had been about 1,800,000 ducats; the Emperor's "fifth" was 360,-

000 ducats. In the following year they were a little over half that amount; by 1547 the total had shrunk to 166,000 ducats, the Emperor's share to 33,000 ducats.[59] Even if all gold and silver were confiscated, it would not suffice to meet the immediate needs.

The Emperor's letter to Philip closed with the following plea: "I again charge you not to lose a moment in doing everything possible to carry out these instructions, as the Grand Commander will tell you. What he advises will be proper to carry out, for I am confident of the care and diligence that he will show in this matter." Cobos did, in fact, act promptly. On May 22, with the members of the Consejo de la Hacienda—Suárez de Carvajal, Fernando de Guevara, Cristóbal Suárez, and Francisco de Almaguer (who had replaced Sancho de Paz on the latter's death in 1543), he signed a contract for a loan with the agents of the Fuggers in Spain.[60]

Inevitably these simultaneous negotiations in several places resulted in confusion. In a letter to Charles which Cobos prepared for Philip, he pointed out the difficulties which had arisen as a result of a loan of 300,000 *scudi* from an Italian banker which the Regent, Queen María, had arranged in Flanders. She had offered as security the income from the military orders and from the subsidy voted by the last Cortes and due in May, 1547. But Cobos pointed out that almost all this income had already been pledged as security for loans which the Emperor had negotiated or had been made in Spain, as a result of His Majesty's instructions. They had tried to patch up a list of securities that would be satisfactory, but the bankers' agents had refused to accept them. They had therefore written to Queen María to explain the situation. In her reply the Queen reminded them of the importance of finding a solution in order to maintain their credit; she was so desperate that she might have to sell her personal property to meet the need.[61]

Once more Cobos tried to solve the problem. Taking out an item here and adding another there he managed to prepare a list of securities, based on *juros* to be sold in the future, and on parts of the expected income from the subsidies, the Cruzada, and the military orders, although they were already committed. This seemed acceptable to the bankers' representatives, but even so, they said that they must consult their principals before taking final action. Again he wrote to Queen Mary and the Emperor, setting forth the situation; he could see no other possibility of a solution in Spain. For the situation there was indeed desperate. Most of the royal income had been sold or pledged up to the end of 1549 and even part of 1550. Part of the income from the Indies was already committed. "To tell the truth"—he went on— "as I should, we are at the end of the rope, unless God Our Lord in his mercy and Your Majesty can find a remedy." There was the further difficulty that there were not enough funds available to meet the current interest on outstanding loans and to pay the operating expenses for the fleet and the armed forces and the defense of the frontiers in 1546 and 1547.

> For all this, or even for the least part of it, there is no way to find money, because we have exhausted everything we could think of. And besides, the season has been so unfruitful in Spain that the people are alarmingly poor, which has caused us all great trouble and concern, and it is a situation which must be remedied. . . . I humbly beg Your Majesty to consider the matter with great care, because although we know the holy enterprise which Your Majesty has undertaken and how important it is for the service of God Our Lord and his Catholic Church and the welfare of Christendom, and your holy zeal and the heavy expenses that are involved, we cannot fail to urge Your Majesty to remember the importance of finding a remedy and relief for these kingdoms, because of the extreme need, for otherwise there could not fail to be serious trouble, because the need is so notorious that not only are the natives of the kingdom aware of it and are refusing to take part in any financial transactions, but even foreigners, both abroad and in Spain, are doing the same thing, because they know that there is no source from which payments can be made.[62]

In spite of his despair, Cobos continued to seek new funds. Once more he prepared a list of persons who could be asked to make loans. The response was discouraging: by the end of September only 30,000 ducats had been offered. Cobos had originally been asked to loan 5,000 ducats; actually he loaned 10,000, a third of the total collected.[63] At the time he wrote to the Emperor: "Just as when I pledged my gold to your service at the time of the Perpignan affair, so now I will pledge my silver and I have taken 10,000 ducats to send with the rest." [64]

Some more drastic steps were necessary and Philip called a meeting of the Consejo de la Hacienda, with the Marqués de Mondéjar, to seek new measures. Philip had already approved of confiscating all the gold from the Indies; he even considered seizing the estate of the Bishop of Badajoz, until the courts reached a decision concerning its disposal.[65] Cobos now came forward with a counsel of despair: the seizure of all specie in Spain and its shipment to the Emperor by way of the Genoese galleys. Even though much of the money was already pledged as security, this step would avoid the payment of interest and would provide ready cash in Genoa, where it was urgently needed. Suicidal as the plan was, it was approved by Philip and the Council. Very secretly they set about putting it into effect; as Philip wrote to his father: "These kingdoms are so bare of gold—for you cannot find a *scudo*—that there will be no lack of complaints and outcries." [66] On October 10 Philip was able to report to the Emperor that they had already gathered 180,000 *scudi* in cash; they hoped to increase it to 200,000.[67] Against his judgment, for he had no sympathy with the Emperor's imperial dreams, Cobos with his unwavering devotion had done his best to provide the sinews of war that made possible the victory of Mühlberg.

Death Comes to the Counsellors

The year that followed the death of the Cardinal Tavera on August 1, 1545, witnessed the disappearance of almost all the men who had been the advisors of Charles and Philip. On September 1, 1545, the Conde Cifuentes, majordomo of the Infantas, died and was replaced by Bernardino Pimentel.[68] The Duque de Alba had already been summoned to service at the Emperor's Court. García de Loaisa, Archbishop of Seville and President of the Consejo de las Indias, who had been failing in health for some time, died on April 22, 1546.[69] Two months later Cobos reported the death of the Vice-Chanciller of Aragon, Miguel Mai.[70] Other old friends and associates passed on: the Conde de Osorno, the Marqués del Guasto, the Marquesa de Lombay, Leonor de Castro. And some enemies were eliminated too: Martin Luther on February 18, 1546 and Barbarrosa on July 4.

Perhaps the most serious loss was that of Juan de Zúñiga, chief personal advisor of Philip, on June 27, 1546.[71] Reporting to the Emperor on July 3, Cobos wrote: "I had such companionship and friendship with him that I have deeply regretted his loss, and more now than ever, when I have been left alone in everything, as Your Majesty knows." [72] Santa Cruz tells us that on Zúñiga's death Cobos and his wife moved into Philip's palace in Madrid, an action so unprecedented that it gave rise to much unfavorable comment.[73] Perhaps Cobos was justified in feeling that he should be close to the Prince; for it was quite literally true that he was left alone as his only counsellor. With the retirement of Siliceo to his see in Toledo, every one of the counsellors that the Emperor had so carefully chosen in 1543 to guide his son had disappeared from the scene. The burden of responsibility and worry proved too heavy for Cobos' aging shoulders.

Growing Ill Health

Save for a brief bout of cold and fever in the summer of 1545,[74] he had been in good health all that year and during the first half of 1546. But in July, 1546, he had a violent attack of fever that left him at death's door.[75] He rallied, however, and on August 10 Philip wrote to him from Guadalajara, advising him to come there for a rest, now that he was feeling better.[76] A few days later Cobos replied that there was nothing that he would like better, but that he could not leave until he had settled the problem of the loans; he would come as soon as possible.[77] The strain of work proved too much and he suffered a relapse in September, which once more brought him to the point of death.

At Ratisbonne, on July 5, 1546, the Emperor had authorized the Marqués de Mondéjar, Cobos, and Zúñiga, or any one of them, to receive the oath of Philip, accepting the investiture of Milan.[78] But Zúñiga was dead and Cobos was too ill to travel to Guadalajara, so the Marqués alone received the oath on September 16; Cobos had sent Gonzalo Pérez to act as notary.[79] On September 27 he wrote to the Emperor:

> Although my health is considerably improved, no small part of my illness is due to my worry over your undertaking in Germany and your involvement in it . . . My fever has been gradually lessening, after being bled five times [this phrase deleted] and I am still in very poor shape, for I cannot get rid of the fever altogether and I am very thin and weak, though even so, I am doing everything I can to provide for Your Majesty's service, as I said above.[80]

In the letter to Charles, already cited, Philip had made a similar comment on the cause of his illness: "It seems certain that his worry over finances has been the principal cause of his ailment and has aggravated his condition." [81]

The final evidence of his breakdown is found in another letter to Charles of the same day (September 27) : "Juan Vázquez has come to see me and since I cannot attend to all the affairs I should, I have entrusted them to him, and so he can take my place, as long as I am in this condition. He comes so well prepared that he can do it well, for it is absolutely necessary that I get away from here for a few days." [82] But new troubles now beset him. On October 10 he wrote again:

My improvement has continued. Though I have been free from fever, I have had an attack of gout in both feet, with so much swelling and pain that it has made me miserable, and now I can understand what Your Majesty has been through, when he had those bad attacks. The pain has subsided since day before yesterday, but it has not wholly gone and I am so weak that the doctors are of the opinion that I must have a change of air, because my illness was so serious and afterwards the gout came on. They say that to recover my health I should get away for a few days and so I have been hurrying to finish up the negotiations for the loans and find some rest, so that I can come back to work again, if it is God's pleasure to restore me to health.[83]

A few days later he wrote to the Ambassador St. Mauris that he had been too ill to read his letter of September 20, but that Gonzalo Pérez had reported its contents to him.[84] On October 21 he was able to go out to the monastery of San Gerónimo, where he reported that his convalescence was slowly continuing, though he had been too weak to see Philip, who had come back from Guadalajara.[85] He seems to have stayed at San Gerónimo during November and December.

During these months of illness, there had been a number of events which he was too weak to notice. On September 27 the Prosecutor of the Consejo de las Indias charged before the Council that Cobos had illegally collected 300,000 ducats as *fundidor* of the Indies, because he had taken his 1 per cent on all the metal assayed and minted, instead of taking it after the royal *quinta* had been subtracted.[86] This was the first charge of malfeasance in office that had ever been brought against him. For thirty years his power and his influence with the Emperor had protected him against any suspicion of wrongdoing. How shall we explain this sudden attack? Was it a reflection of the resentment of the Council at the seizure of all the cash in the Casa de la Contratación? Or was it merely that the old lion was stricken and the jackals were gathering? Let us hope that in his weakened state he was mercifully kept in ignorance of the charge.

Another event that would have been celebrated by letters to all of his friends in better days but now was passed over in silence was the birth of his first grandson, in October, 1546. This first-born of the Marqueses de Camarasa was christened Francisco de los Cobos y Luna, in honor of his grandfather; he lived on into the seventeenth century. Philip, or someone else at Court, must have informed the Emperor, for he wrote to Cobos on November 28 to congratulate him on the birth of an heir to carry on his estate.[87] One other event which Cobos failed to notice was the death in December of Dr. Guevara,[88] the oldest member of the Consejo de Castilla, the last survivor of that group of advisors who had begun their service under Ferdinand the Catholic.

In spite of his weakness, Cobos continued to busy himself with affairs. On January 25, 1547, he wrote to the Emperor, urging him to appoint his friend the Bishop of Coria to the vacancy in the bishopric of Cuenca,[89] and on the same day he reported that he had not been able to find certain documents that the Emperor had asked for; they must have been burned in the sack of García Ruiz de la Mota's house during the rebellion of 1521.[90]

By the beginning of February he was strong enough to travel, and thinking that he might recover his health in the air of his home town he started back to Ubeda.[91] He made the trip very slowly, but he arrived there before the end of February. On February 12, Idiáquez, on his way to Spain on another mission, wrote to Antonio de Eguino, one of Cobos' servants, that he was delighted to know that the Commander was convalescing; he was planning to come to Madrid to see him. In a postscript he asked Eguino where he had better stay, in case Cobos had left town.[92] Though his condition did not improve greatly, Cobos still kept up his correspondence. On February 25 he wrote one more letter to the Emperor with regard to Cazorla, thanking him for his instruction to the Archbishop of Toledo:

It appears that nothing will placate his ill will, for there is no one who says that he has any reason for it. The complaints which he makes against me are contrary to the truth, because I swear to God, by my hope of seeing Your Majesty back in Spain, which is the thing I now most desire, that neither before his appointment nor after have I committed the slightest sin toward him in thought or deed. And before his appointment to Toledo, Your Majesty is a better witness than anyone of all that I tried to do in his behalf. Some things happened for which he thinks that I was to blame, but in truth I was not.

I have been very unhappy that this affair has made me bother Your Majesty, but I could not and cannot overlook certain things, though I should like to forget this whole business, since he is unwilling to do what Your Majesty has requested and ordered. I am informed by good lawyers that I ought to take definite steps, presenting the bulls and confirmations to him, so that if he appeals, I can bring court action or take whatever steps seem best. I have not done this, though there is ample cause, without first letting Your Majesty know. I humbly beg you to approve, assuring you that I will act with the proper consideration and respect; and since the case will have to go to Rome, I beg you to write to his Holiness and the other people to support my cause in respect to the original grant. I no longer need to ask for modifications, since my son now has a son . . . I trust that Your Majesty will pardon my importunity, for I assure you that I would not have done so, if it had not been harmful to fail to do so.[93]

The End

On the same day he wrote a second letter to Charles—it is the last one that has survived:

I left Madrid as soon as I could, because my ill health made it necessary. God knows how it distressed me to have to leave matters there at a time of such need, although everything necessary for the transaction of business had been provided for and ordered and Juan Vázquez is taking good care of it. . . . Although I have been free of fever for several days, I am still weak and suffering the usual difficulties of a slow convalescence. I am better, thank God, and I have nothing to do except to try to get back my health, so that I may return to work, which I think will be soon—God willing. Meanwhile, in addition to the instructions I left, I am writing what I think should be done in matters affecting Your Majesty. Certainly I shall not waste a moment of time.[94]

The letter is signed in a trembling hand; the rubric is hardly more than a scrawl.

Eguino had gone to Ubeda with Cobos and he wrote to Idiáquez on March 3, urging him to stay with Juan Vázquez, who was living in Cobos' house in Madrid, "to dissipate any clouds there may have been," and besides, he knew that it would make the Commander happy to see them on good terms.[95] Again on March 8 he wrote: "The Commander has been ailing these days and especially yesterday, when he did not get up and so did not sign any letters." [96] By March 20 the Emperor had received Cobos' letter of January 25 and he wrote to approve of his departure for Ubeda, urging him to think only of his health, though he added: "Meanwhile I am sure that from there you will direct affairs, as you are wont to do." [97]

Cobos' condition grew worse during April. At the middle of the month he had another attack of double tertian fever and his local physician, Dr. Villarroel, sent for Dr. Zaballos, the Court physician. The latter reported to the Conde de Morata, with whom Cobos' son and daughter-in-law were living in Zaragoza, that he had some hope of his recovery. But on May 1 they received the news that there was little hope, and Diego started at once for Ubeda. His father was unconscious when he arrived, but he rallied enough to sign his last will on May 4. Diego found his sister and her husband, the Duque de Sesa, already there, but there is no evidence that María de Mendoza was with her husband; she did not accompany him when he left for Ubeda, for in his letter of March 8 Eguino had sent his greetings to her in Madrid. In a letter of the Conde de Morata to Gonzalo Pérez he commented: "I am afraid that it was very hard for the Commander that neither you nor Juan Vázquez were with him and that the Duke and Duchess were there. God grant that the Duke may not do something that his servants and kinsmen cannot remedy." [98]

The end came on May 10, in the house where Cobos was born. The official document tersely states: "Francisco de los Cobos died and passed from this life in the city of Ubeda on the morning of Tuesday, May 10, 1547, because on the said day I saw the body of His Lordship in his house, before it was buried." [99] *Sic transit gloria mundi.*

CHAPTER XIV

———————•••◦≈◦•••———————

END OF AN ERA

The news of Cobos' death was carried quickly throughout Spain and the rest of Europe. At Zaragoza it was known on May 16, when the Conde de Morata wrote to Gonzalo Pérez: "For this household it has been the worst news that could come," and on May 18 the Protonotary of Aragon, Climent, wrote to Pérez in the same vein.[1] Far away in Trent, Páez de Castro, who was serving at the Church Council, wrote to Gerónimo Zurita on May 31: "With the death of the Comendador Mayor everything must be seriously upset. Please write me something about what is going on, for here, *multi multa*. I can tell you that the Fiscal felt so badly about it that it is clear what he has lost." [1a] We have already seen how Diego de Mendoza, in Rome, had received the news early in June. From Genoa, on June 7, the ambassador Figueroa wrote to Philip: "The news has grieved me greatly, because His Majesty and Your Highness have lost in him so good a vassal and minister in your service, especially in the affairs of Castile, in which he had such experience that he will be sorely missed in them. God keep him in eternal glory." [2]

A little later (June 24) the ambassador in Portugal, Lope Hurtado, wrote from Lisbon to Francisco de Ledesma: "Now that God has taken our "Boss," it is time that those of us who were his servants should more than ever be brothers and friends. And since I have always considered you such, I shall now regard it as a favor, if you will hold me in the same esteem as before and let me know how you have fared." [3] It is striking that the one who was most grief-stricken was the Marquesa de Camarasa, who was so broken that the Conde de Morata thought that she ought to get away from Zaragoza.[4] Cobos had always been indifferent to her. Yet she must have been attractive, for Rábago, who was a good judge of women, wrote to Ledesma in her praise: "She is very much a woman and very well built," or again: "Our Marquesa was one of the most lovely of the ladies at the party, because she is as sleek as a partridge at Christmas." [5] One wonders if Cobos' lack of interest in her was because she was so poor.

On June 1 Philip wrote to his father announcing Cobos' death:

> I have naturally regretted his passing, for the good will I felt toward him and because Your Majesty has lost in him so great a servant, who served him with such care, love and loyalty and who was so well informed of everything that affected the welfare of these kingdoms and Your Majesty's service that his loss is to be regretted, especially at this time. Although I know that the services and merits of the Grand Commander were so outstanding that Your Majesty will give them proper recognition by showing his son and his family the love and gratitude that is your custom with such persons, I have not wanted to fail to remind Your Majesty that by his death the posts of Contador Mayor and Comendador Mayor de León have become vacant and I beg you earnestly to keep the Marqués de Camarasa in mind, when you come to fill them, and also to grant to Doña María de Mendoza a life pension befitting her station, as an aid in her support. Not only will it seem proper to everyone that Your Majesty should show gratitude to the heirs of one who served him so long and so well, but I shall personally count as a favor anything that you may do for them.[6]

At the same time Philip wrote to Doña María and to Diego, expressing his regret at Cobos' death and his satisfaction that he had died in so Christian a fashion and assuring them that they could count on his favor and that he was writing to his father to request that he reward them as was befitting.[7]

The death of Cobos deprived Philip of the last of his privy counsellors. It was followed closely by another major loss to the Imperial secretariat. As we have seen, Idiáquez was in Madrid on a special mission in March. In spite of delays he was in Barcelona on April 14, when he wrote that he was planning to leave as soon as possible to join the Emperor's Court at Nuremberg.[8] Again there were delays, while he and the Príncipe de Ascoli waited for passage. But by May 20 he was in Genoa, where he picked up the dispatches to the Emperor.[9]

Early in June he had almost caught up with the Emperor, who had left Wittenberg for Halle. Crossing the Elbe on June 8, he was attacked by a band of robbers, who murdered him, his four servants, and the Imperial courier. When Charles heard the news, he sent four hundred cavalry to apprehend the murderers, but they could not be found. They did, however, come upon his body, with four mortal wounds, on the bank of the river, only a league from the Emperor's camp. He was buried in Halle, which the Emperor reached on June 10.[10] When Diego de Mendoza heard of the tragedy, he wrote to Charles, urging him "to provide for his children with his usual clemency and gratitude." [11]

The death of Cobos and Idiáquez reduced the secretariat to a mere skeleton. Only Eraso was left with the Court of the Emperor; in Spain, Juan Vázquez and Gonzalo Pérez were the only experienced secretaries to survive, although Francisco de Ledesma continued to serve as secretary of the Council of War.[12] Even before Cobos' death the Conde de Morata was dismayed at the thought that he might not be able to take part in the Cortes of Aragon which Philip had just summoned: "I doubt whether, without him, anything can be accomplished, because there are few people who have enough experience with a Cortes to be able to tell His Highness what should be done." [13] When we remember that Philip was just twenty years old at the time, the need for seasoned counsellors is the more apparent.

The vacancies left by Cobos' death naturally awakened hopes in many minds. One of them was the Aragonese secretary Comalonga. As soon as he learned that Cobos was gone, he wrote from Madrid, asking the Emperor to keep him in mind. In July he was at Monzón for the Cortes and again he renewed his request. After pointing out that the secretariat was in need of reform, particularly now that Idiáquez was dead, and that men of experience were badly needed, he suggested that he was precisely the man required for the job. He had been in the service twenty-eight years, having received his training under Ugo de Urríes. After the death of Alonso de Valdés he had been in charge of Neapolitan affairs for four years, until Idiáquez wormed his way into the post, as Granvelle could testify.[14] He did not add that he had taken part in the Tunisian campaign nor that he had received his present post as secretary for the Balearic Isles on August 28, 1546, through the influence of Cobos.[15]

Another who thought that he might pick up one of the vacant posts was the Marqués de Aguilar, Viceroy of Cataluña. He too was at Monzón for the Cortes and on July 15 he wrote to the Emperor suggesting that if the position as Comendador Mayor de León had not been filled, he would be glad to receive it; or perhaps, failing that, he could be named *contador mayor* of Castile.[16] As usual, the Emperor was long in making a decision, but at Augsburg, late in 1547 he appointed Diego as Comendador Mayor, and at the same time he granted María de Mendoza a life pension of 1,000,000 *maravedís* a year.[17] Already in 1543 he had made up his mind that Diego was not to succeed his father as *contador mayor,* and he now named Francisco de Almaguer to the post.[18] The decision was a wise one, for Almaguer had been serving as Cobos' chief deputy in the job since the death of Sancho de Paz and had demonstrated his ability as a financial officer.

Last Will and Testament

On the very day of his father's death Diego appeared before the deputy *corregidor* of Ubeda, Alonso Pérez de Arteaga, accompanied by his uncle, Alvaro de Mendoza, and the Dean Ortega, and presented the will which Cobos had signed on May 4, "lying in bed, ill of body but in sound mind and judgment," before the notary Hernán Verdugo de Henao and in the presence of a long list of witnesses, including Dr. Zaballos, Dr. Villaroel, Captain Andrés de Prada, and several servants.[19] It is a long document and it will not be necessary to examine in detail all of its provisions, particularly since all of his real property had been incorporated in the *mayorazgo* set up for his son.

After the usual pious preliminaries, in which he appealed to Our Lady, to San Miguel (patron of Ubeda), and to Santiago for their intercession, that God might forgive his offenses and heed not his sins and weaknesses, he provided that his body should be buried in his chapel of San Salvador; until it was completed, his body should be deposited in the chapel of La Concepción in the church of Santo Tomás. There follows provision for the customary masses for his soul. He has drawn up a statute for his chapel and he calls on his wife and son to see to it that his instructions are carried out. If necessary, he authorizes his executors to use money from his personal property to complete the church.

He next orders his family and servants not to put on mourning for his death. To two monasteries, Guadalupe and La Peña de Francia, he leaves the trifling bequest of ten ducats each. His possessions as Grand Commander of Santiago are to be distributed according to the rules of the Order: his horse and arms to his successor as Grand Commander; a mule and a cup to the Master of the Order; a bed and some of his clothes to the hospitals. His debts are to be paid; his Christian slaves are to be freed, as a reward for their faithful services in his house and in the work at the fortresses of Sabiote and Canena.

For his chapel, he requests that Doña María provide for any additional ornaments, vestments, silver, and tapestries necessary beyond what they had already given. And he provides another benefice, as well as confirming a donation for a monastery.

For his sisters, Leonor and Isabel, he makes special provision. During his lifetime they have been living in his palace in Ubeda and he now asks his wife and son to permit them to continue to enjoy this privilege. He is particularly indebted to Doña Leonor for all that she has done for their parents and he requests that she continue to receive the income she has been enjoying from various properties in Ubeda and from his post as *escribano del crimen.* He also assigns her and Doña Isabel a hundred bushels of wheat a year. If Doña Leonor dies, her sister is to receive these privileges, except the income from the *escribanía,* which is to go to Diego.

He calls on his son to live up to all the provisions for the *adelantamiento* of Cazorla and at all times to show great respect for the Holy See. He hands on to him all the posts which he had held and which the Emperor had authorized him to transfer: as *fundidor* of the Indies, as *regidor* of Valladolid and of Ubeda, as *escribano del crimen* of Ubeda, as *contador mayor* of Granada and *escribano mayor* of Alcaraz and the Campo de Montiel. He explains that he had granted the post of *regidor* of Valladolid to Juan Mosquera de Molina, his deputy as warden of Simancas, but he now revokes that grant.

He had given Diego 15,000 ducats to pay off mortgages on the estates of the Marquesa de Camarasa; these properties are to be incorporated in the *mayorazgo.* His servants are to be paid and fed for two months, while they are finding new jobs. Idiá-

quez, who owes him money collected in fees in the despatch of
Neapolitan affairs, is excused from paying his debt; so too are
the heirs of Francisco de Olaso, for money owed at the time of
his death. Because of his confidence in Almaguer, he orders his
executors to accept without question whatever account he turns
in. Since by the terms of the *mayorazgo* his bequests are limited
to 4,000 ducats, he gives to Diego one of the two rich badges of
the Order of Santiago *(veneras)* which he has, together with
the gold chain on which it hangs (he may chose whichever he
wants); he also leaves to him a sable cloak and any one he
chooses of the three suits of armor he has left.

In accordance with the terms of the marriage contract with
the Conde de Morata, he now confirms that all additions to the
property of the Marquesa shall remain as a permanent part of
the *mayorazgo*. Once more he urges his wife to carry out the
plans for the chapel. He calls on his children to honor, obey,
and care for their mother. In particular he commends his wife
and son to the Duque de Alba, to Granvelle, and to the Marqués
de Mondéjar, whom he has always served, to the Emperor, from
whom he has received so many favors, and finally to the Prince.
He calls on Diego to serve the Emperor and Philip.

He names Diego as his heir, in accordance with the provisions
of the *mayorazgo*. He had already given his daughter a dowry
of 10,000,000 *maravedís* and had added considerable sums out
of the 1,000,000 *maravedís* which the Emperor had bestowed on
her, all this in addition to the gold, silver, horses, clothes, etc.
which he had presented to her and her husband. He now gives
her 15,000 ducats more, out of which there must be taken the
advances of wheat and barley which he had made to the Duque
for the operation of his household in 1546 and 1547; he also
provides for repayment, if no cash is available. If they do not
accept his conditions, the money is to go to Diego. He also leaves
to his daughter a little gold pendant, with an image of God
the Father at the top, under it five large pearls, and in the middle
an enameled figure of Our Lady, with certain lettering and other
polished things, worth six and one-half marks,[20] together with
the little gold chain on which it hangs, and also a drinking-cup,
carved in the Roman style with *veneras,* worth over five marks.
If María dies without issue, these gifts are to revert to the
mayorazgo. That is all she can have from his estate.

Finally he names as his executors his wife, the Duque de Alba, and the Marqués de Mondéjar. Since both these gentlemen are busy men, he also appoints Alvaro de Mendoza, Juan Vázquez de Molina, Alonso de Idiáquez, Juan de Samano, Hernando Ortega, and Francisco de Almaguer. What a revealing list! He needed the support of great lords like Alba and Mondéjar. But the men on whom he counted in the hour of final decision were his associates of all the years in the secretariat. His brother-in-law, Don Alvaro, and the Dean of Malaga were his ties with the Church, as well as long-familiar friends.

Strangely enough, another copy of the will was presented by Diego on May 10 at Ubeda to the deputy *corregidor* of Baeza, Pedro Izquierdo.[21] In this case, however, the will was not opened until the Duque de Sesa had been notified and had sent Juan de Eriales as his representative to be present at the ceremony. And so, after all the witnesses had been called and had sworn that they had seen Cobos sign the will and knew that he was dead, the document was duly opened and read. We have seen that the Conde de Morata was worried lest the Duque de Sesa might cause some trouble. Is it possible that Diego was afraid that his brother-in-law might contest the will, if he, as a person concerned, were not properly informed, and so took this precaution?

On this occasion Diego also presented a brief memorandum prepared by his father, which listed a few special bequests to some of his personal servants—his valet, his butler, his barber. The others were to be content with the generous provisions he had made in his will. This document was signed only by Diego and Andrés de Prada.

The Value of His Estate

Under instructions from María de Mendoza, Verdugo de Henao, his majordomo and business manager, at once set about preparing an inventory of all Cobos' property, as of the day of his death, which was signed at Sabiote on June 26, 1547.[22] It is another long, bewildering document, which need not be analyzed in detail here. But on the basis of it, of the list of his purchases of real estate preserved in the Archivo de Camarasa, and the *juros* that he bought, recorded in the Archivo de Simancas, it is possible to draw up an approximate statement of his assets, his cash balances, and his annual income for 1546. It must be remembered that the record is not complete and that many of the items are only estimates.

Thus, for instance, we do not know the amount of money that he had invested in his palace in Valladolid. But when his grandson sold the property to the Duque de Lerma in 1601, he received for it an annual income of 4,000 ducats, at the rate of 5 per cent of the value. Assuming that prices had doubled in fifty years, an income of 2,000 ducats a year implies a capital of 40,000 ducats, or 15,000,000 maravedís. At the time of the sale, Don Francisco declared that his palace in Ubeda was as good as, or better than the house in Valladolid.[23] We may, therefore, set on it a similar value.

It is well-nigh impossible to estimate the value and income of the adelantamiento of Cazorla. Since the property was under litigation, it is not important to suggest a figure for its total worth, especially since it was granted to Cobos by the Cardinal Tavera without any payment on his part. The income from the alcabalas of Cazorla was 1,838,000 maravedís in 1503; in 1527 it had increased by about a third.[24] By 1546 they must have been yielding at least 3,000,000 maravedís a year. Since the majordomo held a cash balance of 2,218,000 maravedís in the Cazorla account on May 10, 1547, plus a considerable amount of wheat and barley, an estimate of a total annual income of 3,000,000 maravedís from that source is certainly a modest one. It should be added that when the suit was finally settled in 1604, the Archbishop of Toledo granted to the Marqués de Camarasa an annual income of 7,500 ducats a year from the total income of the property.[25] And obviously this 2,812,500 maravedís was only a part of the total.

Similarly there are no precise figures for his income from his post as fundidor. Both Laiglesia and Hamilton give the average receipts of gold and silver from the Indies in the period from 1541 to 1545 as about 440,000,000 maravedís a year.[26] Cobos' 1 per cent may therefore be set as approximately 4,400,000 maravedís a year. In most cases we do not know the exact rates of interest on juros of real estate. In general, however, juros were issued at 7 per cent, and this is the figure that can be used as a basis. In the same way, we may be sure that when Cobos bought a property, as a good business man, he expected to receive a fair income. In fact, in the sale of Torres and Canena, the value of the properties was determined by the royal assessors on the basis of actual income. With these reservations, we may venture to give a rough picture, in round numbers, of his financial position at the time of his death.[27]

Assets	
Real estate	79,193,000 mrs.
Alcabalas	25,495,000
Juros (purchased 1519-1545)	17,100,000
Loans outstanding	8,532,000
Total	130,320,000 mrs.
	(347,000 ducats)

Cash Balances, as of May 10, 1547	
In agents' hands	43,034,000 mrs.
Due on unpaid salaries, fees, etc.	2,595,000
Total	45,629,000 mrs.

Income (1546)	
Real estate	6,050,000 mrs.
Alcabalas	1,764,000
Juros	1,191,000
Mines	1,382,000
Salaries	1,767,000
Grants	7,404,000
Fees	333,000
Total	19,891,000 mrs.
	(53,000 ducats)

It must be remembered that the estimates given here certainly do not provide a complete picture of Cobos' total assets nor of his annual income. No account is given of his large holdings of real estate in Castile and Andalusia. His investments in treasury notes *(juros)* were surely greater than those which chanced to be recorded and preserved in the documents of his time. For these reasons it seems probable that during the last years of his life his annual income was at least 60,000 ducats a year. This would place him in the bracket of the richest nobles in Spain, whose income was estimated at that amount in 1530 [28] by Marineo Sículo—the Condestable de Castilla, the Duque de Escalona, and the Duque de Sesa, the Marqués del Valle (Hernán Cortés), and his wife's cousin, the Conde de Benavente.

In his *Relazione* of 1546 the Venetian ambassador, Bernardo Navagero, reported that Cobos' income was 70,000 ducats a year.[29] Another contemporary, Luis Zapata, tells us in his *Mis-*

celánea that Cobos left an income of 40,000 ducats a year when he died.[30] Their guesses seem to have been well founded. For a penniless boy, Cobos had done well; Horatio Alger could not have invented a more spectacular "success story."

In all this account we have made no mention of Cobos' personal property. It must have been extensive, as we have seen from occasional mention of jewels, suits of armor, tapestries, paintings, and the like which were in his possession. As was the custom of his time, many of his personal effects were sold after his death to provide ready cash for the payment of his bequests. In November, 1547, auctions of his property were held in five cities: Seville, Córdoba, Granada, Madrid, and Valladolid. Somewhere in the Archivos de Protocolos of these cities there must lie hidden the inventories of these sales, but I have not been able to uncover them. As it is, all that we know is that at the auction in Valladolid, which was the poorest of them all, there were silver table-cloths that fetched 4,000 ducats and Prince Philip paid 400 ducats for one of two rugs. It would be interesting to know who bought the buffet with doors filled with large and small silver objects, as well as seven pairs of platters and seventeen cups, goblets and pitchers, all of gold, and other things, "as valuable as any the Emperor might have." [31]

The sumptuous equipment of their palaces, the splendor of their jewels, tapestries, clothes, and appurtenances are a clear reflection of the values that Cobos and his wife held in esteem. Cobos had grown up as a poor boy and Doña María, as a girl, had lived very modestly. They found themselves in a social world where material things were the symbol of status. The example of extravagance in his standard of living set by the Emperor had been quickly followed by the Spanish noblemen like the Duque del Infantado or the Duque de Medinasidonia. Both Cobos and his wife were ambitious; they craved social prestige. And for that, the acquisition of wealth and the things that money can buy were essential, if they were to keep the pace of the people with whom they associated. In that they were successful. They could have found no greater satisfaction than the comparison of their treasures with those of the Emperor himself or the description of their palace in Valladolid as "Imperial." [32]

The Family and Heirs

There is little record of the activities of Cobos' widow in the first years after his death, other than her financial affairs. The threatened suit against Cobos to recover money which he was charged with having collected illegally from the Indies was instituted against Doña María and her son on June 14, 1548, before the Consejo de las Indias. Doña María at once denied the charge and produced the royal *cédulas* to prove her case. The prosecutor, Villalobos, sent an instruction to all the royal officials in the Indies on June 1, 1549, ordering them to report all gold and silver that had been assayed and minted in the Indies since 1522. Villalobos died in 1550, but his successor, Agreda, was ordered to continue the case. There are documents in the file as late as August, 1555, but there the story ends. Perhaps, like so many legal cases in the sixteenth century, the matter never came to a decision.[33]

Certainly, at the time, Doña María was not in financial straits. On July 4, 1548, she bought the towns of Ximena and Recena, which had been dismembered from the Order of Calatrava, for 70,000 ducats.[34] Three years later she purchased for 7,500,000 *maravedís* a *juro* that paid 375,000 *maravedís* a year at 5 per cent.[35] But shortly thereafter she was threatened with a serious reduction of her and her son's income.

When Cobos died he transferred his post as *fundidor* to his son. At Augsburg on July 8, 1548, the Emperor confirmed the appointment for the present, reserving the right to change the conditions at his pleasure.[36] Diego had already promised to pay his mother 1,000,000 *maravedís* a year out of the income (April 16, 1548) and she had accepted the offer.[37] Between 1545 and 1549 the receipts of gold and silver from the Indies had dwindled, but with the return of the Bishop of Palencia, Pedro de la Gasca, in 1550 they suddenly rose to unprecedented figures. The average annual receipts in the next five years were over 2,000,-000,000 *maravedís;* the 1 per cent which went to Don Diego began to be an important item.

On May 31, 1552, the Emperor ordered that, beginning with January 1 of that year, the 1 per cent for the charge of assaying should be transferred to the royal account and that from the total so received, 1,000,000 *maravedís* a year should be assigned to Doña María and 2,000,000 to Don Diego. Of the amount which had recently come from the Indies, Don Diego was to receive one half; if he had already received more than that, he was to make restitution to the Treasury.[38] When Doña María heard of the decision, she promptly addressed a protest to the Consejo de las Indias. Rehearsing the background of the case, she pointed out that she and her son were being wronged on three accounts. First, the *cédula* which Cobos had signed in 1539, authorizing the Emperor to modify the income from the appointment, had been based upon the assumption that he and his heirs were to enjoy the possession of the *adelantamiento* of Cazorla. That was now under litigation in Rome and she and her son were spending more than their income from Cazorla on the costs of the trial. Second, the *cédula* had not agreed that the office should be taken away, but only that the income might be "modified." And finally, an *ex post facto* ruling was unfair; they had received the income in good faith and had spent it; they should not be required to make restitution.[39] She therefore humbly requested that action be suspended until the case had been reviewed.

Early in June she continued to press her cause. She appealed to Eraso, the Regent Figueroa, and the Bishop of Palencia to present the case to the Emperor. "The Duque de Alba"—she remarked—"who is the lord of this household and master of this affair, will suggest what should be done." [40] If the Emperor was determined to deprive Don Diego of the office, let him give him, not a fixed amount of 2,000,000 *maravedís* a year, but two-thirds of the total or one half. She would be willing to have her 1,000,000 mrs. taken out of the total, if such a provision were made. Certainly no change should be made retroactive. She reminded the Emperor, in another letter, that the heirs of Pérez de Almazán and Conchillos were still receiving the income from their appointments as *fundidor,* made by the Reyes Católicos. After all, the amount that her son would receive at 1 per cent was petty, compared with the royal *quinta,* particularly in view of the expected increase in metal shipments from the Indies. He must not give aid and comfort to her husband's enemies by doing an affront to his wife and children. She can only throw herself on his mercy.[41]

The Consejo took up Doña María's protest at its meeting of August 2 and decided to refer the whole question to Philip when he returned.[42] But Philip was still in doubt: at Monzón, on

October 16, he wrote to his father, asking for instructions.[43] The Emperor's final decision was to reaffirm the original order.

It must be said that in this whole affair justice was on the side of Doña María. The Emperor's memory of the agreement of November, 1539, was faulty; in his "Secret Instruction" to Philip in May, 1543, he had written: "Cobos has given me a *cédula* that, if the bulls regarding Cazorla are carried out and his son has possession of the *adelantamiento,* his jurisdiction as *fundidor* can be taken away from him." [44] The *cédula* certainly did not say that, but only that the conditions could be modified. Certainly, too, Diego's possession of Cazorla was in jeopardy as a result of Siliceo's refusal to approve of the transaction. But by this time the Emperor's financial situation was so precarious that justice was no longer important.

In fact, by 1557, the Spanish treasury was bankrupt and payments were suspended. It is not surprising, then, that Doña María and Don Diego were unable to collect even the 3,000,000 *maravedís* a year that they had been assigned. By the end of 1564 they had received only 1,000,000 *maravedís* in twelve years. And so they agreed to a compromise with the Consejo de las Indias whereby they would accept, in lieu of the 35,000,-000 mrs. still due them, a *juro* of 21,750,000 mrs. at 5 per cent, payable in the Casa de la Contratación.[45] We will not speculate as to whether they and their heirs succeeded in collecting even this income.

Doña María

After Cobos' death Doña María spent most of her time in their palace in Valladolid. There, on February 4, 1556, a royal messenger appeared, bringing instructions to her to hand over all of her husband's papers to the Archivo de Simancas. She complied, and ordered Hernando Bernaldo to prepare an inventory and deliver the documents. The inventory has survived and enables us to form some idea of the extent of Cobos' official labors.[46] It is in two parts: the first lists five chests, containing a total of 173 bound volumes, some of which, exquisitely bound in parchment, with leather lacings, are still in the Archivo. The papers begin with the correspondence of Zafra, Gricio, and Conchillos and include materials from the files of Cobos and Juan Vázquez down to 1553. The second part of the inventory lists the contents of 24 chests. Most of these documents are in bundles *(legajos)*—there were 146 bundles in Chest No. 1—but in Chest No. 16 there were 21 bound volumes and a "note book" of damage done by deer at various royal estates. In general, in both parts of the inventory, the documents in each chest are roughly classified by subject, but there are thousands of miscellaneous papers. It is, of course, impossible to estimate the total number of documents included, but surely there must have been well over one hundred thousand, which helps to explain why no one had been sufficiently foolhardy to undertake a biography of Cobos.

Meanwhile, work on the chapel of San Salvador had been continuing. Berruguete had finished carving the *retablo* of the Transfiguration and Alvaro de Mendoza, now Bishop of Palencia, had ordered in 1555, as a gift to his sister, the construction of a *reja* by Francisco de Villalpando, the celebrated creator of the *reja* in the Cathedral of Toledo.[47] The church was consecrated by the Bishop of Jaén, Diego Tavera, on October 8, 1559. We may be sure that Doña María and her children were present at the ceremony and that they stayed on in Ubeda until November 20, when Cobos' remains were transferred from the chapel in Santo Tomás to the crypt in the Capilla Mayor of San Salvador.[48]

In 1563 Doña María was at the monastery of El Abrojo. Perhaps she was seriously ill at the time, for on August 28 she made her will; in those days, people drew their wills only when they thought they were at the point of death. The document contains the usual provision for masses and for gifts to monasteries. The most curious passage is one that provides that on her death her body must not be embalmed, but placed in a coffin, "even though it smelt bad," and carried to Ubeda, accompanied by twenty-four Dominican and Franciscan friars with torches, to be buried in her chapel.[49] One cannot help thinking of another funeral cortège that carried the body of the Empress to Granada in 1539, and even of a funeral procession that Don Quixote met on his adventurous way.

That year Doña María began a series of donations to pious foundations. Outside of Valladolid, on the west bank of the Pisuerga, she built and endowed the Hospital of San Bartolomé at a total cost of 30,000 ducats.[50] Within the next few years she rebuilt and equipped the choir of the church of San Francisco at a cost of 3,500 ducats.[51] For the Hospital de la Resur-rección she secured grants and indulgences from the Pope.[52] In 1570 she donated to the monastery of Santo Domingo in Rivadavia the sum of 150,000 *maravedís* a year in return for the privilege of providing a burial place for her brother, Don Alvaro, and her nephew, Luis Sarmiento, Conde de Rivadavia, for which they had made arrangements two years before.[53]

When Santa Teresa came to Valladolid in 1568 to found an-other house of the Reform, she stayed at first in Doña María's house;[54] she already knew of her through her brother, Don Alvaro, now Bishop of Avila, who had been such a help to her in the foundation of her first house.

Just behind the palace, in the same block, was the little chapel of the Cofradía of El Rosario.[55] As soon as the palace was built, it must have served as a sort of private chapel for the owners. Juan Mosquera de Molina said that he used to attend matins there even before the birth of the Prince (1527). Cobos and his wife were interested in the improvement of the chapel. They provided a new altar, with a *retablo,* a new pulpit, and vestments for the divine services. Cobos' agents in Rome secured from the Pope special favors and indulgences. Between 1536 and 1538 the Empress lived for two years in the palace—it was there that she gave birth in October, 1537 to the Infante Don Juan, who died five months later. During her stay, Cobos had a passageway built from the palace to the chapel and also a tribune especially reserved for the Empress. When she left for Madrid in Septem-ber, 1538, she wrote to the Cofradía, asking them to make no changes in "her chapel" but to leave everything as it was, "until —God willing—I return." The renovated chapel was consecrated by Pedro Manuel, Bishop of Zamora, on March 17, 1539. But the Empress never made her hoped-for return.

Cobos had continued to seek new indulgences for the chapel from the Pope.[56] After the foundation of the Jesuits, Cobos, like Juan de Zúñiga, was regarded as friendly to the members of the new Order,[57] and in April, 1545 Padre Araoz wrote that María de Mendoza had invited him to preach at the chapel of El Rosario.[58] A few months later, the Infante Don Carlos was born in Cobos' palace and was baptized in the chapel on August 2. After the death of the Princess no less than one hundred and thirty-four masses were sung in the chapel for the repose of her soul.[59]

After the death of Cobos, María de Mendoza continued to show her interest in the chapel. When it fell into bad repair, she sent for Luis de Vega to superintend the necessary restorations, including a new sacristy. In recognition of her benefactions, the Cofradía granted her in 1552 the exclusive use of the tribune which had been built for the Empress.[60] It was from this tribune —we learn from one of her companions—that Santa Teresa heard mass during her stay with Doña María.[61]

Another brother of Doña María, Bernardino de Mendoza, now offered Teresa an estate outside the town, called Río de Olmos, as a site for her new foundation. Work was begun at once and the little group of sisters occupied the building on August 15, 1568. Meanwhile, however, Don Bernardino, while visiting in Ubeda, was paralyzed by a stroke and died without being able to make confession. The Saint was sorely troubled that his soul was thus in jeopardy, but Our Lord told her not to worry, because it would be released from Purgatory on the day when the first mass was sung in the new house. It was Juan de Avila who celebrated that mass and as Santa Teresa received the Host, Don Bernardino appeared before her in a vision, with happy, shining face.[62]

The new house of Río de Olmos soon proved unsatisfactory. It was a long way for the sisters who went to beg alms, and besides, it was in an unhealthy situation and many of the sisters fell ill. At this juncture Doña María offered to provide a house in town, in exchange for the other property. To this end she purchased from María Hernández de Isla a house in the Calle Real—now the Rondilla de Santa Teresa—and rebuilt it for the use of the Order. The new monastery was dedicated on February 3, 1569. A year later Santa Teresa wrote to her brother Lorenzo: "About a year ago I had an attack of quartan fever that left me in better health. I was busy at the time with the foundation in Valladolid, where María de Mendoza, who is very fond of me, was fairly killing me with presents." [63] And in her *Fundaciones* she wrote: "Doña María de Mendoza, a good Christian and a woman of great charity, as her abundant gifts of alms make clear, showed great charity toward me. . . . She has provided us with everything necessary up to now and she will continue to do so, as long as she lives." [64] Doña María lived up to her expectations and before her death she endowed the convent in 1585 with 8,000 ducats.[65]

In January, 1568, Doña María had paid a visit to Ubeda to inspect the chapel there.[66] Explaining that because of illness and cares she had not been able to provide for the regular visitations prescribed by the Statutes of the chapel, she now appointed Dr. Bernardino de Carleval and Fray Gerónimo de Aguilera to make the required inspection of the chaplains and she named Antonio Cabero de Valderrábano, *corregidor* of Sabiote, to examine the accounts. The inspectors made their report in May, and on June 2 Doña María approved their recommendations. Most of these dealt with the duties of the chaplains, the sacristan, the organist, and other servants of the chapel, the proper use of the vestments, of which eleven sets are listed, the use of the silver, etc. They also proposed that these new regulations be incorporated in the original Constitution. The last of the recommendations approved by Doña María were: to add four more half-time chaplains to the twelve already provided, to increase the stipends of all the chaplains from 36,000 to 50,000 *maravedís* a year, and to begin the teaching of Latin and rhetoric as part of the plan to establish a university.

When the ordinary of the bishopric of Jaén refused to confirm her nominations to the new posts, calling in question her right as patroness of the chapel, she ordered prepared a long history of its development, beginning with the founding of the chapel of La Concepción in 1525. At the same time she drew up a list of nineteen questions which were to be asked of the witnesses whom she proposed to summon in the suit to establish her right as patroness. These documents, together with the answers of the witnesses, provide us with much of what we know about the chapel. The most impressive part is the list of treasures that she and her husband had lavished on it: 20,000 ducats on its construction, relics, ornaments, vestments, silver, paintings, the alabaster statue of St. John by Michelangelo. In all, she estimated that they had spent over 50,000 ducats.

A few of the items deserve special mention. One of the relics, for example, was four of the heads of the Eleven Thousand Virgins, a gift from the Emperor made at Cologne in 1521. One of the many sets of vestments was made from the robe which Charles had worn at his coronation in Bologna and which he had presented to Cobos. Another gift of the Emperor, a gold goblet, had been converted into a richly mounted chalice; it is one of the few objects that have survived to our day.

During the last few years of her life there is little known of Doña María's activities. Early in 1570 her nephew, Luis Sarmiento, died and the title of Condesa de Rivadavia went to his only daughter, Leonor Sarmiento. The wife of her son, Francisca Luisa, must have died by this time, and Don Diego was evidently betrothed to his cousin, Doña Leonor. But Diego died in 1575 and Doña María was soon involved in a lawsuit with María de Toledo over the guardianship of Doña Leonor. With her death, the last of the male line of Rivadavia was extinguished and the title reverted to Doña María, as the eldest of the sisters in the family.[67]

The last of the financial transactions in which Doña María was involved was the purchase of a mortgage of 5,404,000 *maravedís* in Valladolid on September 6, 1578.[68] On October 1, 1583 she signed a new will.[69] The next years were probably heavy with ill health, but she lived on until she was almost eighty. Death came on February 11, 1587.[70]

Although no portrait of Doña María has survived, there must have been a number of them in her time. We know, for example, that there was once a portrait of her by Titian in the royal collection; [71] perhaps this is the same portrait that Diego de Mendoza once listed as security for a loan.[72] Diego López de Ayala, master of works at the Cathedral of Toledo, wrote to one Juan Mudarra, asking him to have a block of marble sent to Alonso Berruguete, for a bust of Doña María that he was to make.[73] It would be pleasant to think that the lovely female figure above the cornice in the southwest corner of the sacristy in the chapel in Ubeda is an idealized portrait of her from the cunning hand of Jamete, who must have known her when he was working on the palace in Valladolid. But that is mere speculation.

She must have had charm. When she was married in 1522, Salinas called her a "comely lass." Poets later sang the praises of her beauty. Gutierre de Cetina dedicated to her his version of a madrigal of the Italian poet, Luigi Tansillo:

> "Yo diría de vos tan altamente
> Que el mundo viese en vos lo que yo veo,
> Si tal fuese el decir cual el deseo.
> Mas si fuera del más hermoso cielo
> Acá en la mortal gente,
> Entre las bellas y preciadas cosas
> No hallo una que os semeje un pelo,
> Sin culpa queda aquel que no os atreve.

El blanco del cristal, el oro y rosas,
Los rubís y las perlas y la nieve,
Delante vuestro gesto comparadas,
Son ante cosas vivas las pintadas.
Ante vos las estrellas,
Como delante el sol, son menos bellas.
El sol es más lustroso,
Pero a mi parecer no es tan hermoso.
¿Qué puedo, pues, decir, si cuanto veo
Todo ante vos es feo?
Mudad el nombre, pues, señora mía,
Y vos llamad beldad, beldad María." [73a]

Dormer in his *Progreso de la historia en el reyno de Aragón* mentions an epigram of the Flemish poet, Joannes Secundus, dedicated to her.[74] But none of the editions of his erotic Latin verses mentions her. There is, however, no reason to doubt Dormer's statement, for Secundus was in Spain from April to June, 1534, at Toledo, Palencia, and Segovia, and he dedicated poems to Gonzalo Pérez, Diego Hurtado de Mendoza, and Gerónimo Zurita.[75] Another humanist poet, the historian Ambrosio de Morales, also dedicated a poem "In Mariam Mendozam":

Vix primo lux alma diem quae proxima Maio est
    Mostrarat mundo et dispulerat tenebras,
Illustris Maria, Dryades quam mille sequuntur
    Calcabat niveo florida rura pede,
Pallentes violas dum purpureis hyacintis
    Commiscet, rubris lilia et alba rosis
Et sibi de vano connectit flore corollas,
    Ocurrit natus Cypridos omnipotens.
Vidit et obstipuit, nam credidit esse parentem
    Formosis figens lumina luminibus;
Sic Mariam Paphia dum progenetrice salutat—
    "Quo mea, quo,"—dixit—"mater?" et erubuit.[76]

In his *Relazione* of 1546 the Venetian ambassador, Bernardo Navagero, attributes part of Cobos' popularity to the "manners and sweetness of his wife, Doña María de Mendoza, who entertains everyone with great skill and courtesy." [77]

There was, however, another side to her personality. We already mentioned Salinas' obvious reference to her greed, and elsewhere he implies that she kept her husband away from his work.[78] In his "Secret Instruction" to Philip, the Emperor also warned him that Doña María was responsible for Cobos' bad reputation in the matter of accepting gifts by receiving "small

presents" and that it was she who involved him in the factional
rivalries of the Court. On the basis of the Emperor's words some
modern writers have made of her an example of the ambition
and greed of the whole Mendoza family.

There can be no doubt that she was ambitious, that she cultivated the great nobles, that she would have liked to assume control of Philip, that she dreamed of building a chapel which
would rival the royal chapel in Granada. And it is equally certain that she craved wealth. But there is little in the records of
the time to prove that she encouraged bribes. Gifts she undoubtedly accepted. Hernán Cortés gave her and her sister rare gifts
from Mexico when they were at Guadalupe in 1528. When Don
Alonso Enríquez returned from Peru in 1540 he brought her
a chain of little gold beads.[79] But most of the presents she received were trifles from her and her husband's friends—preserves from Andrea Doria, a bolt of silk from Ferrante
Gonzaga, gloves from the Duchess of Mantua, green almonds
from Francisco de Borja, even some unnamed "cosillas" from
Queen Eleanor of France. These are all matters of courtesy,
characteristic of the *mores* of the day.

There is only one gift that is mentioned with the avowed purpose of gaining influence. In 1542, the unscrupulous governor of
Peru, Cristóbal Vaca de Castro, wrote to his wife an astonishing
letter, recounting his exploits and advising her what she should
do to promote their interests. He lists the people at Court whom
she should cultivate, among them Doña María, "for since I am
striving to serve them all, it is right that they should be grateful
to me and pay me for it." And he goes on: "With Doña María de
Mendoza you should be on cordial terms and call on her and
give her some things, for with that you can get what you want;
and also with her mother, the Condesa de Rivadavia, it will be
profitable, because I am her servant." [80] It should be noted that
Vaca de Castro returned to Spain in disgrace.

If Doña María was regarded as grasping and ambitious in
her heyday, the later years of her life completely changed the
picture. In 1568 she described what she had been trying to do in
Valladolid since her husband's death, living an exemplary life as
a servant of God, giving alms, aiding widows and poor prisoners, providing for the care and cure of the sick, "as an example
and model for faithful Christians, so that she was beloved by
the people of the town and by strangers, who found in her com-

fort for their needs." [81] It is in this rôle that Zapata describes
her, among other famous widows, in his *Carlo famoso:*

> "Y ansí alabarte a ti, doña María
> De Mendoça, sería dexarte en niebla,
> Qu'en ser caritativa, amiga y pía
> De la biudez tornaste la tiniebla." [82]

In a similar vein, a little known poet, Gerónimo de los Cobos,
who was probably the son of Pedro de los Cobos and named for
his uncle, Gerónimo Vela de los Cobos, dedicated to her his poem
the *Lágrimas de San Pedro:*

> "De España honor, clarísima María,
> Del nombre de Mendoza primer gloria,
> Que con ejemplo raro y nueva guía
> Al templo enderezáis de la victoria
> Con vida tal que contra la porfía
> Del tiempo durará vuestra memoria,
> Mientras por bien tan alto y sin segundo
> Valiere el ruego universal del mundo;
>
> Ya que en la tierna edad, que por hermosa
> Admirasteis a todo el universo,
> Cantar no pude la beldad famosa
> Con digno ingenio y con estilo terso,
> Agora esa virtud vuestra gloriosa
> Será objeto de mi prosa o verso,
> Consagrando con otras esta historia
> Al nombre inmortal de vuestra gloria." [83]

Of her death in 1587 Cabrera, the biographer of Philip II,
wrote that it brought "great regret because of her good works,
for according to the account-books of her house, during forty
years of widowhood she gave away in alms 500,000 ducats. Her
heir was her grandson, the Marqués de Camarasa, whose *mayorazgo* was thereby increased by almost 70,000 ducats." [84]

During her lifetime her closest friends were naturally in the
circle in which her husband moved—the Duquesa de Alba, Leonor de Castro, Mencía de Mendoza, the Marquesa de Cenete,
Estefanía de Requeséns, wife of Juan de Zúñiga, and her mother,
Hipólita de Liori, Condesa de Palamós. She was evidently popular with her husband's friends, for all his intimates—Italian
noblemen, ambassadors, colleagues, and even servants—never
failed to send her greetings in their letters. The only gentlemen
of the Court who left any personal record of her was Don
Alonso Enríquez de Guzmán. We have seen how constantly de-

voted to her he was; almost the last letter he ever wrote was
addressed to her on April 26, 1547, from the Emperor's camp
outside of Mühlberg. After giving a vivid account of the battle,
he ended:

> I wrote to the Comendador Mayor with the last courier before this. In
> this letter I send my greetings to him and beg him to consider it as his, as
> I am his. I beg Your Ladyship, after she has read it and shown it to His
> Lordship, to send it to the Duquesa de Alba, your great friend, and ask her
> to have it copied in the *Libro de mi vida* which she has, and then send it to
> my wife—better late than never—for when I write to her, it is not as copiously
> as this, but only love and kisses, as good husbands should. The troubles and
> worries here are so numerous that if it were not for the love and respect
> and obligation I feel for Your Ladyship, I could not have written, and it
> has cost me great trouble to do it.[85]

Cobos never saw this letter, for he was dead by the time it
reached Spain. A few months later Don Alonso too had disappeared from the scene. But fortunately the *Libro de su vida,*
with which he was so concerned, has survived. From it, more
than any other source, we can catch a glimpse of Doña María as
she was in flesh and blood—the way she acted, the way she
talked. Perhaps Don Alonso was in love with her, but never
once did he overstep the bounds of due respect. If she was as
generous and considerate of other men as she was of Don
Alonso, she must have had a host of admirers at the Court.

Don Diego and His Children

Don Diego, Cobos' son and heir, must have been a sore disappointment to his father, for there is no evidence that he ever did
anything important. Up to the time of his father's death, prac-
tically every mention of him refers to some appointment his
father had secured for him. When Blasco Núñez Vela arrived in
Lima in May, 1544, bringing the new seal which Diego (or his
father) had ordered, as Chanciller of the Indies, it was Cobos'
agent, Juan de Luna, who led the horse in the ceremony, with
the seal beneath a canopy on the horse's back.[86] One of the
charges that the Archbishop Siliceo brought against Cobos in
1546 was that Diego, as *adelantado* of Cazorla, had failed to
accompany him when he made his first episcopal visit to Alcalá
de Henares.[87] There is no evidence that he made the slightest
effort to defend his claim to the *adelantamiento*. Certainly it was
his mother, not he, who fought to retain his post as *fundidor,*

when it was taken away from him in 1552. In 1568, during the civil war in Granada, he reported that he was too old to serve, but was sending a thousand men.[88] He was then forty-five years old; his grandfather, for whom he was named, had not been too old, at the age of fifty-eight, to take part in another campaign in Granada.

It may be that his lack of force and initiative was the result of his upbringing under a dominating mother and a father too busy to give him any personal attention. But perhaps his indifference was only the natural reaction of a boy, brought up in affluence, to the constant drive of both his parents for power and wealth.

Don Diego's eldest son, Francisco de los Cobos y Luna, born in 1546, inherited the title of Marqués de Camarasa on his father's death in 1575. He had been made a knight of Santiago in 1569 [89] and had served with fifty lances in the war in Granada (1569-1570).[90] There is an amusing story that when he married Ana Félix de Guzmán, daughter of the Condes de Olivares, one of the wedding guests, Diego de Mendoza, brother of the Marqués de Mondéjar, wore a hat stuck full of pens, explaining that it was a festival of pens, not plumes ("de plumas y no de plumajes"), referring to the fact that the contracting parties were both children of secretaries, who had won great estates through their jobs.[91] On his grandmother's death in 1587 he inherited most of her estate, although the title of Conde de Riva-davia went to his younger brother, Alvaro de Sarmiento Mendoza, since by the terms of the *mayorazgo* the Marqueses de Camarasa could not also hold the title in the house of Riva-davia. He was still alive when the courts handed down their final decision with regard to Cazorla in 1604.

It would little profit to trace the rest of the history of the heirs of Don Francisco and Doña María. They were wealthy; they married into noble families; they served their king on occasion. But as usually has happened in Spain, the title of Camarasa was in the end absorbed in another house, that of the Duques de Medinaceli. The present Marquesa de Camarasa, daughter of the Duque, who is also Duquesa de Alcalá, lives with her consort in the magnificent Casa de Pilatos in Seville. And so today their children, the last direct descendants of Cobos and his wife, scamper in the broad patio on sunny mornings, disturbing the small army of cats that drowse against the vine-clad wall.

CHAPTER XV

COBOS AND HIS WORLD

His Career as Secretary

Since all of Cobos' public life was spent as a secretary, it were well to trace the steps by which he rose to power, the methods he used in building a staff, and the practices he followed in performing the duties of his office.

When he arrived in Flanders in 1516 he had already had fifteen years of experience under Hernando de Zafra and Lope Conchillos. If he quickly won the favor of Chièvres, it was undoubtedly because he was well versed in the operation of the secretariat, both in Castile and Aragon, because he was familiar with the leading figures of the Consejo Real and the other government officials, and because, as *contador mayor* of Granada, he knew something of the intricacies of finance. Since 1510, he had had charge of recording all royal grants and favors; Chièvres continued him in that office and extended his responsibility to the similar task of keeping the record of all royal receipts and expenditures.

In Flanders he shared the duties of secretary with Antonio de Villegas and a number of other secretaries. But with the arrival of the Court in Spain in September, 1517, he quickly became the principal member of the secretarial staff, signing almost all royal orders. Responsible at first only for the affairs of the Consejo Real, he soon took over the duties of Conchillos in the

management of Indian affairs. With the reforms of 1523 he became the controlling figure in the new Consejo de la Hacienda.
In this process, Villegas and the other secretaries were reduced
to minor rôles. In February, 1523, Martín de Salinas thought
that Villegas was to be dismissed [1] and López de Gómara
charged that he had crushed Villegas.[2] In reality, Villegas continued to serve for many years, but as Salinas wrote on September 7, 1524, he and Ruiz de Castañeda now had to be content
with the leavings.[3] By this time Cobos' position was secure.

We have already discussed the conflict between Cobos and
Gattinara for the control of the secretariat which began at this
time. With the elimination of Jean Lallemand in 1528, the star
of Gattinara began to decline. When Cobos was appointed a
member of the Council of State in 1529 and Granvelle joined
the staff, a new period began in the career of Cobos, for after the
death of Gattinara in the following year, these two became the
Emperor's chief counsellors. During the next eight years they
accompanied him on all of his travels; they were his principal
agents and representatives in all his diplomatic negotiations. We
know that both Granvelle and Cobos sincerely desired peace
with France; we know too that Cobos had little sympathy with
the Emperor's Imperial interests and constantly urged him to
devote himself to his kingdoms in Spain. Perhaps it was his
failure to exercise any influence on the Emperor, especially
during the negotiations of 1537 and 1538, that led him to withdraw from the diplomatic field, leaving those particular problems
to Granvelle.

When Charles left Spain for Flanders in the autumn of 1539,
Cobos remained behind, with the special responsibility of
straightening out the finances. And again in 1543, when the Emperor sailed from Barcelona, not to return for fourteen years,
he left Cobos, with Tavera and the Duque de Alba, as the chief
counsellors of Philip, who had been appointed Regent. Even during the last years of his life Cobos continued to carry on the
duties of the secretariat as long as he could. Near the end he
reluctantly turned them over to Juan Vázquez. Six months later
he was dead.

The Building of a Staff

Cobos' most important contribution to the administration of Castilian affairs was the development of a staff of public officials with a strong sense of professional solidarity and devotion to duty and of loyalty to their chief. The methods by which he achieved this end are interesting.

The first appointment to his staff of which there is record is that of Juan de Samano, who was assigned duties in the administration of Indian affairs in 1519, after the dismissal of Conchillos. Samano had been one of Cobos' associates when they were both employed in the office of Conchillos and therefore came to the task with considerable experience. He was a man of modest talents, but he remained in the service to the end of his life, and over the years Cobos secured for him a number of favors. In later years he received the title of secretary and served in a variety of functions with the Empress, with the Consejo de la Guerra, even with the Consejo Real. He was Cobos' oldest and most devoted subordinate.

The other of the two men who were appointed to take Cobos' place in the dispatch of Indian affairs, when Cobos left Spain in 1520, was his cousin, Pedro de los Cobos. He had served an apprenticeship as secretary of the Marqués de Olivares and he had been *regidor* of Ubeda. Like Samano, he was a man of small ability; like him, he served in a variety of minor functions for many years and he was even made a knight of Santiago. He was an old man in 1544, when Cobos asked that he be permitted to retire on a pension.[4] He was the first of his many kinsmen for whom Cobos found a berth and a comfortable living, without, however, assigning them any post of responsibility.

As Cobos acquired new appointments and new duties, it was necessary for him to find deputies to perform the tasks of office. Thus we learn that in Flanders, in 1521, Sancho de Paz was serving as his deputy in the job of keeping the record of all the royal grants. Sancho must have proved an efficient worker, for when the Consejo de la Hacienda was established in 1523, he was named "escrivano de finanzas" and given charge of recording all receipts and expenditures, a function that Cobos had been performing. Until his death in 1543 he remained the effective head of the treasury office, member of the Consejo de la Hacienda in 1530, and Cobos' deputy as *contador mayor* in 1541. He married the daughter of the Duque del Infantado and his name became famous through a widely quoted anecdote of the episode at the tournament in 1539, when the Duke slashed a bailiff who had struck his horse and when Diego Hurtado de Mendoza wrote to the Duke: "At the Cortes of Toledo you approved of the nobles' paying taxes; then you slashed a bailiff; and you married your daughter to Sancho de Paz. Speak not of honor, for the King has plenty." [5]

With Sancho de Paz in the operation of the Treasury, Cobos kept Cristóbal Suárez as chief paymaster. Suárez had held that post under Ferdinand the Catholic, and he too remained in office until the end of his life. In later years he was a member of the Consejo with Sancho de Paz and the Bishop of Badajoz, Gerónimo Suárez Maldonado. Like all the other public servants, he seems to have prospered financially; when the Princess María came to Salamanca in 1543, she was lodged in his palace.

None of the men whom Cobos appointed to his staff was drawn from the long list of secretaries who had begun their service under the Catholic Kings. During the first years he turned to people as his protégés who had had experience in other branches of the service and on whom he could count. But once he was firmly established in control of most of the administrative affairs of Castile, he undertook a different course: that of training men for responsibility.

The first of those whom he took on as an apprentice in his office was his nephew, Juan Vázquez de Molina, who appeared as one of his employees *(criado)* in 1523. Like his kinsman, Pedro de los Cobos, he had been appointed *regidor* of Úbeda and he was named a "caballero" of Santiago in 1528. Eventually he became Commander of Estriana and later of Peñaranda in the Order. Not until 1529 did Cobos consider him ready to assume important tasks, when he had him appointed secretary of the Empress during the absence of the Court on the first Italian journey. From then on Vázquez was Cobos' chief assistant. In 1533 he replaced Zuazola as secretary of the Consejo de la Guerra and thus gave Cobos for the first time a foothold in that Council. During Cobos' absence from Spain in 1535 and 1536, and again in 1538, he remained in charge of Castilian affairs. When Charles went to Flanders in 1539 and also in 1543 Vázquez accompanied him as secretary. In 1545 he was sent back to Spain to help carry the burden of his aging uncle. At his uncle's death he succeeded to the post of chief secretary to Philip II. His palace in Ubeda is one of the masterpieces of Vandelvira's latest period.

Another of the men Cobos trained was Alonso de Idiáquez, who also entered his office in 1523. He too was a *regidor* of Ubeda, and he was later a knight of Calatrava and secretary of the Orders of Calatrava and Alcántara.[6] Cobos took him with him on the trip to Italy, Germany, and Flanders (1529-1533). When Alonso de Valdés died in 1532, Cobos placed Idiáquez in charge of Neapolitan affairs and made him his assistant in the Tunisian campaign and in Italy and Provence (1535-1536). But Idiáquez did not receive an appointment as secretary until June 2, 1537; at that time he was already receiving a salary of 200,-000 *maravedís* as an *ayuda de costa*.[7] With Juan Vázquez he accompanied the Emperor to France in 1539; there he received a gift of 1,000 ducats from Francis I.[8] Again in 1543 he left Spain with the Emperor, who sent him back to consult with Philip and the Regents after the Peace of Crépy. In 1547 he was again sent to Spain on a special mission. We have learned how he met his death on the banks of the Elbe.

When Alonso de Valdés died in 1532, he recommended to Cobos that he use the services of one of his assistants, Gonzalo Pérez. Cobos seems to have taken that advice, for he needed a Latinist in his office and Pérez was a man of some learning. In Pérez's correspondence with Pietro Aretino there are frequent references to his *patrón,* the Grand Commander. Cobos used his influence to secure minor ecclesiastical appointments for Pérez, but as with Idiáquez, he did not give him a secretarial appointment until May 1, 1543, when he was named acting secretary to Philip, a post in which he was presently confirmed. It was he who wrote and read Philip's address to the Cortes in Cobos' palace in Valladolid in 1544. In 1545 he acted as Cobos' representative in the negotiations over the *adelantamiento* of Cazorla. After Cobos' death he remained in the service of Philip, where he was succeeded by his notable—and notorious—son, Antonio Pérez.

One of the men who entered Cobos' service fairly late was Francisco de Almaguer. He had been trained in the office of Juan López de Recalde, the *contador* of the Casa de la Contratación in Seville, and he first appears as one of Cobos' employees in 1535,[9] when he was acting as his personal business agent. At first he irritated Cobos by the insistence of his demands for

recognition, but he soon won his chief's favor, and in 1540
Cobos warmly recommended him for appointment as his deputy
in the office of *contador mayor,* pointing out that in addition to
his excellent training, he had another advantage: "He is not a
converted Jew." [10] However, he did not receive the appointment until after the death of Sancho de Paz (November 6,
1543). From then on he worked in the closest collaboration
with Cobos and succeeded him as *contador mayor* under Philip.

The last of the major officials trained by Cobos was Francisco
de Eraso. He was evidently a man of noble family, for he is usually referred to as "Don Francisco," and in a letter the Duque
de Alba addresses him as "My cousin." [11] He was a member of
the Emperor's household as early as 1523, when he was a *contino;* [12] he is first mentioned in connection with the secretariat in
1535, when Cobos, urged by Eraso's friends, tried to secure
some appointment for him from the Emperor. In 1539 he was
living in Juan Vázquez's house in Valladolid; he was with Cobos
at Monzón in 1542. When Vázquez fell ill in Flanders in 1545,
he recommended Eraso to Cobos as a temporary substitute. At
first Cobos was reluctant: he was not yet convinced that Eraso
had the necessary qualifications for the post. But when Vázquez
assured him that both he and the Regent Figueroa had confidence
in him, Cobos gave his approval. His temporary appointment
as secretary was made permanent on January 1, 1546. He too
remained in the service of Charles and Philip until his death in
1570.

These are the men whom Cobos gathered around him to carry
on the tasks of the secretariat. Many others served in minor
posts: Diego de Zárate, a comrade of Cobos' early days under
Conchillos, who for years was his personal messenger and who
ultimately became the successor of López de Recalde in Seville;
Francisco de Ledesma, who had been a secretary of the Cardinal
Tavera and succeeded Vázquez as secretary of the Consejo
de la Guerra; Andrés Martínez de Ondarza, *contador* of Queen
Juana and a handy man for all sorts of temporary assignments;
Pedro de Zuazola, royal treasurer from 1529 till his death in
1536, who had begun his service as secretary in 1520; another
of Cobos' cousins, Juan Mosquera de Molina, who was his
deputy as warden of the fortress of Simancas.

It is noteworthy that in all this staff there were no younger
sons of the nobility and, with the exception of Gonzalo Pérez,

no men of learning or university training. They were, like Cobos, petty gentry from small towns; their vision was circumscribed to the little bureaucratic world in which they operated. Naturally, as became the times, they were anxious for wealth and preferment, and thanks to Cobos' influence, most of them achieved their goal. It is striking that Cobos, like his master the Emperor, remained loyal in his support of his subordinates, once he had found them worthy. There is no record that he ever dismissed one of his associates. To him they were like a family: he did not hesitate to advise them as to proper behavior or to scold them, if they showed poor judgment.

Thus, during the period when he was in Augsburg, he wrote to Juan Vázquez that he had learned he was sending letters requesting the appointment of people to various positions:

> Although it may not seem important at the time, they may cause trouble afterwards. You must be very careful what you do and never approve of anything, no matter how trivial it may seem, without the approval of the Council and Dr. Polanco, and letters of request should not be sent, unless there be special reason. You run the risk of giving little pleasure and causing a lot of shame and damage, part of which will fall on me. Watch what you do, for there are always people who are ready to meddle.[13]

On another occasion he wrote to Vázquez, when there had been a "leak" in the matter of an ecclesiastical appointment, "I have always made it a rule to tell each person only what concerned him, so that he would think that he was the only person receiving a favor," [14] and in August, 1543, he reprimanded him for not having made explicitly clear to the Marqués de Aguilar, Viceroy of Cataluña, his relations to the Captain General, the Duque de Alba.[15]

When Vázquez and Idiáquez were with the Emperor in Flanders in 1541, there was some disagreement between them as to their respective duties. To avoid a continuance of the conflict, when they again left Spain in 1543, Cobos sent an instruction to Figueroa defining precisely their particular duties, and he also wrote to Granvelle, asking him to keep a friendly eye on them.[16] At the same time he wrote to Vázquez:

> You know what I told you, that His Majesty would be pleased if there were great harmony between you and Señor Idiáquez, because this was important for the conduct of his affairs and for his service; and he also instructed me, in order to avoid any future misunderstanding, to give you a written statement of what each one of you was responsible for. After consultation

with His Majesty I did that and I am now sending it to you as the regulation for your operations. I beg you, gentlemen, to have the harmony, friendship and love that I expect of you, for His Majesty will be pleased and you will do me a favor.[17]

The most revealing of these letters of advice is the one that he wrote to Eraso at the time of his appointment.

You are doing well,—*he begins*—to inform me in detail of what is happening, and I wish that you would do so in the future. I approve of the handling of dispatches, during the absence of Juan Vázquez, that you have described and also the work that you are doing that the Regent Figueroa has written about. Even though you are to take care of these matters, as you are doing, I shall be glad if you will inform the Secretary Idiáquez of everything that is written, since he is to countersign the papers during Vázquez's absence. I am confident that that can easily be done; otherwise he might be offended and I am sure that Vázquez will be glad of it . . .

I am writing to Idiáquez, urging him to aid and favor you in every possible way, and so you must place great confidence in him and keep constantly on the watch in all matters and preserve all official papers, serving and following M. de Granvelle in all matters, without pestering him, and likewise the Regent Figueroa, whom I hold in high esteem; and I think that they are good friends, as I am theirs. And so I put my trust in him in all matters. Whatever you do in this respect, let it be without showing that you have any new instructions from me, but going on as you have been, since you say that that is the will of His Majesty. Let this be done with great meekness and frankness. If you do so, we shall better be able to see what people's intentions are, in order to make any necessary provisions, though I do not think that anyone will presume in these matters to do anything against my will. The letter which I am writing to Juan Vázquez you should show to Idiáquez, with the confidence that I have mentioned, since he understands that you are there in the name of Juan Vázquez and acting in his behalf. In all matters that you discuss with His Majesty, be careful to be circumspect, truthful and honest, as I am sure you do, putting great confidence in M. de Granvelle and the Regent Figueroa.

You must watch closely the dispatches that come from Spain, especially those that come from the Cardinal Tavera, because from what they tell me, he is on close terms with Figueroa, though I think that nothing can be to our prejudice. This must be done with great caution, secrecy and judgment.

Let me know particularly whether Don Fernando [the Duque de Alba] is attending to any other matters except war, and how they are operating and whether there are new friendships and with whom, and how they get on with M. de Praet and the other Flemings, and also how our people are treated. You will also inquire to whom His Majesty refers the memorandum about the Church that I am sending and give the Confessor to understand that I am always writing you to be especially careful to serve him.

In your replies that deal with personal matters, referring to people here, be sure and put them down in such a way that I can show them the paragraphs as evidence that I was taking care of them.

You have done well to inform me about the loan for 200,000 or 250,000 ducats that is being negotiated. I have kept it secret, so as not to interfere with the contract that I am trying to settle here, though I should have liked to have you let me know the rate of each ducat and the interest rate. When you finish reading this letter, you will burn it.[18]

It was a tight little world that Cobos and his associates had created. They were bound together by ties of common purpose and common interests. It was important that a newcomer should be initiated into its mysteries!

If Cobos took such care to direct the activities of his comrades when they were absent, he tried by word, as well as by example, to advise them wisely when they were working together. His purpose was clear: to develop in his staff a strong *esprit de corps,* a sense of belonging to a "team." Their interests were not wholly selfish; they must serve the Emperor well. It is not surprising that by his own example of loyalty and devotion to the Emperor, he won the loyalty and devotion of his subordinates to himself; they all referred to him affectionately as "The Boss" *(el Patrón).* Like hundreds of others for whom he had secured appointments, honors, and prestige, they were proud to call themselves his "creatures" *(hechuras).*

While Cobos was dedicated to the formation of his own Castilian staff, he kept rigorously aloof from interference with the secretariat in Aragon. He was on friendly terms with the Vice Chanciller, Miguel Mai, and the first secretary, Ugo de Urríes. If he intervened to take the control of Neapolitan affairs away from the Aragonese group, it was because he believed that Castile should be responsible for Italian affairs, and that he should put an end to the feeling that Naples and Sicily were Aragonese, rather than Spanish kingdoms. In the same way, he never meddled with the secretariat of Gattinara nor, after the downfall of Jean Lallemand, with Anthoine Perrenin and Jean Bave, the secretaries of Granvelle. He was content to exercise his authority in the land that was his.

It is a tribute to Cobos' own integrity and the high standards he demanded of his associates that no one of them was ever convicted of malfeasance in the conduct of his office. Samano, the only one who was investigated, was exonerated. Conchillos, Lallemand, and Dr. Beltrán were convicted of malpractice and dismissed in disgrace. Some of the men whom Cobos appointed to posts in the Indies proved corrupt. But within his own circle, where he could exercise his own influence and control, only the highest standards were acceptable and his associates lived up to them.

The Conduct of Business

When we remember the care with which Cobos provided for every detail in the organization of his chapel in Ubeda, it is surprising that he did not draw up the ordinance of his secretariat, with assignment of duties, maintenance of discipline, and all the provisions necessary for successful operation. We do have, however, brief descriptions of the methods followed by Gattinara and Granvelle in their conduct of the daily routine. From them and from the documents themselves we can form a fairly clear picture of how Cobos and his staff functioned.

From the beginning of his service, his office was responsible for the affairs of Castile, Portugal, and the Indies. After 1530 they also handled Italian matters—the Italian city states, the Vatican, and the kingdoms of Naples and Sicily. Aragonese affairs were in the hands of Vice Chanciller Mai; at first Gattinara and (after 1530) Granvelle were in charge of the rest of the Empire and the other European countries.

Theoretically, the Emperor was supposed to open all correspondence addressed to him, but he was impatient of detail and so almost all the correspondence was referred to the responsible officer. It was, then, Cobos who received the pouches for his area of interest and who opened the letters. If they were in cipher, a confidential clerk deciphered them and prepared a fair copy; for years all the decoded messages were written in the same hand. The letters were then assigned to the proper agency; some were reported directly to the Emperor, others were referred to the proper Council. In each case, Cobos prepared a note of the content to be placed on the agenda, either for consultation with the Emperor or for study and recommendation by the appropriate Council. If the letter was a long one, one of the clerks prepared a summary, covering each of the main topics included.

Each day Cobos prepared a memorandum of all the matters that were to be brought to the attention of the Emperor; the topics were summarized briefly, often with a suggestion for the proper answer. The left margins of the sheet were left wide and Cobos noted there, during the interview with the Emperor, the decision he reached or the answer he wished to give. Once a week, on Friday,[19] the Consejo de Castilla met, and at that time Cobos presented a memorandum of the topics they were to discuss. Again he noted on the margin the recommendations they made and these were carried to the Emperor for final decision. Cobos usually followed the same practice with regard to matters that came before the Consejo de las Indias and the Consejo de la Hacienda, but at times his deputy took his place at the meetings of the other councils. One can always tell whether it was Cobos or Idiáquez or Samano who recorded the decisions by the handwriting in the margin. There are hundreds of these memoranda for the Emperor and the Councils in the Archives of Simancas and the Indies. They cover every phase of the affairs of state. But as a whole, one cannot fail to be impressed by the large proportion which deal with appointments of individuals to fill vacancies in the operation of State and Church.

Official business therefore came to the Emperor thoroughly sifted by Cobos and the Councils. Except for matters of international interest he rarely read correspondence himself. His answers often began: "The Grand Commander has reported to me the content of your letter . . ." When the Emperor had indicated his decision on any issue, Cobos then dictated a reply to one of his clerks, who prepared a rough draft of the answer. This was read to the Emperor, and any changes, deletions, or additions were entered on the draft. The corrected version was then copied, usually in a legible hand, and submitted to the Emperor for his signature, "I the King," and for the countersign of Cobos. Once in a while the Emperor would add a postscript in his own hand, even on the corrected copy.

When the Emperor was in residence at Court he transacted business every day, usually in the morning before mass. But there were frequent periods when no papers were signed: he was fond of hunting, he almost always spent Holy Week in retreat, and he rarely took care of the dispatches when he was traveling. At these times official business would accumulate until there were scores of royal orders, grants, privileges, and letters awaiting his signature. Especially when he was preparing to start on one of his many journeys, there would be such an accumulation that Cobos would have to stay behind for a few days to clear up unfinished business. Perhaps Gattinara was right when he proposed that the Emperor have a stamp made with his signature and authorize someone to use it.

In addition to the correspondence addressed to the Emperor there was an almost equally large correspondence with Cobos personally. Early in his term of office people discovered that it was he who took matters up with the Emperor; hence they started writing to him at the same time, begging for his support. Frequently they addressed their answers to the Emperor's letters directly to Cobos. And in the end many of the ambassadors always sent him a copy of their official communications to the Emperor. On this personal correspondence Cobos often wrote at the top "To me," and these he answered personally, sometimes noting on the back "Answered on (such and such a date)," although the actual letter was almost always prepared by one of the clerks. Only in his letters to Juan Vázquez did he regularly write the letter in his own hand.

The volume of correspondence that he carried on, the number of royal orders, instructions, and regulations which he had to prepare is staggering. It is hard to conceive how one person could have managed to control such a vast variety of details—finances, equipment of the army and the fleet, the defense of the frontiers, conflicts with the Pope, a thousand activities at home and abroad. And amid all the public affairs Cobos somehow found time to write to people, asking them to help his friends, in the Indies, in Italy, and in Spain, promising others that he would do all in his power to favor them.

Although Charles V acknowledged that Cobos knew more about his affairs in general than any other person, he considered that his greatest value was in the field of finances. In view of Ramón Carande's masterly study of *Carlos V y sus banqueros* we do not need to analyze the financial collapse of Spain during the Emperor's reign. The chief cause was the support of his military campaigns in Africa and Europe; for Spain was called upon to finance a large part of these expenditures. A contributing cause was the Emperor's personal extravagance. The operation of the various royal households took a tenth of the national income. And in addition the Emperor spent money with reckless abandon—for tournaments, pageants, and luxuries. When he traveled with the entire Court the costs were enormous. Besides, he had a penchant for making lavish gifts; it was said that he gave away 300,000 ducats at the time of his coronation in

Bologna. And he was constantly buying diamonds and jewels to present to his family and his friends.

It is hard to explain Karl Brandi's statement that Cobos "does indeed seem to have been partly to blame for the deplorable state in which the Emperor perpetually found himself." [20] Each year Cobos and his associates in the Consejo de la Hacienda drew up budget estimates for the following years. They were not always realistic: they failed to include interest on outstanding loans in the estimate of expenditures; they often included in receipts items that were already committed on prior obligations. The real difficulty lay in the fact that at any moment the requirements of a new campaign or a loan of several hundred thousand ducats negotiated by the Emperor without their knowledge made any attempt at a valid estimate impossible.

Cobos was acutely aware of the desperate financial situation. During his last years his letters are filled with his despair at the impossibility of raising new funds. He pled with the Emperor to make peace; he even protested feebly at times at the Emperor's purchase of another diamond or two, when the ones he had bought a few years before had never been paid for. Philip was convinced that his declining health was due to his worry over finances. Cobos' last official act was to seize all the available specie in Spain and ship it to Genoa. That was the road to ruin. In 1558 Philip suspended payment on the national debt.

To Cobos' credit it must be said that he administered the Treasury carefully and honestly. There is no evidence that during his régime there was any embezzlement of public funds. Neither he nor his associates profited personally, except through the large salaries and special grants they received. None of the nobles succeeded in raiding the treasury, as they did in later reigns. There is an illuminating example in the Emperor's refusal, on Cobos' advice, to grant the Duque de Alba permission to receive the income of 5,000 ducats from a second appointment; twenty years later he was receiving a salary of 40,000 crowns (35,000 ducats) from the royal treasury.[21] Of Cobos' record as a whole, we must accept the dictum of Charles V as well founded: "I believe that he will serve well and cleanly."

His Acquaintances and Friends

No Spaniard of his time had as wide a circle of acquaintances and friends as Cobos. Because of his travels in the suite of the Emperor he knew personally, even intimately, most of the leading figures in Spain, Italy, and Flanders. Once he wrote to Idiáquez: "God forgive me for having so many friends." [22] The list of his correspondents ran into the hundreds, even the thousands. Popes and cardinals, kings and princes, ambassadors and nuncios, great lords and humble workers, *conquistadores* and jesters, widows and orphans—people of every walk and condition of life—came within his orbit. Many of those who wrote to him were almost strangers who turned to him because of his influence with the Emperor.

Aside from his associates in the secretariat, his closest relations were naturally with the other counsellors: in the early days with Chièvres, the Bishop Mota, and García de Padilla; later with Loaisa, the Cardinal Tavera, and Juan de Zúñiga. For almost twenty years he worked in the most complete harmony with Granvelle; the letters they exchanged were outspokenly cordial, though formal. With Gattinara, on the other hand, he was never intimate, although he must have had constant dealings with him. His conflict with Bishop Siliceo we have already discussed. But in general he cultivated the friendship and good will of his fellow counsellors; his comments on them were always generous.

Though he was acquainted personally with all the grandees of his generation, he was on intimate terms with only a few—the Duque de Alba, the Duque de Calabria, and the Marqués de Lombay. In the last years of his life he came to know well the Marqués de Mondéjar, whom he named, with the Duque de Alba, one of the honorary executors of his last will. With these men and their wives Cobos and Doña María had close social relations; they shared together the life of the Court; when their duties kept them apart, they carried on a steady correspondence.

Because of his responsibility for the affairs of Portugal and Italy, Cobos was on the closest terms with the ambassadors in those countries. During the first years of his reign Charles had tried the experiment of appointing distinguished noblemen as his diplomatic agents—men like Juan Manuel and the Duque de Sesa, who served in Rome. But as time went on, he more and more chose men of lesser rank. Some were minor nobles, like the Marqués de Aguilar or the Conde Cifuentes; others were petty gentry, among them men of letters as well, like Diego Hurtado de Mendoza or Luis de Avila y Zúñiga. There were even a few who had risen from the secretariat, as had Miguel Mai and Lope de Soria. Only one of them, Luis Sarmiento, was a kinsman of Cobos or his wife.

The correspondence which Cobos carried on with these men is of extraordinary interest because it contains such a mixture of official business and personal affairs. Side by side in the same letter we find subtle analyses of current political events and accounts of amorous escapades, scurrilous, even obscene gossip, and the trials and tribulations of diplomatic life. Pedro González de Mendoza once called Cobos "Father of ambassadors" [23] and his relations with Diego de Mendoza, the Marqués de Aguilar, Luis de Avila, and Lope de Soria bear this out. To all of them he was their "Boss" and he was their mentor in both public and private affairs. When reports came to him from Rome that the Marqués de Aguilar was neglecting his duties and causing criticism by his scandalous relations with the notorious Marchesana di Massa, he did not hesitate to write him a chiding letter. The Marqués defended himself hotly: he had not failed in his duties; people in Rome did not take these *amours* as seriously as they did in Spain. Nevertheless he went on: "To prevent criticism, as you say, I have made up my mind to accept your reproof, as coming from my father and lord, and to behave as you order and advise; and so, though my visits to the Massa woman are already rare, I will cut them down from now on and limit them to what I must do in order not to seem ungrateful." [24] Our chief cause for regret in all this correspondence is that we do not have the letters which Cobos himself wrote, except an occasional outline which he prepared for the file.

During his three visits to Italy Cobos met most of the leading figures of his day. With some of them he established a real friendship. Both Clement VII and Paul III held him in high regard. He was close to the Dukes of Ferrara and Mantua, the Marqués del Guasto, and Ferrante Gonzaga, Viceroy of Sicily. He was in constant correspondence with Andrea Doria, as well as the Imperial generals Antonio de Leiva and Giambattista Castaldo. His contact with intellectuals was slight. He did meet the historian Paolo Giovio in Naples and later he came to know that unprincipled sycophant, Pietro Aretino, who later wrote to him fawning letters couched in his unctuous rhetoric, such as:

I beg Your Distinguished Excellency to be moved to console me in the request which good Gonzalo Pérez will present to you. Meanwhile I shall go about preaching that among all the things that exist only the prudence that governs you in your government of the world has no need of fortune. And then I shall inform men everywhere that the eyes of our time witness two miracles: the deeds of Caesar and the words of Cobos. Both are a cause for admiration, for the valor of one is the sun that illumines the days with every kind of magnanimous emprise; and the wisdom of the other is the moon that lightens the nights with every sort of glorious achievement.[25]

It is regrettable that Cobos did secure him a pension.

At Ferrara, in 1532, Cobos came to know Titian. There too and at Mantua and Correggio he met many of the ladies of the court, among them Veronica Gambara, the leading poetess of the day. He seemed to have had a peculiar charm at this period, for several years later Lope de Soria wrote to Cobos that wherever he went—at Correggio, at Piacenza, at Milan— he was received as a welcome guest, because he was a friend of Cobos.[26] For Cobos himself the most significant of all his contacts in Italy was his relations with Cornelia Malespina and the Condesa de Novellara.

It is not possible to list the names of all the men and women who entered his life, some of them briefly, others through long years. We have mentioned some of them in passing—the conquerors of the New World, Pedro de Alvarado, Hernán Cortés, the Pizarro brothers; artists and architects like Berruguete, Jamete, Siloee, Vandelvira, and Luis de Vega; his chaplain, Hernando Ortega; the adventurer, Don Alonso Enríquez; his associates in the secretariat. By almost all of them he was respected and beloved. It is astonishing, in view of his place as a favorite of the Emperor, that he made so few enemies in his public career. We have mentioned some of those with whom he came into conflict: Gattinara, the Conde de Benavente, Juan de Vega, the Bishop Siliceo. But most men were drawn to him, none more than the Emperor himself.

His Influence and Power

Cobos' contemporaries were quick to recognize the growth of his influence and power. Bartolomé de las Casas commented that when the King came to Spain for the first time, in 1517, Cobos was already the sole advisor of Chièvres in Castilian affairs. As early as 1522 that shrewd observer of people and events, Martín de Salinas, remarked on his importance in the conduct of affairs, and again and again he wrote to King Ferdinand and his secretaries of Cobos' increasing power. Others too repeated the theme—the British ambassador (1523), Antonio de Guevara in the same year. In 1524 Pedro Mexía wrote: "The Emperor was already showing great confidence in his secretary, Francisco de los Cobos, and most of the business of state passed through his hands." [27] When the Venetian ambassador Contarini prepared his *Relazione* he reported that Cobos had become great, since Contarini left Spain (1525). Even the jester, Francesillo de Zúñiga, swore "by the power of Cobos" in 1529.

Before the end of his life, Cobos' dominant rôle was generally recognized. Another Venetian ambassador, Bernardo Navagero, wrote in 1546:

> He knows the nature of Caesar and the time to obtain everything from him; and this is perhaps why he is so completely popular with His Majesty and that the latter never refuses anything that he asks for. When he is with the Emperor, everything goes through his hands, and when the Emperor is absent, in all important matters he is the ruler through the Council and his own judgment.[28]

Salinas echoed something of the same sort when he remarked that Cobos had his way by moulding the Emperor's will in the direction he wanted him to take.[29]

Contemporary historians wrote in the same vein. Sepúlveda, in his Latin life of Charles commented that "men of all ranks vied in cultivating Cobos' favor, the more so because there were no matters of state, except questions of justice, in which Charles did not utilize his advice and assistance." [30] So too López de Gómara wrote:

> He won the favor of the Emperor so completely that for many years all public affairs, of Italy as well as of the Indies and Spain, passed through his hands. In Italian matters he quarreled with Idiáquez, his creature and servant, because he would not have his office in Cobos' house. . . . He was a friend of his friends and so he did favors for many who did not deserve them, not without offence to good men, and he even took away offices, benefices and pensions from people to whom the Emperor wanted to give them and named his own men. As a result he was named and cursed by many. In the end the Emperor realized it, because of the activities of the kinsmen of his son-in-law

and of his wife, Doña María de Mendoza, daughter of the *Adelantado* of Galicia.[81]

As it became generally known that he was the person who had the ear of the Emperor, people who had favors to ask naturally turned to him for support. Perhaps at first they thought that Charles would not understand their Spanish, if they wrote directly to him. The Emperor could not be bothered with details, and as a result, with the exception of a few major appointments, he depended on Cobos for all recommendations. Once they had been approved, Cobos saw to it that it was he who conveyed the news to the successful candidate, a practice to which Gattinara vigorously objected, since he himself wanted that privilege. Siliceo seems to have the same criticism of Cobos in mind, when he suggested to the Emperor that he assign a few thousand ducats to Philip to hand out as gifts, lest people think that it was some official who was dispensing favors, not the Prince.[32] It should be added that in the few cases where Cobos' recommendations were rejected he could always say that he had done his best, but it had proved impossible ("no hubo lugar").

Over the years the number of people who sought his favor and support was legion. They were not all humble folk begging for a job; prelates and princes urged him to back their requests for favors for themselves or their friends. As early as July, 1523, when Pope Adrian VI asked the Emperor to grant to one Diego de Gumiel the privilege of receiving his stipend as a knight of Santiago even when he was not in residence, he wrote at the same time to his "Dilecto filio Francisco de los Cobos, Caesareae Maiestatis secretario," urging him to use his influence to secure the privilege.[33] Andrea Doria, Principe di Amalfi, thanked him for the "multiple favors which every day I receive from you, for myself and for my affairs." [34] In an even more eloquent vein, he wrote to Cobos:

Having placed in Your Lordship the hope of every good and favor which I expect to receive in this world, not only because of your humane benignancy, shown toward me on every occasion, but also because of my ardent desire to serve you, I shall not fear to be importunate, if with that security I have recourse to your patronage, whenever there is need. . . . And because, where the wind of your favor does not blow through your lofty worth, no fruit will ever germinate, as urgently as I can I beg you to be good enough to interpose your favoring arm in this matter.[34a]

On January 11, 1543 the Duke of Savoy wrote to Cobos:

Knowing that in this and in all my other affairs you are the person who can favor and protect me with His Majesty and console me by your aid, wishing to place myself even more deeply under obligation to you, as one in whom I have entire confidence, I have decided to send this letter, begging you, as earnestly as I can, to be favorable and propitious to me in all things, so that I may attain my purpose.[35]

The Emperor's agents abroad expressed the same obligation to Cobos. Thus Pedro de Toledo, Viceroy of Naples, writing to ask for his help in securing the appointment of his son, Luis de Toledo, as archbishop of Santiago, ended his letter: "Since we all, parents and children, have no other protection and favor save you, I beg you to do us the favor of directing this matter to a successful outcome, with the good offices you are wont to use with all your servants." [36] The warden of the castle of Milan, Alvaro de Luna, did not dare to ask for a leave of absence until he had received Cobos' approval and permission.[37] And Gutierre López de Padilla, ambassador at the Court of the Duchess of Savoy, who had been trying desperately to secure a transfer to some other post, wrote: "I believe what you say about my affairs, because you are so virtuous that all your life you have desired to do favors to all men in the world. Why, then, should I think that you do not desire to do one for me, when you know that I am your servant?" [38]

The lesser fry were even more fulsome in the flattery they thought would win Cobos' support. Sebastián de Clavijo, dean of the Cathedral of Cartagena, cites ancient precedents in his plea:

I am sure that neither I nor my merits nor the services which I can perform or have performed deserve your favors. Nevertheless princes and great lords like you have the custom and even the proper function of doing favors for their servants. We have the example of King Alexander, who when someone asked him for ten ducats, gave him a city. And when they asked him why he had done that, he said that the question was not what the man deserved, but what he, the King, could give and what was befitting his authority. I mean that though I do not deserve the favors you will do me, you will be exercising the office of a prince and lord, as is your custom with the servants of your distinguished house.[39]

There must have been a great many people who, like Don Alonso Enríquez and Rábago, felt that he was, in very truth, the "governor," if not the "ruler" of Spain.

Another evidence of his power and prestige is found in the books which were dedicated to him. In those days, in Spain and in the rest of Europe, writers placed their books under the protection of some patron from whom they hoped to gain financial recognition. The first of these dedicated to Cobos was the *Ley de amor* of the great precursor of Santa Teresa, Fray Francisco de Osuna, published at Seville in 1530.[40] "Very magnificent sir"—the Prólogo begins:

> It is the custom of the prudent to lift up their hearts from earthly to heavenly things . . . contemplating in visible things the invisible things they hope for . . . Our Lord gave us understanding that we might sing counterpoint to the plainsong of visible things; and you, sir, must give heed to the singular favor He has granted you with the greatest earthly Lord and seek to provide a good counterpoint, if you contemplate the favor you should enjoy with the greatest Lord of Heaven.

Citing the example of Mardocheo, who won favor with the Emperor because of his loyalty and wise administration, he calls on Cobos to remember that all that he has has come from nature; he must use his gifts of talent, ability and sweet conversation to lift up his soul to heavenly things; his great house and his great possessions can have no firm foundation without God. "Think not"—he continues—"that you received this royal favor, except to provide for those that lack favor, nor did Our Lord give you grace of speech, except that you might defend the cause of the ignorant, nor does He open the doors of secrets, except that you remember those who have gone astray." In a word, like Job, Cobos must be the spokesman for all the dumb and lame, of Spain, of Italy, of the Indies.

Cobos, because of his position, has a special obligation to love God; rightly, then, the author has decided to dedicate to him this book which treats at length this love.

> If Absalom by empty promises held in his hand the heart of King David and the heart of all the people, it is not surprising that you should enjoy the same position by your loyal services, so loyal that I should find it hard to say who has the greater fortune, the Emperor with you, so loyal a secretary, or you with him, so good a master. It seems that there is this dispute between you and him: he calls himself fortunate with you and you count yourself fortunate with him. Hence he persists in granting you greater favors, you in giving him more loyal service. This is a happy strife, a fabric so well woven that only love can preserve it; love preserves service in you, in him, the favors he gives. Oh happy strife!—you in serving, he in rewarding; you in being his, he in being yours. You call him 'My Lord'; he calls you 'My secretary.' On both sides there is a sense of possession and I know not which is greater.

Thus, in almost mystic language, Fray Francisco describes the rôle of love which binds Cobos and the Emperor together. The Prologue closes with an expression of his hope that, through Cobos, this book will even reach the Emperor himself.

Another book dedicated to Cobos, of a very different sort, was the *Seis libros del Delphín de música de cifras para tañer vihuela* of Luis de Narváez (Valladolid, 1538).[41] In his Prologue Narváez explains that he has spent his whole life in the study and practice of music, particularly in the art of the *vihuela* (an older form of the guitar); he calls his book the "Dolphin" because it is a fish which is especially fond of music and sensitive to it. "I beg Your Lordship"—he goes on—"to examine it lovingly and correct it with that discretion and wisdom that you show in all things, for I am so certain a servant of yours that this book may justly be called yours."

There follow six double *quintillas* of very bad verse in honor of Cobos. We need cite only a sample:

> "La virtud más principal
> que al fuego se da y aplica
> es que de su natural,
> echando en él el metal,
> del todo se purifica.
>   Y así quiso daros Dios
> tan gran virtud entre nos
> que a la obra que tocáys
> no sólo purificáys,
> mas toma valor de vos . . .
>   Que porque lo merecéys,
> tantos súbditos tenéys
> ganados, y no por guerra,
> que dó llega vuestra tierra
> aun vos mesmo no sabéys;
>   Y tenéys tal poderío
> que a vos vienen las gentes,
> conosciendo señorío,
> como a caudaloso río
> donde paran las corrientes."

Anglés, in his study of music at the Court of Charles V, has surmised that Narváez was in the employ of Cobos as a *vihuelista*.[42] While there is no specific evidence of this in the Prologue or in the text of the book, the guess may be well founded, for this was a period when the *vihuela* was a favorite instrument and when courtiers were proud to have a musician attached to their household.

In the same year, 1538, Lorenzo de Padilla dedicated to Cobos his *Catálogo de los santos de España* (Toledo, December 12, 1538). The dedicatory Prologue is interesting because of the stress it lays on Cobos' noble ancestry.

Very illustrious sir—*he begins*—though the order of presentation is not elegant, your authority will suffice to make good its defects. I beg of you to examine it, for such an examination is appropriate for illustrious and noble persons such as you. That you have this quality there can be no doubt, for, as Seneca declares, nobility consists in the fact that the ancestors of those who possess it have for long years been free men, as yours have been notoriously in Ubeda, where you were born and where they have been among the principal settlers. The Quarter of Los Cobos bears witness to this, for more than three hundred years ago it received that name from the founder of your house and all your ancestors have always preserved that nobility. And since God and the Emperor our lord have raised you to high estate, as an illustrious person you are under obligation to do favors, that through your intercession we Spaniards may have knowledge of the lives and constancy of our saints, born in our land, and by imitating them may win heavenly glory for evermore.[43]

It should be added that the title page is ornamented with a shield bearing Cobos' coat of arms, but through a blunder on the part of the engraver the five lions are ramping to the right, instead of to the left.

In the following years, two of the works in the first edition of the *Obras* of Antonio de Guevara are also dedicated to Cobos: the *Aviso de privados y doctrina de cortesanos* and the *Libro de los inventores del arte de marear y de muchos trabajos que se passan en las galeras* (Valladolid, June 25, 1539). Each of them begins with a long preface in the typically exaggerated rhetoric of Guevara. A few samples will suffice to illustrate their content.[44]

I, sir—*the Prologue of the* Aviso de privados *begins*—do not want to confess that I am your servant, because that would be rather fearing you than loving you; nor do I want to take pride in being your kinsman, because that would be very importunate; nor do I want to boast that we knew each other long ago, because it would be holding you in slight esteem; nor do I want to boast that I am now your intimate friend, because that would be presuming. What I will confess is that I love you as a friend and you love me as one of your fellow men, although it is true that you, as a man of standing, have shown me your friendship in good works, while I, as a weak person, have shown mine only in good words.

If you consider who you are, what is your power, what your possessions and what your worth, you will find that among the counsellors you are the greatest, among the rich, the greatest, among those who have prestige, the greatest, among the fortunate, the greatest, among the secretaries, the greatest, among the Commanders the greatest [he was Comendador *mayor*]. Since that is so, it certainly is not right that among the virtuous you should be the least. You may be sure that with time your affairs will decline, your friends will leave you, your estate will be scattered, your person will die, your favor with the King will come to an end, those who come in the future will forget you; you know not where the succession of your house will end, above all you know not how your children will turn out. But through what I am writing of your unprecedented favor in the *Royal Chronicle* and what I am doing in your service, as in this book, your memory will remain immortal for centuries to come.

The Prologue of the second book is cast in the form of a letter.[45] Having set forth the opinion of four philosophers as to what are the most uncertain walks of life, Guevara decides that two are particularly applicable to Cobos: his position as the favorite of the Emperor and the frequency with which he travels by sea.

To advise you, sir, not to follow Caesar would be a lack of respect; to persuade you not to return to Italy would be daring. What I will dare to tell you is that you should be as proud of being a Christian as of being the King's favorite and that you should be guided by reason rather than by opinion . . . I wrote for you, sir, a book called *Aviso de privados* for the times when you were on land. I have composed this other treatise on life in the galleys for the times when you are traveling by sea. My purpose was that one of them might be a pastime; the other might help you to profit by your time.

Each of these treatises has a separate title page and at the top of each title, between the coats of arms of the Bishop, are the combined arms of Cobos and his wife—Cobos-Molina, Sarmiento-Mendoza. If the choice of Cobos as sponsor of the *Aviso de privados* has some relevance to his interests and career, there seems to be little reason for naming him as protector of the second treatise, other than the author's hope that he might win Cobos' favor.

One wonders if Cobos found time or had sufficient interest to read any of these books that were so fawningly dedicated to him. Nowhere in his correspondence is there mention of a book; his literary friends did not discuss books when they wrote to him; they talked about women. But it would be safe to hazard a guess that he had them elegantly bound in parchment and that they were an ornament of his drawing room. Like his paintings, they were a visual symbol of his prestige.

Such was the place of power to which he had risen. It is time to ask: what were the personal qualities that made it possible for a man with so unpromising a beginning in life to reach such a position?

CHAPTER XVI

HIS PERSONALITY

Portraits

It is difficult to form any clear impression of Cobos' physical appearance. The only contemporary indications we have are that he was fat and good looking. So Gómara: "He was fat, good looking, merry and gay, and so, pleasant in conversation"; [1] Salinas too remarked that Granvelle was "not as fat as Cobos." [2] For Bartolomé de las Casas he was "good looking and well built." [3]

Two portraits of him have survived. The first,[4] which is in the possession of the Duque de Alcalá, is a copy of an earlier painting, said to have been done by Titian. The three-quarters length figure represents a man in the prime of life, wearing a broad velvet cap and a dark cape over an embroidered tunic. With his right hand he is fingering the *venera* of the Order of Santiago that hangs on a slender chain, while the left hand rests on the pommel of his sword. On the breast of the tunic is the red cross of Santiago. A narrow white neckband peeps out above the high collar of the tunic. The face is stern, almost forbidding, with a heavy moustache and a trimmed, slightly pointed beard.

Several questions at once arise as to the authenticity of the likeness. In the first place, the face and figure are slender, rather than fat, as his contemporaries saw him. In the second place, Cobos did not begin to wear a beard until 1529, when he was about fifty-two years old; the figure in the painting appears to be much younger than that. Moreover, the cut of the pointed beard is quite different from that worn by most men of his time and seems more characteristic of the second half of the sixteenth century. It is possible, of course, that the painter who made the copy is responsible for these details; the inscription in the upper left-hand corner: "D. Francisco de los Cobos. Comendador Mayor de León," is certainly not contemporary with him, for "Cobos" is spelled with a "B," not with a "V," as was the practice in his time. There is, therefore, serious doubt as to how closely the portrait represents Cobos as he really was.

We have already mentioned the other portrait, a medal made at Brussels in 1531 by an engraver whom Habich has identified as Christoph Weiditz of Augsburg.[5] It shows Cobos wearing a flat cap, with fairly long hair, a heavy moustache, and a short, jutting beard. A medal (of Santiago?) hangs on his breast. Around the rim of the medal is the inscription: "Francisco Covo. Magno. Comed. Legionis. Caroli. A. Secret. Cons. A. MDXXXI." The obverse of the medal shows a naked rider on a galloping horse, holding in his upraised hand a long streamer on which is inscribed: "Fata. Viam. Invenient." During this period in Brussels, Weiditz made medals of several other Spaniards. They all bear a certain family likeness, but the face of Cobos looks strong and alert. Another version of the medal, with another "I" added at the end of the date, was described by Armand in his study of *Les médailleurs italiens des quinzième et seizième siècles,*[6] before Habich's identification of the engraver.

In the Museo del Prado there is a splendid portrait of a "Man of 54 years" which was long considered to be that of Cobos.[7] But Sr. Sánchez Cantón has pointed out to me that the wide, crinkled ruff portrayed must belong to the second half of the sixteenth century and so, unless the ruff is a later addition, the figure cannot be that of Cobos. It is too bad, for it would be pleasant to think that the strong, handsome face, rather heavy but kindly, represents the Imperial secretary as he looked to his contemporaries.

There were undoubtedly other portraits of Cobos. We have mentioned in passing the one on the *retablo* in Cobos' palace in Valladolid that was so lifelike that his little girl recognized her "Mamo," and another that hung in the bedroom of the Condesa de Novellara. The will of the Marqués de Poza (1605) listed a portrait of Cobos among his possessions,[8] and at one time the collection in the Royal Palace had a large portrait of him by Titian.[9] Some of these portraits have probably been destroyed, but others, now unidentified, may still grace the walls of some noble family in Italy or Spain. As it is of the portrait of Doña María in the chapel in Ubeda, it is tempting to surmise that the bold, bearded face that looks down from the northwest corner of the sacristy is Jamete's tribute to his patron. But this lies in the realm of mere conjecture.

Without more specific pictorial evidence, we shall have to rest our judgment of the kind of man he was on the comments of the men who knew him. Some of them we have already cited in the course of his story. But even at the risk of repetition it will be well to bring them together here, in order to bring into sharper focus the peculiar traits which impressed his contemporaries.

Contemporary Impressions

The first of the men who knew him that expressed an opinion regarding Cobos was Las Casas, who remarked that he was "soft of voice and speech, and so well liked." [10] Later he inserted in his comment: "in his bearing he showed that he was prudent and quiet." Surprisingly, Martín de Salinas had nothing to say about his personal qualities, but another of his friends, García de Loaisa, frequently identified his outstanding gifts. Writing to the Emperor, he says: "He knows how to make up for your carelessness in your dealing with people and in defense of his master. He loves you with the highest loyalty and he is extraordinarily prudent, and he does not waste his brains saying clever things, as others do, and he never gossips about his master and is the best loved man that we know." [11] In the same vein, Loaisa assured Pope Clement: "He has greater worth and has more influence with His Majesty because he is virtuous, prudent and of sound and solid counsel than because he is a secretary." To that His Holiness assented, saying: "The Emperor is fortunate to have such an official, beloved by all and so faithful and useful in his service." [12]

One of the most significant of the evaluations of Cobos is that of Bernardo Navagero: "He is very affable and very skillful.

The greatest difficulty is in getting to see him, but once you are in, his manner is so engaging that everyone goes away completely satisfied. The favors that he can do, he does quickly. If he refuses something, he explains the reason and cause why he does it, making clear his desire to please." [13] Others, as we have seen, spoke of the difficulty of getting access to him, and in his picture of Cobos, Gómara offers an unusual explanation: "He was diligent and secretive . . . He was very fond of playing *primera* (a card game) and of conversation with women. He often pretended to be sick for many days to get away from business. He showed clearly that he was sorry to die and he did not believe that death was coming. As a result he died with a not very good reputation." [14]

For Sepúlveda, the qualities that stood out in him were loyalty, wise counsel, and industry.[15] Luis Zapata records that there was once an inscription in the chapel of Ubeda, with Cobos' motto: "Fides, labor, et solertia haec et majora donant" ("Faith, hard work, and diligence give these and even greater things").[16] In comparing Cobos' relations with the Emperor and those of Luis de Avila, Zapata pointed out that Cobos' relations were on a business level, while those of Avila were personal.

Fernández de Oviedo, one of the few historians who knew him as a boy, stresses a very different side of his personality, his filial piety and devotion to his father, a trait which we have seen illustrated all through his life.

Of all the analyses of Cobos' personal characteristics the one that gives the clearest picture of what the men of his day thought of him is the *Diálogos de la preparación de la muerte,* by the Bishop Pedro de Navarra (Pierre d'Albret), directed to the secretary Francisco de Eraso. It forms part of his *Diálogos muy subtiles y notables,* published at Tortosa about 1565.[17]

In the introduction to the *Diálogos,* the Bishop explains that in the days when he was at the Emperor's Court in Spain, he used to attend the meetings of an "Academy" which met in the house of Hernán Cortés. Among the others who gathered there he mentions, besides Cortés, several men who knew Cobos well: the Nuncio Poggio, Juan de Zúñiga, and Juan de Vega. It was the custom of the group that the one who arrived last at the meeting should propose a subject for discussion and name some one of the group to keep a record of what was said. It so happened that one day it fell to Juan de Zúñiga to name the topic for the day; the theme he proposed was: "Cobos and the order which every good Christian should follow in preparing himself to die well." The Bishop was named to record the discussion, which he now dedicated to Cobos' successor, Eraso.

The relation between Cobos and the subject of the preparation for death is understandable only if he is assumed to be at the point of death, and this is borne out by the Dialogue. But it is at once evident that the situation is purely fictional, for Zúñiga died almost a year before Cobos died. Besides, the only time when Cortés, Poggio, Zúñiga and Juan de Vega could have been together at the Court was in 1542, five years before Cobos died. Internal evidence in the *Diálogo* reveals that it was written after the death of the Emperor (1558) and after the completion of Cobos' chapel in 1559. But the fiction of the setting is irrelevant. What is significant is Navarra's intimate acquaintance with Cobos, whether from firsthand observation or from the testimony of his friends, and the light that he casts on what was the current opinion of Cobos' character in the years immediately following his death.

The *Dialogue* is presented in a series of conversations and monologues. The two speakers are a priest, Cipriano, and a courtier, Basilio. It is at once apparent that Basilio is the spokesman of Cobos; the priest reflects the ideas of the Bishop. We may pass over the pious generalizations about the inevitability of death and look only at the passages in which the author reveals through the words of Basilio what he believed to be characteristic of Cobos.

At the beginning of Diálogo II, Basilio gives an account of his daily life:

For twenty years I have been living at Court and this is the order of my life. At midnight I go to bed and at eight I get up. Until eleven o'clock I attend to business and from eleven to twelve I have dinner; from twelve to one I amuse myself with buffoons and slanderers or in idle conversation; from one to three I take my *siesta;* from three to six I dispatch business matters; from six to eight I stroll around the streets of the Court or in the countryside; from eight to ten I have supper and rest; from ten to twelve I amuse myself with conversation; from twelve on I sleep, accompanied rather with ambition and greed or fear and malice than with peace and contentment, for this is the garden that we favorites of princes cultivate.[17a]

Of his religious observances Basilio explains:

I hear mass and fast on most of the prescribed days. I give some alms, I say some prayers (though very absentmindedly because I am so busy), I visit the stations of the Cross and I listen to sermons, when I have nothing else to do, especially if some famous preacher is speaking. I make confession and receive communion, when Holy Mother Church requires. For the rest, I follow the common opinion.

After telling how he had risen from humble beginnings to wealth and power through his diligence, vigilance, solicitude, and loyalty and how he had kept his post by prudence and foresight, he continues:

> Thus I came to be a royal favorite, as you see, though with all my intimacy, I never lacked rivals and critics; but with my loyalty to the King and my watchfulness over my personal behavior, I rose to my present state, where I was so firmly established that no one was strong enough to overthrow me, except this present divine summons to death.

Cipriano points out that in spite of his lofty position, no one really held him in honor: "for every word you spoke against them in secret, they published a hundred thousand insults against you in public . . . Who is there, in short, among all those who have offered to serve you and whom you have aided that would not turn his back on you, if he saw the wheel of fortune turning but a jot?"

Basilio now admits that he is troubled by three things in his life: that gravity and personal divinity which he pretended to assume, the general words with which he met all requests, and the direction of public affairs to the profit of the King and to the detriment of the kingdom, not to mention the advice he had given to the damage of the common weal and even of private interests. Cipriano points out that instead of making vague promises to all-comers, he would have done better to dispatch business, with grace or without, as García de Padilla did, rather than hold people off, like a greedy lawyer.

Now Basilio tries to bribe Cipriano to grant him absolution: he will give him fifty thousand, a hundred thousand ducats. Besides, he adds. "I have for you a rich gold clock they brought me from Flanders and ten dozen sable furs they sent me from Poland and there are a couple of Frisian horses for you, when you go hunting." When Cipriano indignantly rejects these offers, Basilio persists: "Absolve me, and when you least expect, some rabbit of a pension may pop up, and it may even happen that, if God rains miters, one may fall on your head." Discouraged by Cipriano's obstinacy, he threatens to find another priest: "I as-

sure you that there is more than one priest, friar and even prelate who would be honored to grant me the sacrament."

When this approach fails, Basilio begins to commiserate with
himself: to think that at the very moment when he expected to
rest, after working all his life, the shock of death should come
upon him! Who would not grieve at giving up all that he had
had:

Being worshipped like a god, ruling kingdoms like a king, treating states
like a lord, being served by so many nobles, enriched with gifts from Araby and
Saba and the New Indies? Who could forget the eagerness of provinces to
please me, the receptions in so many cities to honor me, the visits of so many
nobles to win my favor, the embassies from diverse lands? Or the unprecedented Imperial favor, the holding in my hands the power to give life or death
to whomsoever I would, the control of all important matters, where my word
was the weight and measure in all things? Who can tolerate giving up so
many offices, losing so many titles and all the income I enjoyed and the delight
of the great gifts with which my house was equipped? Of what use now are
the sables of Germany, the paintings and antiquities of Italy, the tapestries
of Flanders, the brocades of Venice, the silks of Genoa, the gold of Calcutta,
the silver of New Spain, the gems of Africa, the pearls of Guinea, the fine
fabrics of Portugal, the gloves from the Canary Islands, save only as new
torments for my body and fuel for the fire of my soul?

In an outburst of misery, he cries:

Oh wretched house, once full of gentlemen and now of moaning; once full
of nobles and now of sighs; once full of songs and now of tears; once crowded
and now—woe's me!—so empty! What has become of my nobles, of all the
company I had at my table, in the Palace, at church, in the Council, on the
road, in visits and banquets and everywhere, that now there is not one? What
has become of my associates, my attendants, my servants, the people of my
household?

Cipriano's only answer is that he must renounce all his wealth
and make restitution for his ill-gotten gains.

Suddenly Death appears. At first Basilio tries to threaten him,
but Death is inexorable: his body will be consumed in the dark
tomb which he has prepared in his chapel. "I will tell you even
more"—he continues—"if the torches of your good works had
been as long as the bars of the *reja* in your chapel, and if the end
of your living had been as pleasing unto God as the top of your
reja is to the sight, you would have received in Heaven as great
a reward as you have received in the world of empty glory."
The twelve benefices with which he had endowed the chapel had
been taken away from twelve parishes and so had deprived these

people of divine services. What was worse, he had secured the Papal bulls through the machinations of his agents at the Vatican. Now he has only four hours to live. And Basilio wanted ten years more of life!

At last, in despair, he begs God for mercy. What has it profited him to gather all of his treasures, only to bury his body in gold and his soul in Hell? What has he gained from his Herculean, gilded buildings, his accumulated income, his lofty estate, except to pile wood on the fire of his guilt? Once he could not slip away from the throng of rich nobles and now there is no one to stay with him except children and paupers. His table was always crowded with bishops and prelates and now chaplains and mendicant friars scorn to come to his burial. He was always surrounded with illustrious dukes, counts, and marquises, with noble cardinals' caps and miters; now even friars' cloaks and cowls scorn to come to his funeral. What more can be said than that he who but yesterday was served by nobles has not found anyone to bear his body to the church, except two or three lowly common folk?

When Basilio at last accepts the inevitability of death, he thinks bitterly of his past misdeeds:

> Oh Lord, how heavy is my heart when I remember all the good I might have done in the Councils, which I failed to do out of self-interest, when a word of mine had more weight in the world than the wealth and pleas of a thousand others, because in all the Councils I never expressed an opinion that was rejected nor uttered a word that was denied nor gave a piece of advice that was not more than law, nor asked for a thing that was refused, so that I could do what I wanted, and I wanted what I should not have wanted. Who can doubt that in such absolute power I was moved by interest, passion or affection, that in providing miters and cardinals' caps, in appointments and judgeships, in offices and presidencies, in the Council of the Indies and the Council of War, where countless people have perished and so many kingdoms have been destroyed, that in the Cortes and their votes, all in favor of my master and to the damage of his vassals, that, in a word, in everything important that occurred, if I had lifted my hand, no one would have dared to thwart me?

How long is the list of his offenses!

> How many opinions in my time I have made men accept as good, though they were bad for the republic, delighting only to keep the King happy and rich, and keep his kingdoms unhappy and poor! How deeply I regret that the great Imperial confidence I enjoyed has only provided the wings to plunge me into the depths, where my master and his Empire, where the miter and the cardinal's cap, the "lizard" of Santiago, the flowers, the banners, the

standards, the helmet and sword, where even the staff of office and my signature have no power to save me, for in Hell there is no redemption!

Basilio now apostrophizes his family. He calls upon his children to live righteously, to carry out the instructions of his will in providing alms and masses, to do deeds of charity rather than spend money on a sumptuous tomb. "Spend what you have to spend on alms, rather than gilded *rejas;* let what you have for burial statues go to hospitals and the needy." Then, turning in fancy to his wife, he bids her farewell:

> I end now with you, my dear wife and lady, no less troubled at your sadness than your are sad at my passing. But I trust in your virtue and nobility that you will be an example among the women of Spain. I shall know that the love you showed me in life was true, because you weary not in doing good after my death.
>
> I will not urge you to be chaste, because among all nations there is none that equals you women of Spain, when you are bereft, nor will I deprive you of your freedom, though I have always been your slave. But I will say what I feel: that all the pleasures of a second marriage will never equal the least pleasure of the first. You can do what you will, but this is how I feel. Be not deceived by your youth, your beauty, your complete freedom, the loftiness of your estate, your great wealth, because each of these may bring you to the mire. I go now in confidence that through your good works I shall see you in the mirror of divinity, that I shall be enhanced in that eternal glory, where I await you, as my own wife, sister and companion.

Written more than ten years after Cobos' death, the interpretation of the Bishop of Tortosa presents a different perspective of his career. There can be no question that it corroborates Gómara's statement that he was not ready to die, that to the very end he fought to live on. As a good churchman, the Bishop was shocked at his lack of true piety; even the chapel that he endowed was a symbol of personal ostentation, not of devotion to God. Perhaps the most striking of his opinions is his feeling that, in his utter devotion to the Emperor, Cobos sacrificed the best interests of Spain. Seeing him thus from a distance, after the lapse of a decade, influenced perhaps by the opinions of men like Juan de Zúñiga or Juan de Vega, who were envious of him or hostile to him, the Bishop believed that Cobos had been guilty of abuse of his power, for his own benefit. But even in his adverse attitude, two traits stand out clearly: his loyalty to the Emperor and his devotion to his wife.

For most of Cobos' contemporaries, the facets of his personality which were most impressive were his prudence, his caution, and his industry. Almost all of them commented on his affability, his pleasant speech, his eagerness to be helpful. Above all they stressed his value as a counsellor of the Emperor and his loyalty to him. These are the qualities that were manifest in the day-by-day activities of his life, as we have traced them from his youth on. There is, however, one question that should be examined in more detail: that of his acceptance of bribes.

His Venality

It is not surprising that in view of his favored position with the Emperor and the wealth that he acquired, he was charged with being venal. In the sixteenth century the practice of bribery was almost the rule in Europe. Charles himself had set a notable example by the brazen bribery with which he had won his election as Holy Roman Emperor in 1519—a title which he later came to consider as a divine mission.

Most of the charges against Cobos came from foreigners. Thus in 1525 Contarini observed that he was not ill-disposed toward Venice, though he had no particular affection for the Serene Republic, nor had any of the other counsellors of the Emperor, because they were not being paid by Venice, as they were by the other Italian princes.[18] Benedetto Varchi, in his *Storia fiorentina,* hinted that Cobos and Granvelle accepted bribes from both the Florentine exiles and from Alessandro de' Medici in 1535. And Du Bellay wrote that during the negotiations with the French in 1535 and 1536 they had asked for a continuance of their pensions in Milan, if the Duchy was finally granted to the Duke of Angouleme.

The most explicit of the statements is that of Bernardo Navagero (1546). The two chief counsellors of the Emperor—he explains—are Cobos and Granvelle,

neither of them of very noble birth, nourished and made great by the Emperor. Together with the greatness he has given them, they have acquired great wealth, part of it from the liberal gifts of the Emperor, part from the important affairs they handle. There is no king, prince, duke or private lord who does not make them liberal gifts and support them. The Emperor knows it and tolerates it. It certainly is a great source of satisfaction for anyone who wants something to have a way of gaining the favor of the man who can grant it to him.[19]

As for the Emperor's acceptance of the practice, Tyler goes

so far as to say that he was aware of the fact that Cobos and Granvelle were receiving money from the French and did not disapprove.[20]

There are a few references to Cobos' venality even among Spaniards. Thus Gómara, who was in general hostile to Cobos, declares: "he was greedy and niggardly and he accepted presents with both hands, which brought him excessive wealth." [21] And Santa Cruz implies the same thing when he remarks that the ministers of Charles V, finding themselves in such favor, were "very absolute in their exercise of authority and very dissolute in their robbing." [22]

As we have seen, the Emperor himself had confidence in Cobos' honesty: "I do not think that he accepts anything important." We should not expect to find evidence of open bribery in the documents of the time. But it is significant that there is record of two occasions when Cobos refused to accept a gift of money intended to elicit his support.

The first of these was in 1531, when Cobos was in Flanders.[23] At that time, Sigismundo della Torre, the agent of the Duke of Mantua, offered him 10,000 *scudi* in return for his support of the Duke's interests. Cobos replied that he served men only because he was fond of them and that he was not a person who sold his services for a price, but that he would not fail to do everything in his power to befriend the Duke. If the latter were so disposed, he would be willing to accept a horse or a jewel or some other little thing from him. When the Duke's representative returned to the same theme a few weeks later, Cobos repeated his earlier statement. And this time he begged his tempter to burn any papers on the subject that he possessed, for if the matter were known, it would bring great shame upon him.

The second time that he refused to accept a cash gift was seven years later, when Martín de Salinas offered in the name of King Ferdinand to give him and Granvelle an annual pension of 2,000 ducats.[24] They were unwilling to accept the money without the Emperor's approval and when the Emperor rejected the proposal the matter was dropped. But almost immediately Salinas proposed to the King that he give them this recognition secretly. It could go to the Grand Commander as the equivalent in sable furs; they were a product of the kingdom and so it would look all right. To Granvelle, because he was not so fat, he could hand the money personally in an Ocaña glove.

This illustrates the difficulty of drawing a line between a gift and a bribe—a difficulty still known in Washington. Gifts he did receive in astonishing numbers, for giving was then conceived, as the Dean Clavijo had observed, not in terms of the receiver's deserts, but as evidence of the giver's magnanimity, a sort of *noblesse oblige*. In this, as in so many ways, it was the Emperor who set the pattern; we have had occasion to mention the numerous gifts he made to Cobos—a gold chain, a silver cannon, a gold nugget from Peru, the ring and robe he wore at his coronation, the rugs from the tent of Barbarossa. And it should be added that many of the appointments and grants that the Emperor made to Cobos, like the 20,000 ducats payable from cochineal, were in reality gifts from the public treasury.

We cannot undertake to list the hundreds of specific gifts to him which are recorded in the documents of his day, but a few deserve mention. The only gifts of cash of which we know were from Francis I, the first of 12,000 ducats which he sent to him after the negotiations at Nice in 1538, and 4,000 ducats in silver which he presented to him, though absent, during the visit of Charles in France in 1540. There were a few gifts of value— a diamond ring from some one in Italy,[25] a gold goblet from Pedro de Toledo, so that every time he gave a banquet he might drink from it and remember Don Pedro.[26]

Among the gifts were a number of works of art—four pictures from Germany, paintings from the Duke of Ferrara, paintings from the municipal council of Lucca, portraits of Diego de Mendoza, of Pedro González de Mendoza and the Princess of England by Titian.[27] The most interesting of these paintings is the *Pietà* of Sebastiano del Piombo, which is still in the possession of the Duques de Alcalá in Seville.[28]

Some time in 1533, Ferrante Gonzaga decided to send a present to Cobos, and he commissioned del Piombo to make a painting—choosing from the two subjects del Piombo proposed a figure of Our Lady holding her dead Son in her arms. Del Piombo was not eager to undertake the task, and even after he had agreed, he dilly-dallied, as was his habit. But the painting was almost completed in 1537. Then there arose a dispute between him and Gonzaga's agent, Niccolò da Cortona, as to the proper price, the painter demanding 1,000 *scudi* and Cortona offering 400. Del Piombo argued that the higher the price, the more highly Cobos would esteem it. But Cortona countered that, on the contrary, Cobos would find it more acceptable, if he knew that it had cost the owner little loss. The poet, Francesco Maria Molza, was called in as an arbiter and he doubted whether del Piombo really wanted to paint the picture: "If Your Excellency" —he wrote to Gonzaga—"had seen the picture of Christ carrying the cross which he painted for the Conde Cifuentes, you would have little hope from him." But a compromise figure of 500 *scudi* was finally reached and the painting was finished by October, 1539.

Now a new problem arose. For the picture was painted on a large slab of slate and was surrounded by a heavy stone frame; it was too heavy to transport by mule-back or in a litter, and so it was necessary to hire a frigate to pick it up at Ostia and carry it to Spain. And it was also necessary to send a special attendant with it, to insure that it was properly handled. At some later date the frame was removed and the slate was cut into two pieces. It is now in process of restoration by its owners.

Another work of art which Cobos had was the head and torso of Apollo that Miguel Mai sent him from Rome together with the fountain for the patio of his palace in Ubeda.[29] In this case, as in some others, it is impossible to tell whether in the end Cobos paid for these treasures or whether they were gifts. This is particularly true of some of the things that Diego de Mendoza sent him from Venice—mirrors, Oriental rugs, tapestries, and the like, and of the suits of armor which the Marqués del Guasto shipped to him from Milan. Among the works of art we should not overlook such an unusual object as the glass bottle, covered with fine straw interwoven with mother-of-pearl, which the General of the Augustinian Order presented to him and which, at Lope de Soria's suggestion, may have landed in the hands of the fair Cornelia at Novellara.

The list of other gifts is endless—horses and hunting dogs, furs and gloves, sable from the Queen of Poland, velvet and cushions, not to mention all the dainties—preserves, marmalade, fresh fruit, cherries, green almonds, quinces, even "roses in sugar" and manna. Some of these edibles may have been intended as medicines, like the four kegs of fresh fruit from the Indies that Lope Hurtado sent him from Portugal, or the dog-rose berries *(escaramujos)* which Francisco de Borja shipped from Barcelona. One gift was certainly medicinal—a barrel of water sent by the warden of the fortress of Florence, Juan de

Luna, which was said to be efficacious in the treatment of gall-stone and kidney trouble, the chief ailments that beset Cobos. Perhaps we should close this list, already too long, with the mention of a box full of *agnusdei* (or is it *agnidei?*), which the Conde Cifuentes sent him from Rome in 1535, with instructions to take one or two dozen for himself, to give as many more to Pedro González de Mendoza, and have the rest sent to the Condesa.[30]

We should, at this point, look at the other side of the picture —the gifts which Cobos made to other people. The list is not long, nor are most of the presents of great value. Some of them we have already mentioned—a box sent to the Condesa de Novellara, the Aztec manuscript he presented to Paolo Giovio, which he in turn had received from Hernán Cortés, the suit of armor he gave to Cortés as he was leaving for Algiers in 1541. Once he sent a horse to the Marqués del Guasto.[31] For the rest, the gifts we know about were trifles, largely gloves, purses, and samplers made by Doña María, that went to Diego de Mendoza, the Duke and Duchess of Mantua, and a few other people in Italy. Once, too, he sent a basket of green almonds from Barcelona to Juan Vázquez.[32]

All the other gifts of which there is record went to his children, particularly to María Sarmiento, and to his chapels in Ubeda. This is not surprising. Cobos had set his heart on handing on to his heirs an inheritance of which they could be proud and on leaving in Ubeda a monument that would forever keep his memory alive. All that he had was devoted to these two ends. It is easy to understand why to Gómara and probably to other people he seemed "niggardly."

Finale

There are certain aspects of Cobos' life that were not mentioned by any of his contemporaries, but which are essential to an understanding of his character. Born in poverty and obscurity, he had no formal education, no background of culture; "the three R's" were the extent of his training. During his travels he must have picked up a speaking knowledge of French and Italian, though already in his time Spanish was becoming the common language of Western Europe. He did not know Latin and hence had no contact with much of the writing of his age.

So far as we know, he had no books, except those that were dedicated to him by their authors; for that matter, there is no evidence that he ever read any books. Although some of his associates, like Diego de Mendoza and Luis de Avila, were men of letters, they never mentioned literature in their communications to Cobos. In all of his correspondence there is only one reference to a literary theme, when he wrote to Juan Vázquez, after the return of Alonso Enríquez from Peru with his wild tales, that if Don Alonso were in Flanders, the courtiers would not find *Amadís de Gaula* and *Esplandián* so entertaining.[33]

He must have known some of the poets of his time. Boscán and Garcilaso were at Court down to the time of the first journey to Italy (1529). But for him, Garcilaso and Gutierre de Cetina were not poets; they were messengers that brought him dispatches in the service of the King. For himself he had no literary pretenses. His letters were written in a terse, matter-of-fact style that often drifted into mere formulae. In a few cases one can detect in his revisions of rough drafts of documents a desire to express himself more effectively, even more elegantly, but usually the changes were dictated by caution or the fear of giving offense. If he dreamed, late in his life, of founding a university in Ubeda, he was not motivated by any desire to promote learning or to train the youth. Cardinal Cisneros had founded a great university at Alcalá de Henares. Why should not he, another King's minister, establish a university in his home town—no modest college, but a university that would vie with Bologna, Paris, and Salamanca?

Again, because of his lack of contact with books, he showed no interest in the great intellectual, political, and religious problems of his age. There is no mention of Erasmus, no intellectual concern with the problems posed by the Reformation in Germany and England, no knowledge of the revival of the Classic past. What is more surprising is that there is no discussion in his letters of the great issues of Church and Empire, with which Gattinara was so passionately concerned and to which Granvelle in later years gave so much thought. In sharp contrast to Galíndez de Carvajal and Gattinara, who were constantly preparing for the Emperor long "opinions" *(pareceres)*, only one such document of Cobos has survived and that deals wholly with people.[33a] In a word, he was not a man of ideas; his talents and his interests lay in action and in personal relations with individual men and women.

Cobos was a collector of works of art; he built two great palaces and a noble church. But there is no reason to believe that he had any artistic taste or any love of beauty. The objects which he included in his *mayorazgo* were not important to him for their artistic merit, but only for their monetary value. He knew artists—great artists—Titian in Italy, Berruguete and Jamete in Spain. He brought painters from Italy to decorate his palaces in Valladolid and Úbeda. He engaged "eagles" as architects to design his buildings—Siloee, Vandelvira, Luis de Vega. To his credit it must be said that he had the wisdom to realize his own lack of competence and to choose expert advisors. But there is nothing to indicate that he had any personal share in the decisions they made. Even in his chapel of San Salvador he left all the details to his chaplain, Dean Ortega, to Luis de Vega, and to the canon of the Cathedral of Toledo, Diego López de Ayala. He may have been responsible for the important place given to his arms and those of his wife on the façade of the church; they are repeated, in diminishing size, four times. Perhaps he got the idea from the similar *motif* on the façade of the church of San Pablo in Valladolid. But it could hardly have been he who chose the Latin inscriptions that interpret the figures of Faith and Justice.

It has been suggested that the use of the two labors of Hercules on the *contre-forts* of the church was a tribute of Cobos to the Emperor.[34] It seems more probable that they are a reflection of Jamete's classicizing taste. The labors depicted are the only two which were reputed to have taken place in Spain; they are copied from plaques made in Italy by Moderno, and the same figures are found in the decoration of other buildings of the period in Spain.

San Salvador is one of the loveliest churches in Spain, a triumph of Vandelvira's most creative and original period, combining structural simplicity with rare decorative grace. Jamete's sculpture, particularly in the sacristy, has a vigor and a beauty almost unsurpassed. But the church is, above all, a monument, not to Our Savior, but to Cobos; his arms, the victory of Santiago over his enemies depicted on the north portal, the red swords of Santiago that decorate the interior walls, the tomb that lies in the crypt beneath the circular dome, all these are a tribute to the founder. Moreover, countless details—the pagan deities, the lush female figures, the Roman centurions who support the shields lend an atmosphere that has little to do with Christian devotion. Both Cobos and his wife were anxious to leave a monument and a burial place that would reflect their wealth and power. In her visit to the church in 1568, Doña María speaks repeatedly of the "sumptuous" character of its treasures and ornaments; she stresses the thousands of ducats that she and her husband had spent on its construction and decoration. There can be little doubt that they both dared to emulate even the King: in his Ordinances of the chapel, Cobos ordered that the divine services be celebrated with the same pomp and dignity as those of the Royal Chapel of Granada, where Ferdinand and Isabel lay buried.

As we have already seen, the qualities which Cobos' contemporaries found in him are precisely those that are revealed in the story of his life. They were all impressed by his tremendous capacity for work. For years he bore a burden of consultation and correspondence that few men could carry. In his most active period it is understandable that he could not find time to see all the people who came to ask him for advice or for favors. As he slowed down in his later years, he may well have used this as an excuse for preserving some privacy. All of the men who commented on him were impressed by his caution and secretiveness. This is also manifest in everything he did—in the care with which he couched his letters, in his instructions to his associates, in the caution with which he eliminated from his files all of his personal correspondence.

Another outstanding trait was his loyal devotion to the people who were closest to him. First of all to the Emperor. From the day that he entered the Emperor's service in Brussels he devoted himself wholly and unreservedly to the promotion of his interests. He did not hesitate to support him at the Cortes, even though it meant the betrayal of the towns, of which he was one of the *procuradores*. He backed the Emperor against the nobles. He wore himself out, working and worrying in the effort to find funds for his far-flung campaigns. Though he profited by the rewards which he received for his faithful service, his feeling for the Emperor was not merely self-seeking. Twenty years the Emperor's senior, he came to have an almost paternal affection for him. He worried over his health; he was terrified at the risks he saw him taking in battle. Cobos had been ill during the campaign in Algiers in 1541; when he heard the glad news that the Emperor was returning in safety, he immediately recovered his health. In one of his last letters to Cobos, written on the eve of his departure for the campaign against the German Protestants, realizing that he was risking his life in the venture, Charles wrote: "I know that this will cause you to shed a few tears, as it has so often in the past." [85] Cobos' devotion to the Emperor was intimate, deeply personal.

His other great loyalty was to his family—his parents, his wife, his children, his own and his wife's kinsmen. Oviedo had expatiated on his care and devotion to his old father; his will bears testimony to his concern for his sisters. Most of the later years of his life were dedicated to assuring for his son Diego an estate and a title, although it must be said that his concern seems less a personal interest in his boy than in the projection of himself into the future. In spite of his amorous interlude in Italy, it is certain that he was devoted to his wife. Both the Emperor and Salinas believed that she dominated him and was responsible for some of his weaknesses. But the tribute to her which Pedro de Navarra includes in his *Diálogo* must be a reflection, not only of what Cobos' contemporaries thought, but also of his actual feeling for her. The long list of appointments and favors he secured for all the members of his family is testimony to his preoccupation with the fortunes of his clan.

Of all the traits of Cobos the most conspicuous was his capacity for friendship. It was not merely a matter of affability, of grace of speech and manner. It was a gift for people. He liked people; he enjoyed conversation and the telling of gay, even ribald tales. His friends in Spain and Italy were constantly writing to him how they missed him after an absence, how they wished he were with them, free from all the cares of state, to make their life gayer, more happy. To them he was a boon companion. He was not free with gifts, but he liked to befriend people, to secure them favors. No doubt he was too anxious to be all things to all men; the "general words" of which Pedro de Navarra complained became a habit. But underneath the conventional words there is always a sense of warmth, of sincerity, of desire to serve. Perhaps it was this gift of winning the affection of the men with whom he had to deal that made him appealing to the Emperor, for this was precisely Charles's most endearing trait.

Cobos' rise to power could have happened only at a time when all authority was vested in a single person. Perhaps it could have happened only under an Emperor who was so involved in the complex problems of his far-flung domains that he was glad to place the responsibility for the administration of his Spanish kingdoms in the hands of a trusted servant. For Cobos this power became the instrument for the attainment of his two great ambitions: wealth and prestige. Wealth he wanted and wealth he attained. But he cared even more for prestige, for social recognition. To win it, he was willing even to sacrifice his treasures. The symbols of his success were the marriage of his daughter to the Duque de Sesa, the ennoblement of his son as Marqués de Camarasa, the endowment of a sumptuous church as his monument.

In the end, he was by no means certain that all his efforts were worthwhile. As his health failed, he saw his dreams slipping away. His daughter's marriage was not happy; she had borne no sons. His own son had failed to win either honor or responsibility. Even the coveted estate of Cazorla was in jeopardy. But to the end he strove to carry on: to win his fight for Cazorla— above all, to remain constant in his service of the Emperor. He had spent his life building and controlling a vast administrative network that would promote the interests of the King in Spain, in Italy, in the New World. That was his true monument. He would have been content to know that, as the years rolled by, he was remembered as Privy Counsellor and Prime Minister of the Emperor, Charles V.

APPENDICES

THE LOS COBOS FAMILY TREE

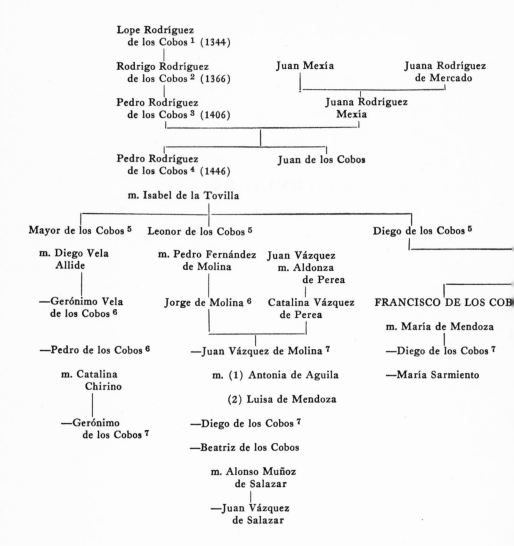

Lope Rodríguez
de los Cobos [1] (1344)

Rodrigo Rodríguez
de los Cobos [2] (1366)

Juan Mexía

Juana Rodríguez
de Mercado

Pedro Rodríguez
de los Cobos [3] (1406)

Juana Rodríguez
Mexía

Pedro Rodríguez
de los Cobos [4] (1446)

Juan de los Cobos

m. Isabel de la Tovilla

Mayor de los Cobos [5]

Leonor de los Cobos [5]

Diego de los Cobos [5]

m. Diego Vela
Allide

m. Pedro Fernández
de Molina

Juan Vázquez
m. Aldonza
de Perea

—Gerónimo Vela
de los Cobos [6]

Jorge de Molina [6]

Catalina Vázquez
de Perea

FRANCISCO DE LOS COB

m. María de Mendoza

—Pedro de los Cobos [6]

—Juan Vázquez de Molina [7]

—Diego de los Cobos [7]

m. Catalina
Chirino

m. (1) Antonia de Aguila

(2) Luisa de Mendoza

—María Sarmiento

—Gerónimo
de los Cobos [7]

—Diego de los Cobos [7]

—Beatriz de los Cobos

m. Alonso Muñoz
de Salazar

—Juan Vázquez
de Salazar

THE MOLINA FAMILY TREE

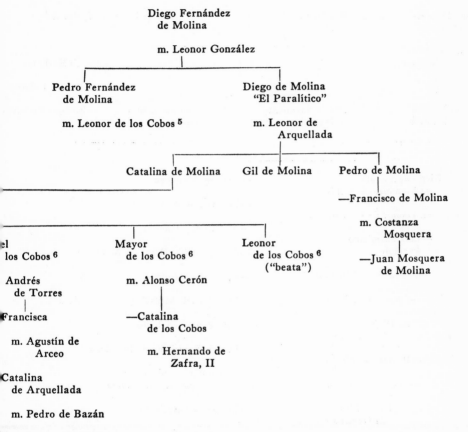

Diego Fernández
de Molina

m. Leonor González

Pedro Fernández
de Molina

m. Leonor de los Cobos [5]

Diego de Molina
"El Paralítico"

m. Leonor de
Arquellada

Catalina de Molina   Gil de Molina   Pedro de Molina

—Francisco de Molina

m. Costanza
Mosquera

—Juan Mosquera
de Molina

el
los Cobos [6]

Andrés
de Torres

Francisca

m. Agustín de
Arceo

Catalina
de Arquellada

m. Pedro de Bazán

Beatriz

m. Pedro de Torres

Mayor
de los Cobos [6]

m. Alonso Cerón

—Catalina
de los Cobos

m. Hernando de
Zafra, II

Leonor
de los Cobos [6]
("beata")

THE MENDOZA–SARMIENTO FAMILY TREE

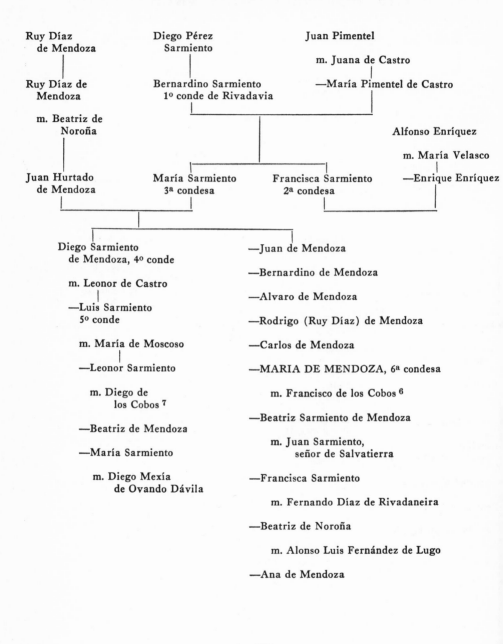

Ruy Díaz
de Mendoza

Ruy Díaz de
Mendoza

m. Beatriz de
Noroña

Juan Hurtado
de Mendoza

Diego Pérez
Sarmiento

Bernardino Sarmiento
1º conde de Rivadavia

María Sarmiento
3ª condesa

Juan Pimentel

m. Juana de Castro

—María Pimentel de Castro

Alfonso Enríquez

m. María Velasco

Francisca Sarmiento
2ª condesa

—Enrique Enríquez

Diego Sarmiento
de Mendoza, 4º conde

m. Leonor de Castro

—Luis Sarmiento
5º conde

m. María de Moscoso

—Leonor Sarmiento

m. Diego de
los Cobos 7

—Beatriz de Mendoza

—María Sarmiento

m. Diego Mexía
de Ovando Dávila

—Juan de Mendoza

—Bernardino de Mendoza

—Alvaro de Mendoza

—Rodrigo (Ruy Díaz) de Mendoza

—Carlos de Mendoza

—MARIA DE MENDOZA, 6ª condesa

m. Francisco de los Cobos 6

—Beatriz Sarmiento de Mendoza

m. Juan Sarmiento,
señor de Salvatierra

—Francisca Sarmiento

m. Fernando Díaz de Rivadaneira

—Beatriz de Noroña

m. Alonso Luis Fernández de Lugo

—Ana de Mendoza

THE FAMILY OF
LOS COBOS–MOLINA — MENDOZA–SARMIENTO

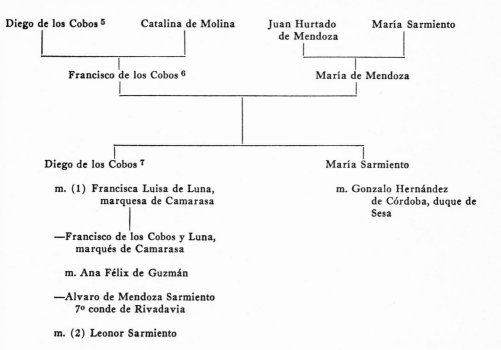

Diego de los Cobos [5]   Catalina de Molina   Juan Hurtado   María Sarmiento
                                                 de Mendoza

Francisco de los Cobos [6]   María de Mendoza

Diego de los Cobos [7]   María Sarmiento

m. (1) Francisca Luisa de Luna,   m. Gonzalo Hernández
    marquesa de Camarasa   de Córdoba, duque de
                                                     Sesa

—Francisco de los Cobos y Luna,
    marqués de Camarasa

m. Ana Félix de Guzmán

—Alvaro de Mendoza Sarmiento
    7° conde de Rivadavia

m. (2) Leonor Sarmiento

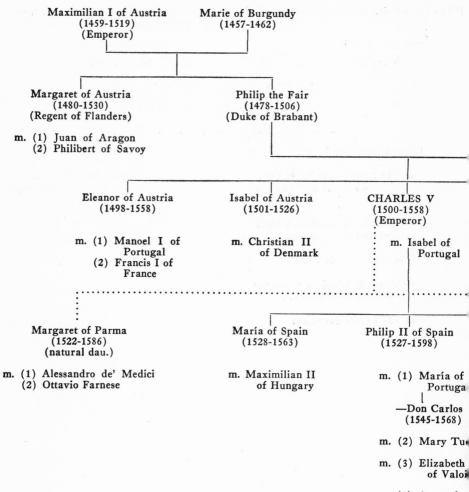

Maximilian I of Austria
(1459-1519)
(Emperor)

Marie of Burgundy
(1457-1462)

Margaret of Austria
(1480-1530)
(Regent of Flanders)

Philip the Fair
(1478-1506)
(Duke of Brabant)

m. (1) Juan of Aragon
(2) Philibert of Savoy

Eleanor of Austria
(1498-1558)

Isabel of Austria
(1501-1526)

CHARLES V
(1500-1558)
(Emperor)

m. (1) Manoel I of
Portugal
(2) Francis I of
France

m. Christian II
of Denmark

m. Isabel of
Portugal

Margaret of Parma
(1522-1586)
(natural dau.)

María of Spain
(1528-1563)

Philip II of Spain
(1527-1598)

m. (1) Alessandro de' Medici
(2) Ottavio Farnese

m. Maximilian II
of Hungary

m. (1) María of
Portuga

—Don Carlos
(1545-1568)

m. (2) Mary Tud

m. (3) Elizabeth
of Valoi

m. (4) Anne of
Austria

—Philip III

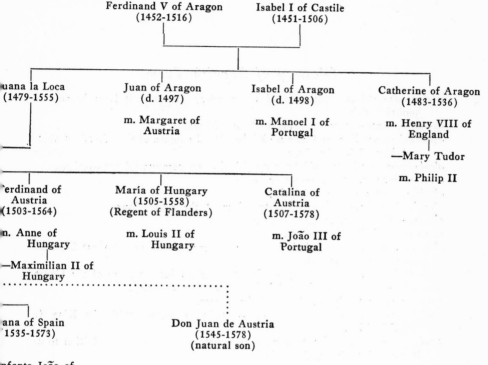

Ferdinand V of Aragon
(1452-1516)
    Isabel I of Castile
(1451-1506)

uana la Loca
(1479-1555)
    Juan of Aragon
(d. 1497)
    m. Margaret of
Austria
    Isabel of Aragon
(d. 1498)
    m. Manoel I of
Portugal
    Catherine of Aragon
(1483-1536)
    m. Henry VIII of
England
    —Mary Tudor
    m. Philip II

'erdinand of
Austria
(1503-1564)
    m. Anne of
Hungary
    —Maximilian II of
Hungary

María of Hungary
(1505-1558)
(Regent of Flanders)
    m. Louis II of
Hungary

Catalina of
Austria
(1507-1578)
    m. João III of
Portugal

ana of Spain
1535-1573)

Don Juan de Austria
(1545-1578)
(natural son)

nfante João of
Portugal

Glossary of Spanish Terms

adelantado—military governor of a (frontier) province; it later became an honorific title.

adelantamiento—office or domain of an *adelantado*.

agnusdei—a small, round wax medal, bearing the figure of the "Lamb of God" and blessed by the Pope.

alcabala—a royal tax paid by a municipality on commercial transactions.

alcaide—warden of a fortress or castle.

alcalde—mayor of a municipality.

alcalde de Corte—a law-enforcing officer of the royal Court.

alcázar—(1) fortress; (2) royal palace.

alguazil—bailiff, police officer.

almirante de Castilla—admiral of Castile, one of the two highest honorific titles of the kingdom.

aposentador—officer in charge of finding lodgings for members of the Court.

argentier—treasurer of Imperial funds (a Flemish title).

asistente—aide to the President of the Cortes.

audiencier—secretary in charge of arranging audiences with the King (a Flemish title).

ayuda de costa—an allowance made to government officials, in addition to or in lieu of their regular salaries.

bachiller—holder of the first degree from a university.

cantero—a master stonecutter serving as an architect.

castellano—unit of currency worth 490 *maravedís*.

cédula—royal order or instruction.

cofradía—religious or charitable fraternity of lay members.

colación—municipal ward or district.

comendador—Commander in a Military Order.

comendador mayor—Grand Commander.

comunero—one of the municipal rebels in 1520-1521.

condestable de Castilla—Constable of Castile, one of the two highest honorific titles in the kingdom.

Consejo de Castilla (Consejo Real, Consejo de Justicia)—Council in charge of internal affairs of Castile and Leon.

Consejo de Estado (Consejo de Cámara)—Privy Council.

Consejo de Guerra—War Council.

Consejo de la Hacienda—Treasury Council.

Consejo de la Inquisición—Inquisition Council.

Consejo de las Indias—Indies Council.

Consejo de las Ordenes—Council of the Military Orders.

consulta—memorandum prepared for presentation to the King or to a Council.

contador—Treasury officer in charge of accounts, a sort of comptroller.

contador de rentas—officer in charge of Treasury receipts.

contador mayor—chief *contador*.

contino—member of the royal household, yeoman of the guard.

converso—a Jew who accepted Christianity after the edict of 1492.

corral—a backyard or lot for cattle.

corregidor—chief municipal magistrate, appointed by the King.

Cortes—assembly of the representatives of the towns; in Aragon, of the representatives of the three "Estates."

Cruzada—money derived from the sale of Papal bulls to support the Crusade against the Infidels.

custodia—monstrance.

encomienda—(1) office of a *comendador* of a Military Order; (2) land and Indians granted to colonists in the Indies.

escribanía—office of an *escribano*.

escribano—scrivener or clerk attached to the royal secretariat.

escribano de finanzas—clerk in charge of recording official financial transactions.

escribano de rentas—clerk in charge of receipts.

escribano del crimen—clerk of a criminal court.

fuero—municipal charter.

fundidor y ensayador—officer in charge of minting and assaying all specie.

garrote—method of execution by strangling with an iron collar.

grande—one of the upper nobility, a "grandee".

infanta—royal princess.

infante—royal prince.

infanzón—one of the nobles of limited rights in the Middle Ages.

juego de cañas—a game played by two teams, in which each side threw wooden wands at the other; it was of Moorish origin.

jurado—juryman, an elected officer in a municipality.

juro—a "treasury note", issued either as a royal grant or in return for a loan, at a definite annual yield and usually based on a specific source of income.

licenciado—holder of the second degree from a university, usually a lawyer.

madrina—sponsor of the bride at a wedding.

maestrescuela—head of a cathedral school.

maestro de obras—chief architect.

maravedí—monetary unit used in all financial transactions; the present value in purchasing power is about two pesetas. A ducat was 375 *maravedís*.

marranilla—a term of scorn applied to converted Jews.
mayorazgo—an entailed estate descending by right of primogeniture.
merced—a special grant or favor from the King.
morisco—a Moor who remained in Spain after the conquest of Granada.

padrino—sponsor of the groom at a wedding.
pascuas—the major religious holidays—Christmas, Easter, etc.
patrón—the "Boss."
peso—a currency unit, used in the Indies, worth 450 *maravedís*.
pliego suelto—a short publication, consisting of a single sheet, folded in quarto.
pragmática—a royal decree providing sumptuary regulations.
procurador—representative of a municipality at a Cortes.
prueba de nobleza—examination of a candidate for appointment to a Military
    Order to establish his qualifications of ancestry.

quinta—the King's "fifth" of treasure derived from the Indies.

regidor—councilman of a municipality.
reja—(1) iron grille covering a window; (2) iron screen separating the
    chancel from the body of a church or chapel.
repartimiento—allotment of Indians to a Spaniard to work as his serfs.
residencia—investigation of the operations of a government official made at the
    end of his term of appointment.
retablo—altar piece.
Reyes Católicos (los)—Ferdinand and Isabel.

sala—main hall or drawing room.
scudo—Italian monetary unit worth 350 *maravedís*.
sisa—general sales tax or excise tax.
sortija—a game which consisted in threading a ring with a lance or wand
    from on horseback.

teniente—deputy to a person holding an office.
trinchante—carver in the royal household.

vara—a measure of length (2.8 feet), a "yard."
veinticuatro—a title given to the *regidor* in many Andalusian towns.
venera—scallop shell used as a badge of the Order of Santiago.
vihuela—older form of the guitar, comparable in many ways to a lute.

Sources

The story of Cobos' life is in large part based upon documents in the Archivo de Simancas and the Archivo de Indias and the Archivo de Camarasa in Seville. There are, however, scattered materials in other archives and libraries which have enlarged the range of documents. Those that have contributed are the following:

Spain
Barcelona. Archivo de la Corona de Aragón.   (ACA)
El Escorial. Biblioteca.   (BEsc)
Madrid. R. Academia de la Historia.   (AcHist)
—— R. Academia Española   (AcEsp)
—— Archivo Histórico Nacional.   (AHN)
—— Archivo Municipal.   (AMadrid)
—— Biblioteca Nacional.   (BN)
Sevilla. Archivo de Camarasa.   (ACam)
—— Archivo General de Indias.   (AInd)
Simancas. Archivo General.   (ASim)
Ubeda. Archivo Municipal.   (AUbeda)
Valladolid. Archivo Provincial.   (AVall)
Belgium
Bruxelles. Archives générales du Royaume.   (ABrux)
England
London. British Museum.   (BM)
—— Public Record Office.   (PRO)
Oxford. Bodleian Library.   (Bodl)
France
Besançon. Bibliothèque de la Ville.   (BBesançon)
Paris. Bibliothèque Nationale.   (BN, Paris)
Italy
Mantova. Archivio di Stato.   (AMantova)
Milano. Archivio di Stato.   (AMilano)
Modena. Archivio di Stato.   (AModena)
Novellara. Archivio Municipale.   (ANovellara)
Parma. Archivio di Stato.   (AParma)

The Archivio of Naples does not contain the papers of the Viceroyalty of Pedro de Toledo. The collections of the Vatican were too vast for me to tackle. I did not have an opportunity to study the papers in the Haus-, Hof- und Staatsarchiv in Vienna.

In addition to these manuscript materials there are numerous printed sources of value, both for particular information about Cobos and for the general background. The most important are the various collections of diplomatic correspondence, such as the *Calendar of State Papers,* Spanish, Venetian, and Foreign and Domestic (Henry VIII), the *Diarii* of Sanuto, the *Venetianische Depeschen,* or the *Nuntiaturberichte aus Deutschland.* There is a dearth of personal letters and memoirs in this period in Spain, but the *Cartas* of Martín de Salinas and the *Libro de la vida* of Alonso Enríquez de Guzmán have provided many picturesque details, and occasionally the *Relaciones* of particular events, usually printed as *pliegos sueltos,* have contributed a touch of color.

Of contemporary historians, the most valuable is Santa Cruz, whose *Crónica* reports hundreds of details nowhere else recorded. His work is supplemented by Sandoval, who had access to many documents no longer available. For the specific chronology, Foronda's *Estancias y viajes* is essential. Among modern historians, the work of Karl Brandi and his school is monumental. For the bibliography of Charles V the second volume of his *Kaiser Karl V* is indispensable and the several volumes of the *Berichte und Studien zur Geschichte Karls V* have added a wealth of information and have made available numerous documents. Brandi was largely concerned with the German rôle of the Emperor, but Tyler, *The Emperor Charles V,* has contributed to our knowledge of his relations with England. There is still no adequate study of the Emperor's activities in relation to Spain.

A number of studies of special aspects of the period have contributed to the story, in particular the work of Carande, Giménez Fernández, González Palencia, Padre March, Ernst Schaefer, and Fritz Walser. The *Notes* record the extent of my indebtedness to them. It should be remarked that in the *Notes* I have given the briefest possible references to identify the works cited; more complete descriptions are given in the *Bibliography.*

Most of the printed materials can be consulted in one or more great libraries: the British Museum, the Harvard College Library, the Library of Congress, and the Biblioteca Nacional in Madrid. But everywhere I have taken advantage of the collections of public and university libraries for the prosecution of my studies. There are a few titles which I have not been able to locate. And I am sure that there are scores, even hundreds of documents and references to Cobos that I have not uncovered. But I like to think that while they would add a detail here and there, they would not change fundamentally the picture I have tried to draw.

It would be impossible to name all of the people who have placed me under a debt of gratitude for their help during this study. It is evidence of their high professional sense that everywhere archivists and librarians gave to me, a stranger, every possible facility and aid. There are, however, a few acknowledgments that I cannot fail to make.

First of all, I must express my gratitude to the Simon N. Guggenheim Foundation for the fellowship which made it possible for me to spend two years in the archives and libraries of Europe and for their generous contribution toward the cost of printing the present volume. To the Duke and Duchess of Alcalá I am indebted for the privilege of utilizing the materials in their family Archivo de Camarasa in the Casa de Pilatos in Seville. To a few friends, José de la Peña in Seville, José Molina Hipólito in Ubeda, Angel de la Plaza in Valladolid, I would express my thanks for their personal interest. Most of all, I want to record my appreciation of the happy afternoons I spent with my colleagues and friends who gathered at the Café León in Madrid. They were tolerant of my questioning, generous in sharing their knowledge, stimulating in their scholarly concern. To Antonio Rodríguez Moñino, who presided over the group from his corner, I cannot hope to give adequate expression of my gratitude for his generosity and friendliness. Finally I must record the decisive part which Agnes Starrett, Director of the University of Pittsburgh Press, has played in the publication of this book. Her interest in the manuscript, her wise judgment and discriminating taste have made possible its appearance in the present form.

NOTES

CHAPTER I

(pp. 1-23)

1. For the early history of Ubeda, see:
   Jiménez de Rada, *Rerum in Hispania gestarum chronicon,* 1545, fols. LXXVI-LXXVII.
   Jiménez Patón, *Historia de la . . . nobleza de la ciudad de Jaén,* 1628.
   Jimena Jurado, *Catálogo de los obispos . . . de Jaén,* [1654], pp. 109 ff.
   Lozano Muñoz, *Crónica de la provincia de Jaén,* 1867, p. 44.
   Cózar Martínez, *Noticias y documentos para la historia de Baeza,* 1884, pp. 112-120.
   Ruiz Prieto, *Historia de Ubeda,* 1906, I, 33-34, 41.
2. For the genealogy of Cobos the chief sources are:
   Argote de Molina, *Nobleza del Andaluzía,* 1588, fol. 282.
   AcHist, MSS. Salazar B-24, B-40.
   Montesinos, *Comentario de la conquista de Baeza,* in AcHist, MSS. Salazar H-13, fol. 146.
   López de Haro, *Casas solariegas de Castilla,* in AcHist, MSS. Salazar C-20, fols. 218-222.
   Padilla, *Nobiliario antiquísimo de España,* in BM, MSS. Add. 12,470, fol. 103.
   Salazar y Castro, [*Comendadores de Santiago*], in BN, MSS. 10,996, fol. 148 ff.
   Los comendadores de la Orden de Santiago, 1949, pp. 431-432, 586-588.
   Historia genealógica de la Casa de Lara, 1696-1697, II, 748.
   Apuntes para el historial de la Casa de Camarasa, 1934, pp. 50-53.
   García Carraffa, *Enciclopedia heráldica y genealógica,* XXVII, 34-41.
   Atienza, *Nobiliario español,* 2a ed., [1954], p. 313.
   See also Appendices, p. 376.
3. Doña Juana was the aunt of the Duque de Alburquerque and thus the Cobos family established a distant tie with the distinguished house of La Cueva.
4. Mejía de Contreras, *Sumario sobre la sentencia arbitraria . . . de Ubeda,* 1613, fols. 24-25.
5. On the Molina family, see especially AcHist, MSS. Salazar, B-24, fols. 73-81, and Salazar y Castro, *Historia . . . de la Casa de Lara,* I, 262 ff. For the family tree, see Appendices, p. 377.
6. Martos López (*Monumentos de Ubeda,* p. 11), also suggests these as the probable dates.
7. Fernández de Oviedo, *Las quinquagenas,* in BN, MSS. 2217-2219, II, fol. 4.
8. *Floreto de anécdotas,* pp. 170-171.
9. In his *De rebus gestis Caroli V,* (*Opera,* II, 93).
10. *Diálogos de la preparación de la muerte,* [1565?], fol. 47.
11. Ruiz Prieto, *Historia,* I, 146-147.

12. Campos Ruiz, *Guía artística e histórica de Ubeda*, I, 26-27.
13. Fernández de Oviedo, *Libro de linaxes y armas,* in AcHist, MSS. Salazar C-24.
14. Reproduced in Schaefer, *Las rúbricas del Consejo . . . de las Indias,* p. 6.
15. Fernández de Oviedo, *Libro de linaxes,* l.c.
16. Fernández de Oviedo, *Las quinquagenas,* 1880, pp. xii-xv.
17. Calamita, *Figuras y semblanzas,* pp. 284-285.
18. ASim, Registro general del Sello.
19. Sevillano Colom, "La cancillería de Fernando el Católico," gives a general account for Aragon. There is no similar study for Castile.
20. Keniston, "Notes on the *De liberis educandis* of Antonio de Lebrija," in *Homenaje a Menéndez Pidal,* 1925, III, 129.
21. Schaefer, *Indice,* II, 46-76.
22. ASim, Registro general del Sello.
23. *Avisos de lo que convendría hacerse para evitar algunos abusos en el gobierno,* in *Codoin,* LXXXVIII, 504-506.
24. Cedillo, *El Cardenal Cisneros,* II, 656-659.
25. ACam, Sabiote 3-8-48.
26. AInd, Indif. general 1961 (I, 6).
27. ASim, Títulos rasgados, 1446-1519.
28. Giménez Fernández, *Bartolomé de las Casas,* I, 284.
29. ASim, Registro general del Sello.
30. AcHist, MSS. Muñoz 75, fol. 248.
31. ASim, Registro general del Sello.
32. ACam, Sabiote 3-4-32.
33. AcHist, MSS. Muñoz 75, fol. 248.
34. ASim, Quitaciones de Corte, Leg. 16.
35. *Idem* (March 3, 1517).
36. In his *Libro de linaxes, ms. cit.*
37. *Memorial dado al cardenal Cisneros de lo que conviene proveer para la buena gobernación de la Isla Española,* in *CodoinAm,* I, 253-264.
38. *Ed. cit.,* I, 56-57, 284.
39. See p. 22.
40. This and the following appointments are recorded in ASim, Registro general del Sello, II.
41. Danvila y Collado, *El poder civil en España,* V, 147.
42. Muñoz de San Pedro, "Francisco Lizaur," in *BAH,* CXXIII, 108 (Logroño, December 12, 1512).
43. ASim, Patronato Real 59, fol. 101.
44. ASim, Cámara de Castilla.
45. AcHist, MSS. Muñoz 75. fol. 248 ff.
46. ASim, Registro general del Sello.
47. ACam, Sabiote 3-4-58; ASim, Registro general del Sello, II.
48. ASim, Registro general del Sello, II.
49. Fuente, *Cartas de los secretarios,* p. 64.
50. ASim, Registro general del Sello, II.
51. ASim, Patronato Real 59, fol. 106; ASim, Estado 6, fol. 72.
52. ASim, Registro general del Sello; ASim, Cámara de Castilla.
53. Keniston, *op. cit.,* III, 130.
54. Sevillano Colom, *op. cit.,* p. 248.
55. *Idem,* p. 241.
56. Salazar y Castro, *Historia de la Casa de Lara,* I, 268.
57. ACam, Sabiote 3-8-74.
58. Giménez Fernández, *op. cit.,* Nota 802.

59. ASim, Patronato Real 69 fol. 28.
60. Fernández de Oviedo, *Libro de linaxes;* ASim, Quitaciones de Corte, Leg. 16.
61. ASim, Contaduría mayor de rentas, 1ª época, 422, fol. 49.
62. ACam, Sabiote 3-8-60.
63. *CodoinAm, passim.*
64. AInd, Indif. general 419 (V, 235-237).
65. Giménez Fernández, *op. cit.,* p. 285 and Nota 804.
66. On the travels of Ferdinand V, see Galíndez de Carvajal, *Anales de los Reyes Católicos,* fols. 51-56. The narrative of the following events is based on familiar sources.
67. Giménez Fernández, *op. cit.,* p. 115. The charges against him are printed in *CodoinAm,* I, 262.
68. Fuente, *Cartas, passim;* ASim, Contaduría mayor de rentas, 1ª época, 422, fol. 52.
69. Fuente, *Cartas,* pp. 51, 62.
70. Cedillo, *op. cit.,* II, 59-60.
71. *Idem,* II, 327-328.
72. Foronda, p. 74.
73. *Segunda parte de los Anales . . . de Aragón,* II, 412-413.
74. *Historia . . . del Emperador Carlos V,* I, 167.
75. Fuente, *Cartas,* p. 208.
76. ACA, Cancillería, No. 3890.
77. ASim, Estado 3, fol. 1; BM, MSS. Add. 28,572, fol. 160.
78. On the activities of the secretaries in Flanders, see Cedillo, *El cardenal Cisneros.*
79. ASim, Estado 12, fol. 233; Fuente, *Cartas,* p. 231.
80. Cedillo, *op. cit.,* II, 370-371; III, 538.
81. ACA, Cancillería, No. 3890.
82. In his *Historia general,* III, 54.
83. *Libro de linaxes,* fol. 37.
84. Cedillo, *op. cit.,* II, 425-426.

CHAPTER II

(pp. 24-43)

1. ASim, Registro general del Sello.
2. ASim, Estado 2, fol. 84.
3. *Libro de linaxes, ms. cit.*
4. *Carlos V,* p. 246.
5. The following paragraphs follow the conventional sources.
6. In Gachard, *Voyages des souverains,* II, 493-494.
7. Rodríguez Villa, *Doña Juana,* pp. 480-481.
8. *Crónica,* I, 143.
9. Brewer, *Letters and papers,* II, I, 623, 648.
10. Fuente, *Cartas,* p. 212.
11. Doussinague, *El testamento político,* pp. 443-444.
12. Fuente, *Cartas,* p. 9.
13. Cedillo, *op. cit.,* II, 654.
14. Fuente, *Cartas,* p. 267.
15. *Idem,* p. 268.

16. ABrux, Etat et audience, No. 788, fols. 136-140.
17. See above; also Gossart, *Notes*, p. 23.
18. ABrux, *ms. cit.*
19. Fuente, *Cartas*, p. 268.
20. Cedillo, *op. cit.*, II, 654.
21. Fol. 46.
22. Cedillo, *op. cit.*
23. ASim, Quitaciones de Corte, Leg. 16.
24. *Idem.*
25. ASim, Quitaciones de Corte, Leg. 16.
26. *Idem.*
27. Cedillo, *op. cit.*, II, 577-578.
28. *Bartolomé de las Casas*, p. 285 ff.
29. Fuente, *Cartas*, p. 43.
30. AInd, Contratación 5784.
31. AcHist, MSS. Muñoz 76, fol. 34.
32. Fuente, *Cartas*, pp. 44, 115-116.
33. *Idem*, p. 237.
34. E. g., Cedillo, *op. cit.*, II, 410-411.
35. Fuente, *Cartas*, p. 44.
36. *Memorias*, fol. 105. There is a brief summary of the *Memorias* in Pedro de Gante, *Relaciones*, pp. ix-xii.
37. *Idem*, fols. 106-107.
38. Foronda, p. 94; Vital, *Premier voyage*, in Gachard, *Collection*, III, 47 ff.
39. Bodleian Library, MSS. Tanner 90, fols. 57-58; Brewer, *Letters and papers*, II, II, 1168-1170.
40. E. g., AUbeda; Ruiz Prieto, *Historia*, I, 157-158.
41. In Gachard, *Collection des voyages*, III.
42. *Brewer, l.c.*
43. Weiss, *Papiers d'état*, I, 105-109.
44. BN (Paris), MSS. Esp. 143, fols. 44-48.
45. Weiss, *op. cit.*, I, 89-100.
46. Sandoval, *Historia*, I, 335-336.
47. *Idem, l.c.*
48. *Idem*, I, 338.
49. *Bartolomé de las Casas*, p. 401 and Nota 1111.

Chapter III

(pp. 44-73)

1. ASim, Patronato Real 69, fol. 33; Ferrer del Río, *Decadencia de España*, pp. 25-26.
2. Garnode, *Le couronnement*, fols. [2], [4].
3. AInd, Indif. general 419 (VII, 23, 36).
4. Las Casas, *Historia*, III, 170; Herrera, *Historia*, Dec. II. 51; Leonardo de Argensola, *Anales de Aragón*, p. 444.
5. AInd, Indif. general 419 (VII, 37); Schaefer, *El Consejo*, I, 34.
6. *Historia*, III, 170-171. Herrera (*Historia*, Dec. II, 51) echoes Las Casas: "M. de Chièvres became fond of him, because he was prudent and likable and

he was helped by his knowledge of the affairs of the kingdom, in which
he had been trained."

7. AcHist, MSS. Muñoz 76, fol. 22; *CodoinAm*, XI, 556-559.
8. AInd, Contratación 5784; AcHist, MSS. Muñoz 76, fol. 84.
9. ASim, Cámara de Castilla; AcHist, *ms. cit.*, fol. 34.
10. ASim, Estado 5, fol. 34.
11. AcHist, MSS. Muñoz 76, fol. 80; *CodoinAm*, I, 356-357; XXXIV, 329-331.
12. AInd, Indif. general 420 (VIII, 15).
13. AInd, Patronato 246, No. 1—1; AInd, Indif. general 419, (V, 248).
14. ASim, Registro general del Sello.
15. AInd, Contratación 5784.
16. ASim, Estado 5, fol. 48.
17. AInd, Indif. general 419 (VII, 82-83).
18. ASim, Estado 7, fol. 107.
19. Las Casas, *Historia*, III, 182.
20. *CodoinAm*, I, 374.
21. *Idem.*
22. ASim, Estado 8, fol. 257.
23. AInd, Indif. general 420 (VIII, 355, 360).
24. ASim, Registro general del Sello (February 23, 1518).
25. ASim, Quitaciones de Corte, Leg. 16 (March 2, 1518).
26. AInd, Indif. general 419 (VII, 48-49, 56).
27. ASim, Estado 4, fol. 100.
28. ACam, Sabiote 3-4-32.
29. This episode is found in ASim, Estado 267, fols. 78-111.
30. Bofarull y Broca, *Historia . . . de Cataluña*, VII, 16-20; Bofarull y de Sartorio, "Festejos y ceremonias," I, 74-83; *Libre de les solemnitats*, I, 390-402.
31. For the story of the negotiations at Montpellier, see Le Glay, *Négotiations*, II, 450-454; Du Bellay, *Mémoires*, I, 94-95; Henne, *Histoire*, I, 285-90; Dansaert, *Guillaume de Croy*, pp. 167-173; Sandoval, I, 408-410.
32. *Manual de novells ardits, vulgarment apellat Dietari*, III, 285.
33. *Idem*, III, 288.
34. *Historia vite*, 405-413.
35. *Libro de la vida*, pp. 9-10.
36. ASim, Registro general del Sello.
37. AInd, Indif. general 419 (IV, 20).
38. ASim, Cámara de Castilla.
39. This episode is from Las Casas, *Historia*, III, 276 ff. See also Remesal, *Historia*, pp. 73-74 and Herrera, *Historia*, Dec. II, 54.
40. Palacio, *Documentos*, IV, 255-258; Santa Cruz, I, 205; Sandoval, I, 413-415 (wrongly dated September 5); Brandi, *The Emperor*, p. 113.
41. *Historia vite*, pp. 414-422.
42. Foronda, p. 159.
43. ASim, Estado 267, fol. 43 (April 1, 1519).
44. *Historia*, p. 136.
44a. On the bribery of *procuradores*, see Martínez Marina, *Teoría de las Cortes*, p. 201.
45. *Cortes . . . de León y de Castilla*, IV, 290.
46. For Cobos' part in these negotiations, see Mejía, *Historia*, p. 139; Danvila y Collado, *Historia . . . de las Comunidades*, I, 116; Leonardo de Argensola, *Anales*, 917; Sandoval, II, 43-50.
47. *Cortes*, IV, 302.
48. ASim, Registro general del Sello.
49. *Historia vite*, p. 280.

394   FRANCISCO DE LOS COBOS

50. *Crónica,* I, 228.
51. Schaefer, *El Consejo,* I, 36.
52. *CodoinUlt,* XIV, 19.
53. Fernández de Oviedo, *Libro de linaxes, ms. cit.*
54. ASim, Registro general del Sello.
55. ASim, Estado 6, fol. 62; Estado 14.
56. Sandoval, II, 75.
57. *CodoinAm,* XXXVII, 212.
58. *Idem,* VII, 65-89.
59. *The Emperor,* p. 84.
60. Dansaert, *Guillaume de Croy,* pp. 164, 194.
61. Santa Cruz, I, 185.
62. Bofarull y de Sartorio, "Festejos," I, 76, Note 1; Vandenesse, *Journal,* in Gachard, *Collection des voyages,* II, 62; Ulloa Cisneros, *Historia,* p. 12.
63. *CodoinAm,* VII, 423-424 (Note 1); Remesal, *Historia,* p. 77.
64. ASim, Estado 65, fol. 325. It is not sure that Recalde accepted the proposal, for on July 23, 1518 he was confirmed in his post as accountant of the Casa de la Contratación (Foronda, p. 126).
65. Dansaert, *op. cit.,* pp. 186-187, Note 291 (October 12, 1519).
66. *Historia,* II, 77.
67. Danvila y Collado, *Historia,* I, 452.
68. *Idem,* II, 431.
69. *Idem,* II, 35.
70. Sandoval, III, 126.
71. Danvila y Collado, *op. cit.,* III, 300.
72. *Idem,* V, 172.
73. ASim, Patronato Real 1, fol. 74.
74. ACam, Sabiote 3-8-16.
75. BN, MSS. 18,697, No. 9.
76. AHN, Encomiendas, Leg. 67: Bastimentos de León, No. 5; BN, MSS. 10,996, fol. 46.
77. ASim, Patronato Real 26, fol. 16; Danvila y Collado, *Historia,* IV, 639.
78. ASim, Registro general del Sello.
79. Danvila y Collado, *op. cit.,* III, 568; IV, 187.
80. ASim, Estado 5, fol. 131.
81. AHN, Encomiendas, Leg. 67.
82. *Idem.*
83. ASim, Obras y bosques 16, fol. 2.
84. Brown, *Calendar,* III, 194, 197, 199.
85. ASim, Estado 10.
86. AInd, Patronato 246, No. 2-2; *CodoinUlt,* XVIII, 29 (May 10?).
87. ACA, Cancillería, No. 3890.
88. Foronda, p. 126.
89. PRO, S.P. 1/24, fols. 168-208.
90. Gachard, *Analectes,* Sér. V-VII, pp. 25-28.

CHAPTER IV

(pp. 74-98)

1. Brandi, *The Emperor,* p. 204.
2. Brown, *Calendar,* III, 395.

3. *Cartas*, p. 64.
4. ACam, Rivadavia 2-1-30.
5. ASim, Contaduría de mercedes 41, fol. 27; 42, fol. 28.
6. ACam, Rivadavia 2-1-28.
7. *Cartas*, p. 77.
8. On the family of María de Mendoza, see López de Haro, *Nobiliario*, II, 89 ff.; AHN, Consejos 37,824, No. 6,324; ACam, Rivadavia 2-1-25 and 26; 3-1-11 to 13. For her family tree, see Appendices, p. 378.
9. Marineo Siculo, *De las cosas memorables de España*, 1530, fols. xxiii-xxv; Laiglesia, *Estudios históricos*, la ed., 721-727.
10. Salinas, *Cartas*, p. 81.
11. ASim, Estado 16, fol. 306.
12. Sandoval, I, 406.
13. ASim, Estado 65, fol. 230; Danvila y Collado, *Historia*, IV, 748.
14. *Floreto*, p. 171.
15. ASim, Estado 10; Danvila y Collado, *op. cit.*, V, 250.
16. Brown, *Calendar*, III, 285-286; Zúñiga, *Crónica*, in *BAE*, XXXVI, 18; Sandoval, III, 255-262.
17. Brandi, *op. cit.*, p. 200.
18. AUbeda.
19. ACam, Sabiote 3-8-50.
20. I am indebted to my friend Don José Molina Hipólito of Ubeda for this information.
21. ASim, Estado 8, fol. 260.
22. Salinas, *Cartas*, p. 45.
23. BEsc, &. II. 7, fol. 122.
24. ASim, Estado 11, fols. 4-6; ASim, Escribanía mayor de rentas 526.
25. Salinas, p. 70.
26. AHN, Encomiendas, Leg. 67: Bastimentos de León, No. 5.
27. ASim, Estado 11, fols. 4-6; ASim, Escribanía mayor de rentas 526.
28. Salinas, p. 104.
29. Claretta, *Notice*, p. 327.
30. ASim, Escribanía mayor de rentas 526.
31. *Cartas*, p. 149.
32. *Idem*, p. 210.
33. *Idem*, pp. 203-204.
34. ASim, Estado 12, fol. 3.
35. *Idem*; Martire d'Anghiera, *Opus epistolarum*, p. 451.
36. *Cartas*, p. 100.
37. ASim, Estado 11.
38. *Cartas*, p. 210.
39. ABrux, Manuscrits divers, No. 156; Gossart, *Notice*, pp. 100-115.
40. Ruiz Prieto, *Historia*, I, 161.
41. ASim, Registro general del Sello.
42. ASim, Quitaciones de Corte 16.
43. ASim, Contaduría de mercedes 92, fol. 2.
44. BM, MSS. Vesp. C.II, fols. 216-217; Brown, *Calendar*, III, II, 1469.
45. Rivera Recio, *El adelantamiento de Cazorla*, p. 102.
46. *Epístolas*, fol. lxviii.
47. *Historia*, p. 352.
48. Sandoval, IV, 96.
49. ASim, Estado 12, fol. 21; Ulloa, *Vita dell'* ... *Imperatore*, fol. 103.
50. ASim, Estado 367, fols. 67, 166.
51. Danvila y Collado, *Historia*, V, 298, 382-383; *Codoin*, I, 286-287.

52. Herrera, *Historia,* Dec. III, 153-154.
53. AInd, Patronato 246, No. 2-1, No. 3-3.
54. *Libro de la vida,* pp. 42-43.
55. ASim, Estado 12, fol. 3.
56. Brown, *Calendar,* III, 376 (August 16, 1524).
57. *Cartas,* p. 205 (August 15, 1524).
58. BM, MSS. Eg. 307, fols. 159-163.
59. ASim, Estado 12, fol. 3.
60. Brandi, "Eigenhändige Aufzeichnungen Karls V," in *Nachrichten der Gesell-schaft der Wissenschaften zu Göttingen.* Phil.-hist. Kl. (1933), pp. 256-260.
61. Brown, *Calendar,* III, 395, 398.
62. See p. 217.
63. *Libro de la vida,* MS. pp. 53-54.
64. *Idem, l.c.*
65. Salinas, *Cartas,* p. 263.
66. Gams, *Series episcoporum,* p. 91.
67. Salinas, p. 131. Charles' former confessor, Jean Glapion, had died at Valladolid on September 14, 1522 (Salinas, p. 43.)
68. *Idem,* p. 245.
69. *Idem,* pp. 251, 270.
70. ASim, Diversos de Castilla 39, fol. 26; Danvila y Collado, *Historia,* V, 562.
71. *Libro de la vida,* p. 47.
72. The account of this trip is found in AUbeda, *Relación verdadera de lo que pasa en el patronato y fundación de la capilla de la Concepción,* and in ACam, Sabiote 3-8-8.
73. ACam, Sabiote 3-8-16, fols. 20-28.
74. *Cortes,* IV, 403-447; Laiglesia, *Estudios históricos,* 2a ed., I, 369.
75. *CodoinAm,* XXXV, 563-564.
76. Danvila y Collado, *Historia,* V, 559.
77. There are many accounts of this tragic event: BM, MSS. Add. 10259; BM, MSS. Eg. 329, fols. 65-72; Santa Cruz, *Crónica,* II, 231; Ferrer del Río, *Decadencia de España,* 318-319, 392 ff.; Sandoval, II, 264.
78. Gachard, *Correspondance de Charles-Quint et d'Adrien VI,* pp. 171-172, ciii.
79. Danvila y Collado, *op. cit.,* V, 408.
80. Salinas, p. 226.
81. BM, MSS. Add. 10,259, fol. 1; Danvila y Collado, *op. cit.,* V, 567-572; Ferrer del Río, *op. cit.,* 392-396.
82. Ortiz de Zúñiga, *Anales . . . de Sevilla,* p. 483 ff.
83. *Lettere,* ed. Serassi, II, 35.
84. AcHist, MSS. Muñoz 56, fol. 299; Gachard, *Correspondance,* pp. 225-226.
85. Braamcamp Freire, *Ida da Imperatriz Isabel para Castela,* p. 79. On April 6 Villarreal reported that Gattinara had told him that he disapproved of the Emperor's action (*idem,* pp. 81-82).
86. AcHist, MSS. Salazar A-39, fols. 188-189.
87. *Lettere,* II, 142-143.
88. BN, MSS. 20214[6], formerly in the R. Academia de la Historia.
89. BM, MSS. Add. 10,259, fol. 2.
90. Gayangos, *Letters and despatches,* III, II, 254.
91. Braamcamp Freire, *op. cit.,* pp. 76-77.
92. Sandoval, IV, 611-612.
93. Santa Cruz, *Crónica,* II, 247; Sandoval, IV, 449-453.
94. Foronda, pp. 280-281.
95. Ruiz Prieto, *Historia,* I, 161-162; Martos López, *Monumentos,* p. 16.
96. See p. 103.

97. ASim, Estado 14.
98. García Chico, "El palacio de los Dueñas," p. 95.
99. Chueca Goitía, *Arquitectura,* p. 80; Camón Aznar, *La arquitectura plateresca,* I, 300. Without any documentary evidence, Agapito y Revilla ("La Capilla Real" in *BSEE,* LXVIII, 131) shrewdly guessed that Vega was the architect of the palace.
100. See p. 188.
101. *Ingeniosa comparación,* pp. 172-173.
102. Bataillon, *Erasme et l'Espagne,* p. 251 and Note 2.
103. BN, MSS. 11599, No. 9; Ortiz de Zúñiga, *Anales,* p. 491.
104. AHN, Santiago, Capítulos 2243 C.
105. Sandoval, V, 10.
106. Brown, *Calendar,* IV, 50.

CHAPTER V

(pp. 99-122)

1. Salinas, pp. 172, 185.
2. Brown, *op. cit.,* III, 369.
3. *Idem,* III, 376.
4. In Albèri, *Relazioni,* II, 55-56.
5. Salinas, pp. 270-271.
6. Brown, *op. cit.,* III, 458 (July 6, 9, 1525).
7. The account of Gattinara's activities in this period is based on ABrux, Etat et Audience 1,471 (4): "Remonstrances et mémoires du Grand Chancelier Mercurin de Gattinaire, faites à l'Empereur, l'an 1526." Another version, in Italian, is found in Claretta, *Notice,* pp. 309-324.
8. ASim, Diversos de Castilla 47.
9. *Cartas,* p. 330.
10. *Idem,* pp. 344, 355; Brown, *Calendar,* IV, 36, 50.
11. *The Emperor,* p. 254.
12. *Idem.*
13. Brown, *Calendar,* III, 383.
14. Martínez Ferrando, *Privilegios,* pp. 121-122.
15. ABrux, *ms. cit.*
16. Salinas, pp. 355 ff.; Brandi, *op. cit.,* 254-257.
17. For accounts of Philip's birth and baptism, see Arriaga, *Historia del Colegio de San Gregorio,* I, 487-494; March, *Niñez,* I, 27-40, 349; Vales Failde, *La emperatriz,* p. 244; Sandoval, V, 43-51.
18. The doorway was later blocked and replaced by a window. There is a local legend that Philip was handed out through this window, when he was carried to his baptism, and that it was then closed. A chain still hangs across the *reja,* as proof of the authenticity of the story.
19. Arriaga, *op. cit.,* I, 493.
20. AInd, Indif. general 421 (XIII, 64-66); Patronato 246, No. 2-2.
21. AInd, Indif. general 421 (XII, 296-297).
22. AInd, Patronato 246, No. 2-2; Brandi, *op. cit.,* 337-338.
23. AHN, Ordenes militares. Santiago, Expediente 1985.
24. *Libro de la vida,* pp. 59-63.
25. AInd, Indif. general 421 (XII, 311).

26. AcHist. MSS. Muñoz 75, fol. 248 ff.
27. See p. 105.
28. Details on Pedro de Alvarado in: Altolaguirre y Duvale, *Don Pedro de Alva-rado, passim;* Remesal, *Historia . . . de Guatemala,* pp. 16-17; *Cartas de Indias,* pp. 708-710; Díaz del Castillo, *Verdadera historia,* II, 241; He-rrera, *Historia,* Dec. IV, 26.
29. See p. 389, Note 3.
30. ASim, Estado 29, fol. 170.
31. AcHist, MSS. Muñoz 75, fol. 248 ff.; AInd, Patronato 246, No. 2-3.
32. AInd, Patronato 246, No. 2-14.
33. AcHist, MSS. Muñoz 78, fols. 268-269.
34. ACam, Sabiote 3-2-23. All the "palace gang" received similar grants.
35. *Idem,* 3-2-24.
36. ASim, Estado 16, fols. 248-249.
37. Santa Cruz, II, 432; Sandoval, V, 125-145.
38. *Codoin,* I, 47 ff.
39. Núñez de Castro, *Historia . . . de Guadalaxara,* p. 178.
40. Martire d'Anghiera, *Opus epistolarum,* p. 338; Madariaga, *Hernán Cortés.* 2a ed., p. 404.
41. *CodoinAm,* XII, 318-326.
42. In his *Cartas y relaciones,* p. 317.
43. *Verdadera historia,* II, 146-147.
44. Brown, *Calendar,* III, 442.
45. *Idem,* II, 482.
46. *Verdadera historia,* l. c.
47. *Idem,* II, 228 ff.; Gómez de Orozco, "El exvoto de Hernán Cortés," I, 221. There is another mention of a jeweled scorpion, sent to Spain by Cortés in 1526, in Cuevas, *Cartas y documentos,* p. 24.
48. E. g., Madariaga, *op. cit.,* pp. 613-615.
49. ACam, Rivadavia 2-1-39.
50. Díaz del Castillo, *l. c.*
51. *CodoinAm,* XII, 379-380.
52. *Idem,* XII, 380 ff.
53. AInd, Indif. general 421 (XIII, 91-93); *CodoinUlt,* XIV, 34.
54. ASim, Registro general del Sello, III; González García-Valladolid, *Datos,* p. 313. See also p. 313.
55. AInd, Justicia 973, 2-2.
56. See p. 259.
57. ABrux, Etat et Audience, No. 29; Labande, *Recueil,* p. 37; *Documents . . . de Monaco,* II, 389.
58. ASim, Guerra y Marina 2, fol. 201.
59. Santa Cruz, II, 462-463.
60. ASim, Estado 77, fol. 84; Bataillon, *Erasme et l'Espagne,* pp. 417-418.
61. ASim, Estado 14.
62. Vandenesse, *Journal,* p. 100.
63. *Cartas,* p. 569.
64. *Anales,* p. 255.
65. *Crónica,* II, 463.
66. *Cartas,* p. 423.
67. See, for example: Bataillon, *op. cit.,* p. 464, Note 5; Fermín Caballero, *Alonso y Juan de Valdés,* pp. 432-437.
68. *Diálogo de Mercurio y Carón,* pp. 118-125.
69. ASim, Registro general del Sello, III; Diversos de Castilla 40, fol. 9.
70. *Essais sur l'administration de la Castille,* p. 335.

71. Pacheco y de Leyva, "Relaciones vaticanas de hacienda española," pp. 113-114.
72. All these documents are found in ASim, Estado 16, fol. 249, and Estado 17-18, fols. 2-5.
73. ASim, Estado 17-18, fol. 193; Brandi, *op. cit.,* p. 274.
74. Brandi, *l. c.*
75. AInd, Patronato 246-2-11.
76. ASim, Registro general del Sello, III (March 1, 1528).
77. AInd, Patronato 246-2-6.
78. *Idem,* 246-2-7. The following list gives the details. Information with regard to salaries is largely from ASim, Contaduría mayor, la época, 422. Items marked with an * are estimates.

Income—1529

Salaries

Secretary for Castile	100,000	*maravedís*
— Ayuda de costa	50,000	
Secretary of Hacienda	100,000	
Secretary for the Indies	50,000	
Secretary of the Order of Alcántara	15,000	
Regidor of Ubeda	*200,000	
Regidor of Valladolid	*200,000	
Escribano del crimen of Ubeda	*150,000	
Alguazil of Talavera	70,000	
Escribano de rentas de Alcaraz	20,700	
Office fees for Castile	?	
Office fees for the Indies	?	

Special grants

Comendador de Azuaga (9,000 ducats)	3,375,000	
Fundidor of the Indies	*1,000,000	
2,000 ducats a year	750,000	
Salt mines of the Indies	?	
Mine rights in Spain	?	
Lost cattle of Alcaraz	6,000	

Investments

Villa de Hornillos	*150,000	
Juro from Juan Hurtado de Mendoza	74,550	
Juros purchased (1519-1529)	376,950	
Land in the Cañada de la Nava	?	
Total	6,688,200	*maravedís*

79. ACam, Sabiote 3-8-8.
80. *Idem,* 3-8-2 and 3; 3-8-16.
81. ASim, Estado 29, fol. 170.
82. ASim, Estado 2, fol. 141; Ruiz Prieto, *Historia,* I, 162.
83. AHN, Encomiendas 67 (January 31, 1523).
84. Danvila y Collado, *Historia,* V, 514.
85. Zúñiga, *Crónica* (*BAE,* XXXVI, 36).
86. AHN, Ordenes militares, Santiago, Expediente 8588.
87. Carande, *Carlos V y sus banqueros,* II, 54; ASim, Registro general del Sello.
88. *Libro de linaxes, ms. cit.*
89. AInd, Patronato 246-2-10.
90. *Cartas,* p. 431.
90a. *Relaciones de los reinados de Carlos V y Felipe II,* II, p. viii.
91. Sandoval, IV, 401; Tyler, *The Emperor Charles V,* pp. 56-57.

92. Santa Cruz, II, 419; Sandoval, V, 126.
93. Sandoval, V, 131.
94. *Documents . . . de Monaco,* II, 397 (October 31, 1528).
95. Dumont, *Corps universel diplomatique,* IV, II, 1-7; Sanuto, *Diarii,* LI, 252; Bodl. MSS. Rawl. D 648, fols. 2-3.
96. BN (Paris), MSS. Fr. 3022, fols. 77-79: "Abertimiento de la Corte del Emperador."
97. *Manual de novells ardits,* III, 407; BN (Paris), *ms. cit.*
98. ASim, Estado 368, fol. 96.
99. *Idem,* fols. 222, 250; *Manual,* III, 409. The Paris manuscript (fol. 78) gives the number of loads as twenty-four.
100. AInd, Patronato 197-5; published in *CodoinAm,* XL, 455-458.
101. AInd, Patronato 246-2-7.
102. AcHist, MSS. Muñoz 78, fol. 185.
103. *Idem,* Muñoz 79, fols. 18, 48; *CodoinAm,* III, 501.
104. ASim, Estado 17-18, fol. 9.
105. Pacheco y de Leyva, *op. cit.,* pp. 113-114.
106. AUbeda ("de mi galera").
107. BN, MSS. 991, 113, 119, 120.
108. *Crónica,* (*BAE,* XXXVI, 53).

CHAPTER VI

(pp. 123-147)

1. *Charles-Quint et son temps.* Pl. 31. Tyler (*op. cit.,* p. 290) says that at the time of his marriage in 1526 he was wearing a beard. If so, he must have shaved it off shortly thereafter. The alabaster portrait of Charles and Isabel in the Château de Gaesbeek (*Charles-Quint,* Pl. 32) is certainly of a later period; the date "1526" is that of their wedding.
2. See, for example, Sanuto, LII, 193: "viso longo con barbuza grande et in fuora, *cum* barba non molto rosa, toso."
3. For the entry into Genoa, see *Cronaca del soggiorno di Carlo V in Italia,* pp. 79-89.
4. ASim, Estado 1362.
5. ASim, Estado 17.
6. AInd, Patronato 246-2-3.
7. *Cronaca,* p. 97; Pastor, *Histoire des Papes,* X, 28.
8. Capella, *Historia de las cosas que han passado en Italia,* fol. xlviii; Santa Cruz, III, 73.
9. ASim, Estado 1454, fol. 168.
10. *Idem,* fol. 170.
11. ASim, Estado 17, fol. 182.
12. *Cartas,* p. 446.
13. ASim, Estado 1172, fol. 64.
14. ASim, Patronato Real 17, fol. 37.
15. ASim, Quitaciones de Corte 16.
16. Santa Cruz, II, 248; Sandoval, IV, 451-452.
17. Albèri, *Relazioni,* I, 60-61.
18. Santa Cruz, III, 66.
19. AModena, A. S. E., Cancelleria, Particolari.

20. There is a very large bibliography of works describing events in Bologna in 1529 and 1530. The most detailed are: *Cronaca*, pp. 100-125; Giordani, *Della venuta e dimora in Bologna di Clemente VII*, pp. 12-152; [Guazzo], *Historie di tutte le cose degne di memoria*, fols. 71-80; Sanuto, LII, 193, *et passim*.

21. Giordani, p. 30.

22. *The entry of the Emperor Charles V into the city of Bologna*, Florence, 1875.

23. Giordani, p. 92.

24. *Idem*, pp. 53-55; Documenti, 30-37; Dumont, *Corps universel*, IV, II, 53-58; Sanuto, LII, 386.

25. Sanuto, LII, 431-432.

26. Varchi, *Storia fiorentina*, II, 278. See also Bodl, MSS. Rawl. D 648, fols. 6-11.

27. ASim, Estado 45, fol. 67.

28. *Breve expedido por S. S. el papa Clemente VII;* ACam, Sabiote 3-8-2.

29. Thus, for example, to the new Condestable (Paz, *Catálogo de documentos españoles*, No. 100—February 2, 1530) and again on February 11 (BN, MSS. 991, fol. 266).

30. *Cartas*, p. 464.

31. *Idem*, pp. 467-468.

32. Giordani, *op. cit.*, p. 92. On Bagnacavallo, see Vasari, *Vite*, V, 175-177; Vaccolini, *Bagnacavallo*, esp. p. 18. He was one of those who painted the decorations for the entry of Charles V (Giordani, p. 18).

33. ASim, Guerra y Marina 2, fol. 265. Printed in *Codoin*, LV, 335-338, and in Zarco del Valle, *Documentos inéditos*, pp. 135-138.

34. Again, they are so numerous that it is not necessary to list them all. I mention only the Bodleian Library MS. Rawl. D. 1142, and the *pliego suelto, La maravillosa coronación*, reprinted in *Relaciones de los reinados de Carlos V y Felipe II*, II, 125-131.

35. Giordani, pp. 101-102.

36. *La maravillosa coronación*, II, 127.

37. Giordani, p. 138.

38. *Crónica*, III, 89-90.

39. *Vita dell' . . . Imperatore Carlo V*, fol. 120.

40. *Cronaca del soggiorno*, p. 231; Salinas, p. 481.

41. González Palencia, *Don Luis de Zúñiga y Avila*, p. 69. I have preferred to call him "Luis de Avila," the name by which he was generally known at Court.

42. *Idem*, p. 60.

43. The chief source is Davolio, *Memorie storiche della contea di Novellara*, 1833. The Archivio Municipale of Novellara has a more complete manuscript of Davolio's *Memorie* in three volumes. See also Veronica Gambara, *Rime e lettere*, 1759, p. xlv.

44. Varchi, *Storia fiorentina*, II, 488 and Note (1).

45. AMantova, No. 1348 (Documenti di Novellara) ; Davolio, *op. cit.*, p. 21.

46. ASim, Estado 1177, fol. 113.

47. ASim, Estado 1310, fols. 79-80.

48. AMantova, No. 1348.

49. ASim, Estado 1310, fol. 48.

50. Davolio, p. 24.

51. ASim, Estado 1369, fol. 132.

52. ASim, Estado 1182, fol. 119.

53. Santa Cruz, III, 431.

54. *Idem*, III, 456.

55. ASim, Estado 49, fol. 202 (December 13, 1540).

56. *Rime e lettere,* 1850, pp. 207-210; *Undici lettere,* 1889, pp. 30-31.
57. González Palencia, *Don Luis,* p. 68.
58. *Rime e lettere,* 1759, pp. 142-144.
59. [Landi], *Paradossi,* fol. 68.
60. Davolio, p. 24. Tiraboschi (*Storia della letteratura italiana,* XII, VII) mentions her among the "donne erudite" of her time.
61. ASim, Estado 1188, fol. 121.
62. *Idem,* fol. 24, and 1187, fol. 12.
63. Gaye, *Carteggio,* II, 220.
64. *Idem,* II, 219-220.
65. Crowe and Cavalcaselle, *Titian,* I, 448.
66. *Idem,* I, 449.
67. ASim, Estado 1366, fol. 160.
68. ASim, Estado 1456, fol. 221. In 1535 Battista degli Strozzi was Governor of Modena (Varchi, *Storia fiorentina,* III, 101).
69. AModena, A. S. E., Cancelleria, Particolari.
70. *Idem.*
71. *Idem.*
72. ASim, Estado 1,310, fol. 98.
73. ASim, Estado 1,366, fols. 191, 211.
74. ASim, Estado 1,310, fols. 48, 79-80.
75. ASim, Guerra y Marina 3, fol. 362.
76. ASim, Estado 863, fol. 64.
77. AMilano, Documenti diplomatici, No. 2.
78. ASim, Estado 1,183, fol. 17.
79. ASim, Estado 866, fol. 41.
80. ASim, Estado 868, fols. 86-87.
81. González Palencia, *Don Luis,* p. 62.
82. *Idem,* pp. 68-70.
83. *Idem,* pp. 70-71.
84. ASim, Estado 1,187, fol. 32.
85. *Idem,* fol. 29.
86. González Palencia, *Vida . . . de D. Diego Hurtado de Mendoza,* p. 129.
87. ASim, Estado 1,187, fol. 26.
88. ASim, Estado 49, fol. 306.
89. ASim, Estado 1,187, fol. 26.
90. ASim, Estado 1,188, fol. 116.
91. ASim, Estado 1,460, fol. 195.
92. ASim, Estado 1,190.
93. AModena, Cancelleria, Particolari.
94. BN, MSS. 991, fol. 271.
95. Brown, *Calendar,* IV, 503; AInd, Indif. general 422 (XVI, 23-24)—June 5, 1530.
96. *Cartas,* ed. Heine, p. 19 (July 6, 1530).
97. *Codoin,* XCVII, 278 (July 2, 1531).
98. Caballero, *op. cit.,* pp. 442-443. The Marcello whom he mentions is probably Antonio Marcello Cervini, who was later secretary of Cardinal Farnese and finally Pope under the title of Marcellus II.
99. ASim, Estado 636, fol. 102.
100. ASim, Estado 1176, fol. 39.
101. Carande, *op. cit.,* II, 388.
102. Dormer, *Progreso de la historia,* p. 22.
103. BN, MSS. 18,634, No. 58; Pastor, *History of the Popes,* X, 154-156.
104. Habich, "Studien zur deutschen Renaissancemedaille. IV. Christoph Weiditz,"

(Tafel V. 8 and 8a). Also in his *Die deutschen Schaumünzen des 16*ᵉ *Jahrhunderts,* No. 396 (Tafel LI, 3.)
105. ASim, Estado 496, fol. 190.
106. Sanuto, LV, 419.
107. *Idem,* LVI, 523, 566.
108. Bataillon, *op. cit.,* p. 465 and Note 1.
109. González Palencia, *Gonzalo Pérez,* I, 18.
110. See p. 336.

CHAPTER VII

(pp. 148-165)

1. ASim, Estado 25, fol. 233.
2. For example, ASim, Estado 24, fol. 354.
3. *Libro de la vida,* MS. p. 117.
4. ASim, Estado 496, fols. 172-173.
5. ASim, Estado 15, fol. 9. At the time of the Empress's death in 1539, Doña María was "guard of the ladies in waiting," (March, *Niñez,* II, 356).
6. ASim, Registro general del Sello, II.
7. ACam, Rivadavia 1-1-45; AHN, Consejos 37,824, No. 6324. At Mantua, on April 17, 1530, the Emperor wrote to the Empress, asking her to show favor to Juan de Mendoza (ASim, Estado 1,455, fol. 24).
8. *Codoin,* XCVII, 238.
9. ASim, Estado 496, fol. 171.
10. AInd, Patronato 246-1-15.
11. AInd, Indif. general 422 (XV, 173-174).
12. *Idem,* XVI, 23-24.
13. AInd, Patronato 246-1-15.
14. ASim, Quitaciones de Corte 16.
15. ASim, Diversos de Castilla 46, fol. 13.
16. ASim, Registro del Sello, II.
17. ASim, Estado 496, fols. 172-173.
18. Carande, *op. cit.,* II, 350.
19. ACam, Sabiote, III-1-18.
20. ASim, Estado 22, fols. 45-46.
21. ASim, Estado 496, fol. 174.
22. ASim, Estado 496, fols. 172-173.
23. AHN, Ordenes militares. Santiago, Expediente 1987.
24. ASim, *ms. cit. supra.*
25. *CodoinAm,* VII, 423-424. On the same day (August 21, 1529) the same privilege was granted to Juan Vázquez (AInd, Indif. general 422 -XIV, 7).
26. ACam, Sabiote 3-8-73.
27. AUbeda, "Relación verdadera."
28. *Libro de linaxes, ms. cit.* See also his *Quinquagenas,* pp. xii-xv.
29. ACam, Sabiote 3-8-55 and 56.
30. ASim, Estado 852, fol. 122.
31. ACam, Sabiote 3-8-76; ASim, Registro general del Sello, II. The Empress confirmed the grant at Avila on August 11, and the Emperor, at Brussels on October 15.
32. ASim, Estado 496, fols. 172-173.

33. ASim, Estado 25, fols. 234, 236.
34. *Idem,* fol. 238.
35. *Idem,* fol. 234.
36. ASim, Patronato Real 35, fol. 10.
37. ACam, Sabiote 3-8-2A.
38. Sanuto, LVII, 150.
39. Tyler, *The Emperor,* p. 290. Titian made a rough pen and ink sketch of his presentation to the Emperor. Could it be that the bearded courtier standing, with folded arms, beside the Emperor's chair is Cobos? (*Charles-Quint,* Pl. 18).
40. *Documents . . . de Monaco,* II; AInd, Patronato 246-1-15; ASim, Estado 636, fol. 84.
41. Campori, "Tiziano e gli Estensi," in *Nuova antologia,* XXVII, 601-604; Crowe and Cavalcaselle, *Titian,* I, 359-364.
42. ASim, Estado 1366, fol. 144.
43. *Idem,* fol. 166.
44. Pastor, *History of the Popes,* X, 221.
45. ASim, Estado 1,457, fols. 247-249.
46. AModena, Cancelleria. Particolari.
47. Weiss, *Papiers d'état,* LL, 7.
48. *Idem,* II, 19; Sanuto, LVII, 610.
49. ASim, Patronato Real 43, fol. 26.
50. *Manual de novells ardits,* III, 463.
51. ASim, Estado 857, fol. 71.
52. AModena. Cancelleria. Particolari.
53. AMantova, No. 587.
54. ASim, Estado 26, fol. 17.
55. Sanuto, LVIII, 474.
56. ASim, Estado 1,178, fol. 58.
57. Foronda, p. 377.
58. ASim, Estado 1,178, *passim.*
59. *Cartas,* p. 536.
60. *Idem,* p. 532.
61. Foronda, p. 388.
62. *Idem,* p. 395.
63. *Cartas,* p. 551.
64. *Idem,* p. 558.
65. AInd, Patronato 194, Ramo 19. Printed in *CodoinAm,* XLII, 69-71. Eventually Cobos built up a vast network of agents all over the Indies to collect his 1%. As late as the end of the 17th century this tax on gold and silver was known as the "rights of Cobos" *(derechos de Cobos)* (AInd, Charcas, Leg. 15); see also Restrepo, *Estudio sobre las minas,* p. 208, Nota (1), and Haring, "American gold and silver production . . . ," XXIX, 445, Note 1.
66. AcHist, MSS. Muñoz 75, fol. 54.
67. Salinas, *Cartas,* p. 553.
68. ASim, Estado 36, fol. 243.
69. *Cartas,* p. 465.
70. These letters are in ASim, Estado 12, fols. 167-177 (January 25 to February 6, 1534).
71. For the history of Cazorla, see Rivera Recio, *El adelantamiento de Cazorla,* 1948.
72. Details in Salazar y Mendoza, *Chrónica de el cardenal don Juan Tavera,* pp. 111 ff.; Salinas, *Cartas,* pp. 594-595.

73. Rivera Recio, *op. cit.*, p. 99.
74. March, *Niñez,* II, 118.
75. ASim, Estado 29, fol. 47.
76. *Cartas,* pp. 600, 608.
77. *Idem,* pp. 529-530.
78. AInd, Lima 565 (II, 60).
79. *Cartas,* p. 571.
80. *Idem,* pp. 591-592.
81. *Op. cit.,* II, 93-94.
82. AcEsp, *op. cit.*
83. *Cartas,* p. 587.
84. *Idem,* pp. 602-603.
85. AUbeda, "Relación verdadera."
86. ACam, Sabiote 3-8-58.
87. ASim, Estado 36, fol. 252.
88. Ruiz Prieto, *Historia,* II, 164.
89. ACam, Sabiote 3-8-9.
90. *Idem,* 3-8-16.

CHAPTER VIII

(pp. 166-193)

1. Santa Cruz, III, 204.
2. AHN, Santiago, Capítulos 1062 C and 1244 C.
3. Walser, "Spanien und Karl V," in *Nachrichten* (1932), pp. 167-171.
4. *Cartas,* p. 634.
5. *Idem,* p. 636.
6. ASim, Estado 268.
7. March, *Niñez,* II, 358.
8. *CodoinAm,* XLII, 498-501.
9. The account of these financial problems is found in ASim, Estado 34, fol. 208 ff. and Estado, 268.
10. AInd, Contaduría 270; Indif. general 1,092.
11. These letters are in ASim, Estado 31, fol. 2 ff.
12. ASim, Estado 496, fols. 297-298.
13. ASim, Estado 271.
14. Santa Cruz, III, 257.
15. *Manual de novells ardits,* IV, 26.
16. Gachet, *Documents inédits,* p. 13.
17. *Cartas,* pp. 625, 645.
18. *Idem,* pp. 632, 645.
19. AInd, Contratación 5,784; AcHist, MSS. Muñoz 80, fol. 159.
20. AInd, Lima 565 (II, 60); Patronato 246-2-19.
21. ASim, Estado 270.
22. ASim, Contaduría de mercedes 41, No. 33.
23. Salazar y Mendoza, *Chrónica,* p. 146; Rivera Recio, *op. cit.,* p. 101.
24. ASim, Registro general del Sello, III; ACam, Sabiote 3-1-23; AHN, Consejos 4,829, No. 4, Pt. 4 (May 2, 1535).
25. AInd, Patronato 246-2-16.

26. There are many contemporary descriptions of the *alarde:* see *Copia de una letra escrita en Barcelona,* (n. p., n. d.) ; *Traslado de la memoria que Su Magestad embió a la Emperatriz,* Medina del Campo, [1535] (BEsc, MSS. V. II. 4, fol. 67), reprinted in Pérez Pastor, *Imprenta en Medina del Campo,* pp. 411-414; García Cerezeda, *Tratado,* II, 7-10; Santa Cruz, III, 25. The tapestry, based on the design of Vermeyen, which depicts the scene is reproduced in March, *Niñez,* I, 192.
27. Bodleian Library, MSS. Rawl. D 648, p. 144.
28. Varchi, *Storia fiorentina,* III, 99.
29. Rivera Recio, *op. cit.,* p. 100.
30. ACA, Cancillería, No. 3,899.
31. In Schardius, *Historicum opus,* II, 1352; see also Sandoval, VI, 193 and Montoiche, *Voyage,* in Gachard, *Collection,* III, 335.
32. ACA, Cancillería, No. 3,899.
33. Dumont, *op. cit.,* IV, II, 128 ; Santa Cruz, III, 291-293.
34. Montoiche, *op. cit.,* III, 370.
35. Sandoval, VI, 358.
36. On Charles' visit to Messina, see Guazzo, *Historie,* p. 234 ff. ; Sala, *La triomphale entrata;* Santa Cruz, III, 294-300.
37. ASim, Estado, 1,111, fol. 122.
38. *Cartas,* p. 663.
39. Santa Cruz, III, 301-303.
40. ASim, Estado 1,111, fols. 122-123.
41. *Idem,* fol. 126.
42. *Idem,* fol. 124.
43. Salinas, *Cartas,* pp. 667, 673 ; Montoiche, *op. cit.,* III., 388 ; Berotius, *op. cit.,* II, 1,379.
44. Salinas, *Cartas,* p. 673.
45. ASim, Estado 1,311, fol. 44.
46. *Cartas,* p. 698.
47. For events in Naples in the winter of 1535-1536, see Rosso, *Historia delle cose di Napoli,* pp. 121 ff.; Giannone, *Dell'istoria . . . di Napoli,* IV, 57-62; Parrino, *Teatro eroico . . . di Napoli,* I, 156-161.
48. In his *Lettere volgari,* [1560], fol. 97.
49. *Historiarum sui temporis tomus secundus,* 1553-1554, II, 171.
50. Berotius, *op. cit.,* II, 1,379-1,380; Montoiche, *op. cit.,* III, 386-387.
51. Rosso, *op. cit.,* p. 126.
52. *Idem,* p. 127 ff.
53. Leti, *Vita dell' . . . imperadore Carlo V,* II, 337.
54. *Cartas,* p. 693.
55. *Idem,* pp. 684, 699.
56. Du Bellay, *Mémoires,* II, 397-398.
57. Varchi, *op. cit.,* III, 198 ; see also Segni, *Storie fiorentine,* pp. 189-190.
58. Gayangos, *Letters and despatches,* V, II, 64.
59. *Op. cit.,* III, 204, 209.
60. *Nuntiaturberichte,* Abt. I, Band I, 562-566.
61. *Die Kaiser-Idee Karls V,* pp. 232-233.
62. Rosso, *op. cit.,* pp. 127-129.
63. Gayangos, *op. cit.,* V, II, 24.
64. *Cartas,* pp. 693-695.
65. Under Cancelleria, Particolari.
66. Salinas, *Cartas,* p. 669.
67. Guazzo, *Historie,* fol. 141.
68. BM, MSS. Vit. B, XIV, fol. 164.

69. Podestà, "Carlo V a Roma," p. 316.
70. *Lettres*, p. 41.
71. *Ordine, pompe, apparati et ceremonie delle solenne intrate di Carlo V,* [1536]; Podestà, *op. cit.*, pp. 325-328; Santa Cruz, III, 326; Rabelais, *Lettres*, p. 20.
72. *Vita*, pp. 192-198.
73. Foronda, p. 421.
74. Du Bellay, *Mémoires*, II, 372.
75. BM, MSS. Vit. B, XIV, fol. 186; Capasso, *Paolo III*, I, 252; Salinas, *Cartas*, p. 712.
76. Pastor, *Histoire des Papes*, XI, 213; Du Bellay, *Mémoires*, II, 390.
77. ASim, Estado 1,183, fol. 7.
78. ASim, Estado 865, fol. 31.
79. Gayangos, *op. cit.*, V, II, 102-103.
80. *Nuntiaturberichte*, Abt. I, Band I, 583-584.
81. Santa Cruz, III, 425-427.
82. ASim, Estado 1,182, fol. 58.
83. *Idem*, fol. 209; Santa Cruz, III, 352.
84. *Nuntiaturberichte*, l. c.
85. Du Bellay, *Mémoires*, II, 393; Pastor, *Histoire*, XI, 214.
86. Vigo, *Carlo Quinto in Siena*, p. 49.
87. ASim, Estado 865, fols. 34-35.
88. Salinas, *Cartas*, p. 722.
89. Montecatini, *Entrata del Imperatore nella città di Lucca*, [1536].
90. Volpi, *Carlo V a Lucca*, pp. 41, 59-61.
91. Salinas, *Cartas*, p. 724.
92. *Idem*, pp. 726-727.
93. *Idem*, p. 742.
94. *Idem*, p. 751.
95. AModena, Cancelleria, Particolari.
96. ASim, Estado 1,181, fol. 68.
97. Salinas, *Cartas*, p. 777.
98. ASim, Estado 1, 183, fol. 136.
99. *Lettere di principi*, III, fols. 44-47; Capasso, *Paolo III*, II, 297.
100. Weiss, *Papiers d'état*, II, 498-499.
101. Salinas, *Cartas*, pp. 789-790.
102. Brandi, *The Emperor*, pp. 381-382.
103. Capasso, *op. cit.*, II, 301.
104. Salinas, *Cartas*, pp. 794-795; Foronda, p. 432.
105. ASim, Estado 1,184, fol. 161.
106. Salinas, *Cartas*, p. 795.
107. *Manual de novells ardits*, IV, 54.
108. Salinas, *Cartas*, p. 796.
109. Domínguez Bordona, *Proceso inquisitorial contra . . . Esteban Jamete*, p. 24.
110. *Arte de la pintura*, II, 42.
111. *Cosas granadinas*, p. 126 ff. See also Bosarte, *Viage artístico*, pp. 359 ff.
112. Bosarte suggests (pp. 129-132) that the paintings of Adam and Eve in the chapel of Fabio Nelli (church of the Agostinos Calzados) may be the work of Aquiles.
113. ASim, Estado 40, fol. 110; Santa Cruz, III, 435.
114. ASim, Quitaciones de Corte 16.
115. ASim, Diversos de Castilla 40, fol. 9.
116. ACam, Sabiote 3-1-6.
117. *Idem, l.c.;* ASim, Estado 40, fol. 53.

118. ASim, Registro general del Sello, III.
119. ACam, Sabiote 3-1-5.
120. ASim, Estado 40, fol. 53; ACam, Sabiote 3-1-9.
121. ASim, Registro general del Sello, III; ACam, Sabiote 3-1-7. There is an illuminated manuscript of this *cédula* in the Archivo de Camarasa.
122. ACam, Sabiote 3-1-8.
123. *Idem,* 3-1-9.
124. *Idem,* 3-1-10. In the following year Charles instructed Cobos to set guards in Sabiote to prevent poaching (*idem.* 3-1-11).
125. *Idem,* 3-1-12.
126. *Cartas,* 888-889.
127. González Palencia, *Vida . . . de Hurtado de Mendoza,* III, 294.
128. ASim, Estado 49, fol. 375.
129. ASim, Estado 1,369, fols. 134, 153; ACam, Sabiote 3-8-16.
130. AInd, Patronato 246-2-16.
131. Gómez Moreno, *Las águilas del Renacimiento,* pp. 202-208.
132. ASim, Estado K 1,642, No. 24 (January 1, 1538).
133. *Idem,* K 1,693, No. 48.
134. ASim, Estado 25, fol. 66.
135. Llaguno y Amírola, *Noticias de los arquitectos,* II, 167. The appointment dates from December 21, 1537.
136. ACam, Sabiote 3-8-22-2º.

Chapter IX

(pp. 194-222)

1. *Nuntiaturberichte,* Abt. I, Band II, p. 116.
2. Gayangos, *Letters and despatches,* V, II, 344.
3. *Cartas,* p. 799.
4. ASim, Estado K 1,642, Nos. 13-14.
5. *Idem,* No. 16.
6. *Idem,* Nos. 18-19.
7. Gayangos, *op. cit.,* pp. 376-377.
8. Salinas, *Cartas,* 815-817.
9. ASim, *l. c.,* No. 20.
10. Salinas, *Cartas,* p. 820; Gayangos, *op. cit.,* pp. 382, 390.
11. Dumont, *op. cit.,* IV, II, 154-157; *Publicatione della tregua & maneggio di pace,* [1538]; BM, MSS. Harl. 282, fol. 261.
12. ASim, *l. c.,* No. 21. Summarized in Gayangos, *op. cit.,* V, II, 393-415.
13. ASim, *l. c.,* No. 36c.
14. ASim, Estado 268.
15. ASim, Estado 1,184, fol. 162; Salinas, *Cartas,* pp. 825-826.
16. The following account is based on ASim, Estado K 1,642, Nos. 24-26, 29-33, 36-40, 47-49; K 1,643, No. 120.
17. Ribier, *Lettres et mémoires,* I, 336; Decrue, *Anne de Montmorency,* p. 334.
18. These two letters (K 1,642, Nos. 48 and 49) are printed, wrongly dated January 15, in Rassow, *Die Kaiser-Idee,* pp. 431-432, with a number of faulty transcriptions.
19. Text in Dumont, *op. cit.,* IV, II, 159.
20. Capasso, *Paolo III,* I, 478.

21. Gayangos, *op. cit.,* p. 377.
22. Foronda, p. 447.
23. Pedro de Gante, *Relaciones,* pp. 15-16; Rassow, *op. cit.,* p. 323.
24. Pedro de Gante, *op. cit.,* pp. 17-19.
25. ASim, Estado 268.
26. *Idem.*
27. ASim, Estado 270.
28. ASim, Estado 25, fol. 66.
29. ASim, Estado 19.
30. ASim, Estado K 1,693, No. 48.
31. ASim, Estado 25, fol. 66.
32. ASim, Estado 866, fol. 57; K 1629, No. 23.
33. ASim, Estado 21, fol. 47. Later, when the Conde Cifuentes asked for the appointment, Cobos commented: "Tell him that His Majesty is grateful for his services and anxious to favor him," (ASim, Estado 1458, fol. 49).
34. ASim, Quitaciones de Corte 16.
35. AInd, Patronato 246-2-18.
36. Schaefer, *El Consejo,* II, 69.
37. ASim, Estado 25, fol. 66.
38. ASim, Estado 19.
39. ASim, Estado 268.
40. After Cobos' death his widow bought Ximena and another nearby fortress, Recena, for 70,000 ducats (ACam, Sabiote 3-6-48).
41. Foronda, p. 457.
42. ACam, Sabiote 3-5-1 to 10; ASim, Mercedes y privilegios 341, fol. 14.
43. *Cartas,* pp. 834, 837.
44. ASim, Estado K 1,484, Nos. 97-98. The instruction to Schepper is summarized in Gayangos, *op. cit.,* pp. 450-454.
45. *Cartas,* p. 837.
46. Rassow, *op. cit.,* pp. 433-437 (ASim, Estado K 1642, No. 51).
47. Gayangos, *op. cit.,* p. 453.
48. There are many contemporary accounts of the events at Nice:
    Pedro de Gante, *Relaciones,* pp. 30-34; 175-180.
    Gayangos, *op. cit.,* pp. 484-486; 537 ff.
    Santa Cruz, III, 507-518.
    ASim, Estado 1,185, fol. 196 (Charles to the Empress).
    ASim, Guerra y Marina 12, fol. 156.
    Cronique du roy François, p. 240 ff.
    Archives curieuses, Série I, Tome 3, pp. 21-28.
    Venetianische Depeschen, I, 22 ff.
    Diarii udinensi, pp. 428 ff.
    Segre, "Documenti ed osservazioni sul congreso di Nizza," pp. 75-94.
    Dumont, *op. cit.,* IV, II, 172-181 (*Relazione* of Tiepolo).
    For later accounts, see:
    Cardauns, *Von Nizza bis Crépy,* pp. 4-6; 361-366.
    Decrue, *Anne de Montmorency,* pp. 352-353.
    Lambert, *Mémoires sur la vie de Charles, duc de Savoye,* col. 891.
    Leti, *Vita dell'* . . . *imperadore* Carlo V, II, 487.
    Pastor, *Histoire des Papes,* XI, 241-242.
    The following narrative presents a summary, with particular reference to the events in which Cobos took part.
49. *Venetianische Depeschen,* I, 22.
50. ASim, Estado 1,185, fols. 109-113.
51. *Venetianische Depeschen,* I, 48.

52. ASim, Estado 1,185, fol. 114.
53. *Venetianische Depeschen,* I, 61.
54. Pastor, *Histoire,* XI, 241, Note 1.
55. ASim, Estado 1,185, fol. 196.
56. *Cronique du roy,* p. 242.
57. Pastor, *op. cit.,* XI, 242.
58. Ribier, *Lettres et mémoires,* I, 167. Text of the truce in Dumont. *op. cit.,* IV, II, 169-172.
59. *Venetianische Depeschen,* I, 170.
60. ASim, Estado 1,371, fols. 80-81.
61. For the interview of Aigues-Mortes there are, in addition to the sources cited for the meeting at Nice, a number of other accounts:

   Accame "Una relazione inedita sul convegno di Acquemorte," (VI, 407-417).

   Relación muy verdadera sobre las paces en la villa de Aguas-muertas, [1538], reprinted in Espinosa y Quesada, *Cosas de España,* pp. 20-31.

   Rivoire, "L'entrevue du roy François Ier et de l'Empereur Charles V à Aigues-Mortes," in *Archives curieuses,* Série I, Tome 3, pp. 29-33.

   Schrijver, *Pacis inter Carolum V . . . et Franciscum primum . . . ad Aquas-Mortuas descriptio,* [1540]. (an allegorical poem)

   Staffetti, "Carlo V e Francesco I a Aigues-Mortes," (XXIII, 216-219)

   Letters of Charles V: in ASim, Estado 276; Estado 867, fol. 55; Lanz, *Korrespondenz,* II, 284-289.

   Letter of Francis I to the Empress, in ASim, Estado K 1484, No. 103.

   Letter of Gamiz to King Ferdinand, in Salinas, *Cartas,* pp. 869-871.

   Letter of Poggio to Farnese, in Cardauns, *op. cit.* p. 363.
62. AInd, Patronato 246-2-17.
63. AInd, Indif. general 423 (XVIII, 150).
64. ASim, Estado 42, fols. 168-169.
65. ACam, Sabiote 3-7-3 and 11; ASim, Registro general del Sello, III.
66. "Objetos artísticos de la iglesia de Velliza," in *BSCE,* I (1903-1904), 323.
67. ASim, Contaduría de mercedes 44, No. 63.
68. BEsc, MSS. V. II. 4, fols. 135-136.
69. Foronda, p. 458.
70. There are accounts in *Cortes,* V, 9-161; Salazar y Mendoza, *Chrónica,* pp. 191 ff.; Laiglesia, *Una crisis parlamentaria en 1538,* reprinted in his *Estudios históricos;* Cánovas del Castillo, "Carlos V y las Cortes de Castilla," in *España Moderna,* III, 73-115.
71. BM, MSS. Add. 5498, fol. 13.
72. *Cartas,* pp. 895-896.
73. *Idem,* pp. 896, 901-902; Santa Cruz, IV, 23-24.
73a. There is a painting by Vermeyen of a *juego de cañas,* at Toledo early in 1539, in Drayton House in England; see Glück, "Bildnisse aus dem Hause Habsburg," VII, 200.
74. *Cartas,* p. 902.
74a. There are many accounts; see, for example, Salinas, *Cartas,* pp. 902-903; Santa Cruz, IV, 21-23; Salazar y Mendoza, *Chrónica,* pp. 203-205; Sandoval, VII, 59-62; Ulloa, *Vita,* fol. 155; Núñez de Castro, *Historia,* pp. 182-183; Arteaga, *La Casa del Infantado,* pp. 332-333.
75. *Venetianische Depeschen,* I, 309-311; Salinas, *Cartas,* p. 906.
76. ASim, Estado 45, fol. 132.
77. ASim, Quitaciones de Corte 16.
78. ASim, Registro general del Sello, III.
79. ASim, Quitaciones de Corte 16.

80. The individual items are:

Secretary of the Council	100,000 *maravedís*
Secretary of State	150,000
Secretary of the Treasury	100,000
Secretary of the Indies	50,000
Secretary of Philip	100,000
Contador mayor	550,000
Teniente of Simancas	100,000
Total	1,150,000 *maravedís*

81. AInd, Patronato 150-51.
82. *Nuntiaturberichte,* Abt, I, Band III, p. 368.
83. *Idem,* Band IV, pp. 147, 417.
84. *CodoinAm,* IX, 453-454 (also XXX, 6).
85. ASim, Estado 45, fols. 238-239; Estado 46; AInd, Indif. general 737; *Codoin-Ult,* XVII, 10.

CHAPTER X

(pp. 223-247)

1. Weiss, *Papiers d'état,* II, 549-561.
2. *Venetianische Depeschen,* I, 382.
3. ASim, Estado 1,113, fol. 10; 1,315, fol. 230.
4. *Cartas,* p. 936.
5. González Palencia, *Don Luis de Zúñiga,* p. 56.
6. ASim, Estado 868, fol. 98.
7. *Idem,* fol. 97.
8. González Palencia, *l. c.*
9. *Idem,* p. 61.
10. ASim, Estado 45, fol. 240.
11. *Idem.*
12. Borja, II, 42.
13. Foronda, p. 457.
14. This story is told by Díaz del Castillo, *Verdadera historia,* II, 256-257. According to Fernández del Castillo (*Doña Catalina Xuárez Marcayda,* p. 29), the *maestre*'s real name was Pedro Muñoz.
15. ASim, Estado 869, fol. 156. Two years later Dr. Villalobos gave a somewhat different picture of the situation, when he wrote to Cobos: "Not many days ago I heard at Court that Your Lordship had sired another filly. I am sorry that it proved to be untrue, because, just as we are great friends, I should have been glad if we were also business associates, even if Doña María had not liked the idea of raising young mares." (*Algunas obras,* p. 150).
16. Fernández del Castillo, *op. cit.,* p. 30.
17. ASim, Estado 49, fol. 326.
18. Santa Cruz, IV, 27-28; Amador de los Ríos, *Historia de Madrid,* IV, Apéndice V.
19. ACam, Sabiote 3-8-22-3°; Gómez Moreno, *Las águilas del Renacimiento,* pp. 208-209; Campos Ruiz, "El contrato para construir la Sacra Capilla," (VII, 326-329, 358-359).

20. ASim, Estado 49, fol. 203.
21. ACam, Sabiote 3-8-16.
22. *Libro de la vida,* p. 183.
23. Sandoval, VII, 112; Amador de los Ríos, *op. cit.,* II, 439, 473.
24. ASim, Estado 49, fols. 44, 77.
25. *CodoinAm,* XLII, 178-179.
26. ASim, Estado 50, fol. 129.
27. ASim, Estado 54, fols. 50-51.
28. ASim, Contaduría de mercedes 48-1.
29. ACam, Sabiote 3-1-14; 3-5-10 and 11.
30. *Nuntiaturberichte,* Abt. I, Band V, p. 73.
31. AInd, Indif. general 423 (XIX, 182).
32. ASim, Estado 1,439, fol. 25.
33. ASim, Estado 868, fol. 152.
34. *Nuntiaturberichte,* l. c., p. 100.
35. *Idem,* p. 352.
36. Gayangos, *op. cit.,* VI, I, 263.
37. *Nuntiaturberichte,* Abt. I, Band VI, p. 164.
38. AParma, Busto 124.
39. ASim, Estado 869, fol. 104.
40. ASim, Registro general del Sello, III.
41. AHN, Consejos 4,829, No. 4, fols. 17-22.
42. ASim, Estado 49, fol. 198; Estado 870, fol. 15; González Palencia, *Vida . . . de Hurtado de Mendoza,* II, 299.
43. Santa Cruz, IV, 134.
44. ASim, Estado 51, fols. 268-269.
45. ASim, Estado 55, fols. 75, 27-28.
46. There are several accounts of the wedding: "Relación de las fiestas y regocijos que se han hecho en las bodas del duque y duquesa de Sesa," in *Relaciones de los reinados de Carlos V y Felipe II,* II, 157-169; Santa Cruz, IV, 134; AcHist, MSS. Muñoz 93. For Philip's part, see March, *Niñez,* I, 247.
47. ASim, Estado 51, fol. 253.
48. ASim, Estado 54, fol. 27.
49. March, *Niñez,* I, 294.
50. ASim, Estado 51, fol. 113.
51. *Idem,* fols. 163, 165, 235.
52. *Libro de la vida,* pp. 210-212.
53. ASim, Estado 52, fol. 31.
54. ASim, Estado 51, fol. 161.
55. ASim, Estado 51, fol. 75.
56. ASim, Estado 870, fol. 81.
57. ASim, Estado 49, fol. 250.
58. *Idem,* fol. 126.
59. ASim, Estado 52, fol. 70. Sarmiento replied on April 24 (Estado 372, fol. 174).
60. González Palencia, *Vida,* III, 310-312.
61. ASim, Estado 51, fol. 80; 52, fols. 93, 114.
62. Alvarez de Toledo, *Epistolario,* I, 4.
63. ASim, Estado 53, fol. 72; K 1698, No. 43.
64. ASim, Estado 1,460, fol. 144.
65. ASim, Estado 52, fol. 73.
66. ASim, Estado 51, fol. 178.
67. *Idem.*
68. ASim, Estado 52, fols. 98, 102.
69. ASim, Estado 51, fol. 233.

70. *Idem,* fol. 176.
71. ASim, Estado 52, fol. 102.
72. ASim, Estado 1,374, fol. 28.
73. González Palencia, *Vida,* III, 314.
74. *Carlo famoso,* fols. 248-257.
75. ASim, Estado 67, fol. 151.
76. *Crónica,* IV, 24.
77. There are several copies of the document: ACam, Sabiote 3-1-16; ASim, Contaduría de mercedes 48-1; AHN, Consejos 4,829, No. 4, Pt. 4. It is summarized in Salazar y Castro, *Historia genealógica de la Casa de Lara,* IV, 578-579, and González Palencia, *Vida,* I, 126.
78. This series, probably from designs by Van Orley, was popular in the 16th century. There are examples (five or six in the series) in the Royal Spanish Collection, the Kensington Museum and the Imperial Palace in Berlin; see Tormo Monzó and Sánchez Cantón, *Los tapices de la Casa del Rey N. S.,* pp. 125-128.
79. ASim, Registro del Sello, III; AHN, Consejos 4,829, No. 4, Pt. 4.

CHAPTER XI

(pp. 248-260)

1. ASim, Estado 280.
2. ASim, Estado 51, fol. 193.
3. ASim, Estado 58, fol. 75; 1,460, fol. 123.
4. ASim, Estado 54, fol. 60.
5. *Epístolas familiares,* fol. xiii.
6. Alvarez de Toledo, *Epistolario,* I, 42.
7. ASim, Estado 54, fol. 88.
8. *Catálogo de los cuadros,* p. 402.
9. ASim, Estado 51, fol. 142; 53, fols. 245, 307; 58, fol. 75.
10. ASim, Estado 53, fol. 309.
11. ASim, Estado 58, fols. 35-36, 39.
12. ASim, Quitaciones de Corte 16.
13. Santa Cruz, IV, 152.
14. Foronda, p. 518.
15. BN, MSS. 18,862 [82]; *Codoin,* XLIII, 240.
16. ASim, Estado 283; K 1,629, No. 22.
17. Foronda, p. 530.
18. Vandenesse, *Journal,* in Gachard, *Collection,* II, 247.
19. *Idem,* pp. 249, 250.
20. *La heroica vida . . . del grande S. Francisco de Borja,* p. 124.
21. ASim, Estado K 1,694.
22. ASim, Estado 287.
23. ASim, Estado 56, fol. 169.
24. ASim, Estado 1,187, fols. 19, 22; 1,188, fols. 115-116; 1,373, fols. 67, 93; 54, fol. 6.
25. ASim, Estado 52, fol. 114.
26. ASim, Estado 1,375, fol. 127.
27. Santa Cruz, IV, 222-236.
28. *Tratado de confirmaciones reales,* fols. 7-9.

29. AcHist, MSS. Muñoz 93, fol. 19.
30. Santa Cruz, IV, 318.
31. Brandi, *The Emperor,* p. 473.
32. Dormer, *Progreso de la historia,* pp. 39-40.
33. PRO, E 30 / 1,038.
34. ASim, Estado 61, fol. 211.
35. *Idem,* fol. 212.
36. Laiglesia, *Estudios históricos,* 2a ed., I, 66-67.
37. The first critical edition is that of Morel-Fatio, based on the original draft, in *Bulletin hispanique,* I (1899), 135-148. Later editions in Laiglesia, *op. cit.,* I, 69-79; March, *Niñez,* II, 11-22; Brandi, *Nachrichten der Gesellschaft der Wissenschaften zu Göttingen,* Phil.-Hist Kl., (1935), pp. 45-67.
38. The best available text is that of Brandi (*l. c.,* pp. 68-107) based upon Maurenbrecher's faulty readings of the original draft, which has disappeared, (*Forschungen zur deutschen Geschichte,* III (1863), 281-310). Also printed in Laiglesia, *op. cit.,* I, 81-92, and March, *Niñez,* II, 23-39, with notes from BN, MSS. 19,699, No. 43.

CHAPTER XII

(pp. 261-286)

1. ASim, Estado 289.
2. *Manual de novells ardits,* IV, 127.
3. Alvarez de Toledo, *Epistolario,* I, 25.
4. ASim, Estado 289.
5. *Idem,* l. c.; Estado 1,190, fol. 97; Estado 61, fols. 29-30, 251.
6. ASim, Estado 1,190, fol. 97.
7. ASim, Estado 286, 289; Estado 61, fol. 9; Alvarez de Toledo, *op. cit.,* I, 36-39.
8. ASim, Estado 289.
9. ASim, Registro general del Sello, III.
10. ASim, Estado 38, fols. 256, 266. (September 27, 1536). Even before this Diego and his sister had been taking dancing lessons from Juan de Araméndez, who was hoping through this contact to secure Cobos' support (Salinas, *Cartas,* p. 546.)
11. ASim, Estado 49, fols. 51, 55, 81. Rábago had already written to Cobos: "It wouldn't be a bad idea to get Doña Mencía for the Adelantado. Excuse my daring in suggesting it," (ASim, Estado 868, fol. 100). The "Doña Mencía" is certainly the famous Mencía de Mendoza, Marquesa de Ceñete, recently widowed by the death of Henry of Nassau and shortly to be married to the Duque de Calabria.
12. Saltillo, *Historia nobiliaria,* I, 107-108.
13. *Libro de la vida,* pp. 233-234.
14. *Idem,* pp. 235-236.
15. ASim, Estado 60, fol. 174.
16. *Libro, l.c.*
17. *Epistolario,* I, 39-42.
18. ASim, Estado 60, fol. 229.
19. ASim, Estado 286.
20. ASim, Estado 60, fol. 174.
21. ASim, Estado 63, fol. 100.

22. ASim, Estado 60, fols. 241, 257-258.
23. *Idem,* fol. 31.
24. There are several detailed accounts of the marriage of Philip and María: "Relación del recibimiento que se hizo a doña María, infanta de Portugal," in *Codoin,* III, 361-418.

   Sanabria, "Le mariage de Philippe II et de l'infante Marie de Portugal," in *Bulletin hispanique* XVII (1915), 15-35.

   AcHist, MSS. Salazar A-48, fols. 34-35.

   "Agasajos que hizo el Príncipe a su esposa," in March, *Niñez,* II, 80-91.

   Enríquez de Guzmán, *Libro de la vida,* pp. 242-243.

   Alvarez de Toledo, *Epistolario,* I, 45.
25. AcHist, MSS. Salazar A-48, fol. 34.
26. March, *Niñez,* II, 85.
27. Martí y Monsó, *Estudios histórico-artísticos,* pp. 443-444.
28. March, *Niñez,* I, 350. Shortly after, Cobos wrote to the Emperor that he had visited the Princess to tell her how the Emperor regretted that he had not been able to attend the wedding and to give her the rich jewel he had sent to her. The Princess expressed her deep thanks (ASim, Estado 68, fol. 359).
29. ASim, Estado 291; Borja, II, 479, 680-682; III, 582-583.
30. *Idem.*
31. BN, MSS. 10,300: "Copia de una carta que Francisco de los Cobos, grandemente estimado del señor emperador Carlos V, y su secretario de Estado, escribió a S. M. Cesárea, respondiendo a otra que tubo de dicho señor Emperador." Published by Walser in his "Spanien und Karl V: Fünf spanische Denkschriften," (*Nachrichten der Gesellschaft der Wissenschaften zu Göttingen,* Phil.-hist. Kl., 1932, pp. 173-177. There is a summary in an 18th century manuscript of the Fundación Lázaro, No. 15,167.
32. Walser, *op. cit.,* pp. 154-155.
33. March, *Niñez,* II, 76.
34. ASim, Estado 64, fol. 403.
35. ASim, Estado 67, fol. 80.
36. *Idem,* fol. 157.
37. *Cortes,* V, 265-343; ASim, Estado 65, fol. 173.
38. ASim, Estado 60, fol. 227.
39. ASim, Estado 68, Fol. 372.
40. *Epistolario,* I, 48-49.
41. *Historia . . . de Guadalaxara,* p. 184.
42. For an account of the preservation of state papers in Spain, see Walser, "Die Ueberlieferung der Akten der castilisch-spanischen Zentralbehörder unter Karl V," in *Nachrichten,* 1933, pp. 93-138, with a full bibliography.
43. AInd, Indif. general, 1,961 (I, 9).
44. Walser, *op. cit.,* pp. 97-98.
45. Romero de Castilla y Perosso, *Apuntes históricos sobre el Archivo General de Simancas,* pp. 18-19.
46. Sandoval, II, 122-123; *CodoinUlt,* VIII, 347; ASim, Estado 75, fol. 315.
47. AInd, Indif. general 420 (IX, 58); *CodoinUlt,* XX, 254.
48. ASim, Cédulas de la Cámara 75, fol. 365; Morel-Fatio, *Historiographie de Charles-Quint,* p. 27.
49. González Palencia, *Gonzalo Pérez,* I, 18.
50. ASim, Libros de copias, II, fols. 122-129.
51. *Guía histórica y descriptiva de los archivos,* I, 137.
52. *Idem,* I, 138.
53. AInd, Indif. general 423 (XX, 53, 99).

416   Francisco de los Cobos

54. Díaz Sánchez, *Guía de la villa y archivo de Simancas,* p. 19; ASim, Estado 49, fol. 81.
55. *Guía histórica,* I, 137.
56. Díaz Sánchez, *Guía,* p. 22.
57. *Idem,* p. 20.
58. Riol, *Informe,* in *Semanario erudito,* III, 81.
59. AInd, Indif. general 423 (XX, 267).
60. ASim, Estado 56, fol. 13.
61. ASim, Estado 500, fol. 6.
62. ASim, Estado 69, fol. 82.
63. Díaz Sánchez, *Guía,* p. 23.
64. Brandi, *The Emperor,* pp. 519-522.
65. ASim, Estado 67, fol. 148.
66. *Idem,* fols. 13-16.
67. *Idem,* fol. 144.
68. ASim, Estado 293.
69. ACam, Sabiote 8-22-4.
70. Domínguez Bordona, *Proceso inquisitorial contra . . . Jamete,* pp. 24-25.
71. ACam, Sabiote 3-8-16, 3-8-6.
72. AcHist, MSS. Salazar M-198, fols. 59-78. See also Campos Ruiz, "La Sacra Capilla del Salvador," VI, 304-306.
73. ASim, Estado 64, fol. 151; Estado 293; Borja, II, 472-473.
74. *Codoin,* XCVII, 238.
75. ASim, Estado 67, fol. 154; Estado 293.
76. ASim, Estado 280; Borja, II, 281.
77. ASim, Estado 52, fol. 98.
78. ASim, Estado 289.
79. ACam, Rivadavia, 2-1-43.
80. ASim, Estado 64, fol. 131; Borja, II, 496, 686-687.
81. *Libro de la vida,* MS., p. 508.
82. *Idem,* pp. 509-510.
83. Arriaga, *Historia del Colegio de San Gregorio,* I, 491-493.
84. Sanuto, LVII, 113.
85. Pedro de Gante, *Relaciones,* pp. 17-20.
86. Foronda, p. 477.
87. ACam, Rivadavia 1-1-4. He had inherited the title and estate of Rivadavia on the death of his mother in April, 1542 (ACam, Sabiote 3-1-14).
88. González Palencia, *Don Luis de Zúñiga,* p. 93.
89. ASim, Estado 51, fol. 78; Estado 52, fol. 114. He was in Mallorca, about to embark for Algiers, in October (Gayangos, *Letters and despatches,* VI, I, 373).
90. Santa Cruz, IV, 261.
91. ASim, Estado 55, fol. 30.
92. ASim, Estado 1,375, fol. 127.
93. ASim, Estado 67, fol. 154.
94. *Idem.*
95. *Idem,* fol. 145.
96. ASim, Estado 25, fol. 66.
97. ASim, Estado 268.
98. *Idem.*
99. ASim, Estado 1,113, fol. 19.
100. ASim, Estado 1,114, fols. 48-49.
101. ASim, Estado 55, fol. 31; Estado 51, fol. 79. On his way back to Naples he

stayed with the Marqués de Lombay. On July 6 Cobos wrote that he was glad he had left.

102. ASim, Estado 1,460, fol. 164; Estado 57, fol. 257.
103. ACam, Rivadavia 2-1-39.
104. ASim, Estado 857, fol. 203 (November 8, 1532).
105. *CodoinAm*, XXII, 406-433; *Libro de la vida*, MS., pp. 237-242.
106. *Historia general*, Dec. V, 149.
107. *CodoinAm*, VII, 432.

CHAPTER XIII

(pp. 287-308)

1. ASim, Estado 13, fol. 56.
2. ASim, Estado 69, fol. 80.
3. ASim, Estado 61, fol. 246.
4. *Libro de la vida*, p. 49.
5. Borja, III, 266; Cienfuegos, *op. cit.*, p. 35.
6. ASim, Estado 373, fol. 294.
7. March, *Niñez*, I, 198.
8. ASim, Estado 61, fol. 248.
9. *Idem, fol.* 247.
10. *Idem,* fol. 248.
11. ASim, Quitaciones de Corte 16.
12. March, *Niñez*, I, 350.
13. Foronda, p. 573.
14. *Vita,* fol. 177.
15. ASim, Casa Real 32.
16. ASim, Estado 69, fol. 54.
17. *Idem.*
18. Martín González, *Guía . . . de Valladolid,* 2a ed., *Addenda.*
19. Santa Cruz, IV, 540.
20. ASim, Casa Real 32.
21. ASim, Estado 69, fol. 133.
22. BBesançon, Collection Granvelle, MSS. 70, fol. 152. There is a copy in BN (Paris), MSS. Fr. 7,122, pp. 364-365.
23. ASim, Estado 69, fol. 54.
24. The chief sources for these events are Recio Rivera, *El adelantamiento de Cazorla,* and Salazar y Mendoza, *Chrónica de el cardenal Juan Tavera.*
25. AHN, Consejos 27,894.
26. Recio Rivera, *op. cit.,* p. 100.
27. *Idem,* p. 109.
28. AHN, Consejos 27,894.
29. ASim, Estado 69, fol. 54.
30. ASim, Estado 70, fol. 81.
31. AHN, Consejos 27,893.
32. Salazar y Mendoza (*Chrónica,* p. 146 ff.) names the lone dissenter as Juan de Vergara.
33. Recio Rivera, p. 110.
34. ASim, Estado 501, fol. 118.
35. ASim, Estado 49, fol. 83.

36. *Codoin,* I, 151.
37. *Felipe Segundo,* II, 11.
38. AcHist, MSS. Muñoz 93, fol. 25.
39. ASim, Estado 69, fol. 69; *Codoin,* I, 151.
40. AHN, Consejos 27,894.
41. ASim, Estado 73, fol. 173.
42. *Idem,* fol. 214.
43. AParma, Busto 125.
44. Recio Rivera, p. 106.
45. *Idem,* pp. 107-117.
46. ASim, Estado 73, fol. 194.
47. *Idem,* fol. 210.
48. González Palencia, *Vida . . . de Hurtado de Mendoza,* III, 334.
49. Döllinger, *Dokumente zur Geschichte Karls V,* p. 132.
50. González Palencia, *op. cit.,* III, 337.
51. ASim, Estado 502, fol. 185.
52. ACam, Sabiote 3-2-4.
53. ASim, Estado 73, fol. 216.
54. *Libro de la vida,* p. 286.
55. ASim, Estado 73, fol. 185.
56. March, *Niñez,* I, 209.
57. ASim, Estado 73, fol. 178.
58. Döllinger, *op, cit.,* 43-47.
59. *Estudios históricos,* 1a. ed., pp. 236-237.
60. Carande, *Carlos V y sus banqueros,* II, 400.
61. ASim, Estado 73, fol. 158.
62. *Idem.*
63. *Idem,* fols. 6, 146.
64. *Idem,* fol. 205.
65. *Idem,* fol. 26.
66. *Idem,* fol. 151.
67. *Idem,* fol. 152.
68. *Idem,* fol. 88.
69. Gams, *Series episcoporum,* p. **73.**
70. ASim, Estado 300.
71. March, *Niñez,* I, 88.
72. ASim, Estado 73, fol. 141.
73. *Crónica,* IV, 541.
74. ASim, Estado 69, fol. 189.
75. Santa Cruz, *Crónica, l. c.*
76. March, *Niñez,* I, 211.
77. ASim, Estado 73, fol. 64.
78. AHN, Estado 2,450, No. 68.
79. ASim, Estado 73, fol. 204; Estado 1,192, fol. 292. The original rough draft
    gave the place as Madrid and Mondéjar and Cobos as the signatories.
80. ASim, Estado 73, fol. 205.
81. *Idem,* fol. 158.
82. *Idem,* fol. 204.
83. *Idem,* fol. 210.
84. ASim, Estado K 1,486, No. 68.
85. ASim, Estado 73, fol. 206.
86. AInd, Justicia 1,020-1.
87. ASim, Estado 642.
88. ASim, Estado 73, fol. 156.

89. ASim, Estado 75, fol. 314.
90. *Idem,* fol. 315.
91. AcHist, MSS. Muñoz 93, fol. 25 ; Santa Cruz, V, 91.
92. ASim, Estado 49, fol. 397.
93. ASim, Estado 75, fol. 310.
94. *Idem,* fol. 311.
95. ASim, Estado 49, fol. 395.
96. *Idem,* fol. 396.
97. ASim, Estado 75, fol. 3.
98. The documents on these last days are found in ASim, Estado 301. See also Campos Ruiz, *Guía . . . de Ubeda,* II, 50.
99. ASim, Quitaciones de Corte 16.

Chapter XIV
(pp. 309-331)

1. ASim, Estado 301.
1a. Dormer, *Progresos,* p. 479.
2. ASim, Estado 1,379, fol. 281.
3. ASim, Estado 374, fol. 45.
4. ASim, Estado 301.
5. ASim, Estado 297.
6. ASim, Estado 75, fol. 77.
7. ASim, Estado 65, fol. 245.
8. ASim, Estado 300.
9. ASim, Estado 1,379, fols. 278, 226.
10. ASim, Estado 300; Registro general del Sello; BEsc, MSS. V-II-4, fol. 310; Cabrera, *Felipe Segundo,* II, 10-11.
11. Döllinger, *Dokumente,* p. 91.
12. ASim, Estado 283 ; Santa Cruz, V, 94.
13. ASim, Estado 301.
14. ASim, Estado 300.
15. *Idem.*
16. *Idem.*
17. ASim, Estado 59, fol. 247 ; Santa Cruz, V, 95.
18. ASim, Escribanía mayor de rentas 517.
19. ACam, Sabiote 3-1-17.
20. There is a pendant of this type in the collection of the Hispanic Society of America, with the figure of the Virgin in enamel, surrounded by small pearls, and with two large pendant pearls.
21. ASim, Hacienda, Contaduría de mercedes 48-1, No. 4.
22. ACam, Sabiote 3-1-18.
23. ASim, Patronato Real, fol. 10.
24. Laiglesia, *Estudios históricos,* la ed., pp. 646-650.
25. ACam, Sabiote 3-2-4.
26. Laiglesia, *op. cit.,* pp. 236-237 ; Hamilton, *American treasure,* p. 34.
27. The following tables give the details. Figures marked with an * are estimates.

Assets (as of May 10, 1547)

Real estate
Valladolid
  Palace   *15,000,000 mrs.
  Huerta de Río de Olmos   —
  Houses   —
Ubeda
  Palace   *15,000,000
  Houses in the city   —
  Orchards, vineyards, etc,   —
Sabiote
  Fortress   18,510,000
  Houses   —
Torres and Canena
  Fortresses   21,796,000
  Houses and lands   —
Velliza
  Town   3,262,000
  Houses   —
Properties of the Marquesa de Camarasa 5,625,000
Cañada de la Nava—Land   —
Cabezón—House   —
Cazorla—Houses   —
Iruela—Houses   —
Quesada—Houses   —
Aguilarejo—Mill   —
    Total   79,193,000 mrs.
Alcabalas
  Sabiote   16,590,000
  Torres and Canena   7,875,000
  Velliza   1,030,000
    Total   25,495,000 mrs.
Juros (purchased 1519-1545)   17,100,000 mrs.
Loans outstanding
  Charles V   6,875,000
  Marqués de Alcaudete   750,000
  Genoese bankers   750,000
  Tomás de Forne   157,000
    Total   8,532,000 mrs.
Total assets (not including the value of houses and lands)
                              130,320,000 mrs.
                            (347,000 ducats)

Cash Balances (as of May 10, 1547)

In agent's hands
  Almaguer, Contador de Castilla   20,264,000 mrs.
  Zárate, Contador de Indias   5,653,000
  Rodrigo de Dueñas, Banker   4,514,000
  Ramírez, Encomienda de León   4,121,000
  Ribera, Mines in Azuaga   395,000
  Baeza, Mines in Cartagena   2,158,000

Ortega, Chaplain	1,343,000
Verdugo de Henao, Majordomo of Valladolid	656,000
Amador, Majordomo of Cazorla	2,218,000
Baeza, Majordomo of Ubeda	53,000
González de la Rua, Chamberlain	168,000
García de Vallejo, Salt mines of Pinilla	325,000
Bernaldo, Simancas	23,000
Biedma, Collector	143,000
Total	43,034,000 mrs.

Due on unpaid salaries, fees, etc.

Royal salaries	
Castile	984,000
Simancas	400,000
Granada	525,000
Orán	102,000
Fuente de Cantos	96,000
Campo de Dalías	8,000
Pension in Milan	480,000
Total	2,595,000
Total balances	45,629,000 mrs.
	(122,000 ducats)

Income (1546)

Real estate	
Cazorla	*3,000,000 mrs.
Sabiote	1,296,000
Torres and Canena	1,526,000
Velliza	228,000
Other houses and lands	—
	6,050,000
Alcabalas	
Sabiote	1,161,000
Torres and Canena	551,000
Velliza	52,000
	1,764,000
Juros	1,191,000
Mine rights	
Azuaga	142,000
Cartagena	1,240,000
	1,382,000
Salaries	
Royal	
Secretary—Castile	100,000
— —Estado	150,000
— —Hacienda	100,000
— —Cámara	50,000
— —Indias	50,000
— —Philip	100,000

Contador mayor	582,000
Alcaide—Simancas	100,000
	1,232,000
Other	
Alguazil de Talavera	70,000
Alcalde de Fuente de Cantos	28,000
Escribano del crimen—Ubeda	187,000
Escribano de Alcaraz	50,000
Regidor de Ubeda	*100,000
Regidor de Valladolid	*100,000
	535,000

Grants, privileges and pensions	
Comendador mayor de León	2,250,000 mrs.
Fundidor de las Indias	*4,400,000
Pension in Milan	480,000
Saltmines of Pinilla	274,000
Saltmines in the Indies	—
	7,404,000
Office fees	
Castile	50,000
Rentas y mercedes	75,000
Granada	82,000
Orán	51,000
Naples	50,000
Indies seal	17,000
Campo de Dalías	8,000
	333,000

Totals	
Real Estate	6,050,000 mrs.
Alcabalas	1,764,000
Juros	1,191,000
Mine rights	1,382,000
Salaries	1,767,000
Grants, etc.	7,404,000
Office fees	333,000
	19,891,000 mrs.
	(53,000 ducats)

28. Marineo Siculo, *op. cit.,* fols. xxiii-xxv; Laiglesia, *op. cit.,* pp. 721-727.
29. In Albèri, *Relazioni,* I, 344.
30. *Miscelánea,* in *MHE,* XI, 241.
31. Saltillo, *Doña Mencía de Mendoza,* p. 51.
32. Villalón, *Ingeniosa comparación,* pp. 172-173.
33. AInd, Justicia 1,180-1-1; Patronato 246-2-20.
34. ACam, Sabiote 3-6-48 ff.
35. ASim, Contaduría de mercedes 93, fol. 17.
36. AInd, Patronato 170-51.
37. *Idem.*
38. AInd, Indif. general 1,093; *CodoinUlt,* XVIII, 82.
39. AInd, Patronato 170-51; ASim, Guerra antigua 41, fol. 258.
40. AcHist, MSS. Muñoz 75, fols. 67-68.

41. AInd, Patronato 170-51.

42. AcHist, *ms. cit.,* fol. 65.

43. *Idem,* fol. 68.

44. Laiglesia, *Estudios,* 2a ed., I, 86.

45. ASim, Estado 12, fol. 171.

46. ASim, Secretaría, Expedientes 20, No. 34; Libros de copias de documentos, II, 233-243.

47. Martos López, *Monumentos de Ubeda, passim.*

48. Ruiz Prieto, *Historia,* II, 165.

49. ACam, Rivadavia, 2-3-15.

50. ACam, Sabiote 3-9-15.

51. AUbeda, *Relación verdadera;* González García-Valladolid, *Datos,* p. 313.

52. *Idem,* pp. 313-314.

53. ACam, Rivadavia 4-1-7, 11 and 13.

54. Agapito y Revilla, "Estancia provisional de Santa Teresa . . . en el palacio de Cobos," in *BSCE,* IV, 529-532; Sangrador Minguela, "Más sobre la estancia de Santa Teresa en Valladolid," in *BSCE,* VI, 573-574.

55. Agapito y Revilla, "La Capilla Real de Valladolid," in *BSEE,* LXVIII (1944), 115-144, 161-203.

56. ASim, Estado 869, fol. 31.

57. Orlandini, *Historiae Societatis Iesu,* p. 160.

58. Borja, II, 496 (Note); March, *Niñez,* II, 394.

59. March, *l. c.*

60. ACam, Sabiote 3-9-14.

61. Agapito y Revilla, "Estancia . . .", p. 530.

62. Santa Teresa, *Libro de las fundaciones,* in her *Obras,* II, 725-731; *Apuntes para el historial . . . de Camarasa,* pp. 91-93.

63. *Apuntes,* p. 95.

64. In her *Obras,* II, 727.

65. ACam, Sabiote 3-9-16.

66. AUbeda, "La visita del año de 68 que hiço Su Señoría Illustrísima, mi señora, en la iglesia del Salvador."

67. López de Haro, *Nobiliario,* II, 90.

68. ACam, Sabiote 3-2-15.

69. ASim, Contaduría de mercedes 48-1, No. 6.

70. Campos Ruiz, "La Sacra Capilla," (VI, 251).

71. Allende Salazar and Sánchez Cantón, *Retratos del Museo del Prado,* p. 44.

72. González Palencia, *Vida . . . de Hurtado de Mendoza,* III, 247.

73. Sánchez Cantón, *Documentos de la Catedral de Toledo,* II, 302-303.

73a. *Obras,* I, 7-8. Two of Cetina's sonnets are addressed to the Duque de Sesa ("Sesenio"), who was also responsible for a *copla* and for a sonnet on the evils of poverty!

74. P. 29.

75. *Opera,* 1619, pp. 38, 76, 118, 201.

76. AcHist, MSS. Salazar A-112, fol. 548.

77. Albèri, *Relazioni,* I, 345.

78. *Cartas,* p. 591.

79. AInd, Justicia 1171 (October 21, 1540).

80. *Cartas de Indias,* pp. 494-502.

81. AUbeda, Relación verdadera.

82. Fol. 139 (Canto XXV).

83. Macías, "Lágrimas del Apóstol San Pablo (!)" (II, 316).

84. *Felipe Segundo,* III, 231.

85. *Libro de la vida,* pp. 295-296.

86. *Zárate, Historia . . . del Perú,* in *BAE,* XXVI, 511.
87. Rivera Recio, *op. cit.,* 114.
88. Ruiz Prieto, *Historia,* I, 173.
89. AHN, Ordenes militares, Santiago, Expediente 1985 bis.
90. Ruiz Prieto, *l. c.*
91. AcHist, MSS. Salazar C-14, fol. 805.

Chapter XV

(pp. 332-355)

1. *Cartas,* p. 100.
2. *Annals,* p. 255.
3. *Cartas,* p. 210.
4. ASim, Estado 67, fol. 164.
5. Paz y Melia, *Sales españolas,* pp. 272, xxix.
6. Foronda, p. 395.
7. ASim, Quitaciones de Corte 16.
8. *Nuntiaturberichte,* Abt. I, Band V, p. 73.
9. ASim, Estado 41, No. 33.
10. ASim, Estado 49, fol. 118.
11. ASim, Estado 61, fol. 266.
12. Carande, *op. cit.,* II, 183-184.
13. ASim, Estado 42, fol. 118.
14. ASim, Estado 51, fol. 253.
15. ASim, Estado 61, fol. 289.
16. ASim, Estado 1,190, fol. 97.
17. ASim, Estado 61, fol. 245.
18. ASim, Estado 64, fol. 158.
19. The rules for the meetings of the Councils are found in ASim, Estado 11.
20. *The Emperor,* p. 463.
21. *The Emperor,* p. 236.
22. ASim, Estado 51, fol. 260.
23. ASim, Estado 867, fol. 124.
24. ASim, Estado 869, fol. 67.
25. *Il secondo libro delle Lettere,* II, 256-257.
26. González Palencia, *Don Luis de Zúñiga,* pp. 68, 70-71.
27. *Historia del Emperador,* p. 352.
28. Albèri, *Relazioni,* I, 344-345.
29. *Cartas,* p. 837.
30. In his *Opera,* II, 93-94.
31. *Annals,* p. 255-256.
32. ASim, Estado 68, fol. 367. Printed by Walser in *Nachrichten* . . . (1932), pp. 177-181.
33. ASim, Patronato Real 62, fols. 9-10.
34. ASim, Estado 1,374, fol. 135.
34a. ASim, Estado 1,458, fol. 213.
35. ASim, Estado 1,376, fol. 207.
36. ASim, Estado 1,440, fol. 53.
37. ASim, Estado 1,189, fol. 37.

38. ASim, Estado 1,179, fol. 151.
39. ASim, Estado 72, fol. 345.
40. Edition of 1530, fols. ii-iv.
41. Edition of 1538, fol. a ij.
42. *La música en la Corte de Carlos V*, p. 89. See also Pujol in his edition of *Los seys libros del Delfín*, p. 11.
43. Edition of 1538 : *Prólogo*, fol. ij.
44. Edition of 1539, fols. [iii]-[v].
45. Edition of 1539, fols. [I]-[II].

CHAPTER XVI

(pp. 356-374)

1. *Annals*, p. 255.
2. *Cartas*, p. 835.
3. *Historia*, III, 170.
4. The best reproduction is in Tyler, *op. cit.*, p. 316. See also Allende Salazar and Sánchez Cantón, *Retratos*, Lámina V^2.
5. See above, p. 177.
6. 2e. éd., II, 185, No. 3.
7. *Catálogo de los cuadros*, No. 528 (p. 753).
8. Pérez Pastor, *Noticias y documentos*, II, 111 (No. 559).
9. Allende Salazar and Sánchez Cantón, *op. cit.*, p. 43.
10. *Historia*, III, 170.
11. *Cartas*, ed. Heine, p. 19. In connection with Loaisa's remark about the Emperor's negligence, it might be noted that in his description of the Emperor Santa Cruz observed: "He was not very fond of official business, and as he had a lot of it, he would unload it on a secretary. As a result, decisions were delayed and there was much complaint" (*Crónica*, II, 38).
12. *Codoin*, XCVII, 278.
13. Albèri, *Relazioni*, I, 344-345.
14. *Annals*, p. 255.
15. *Opera*, II, 94. So too Paolo Giovio described him as "ingenio fideque spectatum."
16. *Miscelánea*, in *MHE*, XI, 184-185. In his *Carlo famoso* (fol. 139) Zapata devotes a stanza to the arms of Cobos:
    "Y en el escudo azul, cinco leones
    De oro, cada qual con su corona.
    De los Cobos, que son nobles varones,
    Estas armas adornan la persona,
    Como las peñas son de los halcones
    Los nidos, y Lybia es de la leona
    Las partes donde aquellos y esta cría,
    Assí de aquestos es la Andaluzía."
    In a manuscript genealogy of the Cobos family in the R. Academia de la Historia (Salazar H-13, fol. 146) there is a verse on Cobos:
    "Es don Francisco, lector,
    de los Cobos el que ves,
    gran comendador mayor
    de León, cuyo valor
    muy claro y sabido es.

Fué varón muy señalado
y de don Carlos amado,
emperador de Alemaña,
por quien los reynos de España
creyeron (?) ser muy preçiado."

17. I have used the copy in the library of the Real Academia Española.

17a. For a similar picture of Court life, see Guevara, *Menosprecio de Corte,* pp. 154-159.

18. Gachard, *Relations des ambassadeurs,* p. xxxii.

19. Albèri, *op. cit.,* I, 344-345.

20. *Op. cit.,* p. 237. He is probably following Rassow (*Die Kaiser-Idee,* pp. 235-236) who misinterpreted a remark in the *Mémoires* of Du Bellay (II, 322).

21. *Annals,* pp. 255-256.

22. *Crónica,* II, 38.

23. AMantova, No. 567.

24. *Cartas,* p. 835.

25. ASim, Estado 54, fol. 212.

26. ASim, Guerra y Marina 6, fol. 111.

27. ASim, Estado 1,317, fol. 32.

28. Campori, "Sebastiano del Piombo," II, 193-198; Vasari, *Le vite,* V, 679; Panofsky, "Die Pietà von Ubeda," pp. 151, 275-280.

29. ASim, Estado 853, fol. 122.

30. ASim, Estado 864, fol. 123.

31. ASim, Estado 49, fol. 221.

32. ASim, Estado 25, fol. 66.

33. ASim, Estado 49, fol. 158.

33a. A long manuscript (81 folios) in the British Museum (Sloane 2, 798) bears the title: *Relación de la passada del rey Francisco 1º de Francia en persona en Italia con gran exército y de su prisión sobre Pavia por las armas del emperador Carlos Quinto, escrita por el Comendador Mayor, Francisco de los Cobos, su secretario de Estado.* The title is repeated on the second folio, but the words "escrita por el Comendador Mayor, etc." are omitted. There is another *Relación* on the same theme in the library of the Real Academia Española, MS. 58. It is hardly credible that Cobos could have written this account; Gayangos has suggested that the word "por," after "escrita," is an error of the copyist for "para."

34. Angulo Iñiguez, *La mitología y el arte español del Renacimiento,* pp. 72, 100-101. On the Hercules theme, see Simone, *Hercule et le Cristianisme,* Paris, n. d.

35. Brandi, *Kaiser Karl V,* II, 373.

BIBLIOGRAPHY

Abarca, Pedro. *Segunda parte de los Anales históricos de los reyes de Aragón.* 2 vols. Salamanca, 1684.

R. Academia de la Historia, Madrid. *Indice de la colección de don Luis de Salazar y Castro.* (in progress) Madrid, 1950-

Accame, Paolo. "Una relazione inedita sul convegno di Acquemorte," in *Giornale storico e letterario della Liguria,* VI (1905), 407-417.

Achiardi, Pietro d'. *Sebastiano del Piombo.* Roma, 1908.

Agapito y Revilla, Juan. "La Capilla Real de Valladolid," in *Boletín de la Sociedad Española de Excursiones,* LXVIII (1944), 115-144, 161-203.

———— "Del Valladolid monumental. La iglesia del convento de San Pablo," in *Boletín de la Sociedad Castellana de Excursiones,* V (1911-1912), 193-199.

———— "Estancia provisional de Santa Teresa de Jesús en el palacio del secretario Cobos en Valladolid," in *Idem,* VI, 529-532.

———— "Objetos artísticos de la iglesia de Velliza," in *Idem,* I (1903-1904), 319-323.

Albèri, Eugenio, ed. *Relazioni degli ambasciatori veneti al Senato.* 14 vols. Firenze, 1839-1855.

Alcocer, Pedro de. *Relación de algunas cosas que pasaron en estos reinos desde que murió la reina católica doña Isabel hasta que se acabaron las Comunidades.* Sevilla, 1872. *(Sociedad de Bibliófilos Andaluces)*

Alcocer y Martínez, Mariano. *Catálogo razonado de obras impresas en Valladolid, 1481-1800.* Valladolid, 1926.

Alenda y Mira, Jenaro. *Relaciones de solemnidades y fiestas públicas de España.* Madrid, 1903.

Allende Salazar, Juan and Sánchez Cantón, F. J. *Retratos del Museo del Prado.* Madrid, 1919.

Altolaguirre y Duvale, Angel de. *Don Pedro de Alvarado, conquistador del reino de Guatemala.* Madrid, 1927.

Alvarez de Toledo, Agustín. *Discursos sobre el govierno de Spaña.* BN, MSS. 904, fols. 99-137.

Alvarez de Toledo, Hernán, duque de Alba. *Epistolario.* 3 vols. Madrid, 1952.

Amadei, Federigo. *Cronaca universale della città di Mantova.* 2 vols. Mantova, 1954-1955.

Amador de los Ríos, José. *Historia de la Villa y Corte de Madrid.* 4 vols. Madrid, 1860-1864.

Andrews, Arthur Irving. *The campaign of Charles V against Tunis.* Ph.D. dissertation, Harvard University, 1905.

Anglés, Higinio. *La música en la Corte de Carlos V.* Barcelona, 1944.

Angulo Iñiguez, Diego. *La mitología y el arte español del Renacimiento.* Madrid, 1952.

Antigüedades de la villa de Simancas, escritas en el año de 1580. AcHist, MSS. Salazar H-3, fols. 103-139.

Antolínez de Burgos, Juan. *Historia de Valladolid,* ed. Juan Ortega y Rubio. Valladolid, 1887.

Apuntes para el historial de la Casa de Camarasa. San Sebastián, 1934.

Archives curieuses, see [Lafist, Louis]

Aretino, Pietro. *Del primo libro delle Lettere.* Parigi, 1609.

———— *Il primo libro delle Lettere,* ed. Fausto Nicolini. Bari, 1913. (*Scrittori d'Italia,* 53)

———— *Il secondo libro delle Lettere,* ed. Fausto Nicolini. Bari, 1916. 2 vols. (*Scrittori d'Italia,* 76-77)

Argote de Molina, Gonzalo. *Nobleza del Andaluzía.* Sevilla, 1588.

Armand, Alfred. *Les médailleurs italiens des quinzième et seizième siècles.* 2e éd. 2 vols. Paris, 1883-1887.

Armstrong, Edward. *The Emperor Charles V.* 2 vols. London, 1902.

Arriaga, Fray Gonzalo de. *Historia del Colegio de San Gregorio de Valladolid,* ed. Manuel María Hoyos. 3 vols. Valladolid, 1928-1940.

Arteaga y Falguera, Cristina. *La Casa del Infantado, cabeza de los Mendoza.* Madrid, 1940.

Atienza, Julio de. *Nobiliario español.* 2a ed. Madrid, [1954].

Avisos de lo que convendría hacerse para evitar algunos abusos en el gobierno. *Codoin,* LXXXVIII, 504-506.

Ballesteros y Beretta, Antonio. *Historia de España y su influencia en la historia universal.* 9 vols. Madrid, [1918]-1941.

Bataillon, Marcel. *Erasme et l'Espagne.* Paris, 1937.

"La batalla de Mühlberg (1547); relación contemporánea ed. J. M. de Garamendi," in *RABM,* 3a época, XXV (1911), 432-450.

Baumgarten, Hermann. *Geschichte Karls V.* 3 vols. Stuttgart, 1885-1892.

Bergenroth, Gustav Adolph. *Calendar of letters, despatches and state papers relating to the negotiations between England and Spain.* Vols. I-II. London, 1862-1868.

Berichte und Studien zur Geschichte Karls V, I-XIII, in *Nachrichten,* etc. 1930-1935.

Bermúdez de Pedraza, Francisco. *El secretario del Rey.* 3a ed. Madrid, 1720.

Bernárdez, Antonio. *Enrique Cornelio Agripa . . . Traducción al castellano de la* Historia de la doble coronación del Emperador en Bolonia, *escrita en latín.* Madrid, 1934.

Bernays, Isaac. "Zur inneren Entwicklung Castiliens unter Karl V," in *Deutsche Zeitschrift für Geschichtswissenschaft,* I (1889), 381-428.

Berni y Catalá, José. *Creación, antigüedad y privilegios de los títulos de Castilla.* Valencia, 1769.

[Berotius, Joannes]. *Commentarium, seu potius Diarium expeditionis tunetanae a Carolo V, Imp. semper augusto, anno MDXXXV susceptae, Ioanne Etropio autore,* in Schardius, *Historicum opus,* II, 1341-1381.

Blázquez, Antonio. "Relación de los corregimientos (1516)," in *Papeles his-*

tóricos inéditos del Archivo de la Secretaría de la R. Academia de la Historia. Madrid, 1920, pp. 300-307.

Bofarull y Broca, Antonio de. *Historia crítica (civil y eclesiástica) de Cataluña.* 9 vols. Barcelona, 1876-1878.

Bofarull y de Sartorio, Manuel de. "Festejos y ceremonias públicas celebrados en Barcelona cuando la primera venida de su XXVIII conde D. Carlos I," in *La Discusión*, I, (1847), 74-83.

Boncompagni Ludovisi, Ugo. *Roma nel Renascimento.* 4 vols. Albano Laziale, 1928-1929.

Boom, Gil de. "Voyage et couronnement de Charles-Quint à Bologne," in *Bulletin de la Commission Hist. Belge,* 101, 55-106.

Borja, Francisco de. *Sanctus Franciscus Borgia.* 2 vols. Matriti, 1894-1903. (*Monumenta historica Societatis Iesu,* III, XXIII)

Bosarte, Isidro. *Viage artístico a varios pueblos de España.* Tomo I. Madrid, 1804. (No more published)

Braamcamp Freire, Anselmo. *Ida da imperatriz D. Isabel para Castela.* Coimbra, 1920. (*Boletim da Classe de Letras da Academia das Sciências de Lisboa,* XIII, No. 2)

Bradford, William. *Correspondence of the Emperor Charles V and his ambassadors.* London, 1850.

Brandi, Karl. *Carlos V; vida y fortuna de una personalidad y de un imperio mundial,* trad. por Manuel Ballesteros-Gaibrois. Madrid, 1943.

———— "Eigenhändige Aufzeichnungen Karls V aus dem Anfang des Jahres 1525; der Kaiser und sein Kanzler," in *Nachrichten* . . . 1933, pp. 219-260 (*Berichte und Studien,* IX)

———— *The emperor Charles V; the growth and destiny of a man and of a world-empire,* tr. by C. V. Wedgwood. New York, 1939.

———— *Kaiser Karl V; Werden und Schicksal einer Persönlichkeit und eines Weltreiches.* 2 vols. München, [1941].

———— "Die politische Korrespondenz Karls V; alte und neue Editionspläne," in *Nachrichten* . . . 1930, pp. 250-258. (*Berichte und Studien,* I)

———— "Die politischen Testamente Karls V," in *Idem,* 1930, pp. 258-293. (*Berichte und Studien,* II)

———— "Die Testamente und politischen Instruktionen Karls V, insbesondere diejenigen der Jahre 1543/44," in *Idem,* 1935, pp. 31-96. (*Berichte und Studien,* XII)

———— "Die Ueberlieferung der Akten Karls V im Haus-, Hof-, and Staatsarchiv in Wien," in *Idem,* 1931-1933. (*Berichte und Studien,* IV, V, VII, XI)

Braudel, Fernand. *La Méditerranée et le monde méditerranéen à l'époque de Philippe II.* Paris, 1949.

Breve expedido por S. S. el papa Clemente VII en la ciudad de Bolonia el 8 de enero de 1530 a don Francisco de los Cobos, caballero de la Orden de Santiago. [Madrid], Imp. de J. M. Ducazcal, [ca. 1880].

Brewer, John Sherren, ed. *Letters and papers, foreign and domestic, of the reign of Henry VIII.* Vols. I-IV. London, 1862-1876. Continued by James Gairdner, Vols. V-XIII. London, 1880-1893.

Brown, Rawdon, ed. *Calendar of state papers and manuscripts relating to*

English affairs existing in the archives and collections of Venice. (1202-1558). Vols. I-VI. London, 1864-1884.

Bruchet, Max, comp. *Archives départmentales du Nord. Répertoire numérique. Série B: Chambre des Comptes de Lille.* 2 fasc. Lille, 1921.

Buff, Adolph. *Augsburg in der Renaissancezeit.* Bamberg, 1893.

Caballero, Fermín. *Alonso y Juan de Valdés.* Madrid, 1875. (*Conquenses ilustres,* IV)

Cabrera y Córdoba, Luis. *Felipe Segundo.* 4 vols. Madrid, 1876-1877.

Calamita, Carlos. *Figuras y semblanzas del Imperio; Francisco López de Villalobos, médico de reyes y príncipe de literatos.* Madrid, [1952].

Calendar of letters and papers . . . Henry VIII, see Brewer, J. S.

Calendar of letters, despatches, and state papers . . . Spain, see Bergenroth, G. A. and Gayangos, Pascual de.

Calendar of state papers and manuscripts . . . Venice, see Brown, Rawdon.

Calvo Sánchez, Ignacio. *Retratos de personajes del siglo XVI relacionados con la historia militar de España.* Madrid, 1919.

Camón Aznar, José. *La arquitectura plateresca.* 2 vols. Madrid, 1945.

Campori, Giuseppe. "Sebastiano del Piombo e Ferrante Gonzaga," in *Atti e memorie delle RR. Deputazioni di storia patria per le provincie modanesi e parmensi,* II (1864), 193-198.

———— "Tiziano e gli Estensi," in *Nuova antologia,* XXVII (1874), 581-620.

Campos Ruiz, Miguel. "El contrato para construir la Sacra Capilla del Salvador de Ubeda," in *Don Lope de Sosa,* VII (1919), 326-329, 358-359.

———— *Guía artística e histórica de Ubeda.* Cuadernos I-II. Ubeda, 1926-1928.

———— "La Sacra Capilla del Salvador de Ubeda," in *Don Lope de Sosa,* VI (1918), 249-251, 304-309, 367-369.

———— *Ubeda.* [Ubeda], 1933.

Cánovas del Castillo, Antonio. "Carlos V y las Cortes de Castilla," in *España moderna,* I (1889). 73-115.

Capasso, Carlo. *Paolo III (1534-1549).* 2 vols. Messina, 1923-1924.

———— *La politica di papa Paolo III e l'Italia.* Camerino, 1901.

Capella, Galeacio. *Historia de las cosas que han passado en Italia (1521-1530) . . . sobre la restitución del duque Francisco Sforcia en el ducado de Milán.* Valencia, 1536.

Carande Thobar, Ramón. *Carlos V y sus banqueros. La Hacienda Real de Castilla.* Madrid, 1949. (II)

———— *Carlos V y sus banqueros. La vida económica de España en una fase de su hegemonía, 1516-1556.* Madrid, [1943]. (I)

Cardauns, Ludwig, ed. *Berichte vom regensburger und speierer Reichstag, 1541, 1542. Nuntiaturen Versallos und Poggios.* Berlin, 1912. (*Nuntiaturberichte . . .* Abt. I, Band VII).

Cardauns, Ludwig. *Gesandtschaft Campeggios. Nuntiaturen Morones und Poggios, 1540-1541.* Berlin, 1910. (*Nuntiaturberichte,* Abt. I, Band VI)

———— *Nuntiaturen Morones und Poggios. Legationen Farneses und Cervinis, 1539-1540.* Berlin, 1909. (*Nuntiaturberichte,* Abt. I, Band V)

———— "Paul III, Karl V und Franz I in den Jahren 1535 und 1536," in *Quellen und Forschungen aus italienischen Archiven und Bibliotheken,* XI (1908), 147-244.

—— *Von Nizza bis Crépy; europäische Politik in den Jahren 1534 bis 1544*. (*Bibliothek des Preussischen Historischen Instituts in Rom*, XV)
—— "Zur Geschichte Karls V in den Jahren 1536-1538," in *Quellen und Forschungen*, XII (1909), 189-211, 321-367.

Carderera y Solano, Valentín. *Iconografía española*. 2 vols. Madrid, 1855-1864.

Caro de Torres, Francisco. *Historia de las Ordenes Militares de Santiago, Calatrava, y Alcántara*. Madrid, 1629.

Cartas de Indias. Madrid, 1877.

Casanova, Eugenio, ed. *Lettere di Carlo V a Clemente VII, 1527-1533*. Florencia, 1893.

Casas, Bartolomé de las. *Historia de las Indias*. 3 vols. Madrid, [1951].

Castan, Auguste. *La conquête de Tunis en 1535 racontée par deux écrivains franc-comtois*. Besançon, 1891.

Castañeda Alcover, Vicente. "La entrada del rey Francisco de Francia en Guadalajara y hospedaje que le hizo el duque del Infantado, D. Diego Hurtado de Mendoza y de Luna," in *Revista de historia y genealogía española*, VII (1918), 307-334.

—— *Indice del Boletín de la Real Academia de la Historia, Tomos I al CXV*. 2 vols. Madrid, 1945-1947.

Castiglione, Baldassare. *Lettere*, ed. Pietro Antonio Serassi. 2 vols. Padova, 1769-1771.

Ceán Bermúdez, Juan Agustín. *Diccionario histórico de los más ilustres profesores de las bellas artes en España*. 6 vols. Madrid, 1800.

Cedillo, Gerónimo López de Ayala y Alvarez de Toledo, conde de. *El cardenal Cisneros, gobernador del reino*. 2 vols. Madrid, 1921-1928.

—— *Toledo en el siglo XVI*. Madrid, 1901.

Cellini, Benvenuto. *La vita, scritta da lui medesimo*. Firenze, 1886.

Cetina, Gutierre de. *Obras*, ed. Joaquín Hazañas y la Rua. 2 vols. Sevilla, 1895.

Champollion-Figeac, Aimé. *La captivité du roi François Ier*. Paris, 1847. (*Documents inédits sur l'histoire de France*, XLIII)

Charles V. *Mémoires*, in Morel-Fatio, *Historiographie*, pp. [155]-356.

Charles-Quint et son temps. Musée des Beaux-Arts, Gand, 1955.

Chueca Goitía, Fernando. *Andrés de Vandelvira*. Madrid, 1954.

—— *Arquitectura del siglo XVI*. Madrid, [1953]. (*Ars Hispaniae*, XI)

Cienfuegos, Alvaro. *La heroica vida, virtudes y milagros del grande S. Francisco de Borja*. Madrid, 1702.

Cipolla, Carlo. *Storia delle signorie italiane dal 1313 al 1530*. 5 vols. Venezia, 1863.

—— —— 2 vols. Milano, [1881].

Claretta, Gaudenzio. *Notice pour servir à la vie de Mercurin de Gattinara*. (*Mémoires et documents publiés par la Société Savoisienne d'Histoire et d'Archéologie*, XXXVII (1898).

Cobos, Francisco de los. "Copia de una carta que Francisco de los Cobos, grandemente estimado del señor emperador Carlos V y su secretario de Estado, escribió a S. M. Cesárea, respondiendo a otra que tubo de dicho señor Emperador." BN, MSS. 10,300. Published by Walser in *Nachrichten* . . . 1932, pp. 173-177.

Colección de documentos inéditos para la historia de España. 113 vols. Madrid, 1842-1895. *(Codoin)*

Colección de documentos inéditos relativos al descubrimiento, conquista y organización de las antiguas posesiones españolas de América y Oceanía. 42 vols. Madrid, 1864-1884. *(Codoin Am)*

Colección de documentos inéditos relativos al descubrimiento, conquista y organización de las antiguas posesiones españolas de Ultramar. 2a serie. 25 vols. Madrid, 1885-1932. *(Codoin Ult)*

Comunidades de Castilla, in *Codoin,* I, 530-563.

Copia de una letra escrita en Barcelona, último de mayo deste presente anno, al señor Gaspar de Mendoza, gentilhombre del Emperador. n. p., [1535]. A *pliego suelto.*

Cordero Torres, José María. *El Consejo de Estado; su trayectoria y perspectivas en España.* Madrid, 1944.

Cortés, Hernán. *Cartas y relaciones,* ed. Pascual de Gayangos, Madrid, 1866.

Cortes de los antiguos reinos de León y de Castilla. 5 vols. Madrid, 1882-1903.

Cota, Sancho. *Memorias de Carlos V.* BN, MSS. 18,186.

Cózar Martínez, Fernando de. *Noticias y documentos para la historia de Baeza.* Jaén, 1884.

Cronaca del soggiorno di Carlo V in Italia (dal 26 luglio 1529 al 25 aprile 1530), ed. G. Romano. Milano, 1892.

Crónica de Alonso XI. 2a ed. Madrid, 1787.

Cronicón de los alcaldes de Ubeda desde 1234 hasta 1326. AcHist, MSS. Abella, Tomo IX.

Cronique du roy François . . . ed. Georges Guiffrey. Paris, 1860.

Crowe, Joseph Archer and Cavalcaselle, G. B. *Titian; his life and times.* 2 vols. London, 1877.

Cuenta de lo que han rentado los indios quitados al secretario Lope de Conchillos, in *CodoinAm,* I, 374.

Cuevas, Mariano, ed. *Cartas y otros documentos de Hernán Cortés.* Sevilla, 1915.

Dansaert, Georges. *Guillaume de Croy - Chièvres, dit le Sage.* Paris, n.d.

Danvila y Collado, Manuel. *La Germanía de Valencia.* Madrid, 1884.

—— *Historia crítica y documentada de las Comunidades de Castilla.* 6 vols. Madrid, 1897-1899. *(Memorial histórico español,* XXXV-XL)

—— "Mercurino de Gattinara, gran canciller de España," in *Boletín de la R. Academia de la Historia,* XXXV (1899), 482-494.

—— *El poder civil en España.* 6 vols. Madrid, 1885-1886.

Davolio, Vincenzo. *Memorie istoriche di Novellara e de' suoi principi.* 3 vols. Manuscript in the Archivio Municipale di Novellara, copied in 1825.

—— *Memorie storiche della contea di Novellara e dei Gonzaghi che vi dominarono.* Milano, 1833.

Decrue, Francis. *Anne de Montmorency, Grand Maître et Connétable de France, à la Cour, aux armes, et au Conseil du roi François Ier.* Paris, 1885.

Description de l'entrée et du couronnement de Charles-Quint à Aix-la-Chapelle, 22 et 23 octobre 1520, in *Bulletin de la Commission Royale d'Histoire,* Série II, XI (1858), 218-223.

20. The Chapel of San Salvador in Ubeda (1536-1559)

Designed by Andrés de Vandelvira from plans by Diego de Siloee. The carving is the work of Esteban Jamete.

21. The Main Door of San Salvador

Based on the Puerta del Perdón in the Cathedral of Granada, designed by Siloee.

22. The North Door of San Salvador

This is the work of Vandelvira.

23. The Interior of San Salvador
The design is Vandelvira's. The *reja* is the work of Villalpando.

24. The Sacristy of San Salvador

The carving is by Jamete.

IOÃNES.MARTÍNEZ.SILICE?.CARD.S

25. Juan Martínez Siliceo

By an unknown painter. Bishop of Cartagena (1541-1546), Archbishop
of Toledo (1546-1557). *Toledo, Catedral*

26. The "Cubo de Carlos V" in the Castle of Simancas

This was the first room of the Archivo, designed by Luis de Vega and constructed under the direction of Cobos between 1541 and 1543.

27. The Castle of Simancas

View from the east

28. Ruins of Cobos' Palace in Ubeda

Diarii udinesi, ed. Leonardo and Gregorio Amaseo and G. A. Azio. Venezia, 1884.

Díaz del Castillo, Bernal. *Verdadera y notable relación del descubrimiento y conquista de la Nueva España y Guatemala.* 2 vols. Guatemala, 1933-1934.

Díaz Sánchez, Francisco. *Guía de la villa y archivo de Simancas.* Madrid, 1885.

Documentos sobre el desafío del emperador Carlos V con Francisco I, rey de Francia, in *Codoin,* I, 47-95.

Documents historiques relatifs à la principauté de Monaco depuis le quinzième siècle. Vols. I-III. Monaco, 1888-1891.

Döllinger, Johann Joseph Ignaz von. *Dokumente zur Geschichte Karls V.* Regensburg, 1862.

Dolce, Ludovico. *Vita di Carlo Quinto.* Venezia, 1568.

Domínguez Bordona, Jesús. *Proceso inquisitorial contra el escultor Esteban Jamete.* Madrid, 1933.

Dormer, Diego José. *Anales de Aragón desde el año MDXXV hasta el de MDXL.* Zaragoza, 1697.

———— *Progreso de la historia en el reyno de Aragón.* Zaragoza, 1680.

Doussinague, José María. *El testamento político de Fernando el Católico.* Madrid, [1950].

Du Bellay, Martin and Guillaume. *Mémoires.* 4 vols. Paris, 1908-1919.

Dumont, Jean. *Corps universel diplomatique.* 8 vols. La Haye, 1726-1731.

Ehrenberg, Richard. *Capital & finance in the Age of the Renaissance; a study of the Fuggers and their connections,* tr. by H. M. Lucas. London, [1928].

Enríquez de Guzmán, Alonso. *Libro de la vida y costumbres,* publ. por H. Keniston. Madrid, 1960.

The entry of the emperor Charles V into the city of Bologna . . . from a series of engravings on wood, printed at Venice, in 1530. Florence, etc., 1875.

Espejo e Hinojosa, Cristóbal. "El interés del dinero en los reinos españoles bajo los tres primeros Austrias," in *Archivo de investigaciones históricas,* I (1911), 397-417, 489-534.

———— *Sobre organización de la hacienda española en el siglo XVI.* Madrid, 1907.

Espejo e Hinojosa, Cristóbal and Paz, Julián. *Las ferias antiguas de Medina del Campo.* Valladolid, 1912.

Espinosa y Quesada, pseud. "Entrevista de Carlos I de España y Francisco I de Francia," in his *Cosas de España,* Sevilla, 1891, pp. 20-31. A reprint of the *Relación muy verdadera sobre las paces.*

Estatutos de la capilla de San Nicolás en Ubeda, fundada por don Fernando de Ortega. Manuscript in the possession of A. Rodríguez Moñino.

Estatutos de la Sacra Capilla del Salvador. AcHist, MSS. Salazar M—198, fols. 59-78.

Feliú de la Peña y Farell, Narciso. *Anales de Cataluña.* 3 vols. Barcelona, 1709.

Fernández de Bethencourt, Francisco. *Historia genealógica y heráldica de la monarquía española.* 10 vols. Madrid, 1897-1920.

Fernández de Oviedo y Valdés, Gonzalo. *Batallas y quinquaxenas.* BN, MSS. 3135.

—— *Historia general y natural de las Indias.* 4 vols. Madrid, 1851-1855.

—— *Libro de linaxes y armas.* AcHist, MSS. Salazar C-24.

—— *Las quinquagenas de la nobleza de España.* Tomo I. Madrid, 1880.

—— *Las quinquagenas de los generosos & illustres e no menos famosos reyes, príncipes, duques, marqueses y condes, & cavalleros . . . de España.* 3 vols. BN, MSS. 2217-2219.

—— *Relación de lo sucedido en la prisión del rey de Francia,* in *Codoin,* XXXVIII, 404-529.

Fernández del Castillo, Francisco. *Doña Catalina Xuárez Marcayda.* México, 1920.

Fernández Duro, Cesáreo. *Armada española.* 9 vols. Madrid, 1895-1903.

Fernández Llamazares, José. *Historia comparada de las cuatro Ordenes Militares.* Madrid, 1862.

Fernández Torres, Eleuterio. *Historia de Tordesillas.* Valladolid, 1914.

Ferrer del Río, Antonio. *Decadencia de España.* la parte. Madrid, 1850.

Floreto de anécdotas y noticias diversas que recopiló un fraile dominico residente en Sevilla, ed. F. J. Sánchez Cantón. Madrid, 1948. (*Memorial histórico español,* XLVIII)

Foronda y Aguilera, Manuel de. *Estancias y viajes del emperador Carlos V.* Madrid, 1895.

—— —— Madrid, 1914.

—— "Fiesta del Toisón de Oro celebrada por Carlos V en Utrecht en 1546," in *Revista contemporánea,* CXXVI (1903), 641-661.

Foulché-Delbosc, Raymond. "Le portrait de Mendoza," in *Revue hispanique,* XXIII (1910). 310-313.

Friedenburg, Walter. *Kaiser Karl V und Papst Paul III (1534-1549).* Leipzig, 1932. (*Schriften des Vereins für Reformationsgeschichte,* Jahrgang 50, Heft 1)

—— *Legation Aleanders, 1538-1539.* 2 vols. Gotha, 1893. (*Nuntiaturberichte,* Abt. I, Band III-IV)

—— *Nuntiatur des Morone, 1536-1538.* Gotha, 1892. (*Nuntiaturberichte,* Abt. I, Band II)

—— *Nuntiaturen des Vergerio, 1533-1536.* Gotha, 1892. (*Nuntiaturberichte,* Abt. I, Band I)

Fuente, Vicente de la, ed. *Cartas de los secretarios del cardenal Cisneros.* Madrid, 1876.

Fuertes Arias, Rafael. *Alfonso de Quintanilla, contador mayor de los Reyes Católicos.* 2 vols. Oviedo, 1909.

Fueter, Eduard. *Geschichte des europäischen Staatensystems von 1492-1559.* München und Berlin, 1919.

Gachard, Louis Prosper. *Analectes historiques.* Série V-VII. Bruxelles, 1856.

—— *Les archives farnésiennes à Naples.* Bruxelles, 1869.

—— ed. *Collection des voyages des souverains des Pays-Bas.* 4 vols. Bruxelles, 1876-1882.

—— *Correspondence de Charles-Quint et d'Adrien VI.* Bruxelles, 1859.

—— *Relation des troubles de Gand sous Charles-Quint par un anonyme; suivie de 330 documents inédits.* Bruxelles, 1846.

—— *Relations des ambassadeurs vénitiens sur Charles-Quint et Philippe II.* Bruxelles, 1856.

Gachet, Emile L. J. B. *Documents inédits relatifs à la conquête de Tunis par l'empereur Charles-Quint en 1535.* Bruxelles, 1844.

Galíndez de Carvajal, Lorenzo. *Adiciones genealógicas a los* Claros varones de Castilla *de Fernán Pérez de Guzmán,* in *Codoin,* XVIII, 423-536.

—— *Anales breves del reinado de los Reyes Católicos D. Fernando y Doña Isabel,* in *Idem,* XVIII, 227-422.

—— *Anales de los Reyes Católicos.* BN, MSS. 1752, fols. 1-50.

—— *Informe que dió al emperador Carlos V sobre los que componían el Consejo Real de S. M.,* in *Codoin,* I, 122-127.

—— *Parecer . . . sobre lo que el Emperador deve hacer para ausentarse y cómo debe quedar lo de los Consejos y quién yrá con el Emperador,* BM, MSS. Eg. 307, fols. 159-163. Also in BN, MSS. 1752, fols. 168-173; published by Walser in *Nachrichten . . . 1932,* pp. 163-167.

—— *Pareceres.* BN, MSS. 1752, fols. 168ff.

Gallardo, Bartolomé José. *Ensayo de una biblioteca española de libros raros y curiosos.* 4 vols. Madrid, 1863-1889.

Gambara, Veronica. *Rime e lettere.* Torino, 1880.

—— *Rime e lettere, raccolte da Felice Rizzardi.* Brescia, 1759.

—— *Undici lettere inedite,* ed. Luigi Amaduzzi. Guastalla, 1889.

Gams, Pius Bonifacius. *Series episcoporum.* Leipzig, 1931.

Gante, Pedro de. *Relaciones . . . (1520-1544).* Madrid, 1873.

García Carraffa, Alberto and Arturo. *Enciclopedia heráldica y genealógica hispanoamericana.* 70 vols. Madrid, 1919-1952.

García Cerezeda, Martín. *Tratado de las campañas y otros acontecimientos de los ejércitos del emperador Carlos V, desde 1521 hasta 1545.* 3 vols. Madrid, 1873-1876.

García Chico, Esteban. "El palacio de los Dueñas de Medina del Campo," in Semanario de Arte y Arqueología de la Universidad de Valladolid. *Boletín de trabajos,* XVI (1949-1950), 87-110.

Garibay y Zamalloa, Esteban de. *Compendio historial.* 4 vols. Barcelona, 1648.

Garnode, Laurens de. *Le couronnement du trespuissant et très redoubté roy catholique Charles, par la grace de Dieu roy d'Espagne, en sa bonne ville de Validolif, avecq le nombre des prinches et grantz seigneurs dudit Castille, le dimenche, vii jour de Fevrier, l'an de grace* 1517. n. p., [1517].

Gattinara, Mercurino Arborio di. *Historia vite et gestarum per magnum Cancellarium, con note aggiunte e documenti,* ed. Carlo Bornate. In *Miscellanea di storia italiana* (Torino, 1915), XLVIII, 231-585.

Gayangos, Pascual de, ed. *Calendar of letters, despatches and state papers relating to the negotiations between England and Spain.* Vols. III-VI. London, 1873-1890.

—— *Catalogue of the manuscripts in the Spanish language in the British Museum.* 4 vols. London, 1875-1893.

Gaye, Giovanni. *Carteggio d'artisti dei secoli XIV, XV, XVI.* 3 vols. Firenze, 1839-1840.

Giannone, Pietro. *Dell'istoria civile del regno di Napoli.* 4 vols. Napoli, 1723.

436   FRANCISCO DE LOS COBOS

Giménez Fernández, Manuel. *Bartolomé de las Casas*. Vol. I. Sevilla, 1953.
(*Publ. de la Escuela de Estudios Hispano-Americanos de Sevilla*, LXX)

Giordani, Gaetano. *Della venuta e dimora in Bologna di Clemente VII per la coronazione di Carlo V, imperatore*. Bologna, 1842.

Giovio, Paolo. *Elogios o vidas breves*. Granada, 1568.

———— *Historiarum sui temporis tomus primus [et secundus]*. 2 vols. Lutetiæ, 1553-1554.

———— *Lettere volgari*, racc. da L. Domenichi. Venezia, [1560].

Glück, Gustav. "Bildnisse aus dem Hause Habsburg. I. Kaiserin Isabella," in *Jahrbuch der kunsthistorischen Sammlungen in Wien*, Neue Folge, VII (1933), 183-210.

Gómez de Orozco, Federico. "El exvoto de Hernán Cortés," in *Ethnos* (México), I (1920-1922), 219-222.

Gómez Moreno, Manuel. *Las águilas del Renacimiento español*. Madrid, 1941.

———— "Obras de Miguel Angel en España," in *Archivo español de arte y arqueología*, VI (1930), 189-197.

Gómez Moreno, Manuel (el Viejo). "Los pintores Julio y Alejandro y sus obras en la Casa Real de la Alhambra," in his *Cosas granadinas de arte y arqueología*, Granada, [1885-1888], pp. 121-147.

González Dávila, Gil. *Teatro de las grandezas de Madrid*. Madrid, 1623.

———— *Theatro eclesiástico de las iglesias metropolitanas y cathedrales de los reynos de las dos Castillas*. 4 vols. Madrid, 1645-1700.

González García-Valladolid, Casimiro. *Datos para la historia biográfica de Valladolid*. Valladolid, 1893.

González Palencia, Angel. *Don Luis de Zúñiga y Avila, gentilhombre de Carlos V*. Madrid, 1932.

———— "Fragmentos del archivo particular de Antonio Pérez," in *RABM*, 3a época, XXXVIII-XXXIX (1918).

———— *Gonzalo Pérez, secretario de Felipe II*. 2 vols. Madrid, 1946.

———— *Vida y obras de don Diego Hurtado de Mendoza*. 3 vols. Madrid, 1941-1943.

Gosellini, Giuliano. *Vita di don Ferrando Gonzaga, principe di Molfetta*. Pisa, 1821.

Gossart, Ernest Edouard. *Espagnols et flamands au XVIe siècle. Charles-Quint, roy d'Espagne*. Bruxelles, 1910.

———— *Notes pour servir à l'histoire du règne de Charles-Quint*. Bruxelles, 1898. (*Mémoires . . . publiées par l'Académie Royale de Belgique*, LV (1897).

Gounon-Loubens, Jules. *Essais sur l'administration de la Castille au XVIe siècle*. Paris, 1860.

Grazzini, Antonfrancesco. "Lettera a messer Bernardo Guasconi in Roma: Entrata della Cesarea Maestà in Firenze," in *Giornale storico degli archivi toscani*, III (1859), 288-294.

Gross, Lothar, ed. *Die Reichsregisterbücher Kaiser Karls V*. Wien, 1934.

Guazzo, Marco. *Historie di tutte le cose degne di memoria quai dal anno MDXXIIII sino à questo presente sono occorse nella Italia, nella Provenza*, etc. Venetia, 1540.

Guevara, Antonio de. *Epístolas familiares*. Valladolid, 1544.

—— *Libro de los inventores del arte de marear y de muchos trabajos que se passan en las galeras* . . . *dirigido al illustre señor don Francisco de los Cobos, Comendador Mayor de León y del Consejo de Su Magestad.* [Valladolid, 1539]. In his *Obras*, [Valladolid]. 1539.

—— *Libro llamado Aviso de privados y doctrina de cortesanos, dirigido al illustre señor don Francisco de los Cobos, Comendador Mayor de León y del Consejo de Su Magestad.* [Valladolid, 1539]. In his *Obras*, [Valladolid], 1539.

—— *Menosprecio de Corte y alabanza de aldea.* Madrid, 1915. (*Clásicos castellanos,* XXIX)

Guía-anuario de Valladolid y su provincia. Valladolid, 1927.

Guía histórica y descriptiva de los archivos, bibliotecas y museos arqueológicos de España. 2 vols. Madrid, 1916-1925.

Guicciardini, Francesco. *La storia d'Italia.* 4 vols. Firenze, 1919.

Guillamas Galiano, Manuel. *Reseña histórica del origen y fundación de las Ordenes Militares.* Madrid, 1851.

Gutiérrez Coronel, Diego. *Historia genealógica de la Casa de Mendoza.* 2 vols. Madrid, 1946. (*Biblioteca conquense,* III-IV)

Habich, Georg. *Die deutschen Schaumünzen des 16en Jahrhunderts.* München, 1929.

—— "Studien zur deutschen Renaissancemedaille. IV. Christoph Weiditz," in *Jahrbuch der königlich-preuszischen Kunstsammlungen,* XXXIV (1913), 1-35.

Häbler, Konrad. *Geschichte Spaniens unter den Habsburgen.* Vol. I. Gotha, 1907.

—— *Die wirtschaftliche Blüte Spaniens im 16. Jahrhundert und ihr Verfall.* Berlin, 1888.

Hamilton, Earl Jefferson. *American treasure and the price revolution in Spain, 1501-1650.* Cambridge, Mass., 1934. (*Harvard economic studies,* XLIII)

Hanke, Lewis. *Bartolomé de las Casas, historian; an essay in Spanish historiography.* Gainesville, 1952.

Haring, Clarence Henry. "American gold and silver production in the first half of the sixteenth century," in *Quarterly journal of economics,* XXIX (1915), 433-479.

—— *Trade and navigation between Spain and the Indies in the time of the Hapsburgs.* Cambridge, Mass., 1918.

Hasenelever, Adolf. "Die Ueberlieferung der Akten Karls V in Pariser Archiven und Bibliotheken," in *Nachrichten* . . . 1933, pp. 437-469. (*Berichte und Studien,* X)

Henne, Alexandre. *Histoire de la Belgique sous la règne de Charles-Quint.* 4 vols. Bruxelles-Paris, 1865.

Herrera, Antonio. *Historia general de las Indias Occidentales.* 4 vols. Amberes, 1728.

Höfler, Constantin von. *Don Antonio de Acuña, genannt der Luther Spaniens; ein Lebensbild aus dem Reformations-Zeitalter.* Wien, 1882.

Hurtado de Mendoza, Diego. *Algunas cartas,* ed. Alberto Vázquez y R. Selden Rose. New Haven, 1935.

438   FRANCISCO DE LOS COBOS

Ibarra y Rodríguez, Eduardo and G. Arsenio de Izaga. *Catálogo de los documentos del Archivo de Lope de Soria.* Madrid, 1931.
Illescas, Gonzalo de. *Jornada de Carlos V a Túnez.* Madrid, 1804.
Isabel, la Emperatriz. *Cartas,* in *Codoin,* I, 140-154.
Itinéraire de Charles-Quint de 1506 à 1531, in Gachard, *Collection des voyages,* II, 1-50.

Jansen, Johann and Ludwig von Pastor. *Geschichte des deutschen Volkes.* 3 vols. Freiburg, 1913-1917.
Jimena Jurado, Martín de. *Catálogo de los obispos de las iglesias catedrales de la diócesi de Jaén y annales eclesiásticos deste obispado.* [Madrid, 1654].
Jiménez de Cisneros, Francisco. *Cartas,* ed. Pascual de Gayangos y V. de la Fuente. Madrid, 1867.
——— "Instrucción según la qual el emperador Carlos Vº, nuestro señor, se habrá de haber en su llegada a España," in *Semanario erudito,* XX, 237-245. Also in BN (Paris), MSS. Esp. 143, fols. 44-48.
Jiménez de la Espada, Marcos. *Relaciones geográficas de Indias.* 4 vols. Madrid, 1881-1897.
Jiménez de Rada, Rodrigo. *Rerum in Hispania gestarum chronicon libri novem.* Apud inclytam Granatam, 1545.
Jiménez Patón, Bartolomé. *Historia de la antigua y continuada nobleza de la ciudad de Jaén.* Jaén, 1628.
Juste, Théodore. *Charles-Quint et Marguérite d' Autriche.* (*Mémoires de l'Académie Royale de Belgique,* VII)

Keniston, Hayward. "Notes on the *De liberis educandis* of Antonio de Lebrija," in *Homenaje a Ramón Menéndez Pidal,* 1925, III, 127-141.

Labande, Léon Honoré, ed. *Recueil des lettres de l'empereur Charles-Quint.* Monaco, 1910.
[Lafaist, Louis, pseud. L. Cimber]. *Archives curieuses de l'histoire de France depuis Louis XI jusqu'à Louis XVIII.* 30 vols. Paris, 1834-1841.
Laiglesia, Francisco de. *Los caudales de Indias en la primera mitad del siglo XVI.* Madrid, 1904.
——— *Una crisis parlamentaria en 1538.* Madrid, 1905.
——— *Estudios históricos, 1515-1555.* Madrid, 1908.
——— ——— 2a ed. 3 vols. Madrid, 1918-1919.
——— *Los gastos de la Corona en el Imperio.* Madrid, 1907.
Láinez Alcalá, Rafael. *Breve guía de Ubeda y Baeza.* n.p, n.d.
Lambert, Pierre de, seigneur de la Croix. *Mémoires sur la vie de Charles, duc de Savoye (1505-1539),* in *Monumenta historiae patriae,* III (1840), col. 839-929.
Lampérez y Romea, Vicente. *Arquitectura civil española de los siglos I al XVIII.* 2 vols. Madrid, 1922.
[Landi, Ortensio]. *Paradossi, cioè: Sententie fuori del comun parere, novellamente venute in luce.* 2 parts. Venezia, 1545.
Lanz, Karl, ed. *Aktenstücke und Briefe zur Geschichte Kaiser Karl V.* Wien, 1853. (*Monumenta habsburgica,* Abt. II, Band I)

——— *Korrespondenz des Kaisers Karl V.* 3 vols. Leipzig, 1844-1846.

——— *Staatspapier zur Geschichte des Kaisers Karl V.* Stuttgart, 1845. (*Bibliothek des litt. Vereins in Stuttgart,* XI)

Las Casas, Bartolomé de, see Casas, Bartolomé de las.

Lasso de la Vega, Miguel, see Saltillo, marqués del.

LeGlay, André Joseph Ghislain, comp. *Négotiations diplomatiques entre la France et l'Autriche durant les trente premières années du XVIᵉ siècle.* 2 vols. Paris, 1845.

Leguina y Vidal, Enrique. *Arte antiguo. Espadas de Carlos V.* Madrid, 1908.

León Pinelo, Antonio de. *El Gran Canciller de las Indias; estudio preliminar de Guillermo Lohmann Villena.* Sevilla, 1953.

——— *Tablas cronológicas de los Reales Consejos ... de las Indias Occidentales.* 2a ed. Madrid, 1892.

——— *Tratado de confirmaciones reales.* Madrid, 1630.

Leonardo de Argensola, Bartolomé. *Primera parte de los Anales de Aragón.* Çaragoça, 1630.

Leti, Gregorio. *Vita dell'invitissimo imperadore Carlo V.* 2 vols. Amsterdamo, 1700.

Lettere di principi. 3 vols. Venetia, 1581.

Leva, Giuseppe de. *Storia documentata di Carlo V.* 5 vols. Venezia, 1863-1896.

Libre de les solemnitats de Barcelona, ed. A. Duran i Sanpere i Josep Sanabre. 2 vols. Barcelona, 1930-1947.

Litta, Pompeo. *Celebri famiglie d'Italia.* Milano, 1819-

Llaguno y Amírola, Eugenio. *Noticias de los arquitectos y arquitectura de España,* ed. J. A. Ceán Bermúdez. 4 vols. Madrid, 1829.

Loaisa, García de. *Briefe an Kaiser Karl V von seinem Beichvater,* ed. G. Heine. Berlin, 1848.

——— *Correspondencia del cardenal de Osma con Carlos V y con su secretario don Francisco de los Cobos.* In *Codoin,* XIV, 5-284; XCVII, 213-284.

Looz-Corsvarem, Otto Adalbert, Graf. "Die römische Korrespondenz Karls V in Madrid und Simancas," in *Nachrichten* . . . 1935, pp. 109-190. (*Berichte und Studien,* XIII)

Loperráez Corvalán, Juan. *Descripcion histórica del obispado de Osma.* 3 vols. Madrid, 1788.

López de Ayala y Alvarez de Toledo, Gerónimo, see Cedillo, conde de.

López de Gómara, Francisco. *Annals of the Emperor Charles V. Spanish text and English translation.* Oxford, 1912.

López de Haro, Alonso. *Casas solariegas de Castilla.* la parte. AcHist, MSS. Salazar C-20, fols. 218-220.

——— *Nobiliario genealógico de los reyes y títulos de España.* 2 vols. Madrid, 1622.

López de Villalobos, Francisco. *Algunas obras.* Madrid, 1886. (*Sociedad de Bibliófilos Españoles,* XXIV)

López de Vivero, Juan. *Tratado del esfuerzo bélico heroico.* Madrid, [1941].

Lozano Muñoz, Francisco. *Crónica de la provincia de Jaén.* Madrid, 1867.

Macías, Marcelo. "Lágrimas del apóstol San Pablo [Pedro]," in *Dogma y razón,* II (1888), 252, 316-317, 364-366, 397-398.

Madariaga, Salvador de. *Hernán Cortés.* 2a ed. Buenos Aires, [1943].

Maldonado, Juan. *El movimiento de España, o sea Historia de la revolución conocida por el nombre de las Comunidades de Castilla,* trad. por José Quevedo. Madrid, 1840.

Manual de novells ardits, vulgarment apellat Dietari del antich Consell Barceloní. Vols. III-IV (1478-1562). Barcelona, 1894-1895.

Marañón, Gregorio. *Antonio Pérez.* 2a ed. 2 vols. Madrid, 1948.

March, José María. *Niñez y juventud de Felipe II.* 2 vols. Madrid, 1941-1942.

Marineo Sículo, Lucio. *De las cosas memorables de España.* Alcalá de Henares, 1530.

Martí y Monsó, José. *Estudios histórico-artísticos relativos principalmente a Valladolid.* Madrid, [1901].

Martín González, Juan José. *La arquitectura doméstica del Renacimiento en Valladolid.* Valladolid, 1948.

——— *Guía histórico-artística de Valladolid.* 2a ed. Valladolid, n. d.

Martínez Ferrando, Jesús Ernesto. *Privilegios otorgados por el emperador Carlos V en el reino de Nápoles.* Barcelona, 1942.

Martinez Marina, Francisco. *Teoría de las Cortes.* Parte I. Tomo I. Madrid, 1813.

Martínez Siliceo, Juan. *Carta al emperador Carlos V . . . sobre la perpetuación del adelantamiento de Cazorla.* BN, MSS. 13037, fols. 52-63.

Martire d'Anghiera, Pietro. *Opus epistolarum.* Amstelodami, 1670.

Martos López, Ramón. *Monumentos de Ubeda. La iglesia de El Salvador.* 2a ed. Ubeda, 1951.

Maurenbrecher, Wilhelm. "Die Lehrjahre Philipp's II von Spanien," in *Historisches Taschenbuch,* 6e Folge, 1er Jahrgang (Leipzig, 1882), pp. 271-346.

Medrano, García de. *Copilación de las leyes capitulares de la Orden de la Cavallería de Santiago del Espada.* [Valladolid, 1605].

Mejía (Mexía), Pedro. *Historia de Carlos Quinto,* in *Revue hispanique,* XLIV (1918), 1-564.

——— *Historia del emperador Carlos V.* Madrid, [1945]. (*Colección de crónicas españolas,* VII)

Mejía (Messía) de Contreras, Diego. *Sumario sobre la sentencia arbitraria que los cavalleros hijosdalgo de la ciudad de Ubeda tienen.* Granada, 1613.

Memorial dado al cardenal Cisneros de lo que conviene proveer para la buena gobernación de la isla Española y denuncia de los abusos e injusticias que en ella se han cometido, in *CodoinAm,* I, 253-264.

Memorial del pleyto entre el señor cardenal don Bernardo de Rojas y Sandoval y el señor Fiscal de Su Magestad . . . de la una parte, y el marqués de Camarasa de la otra, sobre el adelantamiento de Caçorla. Valladolid, 1602.

——— *Appéndice y defensa de la alegación en derecho dada por el ilustrísimo señor cardenal de Sandoval, arçobispo de Toledo . . . y el señor Fiscal con don Francisco de los Cobos, marqués de Camarasa, sobre el adelantamiento de Cazorla.* Valladolid, 1603.

Menéndez Pidal, Gonzalo. *Los caminos en la historia de España.* Madrid, 1951.

Menéndez Pidal, Juan. "Don Francesillo de Zúñiga, bufón de Carlos V; cartas inéditas," in *RABM,* 3a época, XX (1909), 182-200; XXI (1909), 72-95.

Menéndez Pidal, Ramón. *Idea imperial de Carlos V.* [Madrid, 1940].

Meneses, Alonso de. *Repertorio de caminos (1576).* Madrid, 1946.

Merriman, Roger Bigelow. *The rise of the Spanish empire.* Vol. III: *The Emperor.* New York, 1925.

Mesonero Romanos, Ramón de. *El antiguo Madrid.* Madrid, 1861.

Miccio, Scipione. "Vita di don Pietro de Toledo, ed. Francesco Palermo," in *Archivio storico italiano,* Ser. 1, I (1846), 1-89.

Mignet, François Auguste. *Rivalité de François Ier et de Charles-Quint.* 3e éd. 2 vols. Paris, 1886.

Monasterio, José. "La antigua iglesia de Santa María la Real de la Almudena," in *Boletín de la Sociedad Española de Excursiones,* LV (1951), 121-129.

Montares Arias, C. *Manual de Madrid.* [Madrid, ca. 1952].

[Montecatini, Niccolò], *Entrata del Imperatore nella città di Lucca.* n.p., [1536].

Montesinos, Ambrosio. *Comentario de la conquista de Baeza.* AcHist, MSS. Salazar H-13.

Montoiche, Guillaume de. *Voyage et expédition de Charles-Quint au pays de Tunis,* in Gachard, *Collection des voyages,* III, 315-388.

Monumenta habsburgica. Sammlung von Actenstücken und Briefen zur Geschichte des Hauses Habsburg in dem Zeitraume von 1473 bis 1576. 4 vols. Wien, 1853-1857.

Morel-Fatio, Alfred. *Catalogue des manuscrits espagnols de la Bibliothèque Nationale.* Paris, 1892.

——— "Da. Marina de Aragón (1523-1549)," in *Bulletin hispanique,* V (1903), 140-157.

——— *Historiographie de Charles-Quint.* 1e partie. Paris, 1913. (No more published)

——— "L'instruction de Charles-Quint à son fils Philippe II, donnée à Palamós le 4 mai 1543," in *Bulletin hispanique,* I (1899), 135-148.

Mota, Diego de la. *Libro del principio de la Orden de Cavallería de Santiago del Espada.* Valencia, 1599.

Moya e Idígoras, Juan. *Discurso de ingreso en la Real Academia de Bellas Artes de San Fernando.* Madrid, 1923.

Muñoz de San Pedro, Miguel. "Francisco Lizaur," in *Boletín de la R. Academia de la Historia,* CXXIII (1948), 57-170.

Muro García, Manuel. *Ubeda monumental.* Madrid, 1928.

Museo del Prado, Madrid. *Catálogo de los cuadros.* Madrid, 1949.

Nachrichten der Gesellschaft der Wissenschaften zu Göttingen. Philologisch-historische Klasse. Göttingen, 1930-1935.

Narváez, Luis de. *Los seys libros del Delphín de música de cifras para tañer vihuela . . . dirigidos al muy illustre señor, el señor don Francisco de los Covos, comendador mayor de León, adelantado de Caçorla, señor de*

442 FRANCISCO DE LOS COBOS

Saviote, y del Consejo de Estado de Su Magestad Cesárea. [Valladolid], 1538.

—— *Los seys libros del Delphín,* ed. Emilio Pujol. Barcelona, 1945.

Navarra, Pedro de (Pierre d' Albret). *Diálogos de la preparación de la muerte.* Tolosa, [1565?].

—— *Diálogos muy subtiles y notables.* Tolosa, [1565?].

Núñez de Castro, Alonso. *Historia eclesiástica y seglar de . . . Guadalaxara.* Madrid, 1653.

Nuntiaturberichte aus Deutschland. Gotha, Berlin, 1892-1912. Abt. I, Band I-VII.

Orano, Domenico. *Il sacco di Roma del 1527; studi e documenti.* Roma, 1901.

Ordine, pompe, apparati et ceremonie delle solenne intrate di Carlo V. Imp. sempre aug., nelle città di Roma, Siena, et Fiorenza. n. p., [1536].

Orlandini, Niccolò. *Historiæ Societatis Iesu.* Romae, 1615.

Ortiz de Zúñiga, Diego. *Anales eclesiásticos y seculares de Sevilla.* Madrid, 1677.

Orueta, Ricardo de. *Berruguete y su obra.* Madrid, n. d.

Osuna, Francisco de. *Ley de amor, dirigido al muy magnífico señor Francisco de los Cobos.* [Sevilla, 1530].

—— *Ley de amor, y quarta parte del Abecedario espiritual.* [Burgos], 1536.

Oviedo y Valdés, Gonzalo Fernández de, see Fernández de Oviedo y Valdés, Gonzalo.

Pacheco, Francisco. *Arte de la pintura.* Madrid, 1866. 2 vols.

Pacheco y de Leyva, Enrique. *La política española en Italia. Correspondencia de don Fernando Marín, abad de Nájera, con Carlos V.* Madrid, 1919. Tomo I: (1521-1524).

—— "Relaciones vaticanas de hacienda española del siglo XVI," in *Cuadernos de trabajos de la Escuela Española de Arqueología e Historia en Roma,* IV (1918), 45-124.

Padilla, Lorenzo de. *Catálogo de los santos de España.* Toledo, 1538.

—— *Crónica de España.* n. p., [ca. 1570].

—— *Nobiliario antiquíssimo de España.* BM, MSS. Add. 12470.

—— *Tratado de nobleza.* BN, MSS. 3260.

Palacio, Timoteo Domingo, ed. *Documentos del Archivo General de Madrid.* 4 vols. Madrid, 1888-1906.

Palomo, Francisco de Borja. *Historia crítica de las riadas o grandes avenidas del Guadalquivir.* Sevilla, 1878.

Panofsky, Erwin. "Die Pietà von Ubeda," in *Festschrift für Julius Schlosser.* Zürich, [1927], pp. 150-161.

Panzano Ibáñez de Aviz, José Lupercio. *Anales de Aragón desde el año 1540 hasta el año 1558.* Zaragoza, 1705.

Pareceres que en diversos tiempos el Consejo ha dado en cosas generales. BM, MSS. 904, fols. 208-266.

Parrino, Domenico Antonio. *Teatro eroico e politico de' governi de' vicerè del regno di Napoli.* 3 vols. Napoli, 1692-1694.

Parry, John Horace. *The Spanish theory of Empire in the 16th century.* Cambridge, 1940.

Pastor, Ludwig von. *Erläuterungen,* etc. 10 vols. Freiburg im Breisgau, 1898-1920.

―――― *Histoire des Papes, depuis la fin du Moyen Age,* tr. par Furcy Raynaud [et al.]. 6e. éd. 15 vols. Paris, 1925-[1933].

―――― *The history of the Popes.* 40 vols. London, 1891-1953.

Paz, Julián. *Archivo General de Simancas. Catálogo I.* Madrid, 1904.

―――― *Archivo General de Simancas. Catálogo II: Secretaría de Estado.* 2a ed. Madrid, 1942.

―――― *Catálogo de documentos españoles existentes en el Archivo del Ministerio de Negocios Extranjeros de París.* Madrid, 1932.

―――― *Catálogo de manuscritos de América existentes en la Biblioteca Nacional.* Madrid, 1933.

―――― *Documentos relativos a España existentes en los Archivos Nacionales de París.* Valencia, 1934.

Paz y Melia, Antonio. "El embajador polaco J. Dantisco en la Corte de Carlos V," in *Boletín de la R. Academia Española,* XI-XII (1924-1925).

―――― *Sales españolas, o Agudezas del ingenio nacional.* la serie. Madrid, 1890.

―――― *Series de los más importantes documentos del . . . señor duque de Medinaceli.* 2a serie. Madrid, 1922.

Pérez Pastor, Cristóbal. *La imprenta en Medina del Campo.* Madrid, 1895.

―――― *Noticias y documentos relativos a la historia y literatura españolas.* Madrid, 1910-1926. 4 vols. (*Memorias de la R. Academia Española,* X-XIII)

Perrenin, Antoine. "Expédition de l'Empereur contre Barberousse et Thunes," in *Bibliothek des Litterarischen Vereins in Stuttgart,* XI (1845), 523-581.

Pfandl, Ludwig. *Felipe II; bosquejo de una vida y de una época.* 2a ed. Madrid, 1942.

―――― *Juana la Loca; su vida, su tiempo, su culpa.* Madrid, [1943].

Piferrer, Francisco. *Archivo heráldico.* 2 vols. Madrid, 1863-1866.

―――― *Nobiliario de los reinos y señoríos de España.* 2a ed. 6 vols. Madrid, 1857-1860.

Pinheiro da Veiga, Tomé. *Fastigiana; o Fastos geniales,* tr. N. Alonso Cortés. In *Boletin de la Sociedad Castellana de Excursiones,* VI (1913-1914), 57 ff.

Piot, Charles, ed. *Correspondance politique entre Charles-Quint et le Portugal de 1521 à 1522; Gattinara et Barroso.* In *Bulletin de la Commission Royale d'Histoire,* Série IV, VII, 11-110.

Podestà, Bartolomeo. "Carlo V a Roma nel 1536," in *Archivio della Società Romana di Storia Patria,* I (1878), 303-344.

Ponz, Antonio. *Viaje de España.* Madrid, 1947.

Publicatione della tregua & maneggio di pace tra la Cesarea Maestà e'l Christianissimo Re di Francia, n. p., [1538].

Puente y Olea, Manuel de la. *Estudios españoles. Los trabajos geográficos de la Casa de Contratación.* Sevilla, 1900.

Rabelais, François. *Les lettres escrites pendant son voyage d'Italie.* Brusselles, 1710.

Ranke, Leopold von. *Pueblos y estados en la historia moderna*. México, [1948].

Rassow, Peter. *Die Chronik des Pedro Giron und andere Quellen zur Geschichte Kaiser Karls V*. Breslau, 1929. (*Abhandlungen der Schlesischen Gesellschaft für Vaterländische Cultur. Gewissenschaftliche Reihe*, No. 2)

——— *Die Kaiser-Idee Karls V*. Berlin, 1932.

Recopilación de las Ordenanças de la Real Audiencia y Chancillería . . . de Valladolid. Valladolid, 1566.

Recopilación de leyes de los reynos de las Indias. Madrid, 1791.

——— Madrid, 1943. 3 vols.

Regla de la Orden de cavallería de S. Santiago de la Espada, con la glose y declaración del maestro Ysla. Anveres, 1598.

Die Reichsregisterbücher Kaiser Karls V, see Gross, Lothar.

Relación de las fiestas y regocijos que se han hecho en las bodas del duque y duquesa de Sesa, in *Relaciones de los reinados*, II, 157-169.

Relación del recibimiento que se hizo a doña María, Infanta de Portugal . . . cuando vino a España a desposarse con Felipe II en el año 1543, in *Codoin*, III, 361-418.

Relación muy verdadera sobre las paces y concordia que entre Su Magestad y el Cristianíssimo Rey de Francia passaron . . . en la villa de Aguasmuertas a xiiij y xv de julio, año de 1538. n. p., [1538]. A *pliego suelto*.

Relación verdadera de lo que pasa en el patronato y fundación de la capilla de la Concepción de Santo Tomás e yglesia de Sant Salvador desde el año 1525 hasta este de 1570 años. AUbeda.

Relaciones de los reinados de Carlos V y Felipe II, [ed. Amalio Huarte]. 2 vols. Madrid, 1941-1950.

Rem, Lucas. *Tagebuch aus den Jahren 1494-1541*, mitgetheilt von B. Greiff. Augsburg, 1861. (*Jahres-Bericht des Historischen Kreis-Vereins im Regierungsbezirke von Schwaben und Neuburg*, 26)

Remesal, Antonio de. *Historia de la provincia de San Vicente de Chiapa y Guatemala*. Madrid, 1619.

Restrepo, Vicente. *Estudio sobre las minas . . . de Colombia*. 2a ed. Bogotá, 1888.

Ribier, Guillaume, ed. *Lettres et mémoires d'estat des roys . . . ambassadeurs et autres ministres . . . contre les menées de Charles-Quint*. 2 vols. Paris, 1666.

Rinaldi, Odorico. *Annales ecclesiatici*. 15 vols. Lucæ, 1747-1756.

Riol, Santiago Agustín. "Informe que hizo a Su Magestad en 16 de junio de 1726 [sobre los papeles de los archivos]," in *Semanario erudito*, III (1787), 73-234.

Rivera Recio, Juan Francisco. *El adelantamiento de Cazorla; historia general*. Toledo, 1948.

Robertson, William. *History of the reign of Charles the Fifth*. London, [1882].

Rodericus Toletanus, see Jiménez de Rada, Rodrigo.

Rodríguez Villa, Antonio. *El emperador Carlos V y su Corte, según las cartas de Martín de Salinas (1522-1539)*, Madrid, 1903. (*Boletín de la R. Academia de la Historia*, XLIII-XLIV)

——— *Italia desde la batalla de Pavía hasta el saco de Roma*. Madrid, 1885.

——— *Memorias para la historia del asalto y saqueo de Roma en 1527.* Madrid, 1875.

——— *La reina doña Juana la Loca; estudio histórico.* Madrid, 1892.

Romano, Giuseppe. *Cronaca del soggiorno di Carlo V in Italia (1529-30), documento . . . estratto da un codice della Regia Biblioteca Universitaria di Pavia.* Milano, 1892.

Romero de Castilla y Perosso, Francisco. *Apuntes históricos sobre el Archivo General de Simancas.* Madrid, 1873.

Rosso, Gregorio. *Historia delle cose di Napoli sotto l'imperio di Carlo Quinto, cominciando dall'anno 1526 per insino all'anno 1537.* Napoli, 1635.

Ruble, Alphonse de. *Le mariage de Jeanne d'Albret.* Paris, 1877.

Ruiz Prieto, Miguel. *Historia de Ubeda.* 2 vols. Ubeda, 1906.

[Sala, Andrea]. *La triomphale entrata di Carlo V, imperadore augusto, in la inclita città di Napoli e di Messina, con il significato delli archi triomphali e de le figure antiche in prosa e versi.* n.p., [1535].

Salazar y Castro, Luis. [*Comendadores de Santiago*]. BN, MSS. 10996.

——— *Los comendadores de la Orden de Santiago.* 2 vols. Madrid, 1949.

——— *Historia genealógica de la Casa de Lara.* 4 vols. Madrid, 1696-1697.

Salazar y Mendoza, Pedro. *Chrónica de el Cardenal don Juan Tavera.* Toledo, 1603.

——— *Origen de las dignidades seglares de Castilla y León.* Toledo, 1613.

Salinas, Martín de. *Cartas (1522-1539),* in Rodríguez Villa, *El emperador Carlos V y su Corte.*

Saltillo, Miguel Lasso de la Vega, marqués del. *Doña Mencía de Mendóza, marquesa del Cenete (1508-1564).* Madrid, 1942. *(Discurso de recepción en la R. Academia de la Historia)*

——— *La embajada a Roma de Juan de Vega (1543-47).* Zaragoza, [1944].

——— *Historia nobiliaria española.* Vol. I. Madrid, 1951.

——— "El retrato del Comendador Mayor, don Juan de Zúñiga," in *Arte español,* 3a época, I, No. 2 (1941), 4-7.

Salutati, Coluccio. *De laboribus Herculis,* ed. B. L. Ullman. 2 vols. in 1. Turici, [1951].

Salvá y Mallén, Pedro. *Catálogo de la biblioteca de Salvá.* 2 vols. Valencia, 1872.

Sanabria, Alonso de. "Le mariage de Philippe II et de l'infante Marie de Portugal, [ed. René Costes]," in *Bulletin hispanique,* XVII (1915), 15-35.

Sánchez Cantón, Francisco Javier. *Dibujos españoles.* 2 vols. Madrid, 1930.

——— *Documentos de la catedral de Toledo; colección . . . donada al Centro en 1914 por D. Manuel R. Zarco del Valle.* 2 vols. Madrid, 1916. (*Datos documentales para la historia del arte español,* II)

——— *Fuentes literarias para la historia del arte español.* Tomo I. *Siglo XVI.* Madrid, 1923.

Sánchez Montes, Juan. *Franceses, protestantes, turcos; los españoles ante la política internacional de Carlos V.* [Pamplona], 1951.

Sandoval, Prudencio de. *Historia de la vida y hechos del emperador Carlos V.* 2 vols. Amberes, 1681.

——— *Historia del emperador Carlos V.* 9 vols. Madrid, 1846.

Sangrador Minguela, Federico. "Más sobre la estancia de Santa Teresa en Valladolid y en el palacio del secretario Cobos," in *Boletín de la Sociedad Castellana de Excursiones,* VI, 573-574.

Sangrador Vitores, Matías. *Historia de . . . Valladolid.* 2 vols. Valladolid, 1851.

Sansovino, Francesco. *Origine e fatti delle famiglie illustri d'Italia.* Venetia, 1670.

Santa Cruz, Alonso de. *Crónica del emperador Carlos V.* 5 vols. Madrid, 1920-1922.

Sanuto, Marino. *Diarii.* 58 vols. Venezia, 1879-1903.

Schäfer, Ernst. *El Consejo Real y Supremo de las Indias.* 2 vols. Sevilla, 1935.

———— *Indice de la Colección de documentos inéditos de Indias.* 2 vols. Madrid, 1946.

———— *Las rúbricas del Consejo Real y Supremo de las Indias.* Sevilla, 1934.

Schardius, Simon. *Historicum opus.* 4 vols. Basileae, 1574.

Schrijver, Cornelius (*alias* C. Scribonius Grapheus). *Pacis inter Carolum V . . . Imp. Caes. Aug., et Franciscum primum ad Aquas Mortuas in agro Narbonis initae descriptio.* [Antuerpiae, 1540].

Secundus, Iohannis. *Opera.* Parisiis, 1561.

———— *Opera.* Lugduni Batavorum, 1619.

Segni, Bernardo. *Storie fiorentine dall'anno 1527 al 1555.* Augusta, 1723.

Segre, Arturo. *Carlo III di Savoia,* 1536-1545. In *Memorie della R. Accademia di Torino,* 2a serie, LII (1902).

———— "Documenti ed osservazioni sul Congreso di Nizza (1538)," in *Rendiconti della R. Accademia dei Lincei,* Classe di scienze morali, Serie 5a, X (1901), 72-98.

Sepúlveda, Juan Ginés. *Opera.* 4 vols. Matriti, 1780.

Serrano, Luciano. *Correspondencia diplomática entre España y la Santa Sede durante el pontificado de S. S. Pío V.* Madrid, 1914.

Serrano y Sanz, Manuel. "Una carta de Fr. Juan de Zumárraga, obispo de México, al secretario Francisco de los Cobos," in *Boletín de la R. Academia Española,* XVII (1930), 696-704.

Sevillano Colom, Francisco. "La cancillería de Fernando el Católico," in *Estudios del V. Congreso de Historia de la Corona de Aragón,* I, 217-253.

Simon, Marcel. *Hercule et le Christianisme.* Paris, n.d.

Sousa, Antonio Caetano de. *Historia genealogica da Casa Real portugueza.* 12 vols. Lisboa, 1735-1748.

Spreti, Vittorio. *Enciclopedia storico-nobiliare italiana.* 8 vols. Milano, 1928-1935.

Sumario de algunos sucesos del reinado de Carlos V, in *Codoin,* IX, 543-566.

Tamara, Francisco. *Suma y compendio de todas las chrónicas del mundo . . . Es la Chrónica de Juan Carión, quitado todo lo superfluo y añadidas muchas cosas notables de España.* Anvers, 1555.

Teresa de Jesús, Santa. *Cartas.* Çaragoça, 1671.

———— *Obras completas.* 2 vols. Madrid, 1951-1954.

Tiraboschi, Girolamo. *Storia della letteratura italiana.* 16 vols. Milano, 1822-1826.

Toda y Güell, Eduardo. *Bibliografía espanyola d'Italia.* 5 vols. Castell, 1927-1931.

Tormo Monzó, Elías. *En las Descalzas Reales.* Madrid, 1915-1917.

―――― and F. J. Sánchez Cantón. *Los tapices de la Casa del Rey N. S.* Madrid, 1919.

Traslado de la memoria que Su Magestad embió a la Emperatriz. Medina del Campo, [1535]. A *pliego suelto,* reprinted in Pérez Pastor, *La imprenta en Medina del Campo,* pp. 411-414.

Tyler, Royall. *The Emperor Charles the Fifth.* Fair Lawn, N. J., 1956.

Ulloa, Alfonso de. *Vita dell'invittissimo . . . imperatore Carlo V.* Venetia, 1574.

Ulloa Cisneros, Luis. *Historia de España.* Vol. IV. *La Casa de Austria (siglos XVI y XVII).* Barcelona, [1936].

Vaccolini, Domenico. *Biografia di Bartolomeo Ramenghi, pittore, detto il Bagnacavallo.* 4a ed. Bagnacavallo, 1848.

Valdés, Alonso de. *Diálogo de Mercurio y Carón,* ed. José F. Montesinos. Madrid, 1929. *(Clásicos castellanos)*

Vales Failde, Javier. *La emperatriz Isabel.* [Madrid, 1944].

Vandenesse, Jean de. *Journal des voyages de Charles-Quint de 1514 à 1551.* In Gachard, *Collection des voyages,* II, 51-464.

Varchi, Benedetto. *Storia fiorentina,* ed. Lelio Arrib. 3 vols. Firenze, 1838-1841.

Vasari, Giorgio. *Le vite de' più eccellenti pittori, scultori ed architettori,* ed. Gaetano Milanesi. 9 vols. Firenze, 1878-1885.

Venetianische Depeschen von Kaiserhofe. 4 vols. Wien, 1889-1895.

Vignau, Vicente and Uhagón, Francisco R. de. *Indice de pruebas de los caballeros que han vestido el hábito de Santiago desde el año 1501 hasta la fecha.* Madrid, 1901.

Vigo, Pietro. *Carlo Quinto in Siena nell'aprile del 1536; relazione di un contemporaneo.* Bologna, 1884. *(Scelta di curiosità letterarie,* 199)

Villalón, Cristóbal de. *Ingeniosa comparación entre lo antiguo y lo presente.* Madrid, 1898. *(Sociedad de Bibliófilos Españoles)*

Villena, Enrique de. *Los doze trabajos de Hércules.* Burgos, 1499. (Edición facsímile)

Villuga, Pedro Juan. *Repertorio de todos los caminos de España.* [Medina del Campo], 1546. (Edición facsímile)

La visita del año de 68 que hiço Su Señoría Illustrísima, mi señora, en la yglesia del Salvador. AUbeda.

Vital, Laurent. *Relation du premier voyage de Charles-Quint en Espagne,* in Gachard, *Collection des voyages,* III, 1-314.

Vitale, Vito. "Trapani nelle guerre di Carlo V in Africa e contro i turchi," in *Archivio storico siciliano,* XXIX (1904), 255-323.

Volpi, Giovanni. *Carlo V a Lucca nel MDXXXVI; lettera di Niccolò Montecatini.* Lucca, 1892.

Walser, Fritz. "Spanien und Karl V. Fünf spanische Denkschriften an den Kaiser," in *Nachrichten. . . .* 1932, pp. 120-181. *(Berichte und Studien,* VI)

———— "Die Ueberlieferung der Akten der kastilisch-spanischen Zentral-behörden unter Karl V," in *Nachrichten*. . . . 1933, pp. 93-138. (*Berichte und Studien*, VIII)

Walther, Johann E. Andreas. *Die Anfänge Karls V*. Leipzig, 1911.

———— "Kanzleiordnungen Maximilians I, Karls V und Ferdinands I," in *Archiv für Urkundenforschung*, II (1909), 335-406.

Weiss, Charles, ed. *Papiers d'état du Cardinal de Granvelle*. 9 vols. Paris, 1841-1852.

Zapata, Luis. *Carlo famoso*. Valencia, 1566.

———— *Miscelánea*. [Madrid, 1859]. (*Memorial histórico español*, XI)

Zárate, Agustín de. *Historia del descubrimiento y conquista de la provincia del Perú*. In *Biblioteca de autores españoles*, XXVI, 459-574.

Zarco Cuevas, Julián. *Catálogo de los manuscritos castellanos de la Real Biblioteca de El Escorial*. 3 vols. Madrid, 1924-1929.

Zarco del Valle, Manuel Remón. *Documentos inéditos para la historia de las Bellas Artes en España*. Madrid, 1870.

Zúñiga, Francesillo de. *Crónica*, in *Biblioteca de autores españoles*, XXXVI, 9-54.

———— *Epistolario*, in *Idem*, XXXVI, 55-62.

Zurita y Castro, Gerónimo. *Anales de la Corona de Aragón*. 6 vols. [Çaragoça, 1578-1585].

INDEX OF PERSONS

449

Rivadavia, Conde de, *see* Sarmiento, Bernardino
Rivadavia, Condesa de, *see* Sarmiento, María
Rivas, Lic., governor of Cazorla, 291
Rivoire, Archambaud de la, 214
Roa, Maestre de, 225, 226, 411
Robertel, French ambassador, 52
Rodericus Toletanus, *see* Jiménez de Rada, Rodrigo
Rodrigo, Lic., royal accountant, 7
Rodríguez de Fonseca, Juan, 13, 41, 46, 55, 58, 119
Rodríguez (Roiz) de los Cobos, Ferran, 3
Rodríguez de los Cobos, Lope, 3
Rodríguez de los Cobos, Pedro, (I), 3
Rodríguez de los Cobos, Pedro, (II), 4
Rodríguez (Ruiz) de los Cobos, Rodrigo, 3
Rodríguez de Mercado, Juan, 4
Rodríguez Mexía, Juana, 4, 389
Rojas, Antonio de, 19, 20, 41, 60, 66, 69, 119
Rojas, Margarita de, 230
Rojas, Pedro de, 16
Rojas y Sandoval, Archbishop of Toledo, 298, 316
Romain, Martín, de, 228
Romano, Giulio, 132
Ronquillo, Rodrigo, *alcalde de corte,* 72, 92, 93, 219
Rua, Gonzalo de la, 421
Ruiz, Alonso, 90, 192, 193, 227
Ruiz de Avendaño, Martín, 67
Ruiz de Calcena, Juan, 10, 11, 21
Ruiz de Castañeda, Bartolomé, 17, 45, 66, 67, 84, 333
Ruiz de la Mota, García, 60, 61, 275, 306
Ruiz de la Mota, Pedro, 24, 29, 30, 35, 37, 43, 45, 52, 56, 59, 60, 63-66, 71-74, 119, 275, 345
Rye, Joachim de, 256

Saavedra, Juan de, 220
St. Mauris, Imperial ambassador, 305

Salamanca, treasurer of Ferdinand of Austria, 89
Salazar, Juan de, servant of Cobos, 213
Saldaña, Conde de, 130, 131
Saldaña, Cristóbal de, 96, 128, 243
Salinas, Condesa de (María de Ulloa), 263
Salinas, Martín de, 75, 77, 80-82, 86, 89, 91, 100, 112, 129, 156-158, 161, 162, 167, 169, 172-175, 179, 184, 186, 190, 191, 194, 197, 206, 217, 218, 223, 326, 327, 333, 348, 356, 358, 366, 373
Salmerón, Lic., member of the Consejo Real, 275
Salvatierra, Conde de (Francisco de Ayala), 89, 243
Salviati, Jacobo, Cardinal, 154, 173
Samano, Juan de, 46-48, 62-66, 84, 106, 117, 119, 121, 124, 128, 148-150, 169, 170, 249, 255, 256, 277, 283, 315, 334, 342
Sampson, British ambassador, 83
Sanabria, member of the Consejo Real, 272
Sánchez, Luis, treasurer for Cataluña, 52
Sánchez Cantón, Francisco Javier, 357
Sánchez de Araiz, Martín, 88
Sánchez de Orihuela, Gaspar, 32
Sánchez de Salamanca, Juan, 71
Sandoval, Gonzalo de, 109
Sandoval, Prudencio de, historian, 22, 65
Santa Cruz, Alonso de, historian, 29, 58, 62, 63, 108, 218, 241, 255, 303, 366, 425
Santa María, Fray Tomás de, 291
Santernas, Perico de, 249
Santiago, Archbishop of, *see* (1) Tavera, Juan, (2) Sarmiento, Pedro
Sarmiento, Bernardino, (Conde de Rivadavia), 76
Sarmiento, Francisca, (I) (Condesa de Rivadavia), 77, 282
Sarmiento, Francisca, (II), sister of Doña María, 110, 263, 286

Francisco de los Cobos

Set in Caslon, printed, and bound by American Book-
Stratford Press, Inc.—designer, Sydney Feinberg;
editorial adviser, Larry Cone.
Front endpaper by Henry Castner, graduate student,
department of geography, University of Pittsburgh;
back endpaper by Barbara Effron of Pittsburgh.
Coordinated and edited by Agnes Lynch Starrett,
University of Pittsburgh Press

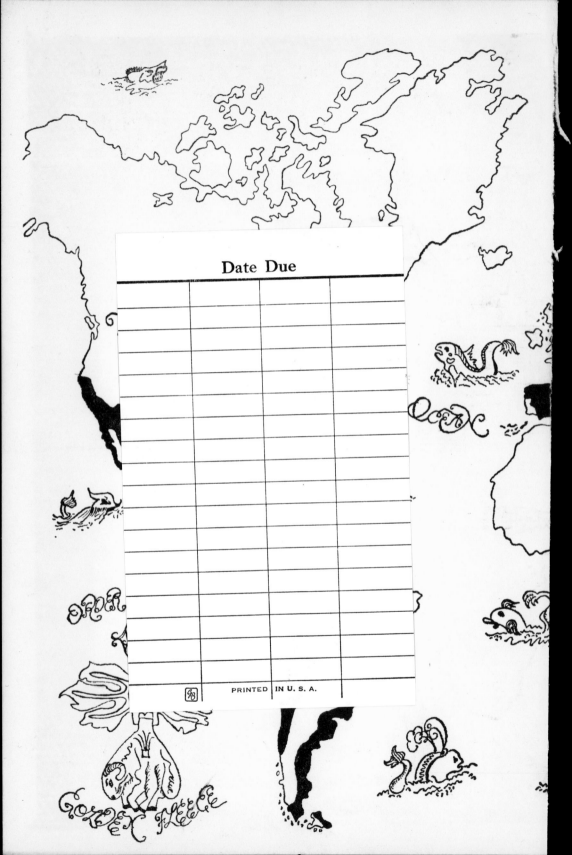

Date Due
